Rwanda and Burundi

PRAEGER LIBRARY OF AFRICAN AFFAIRS

The Praeger Library of African Affairs is intended to provide clear, authoritative, and objective information about the historical, political, cultural, and economic background of modern Africa. Individual countries and groupings of countries will be dealt with as will general themes affecting the whole continent and its relations with the rest of the world. The library appears under the general editorship of Colin Legum, with Philippe Decraene as consultant editor.

Already Published

T. A. BEETHAM	Christianity and the New Africa
ALFRED G. GERTEINY	Mauritania
RICHARD GREENFIELD	Ethiopia: *A New Political History*
RICHARD HALL	Zambia
ALEX HEPPLE	South Africa: *A Political and Economic History*
JAMES R. HOOKER	Black Revolutionary: *George Padmore's Path from Communism to Pan-Africanism*
GUY DE LUSIGNAN	French-Speaking Africa Since Independence
HORACE MINER (ed.)	The City in Modern Africa
JOHN G. PIKE	Malawi: *A Political and Economic History*
WALTER SCHWARZ	Nigeria
RICHARD P. STEVENS	Lesotho, Botswana, and Swaziland: *The Former High Commission Territories in Southern Africa*
CLAUDE WAUTHIER	The Literature and Thought of Modern Africa: *A Survey*

Rwanda and Burundi

RENÉ LEMARCHAND

PRAEGER PUBLISHERS
New York · Washington · London

PRAEGER PUBLISHERS, Inc.
111 Fourth Avenue, New York, N.Y. 10003, U.S.A.
5 Cromwell Place, London, S.W.7, England

Published in the United States of America in 1970
by Praeger Publishers, Inc.

Library of Congress Catalog Card Number: 73-77303

Printed in Great Britain

To My Father

In Memoriam

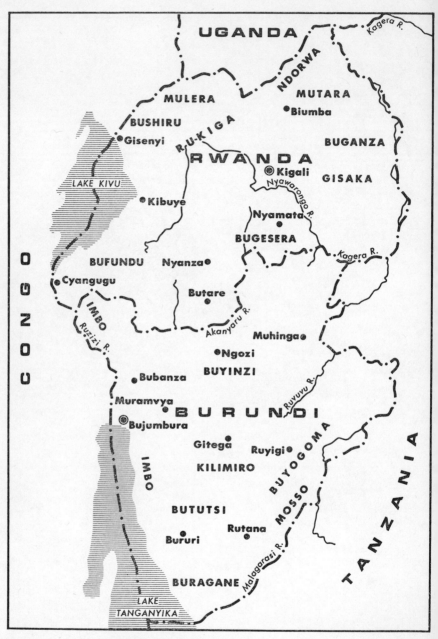

Map 1. Rwanda and Burundi: Regions and Towns

Contents

Contents

Maps

Illustrations   *Facing Page*

Preface

The purpose of this book is to acquaint the reader with the past and recent history of those two states of Africa about which Western observers seem to know least. Apart from whatever merits the book may have from the standpoint of political historiography, it is also meant as a trial essay in the sociology of revolutionary change in contemporary Africa. No attempt has been made, however, to match or supersede the theoretical studies already available on the general theme of revolution. This is no more than a case study intended to suggest new perspectives and foci of investigation, and, hopefully, new avenues for further research.

A personal note is perhaps not entirely out of place at this point. My interest in Rwanda and Burundi goes back to the autumn of 1960, when I first had occasion to visit what was then officially known as the United Nations Trusteeship Territory of Ruanda-Urundi. My trip to Rwanda, occurring at a particularly crucial juncture of the country's recent evolution, gave me the opportunity to witness violence on a scale which, by comparison, made the Congo look almost like a haven of tranquillity. The reasons for writing this book are thus more than a reflection of my own professional interest in the theme around which it is constructed; they stem from a rather unique personal experience—from what can only be described as a sense of cultural shock in the face of wanton killings. Whether this has in any way prevented me from keeping an appropriate distance from my subject is for the reader alone to decide; but I probably would not have embarked upon this task had I not been in a position to measure the appalling character of the events I witnessed against the general indifference they seemed to evoke from the outside world.

My greatest debt is to the many Barundi and Banyarwanda who patiently shared with me their knowledge of the history and political life of their respective countries, and sometimes their anxieties in the face of a still uncertain future. For some, these premonitions proved only too well-founded. It is with a sense of deeply-felt grief that I recall the help and friendly hospitality that were once extended to me by the late Patrice Mayondo, Paul Nibirantiza and Paul Mirerekano from Burundi, and Prosper Bwanakweri from Rwanda. Their names, however, represent but a fraction of the list of those to whom I am personally indebted.

Rwanda and Burundi

A number of friends and colleagues have read portions of the manuscript and kindly proffered their advice and criticisms. Special thanks are owed to Professor Albert Trouwborst for his sustained interest in my work, and in particular for his judicious comments and criticisms of chapter 1; to Professor Jan Vansina for patiently answering the many questions put to him in the course of a lengthy correspondence; and to Rachel Yeld for giving me the benefit of her first-hand experience of the complexities of the Rwandese refugee problem. Professor Henri-Philippe Cart's assistance during the last stages of the manuscript was invaluable; without his kind co-operation, my efforts at penetrating the arcana of contemporary Burundi politics would have been largely in vain. To Professor Arnold Heidenheimer, who learned more about the Burundi monarchy than he had initially bargained for, I also wish to express my thanks for his valuable criticisms of chapter 10. To another friend and colleague at the University of Florida, Professor David Chalmers, goes a similar debt for his comments on the Introduction and Conclusion of this book.

My stay in Belgium would have been decidedly less pleasant, and my research there far less fruitful, had it not been for the charming hospitality of Denise and Jean-Pierre Derscheid. As much as their kindness and generosity, their help in making available to me the papers of Jean-Pierre's father, the late Jean-Marie Derscheid, deserves an acknowledgement which no words can properly express. My sense of gratitude to them, therefore, is also a reflection of the posthumous debt I—as well as any other scholar for whom the names Rwanda and Burundi mean anything—owe to Jean-Marie Derscheid, whose wide-ranging intellectual interests and life-time devotion to Africa are amply reflected in the collection of documents he has left to posterity, and on which part of this work is based. At one time Professor of Colonial Law of the Institut des Territoires d'Outre-Mer at Antwerp, Secretary-General of the Parc Albert, co-founder of the Institut International pour la Protection de la Nature, he combined the talents of the administrator, the meticulousness of the scholar, the zest and stamina of the explorer, to which he added, towards the end of his life, the gallantry of a 'résistant de la première heure'. Until his decapitation by the Gestapo at the Brandenburg prison, on March 13, 1944, he was a leading figure of the Belgian underground—and had been entrusted with, among other things, the elaboration of a secret transmission code based on an adaptation of the Bantu and Sudanese languages.

This study could not have been written without the generous financial support of the Social Science Research Council, and of the African Studies Center of the University of Florida; I am equally grateful for the financial help I was able to secure through a Fullbright-Hays Fellowship in the summer of 1966.

Portions of the research for this book were published earlier in article form. For permission to use and reprint part of this material I wish to express my thanks to the Editors of *Africa Report*, *The Journal of Modern African Studies*, *Civilisations*, and *Cahiers d'Etudes Africaines*. I am equally indebted to Oxford University Press for permission to reproduce segments of my essay on Rwanda published in Robert I. Rotberg and Ali Mazrui, eds., *Traditions of Protest in Black Africa*, Oxford University Press, London and New York 1969. I wish to express my thanks to the Centre Militaire d'Information et de Documentation pour l'Outre-Mer (CMIDOM) for permission to reproduce photos 1 and 3; to Infor-Burundi for photos 2, 4, 14 and 17; to the Ministry of Information of Rwanda for photos 7, 8, 9 and 10; to Jean-Pierre Derscheid for photos 5 and 6. Photos 11, 12, 13, 15 and 16 are from my own collection.

Thanks are also owed to Jan Smith for her exemplary patience in drawing and redrawing most of the maps which appear in this book; to Professor Peter Nixdorff, and Ernst Wittig, for their help in translating various passages quoted from German works; to Ross Pye, of the Pall Mall Press, for his meticulousness in giving final form to the manuscript; last but not least is the debt I owe my wife for her graceful resignation while much of my time was being spent, mentally and physically, in the hills of Central Africa. Bringing me back from time to time to another level of reality was not the least of her contributions.

With all this help any error of fact or interpretation contained in this book must clearly be my own and sole responsibility.

A NOTE TO THE READER

The names of the countries discussed in this book are Rwanda and Burundi. Their inhabitants are known as, respectively, Banyarwanda and Barundi, and in the singular as Munyarwanda and Murundi. The languages spoken are Kinyarwanda in Rwanda and Kirundi in Burundi. The caste names are, in each country, Tutsi, Hutu and Twa. Although the forms Batutsi, Bahutu and Batwa are also encountered, the Bantu prefix 'ba-' has been dropped, in accordance with the prevailing usage. Place names have been standardised in accordance with the new appelations devised after independence, but to avoid possible confusions (as in the case of a radically different spelling) the old place names have sometimes been indicated in parentheses next to the new ones.

'There are general causes, whether moral or physical . . . which operate in every monarchy, to bring about its rise, its duration and its fall. All accidents are subject to these causes, and if the outcome of a single battle—i.e. a particular cause —was the ruin of a state, there was a general cause which decreed that that state was destined to perish through a single battle. In short, the main impulse carries all the particular accidents along with it.'

Montesquieu, *Considerations on the Causes of the Grandeur and Decadence of the Romans.*

Introduction

OF ALL the strange syllables recently added to the roster of newly-independent African states few have a more esoteric connotation than Rwanda and Burundi, or, to use the old terminology, Ruanda-Urundi.* Except for a small circle of initiates these countries are still terra incognita for the general public. If there is a touch of unreality about their Lilliputian dimensions, the paucity of their economic resources and the quaintness of some of their traditions, theirs is a history which in its events and motivations is very much part of the real world. It is the history of two semi-feudal societies caught up in the turmoil of a swiftly changing environment, in which traditional bonds are suddenly ruptured or loosened to give birth to new social groupings and values. It is the tale of two archaic kingdoms, both undergoing a drastic alteration of their traditional structures and symbols of legitimacy, yet each proceeding towards the goal of political modernisation at a different pace and through different paths. Here, as elsewhere in Africa, the familiar themes of accommodation and conflict, continuity and change, provide the key leitmotivs.

That these themes are susceptible to major variations is nowhere more apparent than in the contrasting patterns of development displayed by these two states. What makes the analysis of their recent history both interesting and rewarding is that we are here dealing with societies which, however similar their traditional political institutions and social structures, have responded in radically divergent ways to the challenge of nation-building. And in both cases the developments have been rather different from what one has come to expect of most African states.

In Rwanda the transition to independence was accompanied by one

* In this study, the terms Rwanda and Burundi are used to refer both to the traditional African kingdoms in existence before colonial rule and to the independent states established on July 1, 1962. Though at first an integral part of German East Africa, after the First World War Rwanda and Burundi were entrusted to Belgium as a League of Nations Mandate, and, after the Second World War, as a United Nations Trust Territory. The term Ruanda-Urundi has been reserved for the territorial and administrative unit born of the amalgamation of the two kingdoms under Belgian rule, in line with the official usage. Except where quotations have maintained the old spelling, and where the historical context of the discussion requires that it be preserved, the terms Rwanda and Burundi have been substituted.

of the most terrifying upheavals thus far recorded in the annals of decolonisation, and by what, on the surface, seems a fundamental break with the past. Hard on the heels of a peasant revolt in 1959 came the abolition of the monarchy. The traditional ruling elites were forcibly ejected from the seats of power, and in the process thousands of their kinsmen were massacred or forced into exile. For months on end, swelling waves of terrorism swept through the countryside, causing untold casualties. From this shattering experience Rwanda emerged transfigured—openly committed to socialism, thoroughly imbued with a sense of republican austerity, and, significantly, genuinely pro-Western. To the West's 'liberating' impact, Rwanda's revolutionary elites have responded with a gratitude matched only by their continuing aversion for the ancien régime.

In Burundi, by contrast, passage to self-government was relatively smooth. Although the monarchy has been abolished, its staying power has nonetheless been remarkable by comparison with Rwanda.* Not only was the timing of change different, but also the circumstances. Even if violence did occur on some occasions, and in some places on a substantial scale, the passing of the Burundi monarchy did not produce anything comparable with the Rwandese chaos; more surprising still, the final blow was not delivered by the representatives of the 'lower orders', as in Rwanda, but by the army acting at the instigation of a rather diverse group of youth leaders, university students and civil servants, for the most part ethnically related to Burundi's traditional ruling oligarchy. Although the extent to which the political style and methods of the new regime differ from the old is not as yet fully discernible, the general impression is one of far less drastic change than in Rwanda.

In these contrasting patterns of development lies a unique opportunity for the study of revolution: unique in terms of the comparability of the political units concerned, as both claim roughly the same population figures, have similar geographical size and topographical features, and have the same general type of social structure and colonial heritage; unique, too, in terms of the paradoxical nature of the outcome. The purpose of this book is to explain this paradox.

Part of the endeavour involves shedding light on a set of historical

---

* The Rwandese monarchy was formally abolished in September 1961, and the Burundi monarchy in November 1966. Although the respite accorded to the Burundi monarchy may not seem all that significant against the total span of its previous history, the juncture at which it occurred deserves attention. That Burundi managed to weather the crisis of independence while retaining the outer shell of its monarchical institutions is in itself a significant index of its greater stability in the face of social and political changes.

2

events which have not yet received as much attention from social scientists as they deserve. As one reflects on the volume of printed material dealing with the concept of revolution in Africa, one cannot help being astonished at the paucity of informed references to Rwanda. Yet Rwanda provides one of the very rare examples of a genuine social revolution accompanying the accession of an African state to independence, the only other example of its kind being Zanzibar.[1] And it is the only case of a large-scale, thorough-going transformation occurring under the auspices, and indeed with the positive help and encouragement, of a colonial power. These, presumably, are sufficient reasons for giving Rwanda a more careful consideration than some might otherwise be willing to concede.

The concern of this study, however, is not only the reality of a specific revolutionary experience but what this reality tells us about processes of social change in general. What are the relationships between traditional social structures and their capacity to absorb modernising influences? In what ways does social structure 'connect' with the political system? Why is it that in some cases revolutionary change becomes a sine qua non of political modernisation and not in others? If and when revolutionary change overtakes a society how does a society reconstruct itself? What are the concepts and categories which seem best suited to carry the analytic burdens imposed upon them? To attempt definitive answers to these questions would be presumptuous at this preliminary stage; indeed, one wonders whether the answers can be formulated at all, other than in the most tentative fashion. Even so, one must at least try to delineate the general assumptions which underlie this study and which in turn have dictated the choice of material for emphasis.

A NOTE ABOUT ASSUMPTIONS

That most of these assumptions should imply a partial rejection of earlier ones about the nature of social change in contemporary Africa is perhaps a reflection of the very special conditions encountered in each state; but it also suggests possible shifts in the intellectual perspective from which most theories of social change have thus far proceeded. First and most obviously, the countries selected for analysis provide rather poor illustrations of the popular contention that national unity is the product of many centuries of shared historical experiences, and hence that 'the prime condition for the building of [modern] nations is that they have an opportunity to age in the wood'.[2] If this were so, how could one explain that neither Rwanda nor Burundi was able to make significant headway toward the building of a modern, integrated, national community—except, in one case, through a major political surgery, and, in the other, through the application of increasingly stringent penalties on all 'dissident' elements? Clearly, the processes of adaptation and innovation involved in nation-building may be just as arduous in the case of 'historic' states like Rwanda and Burundi as in the case of the newly-emergent national communities artificially brought together under the aegis of Western imperialism. There are many ways in which history and tradition may conspire to impede otherwise feasible economic integration, to impose political institutions ill-suited to meet the expectations and material needs of the masses, and to perpetuate or intensify traditional cleavages among them, and all this regardless of whether or not a state has been given an opportunity to 'age in the wood'. Nor is there much evidence to be gleaned from the recent history of Rwanda and Burundi to support the contention that a traditional system's capacity to innovate varies in direct proportion to its degree of political centralisation. Or else how should one account for the fact that the more centralised of the two, Rwanda, was the first to succumb to the challenge of political modernisation?

Both states emerged from the recesses of the pre-colonial past with reasonably stable boundaries, definable 'national' cultures, and with political institutions whose legitimacy had long been established— in short, possessing those very features which some have singled out as the principal determinants of political modernisation.[3] The other side of the coin, however, is that the same historical factors which in the past gave territorial unity to each state were also responsible for the elements of disunity discernible in their social structures. The results were poly-ethnic, hierarchically-organised societies, in which power and influence were concentrated in the hands of a small oligarchy, and wherever social and economic differences tended to coincide with ethnic divisions the cohesiveness of the system was directly threatened. Thus if the complex of events and forces that went into shaping their national identities differed substantially from those which have conditioned the building of most other African states, this in itself cannot be regarded as an unmixed blessing.

Broadly speaking, the traditional social context of Rwanda and Burundi is that of caste societies in which social change, or the absence of change, takes place within and against the limits of separated social systems.*

---

* Neglect of this cardinal feature is one reason why Ethel Albert's attempt to investigate differences in the degree of 'receptivity to change' between Rwanda and Burundi seems generally unsatisfactory. Unless one is prepared to recognise at the outset that in each society change has operated selectively, depending on both the sources and implications of change, and the cultural predispositions

The crucial variable in this case lies not so much in the degree of centralisation or decentralisation of the traditional authority system as in the degree of separateness which exists between different status groups. Thus we may encounter a situation—as in Rwanda—where political centralisation would normally favour the acceleration of change throughout society, but where, in fact, the rigidity of the caste system imposes severe limitations on how far down the social pyramid change can be tolerated without at the same time endangering the legitimacy of the political order. On the other hand, where the degree of social mobility between various strata is such that the political system need not be radically altered to accommodate social change—as initially happened in Burundi—the survival of traditional institutions and symbols of legitimacy is not immediately called into question.[4] In other words, whatever adaptiveness a political system may derive from its structural properties ultimately depends on the degree of flexibility and openness of its social structure.

When speaking of closed and open systems of stratification, one must inevitably consider the ingredients which enter into the definition of these situations, i.e. castes, classes and elites. In this study, the word 'caste' is used in the anthropological sense to refer to predominantly endogamous, hierarchically-organised groups with specialised occupations. This is about as accurate a definition as can be devised for the purpose of this discussion. Experience shows an amazing range of variability in caste situations. Ideally, a caste system implies inequality of status as well as the absence of vertical mobility between various strata; yet the way in which the system is supposed to work and how it actually works are two different things. Gerald Berreman's remark that 'there is a considerable variation in the characteristics of, and relation among, the groups to which the term "caste" is applied' has particular relevance to this discussion.[5] Because of differences in the caste relationships in Rwanda and Burundi, the word 'caste' is here applied cross-culturally to refer to quite different sets of conditions. The varieties of cultural and social pluralism it covers range from situations of relatively

---

of the constituent sub-units of each society, the socio-political realities of Rwanda and Burundi are bound to remain something of an enigma. Instead of asking ourselves to what extent Rwanda and Burundi, as distinct analytical units, are amenable to change in general, as does Professor Albert, a more fruitful way of approaching the question is to look at each society in terms of behavioural and normative variations among castes as well as within each caste, taking into account the nature of the changes confronting these different sections of each society at any given time. See Ethel Albert, "Socio-political Organization and Receptivity to Change: Some Differences between Ruanda and Urundi", *Southwestern Journal of Anthropology*, Vol. XVI, 1960, pp. 46–74.

high cultural integration—where different groups are held together by the same language, political culture, religious and political symbols—to the much more narrow definition offered by M. G. Smith, where pluralism denotes institutional discreteness.[6]

The concept of 'class' is even more elusive in its connotations. Not only is it susceptible to a wider range of correlations, but to very different theoretical formulations. For the sake of clarity one may start with the trivial but nonetheless essential postulate that 'class' and 'caste' are both concerned with social differentiation, and that whereas one's membership in a 'caste' usually depends on one's birth, a 'class' is normally considered to be the outgrowth of social and economic transformations that are typically modern in character. But this is a very crude and approximate characterisation, and, depending on whether one chooses to place the emphasis on the presumed rigidity of class divisions or their fluidity, one can elaborate this definition in one of two ways.

If one approaches the concept of class from a Marxist perspective to refer to groups based on relations of productivity, the boundaries between 'caste' and 'class' are liable to become extremely hazy. Thus in his more recent interpretation of Rwandese society Professor J. J. Maquet does not hesitate to identify the caste system of Rwanda with a class system, arguing in effect that the relations of dominance and subordination between castes were but a reflection of the uneven share of economic resources between different social 'classes'.[7] In this sense Maquet's thesis provides an important corrective to P. C. Lloyd's contention that 'classes in the classic Marxist sense of property-owning and non-owning groups exist neither in traditional or modern Africa'.[8] A major difficulty about this line of analysis, however, is that it necessarily conceals the social transformations that have taken place over time *within* each caste and hence tends to exaggerate the degree of consistency between 'class' and 'caste'; another is that it suggests an element of conflict between castes which has not always been present in the traditional society. Despite the acuity of the social conflict of which Rwanda became the scene, neither the timing nor the scale of conflict lends the slightest credibility to the notion of a class struggle between 'haves' and 'have-nots', at least in the sense in which Marx might have used these terms.

Another way of looking at the notion of class is to follow Weber's footsteps and emphasise the possibility of vertical mobility between different layers of society. Not only does this call attention to a major difference between 'caste' and 'class', but it also helps to explain the nature of the change which overtakes a society when the emergence of

6

new reference groups and values brings about a reversal of traditional statuses. In this sense the concept of class uncovers a major aspect of the conflict between traditionalism and modernity in each country. Yet it would be misleading to attribute to the emergent social structure of Rwanda and Burundi the characteristics of a fully developed class structure, for at least three reasons. Firstly, the degree of social mobility from one social stratum to the other is as yet extremely limited, and in some cases severely circumscribed by the persistence of caste divisions. Furthermore, is it at all legitimate to speak of a class structure in the absence of a substantial internal differentiation beyond the usual cleavage between a small and relatively affluent elite of bureaucrats and politicians on the one hand, and a vast rural stratum on the other?* Finally, and to the extent that an embryonic class system can be said to exist, its roots today are still primarily political and bureaucratic. The result, then, is a heavily top-sided social pyramid, almost entirely dominated by what René Dumont aptly refers to as 'a bourgeoisie of civil servants'.[9]

This said, it is equally pertinent to note that in each country has arisen a group of rural wage-earners or salaried workers which, for want of a better term, may be said to represent an emergent middle-class. In view of their low economic standing and continuing close ties with their rural milieux, the expression 'rural proletariat' might better reflect their socio-economic position and residential ties. Nonetheless, insofar as they stood mid-way between the peasantry on the one hand, and the traditional and modern educated elites on the other, they formed a kind of 'middle sector' which, however narrow its base and ambivalent its 'class' consciousness, in both countries provided the crucial connecting links between the emergent elites and the peasantry. Thus if the word 'class' has any relevance in the context of this discussion, rather than to the traditional elites (whom Mosca might have called a 'ruling class'), or the new elites of intellectuals and literati trained under the auspices of the Church, it is to this embryonic category of rural sans-culottes that the term can best be applied.

The term 'traditional elites' has been reserved to holders of traditional offices whose claims to superiority and sense of corporateness were based largely on birth, that is on their membership of an upper caste. While

---

* Balandier suggests that it might be more accurate to abandon the notion of a class structure for that of a class in process of formation: 'Seldom does contemporary political life [in Africa] reveal the existence of an established class structure, but appears, rather, as the instrument of a class in the process of being born.' G. Balandier, "Problèmatique des Classes Sociales en Afrique Noire", *Cahiers Internationaux de Sociologie*, Vol. XXXVIII, 1965, p. 139.

many of these elites were 'modern' in the sense of being westernised, reasonably well-educated and affluent, their distinguishing characteristic is that their claims to authority as well as the character of their offices were primarily rooted in tradition. By 'modern elites', on the other hand, is meant a group of people who may or may not occupy modern political roles but who in any event claim as their main characteristic a relatively high degree of education in relation to both the masses of the population and the traditional elites.[10]

Like all generalisations, this scheme is inevitably limited by the contextual specificities of each state. Hence certain qualifications must be interposed. In Rwanda the percentage of incumbent elites whose level of education meets the requirements of a 'modern' elite is relatively small compared to Burundi, because of the timing of the revolution and the long denial of educational opportunities until then faced by members of the ethnic stratum from which the revolution derived its impetus. Moreover, the distinction between 'traditional' and 'modern' elites is complicated by the existence in northern Rwanda of a special category of traditional authorities: special in that they all belonged to the lower caste, i.e. to an ethnic stratum which, by virtue of its revolutionary commitment, might otherwise be regarded as 'modern'; special, too, in that their traditional claims to authority were temporarily suspended during the colonial period by the counter-claims of the upper-caste traditional elites, and the support which the latter received from the colonial authorities. This in turn underscores the need for adducing yet another variable in explaining elite differences, based on inter-caste variations. As we shall see, while in Rwanda inter-caste differences have now largely lost their relevance insofar as intra-elite tensions are concerned, in Burundi these differences remain the single most important factor in an understanding of present and future developments.

The problem of defining general analytical categories inevitably raises the question of how much emphasis should be given to the unique features of these societies as against their common characteristics. In the light of what has already been said, a convincing case could be made for treating both countries within the same general analytical framework; instead, however, each country has been treated separately in regard to recent political developments. The justification for this approach lies in the radically divergent patterns of evolution exhibited by each state. In one case a violent, genuinely revolutionary change has taken place, involving 'a drastic, sudden substitution of one group in charge of the running of a territorial political entity for another group'.[11] In the other a process of evolution has occurred which, however close it may have come to the threshold of revolution, focuses attention on very different forces, institutions and events. For some, this approach may be regarded as proof of an unwarranted predilection for historicism. The only reply to this is that historicism is not without certain virtues. To the extent that it invites empirical observations from which more general propositions can be derived, historicism may well be a precondition to sound systematic analysis.

Because Rwanda and Burundi are among those countries of Africa about which 'hard' data is extremely scarce, at least insofar as recent developments are concerned, there has been heavy dependence for information on interviews with officials and non-officials from each country. From the very beginning, however, it became evident that such information was frequently biased or incomplete. This was perhaps inevitable in a cultural environment in which concealing or distorting the truth are traditionally regarded as both a virtue and an art; but it also reflects the degree to which political convictions and group loyalties, when carried to an extreme, may inhibit the exchange of objective information.

Whenever possible, therefore, an attempt has been made to cross-check interviews by drawing informants from different ethnic strata. A similar procedure has been employed to verify translations of the vernacular press and documents written in Kinyarwanda and Kirundi. Several administrators have kindly proffered their assistance in making certain documents available, but they have requested that their names should not be revealed. There is a similar obligation towards a number of Africans and Europeans who allowed me to see the petitions they wrote to the United Nations visiting missions. Sources have been cited which have not been fully identified; references are made to interviews with respondents whose names have not been disclosed. It is hoped, however, that in spite of its obvious limitations and shortcomings this book may cast a few rays of light on what, until not too long ago, was still regarded as 'the darkest of Africa'.

Part One

Rwanda and Burundi:
The Background

1. The Lands and the People

'A LAND of almost ideal beauty'; 'The Switzerland of Africa'—these were the words used by early European travellers to describe the mountain kingdoms that have since become the republics of Rwanda and Burundi. Decades of contact with the West have done little to alter the truth of these comments. For all the turmoil and political convulsions suffered by each state, the physical landscape remains essentially what it was when the first Europeans trudged up the rolling hills—a kind of tropical Switzerland, whose geographical outline, shaped in the form of a human heart, is an appropriate reminder of the countries' central location on the map of Africa.

THE SETTING

Of approximately equal size and contiguous to each other, Rwanda and Burundi are located in the Central African rift valley, slightly south of the equator, in one of the highest-lying areas of the continent. They form an elongated block of highlands of some 34,000 square miles (about twice the size of Belgium), bounded on the east and west by the converging frontiers of Tanzania and the Congo, and in the north by Uganda. Rwanda is separated from Burundi by the Akanyaru river, and in the extreme east by the Kagera river valley, which, after a sharp northward bend, becomes Rwanda's eastern border. Except for the lakeshore region of Burundi, generally hot and humid throughout the year, the annual average temperature for both countries fluctuates around 68°F, with only small seasonal variations. The average rainfall for the area varies between 40 and 50 inches a year, but the volume and frequency of precipitations varies markedly according to the season, and heavy rainfalls are often succeeded by severe droughts.

There is bucolic charm as well as a touch of grandiose beauty in the physical environment of both countries. East of Lake Kivu, and traversing the entire region from north to south, surge the giant peaks of the Congo-Nile crest, reaching a maximum of 14,000 feet in the Virunga chain. This great volcanic massif, covered with thick tropical woodlands, merges into an undulating plateau with altitudes varying between 4,500 and 6,500 feet. The typical landscape consists of hills and valleys scattered with eucalyptus trees and banana groves, alternating with patches of luxuriant pasture. It is a fertile region, ideal for herding and the cultivation of food crops. But it quickly shades off in the east into the savannah zone, where the vegetation may range from vast stretches of arid and treeless grassland to acacia scrublands and bamboo forests. A similar type of savannah-like vegetation is found in the Imbo region, a narrow strip of denuded territory which runs parallel to the Ruzizi valley and along the eastern shore of Lake Tanganyika. If one compares this environment with what the early German travellers saw in other parts of East Africa, one can easily understand their enthusiastic reaction upon discovering the area. 'It is a land flowing with milk and honey', wrote the Duke of Mecklenburg in 1910, 'where the breeding of cattle and bee culture flourish, and the cultivated soil bears rich crops of fruit. A hilly country, thickly populated, full of beautiful scenery, and possessing a climate incomparably fresh and healthy; a land of great fertility, with watercourses which might be termed perennial streams; a land which offers the brightest of prospects to the white settlers.'[1]

Despite this surface impression of lushness and prosperity, Rwanda and Burundi are among the poorest countries in the whole of Africa. Partly because of the lack of any significant mineral resources, and partly because of the absence in the past of incentives for development, their economies have not progressed very far beyond the subsistence level. The only important cash crop is coffee (of the 'arabica' variety), first introduced by the Belgians in 1932 under a compulsory cultivation system. Combined production for both countries increased from 10,000 metric tons in 1942 to 33,629 in 1961, but declined sharply after independence. Although cotton growing has been tried with some success in Burundi, in the Mosso region and along the Ruzizi valley, thus far it accounts for only a small fraction of total cash exports. Secondary commercial crops also include palm plantations along the shores of Lake Tanganyika, and tobacco, barley and wheat in the regions of higher altitude. Experiments in rice growing are at present being conducted in the central region of Rwanda, under the supervision of Nationalist Chinese agronomists; as yet, however, the results do not seem so encouraging as to warrant large-scale production. The main crops are beans, peas, sorghum, cassava, maize, and bananas for the brewing of beer. While these are now grown in sufficient quantities to satisfy the needs of domestic consumption in both countries, one needs only to recall the famines of 1916 and 1943, which caused 50,000 and 36,000 deaths respectively, to realise the limits and vulnerability of their economic resources. This, in turn, may help to explain why Mecklenburg's dreams of white settlement never materialised, at least on a substantial scale. An official report, written in 1920, stated: 'The current estimate is that in Rwanda a maximum of a dozen serious and reasonably well-off farmers could settle down on the land without causing prejudice to the natives.'[2] By 1958, there were 1,218 bona fide settlers in Rwanda and Burundi, of whom 550 lived in Bujumbura (Burundi).[3]

Apart from the sheer paucity of natural resources, a major source of economic stagnation lies in the perennial pressure of over-population on the land. With a total of roughly 5 million people, almost evenly distributed between the two countries, the area has the highest population densities in Africa: census figures for 1955 indicate an average density of 227 per square mile in Rwanda and 185 in Burundi. At the present rate of increase (3·3 per cent per annum), their populations are likely to double in about thirty years. Over-population has led to a continued exodus of African labourers to the neighbouring territories: over 300,000 Banyarwanda seek employment in Uganda every year during the cotton-picking season, and many of them are now permanently settled in and around Kampala. But the flow of emigration has not been commensurate with the growth of the population, and, while it may have provided temporary relief to some saturated areas (especially in Rwanda), it did not occur on a sufficient scale to alleviate the growing social and communal tensions arising from the scarcity and unequal distribution of cultivable areas.

A further strain on land resources is the high density of the cattle population, numbering nearly 3 million in 1956. As in most other pastoral societies of East Africa, the herding of cattle had more than just an economic significance; the ownership of cows was not only an important status symbol, but an essential ingredient in the traditional socio-political systems of Rwanda and Burundi. Although their role in contemporary society is no longer what it used to be, the sleek, lyre-horned Ndanga cows are still an all too familiar sight. Their sheer number tends to accelerate the process of erosion on deforested hillsides, having disastrous effects on soil productivity. Moreover, the importance attached in the past to the ownership of cattle is one reason why the adjustment of agricultural production to the requirements of a fast-growing population has proved such a difficult task, and why, until recently, the most fertile areas remained overstocked and overcropped.

The same factors which have tended to limit economic intercourse also inhibited the growth of an economic infra-structure. Because of the mountainous nature of the terrain and the absence of incentives for large-scale industrial development, communication facilities are still very inadequate, even by African standards. Railways are non-existent, and until 1922 there were no roads for vehicles. The main axis of communication between the two countries (Bujumbura-Kigali-Kakitumba) was not completed until 1931. At present there are about 5,400 miles of fair weather roads, but virtually no tarred roads. Despite the improvements envisaged by the administering authorities after the Second World War, an official publication lamented in 1959 that 'the building of arterial and feeder roads provided for in the Ten-Year Plan [had] progressed very little'.[4] Since then, neglect of regular road maintenance work has, if anything, tended to further restrict access to the interior.

With a population of 55,000, Bujumbura is both the capital city of Burundi and the main port of entry from the south. The new port, completed in 1960 at the cost of 149 million Belgian francs, has a handling capacity of approximately 5,000 tons of merchandise annually. It is the only trading centre of some importance, as well as the main processing centre for coffee and cotton. Although trading and manufacturing activities are no longer as prominent as they were before independence, the bustling atmosphere of Bujumbura offers a striking contrast with the air of puritan austerity that one encounters in Kigali, Rwanda's capital city. With a population of 4,000 and only one asphalt road, Kigali shares none of the characteristics of large, cosmopolitan towns. So minimal is the rate of urbanisation in and around Kigali, so limited is the incidence of commercial and industrial activities, that it is perhaps better described as an overgrown village.

From these considerations emerges a significant and paradoxical relationship between the rate of urbanisation and commercialisation in each country and the capacity of their respective political institutions to withstand the impact of modernisation. However limited and peripheral in their incidence, that processes of social mobilisation were carried out on a comparatively more intensive scale in Burundi provides an interesting index of the greater pliancy of its monarchical institutions.

Nonetheless, the social environment has set definite limitations on the 'staying power' of the Burundi monarchy. In the course of the last few years Bujumbura has provided the setting for the emergence of something very close to an urban 'mob', or at least of new elite groups, eager to exert their influence and in time to challenge the legitimacy of monarchic rule. This, coupled with the fact that Bujumbura happened to be the seat of the monarchy, of the government and of parliament, has operated to focus processes of change on the capital city, and to make it the epicentre of Burundi politics. That the fate of the monarchy should have twice depended on the outcome of a power play staged in Bujumbura is indeed symptomatic of the extent to which, in recent times, national politics have become polarised around the capital city. Nothing of this sort has yet happened in Rwanda. This does not mean that there has not been a lack of balance in processes of social change, only that this unevenness has had little to do with the rural-urban split. There are no towns in Rwanda of a size comparable with Bujumbura, and hence no scope for the kind of social and economic forces which in Burundi have affected political processes and institutions. Social change in Rwanda has been a primarily rural phenomenon.

Yet in each country the same ecological factors have tended to impede the promotion of systematic change in the society as a whole. Real villages do not exist. Today, as in the more distant past, the hill remains the primary focus of political activity in the countryside. Beyond the hill there is relatively little sense of unity among the rural communities; even where caste solidarities are most in evidence, fragmentation and parochialism are the rule rather than the exception. And in the absence of adequate communications, the forbidding nature of the topography raises further obstacles in the way of any large-scale political mobilisation. Thus one might be tempted to dismiss the significance of the ecological factor as an independent variable and instead argue that in Rwanda the traditional political institutions produced an awareness of the need for change, as well as an orientation to change, which did not exist in Burundi.

This is only partially true, however. In Rwanda as in Burundi change has been extremely slow to penetrate into the fabric of the traditional societies. This is why the Rwandese revolution has been so violent and so untypical in many ways of what has happened elsewhere in Africa: violent because the very slowness of the changes attempted through constitutional reforms made it necessary at one point to substitute intimidation for persuasion; untypical because of the peculiar circumstances under which violence was used, i.e. under the auspices or at least with the tacit approval of the Belgian authorities. Yet neither of these factors provides an adequate explanation for the contrasting patterns of change, for these, in fact, reflect the radically different ways in which change has been contained within the limits of their respective traditional systems. It is to these differences that we must now direct our attention.

THE INDIGENOUS SOCIETIES

The dominant impression conveyed by much of the literature dealing with Rwanda and Burundi is that their societies were essentially feudal in character. Certainly, to the extent it stresses the personal nature of relationships among individuals, or, to use Marc Bloch's expression, 'the ties of obedience and protection which bind man to man',[5] the feudal analogy draws attention to an important feature of their traditional societies. By emphasising certain common characteristics, however, the term 'feudalism' tends to obscure the crucial differences that have developed over the years between these two kingdoms, and thus conveys a degree of uniformity in the sphere of social and political relations which did not always exist in either society.[6] In attempting to reconstruct the traditional political systems of Rwanda and Burundi the terminology associated with European feudalism cannot serve as a substitute for historical investigation, for only by reference to history can one explain the structural and cultural variations which in recent years have shaped the course of their political evolution.

Historical Perspectives

As in the case of many other African societies, the kingdoms of Rwanda and Burundi developed their present territorial base partly through conquest and partly through peaceful assimilation. The pattern of expansion seems to have been the same throughout the interlacustrine area: under the leadership of a royal clan, successive waves of nomadic pastoralists spread their domination over the indigenous Bantu societies, whose customs and traditions they gradually assimilated into their own culture. This is admittedly an exceedingly simplistic view of historical realities; the 'conquest-and-assimilation' theory of state formation has been convincingly discredited by a number of historians, notably Herbert Lewis and Jan Vansina. There is indeed every reason to believe that the emergence of centralised state structures in both countries must have occurred in part through the stimuli or conditioning influences of pre-existing 'primary' kingdoms of Bantu origins. Nontheless, the decisive expansion in the territorial scale of each kingdom took place under the aegis of an 'alien' minority.

In both kingdoms the invading tribes were Tutsi or Hima pastoralists. Although their origins are not firmly established, their physical features suggest obvious ethnic affinities with the Galla tribes of southern Ethiopia. Commenting on their proverbial tallness and graceful stature, Mecklenburg observed: 'They possess that same graceful indolence in gait which is peculiar to Oriental peoples, and their bronze-brown skin reminds me of the inhabitants of the more hilly parts of northern Africa. Unmistakable evidences of a foreign strain are betrayed in their high foreheads, the curve of their nostrils, and the fine, oval shape of their faces.'[7] Dr Richard Kandt, the first German Resident in Rwanda, was equally impressed by 'their gigantic stature, the sublimity of their speech, the tasteful and unobtrusive way of their dress, their noble traits and their quiet, penetrating, often even witty and irritating eyes'.[8] As they drifted southward into the plateau area they came in contact with the indigenous Hutu peasant populations. Generally short and stocky, the Hutu share the physical characteristics of other Bantu tribes of Central Africa. 'They are a medium-sized type of people', wrote Mecklenburg, 'whose ungainly figures betoken hard toil, and who patiently bow themselves in abject bondage to the later arrived yet ruling race, the Tutsi.'[9] Although their density in relation to the Tutsi group varies greatly from one region to the next, they make up between 83 and 85 per cent of the total population in each country. If the exact date of their arrival is impossible to determine, there is no question that the first inhabitants to settle in the area were not the Hutu but the Twa, a group of pygmoid forest dwellers who constitute less than one per cent of the present population.

How the Tutsi minority managed to extend their hegemony over the mass of the Hutu peasants is a question to which different people have given different answers. For Hans Meyer, the German authority on Burundi, the secret of Tutsi domination lay in their innate superiority— in 'their superior intelligence, calmness, smartness, racial pride, solidarity and political talent'.[10] A more widely accepted explanation is that the Tutsi used their cattle as a lever of economic power to subdue the indigenous tribes; according to this view, the key to the whole situation was a special form of cattle clientship, or cattle-contract, through which the Tutsi oligarchy acquired sovereign political rights over their Hutu clients. Historically, however, the situation appears to have been much more complex. At some time in the remote past wandering bands of Tutsi and Hima pastoralists infiltrated among the indigenous tribes, with whom they established a symbiotic relationship. In some places these intruders set themselves up as minor chiefs controlling a few hills; elsewhere, relations between the two communities were essentially of a commercial nature, involving the exchange of cattle for agricultural products. The little that is known of this early period suggests that the predominant form of political organisation was the clan or lineage group.

The transition from 'statelessness' to kingship was achieved by the amalgamation of a few autonomous chieftaincies into a small nuclear kingdom, under the leadership of a royal clan. In Rwanda this critical step took place in the Bwanacambwe region (near Kigali) under the reign of a Tutsi king named Ruganzu Bwimba, probably in the fifteenth century.[11] In Burundi the creation of the nuclear cell seems to have taken place somewhat later, toward the middle of the seventeenth century, and under the guidance of a Hima king who came from the neighbouring kingdom of Buha. According to one informant: 'The

19

Hutu had taken over the country and divided it into several parts. . . .
It was at that time that foreign kings entered the country. The first king
was Ntare, whose name means "rock". . . . Ntare belonged to the same
family as the kings of the Ha country, of the Shuubi country, of the
Nyoro country, of the Toro country. He was a Muhinda of the clan of
the Bahinda. His mother was Inanjonaki. His father is unknown.'[12]

A final stage of development saw the gradual incorporation of the out-
lying areas into an expanding territorial unit. In Rwanda this process
began in the sixteenth century, with the absorption of what is today the
central region of Rwanda (Nduga-Marangara) into the nuclear kingdom.
With the accession of Ruganzu Ndori to power, in the seventeenth
century, a series of invasions was launched against formerly independent
Hutu communities which resulted in a further expansion of Rwanda's
boundaries, but the ultimate stage in this process of territorial accretion
was not completed until the latter half of the nineteenth century, under
the reign of Mwami Kigeri Rwabugiri, one of Rwanda's most prestigious
historical figures.

Rwabugiri has been credited with a spectacular series of conquests
and political reforms. In a lecture to the Université Coloniale de Belgique, in 1929, J. M. Derscheid described 'the essential characteristics
of Rwabugiri's policies' as follows:

> To strengthen the military power of the nation; to rest the central
> institutions of the realm firmly upon the support of agricultural
> elements, hence of plebeians; to sap the power of the clans, of the
> great feudatories and provincial chiefs at home, and at the same
> time divert the energies of the Batutsi from internal matters to
> military expeditions abroad. . . . I cannot think of a better comparison
> of Rwabugiri's policies than with those pursued by Louis XI in
> the domestic realm and Charles the Bold in the foreign realm.[13]

Mgr Léon Classe, one of Rwanda's first Apostolic Vicars, gave the
following interesting account of Rwabugiri's reign:

> Rwabugiri was a conquering monarch, benevolent towards the masses,
> ruthless towards the Batutsi. The masses loved him because anyone
> could approach him and lay his claims and grievances before him.
> The Batutsi feared him because of his utter disregard for human
> life. . . . Ceaselessly at war with his neighbours, Rwabugiri led the
> Banyarwanda almost everywhere, providing them with unparalleled
> opportunities to acquire abundant loot. . . . We had come a long way
> from the time when the kings of Rwanda stood within the narrow
> confines of the Nduga and Marangara regions.[14]

Where the conquered populations were already organised under a dominant Tutsi lineage (as in the case of the Mubari, Bugesera and Nduga regions), ethnic affinities provided a major integrative bond and made for rapid assimilation. The case of the kingdom of Gisaka is the only notable exception: according to A. d'Arianoff, no less than seven expeditions were launched against the Tutsi chiefs of Gisaka between 1835 and 1852, before they were finally brought to heel by Rwogera's warriors.[15] But in those areas occupied by autonomous Hutu communities, the conquering tribes were faced with a very different situation. Where these communities had already evolved a state system of their own (as in the north*),[16] or where natural obstacles hampered Tutsi penetration, the extension of the Tutsi imperium proved very long and difficult. Thus the effective annexation of the small Hutu kingdoms in the northern and eastern 'marches' was not completed until the early 1920s, and would probably have taken even longer if it had not been for the military assistance proffered first by the German and later by the Belgian authorities.

The story of Burundi's quest for 'lebensraum' is remarkably similar. From a small core area situated in the central region (Nkoma), King Ntare Rushatsi (c.1675–1705) extended his rule over the Bututsi, Kilimiro and Buyenzi regions. His successors saw their territorial ambitions temporarily thwarted by the concommitant expansion of the neighbouring kingdoms of Bugesera in the east, Buha in the south-east and Rwanda in the north. But in the first half of the nineteenth century a new wave of conquests brought most of the peripheral areas into the fold of the central kingdom; this was accomplished under the reign of Mwami Ntare Rugaamba (c.1795–1852), who played for Burundi a role somewhat similar to that played by Kigeri Rwabugiri for Rwanda. Through his conquest of approximately half of Buha, the Buyogoma, Ruyigi and Bugesera regions, Ntare Rugaamba expanded the original boundaries of his kingdom on a wide scale, incorporating into his domains sizable chunks of present-day Rwanda and Tanzania.

By then, however, the two kingdoms had spawned entirely different

* The Hutu populations of northern Rwanda are also referred to as Kiga (or Chiga) and are ethnically related to the Kiga of the Kigezi district of southern Uganda. Unlike their Uganda kinsmen, however, described by Professor Edel as possessing a 'basically anarchic structure', the Kiga of northern Rwanda developed fairly centralised political structures, in which the key figure was a 'king' (*muhinza*). This process of political centralisation seems to have occurred in response to the forays of invading Tutsi tribes, or in opposition to the existing threat of a Tutsi centralised system in the south. (I am grateful to Miss Rachel Yeld for drawing my attention to this point.)

types of political organisation. By 1900 Rwanda had achieved a remarkable degree of centralisation. Except for the northern region, still awaiting incorporation, all major administrative offices at the local level came under the direct control of the king (*mwami*). As in Buganda, where the authority of the clan heads (*bataka*) was gradually curtailed in favour of chiefs appointed by the king (*kabaka*), the Rwanda kings consolidated their rule by suppressing the autonomy of the local hereditary chiefs and by replacing them with loyal retainers of Tutsi extraction. Although we know virtually nothing of how and when this major structural transformation occurred, it is difficult to see how it could have happened in the absence of a strong military establishment. The authority devolved upon the army chiefs in the traditional political structure of Rwanda bears testimony to the crucial role they must have played in bringing about national unification. In Burundi, on the other hand, where the military structure was conspicuously weak, the contest between the monarchy and corporate descent groups resulted in far greater political decentralisation. There was no parallel in Burundi for the centralised, hierarchical pattern of authority found in Rwanda. Instead, power was fragmented among relatively autonomous political units, each under the authority of a prince. This authority was directly related to the rules of royal succession, as the strength of a prince's claims ultimately depended on the genealogical remoteness or proximity of the dynasty from which he claimed descent. The dynastic names of the Burundi kings were fixed by tradition as Ntare, Mwezi, Mutaga and Mwambutsa—in that order—and their immediate descendants were known, respectively, as Batare, Bezi, Bataga and Bambutsa. According to a tradition introduced under the reign of Ntare II Rugaamba (*c.* 1795–1852), the descendants of Ntare would hold office as *ganwa* until the reign of the second Ntare, when a new generation of *ganwa* would come to power; likewise, the offspring of Mwezi would remain in office until another Mwezi became king, and so on. But these rules never became firmly institutionalised, and thus the accession of each new king released new opportunities for conflict. Not only were the incumbents disinclined to surrender their authority to new aspirants, but their power was by that time so firmly entrenched that they could easily face a trial of strength with the monarchy.*

* In Rwanda, as in Burundi, the kings assumed the dynastic names prescribed by tradition—Cyilima, Kigeli, Mibambwe, Yuhi and Mutara—but the sons who failed to become kings never acquired a position comparable to that of the *ganwa*. The ruthless punishment dealt to potential challengers was enough to deter even the most ambitious of the royal princes. While the heirs to the throne were all selected from the same paternal clan (Banyiginya), their maternal clans could be any one of four; thus, in those rare instances where royal succession

This state of affairs calls to mind a sequence of events of considerable historical significance to an understanding of subsequent developments in Burundi. Since the story has already been told elsewhere in greater detail,[17] the following brief summary will suffice. During the first half of the nineteenth century, Mwami Ntare II Rugaamba (*c.* 1795–1852) established his reputation as one of Burundi's most illustrious kings. He owed much of his fame to his spectacular territorial conquests, having successively incorporated into his domain the Bugufi region in the east, parts of Buha and Buyogoma, and a substantial portion of southern Rwanda. The spoils of victory went to his sons, however, and in particular to Rwasha and Twarereye, who, after taking over the administration of the new provinces, proceeded to assert their independence from the crown. This act of rebellion (for this is what it amounted to) led to bitter conflicts between Ntare's sons and his successor on the throne, Mwami Mwezi Kisabo (*c.* 1852–1908), culminating with the death of Twarereye at the battle of Nkoondo, fought near the traditional capital of Muramvya around 1860. The dynastic feuds between the king and the princes went on unabated for many years, and by 1900 Mwezi Kisabo could claim effective control over only half his kingdom, while the other half remained in the hands of Ntare's rebellious sons, from then on known as the Batare. Thus what had initially begun as a series of territorial accretions led to violent rivalries among the representatives of different dynasties. By appointing his sons to rule as his deputies over conquered territories, Ntare unwittingly sowed the seeds of a bitter opposition among the princes of the blood, which in recent times found expression in a resurgence of political antagonisms between certain members of the Batare family and the descendants of King Mwezi, the Bezi.

From this brief incursion into the past one can detect some significant differences in the process of cultural amalgamation which have taken place in each kingdom. By far the most important concerns the very prominent status achieved by the princes of the blood, or *ganwa*, in the political system of Burundi. Because of the special eminence conferred upon them by the accidents of history, they became identified as a separate ethnic group, whose prestige in society ranked far above that of the ordinary Tutsi. If, in addition, one remembers that there are in Burundi two distinctive categories of Tutsi—the 'low-caste'

---

was attended by intrigue and conflict, disturbances stemmed from competition among the maternal clans of the eligible princes—as happened at Rucuncu in 1896. See *infra*, chapter 2, p. 57–8. For an excellent discussion of the dynastic implications of the Rucuncu coup, see M. d'Hertefelt and A. Coupez, *La Royauté Sacrée de l'Ancien Rwanda*, Tervueren 1964, pp. 333–4.

Tutsi-Hima and the 'upper-caste' Tutsi-Banyaruguru—the total picture of society appears decidedly more variegated than in Rwanda.* This greater variety of status groups, ranging from prince to commoner, is one major reason why in the past Burundi society was relatively free of racial tensions; just as the degrees of social distance within the Tutsi stratum were at times far more perceptible than between Tutsi and Hutu, the distance between them and the princely families was equally if not more conspicuous.

Another factor of social cohesion associated with *ganwa* rule lies in the very nature of the competitive relations that have developed among them. Simmel's observation that 'conflict may also bring persons and groups together which otherwise have nothing to do with each other'[18] gives a clue to an understanding of the changing patterns of Hutu-Tutsi relations created by princely rivalries. These rivalries caused the contestants, including the *mwami*, to seek the support of both Hutu and Tutsi, and this could hardly have occurred in a situation of unadulterated harmony among the ruling elites. Since neither the *mwami* nor the *ganwa* could hope to exercise a monopoly of power, and since their security depended ultimately on their ability to generate support from below, they had to adopt a far more conciliatory attitude towards the 'lower orders' than might have been the case. In Rwanda, by contrast, there was no need for the chiefs to pander to the masses because the army was not only powerful but entirely loyal to the Tutsi cause. While in Rwanda monarchical absolutism was a major determinant of the rigidity of the caste structure, in Burundi the institutionalisation of rebellion gave the social system a greater measure of internal cohesion at the local or regional level.

Equally noteworthy are the chronological variations relating to the different stages of Tutsi expansion. As one might expect, in both countries the most recently incorporated areas are also those where regional

* Another factor contributing to the greater flexibility of Burundi's social structure concerns the different rankings of social prestige attached to the various patrilineages (*imiryango*) within each caste. Thus, within the Tutsi-Banyaruguru (literally, 'the people from above'), by far the most prestigious ethno-cultural segment within the Tutsi caste, the usual distinctions made by the Barundi are between the very good families (*imiryango myiza*), those that are rather good (*imiryango myiza cane*), neither good nor bad (*imiryango si myiza si mibi*) and bad (*imiryango mibi*). No less than forty-four different patrilineages thus enter into the Tutsi-Banyaruguru segment, each in turn falling into a specific social category. Very much the same type of classification and terminology applies to the Hutu. In this fashion lineage affiliations could substantially rectify and even reverse the formal rank-ordering established through the caste system. For further information, see J. Keuppens, *L'Urundi Ancien et Moderne*, Bujumbura 1956, mimeo.

sentiments are the most noticeable. In Burundi, for instance, the inhabitants of the Mosso and of the northern parts of the Imbo and Mugamba regions still have a strong sense of regional consciousness. But there is no equivalent in Burundi for the rugged individualism and fierce sense of autonomy which characterise the Hutu populations of northern Rwanda. Nor is there any precedent in Burundi for such a late annexation as that of northern Rwanda. That this area was one where the duration and intensity of contact between Hutu and Tutsi was minimal helps to explain why even to this day it represents a distinctive sub-culture within the broader context of Rwanda society.

Finally, differences in the patterns of Tutsi immigration have affected the geographical distribution of ethnic groups in different ways. In Burundi, the bulk of Tutsi elements are found, logically enough, in the Bututsi region, where they make up between 80 and 85 per cent of the local population. Most other areas have only a sprinkling of Tutsi. About one-third of the country is inhabited by a mixture of Hutu and Hima populations, with virtually no Tutsi. In Rwanda, however, Tutsi elements were spread almost evenly throughout the country. The only notable exception was the northern region (Ndorwa, Mutara, Mulera), where the Tutsi never accounted for more than a tiny fraction of the total population. In practice this meant that the caste structure of Rwanda was fairly rigid throughout the area, while in Burundi local variations dictated a much greater flexibility in the application of the caste system. And just as in Rwanda the uniformity of the caste structure invited a similar uniformity of political organisation, in Burundi regional differences in the pattern of social stratification called for a greater political diversification.

Whatever factors and circumstances have contributed to shape Burundi's traditional social structure, evidences of inter-caste mobility are undeniable. In Professor Albert's words: 'The life history of an individual is limited but not fully determined by the formal structures of the society. The dynamics of the social system make provision for political and economic mobility by which all but the most wretched Barundi know how to profit.'[19] Applied to Rwanda, this characterisation would amount to a travesty of socio-political realities. Seldom have the threads of migrations, history and cultural evolution produced such striking differences—and similarities—of social structure as between Rwanda and Burundi, and it is from that perspective that one must elucidate the divergences of structure and orientation apparent in their traditional political systems.

The Traditional Polities

That the kingdoms of Rwanda and Burundi differed from each other in some essential ways was clearly sensed by early European observers. Hans Meyer, for example, noted that 'under Mwezi Kisabo's predecessors, and Kisabo himself, Urundi did not progress towards a united state to the same extent as Rwanda. The kingdom had not yet created such a supreme position of power over all the Tutsi chiefs as in Rwanda, although Kisabo had concentrated his long and active life on this task with great energy and much success.'[20] The best summary of the relative positions of the kings (*bami*) is found in a 1921 report of one of Belgium's greatest colonial governors, Pierre Ryckmans:

> From time immemorial the policy of the *bami* of Rwanda followed a course of parcelling out the country to infinity, since large homogeneous provinces could easily become centres of resistance. Instead of giving large domains to his favourites, the *mwami* preferred to grant his vassals separate hills, distributed about the country. Within the large fiefs, he carved out small dependencies where devoted persons who owed him everything found excellent observation posts from which to watch vassals who were very powerful, and thus to counterbalance their influence. Besides, he encouraged rivalries by giving to one vassal administration of Hutu lands, to the other, authority over the Tutsi and the disposition of cattle. Finally he drained off the power of the great lords by making of his capital a centre where chiefs came to pay court. . . .
>
> The situation was different in Urundi. Here as in Rwanda power is a family affair. But in Urundi the family of the *mwami* possesses a special and separate existence. It is united by strong bonds and enjoys a special status. All its members, whatever the branch to which they belong, have the generic name *baganwa*. In place of the policy of splintering to infinity pursued by the *bami* of Rwanda, those of Urundi sought on the contrary to reconstitute periodically extended blocs to the profit of their sons. These, placed as often as possible in distant provinces, were the strongest support of the *mwami*, as much against enemies from outside as against possible revolts of the princes of an older branch.[21]

One is reminded here of the classic distinction between 'pyramidal' and 'hierarchical' patterns of authority. Burundi, with its highly decentralised organisation and its different levels of segmentation, was the example par excellence of a pyramidal system. The political fragmentation engendered by *ganwa* rivalries produced a constellation of independent territorial units, each constituting 'a kingdom in miniature, owing only a conditional allegiance to the larger unity of which it formed a part'.[22] In Rwanda, on the other hand, where political centralisation was carried to an extreme, the *mwami* was the source and symbol of all authority. He alone could confer legitimacy upon subordinate ranks. Whereas the *mwami* of Burundi was little more than primus inter pares in relation to the princes of the blood, the *mwami* of Rwanda came as close to the image of an absolute ruler as any other African monarch.

The despotic character of the Rwanda kingship was nowhere more clearly evidenced than in the bureaucratisation of subordinate political roles, and the precarious tenure of the occupants. The political system was one in which a triple hierarchy of army chiefs, land chiefs and cattle chiefs—all recruited from the dominant stratum—radiated from the provincial capital to the provinces, and from the provinces to the districts. Each province was entrusted to an army chief, and each district to a land chief and a cattle chief who were responsible for the collection of tithes in produce and cattle. Beneath this triumvirate spread a vast network of subchiefs from whom tribute was exacted for the higher chiefs and the kings. How much power the chiefs and subchiefs claimed for themselves, and for how long, was entirely dependent upon the *mwami*'s grace. They were 'bureaucrats', as Lucy Mair noted, 'in the sense that they did not claim their position by right or inheritance or by virtue of any prior connexion with the area to which they were appointed',[23] but from the *mwami*'s will.

By contrast Burundi tended to look at best like a loose aggregate of semi-autonomous chiefdoms; at worst like a cluster of warring principalities. Commenting on the state of affairs in the early days of German rule, Hans Meyer observed: '[The king's] absolutism is only pretence and the true rulers are the heads of the royal kin, the *baganwa*, who let the royal puppet dance according to their wishes.'[24] Even those *ganwa* who paid formal allegiance to the king retained sovereign powers within the limits of their domain. They were free to appoint their own subchiefs, to raise their own armies in time of war, to exact tribute and administer justice as they deemed fit. So circumscribed were the powers of the *mwami* by princely prerogatives that one may indeed wonder whether his writ was ever more authoritative or extensive than any of the *ganwa*'s. Below the *ganwa*, the administrative structure resembled that of Rwanda, with power fragmented among relatively small territorial units, each under the leadership of an appointed subchief; but the pattern of recruitment was substantially different. In Burundi the subchiefs were often recruited from the same clans but not necessarily from the same caste. Indeed, a remarkable feature of the traditional system was the comparatively high proportion of Hutu chiefs who held office in the royal domains (the so-called *ivyivare*). One administrative report, for example, notes that 'there existed in the territoire of Rutuna [prior to the arrival of the Belgians] several estates depending directly on the *mwami*. These estates were administered by some Bahutu who were not subject to the *baganwa* but acted like independent chiefs.'[25] The same report goes on to recount how, after these Bahutu chiefs were dismissed by the administration, in 1931, and their estates amalgamated with those of a neighbouring *muganwa*, the latter was unable to command obedience from the incorporated local population. He, too, had to be dismissed. That the king relied so heavily upon Hutu elements for administering the crown lands helps to explain the long-lasting attachment of the Hutu peasantry to the cause of the Burundi monarchy.

This tendency to extend the bases of political recruitment to different ethnic strata also applied to a wide array of advisory roles for which there was no equivalent in Rwanda. The officials in charge of performing these roles were found at each level of the political hierarchy and were collectively known as *bashigantahe*. There were three categories of *bashigantahe*: at the lowest level, were the so-called *bashigantahe bo ku mugina*, entrusted with the task of settling disputes among families or individuals on a hill; at the *ganwa* level, disputes for which local remedies proved of no avail were handled by the *bashigantahe bo ku nama*; still higher up in the hierarchy were the *bashigantahe bo mu rulimbi*, attached to the royal court.[26] Even though their functions were essentially judicial, the *bashigantahe* could wield considerable political influence. As one report explains: 'The *mushigantahe* is the natural counsellor of his countrymen and of the traditional political authorities, because of his wide knowledge of the country, his judgement, his foresight and his sense of justice.' Whether by virtue of their training and personal experience, or because of the nature of their office, they generally enjoyed considerable esteem in society—'the *mushigantahe* of the *baganwa* was always held in higher repute than an ordinary chief, and those who were in the entourage of the *mwami* were more influential than the *ganwa* themselves'.[27] Equally significant in terms of inter-group relations is that they were often selected on the basis of their own merits, which meant that even a Hutu could qualify for office and thus achieve higher status than many ordinary Tutsi.

In a sense, the *bashigantahe* formed the democratic core of Burundi society, a built-in hierarchy of political roles which contained within itself the making of a parliamentary body. That the deputies to the

National Assembly should have been called *bashigantahe* is not mere coincidence. The political beliefs associated with this traditional class of officials, and in particular the belief that it performed a legitimate and useful function in society, expressed the deep affective commitment of the Barundi to the notion of limited government. According to André Makarakiza, 'the dignity and office of *bashigantahe* are accessible to all capable subjects regardless of their social background. Only the Batwa, living on the margin of civil life, are excluded. The institution of the *bashigantahe* . . . therefore insures the advantages of a democratic government, despite the fact that the executive power is almost entirely in the hands of the *baganwa*.'[28]

This is not to say that conciliar organs were unknown in Rwanda. The more important chiefs of the realm, the so-called *batware w'intebe* (chiefs of the stool), did act on occasion as a 'supreme council'. Yet the expression conveys an impression of formalism and efficiency which hardly fits the contextual realities of traditional Rwanda. These 'supreme councillors' were in fact little more than a coterie of self-seeking sycophantic courtiers. As client-chiefs they had no hereditary claims to authority. Their tenure in office depended largely on the whims of the sovereign, or, better, on their ability to turn his whims to their advantage.

What is one to make of these differences in the structure of authority in each kingdom? The first point to note, somewhat in the nature of a paradox, is that the very weakness of the Burundi monarchy has operated to strengthen its legitimacy to an extent virtually unparalleled in Rwanda during the years immediately preceding independence.

Unlike the situation which developed in Rwanda, where all attempts at constitutional reform were generally interpreted by the crown as a threat to its legitimacy, in Burundi the monarchy had already been weakened to the point where the central issue no longer centred upon whether or not the crown should be maintained as symbol of legitimacy but on what particular group of princes should be allowed to gain power. The issue of monarchic versus republican legitimacy did not intrude upon the political scene until after independence, and, characteristically, not until the monarchy had again shown tendencies towards royal absolutism. Before then the key issue was the Bezi-Batare conflict. Although the Bezi did use the symbol of the crown to fortify their claims to authority, at no time before independence did the fate of the monarchy become a major bone of contention between Bezi and Batare. It is not only that the saliency of the Bezi-Batare rivalry tended to overshadow the more fundamental issue of monarchic versus republican rule; the constitutional issue had already been settled, for on one point at least there seemed to be unanimous agreement among the contestants:

the position of the *mwami* in the future political system should be that of a constitutional monarch. Whatever opposition the crown might have otherwise attracted unto itself was automatically deflected against the *ganwa* or the parties with which they became identified, as it had never become as closely associated with either chiefly rule or caste supremacy as in Rwanda.

Thus there occurred in Burundi a phenomenon somewhat similar to that which elsewhere in the world has enabled constitutional monarchies to survive the surge of modern political competition, a phenomenon which Edward Shils and Michael Young have described in the following terms:

> Whereas the lands where personal or absolute monarchy prevailed were beset by revolution, countries of constitutional monarchy became politically stable and orderly. . . . When protected from the full blast of destructiveness by its very *powerlessness* royalty is able to bask in the sunshine of an affection unadulterated by its opposite. The institution of the constitutional monarchy is supported by one of the mechanisms by which the mind defends itself from conflict, namely, by the segregation of mutually antagonistic sentiments, previously directed towards a single object, on to discrete and separate objects.[29]

To the element of powerlessness must also be added the relative openness of Burundi's caste structure. Indeed a major reason why the Burundi monarchy was able to direct 'mutually antagonistic sentiments' to institutions and agencies other than itself is that it never became as closely associated with either chiefly rule or caste supremacy as in Rwanda.

We have seen how in Burundi princely rivalries had the effect of encouraging social cohesion between Hutu and Tutsi while in Rwanda the absence of such rivalries tended to preserve or intensify the rigidity of the caste structure. In Rwanda chiefly rule and caste supremacy were both so intimately associated with the pure authority of the crown that any statutory limitation on the privileges of the dominant caste other than those decreed by the *mwami* implied a corresponding limitation of the powers of the crown. This, however, is precisely what the system could not tolerate. In contrast Burundi showed a much greater flexibility. Tutsi hegemony never became a critical issue (at least, not until after independence) for the simple reason that it had never been firmly institutionalised. Moreover, whatever limitations were placed on the powers of the chiefs were more likely than not to enhance, rather than restrict, the authority of the crown. A last point, implicit in what has already been said, is that the Burundi monarchy was relatively free of ideological constraints, and hence all the more adaptable. Compared to Rwanda, where ideological symbols and myths carefully specified the limits beyond which the monarchy could not innovate without at the same time endangering its own legitimacy, Burundi had very little in the way of precisely articulated ideology. The climate of ideological vagueness surrounding the monarchy made it all the more receptive to ideological change.

In view of the very different operative ideals shared by each society, and of the different kinds of limitations they have placed upon institutions, it may be useful at this point to investigate in somewhat greater detail their respective political cultures, belief-systems and mythologies.

*Ideologies and Norms**

All cultures are myth-sustained in that they derive their legitimacy from a body of values and beliefs which tend to embellish or falsify historical truth. But some more so than others. If there is any validity to Malinowski's argument that 'the function of a myth is to strengthen tradition and endow it with greater value and prestige, by tracing it back to a higher, better, more supernatural reality of initial events',[30] Rwanda is clearly the more cogent example.

What is particularly noteworthy about the social systems of Rwanda and Burundi is not so much that they were both sustained by mythical representations but that myth should have operated selectively, as if by caprice tradition had given a differential value to some of the features shared by each society. There was no equivalent in Burundi for the wealth of traditional literary genres pertaining to the Rwandese monarchy, and even if such material did exist at one point it was obviously not in the interest of the *ganwa* that it should be preserved. Conscious as they were of the circumstances which brought them to power, the *ganwa* naturally feared the verdict of history. For these reasons, as Professor Vansina points out, Burundi was characteristically prejudiced

---

* I am aware that much of what follows suffers from a 'functionalist' bias insofar as primary stress is placed on the static, self-equilibrating aspect of the political systems discussed—and of Rwanda in particular—at the expense of the more dynamic, conflictive elements of their political culture. My only excuse is that the limitations involved in this approach (R. Lemarchand, "Power and Stratification in Rwanda: A Reconsideration", *Cahiers d'Etudes Africains*, Vol. VI, 1966, pp. 592–610) are partially compensated by the advantages it offers from the standpoint of comparative analysis. For a corrective to what some might regard here as a pseudo-historical reconstruction, see, in addition to the article cited above, R. Lemarchand, "Political Instability in Africa: The case of Rwanda and Burundi", *Civilisations*, Vol. XVI, 1966, p. 310 ff.

against history.* This is not to say that the field of oral traditions was completely barren; a variety of folktales and legends filled the gaps of history, of the same kind that one finds in Rwanda under the names of *umugani* and *igitekerezo*. But in Rwanda these sources were supplemented by the memory of court historians whose task was to hand down to posterity the glorious traditions of the realm—not as history might have it but, rather, as royal ordinance prescribed.

Not unnaturally, in Rwanda kingship was the focal point around which mythical imagery clustered, as if to reinforce the exalted position the monarchy already enjoyed in the political system. Three major types of traditions aimed at magnifying the office of the king: the *ubwiru*, the *ubucurabwenge* and the *ibisigo*. The last, transmitted by a category of official bards known as *abasizi*, sought to re-enact the story of the monarchy in a supernatural context, one in which the Rwanda kings were inevitably cast in the mould of supermen. Something of the same epic quality transpires from the *ubucurabwenge*—a collection of traditions which preserved the genealogy of the *bami*—and from the *ubwiru*—an elaborate body of ceremonial prescriptions, described by Alexis Kagame as the 'esoteric code' of the Rwanda monarchy.[31] Although the text of the *ubwiru* is no longer a secret, much of it remains esoteric, at least to the uninitiated reader. Despite or because of its obscurities, the *ubwiru* played a central role in the myth-system of Rwanda.

The *ubwiru* was the ritual code of the monarchy, and the guardians of the code, the *biru*, were its sole authoritative interpreters. But the significance of the code extended far beyond the sphere of ritualised knowledge. Since it also enshrined the testament of the departing king and the choice of his successor, the interpreters of the code were also the interpreters of the *mwami's* will, and in this capacity they tended to act more like a constitutional court than a Delphic oracle. As Professor Maquet observed: 'That traditional body was not unlike a constitution in a modern state and the *biru* institution can be said to have had a role similar to that of a supreme court judging whether a new rule is compatible with the fundamental charter of the country.'[32] Although history

---

* See Jan Vansina, *De la Tradition Orale: Essai de Methode Historique*, Tervueren 1961, passim. Some Belgian administrators admitted that this paucity of reliable oral traditions imposed major handicaps on their work. As one of them lamented, in 1935: 'It is extremely difficult to obtain any sort of reliable information about the *bami* (of Burundi). Even those natives who gravitated around Mwezi Kisabo ignore the feats of his predecessor. . . . How much easier would our work be, including genealogical research, if the court of Burundi had anything like the *ubucurabwenge* of Rwanda!' Letter of Resident Oger Coubeau to J. M. Derscheid; in the Derscheid Collection.

shows that their influence in the sphere of 'power politics' was frequently overshadowed by the countervailing pressure of the great Tutsi lineages, this does not mean that they had no political influence. Even though they may not have had any control over a particular course of events, they alone had the authority to sanction political change. In this respect, perhaps no other institution did more to keep alive the 'myth' of the monarchy, or, for that matter, to thwart any innovation likely to endanger its primeval purity.

A content analysis of traditional sources shows the recurrence of three dominant themes, which together formed the mythical axis of Rwanda society. One such theme was that of a divinely ordained social structure in which each individual was assigned a specific caste, and each caste a specific rank. According to a dynastic poem entitled "The Story of the Origins", the history of Rwanda begins with the reign of Kigwa, who descended from heaven and sired three sons—Gatwa, Gahutu and Gatutsi. To choose his successor Kigwa decided to entrust each of his sons with a pot of milk to watch over during the night. When dawn came it turned out that Gatwa had drunk the milk; Gahutu had gone to sleep and spilt his milk; only the watchful Gatutsi had stayed up through the night to keep guard over his milk. To Kigwa this was conclusive evidence that Gatutsi should be his successor and be forever free of menial tasks. Gahutu was to be his serf. As for Gatwa, who showed himself so utterly unreliable, his station in society was to be that of a pariah. This myth, as Malinowski would put it, was for the Rwandese 'neither a fictitious story, nor an account of a dead past, it was a statement of a bigger reality still partially alive . . . through its precedents, its law, its moral'.[33] As such it provided a moral justification for the maintenance of a system in which a tiny minority assumed the status of a leisure class through the exploitation of the masses.

Next came the theme of royal omnipotence. The typical image of the king conveyed through the lore was that of a Homeric figure. The king was the incarnation of the deity (Imana), the embodiment of ancestral virtues, and the source of all prosperity. In the words of a dynastic poem dedicated to the memory of Mwami Mutara Rwogera (*c.* 1810), the popular view of the monarch was that of 'a faultless work of art, chiselled by chosen tools. . . . The nobility issued of the sacred groves of Rwaniko. . . . The hero of manifold beauty whose decision cannot be swayed, and whose memory will live forever in Rwanda.'[34]

Even though the king stood apart from Tutsi, Hutu and Twa, the theme of kingship was inextricably bound up with the theme of Tutsi supremacy. To rebel against the established order was no less sacrilegious than to rebel against the Mwami himself. According to a popular legend 'the King and the Tutsi [were] the heart of the country. Should the Hutu chase them away, they would lose all they have and Imana would punish them.'[35] The fear of divine punishment, however real it may have been, was not the only factor which helped the Tutsi to stay in power; equally important was the popular notion that the Tutsi were in fact a master race. From the accredited body of myths and super-stitions the Tutsi emerged as Imana's elect, endowed with superior military skill, extraordinary courage, great wealth and commensurate intelligence. Thus, the 'official' history of Rwanda reads like a great success story—like a saga of a few exceptional men performing remark-able deeds. Moreover, Rwanda has no 'official' history prior to the arri-val of the Tutsi, for in those dark ages apparently nothing seemed worth recording. The significance of the transition to Tutsi rule is tersely summed up in the opening sentence of a folktale of central Rwanda: 'Dead are the dogs and the rats, giving way to the cows and the drum. . . .'[36]

As one compares the mythology of Rwanda with that of other inter-lacustrine societies, one discovers that none of its constituent elements was peculiar to Rwanda. The myth of origin of Bunyoro is strikingly similar to that of Rwanda; Bunyoro and Ankole both possessed a myth-conveyed scheme of values to explain the division of their societies into distinctive social categories. As far as the principle of kingship is concerned, one could easily match the omnipotence of the *bami* with the despotic powers of the Kabaka of Buganda prior to 1900. But Rwanda is unique in the sheer abundance of traditions purporting to show the superiority of the Tutsi over the other castes, and in the cumulative impact of these traditions on society as a whole.

To infer from the foregoing that Rwanda society was in a state of permanent racial tension would be as far from the truth as to imagine that Burundi was totally free from such tension. Professor Codere's argument that the Tutsi of Rwanda maintained themselves in power only through the application of naked force, and that the Hutu were everywhere 'powerless', 'oppressed' and 'terrorized',[37] overlooks a basic aspect of stratificatory phenomena—namely, that they are almost always rooted in a universally accepted code of values. This is where Rwanda's mythology played such a crucially important role in the ordering of socio-political relations. The caste structure of Rwanda was based on a shared and 'culturally elaborated' image of society,[38] involv-ing a combination of exclusiveness and reciprocity, of inequality and solidarity. However instrumental the solidaristic features of the system may have been in holding society together, one can hardly escape the conclusion that it was the widespread adherence to what Maquet refers

34

to as the 'premise of inequality' which allowed the caste structure of Rwanda to retain its stern rigidity over the years, until it could no longer withstand the impact of egalitarianism.*

But if Rwanda was fundamentally averse to egalitarian influence, this does not mean that it has always and unconditionally rejected modernisation. As long as the principle of Tutsi supremacy was maintained, modernisation could be easily tolerated. Although the very centralised nature of the traditional polity tended to encourage modernisation, its limits were very sharply delineated by the boundaries of the caste system. Modernisation left off where caste distinctions began, at the point where it threatened to negate the premise of inequality.

In sum, although each society shared a certain consensus, certain common understandings regarding the legitimacy of its social hierarchy, the character and limits of this consensus varied widely from one state to the other. Not only was the premise of inequality less prominent in Burundi than in Rwanda; the lines of demarcation between groups were drawn at different levels in each society. Whereas the main line of cleavage in Rwanda was between Hutu and Tutsi, in Burundi the crucially important distinction was between the princes, on the one hand, and the Hutu and Tutsi on the other. The criteria of ranking, in other words, did not involve ethnic differences as much as differences of lineage and power.

Which brings us back to the main point of this discussion: whereas in Rwanda a challenge to the operative norms of the system was really a challenge to the entire socio-political structure, in Burundi there were

* This is not meant to deny the part played by religious sanctions—in particular by the cult of Ryangombwe and the Kubandwa sect, to which it gave rise—in promoting inter-caste cohesion. In his recent work on Rwanda, Luc de Heusch advances the hypothesis that the Kubandwa sect, by ritualistically reversing the established hierarchy among castes, inaugurated at periodic intervals a kind of fictitious egalitarian order which in turn served as a safety valve for accumulated tensions and antagonisms among castes. 'The Kubandwa introduces a democratic religion which negates the divisions of the real society founded on the ownership of cattle. . . . We do not accept the functional interpretation offered by Maquet, according to which the Ryangombwe cult would only serve as an additional factor of cohesion, uniting into a single belief system members of different castes . . . The ritual of the Ryangombwe rested on a mystical and radical negation of the established order': Luc de Heusch, *Le Rwanda et la Civilisation Interlacustre*, Institut de Sociologie, Brussels 1966, p. 172. This interpretation of the Kubandwa sect, as providing its adherents with a *rite d'inversion* through which a temporary flight from reality could be achieved, is challenged by Claudine Vidal in "Anthropologie et Histoire: le cas du Rwanda", *Cahiers Internationaux de Sociologie*, Vol. XLIII, 1967, pp. 143–57.

relatively few ideals to challenge, save that of the monarchy, and even then, as we have seen, the motives for contesting its existence were not particularly compelling. Questioning the premise of inequality merely meant questioning the legitimacy of the chiefs qua chiefs, that is of a tiny minority of princely families; similarly, to call into doubt the legitimacy of the social hierarchy did not imply a threat to the privileges of a particular caste, but to the prebends of particular individuals.

The Clientage System

In each kingdom the ties of clientship ran like a seamless web, linking men in a relationship of mutual dependence. At the core of this relationship lay an institution called *buhake* in Rwanda and *bugabire* in Burundi, translated alternatively as 'cattle contract' or 'contract of pastoral servitude'. But as Maquet points out, the Western conception of contract, involving specific obligations on both parties, 'is not understood or acted upon even by Banyarwanda who have long been familiar with our culture'[39]—which, of course, is also a commentary on the difficulties faced by Western observers when trying to elucidate the meaning of clientage.

In essence, the clientage relationship was a highly personalised, precarious relationship between a client and a patron, involving the exchange of certain commodities and services. The procedure through which this relationship was established is a familiar one to the student of interlacustrine cultures. A client would commend himself to a more wealthy patron by way of certain ritualised formulae—'always think of me; make me rich; I ask you milk; etc.' If the patron accepted the cue, the client was from then on entitled to certain privileges, usually in the form of cattle and pasture land. But his rights were only those of usufruct: he was entitled to the cow's milk and their calves, and that was all; by the same token, the pasture rights enjoyed by the client did not make him a land owner but only a tenant at the mercy of his lord. In return for these privileges the client owed his patron whatever goods and services had been agreed upon by the parties.

But clientship involved more than just an economic transaction between an inferior and a superior. It also involved a close personal relationship, in some ways reminiscent of the ties of fealty which linked the medieval lord to his vassal. The reciprocal bonds of loyalty between client and patron meant that one became the other's 'man', just as in feudal Europe the lord was the 'man' of the king, and the serf the 'man' of his lord. In return for this act of homage the patron owed protection to his client in every circumstance of life. In a society like Rwanda, where centralisation of authority was carried to an extreme, the need for protection was all the more deeply felt by the subordinate stratum, and so, also, the need to establish reciprocal ties of obligation between inferior and superior. 'Any superior is a protector', writes Maquet, 'and his protection is of the same character as his authority: all-embracing and limited only by his own convenience.'[40] This was true not only of the *mwami* towards the chiefs but of the latter towards the subchiefs. And just as the precariousness of tenure associated with royal absolutism often induced a sense of obligation on the part of the average office-holder towards his superior, the vicissitudes of everyday life on the hills made it mandatory for the average commoner to seek the protection of a superior. In most cases this meant the protection of a Tutsi since by definition the Tutsi were the prime holders of power and influence. Very different was the situation in Burundi, if only because political office was so deeply rooted in hereditary claims. Here the pattern of reciprocity showed little or no coincidence with the political hierarchy, and moreover, the obligations arising from the clientage relationship fell evenly upon Hutu and Tutsi.

The roles of client and patron were not mutually exclusive. For example, a man who had several clients could himself be the client of a more wealthy patron, who in turn would be the client of an even wealthier individual, and so forth. In this fashion, client-patron relationships formed a web of reciprocities embracing a wide segment of the population. Its only limits were the *mwami* at the top, who was the sole proprietor of cattle and land and hence the supreme patron, and, at the other extreme, the ordinary Hutu peasant who was too poor to impose his vassalage upon anyone but the members of his own family.

One can easily imagine the difficulties that were liable to arise from the juxtaposition of clientage and chieftaincy. Did allegiance to a patron exonerate an individual from his obligations towards his chief? If not, how were the conflicting claims of patron and chief reconciled? At what point in the hierarchy would the authority of a chief supersede the claims of a patron?

In Rwanda these questions were never posed in such clear-cut terms, for chieftainship and clientage were but two faces of the same coin. Political office was granted by the *mwami* or a chief as a 'privilege' (*amarembo*) in return for an act of homage on the part of the recipient. One finds in Max Weber's discussion of patrimonialism in medieval Europe an obvious parallel with what happened in Rwanda: 'The community was transformed into a stratum of aids to the rulers and depended upon them for maintenance through the usufruct of land, office fees, income in kind, salaries, and hence through prebends.

The staff derived its legitimate power in greatly varying stages of appropriation, infeudation, conferment, and appointment. As a rule this meant that princely prerogatives became patrimonial in nature.'[41] Similarly, in traditional Rwanda chiefly positions became 'patrimonial' insofar as they were the prebends distributed by the king to retain the loyalty of his 'men'.

There were some instances where a man owed a dual allegiance—to his chief, for example, as well as to his patron, who might or might not reside on the same hill. But this was the exception rather than the rule. Since economic and political power tended to gravitate into the same hands, the ties of clientship also tended to set the pattern of political relations. As Pierre Gravel points out, '*buhake* was identified with the administrative system in that a chief was by definition a person who was a vassal to some more powerful person, or to the *mwami* himself, and he usually had received the hill as a fief, in which case he was not likely to become the lord of all the notables of his hill, and indirectly through them—or directly—that of the peasants of his hill'.[42] The average office holder would in effect combine a variety of roles: as a patron he could always use his 'feudal' privileges to reinforce his authority as chief, or vice-versa; as a client of a higher chief, however, he was also made aware of his obligations towards both his superiors and his subordinates. It was this network of interlocking roles which gave Rwanda a measure of cohesion and stability.

The political system of Rwanda was stable but not static. Since the patron-client relationship could be terminated at any time by either party if, for some reason or another, the arrangement proved unsatisfactory, the system made allowance for occasional shifts in the balance of forces. These transformations were especially noticeable at the hill level, because the hill was the weakest link in the chain of command and because at this level the structure of power was in some ways quite different from what it was at the other echelons. Political competition on the hill centred on three major institutions: the lineage, the chieftainship, and the nuclear feudal cluster (the patron and his clients). As noted earlier, more often than not the chieftain was also the head of the nuclear feudal cluster, and the combination of these two roles evidently weakened the influence of the lineage. But in some cases the strength of the local Hutu lineages was such that the Tutsi found it expedient to absorb these meddlesome 'upstarts' into their own caste. In a fascinating discussion of the power struggle that took place in Remera, in eastern Rwanda, Gravel notes that 'the Hutu lineages which have been in situ longest have acquired some sort of priority of rights on the hill. Their members are respected and the heads of the lineages have much influence on their neighbors, and have an important voice in the local administration. . . . The powerful lineages keep the power of the chieftain in check. If, however, they become powerful enough to threaten the chieftainship, they are absorbed into the upper caste. Their Hutu origins are "forgotten".'[43]

This last point is central to an understanding of social stratification in Rwanda. Besides showing the existence of opportunities for mobility across caste lines, Gravel's findings suggest that the 'play for power' was not confined to the Tutsi caste, nor bound to result in further Tutsi oppression, despite some assertions to the contrary. Yet, the very fact that a Hutu who successfully made his way up the social ladder should ipso facto be assimilated into the Tutsi caste, and henceforth regarded as a Tutsi, shows that as a group the Hutu were inevitably destined to remain in an inferior position. A Tutsi could be both client and patron; but a Hutu could only be a client.*

In Burundi the clientage system was separate from, and subsidiary to, the political structure. It is true, of course, that office holders sometimes used their prerogatives to build up bodies of loyal retainers whose position resembled that of a client towards his lord. And there were some instances in which a chief would receive an estate from the king as a 'benefice', as often happened in the case of those royal domains that were scattered about the country like so many enclaves of royal authority. But at the *ganwa* level at least political office was rooted in hereditary claims, and no amount of patronage could possibly destroy the local corporateness and autonomy resulting from hereditary succession. Indeed, if any lesson can be drawn from the turbulent history of Burundi, it is that the *mwami* had no effective device at his disposal to curb the excesses of rebellious princes. Recognition of hereditary rights as the main source of authority carried some important consequences. For one thing, the hierarchy of power and prestige associated with political office was by no means co-terminous with the clientage structure. While there were definite territorial limits to the scope of

---

* It should be emphasised at this point that the clientship pattern just described was confined to the central region of Rwanda. In the predominantly Hutu areas of the north there developed a somewhat different kind of clientage, based not on cattle but on a land-lease contract between the original owners of the land (*bakonde*), for the most part of Hutu or Twa extraction, and the Hutu lineages who opened it up for cultivation (*bagererwa*). According to this so-called *ubukonde* system, the *bagererwa* offered a tribute in kind to the 'landlord' in exchange for usufructuary rights over the land. It is both ironic and indicative of the strength of indigenous Hutu traditions that this particular system of land tenure, despite its obviously 'feudal' character, should still be practised in republican Rwanda.

political authority, the ties of vassalage paid no heed to such boundaries. A man could be the client of a wealthy chief and yet evade all political allegiance to him; conversely, within the limits of his jurisdiction a chief exercised authority over a number of individuals who were not treated as his clients but only as his subjects, although some could conceivably be treated as both.

This in turn suggests that the dividing line between the economic and political spheres was much more sharply delineated than in Rwanda. In Rwanda a wealthy patron was by definition a powerful man, and since a client's rights were largely dependent upon the solicitude of his patron, it was obviously to his advantage to seek the protection of the wealthy. Inferentially, the wealthier a patron the greater were the chances that he might also be a chief. In Burundi, on the other hand, whether a *muganwa* had a large or small retinue of clients had little effect on his authority as a chief; by the same token, whether a patron was more or less affluent did not substantially alter his bargaining position vis-à-vis his chief, or at least not to the same extent as in Rwanda. In practice, therefore, a client would usually turn to his chief, rather than to his patron, to obtain redress for the wrongs that might have been inflicted upon him. Even in the case of disputes between a client and his lord, the chief remained the supreme arbiter.

Finally, because of the special context in which it was embedded, the clientage system of Burundi operated within a fairly limited framework of expectations. Thus the services expected from a client were not nearly as burdensome as in Rwanda. 'As for the Hutu clients', one report noted, 'their obligations towards their *shebuja* amount to precious little —to pay court from time to time, to bring gifts of beer on even rarer occasions, and that is all.'[44] Moreover, relatively few Hutu were actually involved in clientage relations. In the central region, for example, the vast majority of the Hutu population lived in small, self-contained communities that were virtually immune from contractual obligations. If clientship served any purpose at all for the Hutu it was primarily as an avenue for social mobility, rather than as an instrument of Tutsi domination. Thus, if one were to generalise about the effects of client-patron relationships on social stratification, one could argue that in Burundi the *bugabire* tended to blur caste differences whereas in Rwanda the *buhake* merely served to reinforce social and political inequalities between Hutu and Tutsi.*

* The bonds of subjection created by the *buhake* are nowhere better described than in the following statement, by a group of Tutsi évolués: 'The *buhake* system is the means par excellence through which the Batutsi have managed to maintain and safeguard their ascendency over the masses. The indefinite dura-

Here we touch upon one of the most paradoxical aspects of Rwanda's recent political past. While there can be no question that the obligations of clientage weighed heavily upon the masses, and that the solidaristic features of the institution had been largely corrupted by the environmental and administrative changes introduced by the Pax Belgica and its legitimacy called into question by the more educated segments of the Hutu elites, the clientage relationship served as the chief instrument through which the Hutu leadership managed to enlist the support of the peasantry. As we shall see, the key to this paradox lies in part in the growing inability of the Tutsi patrons to properly fulfil their protective roles as patrons, and in the persistence of a deeply felt need for such protection—in particular for the psychic gratifications which presumably arise from a relationship of dependency of the client-patron type—among the masses. This double-edged aspect of the clientage system, creating as it did a web of inter-caste solidarities as well as the conditions of its rupture, is central to an understanding of the 'play for power' in revolutionary Rwanda. This is also where the legacy of the traditional system intrudes itself most forcefully upon the contemporary political scene.

Traditional Patterns of Behaviour

The writings of early European visitors show a remarkable consensus about the individual deportment of Hutu and Tutsi as well as about their attitudes towards each other. They all seem to have been very forcefully impressed by the extreme reserve of the Tutsi, which seemed so strange when compared with the spontaneous effusions of other African tribes. Of the Tutsi of Rwanda, Mecklenburg wrote that 'one received the impression of being in the presence of an entirely different class of men, who had nothing further in common with the "niggers" than their dark complexion'.[45] After his visit to Burundi Hans Meyer commented in a

---

tion of contractual ties it creates at each echelon of the hierarchy implies a constant obligation to obey the dominant caste; through pure and simple spoliation an instant remedy is found against the danger of over-rapid social mobility or the emergence of competitive centres of power, while intrigue and delation, both of which are encouraged by the system, maintain the omnipotence of the powerful by fostering rivalries among the weak. Thus the system has really become impractical and obsolete for all who have managed to evade the constraints of the dominant caste. For these people—but not the masses!—that is for those who are gainfully employed by Europeans, who live in townships, in brief for a great many évolués, the system is no longer acceptable.' See Christophe Ruhara, Chrysologue Rwamasirabo, Gratien Sendanyoye, "Le Buhake: Une coutume essentiellement munyarwanda", *Bulletin de Jurisprudence des Tribunaux Indigènes du Ruanda-Urundi*, No. 3, May 1947, pp. 103–136.

similar vein: 'The longer one has travelled in negro countries, and the better one has got acquainted with the negro character, the more one is impressed with the proud reserve of the Tutsi. There is no restless curiosity, no noisy, partly fearful, partly good-hearted welcome, as with most other negroes. The tall fellows stand still and relaxed, leaning over their spears while watching the Europeans pass or approach, as if this unusual sight did not impress them in the least.'[46] But Meyer also noted the reverse side of the picture, and in particular their laziness, opportunism and dissimulation: 'The Tutsi never or only seldom says what he thinks; one has to guess it. Lying is not only customary with strangers but a permanent and deeply rooted defect.' He also noted that, for all their mendacity, the Tutsi never concealed the fact that they regarded themselves as the salt of the earth: 'The Tutsi consider themselves as the top of the creation from the standpoint of intelligence and political genius.' Summarising the Tutsi philosophy of life, Meyer concluded: 'To be rich and powerful and to enjoy life by doing nothing is the symbol of all wisdom for the Tutsi, the ideal for which he strives with utmost shrewdness and unscrupulousness.'[47] By contrast the Hutu seemed a singularly servile, boisterous and cowardly people, whose sense of dignity and amour propre had been dulled almost to extinction by centuries of bondage. Of the Hutu of Burundi, Meyer wrote: 'Due to four centuries of terroristic rule, they have become slaves in thinking and acting, though not so slave-like in character as the Banyarwanda under their Hamitic despots.'[48] If this last qualifier sounds like an after-thought, subsequent observations show that this was not Meyer's intention.

Contrasting the behaviour of the Banyarwanda with that of the Barundi, he pointedly stressed the fact that 'in Burundi the Tutsi are neither so pleasure-seeking, lazy, mendacious, violent and opportunist as in Rwanda; nor are the Hutu so servile and hypocritical toward the mighty and so impertinent toward the weak; nor is the king and his court so addicted to idleness, wastefulness, intrigue, and so eager to satisfy their depraved and cruel instincts'. He added that 'despite great differences in status', in Burundi '. . . Tutsi and Hutu conduct friendly social intercourse', and that 'the Hutu who is better off [economically] considers himself socially on the same level as the ordinary Tutsi who has no property'.[49]

Since these lines were written many observers have had occasion to confirm the accuracy of this judgement. But how does it relate to contemporary patterns of behaviour? Two preliminary observations are in order. Firstly, it would be profoundly misleading to ignore the fact that in each society ethnic differences were associated with certain cultura stereotypes. In Rwanda as in Burundi, Hutu and Tutsi were divided into readily recognisable categories, definable in cultural terms; thus in each state a genuine potential existed for a sharp polarisation of group loyalties and identifications. Nonetheless the hierarchical ranking attached to cultural differences was infinitely more pronounced in the case of Rwanda. Thus the next important point to remember is that the attitudinal variations described above were reducible not merely to cultural discontinuities, nor even to disparities in the extent of inter-caste mobility, but to the different moral scales by which the Hutu as a group were measured in each state. There was no equivalent in Burundi for the moral and psychological inhibitions faced by the Hutu of Rwanda in their effort to reverse the 'premise of inequality', no equivalent either for the willing support and co-operation they once gave their masters. Such inhibitions may conceivably provide a retrospective justification for the stolid obduracy displayed by the dominant stratum while trying to maintain its traditional supremacy; but they also offer a plausible explanation for the psychological traumas, insecurities and retreats generated among the masses of Rwanda by the advent of freedom.

The persistence of stereotyped conceptions of inferiority among the Hutu of Rwanda goes far in explaining their general reluctance to even consider the possibility of changing the status quo—in short their long-lasting political apathy. Since the Tutsi were culturally defined as highly intelligent, refined and courageous, and the Hutu as dim-witted, gross and cowardly, the corollary proposition was that the Tutsi were born to rule and the Hutu to be ruled. And because many of the Hutu actually saw themselves with the eyes of the Tutsi, they had understandably little incentive to compete with their overlords. Hence the attitude of sullen resignation which long characterised the Hutu of Rwanda, and which gave currency to the stereotype that 'like almost all negro peoples they have the natural desire to serve and be subjected to a strong and leading hand'.[50]

While this 'natural desire to serve' did not last forever, submissiveness and self-doubt remained the most enduring characteristics of Hutu behaviour. Indeed, one of the most arduous tasks facing the Hutu intelligentsia on the eve of independence was to break this habit of passive obedience which even then continued to paralyse political initiative. What made this task so difficult was not only that it violated some basic cultural norms, but that the breaking of these norms released tremendous psychological insecurities among the Hutu peasantry. As they were suddenly asked to turn against the men and institutions which for centuries had been their sole guarantee of security, many Hutu felt hapless and bewildered. Even those who had nothing but

43

genuine contempt and hatred for the old regime displayed an almost pathological fear of being outsmarted at every turn by Tutsi, as if the latter had been endowed by nature with superior gifts of shrewdness, treachery and cunning. While there can be little question that this stereotype lay at the root of all the insecurity and suspicion the Hutu elites felt toward their former masters, the reverse image of the Hutu as an inferior people, forever destined to be hewers of wood and drawers of water, explains the intransigence of the conservative wing of the Tutsi oligarchy in the months preceding independence. Commenting upon this polarisation of attitudes, a prominent Hutu leader contrasted the Rwanda revolution with the events of 1789 by pointing out: 'In France, during the revolution, at least some noblemen saw the handwriting on the wall. Danton, for example, became one of the staunchest supporters of the revolution. But in Rwanda not a single Tutsi ever committed himself, by word or action, to our democratic ideal.'[51]

If insecurity bred suspicion, both led to aggression. The recent history of Rwanda is punctuated with countless examples of bloodshed and violence; but there are no precedents for the appalling brutality employed after independence by some Hutu officials. In late 1963 and early 1964 thousands of innocent Tutsi were wantonly murdered in what has been described as an act of genocide. Although the massacre was in part the result of repeated provocations on the part of the exiled Tutsi population, the scale and methods by which it was perpetrated suggest that it can only be regarded as an extreme example of pathological behaviour, as the blind reaction of a people traumatised by a deep and lasting sense of inferiority. The heritage of humiliation created by previous centuries of bondage, coupled with the frustration of trying to adjust to new conditions while encountering new interferences, provided an ideal environment for aggressive behaviour.

All this is not meant to imply a situation of unadulterated harmony among the castes of Burundi. Ethnic violence did occur in Burundi, though never on a scale comparable to Rwanda. What was involved here, moreover, was not so much an attempt on the part of a specific group to reject or maintain a status of social inferiority as the expression of a growing political competition between two culturally differentiated segments of society. As one prominent *ganwa* observed, in 1957, 'in Burundi social rank was determined by individual merit, regardless of race, except for the Twa. . . . Many *ganwa* gave their daughters in marriage to Tutsi and Hutu alike.'[52] Likewise, speaking on behalf of his kinsmen, another famous scion of a princely family once confided to Mgr Gorju: 'Do not be mistaken about our origins; our first ancestor was a Hutu; we are all Bahutu.'[53] From a Rwanda chief of similar rank such a statement would have been inconceivable. Thus to associate the occurrence of violence in Burundi with the outburst of a group whose long-suppressed aspirations were bound sooner or later to lead to a racial cataclysm would be profoundly misleading. Ethnic violence in Burundi expressed a relatively low revolutionary quotient, and in any event one that was so evenly shared by the protagonists as to make it difficult at times to tell the insurgents from their opponents.

This said, one is nonetheless struck by the persistence in each state of certain traditional patterns of behaviour. These are most clearly visible in the mechanisms by which political clienteles are formed and cemented. In each state the building-up of a clientele remains the essential prerequisite of influence. In each state the process involves a constant probing of power relationships; it expresses itself in the judicious dispensation of gifts to strategically placed individuals and the extension of special favours in return for gifts; and it is generally governed by certain tacit assumptions: that personal trust deserves a reward, either in terms of political 'benefice' or monetary gains, and that a higher reward may well justify a change of heart from the recipient. Although they unfold in different ethnic contexts and at different hierarchical levels, the byzantine manoeuvrings involved in this kind of gamesmanship remain the constant preoccupation of the aspiring and the ambitious.

It may be that by emphasising the differences discernible between each state their similarities have been unconsciously glossed over. If so it is worth reiterating that Rwanda and Burundi did share many affinities, at least as great and as important as their differences. Both were elitist, hierarchically-organised societies, in which power was concentrated at the top in the hands of a small oligarchy; both attached certain physical and moral stereotypes to castes, and tended to associate qualities of intelligence and resourcefulness with the upper strata; both tended to equate power with wealth and wealth with cattle and land; and in both societies the ties of clientage formed the basis of social and/or political relations. Such being the case it would be naive to argue that none of the problems that have arisen in Rwanda were ever likely to be duplicated in Burundi. Nonetheless, that their initial patterns of development after independence should have differed so strikingly from each other has made it necessary for the purpose of this discussion to play down their similarities and instead focus attention on their differences. Moreover, many of these differences were significantly enhanced as a result of the policies and practices of the colonial powers. There is scant evidence in support of the argument that the divergent paths to independence followed by Rwanda and Burundi were necessarily foreordained, as it were, by the structural and normative disparities of their traditional political systems. That these have had a bearing on the course of subsequent developments is beyond question; but this occurred largely as a consequence of European interpretations, or misinterpretations, and of the policies they have inspired. What these policies were, and the effect they have had on the social structure of each society, is what must now be examined.

2. Historical Survey

In THE perspective of their recorded history, the period of foreign rule experienced by Rwanda and Burundi was exceedingly brief. The scramble had already engulfed most of Africa before the exploration of the area even commenced. Subsequent efforts at penetration proceeded so slowly as to prompt one scholar to remark, with perhaps only a touch of exaggeration, that 'the beginning of the twentieth century saw the passing of Ruanda-Urundi as the unexplored territory'.[1] Yet, despite the brevity of the colonial interlude, its impact was overwhelming. In Rwanda it unleashed one of the most violent upheavals ever witnessed by an African state at a similar stage of its evolution; in Burundi it sowed the seeds of a racial conflict that may well prove equally devastating. It is one of the ironies of history, however, that the country which has so far suffered the most radical transformation should also be the one where traces of modernisation are least in evidence, and where the support of traditional institutions was pursued with the greatest consistency by successive administering authorities.

Although each society did not display the same degree of vulnerability to Western influences, the fact that both escaped the thrust of the Arab intrusion made their initial contacts with the West all the more shattering. At a time when the Zanzibar Arabs were already plying their trade deep into the Congo, the people of Rwanda and Burundi continued to live in a state of splendid isolation, owing as much to the natural bulwark of swamps and mountains as to the fearsome reputation they had earned among their neighbours. During his visit to Karagwe in 1876, Stanley was told by one Ahmed Ibrahim that the Banyarwanda were 'a great people, but covetous, malignant, treacherous, and utterly untrustworthy.... They have never yet allowed an Arab to trade in their country, which proves them to be a bad lot.'[2] Before long the Barundi established a similar reputation for themselves: the first White Fathers to set foot in Burundi were ruthlessly massacred at Rumonge in 1881.

Some ten years elapsed before the Austrian explorer Oskar Baumann decided to venture into what later became known as Ruanda-Urundi— this time with considerably more luck than his unfortunate predecessors. In 1892 he crossed the Kagera into northern Burundi, and, after a quick swerve through Rwanda, reached the Ruvubu river, which he mistook for the source of the Nile. Baumann's was the first of a series of similar explorations by German officers, the most important of which, historically, was Count von Goetzen's expedition through Rwanda in 1894. It was during his stay in Rwanda that von Goetzen met Mwami Rwabugiri for the first time. The friendly welcome extended by Rwabugiri came as a disappointment to von Goetzen, who apparently felt robbed of a splendid opportunity to display his martial qualities; at the time a lieutenant in the Second Royal Regiment of Ulans, von Goetzen's comments were indeed worthy of his calling: 'Feeling strong and being moderately equipped with weapons, we certainly would have liked to cope once with a more serious enemy.'[3] This opportunity would soon present itself in Burundi, where the continuing struggle of the king against rebellious princes confronted the Germans with a much more difficult situation. The first encounter of Captain von Goetzen with Mwami Mwezi Kisabo of Burundi took place in 1899; but the pacification of the country by the Germans was not achieved until several years later, at the cost of numerous military expeditions.

By then, however, von Goetzen occupied the more enviable position of Governor-General of the East African Protectorate, in Dar es Salaam, some six hundred miles away from the scene of operations. The importance of his new post was a fair measure of his previous accomplishments. The results of his peregrinations across the continent appeared in 1895, in his monumental *Durch Afrika von Ost nach West*, which contained the first detailed account of Rwanda's geography. Eventually, the dictum quoted in the preface of his book—'Initium Scientiae Politicae Geographica'—found its justification in the founding of the 'Militärstation' of Bujumbura in 1899. However, the newly-founded military station was nothing more than a precarious outpost, and a full decade had passed before the German government could make a reasonable claim to effective control over the area.

THE GERMAN PHASE

Unlike the rest of German East Africa, where tribal dislocation offered no other alternative but to rule through appointed local officials, regardless of their traditional claims to authority, Ruanda-Urundi was to be administered on the basis of indirect rule.[4] This meant that 'by degrees, and almost imperceptibly to the people . . . the sultans [would] eventually become nothing less than the executive instruments of the Residents'.[5] The attractions of this policy were practical and psychological. Apart from the fact that the centralised political systems of the indigenous societies were admirably suited to indirect rule, any attempt to displace the traditional rulers would probably have met with considerable resistance from the local populations; at all events, it would have required a far greater number of European administrators than was available at the time. This consideration takes on added weight when one recalls that of all colonial administrations Germany's was among the most grievously understaffed: as late as 1913, the whole of German East Africa—a territory larger than Nigeria—was administered by seventy European officials.[6] Moreover, to the German officers on the spot, virtually all of them of patrician origins, the claims of the Tutsi aristocracy were no less sacrosanct than the privileges of the Junker aristocracy in Bismarck's Germany. Their aristocratic leanings were fully concordant with the postulate of indirect rule.

One of the earliest formulations of German policy is found in a report of November 1905, by Captain von Grawert, then Resident of Burundi: 'The ideal is: unqualified recognition of the authority of the sultans from us, whether through taxes or other means, in a way that will seem to them as little a burden as possible; this will link their interests with ours. This ideal will probably be realised more easily and earlier in Ruanda, which is more tightly organised, than in Urundi, where we must first re-establish the old authority of the sultan, which has generally been weakened by wars with Europeans and other circumstances.'[7] This evaluation was based on more than mere conjecture however, for by the time these lines were written von Grawert had already learned by experience that this 'ideal' would not be realised with equal success in each territory. While in Rwanda the implementation of indirect rule came to reflect the logical forethought of von Grawert's formulation almost to the letter, in Burundi German policies showed from the very beginning a mixture of expediency and improvisation which in the end led to surprising contradictions. The key to the situation lies in the very different conditions then prevailing in each kingdom.

The Burundi Residency

When the Germans arrived in Burundi they found a situation bordering on chaos. Internecine struggles between the ageing king, Mwami Mwezi Kisabo, and the rebellious chiefs had reached the point where power was divided among a host of princely factions, with the king assuming the position of a 'potentate of limited power'.[8] His very weak position at first prompted Kisabo to adopt a conciliatory attitude towards the Germans, but his promise of co-operation later turned out to be nothing more than a façade. His real aim, as far as can be determined, was to avoid a direct confrontation with the German colonial troops so as to concentrate his energies against his domestic foes.

His principal challengers at the time were for the most part *ganwa* of the Batare branch, the descendants of Mwami Ntare Rugaamba. Mwezi Kisabo himself was one of Ntare's younger sons, but, as has been noted already, his accession to the throne in 1860, so far from muting the claims of his elder brothers, resulted in a long yet inconclusive fratricidal strife between Bezi and Batare—between Mwezi's supporters and Ntare's marauding minions. The Batare were now firmly entrenched on the periphery of the realm: Chiefs Kanugunu, Mbanzabugabo and Busokoza controlled the eastern and north-eastern marches; Chief Maconco held an important fief in the north;* but by far the most formidable of Kisabo's rivals was Chief Kilima, whose rule now extended over a large chunk of territory in the north-west. And here and there on the fringes of the realm stood a number of lesser chiefs whose authority was exercised more or less independently of the crown.

The real identity of Kilima is somewhat obscure. According to his own version, corroborated by the testimonies of his sons and subchiefs, Kilima was the descendant of one of Ntare's sons named Nyanamusango, who at one time had found refuge among the Bafulero in the Congo. One of Nyanamusango's sons, Njitshi, married a certain Nabakile, probably a Bafulero girl (said to have been 'presented' to him by the king of Rwanda) who bore him a child named Kilima. In later years Kilima concluded an alliance with a group of semi-independent chiefs of the Ruzizi valley and with their assistance established his claims over the north-western region of Burundi. According to one report: 'When he learned that the Belgians had arrived, Kilima came down from the high-lying mountain area between Kagobwami and the Ruzizi to meet them. Since then his territory has stretched, in fact and by tacit agreement, all the way to the Ruvubu.' At the time this report was written (1918), Kilima was said to have been approximately sixty years old, 'with regular features, though slightly chubby'. His sons, Ruhabira, Rusimbi, Kalibwami and Rwasha ('much less vulgar-looking than their father'), were each given extensive tracts of land by the Belgian administration; in 1918, Kilima claimed among his vassals Chiefs Gwinzo and Kana, 'who boast about their Tutsi origins and look down upon (Chief) Mugwaruso, whom they call "Muhutu"; they are themselves descendants of Rukara, to whom King Ntare is said to have given land'.[9]

---

* Maconco was the only rebellious chief who did not claim direct descent from King Ntare: he is said to have been the son of a certain Kagaanza, maternal uncle of King Mwezi. Kanugunu and his son, Mbanzabugabo, were the descendants of King Ntare, through his son Ndivyariye. Busokoza was a cousin of Kanugunu. For further information see the genealogical table in Appendix II, pp. 504–8.

According to Hans Meyer,* Kilima reconquered the northern region in part with the help of his Congolese followers (whom he calls the 'Banyambungu'), and in part by enlisting the support of local Hutu populations: 'When he was grown up, [Kilima] returned to his homeland, in north-west Urundi, thanks to the support he had gained from the Banyambungu. He quickly found followers among the Bahutu too, and murdered all existing Batutsi there; that is why he is called "Batutsi-killer".'[10]

The essence of the dilemma facing the German authorities was to reconcile the conflicting claims of the king and the chiefs in a way that would satisfy both. Yet by supporting the chiefs against the king they risked the possibility of causing irreparable harm to the prestige of the crown; and by throwing their weight behind the king they were bound to antagonise the chiefs. In either case a trial of strength seemed inevitable. But if the difficulties arising from these internal rivalries were serious enough, the absence of co-ordination between the Government-General in Dar es Salaam and the Residency in Bujumbura made the situation even more intractable.

German policies in Burundi fall into three distinctive phases, each reflecting a different assessment of how best to preserve the balance of forces between the crown and the chiefs:

(i) *From 1899 to 1903*: a period of 'non-intervention', abruptly terminated in 1903 by Captain von Beringe's military expedition against Mwami Mwezi Kisabo and the recognition of Kilima and Maconco as independent chiefs.

(ii) *From 1903 to 1908*: a period of consolidation, marked by a partial curtailment of the chiefs' independence, and culminating in 1905 with the defeat and capture of Kilima.

(iii) *From 1908 to 1915*: a period of 'divide and rule', characterised by an attempt to 'freeze' the status quo in such a way as to prevent the crown from gaining a permanent ascendancy over the chiefs, and vice versa.

From the outset, German policies revealed some fundamental disagreements between Bujumbura and Dar es Salaam. For the German Resident in Bujumbura, Captain von Beringe, the policy of non-intervention repeatedly advocated by von Goetzen was self-defeating. In the context of Burundi politics, argued von Beringe, indirect rule could not be applied effectively until the king had made his submission to the Residency, for only then would there be 'a basis on which to build in

---

* Meyer's *Die Barundi*, largely corroborated by oral traditions, provides an important clue to an understanding of the roots of anti-Tutsi sentiments currently encountered in northern Burundi; see *infra*, chapter 13.

Urundi an authority as strong and effective as the one in Ruanda'.[11] Meanwhile the sporadic incursions of the king against his neighbours would probably result in further anarchy. In a report of July 1902, von Beringe described Kisabo as 'the sworn enemy of the Europeans' and went on to request permission to launch a military expedition against the Mwami. The object, he said, was not to depose Kisabo but to force him once and for all to submit to the German authorities. Von Goetzen withheld approval however, whereupon the Resident decided to act on his own initiative. After securing reinforcements from Bismarcksburg (Kasenga), von Beringe opened the hostilities against Mwezi Kisabo in June 1903, and a few weeks later, on June 23, he triumphantly reported to Dar es Salaam the story of his 'great success'. At long last Kisabo had been brought to heel. In the course of the engagement two hundred of Kisabo's men had lost their lives. In reparation Kisabo consented to surrender 424 head of cattle; he was to open a road from Bujumbura to Muyaga, and give all caravans free passage through his domain. More important still, he was to recognise the independence of Chiefs Kilima and Maconco, as well as the latter's claims over the royal fief of Muramvya.[12] As a result, 'the kingship, but, curiously enough, not the country, was divided among three claimants—Kilima in Bukeye, Maconco in Imbuye, and Mwezi [Kisabo] in the Kiganda region'.[13]

Von Goetzen's reaction to the news was one of unmitigated fury.[14] As one might have expected, von Beringe was 'called to other functions', while his successor, Resident von Grawert, was asked to redress the situation as best he could. More than ever von Goetzen was determined to restore the authority of the crown; this, he thought, could best be accomplished by gradual steps, with patience and diplomacy. Above all, it was imperative to avoid 'brutal interventions'. However, this was more easily said than done. In fact, von Goetzen's policy, while in theory unexceptionable, ran foul of several unforeseen developments. For one thing, by granting Kilima and Maconco their independence, von Beringe had led some lesser chiefs, like Lussokossa in the northeast and Lusengo in the Bugofi, to claim a similar status for themselves. Before von Grawert even realised what was happening, the kingdom was fragmented into half a dozen independent fiefdoms. Moreover, it became increasingly clear that, as long as Kilima and Maconco insisted upon enlarging their territorial holdings at the expense of the crown, local resistance to these encroachments would result in further bloodshed. As the situation threatened to deteriorate into complete chaos, the intervention of the colonial troops became unavoidable. The most brutal of such interventions was conducted against Kilima and Kanugunu, in 1905. In October 1905 von Grawert penetrated Kilima's fief and destroyed every village in his path. Von Grawert handled this task with professional conscience: 'The villages we occupied', he later admitted, 'were all burned down; and to make sure the job was well done I stayed in the region for a whole day.'[15] Kanugunu's fief in the north-east was subjected to similar treatment a few months later. In 1908 'a terribly bloody expedition', according to Pierre Ryckmans, 'was launched against Chief Busokoza [Kanugunu's cousin], but came to nought'.[16]

The defeat of Kilima marked the beginning of a new course in Burundi politics. Kisabo's most dangerous adversary was now in gaol; in May 1905 Maconco met his death in a suicidal attempt against von Grawert's life. In October of the same year the Residency formally recognised Mwezi Kisabo as the 'Sultan' of Burundi, with the assurance that 'as long as he met the wishes of the Germans they would regard his enemies as [their] enemies'.[17] Despite the continued resistance of Chiefs Mbanzabugabo and Busokoza in the north-east, Burundi seemed well on its way toward consolidation. The founding of the Burundi Residency, in 1906, signalled the restoration of Kisabo's authority and the beginning of civilian administration.[18]

But this was to be no more than a brief lull before the outbreak of new turbulence. With the death of Kisabo in August 1908, Burundi politics entered another phase of turmoil and confusion. Kisabo was succeeded by his fifteen-year-old son, Mutaga. Though formally recognised as the new Mwami of Burundi by the Residency, the adolescent king was unable to check the centrifugal forces suddenly released by Kisabo's death. In the north-east, Chiefs Lussokossa and Mbanzabugabo took advantage of the situation to reassert their claims to independence; simultaneously, many of the chiefs who had pledged allegiance to the departed king now joined the ranks of the 'rebels'. Adding to the confusion, Mutaga's own relatives wasted few opportunities to increase their power at the expense of the crown. Among them were the regent chiefs appointed by Kisabo on his deathbed to assist the new ruler— Chiefs Ntarugera and Nduwumwe, two of Mutaga's elder brothers. According to Hans Meyer 'these two and the Queen Mother [Ndiri-kumutima]* took full advantage of their position to seize as much land

---

* Ndirikumutima, one of the key figures in the entourage of the Mwami, was later described by Ryckmans in these terms: 'An old woman, with all the vices typical of her age, and endowed with a keen intelligence, she also displays a stubborn obstinacy. Nothing can possibly pry her loose from her blissful inertia. Once the wife of King Mwezi, who never cared much for contacts with the whites, she represents with indomitable tenacity the spirit of the old autocracy. She feels that the established order is the ideal and that everything we do can only upset this order. Her life's sole and constant preoccupation is to plunder

and property as was reasonably possible'.[19] Eventually Ntarugera became 'the greatest and richest man in Burundi, whose views [were] listened to at Mutaga's court because he was feared'.[20]

By a curious coincidence, 1908 also marked a transition for the German East African government. In that year von Rechenberg replaced von Goetzen as Governor-General, and Resident von Grawert went back to Germany on home leave. He was succeeded in Bujumbura by Captain Fonck, whose diagnosis of the situation suggested a radically different course of action from the one pursued by his predecessor. The monarchy, said Fonck, was a pushover: under the circumstances the only sensible policy for the Residency was to withdraw its support from the Mwami and deal directly with the chiefs. Instead von Rechenberg opted for a middle course, aiming at 'freezing' the status quo through recognition of both the Mwami and the chiefs—of *all* chiefs. Accordingly, Fonck was instructed to recognise, in addition to the Mwami, three categories of chiefs: (i) those who were in fact independent, i.e. Mbanzabugabo, Busokoza and Rwasha, Kilima's son; (ii) those who had earlier recognised the authority of Mwami Mutaga and would presumably continue to do so; and (iii) those who were 'more or less independent'—a phrase covering a number of border-line cases to be decided on the basis of their own merits.[21]

This policy, however, was difficult to reconcile with the rapid sequence of events taking place in Burundi. Neither the king nor any of the chiefs was willing to keep the static arrangement that von Rechenberg wished to introduce. Nor was it always compatible with the attitude of the German Residents: 'The Residents had little sympathy for the royal

---

other people's patrimony for the benefit of her sons. In her eyes the exercise of power is reducible to taking property away from those who seem weak enough to let her get away with it. . . . She sees to it that the burden of our requisitions falls upon the weak, so as to spare her favourites, her sons and the royal domain; she plays host and gives moral support to rebellious elements. . . . And when she senses that our patience is nearing the breaking point, she begins acting like a poor old woman, sick and tired of the responsibilities of power. . . .'

Nduwume was said to be 'the most influential of her sons' and 'a worthy heir to his mother's sentiments'; of Ntarugera, Ryckmans had a much higher opinion: 'The administration could not find a more qualified regent during Mwambutsa's minority than his great uncle Ntarugera. Once Mwezi's favourite son, more knowledgeable than anybody else of the affairs of the realm, having already exercised power over the region during his father's old age and at the beginning of his brother's reign; . . . loved by all who feel threatened by the ambitions of the ruling family (if only because he himself is the first to sense the threat), this man [Ntarugera] will lend us the prestige of his authority because he needs us in order to preserve it.' *Observations sur le Rapport du 1er Trimestre*, extract from a report by P. Ryckmans, 1918; in the Derscheid Collection.

family; they tried to "divide and rule", to "play one chief off against the other" ',[22] and although they frequently intervened on behalf of the chiefs, they did not make the faintest effort to restore the authority of the crown. The standard argument advanced by one Resident after the other was that the Mwami should first demonstrate the extent of his authority by his capacity to resist aggression; only then could they decide how much support should be given to the monarchy. That the Residency in fact had no intention of helping the crown reassert its authority was made abundantly clear by the release of Kilima in 1910: once regarded as a dangerous 'rebel', Kilima was now welcome as a 'salutary counterweight to the disruptive influences of Mutaga'. The result was a further weakening of the crown, a situation which Resident von Stegmann later acknowledged with secret satisfaction—and no little exaggeration: 'The Mwami has nothing to say except in his own village. . . . His political influence is non-existent; he exists because tradition says that he must; but he is not the ruler of the country.'[23] What von Stegmann neglected to mention was that this state of affairs was the normal outcome of the policy of 'divide and rule' consistently pursued by the Residency since Kisabo's death.

Despite subsequent attempts to reverse the trend, the situation showed few signs of improvement. For a while the transfer of the Residency from Usumbura to Kitega, in 1912, into the very heart of the country, made it easier for the Germans to control the hinterland; it also brought the administration closer to the court, and thus led to a more active collaboration between the Resident and the Mwami. Mutaga was now a grown man, and as his personal influence increased so did his willingness to share in the responsibilities of government. But the terminal years of the Burundi Residency also saw the recurrence of familiar difficulties. The continued rivalry between the Queen Mother, Ndirikumutima, and Ntarugera sapped the little that was left of Mutaga's authority, until he himself became the victim of one of his nearest relatives, in November 1915. The circumstances of Mutaga's death are unclear, but according to Ryckman's version, which is the most reliable, it probably came about as the result of a love affair between one of Mutaga's wives and his brother: 'Prince Bangura had become the lover of one of his sisters in law, married to King Mutaga. The latter eventually became suspicious. He kept a close watch over his brother and one day struck him in the chest with his spear. While trying to defend himself, Bangura speared his assailant in the abdomen. Bangura preceded his brother into the tomb by only a few days.'[24]

Burundi politics had reached their lowest ebb. In what seemed a perfect re-enactment of the events following Kisabo's death, Mutaga was succeeded on the throne by his infant son, Mwambutsa, with Ndirikumutima, Ntarugera and Nduwumwe in charge of the regency. By the end of 1915, as the days of the German protectorate were quickly drawing to an end, 'the situation in Burundi was perhaps worse than at any time during the German era'.[25]

In his lucid commentary on German colonial rule in Burundi, Pierre Ryckmans laid bare its essential shortcomings: 'On the eve of the [First] World War the European administration was in a state of avowed bankruptcy because it had worked toward the disintegration of a kingdom whose traditions, mores and religion were unknown or ignored; because in tolerating successful revolts, it had encouraged intrigues instead of suppressing them; because each blow against the prestige of the monarchy had rendered the white man more odious to the masses, attached above all to the traditions of their divine monarchy.'[26] In pointing out the reasons for the unqualified failure of German policies in Burundi, Ryckmans also hints at some of the more paradoxical consequences of these policies. While the Residency undeniably encouraged the fragmentation of the realm into a mosaic of independent fiefdoms, it also laid the foundation for a nationalist revival centred on the crown. The dynastic implications of German policies were no less important. As we shall see, much of the nationalist aura which in later years surrounded the claims of the Bezi against the Batare can be traced back to the resistance of their forefathers, and Mwezi Kisabo himself, against the policy of favouritism pursued by the German Residents towards the Bezi's arch-enemies, the Batare. In the minds of most Barundi, the cause of national unity and monarchic legitimacy became indissolubly linked with the cause of the Bezi.

The Rwanda Residency

The German record in Rwanda contrasts sharply with the erratic course of their Burundi policies—a contrast perhaps over-emphasised by Governor Schnee when he wrote, in 1913: 'The history of Urundi since the German occupation is unfortunately not pleasant and contrasts with the peaceful and pleasant state of things in Ruanda.'[27] Those who are familiar with the history of Rwanda know that Schnee's statement cannot be taken too literally: only a year and a half before these lines were written, the Rwanda Residency had launched an extremely brutal expedition against a certain Ndungutse, until then one of the most serious challengers of royal supremacy. But if German policies in Rwanda were not always peaceful, violence was, in a sense, used more 'constructively' and hence less frequently than in Burundi. Instead of dithering between the extremes of support and suppression of the chiefs against the king, the administering authorities consistently and successfully sought to bolster the authority of the king against his rivals.

Unlike Burundi, Rwanda was a centralised state, in which the Mwami was in fact and in theory the supreme ruler of the land. This overwhelming concentration of power in the hands of a single individual spared the Germans many of the difficulties they faced in Burundi. Although the Mwami's authority did not go unchallenged, the contestants were neither so numerous nor so powerful as in Burundi; there was no princely caste comparable to the *ganwa*, whose entrenched rights and privileges might act as a counterpull to the powers of the crown; and as long as the Mwami was willing to recognise the German protectorate there was no need for the Residency to capitalise upon internal divisions. Nor was the willingness of the court to co-operate with the Germans entirely accidental. Given the circumstances of Rwanda politics, the establishment of German rule was not without certain reciprocal benefits. Just as the Mwami needed the support of the Germans to enlarge the territorial bases of his authority, the Germans needed the support of the Mwami to consolidate their protectorate over the country and proceed with the tasks of administration. As it turned out, the terms of the quid pro quo made it possible for the crown to expand its hegemony far beyond the limits of its original jurisdiction.

It will be useful, for the sake of clarity, to take a brief glance at the internal situation prevailing in Rwanda at the turn of the century— a very unusual situation in many respects. Shortly after von Goetzen's visit, in 1894, a period of factional strife set in, centred upon a disputed succession to the throne and culminating in 1896 with the famous coup of Rucuncu. In the annals of Rwandese history, Rucuncu marks the beginning of a long civil war between the Bega and the Banyiginya clans, in a way reminiscent of the protracted struggle between the House of York and the House of Lancaster in fifteenth-century England.

The facts, briefly stated, are as follows. The death of Mwami Kigeri Rwabugiri in 1895 had set the stage for a bitter struggle for the kingship between the Bega and Banyiginya families. While being one of the most prestigious of the several maternal clans from which a future Mwami could be chosen, the Bega had fallen into disgrace under the reign of Rwabugiri. Neither he nor his successor on the throne, Mibambwe Rutalindwa, had any ties with the Bega, and although Rwabugiri had consented that a Mwega named Kanyogera be appointed Queen Mother, this concession apparently failed to satisfy the ambitions of her clan. The Bega would not rest content until Kanyogera's own son, the future Mwami Musinga, had taken Rutalindwa's place. In November 1896, at Rucuncu, the succession was finally settled to the advantage of the Bega after a brief but bloody 'palace revolution' during which Ruta-lindwa, his wife and three children lost their lives. Since the new Mwami, Yuhi Musinga, was a minor at the time, his mother, Kanyogera, acted as regent, together with his maternal uncles, Chiefs Kabare and Ruhinankiko. With this triumvirate at the helm, the Bega then proceeded to consolidate their hold over the country.[28]

As a first step towards this goal—and after the extermination of those *biru** who did not at once recognise the authority of the new Mwami— the Banyiginya clan was systematically purged of its most influential elements. At the same time every effort was made to 'fill the vacancies' with trustworthy chiefs, most of them of Bega extraction. According to Kagame, 'countless members of the defeated party were massacred on the orders of Kabare and his acolytes . . . and new chiefs were appointed to fill the posts vacated by the death of the incumbents'.[29] Yet the very stringency of the repression led to the defection of some chiefs who had initially cast their lot with usurpers, while others, whom Kagame refers to as 'legitimists', i.e. pro-Banyiginya, sought refuge in the north and the east.

With the spread of legitimist sentiment to the north, swells of unrest began to penetrate into the region, culminating in 1911–12 with the famous rebellion associated with the names of Muhumusa, Ndungutse and Bassebya. Northern Rwanda, it must be remembered, was still more or less independent from the crown. The 'annexation' of the region had taken place a decade or so before the coup, under the reign of Mwami Rwabugiri, and although Rwabugiri seems to have extracted a formal pledge of allegiance from some of the local Kiga chiefs, their loyalty to the monarchy was nonetheless highly questionable. Hardier and sturdier than most ordinary Hutu, the Kiga people of northern Rwanda have always been looked upon by their neighbours as a rebellious lot, fiercely individualistic and contemptuous of established authority. It was among these rugged mountaineers that one of Rwabugiri's wives, a presumably full-blooded Munyiginya named Muhumusa, found refuge. She sought to crystallise the support of a few local clans around a hard core of legitimist chiefs, with a view to restoring her son Bilegeya to the throne in Rwanda. The surprising thing about Muhumusa is not that she ul-timately failed to carry out her plans but that she should have come so

---

* The *biru* were the guardians of the esoteric code of the monarchy (*ubwiru*), and thus it was especially important in order to establish the legitimacy of Musinga that his claims be recognised by these officials. No matter how power-less they may have been in deciding the outcome of the struggle, they alone could give it a sanction of legitimacy. (See *supra*, chapter 1, pp. 32–3.)

near to realising them. 'Herself an outstanding personality', writes J. M. Bessel, 'possessing great powers of leadership and organization, and far more brains than probably any Mututsi woman before or since, she was in intelligence quite up to the standards of her late husband.'[30] Not only in intelligence but in ambition: in 1911 she proclaimed herself Queen of Ndorwa and promised her followers that she would soon liberate the country from the yoke of the Europeans.

Although Muhumusa may have been the most prestigious representative of the legitimist faction, she was by no means the only one. Among the Banyiginya chiefs who had sought asylum in the north, the most famous was a certain Ndungutse, presumably Bilegeya's half-brother through Muhumusa.* He and a Twa chief named Bassebya—described by Father Dufays as 'a famous and fearsome brigand, rapacious and sanguinary'[32]—instigated sporadic insurrections throughout the Rukiga and in particular in the marshy country surrounding Lakes Bulera and Luhondo, aided in this task by a Tutsi chief named Lukarra, better known as the murderer of Father Loupias.[32] After Muhumusa's capture in September 1911, when she and a group of her followers were forced to surrender to the British authorities of Bufumbiro (Uganda), Ndungutse emerged as the chief spokesman of the legitimist faction, insisting time and again that Bilegeya was the sole legitimate heir to Rutalindwa. He also claimed considerable authority in his own right. He came to be viewed by the local populations as their saviour, as the prophet who would restore peace to the country and free the labouring masses from the servitude of the corvée (*ubuletwa*), a servitude made all the more intolerable after the additional tribute which the Bega had apparently tried to extract from the northern populations.† Though himself a

---

* Ndungutse's identity has been—and still is—a source of controversy among historians. Some have claimed that he was the son of a princess from Ndorwa named Nyiragumuhusa, sired by Mwami Rwabugiri; others have regarded Bilegeya and Ndungutse as the same person, known first under the name of Bilegeya and later as Ndungutse. The consensus of informed opinion, however, is that Bilegeya and Ndungutse were two different persons. Though Ndungutse's identity is still open to question, most historians seem to agree that Bilegeya was indeed the son of Rwabugiri and Muhumusa.

† As Sandrart noted, in 1929, in his *Rapport sur le territoire de Kigali*, p. 45 (in the Derscheid Collection): 'The coming to power of the Bega led to a recrudescence of corvées and taxes; the new chiefs they had installed sought only to enrich themselves at the expense of their people. Undoubtedly the Bahutu did not voluntarily accept this somewhat burdensome fiscal regime. The most telling proof of this is the enthusiastic response of the local populations to Ndungutse's call in 1912, when he threatened to invade the [central] kingdom, and the unanimous rallying of the peasantry to his cause at the mere mention of suppressing the corvée.'

Tutsi, Ndungutse's name became a symbol of anti-Tutsi sentiment, and by implication of anti-European sentiment as well.

Ndungutse's appeal as a leader was closely linked to the emergence in the north of the Nyabingi cult, a magico-religious cult which Muhumusa had used as a vehicle for propagating her ideas and solidifying her support among the people of the Mulera, Bukonza and Buberuka regions (often collectively referred to as the Kiga). Quite apart from its original eschatology, the Nyabingi developed a strong political attraction for the Kiga, which became apparent not only in Rwanda but in parts of Uganda. 'It seems clear', notes Professor Edel in her discussion of the Nyabingi movement in Kegezi (Uganda), 'that this force had become a military arm, in rebellion against the constituted authority of the attempted conquest by the Court of Rwanda.'[33] More will be heard in a subsequent chapter about the Nyabingi movement (see chapter 3, pages 100–102); suffice it to note, for the time being, that it is against this background of messianic activity that the roots of Ndungutse's popularity must be understood, for not only did he pose as the safest ally of the Kiga against the exactions of the ruling dynasty, but because of the skill with which he managed to exploit the religious superstitions of his followers a close organic relationship developed between certain segments of the northern populations and the survivors of the Banyiginya clan.

As the movement became increasingly xenophobic in character and aggressive in its methods, the 'hands-off' policy which the Residency had heretofore advocated was no longer tenable. After the murder of Father Loupias by Lukarra in 1910, the acting Resident, Gudovius, decided to organise a punitive expedition in the north. The purpose was 'punishment of the insubordinate districts and their peoples and chiefs by causing the greatest possible damage until complete submission; otherwise destruction of crops and settlements, and occupation of the theatre of operations by chiefs appointed by the Resident who are faithful to Musinga'.[34] The expedition turned out to be an unqualified success on both counts. In April 1912 Gudovius's troops attacked Ndungutse's village, near Ruhengeri, killing about fifty defenders including Ndungutse himself. Military operations were later prosecuted by Lieutenant Linde, who carried out his grim assignment to the letter: villages were burned down, crops and settlements were destroyed, and all who resisted were massacred. After the appointment of 'loyal' chiefs to rule over the devastated area, Gudovius could boast that 'complete peace had been restored to the country where Ndungutse and Bassebya and their followers rebelled against Musinga'.[35]

Subsequent events demonstrated the precariousness of the Pax Germanica in northern Rwanda. For many years after the Belgian 'reprise' the northern region remained the scene of recurrent outbreaks against the chiefs and the administration. However, Gudovius's expedition did consolidate the position of the monarchy in an area where it had never been firmly established. In return the Germans 'could continue to count on the complete loyalty of Musinga, and could be assured that he would try to fulfil every wish of the Resident'.[36]

More than anything else, the German Residents wished to use the presence of European missionaries to educate the Tutsi chiefs and thus convert them not only into good Christians but into efficient administrators. This, however, is precisely where the Residency ran into difficulties. At first the German Residents felt obligated to heed Musinga's request that missionary activities be kept at a safe distance from the court, lest the influence of Christianity weaken the authority of the crown. But as they came to realise that the appeal of Christianity was strongest among the Hutu, and discovered that the missionaries, on humanitarian or religious grounds, endeavoured to restrain the abuses of the chiefs, the Residents became understandably concerned over the possible repercussions of missionary work. In their view 'missionary interference' threatened the very basis of indirect rule, if only because the priests sometimes meddled in 'the entirely internal disputes of the natives', as Resident Kandt once put it.[37] Furthermore, the predominance of French elements among the Catholic clergy naturally held disquieting implications for the German administrators, and in turn some of the French missionaries became extremely suspicious of the Residents' motives.* Apart from having led to a number of very ungainly incidents between the Catholic Church and the secular administration, some of which received abundant coverage in the writings of certain missionaries,[38] the foregoing circumstances also help to explain the more or less systematic effort made by the German Residents to keep Catholic missionary activities confined to the outer fringes of the realm—to those

---

* And this not only on grounds of nationality but sometimes on cultural and religious grounds. Commenting on Richard Kandt's Jewish origins, Father A. Van Overschelde, gives this revealing portrayal of the German Resident: 'Richard Kandt was a Jew, very intelligent, occasionally dabbling in poetry, short, anaemic-looking, olive-complexioned. The bile, to which he owed his complexion, did not run only under his skin: he was evil-minded. His small stature, and perhaps also his ancestral habits, did not predispose him to act in a straightforward manner. He excelled at tearing things down in the dark, slyly, gingerly, like a cat.' A. Van Overschelde, *Un Audacieux Pacifique: Monseigneur L. P. Classe, Apôtre du Ruanda*, Grands Lacs, Namur 1948, p. 70.

For an excellent discussion of the relationships between the Church and the European administration, both German and Belgian, see Alison Des Forges, "Kings Without Crowns: The White Fathers in Ruanda", in *Boston University Papers in African History*, Vol. III, Boston University Press, Boston 1967.

regions where Tutsi rule was least stabilised. Except for the Save mission, located near Butare (formerly Astrida), the first Catholic missions were established in 1900 in Nyundo and Zaza, both in the extreme north. Because the missionaries were at times mistaken by the local populations for the agents of the court, some of them (like Father Loupias) became the target of the rebellious movements; at this point, however, European solidarity prevailed over sectarian differences to induce the Residency to take 'protective measures', usually in the form of punitive expeditions. Thus, directly or indirectly, the missionary presence became a major factor in the pacification of Rwanda. However, if the circumstances of missionary penetration at first contributed to strengthen both European and Tutsi over-rule in the north, in later years the spread of Christianity among the Kiga served as a powerful vector of revolutionary sentiment.

In sum, the impact of German rule upon the traditional political structure of Rwanda was precisely the reverse of what happened in Burundi. We have seen how, in Burundi, the policies of the Residents tended to accentuate the trend toward fragmentation already present in the traditional political organisation; how they favoured the emergence of a pleiad of more or less independent fiefdoms and eventually reduced the position of the *mwami* to that of a minor chief. In Rwanda, on the other hand, every effort was made to strengthen and consolidate the position of the crown. In either case punitive expeditions were the chief instrument of German policy, but in Rwanda these were directed against the *mwami*'s opponents whereas in Burundi the *mwami* was more often the victim than the beneficiary of German militarism. In Rwanda the very success of indirect rule reinforced the absolutism of the monarchy, and hence the hegemony of the ruling caste; in Burundi the initial shortcomings of indirect rule enhanced the pluralistic bent of the political system, and in the long run contributed to the softening of caste antagonisms.

Since the entire period of German over-rule was so largely devoted to the conduct of punitive expeditions, it is small wonder that relatively little was accomplished in the realm of civil administration. True, an effort was made to organise an administrative superstructure patterned on the subdivision ('bezirken') already in existence in other parts of the protectorate; separate Residencies were eventually established for each kingdom; a rudimentary judicial system was implanted; and, beginning in 1912, some partially fruitful attempts were made to collect taxes. In fact, however, the administrative machinery set up by the Germans did not amount to more than a few strategically located 'police posts'. The very paucity of administrative personnel employed by the German government illustrates better than any lengthy enumeration how little was done during this period: by 1914 the entire administrative-military staff of the Rwanda Residency consisted of ten German nationals; the Burundi Residency had only six civil authorities. Under the circumstances one is inclined to agree with Professor Louis that the successes of German colonialism are more surprising than the failures.[39] But the failures cannot be overlooked. The geographical remoteness of Ruanda-Urundi, the dearth of administrative personnel, along with the incurable tendency of most Residents to resort to force rather than persuasion, account for the more prominent shortcomings of German colonialism: the absence of a viable administrative machinery at both the central and local echelons, the crudeness of the judicial system, the inadequacy of the economic infrastructure and the limited extent of the communication network. These in turn lend a measure of justification to Professor Marzorati's statement that 'owing to its out-of-the-way position Ruanda-Urundi had not received any methodical care until the arrival of the Belgians. The Belgian government had therefore been obliged to work on virgin soil.'[40]

The Belgian Mandate

The establishment of military rule through Ruanda-Urundi in 1916 was not only a normal epilogue to Belgium's victories in East Africa but a necessary condition for the realisation of its ultimate political objectives. 'One of the goals of our military effort in Africa', said the Belgian Minister of Colonies, Jules Renkin, in 1916, 'is to assure possession of German territory for use as a pawn in negotiations. If, when the peace negotiations open, changes in possession of African territories are envisaged, the retention of this pawn would be favourable to Belgian interests from every point of view.'[41] Prior to the Peace Conference, the Belgians had cast about for territorial concessions from Portugal, on the southern bank of the Congo river, in exchange for the territory they had conquered during the East African campaign. But their hopes failed to materialise. To the chagrin of Belgian statesmen, who thought it rather meagre compensation for their contribution to the war effort, the Milner-Orts agreement of May 30, 1919, left Belgium with Ruanda-Urundi and gave Britain the lion's share.

It was not until 1925, however, that the administrative status of the mandated territory was finally settled. On August 21, 1925, the Belgian government enacted a law providing for an administrative union between their newly-acquired mandate and their Congo colony. Commenting upon the practical implications of the merger, the Belgian representative to the Permanent Mandates Commission stated in October 1925: 'Ruanda-Urundi will take its place on a footing of the most complete equality side by side with the four Congo provinces and will enjoy all the benefits of the large measure of decentralisation possessed by those provinces. . . . The Belgian government thought it good, in the interests of the population of Ruanda-Urundi, not to double the already large central services and the technical and medical services established at Boma, but, thanks to the administrative union, to extend the working of these services to the mandated territory.'[42] Although Ruanda-Urundi was now for all intents and purposes an appendage of the Belgian colony, five or six more years would elapse before it could enjoy the full benefits of a civil administration.* In the meantime the day-to-day tasks of administration remained largely in the hands of the military and at first did not extend very far beyond the immediate requirements of peace and order.

There are several reasons for the incredibly slow pace at which Belgium moved along the road to initiating administrative reforms. The customs and institutions of the indigenous societies of Ruanda-Urundi were unlike any found in the Congo; their social and political organisation seemed unusually, perhaps unnecessarily, strange to the Belgian officers on the spot; the latter, moreover, by virtue of their training and background showed little concern for the social and political problems connected with the tasks of colonial administration. In addition— and this is a point which Belgian officials repeatedly stressed before the Permanent Mandates Commission—the administrative machinery

---

* The first systematic attempt towards the introduction of a uniform system of administration was made in 1929, when, at the request of the Minister of Colonies, a series of general administrative inquiries was conducted in each of the administrative subdivisions (territoires) of Rwanda and Burundi. (These documents, many of which can be secured through the Derscheid Collection, constitute one of the most valuable sources of information for the student of 'native administration' in Ruanda-Urundi.) As a result of this investigation a set of general instructions was issued by Vice-Governor General Voisin, in 1930, which specified the goals of Belgian policies in Ruanda-Urundi in these terms:

1. To respect and reinforce native authority insofar as it is exercised in harmony with civilising directives.

2. To exercise a close check on possible abuses regarding customary tithes [présentations] and compulsory labour [corvées].

3. To replace incapable chiefs with candidates designated with the accord of the Mwami.

4. To regroup chiefdoms in such a way as to suppress the dispersion of fiefs and make the administration easier and more efficient. The European personnel must realise that without the collaboration of native authorities the occupying power would be impotent and faced with anarchy.

See *Historique et Chronologie du Ruanda*, Kabgaye?, n.d., p. 25 ff.

Germany had left behind was so rudimentary and inadequate that it could serve only as a makeshift arrangement pending the introduction of a new system. One Belgian spokesman carried the argument a step further, intimating that the German record in Ruanda-Urundi did not show a single creditable achievement, and that, consequently, Belgium had been forced to make a completely fresh start: 'The Belgian mandate had been set up in a country which had for practical purposes never really come under European supervision—where there was but the embryo of an administrative occupation and no European business interests at all. It was the only mandated territory whose history had commenced for all intents and purposes with the inauguration of the mandate, and where the mandate experiment was not influenced by any colonial past.'[43]

Nevertheless, the early years of the Belgian mandate bore the unmistakable imprint of the German legacy. As in the days of the German protectorate the military was entrusted with a wide range of administrative functions; and, like their German counterparts, the Belgian Residents were forced into a variety of roles, acting as trouble-shooters, judges, counsellors and law-enforcing agents, and relying for assistance on a mere handful of European deputies, 'whose sphere of action depended on the Resident and varied according to political circumstances'.[44] While new regulations were eventually introduced to replace the German legislation, until 1925 the fundamental law of Ruanda-Urundi was German law (even though some Belgian officers candidly admitted that they knew nothing of the German legal system). The same heavy reliance of precedent can be seen in the early statements of Belgian policy. 'Belgian policy', stated an official report of 1921, 'draws its inspiration from the line of conduct followed earlier by the German authorities: to insure peace and public order while maintaining the existing balance between native groups.'[45] One finds here an echo of the principles earlier enunciated by Richard Kandt: 'Our political and colonial interests require that we support the king[s] and uphold the extreme dependence of the great mass of the population. Considering the nature of the country and the character of its people, this arrangement can be reconciled with those humanitarian imperatives which require the elimination of abuses of power and arbitrary rule over subject populations.'[46]

Not until 1925 did the Belgian version of indirect rule receive something approaching an official formulation. The core of the Belgian doctrine is found in the 1925 *Rapport sur l'Administration du Ruanda-Urundi*, in a passage which clearly reveals the authorship of Pierre Ryckmans, Belgium's first Resident in Burundi:

The co-operation of the kings constitutes an indispensable element of progress and civilisation. . . . Without them the problem of government would remain insoluble. There are among the chiefs some who are incapable, imbecile, who will never gain authority. . . . There are some who are irreducibly hostile and who will never accept civilisation. . . . These chieftaincy crises are everywhere the great stumbling block of native policies. To resolve them by dismissing a bad chief and appoint in his stead one more amenable to European influences is tantamount to substituting impotence for insubordination. Legitimacy is a moral factor of incalculable importance.[47]

These ideas were further elaborated upon in an article which appeared in the *Bulletin* of the Société Belge d'Etudes et d'Expansion, in 1925, in which Ryckmans again emphatically stressed the importance of legitimacy: 'Legitimacy is more powerful than violence. The only smoothly functioning organ between us and the masses is the *legitimate* chiefs. They alone, *because they are legitimate*, can induce acceptance of necessary innovations.' While again conceding that some chiefs may well turn out to be 'incapable', 'imbecile' or 'irreducibly hostile', he also urged the greatest caution in the handling of these situations. Removal from office was an extreme measure, to be adopted only in the very last resort, after all other solutions had failed. In any event, every effort should be made to respect the *bami*'s authority and personal prestige:

The presence of the king, the only one capable of conferring a legal, customary investiture upon a candidate of our choice, makes it possible for us to go forward without running the risk of being faced with a fatal impasse, without having to make an impossible choice between a rebellious legitimacy and an impotent submission. . . . It is therefore not because of a pure love for tradition or local colour that we keep the native kings. Let their powers be curtailed if necessary, but let no one challenge their existence and outward prestige.[48]

In arguing his case Ryckmans had constantly in mind the example of previous Belgian policies in the Congo, where the wholesale removal of legitimate chiefs and their replacement by what he called 'chiefs of the whites' had had disastrous consequences for the European administration as well as for the Africans. In contrast, he regarded the Belgian position on Ruanda-Urundi as 'a privileged one'—'for we have kings'. The kings would act as the prime legitimisers of Belgian colonial policies and practices, or, as Ryckmans put it, 'as the familiar décor which permits us to act in the wings without alarming the masses'.[49]

Yet only a year after his plea, hundreds of Rwandese chiefs were dismissed from office and in some cases temporarily replaced by chiefs of Hutu extraction. In 1931, Mwami Musinga of Rwanda was deposed and replaced by his son, Mutara Rudahigwa. Meanwhile, in Burundi a number of Batare chiefs—those very chiefs who only a few years earlier had openly flouted the authority of the crown—were officially recognised by the Belgian administration and granted a status of legitimacy similar to the chiefs of the Bezi branch.

How should one account for such radical departures from the Ryckmans doctrine of legitimacy? First, by pointing to a fundamental flaw in his reasoning, based as it was on the mistaken assumption that the sanction of legitimacy expected of the kings would always be forthcoming, almost automatically and regardless of the circumstances. In evaluating the role of kingship—and chieftainship—he drew heavily from his own experience and knowledge of the Burundi situation, assuming in effect that the king and the chiefs formed two distinctive political entities, which could be dealt with and manipulated more or less independently of each other. While this may have been true of Burundi, in Rwanda no such rigid dichotomy could be drawn, at least as long as Musinga was in power. Moreover, Ryckmans greatly overestimated the area of compatibility between his own definition of legitimacy and the requirements of administrative efficiency, here again basing his estimate almost exclusively on what he had learned in Burundi. Thus it is not entirely by accident if the Ryckmans doctrine should have worked out so much better in Burundi than in Rwanda, though not always in the way that one might have imagined.

Before going any further it will be useful to distinguish at least three levels at which Belgian policies have operated—the levels of kingship, of chieftainship and of caste relations. In practice these different areas of policy-making were not always clearly distinguishable, but for purposes of analysis the institutions to which they refer must nevertheless be treated as separate entities.

If, in Rwanda, the application of the Ryckmans doctrine was challenged from the outset by the all-encompassing, absolutist character of the kingship, and the personal obduracy of Mwami Musinga, in Burundi, where the kingship was already very weak and the office-holder still in his teens, the results were decidedly more encouraging. As mentioned earlier, the institution of kingship in Burundi was almost subsidiary to, or at least on an equal footing with, that of *ganwa*-ship. Thus the really important question was not so much whether or not to recognise the authority of the incumbent king as to decide which of the two principal dynasties—the Bezi or the Batare—should prevail over the other.

Moreover, since Mwambutsa was as yet too young to assume the responsibilities of kingship, a regent had to be chosen. Having learned the lessons of the German experience, Ryckmans correctly saw that on each of these counts political stability depended on reconciling the conflicting claims among the princes. For him this meant recognising the authority of the princes (Bezi and Batare) in their respective fiefs while at the same time working towards a compromise at the centre. To achieve this objective he resorted to a device rooted in tradition but modified to suit the purposes of his policy; this was the Regency Council, whose membership, after the death of Regent Ntarugera, in 1921, was enlarged to include representatives of both the Bezi and Batare dynasties. Ryckmans's initiative provided a basis for institutionalising the interests of the princes in a way which at first led to compromise and co-operation: 'The results obtained in Urundi are quite remarkable', stated an official report in 1925; 'this kingdom, so profoundly divided at the inception of Belgian occupation, has now regained its former boundaries. Five years of peaceful efforts have accomplished what six years of warfare had failed to produce.'[50] However, a closer look at the situation suggests a somewhat more guarded optimism. Though obviously less apparent than in earlier times, the divisions between Bezi and Batare were nonetheless real. By extending recognition to the Batare chiefs— and admitting one of their representatives (Mbanzabugabo) to the Regency Council in 1922—Ryckmans pursued a policy which most of the Bezi viewed as contrary to their interests, as well as to the interests of the crown. They felt, with justice, that the status quo enforced by the Residency had been made 'legitimate' by the force of circumstances (i.e., by the fiat of the administration and Mwambutsa's minority), not by a royal ordinance from above. To revise this status quo and tilt the balance of forces to their advantage became the main preoccupation of the Bezi chiefs in subsequent years.

In Rwanda, the centralised character of the political system made administrative control at the top relatively easy. On the other hand, the imposition of administrative limitations upon the kingship was rendered extremely difficult by the despotic nature of the office, the quasi-pathological suspicion of the king towards Europeans in general, and the maze of intrigue and double-dealings surrounding the court. As long as this situation was allowed to persist, one Belgian administrator contended, nothing but chaos would result.

The root of chaos lies in the existence of an autocratic, powerful monarchy which, moreover, remains captive to the whims of a band of sycophantic courtiers. The power of the crown has fluctuated back and forth in the hands of an ensnaring circle of favourites, and the constant pressures arising from their sedulous courtship has brought them lavish favours in return. Always close to the eyes and heart of the sovereign, he who wished to hold on to what he had gained by dint of attentions and vile flattery would take painful care to stay exposed to the generous if inconstant rays of the monarchical sun. Being absent from the court inevitably entailed all kinds of accusations and slanders, which in turn led to spoliations and often to the absentee's physical liquidation. The result: a cabal of paramount chiefs permanently stationed at the court who meanwhile found it convenient to entrust the administration of their lands to their delegates ['intendants concessionnaires'].[51]

The crisis came to a head in 1931, with the dismissal of Musinga and the accession to the throne of his eighteen-year-old son, Rudahigwa, thenceforth known as Mwami Mutara. The origins of the crisis, according to one version, can be traced back to 1926; in that year 'Musinga had attempted sodomy with sons of his nobles serving at the palace; this caused a breach between him and the chiefs, for which he blamed the White Fathers, saying they had exaggerated the facts'.[52] Whether there is any truth to these claims is difficult to say, but what is beyond question is that Musinga's relations with the Catholic Church had never been very cordial; according to Kagame, 'Musinga was bitterly opposed to missionary enterprise, on the grounds that it undermined his authority'.[53] Interestingly, Musinga is reported to have said to one of his *biru* that 'the Catholics were the most dangerous because they had adopted the practice of making sacrificial offerings to God, unlike the Protestants who recognised the authority of a supreme chief'.[54] While openly distrustful of Catholic missionaries, Musinga had all along adopted an attitude of passive resistance towards the administration, an attitude which Professor Marzoratti attributed to the fact that 'at the time of the occupation [Musinga] had been long subject to native influence': 'It has therefore been difficult to change his mental outlook; the limitation of power which the administration had imposed upon him had contributed to his hostile attitude and latent surliness.'[55]

In support of Marzoratti's argument one might point to the much more 'co-operative' attitude later displayed by Mwami Mutara, and this in spite of certain personality traits and inclinations clearly reminiscent of his father's. At a time when Rudahigwa was still an ordinary chief, in the Marangara province, a Belgian administrator gave the following revealing portrayal of the future *mwami*: 'Very intelligent but is totally lacking in character. Knavish and devious. Has been too long under the pernicious influence of the court. Cleverly conceals his true feelings towards Europeans. . . . Remains deeply attached to old traditions and to a conception of power which claims for those who hold it all conceivable rights over their subjects and no corresponding obligations and responsibilities. While feigning indifference towards the missionaries it is safe to say that Rudahigwa, without ever admitting it, entertains considerable hostility towards them.'[56] Although, in general, Rudahigwa displayed no more sympathy towards Europeans than his predecessor, his methods were very different. Where Musinga openly challenged missionaries and administrators, Rudahigwa had a special talent for working within the confines of the established superstructure, rather than against it. He had come of age at a time when European rule was already firmly established, and was better able to accommodate himself to the norms of the new system. More important still, being himself the product of mission schools, he shared with the up-and-coming generations of Tutsi elites the Western training and education which his predecessor so conspicuously lacked.

Musinga had never been able or willing to work out a mutually satisfactory relationship with the incipient 'class' of mission-educated Tutsi chiefs and subchiefs, and the resulting tensions also played a part in his dismissal. The new generations of chiefs had fully sensed the significance of the social forces that lay behind the spread of Christianity. They felt that the preservation of their traditional claims ultimately depended upon their endorsement of the new creed. For Musinga, however, the adoption of Christianity was seen as nothing short of a betrayal of his authority. Christianity meant the desacralisation of *mwami*-ship, and the relegation of the office-holder to a subordinate position. He believed that, 'since he was no longer able to kill whom he pleased, or even retain his followers in the traditional cult, he had lost all his powers, and the missionaries were now more powerful than himself'.[57]

Musinga's obduracy stemmed from his own unwillingness to accept any sort of limitation that would alter either the sacredness of his office or the structure of authority from which kingship derived its omnipotence—a structure which, with its overwhelming concentration of power at the top and multiple hierarchies of offices, leading to an extraordinary atomisation of power at the base, was quite unsuited to carry the burdens imposed upon it by the administration. The drastic alterations eventually wrought into the system in the name of administrative efficiency (and for which there has been no parallel in Burundi) made Musinga all the more suspicious of Belgian intentions.

It is at the chieftaincy level that the impact of administrative reform had its most devastating effects. In Burundi, the issue of chief-taincy was settled at an early date and, in the beginning at least, without too much difficulty. As a corollary of the Ryckmans doctrine of legitim-acy, the *ganwa* were given a relatively free hand to administer their fiefs as they pleased; and, since chiefly rule was synonymous with *ganwa* rule, this meant that the authority of the chiefs was never directly threatened by the administration. Some chiefs in fact managed to arrogate to themselves almost absolute powers in their provinces: whether they paid or did not pay their taxes was entirely up to them.* And, while the European administrators could generally tell the 'good' chiefs from the 'bad' ones—a favourite dichotomy of Belgian officials— the impression one gets is that, at least until 1929, the sphere of *ganwa* politics was entirely beyond the ken of the administration. For many years thereafter, 'non-interference' remained one of the guiding prin-ciples of the Belgian administration.

In Rwanda, however, non-interference spelled protracted chaos. There the triple hierarchy of political office at the local level confronted the administration with a host of difficulties. The Belgians had no pre-cise understanding of the functions ascribed to the land chief, the cattle chief and the army chief; a rather illuminating, though not entirely accurate, view of the system is found in the following administrative report:

* Chief Nduwumwe, Mwambutsa's uncle, is a case in point. According to Pierre Ryckmans: 'Because of his close relationship with the king, he is virtually exempt from corvées. Not a single carrier, not a single load of food, not a single head of cattle, not a single tax-payer, comes from his immense domain. His only contacts with the administration concern the prestations asked by the "chef de poste" of Kogamwami, which he takes great care in presenting as harmful to the king's authority and incompatible with the dignity that is expected from the "chef de poste" of Kitega.' *Observations sur le Rapport Politique du 1er Trimestre*, extract from a report by P. Ryckmans, 1918; in the Derscheid Collection.

Besides being the object of greater deference on the part of the Belgian administrators, the very high rate of turnover among Belgian officials made it extremely difficult for them to familiarise themselves with *ganwa* politics. Which, incidentally, prompted one official to lament: 'The Governor has explained to me that in the general interest and in the interest of colonial civil servants it was advisable to see that territorial administrators and district commissioners do not stay too long in office in their respective territories and districts. I am flabbergasted by this theory which, I am given to understand, is currently applied by the British in their territories, where the Governor has just spent a week. . . . This is, of course, the theory of the interchangeability of civil servants, which tends to transform the administration into an impersonal, rigid organism, lacking all drive and enthusiasm, and yielding negligible results. . . . I would be less than frank if I did not say that I feel rather disenchanted and that my enthusiasm for the colony is waning.' Personal letter of Oger Coubeau to J. M. Derscheid, July 21, 1933; in the Derscheid Collection.

71

A greater or lesser number of hills falls under the jurisdiction of a provincial chief, but the hills are in turn entrusted to say, 5, 8 or 15 subchiefs who keep him under their surveillance, always ready to report to the king the slightest of his mistakes. Next to the provincial chief, called the *ubutaka* chief, one finds another provincial chief who, like the previous one, is entirely dependent upon the king but whose authority concerns the cattle, the land and the Batutsi. He too is subject to the surveillance and denunciations of his subordinates. He is the *umukenke* chief. This duality of commands inevitably leads to chaos. Finally there emerges a third fellow next to the others, the *ingabo* chief. In theory he is an army chief; in fact he is merely another patron who will also demand prestations and who, in return for gifts, will act as an amicus curiae in the course of judicial proceedings and as an intermediary to the king.[58]

Because the Belgian administration believed that the division of authority would lead inevitably to conflict and anarchy, in the interests of administrative efficiency the Residency decided in 1926 to 'streamline' the structure of local government, and to replace this cumbersome trinity of powers by the rule of a single chief.[59]

This measure struck at the very roots of Rwanda society. While it did provide a temporary solution to the immediate problems, it is a moot point whether the short-run benefits were worth the ultimate risks it implied. For Kagame, it was the elimination of the army chiefs from the traditional power structure, and the resultant abeyance of the military code, which led to all the abuses associated with the *buhake*: 'The army was the basic social organisation which ensured to each individual the enjoyment of his property, in return for certain obligations; it gave him the ready assistance of a public defender [avocat] in the person of the army chief, who was obligated to defend him before every tribunal, including the *mwami*'s.'[60] If this picture seems somewhat overdrawn, it is entirely plausible to assume that, by destroying the pre-existing balance of forces on the hills, the 1926 reform prepared the ground for the emergence of a more starkly authoritarian system, centred on the rule of a single and virtually omnipotent chief. That it dealt a telling blow to the prestige of Musinga is equally clear. Not only did it deprive him of further opportunities to play off one chief against another, but it also gave him a clear hint that from now on his authority would depend upon the will of an alien power.

Far more significant historically—and infinitely more disquieting in terms of the overall objectives of Belgian policies—was the concommittant attempt made by the Residency to substitute Hutu chiefs and subchiefs for the Tutsi incumbents, a move apparently dictated by the resistance of the more conservative chiefs to the 1926 reform.[61] However, the revolutionary implications of this initiative caused the greatest misgivings among Catholic missionaries, some of whom did not hesitate to voice their concern over 'the vacillation of the colonial authorities with regard to the traditional hegemony of the well-born Tutsi'.[62] In 1930 Mgr Classe issued a categorical warning to the administration against any attempt to 'eliminate the Tutsi caste':

A revolution of that nature would lead the entire state directly into anarchy and to bitter anti-European Communism. Far from furthering progress, it would nullify the government's action by depriving it of auxiliaries who are, by birth, capable of understanding and following it. This is the view and the firm belief of all superiors of the Ruanda mission, without exception. Generally speaking, we have no chiefs who are better qualified, more intelligent, more active, more capable of appreciating progress and more fully accepted by the people than the Tutsi.[63]

In view of the radically different attitude adopted by the Catholic Church after the Second World War, this statement has a peculiar ring to it. For the time being, however, the Church posed as the strongest advocate of Tutsi supremacy, largely on grounds of political expediency. That due attention was paid to Mgr Classe's 'profession of faith' was made abundantly clear by the subsequent direction of Belgian policies. Not only were the Hutu chiefs and subchiefs all dismissed from office and replaced by 'well-born Tutsi', but a positive effort was made to preserve Tutsi hegemony in every walk of life.

The preservation—indeed the strengthening—of Tutsi supremacy was achieved in three major ways, and in the following chronological order: (i) by facilitating the territorial expansion of Tutsi political hegemony; (ii) by a rigorous control over all educational opportunities; and (iii) by the introduction of a judicial machinery designed to perpetuate the subjection of the Hutu caste.

As a result of Belgian efforts to extend Tutsi domination to northern Rwanda, a number of indigenous Hutu chiefs (*bahinza*) were summarily removed from office in the early 1920s and replaced by Tutsi appointed by the administration. This policy found its most systematic application in the Ndorwa, Mutara and Mulera regions in the north (roughly corresponding to Ndungutse's sphere of influence) and in the Busozo, Bukinzi and Bushiru in the north-west. While this parachuting of Tutsi chiefs into predominantly Hutu areas was but the continuation of a trend initiated under the German protectorate, it is also true that in many places 'the Belgians helped to install the first Batutsi chiefs in the country, the *bahinza* lacking competence to enforce the methods advocated by the occupying authority'.[64] Here as elsewhere in Rwanda the Belgian authorities were led to perpetuate and systematise the policies inaugurated by their predecessors.

Similarly, just as the education of the Tutsi caste became a special concern of the German Residents, on the grounds that they were the natural auxiliaries of the protectorate, by the early 1930s and until well after the Second World War, the consensus of opinion among Belgian administrators was that the Tutsi should remain the sole recipients of secular and missionary education. At an early date the government schools of Nyanza, Ruhengeri, Gatsibu and Cyangugu became training grounds exclusively for Tutsi (sons of chiefs as well as 'commoners') who later served the administration in the capacity of 'secrétaires indigènes' (i.e., interpreters, clerks, tax collectors, etc.). Many of these educated Tutsi were later appointed chiefs and thus constituted the embryo of a new category of functionaries which the administration used as a counterweight to the apathy or resistance of the older generations. As one administrator put it:

> The mass of the Ruanda chiefs and subchiefs has thus been infiltrated [noyautée] by valuable elements, trained by us and influenced by our methods and ideas. . . . A sense of emulation has gradually emerged among native leaders. . . . For those 'notables' whom we found incapable or unwilling to accept our ideas we were thus able to substitute some of our trainees. In this fashion the oppositional mentality which Musinga himself had tried to foster among the nobility was kept in check. Thanks to the Nyanza school, we were able to create an elite of intelligent chiefs, and, especially in the last few years, to record genuine progress throughout the country.[65]

But only in 1929, with the creation of the Ecole des Frères de la Charité (better known as the Groupe Scolaire) in Astrida (now Butare), was a special effort made to recruit students from among the sons of Tutsi chiefs and to tailor the curriculum to the functions and skills expected of a chief. In subsequent years the Groupe Scolaire became the grace-giving institution through which the Tutsi elites managed to perpetuate themselves in the seats of power, through which they gained the technical skills and training necessary for the preservation of their traditional claims to supremacy.

Although the Groupe Scolaire recruited students from both territories, the standards of admission were not nearly as restrictive in Burundi as in Rwanda. As R. E. S. Tanner recently observed, 'in the development of local government in Urundi it has often been assumed that the Belgian government educated the Tutsi . . . as a deliberate policy of maintaining the Tutsi-dominated status quo. There was in fact no such deliberate preference, but the Tutsi saw early the advantages of education, principally in terms of French and its political uses, and purposefully pursued it.'[66] Nonetheless, the inducements arising from the pressure of the caste system were never quite as pronounced as in Rwanda. The Tutsi of Burundi never felt the same psychological urge to maintain their position of dominance, socially and politically, as their Rwandese kinsmen. This, coupled with the more 'liberal' educational policies of the Burundi Residency, helps to explain why the proportion of Hutu students enrolled at the Groupe Scolaire during the 'thirties and early 'forties was markedly higher for Burundi than for Rwanda. It is also interesting to compare the enrolment figures for the early government schools of Nyanza, in Rwanda, and Muramvya, in Burundi. In 1925, the Nyanza Ecole pour Fils de Chefs had 349 students, all of Tutsi origin; in 1928, the Muramvya Ecole pour Fils de Chefs had 177 students, of whom fifty were described as 'sons of chiefs or belonging to the high aristocracy', sixty-seven were Tutsi, fifty-three Hutu, one mulatto, one Asian and five 'sons of soldiers'. The report from which these figures are extracted goes on to note that 'the educational establish-ment of Muramvya is far less frequented by the sons of paramount chiefs than its counterpart in Rwanda. The influence of the court is far less apparent in Burundi, and a good many chiefs prefer to send their sons to the district schools.'[67] As a group, the Tutsi of Rwanda were relatively better educated than their counterparts in Burundi, which in turn reinforced their sense of collective superiority vis-à-vis the Hutu and gave further justification to the Belgian contention that 'the Tutsi were the pick of the natives and [thus] should be retained in commanding positions in the native social organisation'.[68]

In time some of the policies adopted in the Congo provided a new pole of attraction for the testing and sorting out of native institutions. This is best illustrated by the introduction of 'native tribunals' in 1936. Despite the disastrous results of earlier experiments along these lines, it was assumed that in the context of the mandated territory the native tribunals would become the most effective instrument of indirect rule. In the mind of the Belgian Resident the native court system would provide the master key to every problem of native administration. The native tribunals would act at one and the same time as 'a safeguard of traditions and a brake upon their evolution', as 'a melting pot in which past and present tendencies [would] coalesce', and as 'the means where-by a progressive and progressist, yet slow and smooth, assimilation could be achieved'.[69] In fact, these tribunals became the instruments through which the ruling Tutsi oligarchy not only retained but abused its privileges. Their function was not so much to dispense justice as to legitimise abuses and wrong-doings. Since they were in every case headed by Tutsi chiefs it is difficult to imagine how they could have served a different purpose. Although the *mwami*'s tribunal was intended to serve as a court of appeal the long delays resulting from the accumulation of pending litigations often amounted to a denial of justice. Thus, with an average of only sixty cases handled each year, by 1949 the *mwami*'s tribunal was faced with a backlog of some 900 untried cases, a situation described as 'clearly alarming'.[70] If further evidence were needed to dispel illusions about the true nature of the Rwandese court system one could cite the following statement, by a former Belgian official: 'The native tribunals never played a moderating role because they were intimately linked to the political authorities. In many cases these tribunals were the organs used by the Tutsi to give a semblance of legality to their exactions. . . . The only way to redress these injustices was to seek the annulment of iniquitous decisions from the Parquet, but the number of applications was so great that it was impossible to examine each demand.'[71]

Although abuses were by no means unheard of in Burundi, justice was never quite as grossly miscarried as in Rwanda. There were fewer opportunities for abuses, as the customary obligations arising from the clientage system were less burdensome and encompassing. Moreover, the *mwami*'s tribunal acquired a reputation for efficiency and impartiality which was never matched by its Rwanda counterpart. Last, the traditional institutions of Burundi offered several alternative arenas for the settlement of litigations, for which there was no equivalent in Rwanda; particularly significant was the arbitrating role played by the *bashigantahe* at each level of the political hierarchy.

From the foregoing observations emerge two major points of difference in the working and implications of indirect rule in Rwanda and Burundi. In Rwanda the political monopoly of the Tutsi oligarchy was identified with the retention of caste privileges to a far greater extent than in Burundi; furthermore, in the context of Rwanda society the institution of the monarchy was inextricably bound up with the actions, values and instrumentalities employed by the Tutsi to maintain themselves in power. In Burundi, where administrative control was effected largely through the heads of the princely families and only marginally through the *mwami*, the crown was a minor element in the institutional matrix of the country, and therefore never became the target of social and economic grievances. One could even argue that, insofar as popular grievances were associated with the perpetuation of *ganwa* rule, the opposition of certain princely families to the *mwami*'s person served merely to reinforce the legitimacy of the crown. In Rwanda, on the other hand, political conflict expressed itself in the form of a violent clash between the crown, which stood as the symbol of Tutsi hegemony, and the egalitarian aspirations of the Westernised Hutu elites. The roots of the conflict are to be found in part in the specific pattern of social stratification and traditional institutions of Rwanda, and in the very nature of the policies pursued by Belgium in the years preceding the Second World War.

In spite of these differences, enough uniformity can be found in the principles underlying the Belgian version of indirect rule to warrant a brief comparison with the British model. The contrast between the Belgian and the British conception of 'native administration' is nowhere better illustrated than by Lord Lugard's definition of the role of the chief in the British colonial context, and his later comments about the chiefs of Ruanda-Urundi. In his classic work, *The Dual Mandate*, Lugard wrote:

> The essential feature of the system is that the native chiefs are constituted as an integral part of the machinery of the administration. There are not two sets of rulers, British and native, working either separately or in co-operation, but a single government in which the native chiefs have well defined duties and an acknowledged status equally with the British official; their duties should never conflict and should overlap as little as possible.[72]

When, some ten years later, Lord Lugard served as the accredited British representative on the Permanent Mandates Commission, he was visibly at a loss to reconcile the Belgian conception of the 'Dual Mandate' with his own theoretical formulation. In his address to the Commission, in December 1939, Lugard noted: 'At present the chiefs [of Ruanda-Urundi] have no right to give any order that had not been previously sanctioned by the Administration. They had no criminal jurisdiction; their treasuries were under the direct control of the Administrator.' 'The present system', he said, 'did not seem to allow of any personal responsibility for the chiefs.' When he asked the Belgian representative, Halewyck, about the future native policy of Belgium, he was told that 'the administration was confronted with a certain number of excellent chiefs, some bad ones, and others who only reached a mediocre or indifferent standard. If an attempt were made immediately to so organise all-round indirect administration on the strength of the experience gained with a few very good chiefs , serious disappointments would be in store.' Which in turn prompted Lord Lugard to observe, with flawless logic, that 'the administration did not see its way at present to entrust any personal responsibility to efficient chiefs because there were also bad chiefs. . . . The logical conclusion to be drawn from the explanations given by the accredited representative was that the grant of wider powers might be delayed indefinitely.'[73]

Regardless of the motives then actuating Belgian policies, the abiding fact which emerges from the record is that the authority of the chiefs suffered some crippling limitations from the omnivorous character of the European administration. By comparison with the British model, a former District Commissioner who served in Tanzania found the Ruanda-Urundi administration 'both complicated and interfering', further noting that 'while the British could not be said to have a laissez-faire system Belgium administered a "rule of law" system, imposed from above which involved no predisposing process of change within the people to whom it was applied'.[74] For most Belgian administrators all that was really needed for a satisfactory functioning of indirect rule was 'to organise the outward prestige of the *bami*';[75] that is the kind of 'window-dressing' the Belgian representative to the Permanent Mandates Commission had in mind when he stated, in 1929, that 'by means of establishing a court and a guard of honour [for the *bami*], the administration would increase their authority'. In support of his views the Belgian spokesman cited the example of Uganda, 'where much dignity had been conferred upon certain chiefs by organising their prestige',[76] but neglected to mention that in Uganda, as Lord Lugard later emphasised, 'the chiefs and the subchiefs formed, in effect, a native civil service under the Paramount's government'.[77] In Ruanda-Urundi, by contrast, the chiefs and subchiefs formed a corps of native functionaries under the immediate and permanent supervision of the European administration.

To conclude that the *bami* have always acted as puppets, as docile 'yes-men' in the hands of the coloniser, would be inaccurate. Depending on the attitude of the Residents—and the political conjuncture—they were occasionally deferred to over the appointment of chiefs and, while they were made increasingly aware of the limits of their powers, they also knew how to make the most of the opportunities offered by the system to play one official off against another, how to conceal their real intentions behind a façade of outward submissiveness, and how to put into practice the *kinyarwanda* dictum that 'the Europeans are not clever' (*abazungo ntibaze ubwenge*). But once this is said, it is equally plain that the 'native authorities' of Ruanda-Urundi were by and large denied the prerogatives and freedom the British version of indirect rule presupposed. As we shall see, the constitutional reforms introduced after the Second World War did little to alter this state of affairs.

FROM TRUSTEESHIP TO INDEPENDENCE

After the Second World War, the mandated territories, including Ruanda-Urundi, became trusteeship territories under the United Nations. Belgium's commitment to the aims of the trusteeship (politically far more significant than those stipulated under the mandates system) implied a major departure from its previous policies. Whereas in 1931 the Belgian representative to the Permanent Mandates Commission candidly admitted that 'the mandatory power's policy was not at all directed at the abolition of the feudal system of Ruanda-Urundi, which, with its hierarchy of chiefdoms and sub-chiefdoms, could quite well be adapted to the government of the territory', but merely 'to regroup the areas dependent on one chiefdom which had not been previously united', after the Second World War the official viewpoint of the trust authorities was that 'Belgian policy sought to bring to an end the feudal regime', a major advance over the mulishly static posture of previous years.[78] Moreover, if the Trusteeship Council's visiting missions undoubtedly played a part in hastening the political awakening of the indigenous populations, the repeated criticisms voiced against Belgium in the United Nations were equally instrumental in creating a climate of world opinion which had a direct influence on the pace and direction of its trust territory policy.

Nonetheless, constitutional reforms proceeded slowly and half-heartedly, owing to the characteristic caution with which the Belgian authorities approached the subject of political change, and, initially at least, to the absence of modern forms of political self-expression in each of the territories concerned. Only when confronted with what suddenly appeared an irresistible popular pressure for change did the Belgians actively and deliberately seek to synchronise constitutional reforms with political change. At this late stage, however, synchronisation was no longer possible. As in the Congo, Belgian policies in Ruanda-Urundi were a classic example of 'too little and too late'.

The visit of the first UN mission to Ruanda-Urundi, in 1948, revealed some familiar themes in the credo of Belgian colonial policy. Absolute priority was to be given to the economic progress and moral uplift of the indigenous populations; not until these preconditions were met could one envisage a democratisation of existing political institutions. In a personal statement submitted to the UN delegation, the Burundi Resident, Robert Schmidt, explained the views of his government (the following are Schmidt's own words): 'In this process of changing the whole political machinery [of Ruanda-Urundi], the degree of evolution, the aspirations and faculty of assimilation of the people must be taken into consideration. It would be harsh and unfair to render unhappy, or in a state bordering on social anarchy, one or two generations by imposing premature reforms by virtue of a political ideology or on the excuse that we are hoping to bring happiness in this fashion to future generations.'[79] The election of chiefs was envisaged as a conceivable yet distant possibility, for it would 'require from the masses an understanding of electoral procedures, and from the chiefs a moral preparation which neither has yet attained'. Furthermore, said Schmidt, the setting up of a democratic regime did not necessarily require the election of local officials, a notion which, as he chose to phrase it, might have caused mild consternation among some of his countrymen: 'Concerning the question raised about electing chiefs and subchiefs, may I repeat a remark that I made previously, I think, to one of you on this subject. Belgium, as you will recognise, is an old democratic country. Very much so. Yet our provincial burgomasters and governors (comparable to chiefs and subchiefs here) are appointed by the king and not elected.'[80] On the question of 'Hutu emancipation' the Resident voiced similar reservations: 'It has been found that in many cases as soon as a man taken from the people is given a position of trust, he generally misuses it, being very liable to bribery and embezzlement. He is worse than any of the old class of chiefs in corrupt practices detrimental to his brethren. This is one of the things that has made us wary in bringing about too drastic democratic reforms before the people are sufficiently educated to higher standards and really understand what responsibility means and implies.'[81] The Resident's qualifying remarks that 'this of course does not mean that we must or are ready to remain static' did not seem to augur a more dramatic change of tempo than was then envisaged for the Congo; in time, however, the pressures arising from Belgium's international obligations prompted it to initiate political reforms in Ruanda-Urundi long before similar steps were anticipated for its colony.

For our purpose it may be convenient to look at the constitutional evolution of Ruanda-Urundi after the Second World War as falling into two broad periods:

(i) *From 1952 to 1959*: a period of limited constitutional reforms, resulting in the introduction of advisory councils at each level of the administrative hierarchy.

(ii) *From 1959 to 1962*: a period of accelerated democratisation, inaugurated by the government's declaration of November 10, 1959, which led in 1960 and 1961 to the establishment of popularly elected organs of government both at the local and central levels, and ultimately to the independence of each territory as a separate political entity.

From the radically different responses elicited by the more recent of these constitutional transformations one can detect some equally striking variations in the political cleavages and pressures operating in each territory. In Rwanda, where the internal conflict between Hutu and Tutsi tended to over-ride the conflict between the colonial society and the coloniser, nationalism, as a cohesive force, has never been more than an epiphenomenon; in Burundi, by contrast, where internal divisions had not yet reached a comparable pitch of intensity, or a comparable ethnic quotient, nationalist assertions came to the fore much more vigorously and cohesively than in Rwanda.

Yet relatively little effort was made to accommodate the processes of political transfer to these different patterns of change. Unlike British policy, formulated in reaction to and through 'a process of inter-related pressures',[82] Belgian policy in Ruanda-Urundi was more in the nature of a generalised response to a specific challenge, the challenge of the Rwandese revolution. Just as in the early days of colonial rule Rwanda had served as the model for German policies in Burundi, half a century later it once again set the tone of Belgian policies in Burundi.

In 1952, for the first time, the decision was made to introduce a glimmer of democracy in the sphere of native administration. On July 14, 1952, a decree was issued providing for the establishment of representative organs at each level of the administrative pyramid: advisory councils were set up at the subchiefdom, chiefdom, district and territorial levels, in the form of 'conseils de sous-chefferie', 'conseils de chefferie', 'conseils de territoire' and 'conseils supérieurs du pays' (CSP).* But, apart from the fact that the powers devolved upon the councils remained strictly advisory, the complicated procedure of co-opting introduced by Belgium cast immediate doubts on the value of the experiment. As Professor Maquet pointed out, 'the system was only very moderately elective and representative . . . at each level there were unofficial members but they constituted only a fraction of the council's membership and were elected (i.e., co-opted) from among unofficial members of the lower councils, which meant that the choice was very restricted'.[83]

* To avoid possible confusions, it is well to bear in mind that the French term 'territoire' is by no means synonymous with 'territory'. In this study 'territory' refers to each of the countries that were amalgamated into the Trusteeship Territory of Ruanda-Urundi, i.e. what the Belgians referred to as 'pays'. The 'territoires', in the official Belgian terminology, were administrative subdivisions roughly similar to the 'districts' in the British possessions.

That the system was indeed 'only very moderately representative' was made patently clear by the outcome of the 1953 elections. In Rwanda 52 per cent of the seats in the subchiefdom councils fell into Tutsi hands, against 39 per cent in Burundi, with the Tutsi gaining an increasingly larger representation at each ascending step in the administrative ladder. Thus Tutsi controlled 90·6 per cent of the seats in Rwanda's Conseil Supérieur du Pays, as against 80·7 per cent in Burundi. Nor was the situation markedly improved by the introduction in 1956 of universal male suffrage for the election of the lower councils. In Rwanda, the results of the 1956 elections showed a slight drop (7 per cent) in Tutsi representation in the subchiefdom councils but further gains at the top; in Burundi, the Tutsi consolidated their position at each level.* Except for the subchiefdom councils, reflecting in each country a Hutu majority, in the last analysis the composition of the higher councils continued to show an overwhelming majority of Tutsi.

A study published in 1959[84] gives the following ethnic breakdown of administrative offices in Ruanda-Urundi:

	Offices	Ethnic Distribution					
		Tutsi		Hutu		Total	
		Total	%	Total	%	Total	%
I.	*Chiefs*	81	98·8	1	1·2	82	100
II.	*Subchiefs*	1050	95·5	50	4·5	1100	100
III.	*Conseil Supérieur du Pays*						
	1. Rwanda	31	94	2	6	33	100
	2. Burundi	30	91	3	9	33	100
IV.	*Conseils de Territoire*						
	1. Rwanda	125	80·7	30	19·3	155	100
	2. Burundi	112	81·2	26	18·8	138	100
V.	*Administrative Auxiliaries*	284	67	122	33	406	100

The hopes raised by these early constitutional reforms, and the bitter disappointment caused by the subsequent realisation that these would

---

* The statistics available for Burundi make no distinction between Tutsi, Hima and *ganwa*; all three are apparently lumped together under the same rubric as 'Tutsi'. If for no other reason one is led to suspect a serious distortion in the tabulation of the results of the 1953 and 1956 elections made by J. J. Maquet and M. d'Hertefelt in their otherwise excellent study, *Elections en Société Féodale*, ARSC, Brussels 1959, Vol. XXI, fasc. 2. In the absence of contrary evidence other than what has been gleaned in the course of interviews, I had no choice but to fall back on the data contained in the above study. The same reservation applies to the figures in the table.

hardly alter the privileged position of the ruling caste, were crucial elements in the background of the Rwandese revolution. The electoral processes were introduced at a time when the Hutu educated elites constituted a very tiny minority, and when little fundamental change had yet occurred in the traditional social structure. No parties in the modern sense of the word had emerged in either Rwanda or Burundi. In Maquet's own words, 'an elective system meant to give the people a share in their own government had been introduced in a culture founded on opposite premises, those of inequality, of the idea of born rulers, of stratified society'.[85] In these conditions it would be misleading to speak of a distortion of the vox populi through the electoral system. More than anything else the popular vote expressed the continued attachment of the masses to a value system based on deference towards the ruling caste. This fundamental fact, however, is precisely what the nascent educated Hutu elites refused to accept. In their minds, as Maquet remarked, 'the new institutions were understood in the perspective of a democratic system of representation',[86] one that would presumably 'enthrone' the representatives of the Hutu majority; instead, and to their utter dismay, they saw these institutions converted into modern arenas for the expression of Tutsi supremacy. It is against this background of disillusion and bitterness over the failure of constitutional reforms to meet expected changes that one must seek the origins of the Rwandese revolution.

It would be both an oversimplification and a travesty of facts to infer from the foregoing that the Hutu of Burundi viewed the effects of these reforms in their own territory with nothing but blissful contentment. The predominance of upper caste elements in the higher councils raised considerable anxieties among certain educated Hutu. The late Pierre Ngendadumwe (who twice held the prime ministership, before his assassination in January 1965) expressed his concern that 'the *bami* and the chiefs' had emerged as 'the great beneficiaries of the decree of July 1952', adding that 'the measures taken by assemblies that are dominated by traditional elements are automatically suspect and discredited by public opinion'. 'The present tragedy in Ruanda-Urundi', wrote Ngendadumwe in 1959, 'does not consist only in the fact of white colonisation but also in the paradox that in spite of representing a minority the near totality of offices of chief, subchief and judge are in the hands of the Tutsi'.[87] In spite of this and other evidences of anti-Tutsi sentiment, the fact is, however, that the animus of the educated Hutu of Burundi was at first primarily centred on the princely families (i.e. the *ganwa*) rather than on the Tutsi as a group. What is more, not only did the monarchy manage to escape the stigma of ethnic

83

favouritism; it emerged as the central focus of popular loyalties, and, for a while at least, provided a major unifying bond for society as a whole.

The metropolitan Belgian government's declaration of November 10, 1959, ushered in a new phase in the constitutional history of Ruanda-Urundi, in a way characterised by the same mixture of blindness and naivety as had already been revealed in the Congo—and would soon become even more painfully apparent. The appointment of a parliamentary study group (groupe de travail) in April 1959, to investigate the conditions under which a transfer of authority could safely be accomplished; the issuance of a formal declaration, in November 1959, concerning the character of the future political institutions of Ruanda-Urundi; the subsequent decision to call a Round Table conference to explore possibilities of agreement among the newly-created political parties: all were indicative of how far the metropolitan authorities leaned on the precedents established in the Congo in their effort to transfer power in an orderly manner. And as in the case of an earlier policy statement on the future of the Congo, the government's declaration of November 1959 was quickly outstripped of its contents by the pace of political developments in the trusteeship territory.

It is not only at the level of official policies that a pattern of interaction can be discerned between the Congo and Ruanda-Urundi. Political events within the Congo also had immediate repercussions on the attitudes and expectations of local politicians in both Rwanda and Burundi. Whereas in the mid-'fifties the more politically conscious of the Congolese 'évolués' readily cited the example of Ruanda-Urundi as a justification of their claims for constitutional advance, by early 1959 (and even more so after the Brussels Round Table Conference of January 1960) it was the turn of the Barundi and the Banyarwanda to take their cues from the Congolese, now regarded as the more privileged. Just as there were differences of orientation and ideology among Congolese leaders and parties, the projection of these differences into the context of Ruanda-Urundi has had a direct impact on the internal politics of each country.

By its declaration of November 1959 the Belgian government committed itself to a two-fold programme of political reform. First, to a fundamental revamping of the local political structures of each territory. The aim was to convert the subchiefdoms into communes, headed by a burgomaster assisted by a popularly elected communal council. While the communes were to form the basic political infrastructure, the chiefdoms would be transformed into purely administrative units. In each country legislative powers were to be gradually devolved upon the Conseils de Pays, with the *mwami* relegated to the position of a constitutional head of state. Second, a positive effort was to be made to encourage the creation of a broad political community, 'l'entité Ruanda-Urundi', through 'judicious consultations and with the assistance of the newly established Conseils de Pays'.[88]

By the time the statement was issued, much of its substance had already been reduced to wishful thinking—at least so far as Rwanda was concerned. As the first stage of the revolution got under way, there seemed little prospect of anything but a protracted period of searing civil strife. In any case, from then on the initiative lay almost entirely with the local European administration. At first a Conseil Spécial Provisoire was installed (in January 1960) to replace the Tutsi-dominated Conseil Supérieur du Pays, in the hope that it would 'smooth the transition between yesterday's autocratic system and tomorrow's democratic regime'.[89] By October 1960, however, a new set of provisional organs was introduced, in the form of a forty-eight-member assembly and a government, both appointed by the Residency after taking into account the results of the recently-held communal elections. But their life-span was to be even shorter than that of their predecessor. In January 1961 a Hutu-inspired and Belgian-assisted coup d'état was launched in Gitarama, in central Rwanda, which led to the proclamation of a republic and the installation of a new provisional government and an assembly, both firmly under Hutu control. Despite the vehement protestations raised in the United Nations, the Belgian administration (as well as the metropolitan government) took the view that the authors of the coup represented in effect the only legitimate provisional government of Rwanda. With the local administration now acting as the effective power underpinning the newly-established government, the legislative elections of 1961 merely confirmed the de facto situation engendered by the previous political upset.

The timing and forms of political transfer dictated by the Rwandese situation were paralleled in Burundi by the organisation of communal elections in September 1960, leading in January 1961 to the establishment of a provisional government and a provisional council. Like its Rwandese counterpart, this government was to serve 'as a purely transitional organ, to be replaced by a permanent institution after the [legislative] elections';[90] and, as happened in Rwanda, the permanent organs set up after these elections came to reflect a political complexion quite unlike that of the interim institutions. But apart from the fact that in Burundi political change was effected through the ballot box, and not through a coup d'état, the direction of change was very different. The results of the legislative elections of mid-1961 legitimised the claims of an ethnically-mixed, 'neo-traditionalist' party which, for the time being at least, posed as the strongest supporter of the monarchy.

Rwanda and Burundi

In these circumstances one can better appreciate the difficulties facing the United Nations as the question of the future of Ruanda-Urundi came before the General Assembly's Fourth Committee, in January 1962. Apart from the persistent threats of instability posed by the sporadic incursions of armed bands of Tutsi refugees into Rwanda, and the technical problems involved in the transfer of administrative services heretofore shared with the Congo, the immediate preoccupation of the United Nations was to devise a mutually acceptable formula to keep Ruanda-Urundi a single political entity.

Hyphened together by an accident of history, yet lacking a central institutional focus around which a common political consciousness could be developed, there were ample grounds for questioning the prospects of a durable union between the two states. Now that their recent political evolution had drawn them further apart from each other, their unification into a single independent state seemed even more improbable. It was the attractiveness of the ideal of Pan-Africanism rather than the immediate interest of the people of Ruanda-Urundi which led most of the African delegates to support the eleven-point resolution endorsed by the UN General Assembly on February 13, 1962, a resolution which 'reaffirmed the [General Assembly's] conviction that the best future of Ruanda-Urundi lay in the emergence of a single state with economic unity, common defence and external relations, without prejudice to the internal autonomy of each entity'.[91] Thus, under the terms of the same resolution, the General Assembly entrusted to a five-member commission (better known as the Brooks Commission) the task of convening 'as soon as possible, at Addis Ababa, a high-level conference . . . with a view to finding a mutually acceptable formula for the creation of the closest form of political, economic, and administrative union, the role of the commission being to endeavour to reconcile the two points of view of the two Governments'.

The failure of the Addis Ababa conference to achieve its proposed objective cannot be ascribed to a want of persuasiveness on the part of its chairman, Miss Angie Brooks of Liberia. In presenting her case for unity she reminded her audience that 'the balkanisation of Africa is dangerous to the African cause of unity and solidarity', and that 'close association between the two parts would enable the problems to be tackled more effectively and would at least allow substantial budgetary economies'. Certainly, much could be said for the argument that 'today large economic units can better face the complex problems of development and also better afford to take the independent economic and political stand which alone is a serious guarantee of national independence'.[92] The real question, however, was whether the prospects of economic

86

benefits attendant upon a continued territorial union could be made to prevail over the feelings of mutual repulsion arising from political differences. By dismissing as 'superficial' the objection that the existence within a single entity of a monarchy and a republic would be unworkable, Miss Brooks deliberately dodged the issue.

The statement issued by the Rwanda delegation on April 12, 1962, dashed whatever hopes still remained for a political union of the two countries. 'Political union is, for the time being, an ideal in the haziest sense of the term. . . . The Rwandese government would deplore anything so unrealistic as a forced political union, and considers it necessary to take into account the consequences of events [sic] that have left their mark on our countries' history.'[93] The views of the Burundi delegation were even more to the point: 'The recent political evolution of the two countries has been in diametrically opposite directions, democratisation having progressed in one of them by revolutionary methods and in the other by peaceful methods. The result has been a mutual hostility which leaves no room for any hope of political union in the near future.'[94] The eleventh-hour attempt of the Brooks Commission to elicit a more flexible attitude on the part of the two delegations, by submitting for their consideration a preliminary draft of a federal constitution of the United States of Rwanda and Burundi, ended in total failure.[95]

The only tangible, albeit rather ephemeral, achievement of the conference was the signature, on April 19, of an 'Agreement on Economic Union' between the governments of Rwanda and Burundi, providing for the maintenance of the monetary union and customs union after the attainment of independence, the joint management of such para-statal agencies as the Office des Cafés Indigènes du Ruanda-Urundi (OCIRU), the Institut National des Etudes Agronomiques au Congo (INEAC), and the Institut pour la Recherche en Afrique Centrale (IRSAC); the appointment of a civil service commission to study the administrative and budgetary problems involved in operating these common services; and the establishment of an economic council 'to assist the two governments in co-ordinating the main lines of their economic, financial and trade policy'.[96] Thus the closest possible form of union achieved by the conference was in fact a very loose type of association, based on a half-hearted compromise over the joint management of certain economic and fiscal matters. Even this was at best a precarious formula. Subsequent events made it abundantly clear that there were no possible grounds for such co-operation in a climate of growing political tension.

By way of an explanation for this unhappy state of affairs, the Brooks Commission reported:

87

A whole complex of historical and social conditions, under which their peoples had long been suffering, the unjustified fear that unity might jeopardize what each side had come to regard as a dearly-won prize to be defended at all costs, a deep-seated and almost morbid reluctance on both sides to try a new approach to the old problems in the broader context of their historic evolution—these, among others, were the factors which appeared to be compelling the two delegations to try to preserve at any price what they regarded as the future vehicle of the freedom of action and of identity they had at last regained.[97]

But it remained for Max H. Dorsinville, Chairman of the UN Commission for Ruanda-Urundi, to stress the share of responsibility borne by the administering power:

I have never concealed the fact that in my opinion the record of the administering authority was not good. Decades of political stagnation were followed by an inconsistent and biased policy following the incidents of 1959 in Rwanda. There is justification for thinking that a more straightforward, objective and perspicacious attitude on the part of the administering authority, at least during the past ten years, might have avoided or at least mitigated the crisis through which Ruanda-Urundi is now passing and would have made it possible today to contemplate the future with greater optimism.[98]

It is worth recalling here the absolutely rigid position of the Belgian authorities on the issue of a time-table for independence. As late as 1956, the Trusteeship Council by an eight to five vote recommended the fixing of intermediate target dates for the social, economic and political advancement of Ruanda-Urundi; but the Belgian delegate insisted that this was impossible and dangerous because of the consequences of an inaccurate forecast. One may wonder whether anything could have created a more dangerous situation and shown a more inaccurate estimate of political realities than the hasty improvisations that were forced upon Belgium by the accelerating pace of events in Rwanda.

Yet the character of Belgian policies is not enough in itself to explain the radically divergent paths to independence followed by Rwanda and Burundi. If one accepts the view that Belgian policy was a constant variable in the political history of the two kingdoms, their different evolution must have been conditioned by other factors as well, social and structural differences that had crystallised long before the inception of colonial rule. As noted earlier, however rigid the framework of Belgian administration and however uniform its principles, it was initially bent to accommodate itself to the structural characteristics of each kingdom. Relatively little was done to alter traditional role relationships; indeed, if anything, the result has been to enhance rather than diminish structural disparities between each state. But by the time Belgium found it appropriate to initiate a transfer of power, there occurred a sudden and drastic revision of the policies which had heretofore governed the relationships of the administering authorities with the indigenous groups, as well as the relationships among these groups. At this point the differential impact of previous policies was dramatically brought to light by the course of political developments in each territory. In Rwanda the forcible reversal of traditional role relationships set the stage for violent ethnic strife. In Burundi, where caste cleavages were more numerous and fluid, and less 'consistent' with ethnic differences, the abandonment of indirect rule held no such implications; only after the consummation of independence, with the emergence of a new type of stratification, much closer to the Rwandese pattern, could one detect in the political climate of Burundi signs of an incipient ethnic struggle.

Thus the processes of change set in motion by the approach of independence must be seen in the two-fold perspective of the temporal variations that have affected Belgian policies since the Second World War and of the variant responses these elicited from the indigenous groups. That this pattern of challenge and response should have expressed itself in such radically different ways in each territory is as much a reflection of the political 'immobilisme' which characterised previous Belgian policies as of structural and cultural variations inherent in the political system of each kingdom.

Part Two

Rwanda

'Il faut raccourcir les géants
Et rendre les petits plus grands;
Tout à la vraie hauteur
Voilà le vrai bonheur!'

(We must shorten the giants
And make the small folk taller;
Everything at its true height—
That is real happiness!)

French Revolutionary song, 1793

3. The Peasant Revolution: Myths and Realities

'THE PEASANTS alone are revolutionary, for they have nothing to lose and everything to gain. The starving peasant, outside the class system, is the first among the exploited to discover that only violence pays. For him there is no compromise, no coming to terms.'[1] Seldom anywhere has Frantz Fanon's dismal diagnosis of the revolutionary potential of the peasant masses received greater supporting evidence than in Rwanda during the terminal years of Belgian colonial rule. In no other African state, not even in the Congo during the 1964-65 rebellion, have the underpinnings of a revolutionary movement been so overwhelmingly rural, and its political orientation more plainly illustrative of the phenomenon of 'rural radicalism'. What better example could one cite of a peasant society revolting against the suffocating constraints of the caste system in which it had been enclosed for centuries? Where else in Africa has the defenestration of a ruling aristocracy been more obviously linked to a fundamental change in the political ordering of society?

Yet by formulating the issues in such sweeping rhetorical terms, one runs the risk of giving Fanon's argument more credit than it actually deserves, and of dismissing as irrelevant certain specific aspects of the Rwanda revolution which do not fit the usual pattern of peasant revolution. To grasp the nature of the forces that have demolished the Tutsi monarchy one must first try to demolish the fallacies that have grown around the Hutu revolution.

THE MYTHS EXPOSED

Of all the shibboleths that have gained currency about the Rwanda revolution, none has been more detrimental to sound analysis than the presumption of social and cultural homogeneity among Hutu 'peasants'. Either because the word 'peasantry' implies certain social uniformities, or because 'Hutu' has tended to become almost interchangeable with 'peasantry', relatively little attention has been paid to the degree of internal differentiation that has occurred over the years within this particular stratum, and how this, in turn, has affected the dynamics of

93

revolutionary change.* Thus, it has generally been concluded that, since the revolution received its impetus from Hutu elements, it could only be characterised as the expression of a peasant protest movement. Another misconception is what one might call the 'spontaneous combustion' theory of revolutionary change. According to this view, the advent of republicanism in Rwanda was the result of a spontaneous and massive display of revolutionary fervour, obeying, as it were, its own inner dynamic. Professor Helen Codere's categorical statement aptly sums up the essence of the argument: 'The revolution in Ruanda is a Ruandese revolution. While a host of factors connected with the presence of Europeans in Ruanda during the past six decades enabled the revolution to take place, the revolution was neither inspired, created, nor engineered by outside forces, Belgian, United Nations, African or any other.'[2] Finally, it is generally held that, since the system against which the Hutu peasantry rebelled was a closed feudal oligarchy, it could give way only to a type of polity exhibiting precisely opposite features—an open, democratic, consensual society. Again, to quote from Professor Codere: 'The [Ruanda] revolution [was] an attempt on the part of the majority to achieve a social and political order based on consent.'[3]

No matter how prevalent, none of these assumptions can be accepted without the strongest qualifications and reservations. To argue that, since all Hutu were by definition 'peasants', the revolution could not be anything but a peasant revolution would be just as unwarranted as to ascribe identical status and political aspirations to the Tutsi as a group. Apart from the fact that there is little justification in Rwanda for associating peasant status with uniform cultural traits, on the eve of the revolution the term 'Hutu' could no longer be used interchangeably with a single social category. However limited the scope of the social transformations introduced by Belgium, at least some degree of upward social mobility did take place across caste lines, and, with the emergence of new reference groups within the Hutu stratum, a new basis of relationships was created not only between Hutu and Tutsi, but, even more importantly, among the Hutu themselves. Thus if it can be reasonably

* On the definitional and conceptual problems raised by the use of the term 'peasant' in the African context, see Lloyd A. Fallers, "Are African Cultivators to be called 'Peasants'?", *Current Anthropology*, Vol. II, 1961, pp. 108–11. Although the Hutu of Rwanda come closer than any other African group to meet Fallers' criteria of a 'peasant society'—if only because they possess to a remarkable degree the sense of cultural autonomy or 'folk culture' which Fallers does not 'feel justified in attributing to the African villager'—their social structure exhibits patterns of differentiation, based on residential or lineage segmentations, which deviate markedly from the conventional view of peasant societies.

maintained that all Hutu were by definition of peasant background, it is equally true that those elements who formed the spearhead of the revolution shared occupational statuses and psychological dispositions substantially different from those of ordinary bush peasants.

Nor is the tendency to perceive the Hutu as being all one, culturally and socially, compatible with the persistence in the north of such traditional status differences as can still be discerned between the descendants of traditional land-owning families and their clients. These differences, as we have seen, were part of a system of stratification indigenous to the northern Hutu subculture. The superimposition of Tutsi rule did much, of course, to obscure or modify its original contours, but seldom to the point of obliterating all previous distinctions. Inasmuch as they were allowed to perpetuate themselves, these traditional cleavages played no less important a role in shaping contemporary leadership patterns, during and after the revolution, than modern 'class' cleavages of the type noted above; by the same token, the discontinuities of culture and history associated with the juxtaposition of both types of cleavages— together with the different 'vested interests' which Tutsi rule tended to create within the interstices of such traditional and modern status differences—are just as crucial to an appreciation of intergroup tensions which have developed among the insurgents.

Far from being the massive, irrepressible uprising that some might imagine, the Hutu revolution was a long and painful enterprise, which may not have succeeded without the auxiliary support extended by the Belgian administration to the insurgents. The upheaval began as a jacquerie, transformed itself into a localised rebellion, and finally wound up as a social and political revolution directed against both Tutsi hegemony and monarchical rule. In this process the Belgian administration played a determining role, gradually destroying or neutralising all sources of resistance to the revolutionary movement, while at the same time creating new institutions through which further changes could be generated.

Only by reminding ourselves of the exceedingly circumscribed position of the Hutu peasantry in traditional Rwanda society can we appreciate the tremendous obstacles placed in the way of revolutionary activity. These obstacles were in part those encountered in peasant societies all over the world; they were inherent in the closed, atomised character of rural communities in general.[4] But one could also point to other limiting factors and circumstances more specifically related to the social and physical environment of Rwanda—for instance, the psychological ties of dependence that once linked the Hutu peasant to his lord, a relationship reminiscent of what O. Mannoni refers to as 'the dependence complex'.[5] Based on the need for psychological attachments of the kind that a child is expected to display towards his parents, this relationship was further reinforced by the incidence of the caste system, and in particular by the division of labour and normative expectations perpetuated through caste affiliations. Just as restrictive were the limitations arising from the persistence of clientage ties between Hutu and Tutsi. Because of the very nature of dyadic relationships (i.e., those based on reciprocal obligations between patron and client), the Hutu masses had little consciousness of themselves as a group. The roles, norms and statuses associated with the clientage structure tended not only to block the emergence of a separate Hutu consciousness but to positively reinforce the attachments of the individual Hutu peasant to his lord. The result, up to a point, has been to hamper the development of any sort of corporate ties other than those based on feelings of personal allegiance.[6] Finally, Rwanda's mountainous terrain, the absence of large-scale concentrations of population, and the relative inadequacy of the communications network were all enormous obstacles to effective political mobilisation and made the other handicaps all the more difficult to overcome.

Given these conditions, it would clearly be unrealistic to try to dissociate the course of revolutionary events in Rwanda from the 'supportive' role played by the trust authority after the initial outbreaks. The quotient of democracy exhibited by the republican regime has never been very high and may indeed become even more negligible as years go by. Although the concept of democracy has become officially identified with the temper of the Hutu revolution, and with the inevitability of its triumph, the revolution was primarily, though not exclusively, an ethnic phenomenon. And because the Hutu as a group shared many of the disabilities which elsewhere have hampered peasant political action and influence, its ultimate success, far from being inevitable, appears all the more surprising.

THE SOURCES OF REVOLUTIONARY CHANGE

Given the complexities and ambiguities of the sources of change in pre-revolutionary Rwanda, one can do little more in this chapter than offer a brief sketch of the complex of forces that have shaped the growth of revolutionary sentiment and activity, and, in the light of these conditioning influences, map out the main stages of revolutionary development.

But before embarking on this preliminary exploration, there is yet another myth to be exposed—the notion that Western ideas and influences were the sole motive force behind the upsurge of revolutionary sentiment. While there is no denying the importance of such external stimuli, the questioning of fundamental allegiances brought to light during the revolution was at least as much an expression of disharmonies inherent in the traditional texture of Rwanda society.

There are two points to consider here. Firstly, much of the momentum gained by the revolution after the initial outbreaks came from the resurgence or reactivation of long-standing inter-group tensions which the ruling oligarchy had either failed to dissipate or could no longer manage with the same degree of efficacy as it had in the past. These tensions were of different kinds. While some were essentially cultural and historical, pitting caste against caste and region against region, others were the product of social and economic transformations brought in the wake of Tutsi 'colonisation', and tended to oppose not only Tutsi against Hutu but Hutu against Hutu. In each case, however, predispositions to engage in violence stemmed from social disruptions that can be traced to specific historical conditions.

The next point, implicit in the foregoing, is that the potential for revolutionary change thereby offered by the traditional society could best be tapped through the use or adaptation of traditional relationships and in particular through a redefinition of clientage ties. Tradition, in other words, served both to inhibit and accelerate societal transformations. If so, certain major reservations must be introduced to what was said earlier about traditional sources of resistance to change. Firstly, the strength of the 'dependence complex' varied enormously from one region of Rwanda to another, and the kinds of inhibitions it entailed were largely absent from those areas where Tutsi hegemony was too recent a phenomenon to command widespread allegiance from the Hutu communities. Secondly, it is all too easy, and unwarranted, to exaggerate the stabilising properties of the clientage relationship. One must also take into account the reversibility of this relationship and note the very rich potential for revolutionary change arising from the proper manipulation of the client-patron dependency. Once inserted into the context of ethnic solidarities, the client-patron nexus could easily be transformed into a leader-follower relationship aiming at a total transformation of established hierarchies.

The Incidence of Traditional Cultural Variations

Leaving aside for the time being the more recent changes effected through Western influences, attention must be drawn to certain major variations in the type of social structure encountered among the populations of northern and central Rwanda, for in these variations lies the key to an understanding of their differing degrees of receptivity to revolutionary change. Not only have the northern Hutu populations been subject to very different conditioning influences and institutions, owing to their relatively brief exposure to the Tutsi imperium, but, for this very same reason, their relations with the Tutsi oligarchy have been marked by far greater tensions.

Broadly speaking, these differences are reducible to a juxtaposition of two distinctive patterns of stratification—one characterised by a situation of optimum functional integration, of the kind that one might expect from a fully developed caste society, and the other by what Max Weber referred to as a situation of mere 'ethnic coexistence'.[7] The former, typical of central and southern Rwanda, produced a relatively well-integrated society, even though its legitimacy owed much to the supremacist implications of its traditional mythology; the latter, characteristic of northern Rwanda, was typical of the 'plural society' described by J. S. Furnival, in which 'different sections of the community [live] side by side but separately within the same political unit'.[8] In the latter case the maintenance of the social order had virtually nothing to do with normative sanctions and depended to a considerable extent on the dominant oligarchy's capacity for coercion, thus creating a situation eminently congenial to the growth of revolutionary sentiment.

History shows that neither situation remained static. Absorption of the 'peripheral' Hutu communities into the caste structure of the Tutsi invaders was an almost continuous process, involving as a result a partial loss of cultural identity for the absorbed group and its reintegration into a new system of social action. The process has been described by Weber as follows:

> The caste structure transforms the horizontal and unconnected coexistences of ethnically segregated groups into a vertical system of super- and sub-ordination. Correctly formulated: a comprehensive societalization integrates the ethnically divided communities into specific political and communal action. In their consequences they differ precisely in this way: ethnic coexistences condition a mutual repulsion and disdain but allow each ethnic community to consider its honor as the highest one; the caste structure brings about a social subordination and an acknowledgement of 'more honor' in favor of the privileged caste and status groups. This is due to the fact that, in the caste structure, ethnic distinctions as such have become 'functional' distinctions.[9]

The important point to note here is that the conversion from 'ethnic coexistence' to 'functional distinctions' did not everywhere proceed at the same speed. Because of the time-lag involved in the process of territorial expansion of Tutsi hegemony, the solidity of the caste structure tended to diminish in proportion to the distance from the central to the peripheral regions. This is why in the north 'ethnic coexistence' was the rule rather than the exception, whereas in other regions the indigenous social structure shared the qualities of a society in which ethnic differences tended to reflect a functional division of labour among groups.

This distinction is not only of academic interest; it is absolutely fundamental to an understanding of contemporary issues. Unlike what happened in the north, the revolution in central Rwanda was a social revolution in the sense that it developed its dialectic from the social inequities of the caste system. Such a revolution could not have taken place unless the old particularistic ascriptive order had already been partially undermined by the spread of universalistic egalitarian values. In the north, however, this type of conflict was probably not the most decisive force behind the revolution, for in seeking to evict the Tutsi oligarchy from its position of power the northern Hutu did not aim so much at the creation of a new social order as to revert to the social order in existence prior to the intrusion of Tutsi conquerors.

This curiously 'retrogressive' attitude of the northern Hutu populations is inseparable from the sense of cultural pride which to this day permeates their outlook and gives their political loyalties a distinctively parochial bent. Though ordinarily referred to as Hutu by Westerners, the populations indigenous to northern Rwanda are better known among themselves as Kiga or Bakiga. They form a distinctive cultural complex, the boundaries of which are roughly co-terminous with the former territoires of Ruhengeri, Gisenyi and Biumba. Despite obvious affinities with the Iru populations of Ankole and the Hutu of central Rwanda, they insist that they are culturally distinct from either group. Above all they take great pride in the fact that they managed to hold their Tutsi and Hima neighbours at bay for so long. 'The proud boast of the Kiga', wrote P. T. W. Baxter, 'is that they never were, as a people, subjugated by either Tutsi or Hima.'[10] Although Baxter's reference was to the Kiga of Uganda,* his statement might have applied equally well to the Kiga of Rwanda had it not been for the timely assistance proffered

---

* The Kiga of Uganda are heavily concentrated in the Bufumbiro region, sometimes referred to as 'British Rwanda', one of the four counties of the Kigezi district of Uganda. The area was formally incorporated into the Uganda Protectorate by the International Boundary Commission of 1912. Although the area was never fully assimilated to the Rwanda monarchy, many Tutsi still claim it as an integral part of their national territory.

by the European colonisers to Tutsi invaders. All this, of course, does not mean that the Kiga had approached anything like a 'national' consciousness prior to the Tutsi invasion; although a temporary defensive grouping of clan heads did occur on many occasions, for most Kiga the clan was, and probably still is, the beginning and the end of political authority. But this much at least is clear: not having had the same closeness and duration of contact with Tutsi culture as the Hutu of central Rwanda, the Kiga have all along retained a far deeper attachment to their respective ruling clans than to the chiefly authorities imported by the Tutsi invaders. To this day the heirs of the old Kiga ruling families retain considerable prestige within their region, a fact which many of them have tried to exploit, albeit with varying degrees of success, to regain a measure of authority within the institutions of republican Rwanda.

In this combination of cultural pride and deep attachment to their indigenous political institutions lies part of the explanation for the rich heritage of messianic activity produced among the northern populations by the imposition of both Tutsi and European over-rule. At some time early in the nineteenth century northern Rwanda became the scene of the spirit-possession Nyabingi cult.* Although relatively little is known of its origins, the cult's rapid development among the Kiga seems closely related to the expansionist drive of Mwami Rwabugiri in the late nineteenth century. In time, the Nyabingi added to its magico-religious trappings the qualities of a politically subversive sect directed against all established authority, and in particular against Tutsi authority. J. E. T. Philipps described it as 'revolutionary in method and anarchic in effect. Every attempt is made to surround the simplest actions with supernatural significance. The whole appeal is to fear and the lowest instincts, to the masses, Bahutu, against the classes, Batutsi and Batwa.'[11] But for all its anarchic, nihilistic coloration, it was the Nyabingi cult which provided various political outlaws from the court of Mwami Musinga

---

* 'Nyabingi', meaning literally 'one who possesses great riches', is believed to have been the title of a queen of Karagwe who reigned in the eighteenth century, until she was murdered by a Hamitic chief of Mpororo named Ruhinda. According to one tradition, the Nyabingi sect served as the vehicle through which the queen's spirit enacted vengeance upon her murderers and disloyal subjects. Subsequently, the Nyabingi evolved into a magico-religious sect acting primarily as a protecting authority for its devotees. A British colonial civil servant, who acquired first-hand knowledge of the sect while serving as District Commissioner in Kigezi, reported: 'An outstanding feature of the Nyabingi methods was the alleged power of self-transformation of personality and appearance exercised by its individual priests, of which I have witnessed some astonishing and apparently inexplicable examples.' J. E. T. Philipps, "The Nyabingi: An Anti-European Secret Society in Africa", *Congo*, Vol. I, 1928, p. 318.

with an organisational base against the ruling dynasty; it was through the Nyabingi that Muhumusa achieved political authority in Ndorwa and managed to 'bend to her will all but the most courageous and independent characters among the Bakiga';[12] and it was in part through the Nyabingi that a 'social bandit' like Ndungutse recruited his large following of Kiga. By then, however, the sect had transferred much of its animus against Europeans in general, causing British, Belgian and German administrators countless difficulties. At the outbreak of the First World War, the sect, now under the leadership of a certain Bichu-Birenga, brought the whole northern region to the verge of chaos: 'The caravans of the Mission des Pères Blancs were attacked in the Mlera district; German patrols were murdered in the Kivu area; Belgian lines of communication through Buita were cut; rebellion was organised in the newly-founded British district of Kigezi.'[13] Not until several years later, and at the cost of numerous repressions, was a measure of tranquillity restored to the region.

In what specific ways did all this affect the sources, tempo and direction of revolutionary change? First, and most obviously, the climate of messianic unrest experienced by the northern populations made them all the more receptive to subsequent forms of protest against established authority. Precisely because of this situation, the constraints originating from the 'external' forces of control (i.e., Tutsi chiefs and subchiefs) were all the more difficult to endure. Something of a vicious circle developed: while the northern Hutu were from the outset psychologically conditioned to rebel against the power of the chiefs, for this very reason the chiefs were given a far greater freedom of repression than was ordinarily tolerated, which in turn invited further attempts at rebellion. P. T. W. Baxter's comment, that 'the permanent effect of the [Nyabingi] cult [in the Kigezi District of Uganda] may be said to be the influence it had in strengthening the arbitrary powers of the chiefs',[14] is even more applicable to Rwanda. The very stringency of chiefly rule made rebellion against it all the more probable, once the precipitants of violence became operative.

Second, given the nature of the social and political forces at work in the region, it is not by pure coincidence if the earliest and strongest reaction against Tutsi supremacy should have occurred in the north. This differential timing in the surge and intensity of revolutionary sentiment enabled the northern revolutionary elites to mobilise support more quickly and effectively than elsewhere; and, once this had happened, they were able to accelerate the spread of revolutionary sentiment and activity to areas where there had been little evidence of either phenomenon. The revolutionary contagion emanating from the north considerably strengthened Hutu solidarity throughout the country, at the same time intensifying inter-caste antagonisms.

Third, the same factors which propelled the northern populations to the forefront of the crusade against Tutsi hegemony conspired to give their political awakening a distinctly 'conservative' bent—yet a conservatism shot through with anarchistic overtones. Chalmers Johnson's contention that 'anarchistic revolutions occur in order to reverse changes which are themselves well along towards producing a new status quo', and, more specifically, 'in order to counteract a change from pre-national to national community',[15] is nowhere more aptly illustrated than by the recent history of northern Rwanda. As we shall see, like most earlier examples of 'primary resistance' against Tutsi penetration, revolutionary developments in the north took the form of a reaction against the social and political changes produced by the forceful incorporation of the indigenous populations into a new 'national' framework—against the intrusion of alien minorities (Tutsi and Europeans), and with a view partially to restoring the political status quo in existence before the Tutsi conquest.

The northern uprisings added a special ideological twist to the Hutu revolution, characterised by a curious mixture of elitism and xenophobia. Out of this combination of seemingly incompatible features —elitist and egalitarian, xenophobic and fraternal—has emerged a similarly hybrid, ambivalent polity, in which the notion of democracy takes on very special connotations.

The Reversal and Rehabilitation of Traditional Statuses

The social tensions experienced by Rwanda society on the eve of the revolution should now be looked at from a somewhat narrower perspective—that of the motives behind the behaviour of the revolutionary actors. Two points ought to be emphasised at the outset. For all that has been said about the carry-over of historical influences, the men who assumed the leadership of the revolution in the north are by no means to be identified with the 'social bandit' or 'Robin Hood' type; no matter how prevalent this kind of leadership may have been at one time, theirs was a very different one in terms of its social bases and ideological orientation. The northern leaders were recruited exclusively from Kiga clans indigenous to northern Rwanda; and while many looked back with nostalgia to the pre-Tutsi past, and indeed consciously used their traditional kinship ties and status positions to mobilise the support of the peasantry, their ultimate goal was not purely and simply to turn the clock back to the pre-conquest stage, nor merely to ease the fiscal burdens of the masses—as had been the case in the days of Ndungutse

—but to salvage and adapt specific features of their traditional political culture to the context of a new polity. Unlike the 'social bandits' of an earlier period, they were decidedly more Western in outlook; unlike their revolutionary counterparts in southern Rwanda, however, their residual commitment to their indigenous subculture led them to display a far greater selectivity in their ultimate choice of political formulas and institutions. Just as important to bear in mind, therefore, are the variations of leadership patterns brought to light during the revolution between north and south. Despite the common denominator of their shared opposition to Tutsi rule, the revolutionary zeal of the northern and southern leadership groups stemmed from radically different sets of motivations.

In central and southern Rwanda, the men who took the lead in the fight against the monarchy were drawn from a group of Hutu intellectuals whose perception of themselves in relation to their traditional environment had become the source of intense frustration. Although their 'objective' status in society was intended to remain one of unmitigated subservience to the ruling caste, their comparatively high educational achievements, along with the general socio-economic transformations introduced by Belgium, invited them to drastically redefine their position in society. They now felt an irrepressible urge to align their 'environment' with their levelling aspirations. From their efforts to eliminate the growing discrepancy between Western egalitarian values, on the one hand, and traditional Tutsi values and institutions, on the other, a kind of social disequilibrium developed between the norms of the traditional society and the aspirations of this new group of 'emancipated' intellectuals, which in turn invited a violent reaction against the regime. To put it in more general terms, revolutionary change in central and southern Rwanda was a function of a perceived discrepancy between 'objective' and 'subjective' statuses: the wider the gap between them, and the more insuperable the obstacles in the way of a peaceful adjustment of status, the greater the chances of a revolutionary upheaval.

Far more ambiguous were the motives of the northern leadership. Although Western acculturative influences undoubtedly played a part in fostering new expectations about the future, what was involved here was a desire not so much to bring the existing political system in line with egalitarian norms as to adapt it to pre-Tutsi norms, to standards of behaviour patterned along an indigenous 'clanic' tradition. More was contemplated than a mere reversal of Tutsi-enforced statuses; the aim was nothing less than a rehabilitation of traditional, pre-Tutsi, statuses.

For the sake of clarity, it may be useful to distinguish at the outset the type of social hierarchy in existence in the north prior to the Tutsi conquest from that to which it subsequently gave way. The former consisted essentially of the traditional lineage heads, who originally owned the land (*bakonde*), and their clients (*bagererwa*); the latter included the Tutsi chiefs and subchiefs, now arrogating to themselves the authority of the *bakonde*, plus their own landed clientele, in most cases recruited from among the local Hutu populations. These new clients became known as 'political *bagererwa*' to distinguish them from their predecessors, usually referred to as 'traditional *bagererwa*' ('*bagererwa* coutumiers'). To further complicate matters, the substitution of one hierarchy for the other did not, of course, occur overnight; nor was it everywhere carried out with the same degree of completeness. Situations were thus encountered where the two hierarchies tended to coexist side by side with each other, though seldom peacefully; but even where an entirely new hierarchy seemed to have supplanted the old, traditional claims tended to persist.

Out of the dislocations engendered by this changing political context, the focus of conflict increasingly centred on economic antagonisms between political and traditional *bagererwa*. As clients of the local Tutsi oligarchy, the former had a strong 'vested interest' in maintaining the Tutsi presence; for the traditional *bagererwa*, however, this situation was not only detrimental to their economic interests but hardly compatible with their traditional claims. As they saw themselves forced into surrendering more and more of their usufructuary rights over the land to the political clientele of the Tutsi chiefs, elements of a class struggle were injected into the situation. This, however, was not only a struggle between 'rich' and 'poor', but one in which two different conceptions of legitimacy were at stake: one was identified with the resuscitation of a political order which the Tutsi presence threatened to extinguish; the other with the 'new' order which this presence had forcefully superimposed upon the old.

This is where a genuine identity of interests eventually developed between the *bakonde* and their traditional clients. In a sense, of course, this identity of interests had always existed; but not until the coming of Western economic and educational influences to the north, and the emergence of a new political climate, were the *bakonde* able to translate this relationship into a revolutionary nexus. As long as they were denied all educational opportunities, and as long as the Tutsi oligarchy enjoyed the unconditional support of the European authorities, their attempts to turn back the tide stood little chance of success. When they chose to cast themselves in the roles of 'social bandits', the *bakonde* suffered from the disabilities generally associated with 'social banditry'—no firm organisational apparatus or ideological framework with which to sustain their goals. Only with the emergence of a new generation of *bakonde*, substantially more Westernised and better-educated than their predecessors, could their traditional claims be successfully integrated into a revolutionary movement. Being denied the positions of power and influence to which they felt entitled both by virtue of tradition and, even more importantly, by the conferments of their education and training, they were doubly anxious to challenge the legitimacy of Tutsi over-rule. All the more so, indeed, now that they had the weapons to make good their claims to power. Not only could they use the symbiotic relationship which linked them to their traditional clientele to build up a revolutionary following; they also possessed the manipulative skills and intellectual vision that enabled them to relate this political leverage to the attainment of nationwide goals.

But this was scarcely sufficient to offset the gravitational pull which their local bases of support exercised upon the leadership. Their continued dependence upon their traditional clientele led them to adopt an even more traditional stand on certain issues than they themselves felt to be justified. Their style of leadership also bore traces of this relationship. Thus, in the north, the crusade against Tutsi hegemony took on some of the qualities of an anarchistic movement, conducted, in characteristic fashion, under the aegis of an alliance of the *bakonde* 'aristocracy' and the peasantry. By contrast, the style of protest brought to light in other areas seemed much more typical of a 'modern' egalitarian movement, led by coalition of Westernised intellectuals and rural proletarians.

When the time came to generate support from 'below', however, the Hutu leaders showed themselves very much the captives of tradition, regardless of where they came from. As has already been hinted, revolutionary mobilisation in Rwanda took the form of a reactivation or transfer of clientage ties from one ethnic group to another, with the implication that the elite-follower nexus was but the modified expression of the traditional peasant-lord or *bakonde-bagererwa* relationship. But this conversion of clientage ties could scarcely be effected with the same ease in central Rwanda—where the values underlying the caste system had been operative over a much longer period of time—as in the north —where clientage relationships between Hutu and Tutsi had only the most fragile basis of legitimacy, and where the traditional clientele of the local ruling clans remained acutely conscious of their customary rights and privileges. Clientship in the north was not only strongly anchored in tradition; it was intimately bound up with the land problem

—a problem associated with extraordinarily complex and explosive issues, some of which are still awaiting solution. In these conditions, the *bagererwa-bakonde* relationship could be all the more easily reactivated and the human solidarities thereby established, or re-established, all the more quickly mobilised for revolutionary purposes.

The Accelerators of Change

Of all the external factors which have helped intensify and enlarge revolutionary consciousness and activity, the role of the United Nations visiting missions is the first, chronologically, to have come into play. The opportunities offered by the triennial visits of UN officials for articulating grievances and establishing informal contacts with presumably impartial observers acted as intermittent prods to the nascent revolutionary elites, who, at a later stage, were also able to use the arena of the Trusteeship Council as a forum for ventilating their grievances. Yet this is not where the ultimate significance of the trusteeship machinery lies. The mere fixing of a target date for independence was perhaps even more instrumental in forcing political activities into revolutionary channels. It was their intense fear that self-government might be thrust upon them before they could reap the benefits of majority rule (in which case self-government could only mean the perpetuation of Tutsi over-rule) which prompted the Hutu leadership to engage in revolutionary activity. Similarly, by insisting on the introduction of 'democratic' procedures that would pave the way for independence—i.e., the holding of general elections before the setting up of a provisional government, the presence of UN observers during the elections, amnesty measures for all political prisoners—and insofar as these measures happened to favour the Tutsi oligarchy, the United Nations, albeit unwittingly, caused the Hutu leadership to become increasingly attracted to violence. As we shall see, violence became the principal means through which the insurgents managed to circumvent the legal and constitutional obstacles raised by UN-sponsored resolutions.

By then, however, the insurgents could count on the overwhelming support of the European Catholic clergy and the European administration. Not only did the Catholic Church make it possible for the Christianised Hutu elites to gain a new perception of themselves as human beings, causing them to develop a strong sense of disaffection towards their rulers, but it also provided them with the psychological stimulus and indeed the political weaponry to bring reality in line with their aspirations.

The attitude of the European clergy underwent a major reorientation in the mid-'fifties, partly as a result of impending changes in the policies of the administration, and also because these changes tended to coincide with the arrival in Rwanda of a new category of missionaries. Unlike their predecessors, these newcomers were of relatively humble social origins and hence generally predisposed to identify with the plight of the Hutu masses. They belonged to what is known in Belgium as 'le petit clergé' (minor clergy), and in many cases their previous experience of social and political conditions in the French-speaking provinces of Wallonia enhanced their solicitude for the 'underdog'. Their emotional and psychological involvement in the affairs of Rwanda betrayed a sense of democratic commitment typical of the left-wing Christians ('Chrétiens de gauche'), a tendency associated in Belgium with the 'progressive' wing of the Parti Social Chrétien (PSC). But perhaps the really determining factor was the arrival in Kabgaye, in 1955, of Mgr Perraudin, a Swiss citizen, who, shortly thereafter, became Apostolic Vicar for Rwanda. Whether because of his national origins, or because of his own personal predispositions, Perraudin's democratic convictions found expression in what can only be described as a flagrant parti pris for the Hutu. To this day the name of Perraudin evokes diametrically opposed, though equally emotional, reactions from Hutu and Tutsi, being viewed by the former as nothing short of a saviour, and by the latter as a hateful sycophant, guilty of spreading racial hatred and violence among the people of Rwanda.

The Hutu elites were conscious of the tactical advantages offered by the support of the Church. To begin with, through its links with Church-affiliated metropolitan associations, the European clergy of Rwanda made it possible for these new Hutu elites to establish a wide range of connections outside Rwanda, which enabled them to come in contact with Belgian personalities and interest groups, to present their case, and to seek and receive the moral and financial backing so badly needed to sustain their fight for equality. While in Europe they met representatives of the pro-Catholic PSC and of PSC-affiliated student organisations and trade unions—such as the Jeunesses Etudiantes Catholiques (JEC) and the Confédération des Syndicats Chrétiens (CSC)—and the story they told invariably brought forth a sympathetic response from their audience. Equally important for these elites were the connections of the European clergy of Rwanda with the metropolitan press. Newspapers like *La Cité*, and, to a lesser extent, *La Libre Belgique*—both well-known for their pro-Catholic orientation—and journals like *La Revue Nouvelle* and *Les Dossiers de l'Action Sociale Catholique* provided the Hutu leadership, directly or indirectly, with an ideal platform for airing their views, sensitising Belgian public opinion to the problems of Rwanda, and applying pressure on the metropolitan government to hasten their solution along 'democratic' lines. Nor was the support they won limited to mere gestures of sympathy. Though the exact figures are unknown, the Hutu movement is said to have received substantial financial assistance from the Boerenbond, the powerful, pro-Catholic, Flemish-led agricultural union, as well as from the CSC.

In addition to facilitating their contacts with the outside world, the Catholic Church also played a decisive role in articulating and propagating the demands of the Hutu leadership. Certain missionaries, for example, did not hesitate at one point to write pieces of special pleading on behalf of certain Hutu leaders—to which were subsequently added the latter's signatures;* and it was the same missionaries who, at a later stage, acted as 'ghost writers' when speeches had to be delivered before the Trusteeship Council and petitions submitted to its visiting missions.

However useful the expressional skills of European priests in enlisting the support of Belgian and international public opinion, just as important in arousing the political consciousness of the Hutu masses was the decision to allow control over the local channels of communication to pass into the hands of Hutu politicians. This proved one of the most useful forms of missionary co-operation available to the Hutu elites, for even though the peasant masses were largely illiterate there were enough literate Hutu around to read the vernacular press to their kinsmen. From 1957 onwards, the Church-sponsored *Kimanyateka*, the only really significant newspaper printed in the vernacular, gave increasing coverage to Hutu grievances. Under the editorship of Grégoire Kayibanda (who took over from the Abbé Kagame in late 1956), *Kimanyateka* became the official mouthpiece of the Hutu movement, relentlessly hitting at the privileges of the 'féodalité néo-Hamitique'. At the same time the now-defunct *Temps Nouveaux d'Afrique*, a weekly newspaper published in Bujumbura under the auspices of the White Fathers, echoed many of the protests expressed in the vernacular press. Once in control of both the European and vernacular press, the Hutu leaders had every reason to face the future with greater confidence; not only did they possess a valuable instrument of political mobilisation at home, but they also knew that their voice was being heard abroad and

* Thus the lengthy and illuminating article by G. Cymana, entitled "Plaidoyer pour le Menu Peuple", which appeared in the November 1968 issue of *La Revue Nouvelle*, was apparently written by Canon Ernotte, like many others erroneously attributed to the pen of a Hutu politician. Reprints of the article were sent in large quantities to PSC members of the Belgian parliament through the 'good offices' of the Church. One may also note in passing that the now-famous *Bahutu Manifesto* was presumably written by a Catholic priest from Kabgaye (which, of course, is not meant to imply that the substance of the ideas expressed in it were not actually shared by its signatories).

that their plea for democracy would therefore not go totally unnoticed at the United Nations.

That the Catholic Church could have played such an active political role without eliciting any reaction from the Belgian administration other than one of tacit approval is indicative of where official sympathies lay. This is all the more remarkable if one remembers that the Vice-Governor General between 1955 and 1962 was Jean-Paul Harroy, a well-known freemason and hence supposedly anti-clerical. But since the administration was just as partial in its commitment to the Hutu cause, one can better understand the grounds for the alliance. In sharp contrast with the situation prevailing in the Congo at the time, throughout the late 'fifties and until independence relations between the Church and the administration were not only surprisingly free of strain but marked by a spirit of close and constant co-operation.

The methods used by the administration to accelerate the revolution were in some ways more subtle than those of the Church, but in the end far more effective. The element of subtlety—if not of plain deviousness—lies in the underhand manoeuvrings that went on behind the scenes in late 1960 and early 1961 between the Belgian administration and the Hutu leadership on the one hand, and the metropolitan government on the other, in a deliberate attempt to paralyse the action of the UN representatives in Rwanda and take whatever steps were deemed expedient to circumvent the resolutions of the Trusteeship Council. Seldom has the record of a trust authority shown greater disregard for its international responsibilities; seldom has there been such utter lack of co-operation and mutual understanding between a colonial power and an international organisation as between Belgium and the United Nations during the terminal stages of the trusteeship. Of this there is overwhelming evidence. It emerges with glaring clarity from the proceedings of the 'réunions de cadres' (staff meetings) held in Rwanda in 1960 and 1961, and also from the 1961 report of the UN Commission for Ruanda-Urundi, which was one of the most devastating exposés of the responsibility borne by the Belgian administration in surrendering control of the government to the insurgents, in violation of the procedure laid down by the United Nations.

Apart from having positively encouraged and assisted the seizure of power 'from above', through its own receptivity to the demands of the Hutu elites for 'internal autonomy', in flagrant violation of its international obligations under the UN Charter, the Belgian administration also contributed, directly or indirectly, to the revolution 'from below'. At the same time that the Hutu elites were allowed to seize control of the central machinery of government, every effort was made to prevent the remaining local Tutsi incumbents from using violence against their opponents in the countryside. Of all the factors that favoured the insurgents, this was probably the most critical: had the Tutsi been given a free hand to pursue the repression after the initial outbreaks, had they been able to use repression with sufficient ruthlessness and efficacy, the revolution might not have succeeded. Instead, whatever attempts were made by Tutsi incumbents to repress the insurgents were immediately nipped in the bud by the administration. Whatever repressive actions actually took place merely served to infuriate the Hutu masses; meanwhile the protective shield of the administration enabled the Hutu elites to capitalise upon these feelings of hatred and exasperation to the maximum extent. The results of the repression, in short, were precisely the reverse of what its instigators had intended.

True, the 'tutelle'* did not exercise its options in a total vacuum. One cannot underestimate the gravity of the dilemma confronting the Belgian administrators when it suddenly dawned upon them that they could no longer defer their commitment to 'democracy'. Inaction would have spelled protracted insecurity, perhaps chaos, and, inevitably, severe condemnations from various international quarters. The only viable alternative was to activate the revolutionary process by every conceivable means short of outright intervention.

The attitude of the Belgian authorities in the days which followed the initial disturbances comes out with painful clarity from the terms of a semi-official memorandum submitted to the United Nations in late 1960, entitled *L'Attitude de l'Administration Belge à l'égard de l'Unar.* Commenting on the 'social and political upheaval of November 1959', the administration admitted finding itself 'faced with a redoubtable alternative: either to crush the authentic democratic drive animating the masses of Rwanda, in collaboration with the indigenous authorities ... or else to canalise this claimant movement while publicly recognising its existence'. The first alternative was automatically ruled out, as it was 'in contradiction with the programme of emancipation adopted by Belgium'; the only conceivable course of action, therefore, was to 'inaugurate an "educative protectionism" by no means intended to eliminate once and for all the representatives of the old order but to permit the popular forces to organise themselves, free of the old feudal constraints'.[16] In practice, however, this so-called 'educative protectionism' was overwhelmingly one-sided. As for its presumed educational

---

* In Belgian colonial usage, the term 'tutelle' referred both to the trusteeship authorities and the type of international status associated with trusteeship. It is here (and elsewhere in this book) used as a short-hand expression to designate the former, i.e. the Belgian officials in charge of administering the territory.

virtues, one wonders whether these are appropriate terms to describe the incitements to destructive action and mutual hatred which so prominently figure in the record of Belgian activities in Rwanda. What was actually involved was a gradual elimination of the Tutsi elites from all positions of influence through a series of measures—ranging from sheer coercion to manipulation—intended, first, to weaken or suppress the influence and capacity for repressive violence of the incumbents, and, second, to guide the entry of insurgents into the political arena. The point is *not* that Hutu revolutionary sentiment was an artificial creation of the Europeans, but rather that the European presence served as a guarantee of success for the revolutionary elites. Here, then, lies the supreme paradox of the Hutu revolution: directed against an indigenous form of imperialism, it drew its sustenance and inspiration from one of the imperial powers which had been the strongest supporter of the old regime.

Thus, to argue that the revolution in Rwanda was a 'Ruandese revolution . . . neither inspired, nor created, nor engineered by outside forces, Belgian, UN, African or any other', seems somewhat inconsistent with the facts. Moreover, to speak of a 'Ruandese revolution' to designate such disparate movements as those in northern and central Rwanda raises some obvious difficulties. How much ideological unity did the revolutionaries actually claim for themselves? How much organisational cohesion? To what extent have historical and societal differences between north and south conditioned the political orientations of the revolutionaries?

THE STAGES OF REVOLUTIONARY DEVELOPMENT

In modern times the term 'revolution' has come to denote a conscious attempt at total renovation. 'The modern concept of revolution', wrote Hanna Arendt, 'is inextricably bound up with the notion that the course of history suddenly begins anew, and that an entirely new story, a story never known before, is about to unfold.' As for the plot, 'it is unmistakably the emergence of freedom'.[17] While this usage of the term is commonly associated in European history with the birth of Jacobinism, in the African context it is best illustrated by the growth of egalitarian sentiments among the Hutu elites of central and southern Rwanda. Just as the Jacobins felt the irrepressible urge to make a clean sweep of monarchic absolutism, the Hutu elites saw in the establishment of republican rule the dawn of an entirely new era, one that would bring about the fulfilment of their dreams of justice and equality. Echoes of this can be found in the proclamations made each year on the anniversary of the republic, in the endless litanies celebrating January 28, 1961, as 'the dawn of a new era', 'the day when the Rwandese people chose with enthusiasm and determination to become a free society'.[18]

Yet, in another sense—in the Copernican, astronomical sense of the term—'revolution' implies something quite different—a revolving, cyclical movement that tends to swing back to a pre-existing point. Extended to the social realm, this connotation gives us a clue to the conservative qualities of certain types of revolution, for in this sense 'revolution' becomes largely synonymous with 'restoration'. The restoration of the English monarchy in 1660, after the defeat of the Rump Parliament, is an obvious example. A less obvious but equally pertinent illustration of this type of social movement can be found in the events that took place in northern Rwanda before and after 1959.

To draw attention to this Janus-faced quality of the Rwanda revolution does not mean that each set of motivations has always operated independently from the other. The political awakening of the northern populations had a contagious effect on the growth of revolutionary sentiment in the south, and for a time their awareness of a common enemy helped mitigate ideological differences between north and south. Nonetheless, these differences of orientation must be borne in mind if one is to grasp the dynamics and direction of societal change in contemporary Rwanda.

As shown by the typology in Table 3.1 (page 113), two separate types of protest can be distinguished which, though originating from different localities and at different points in time, converged in the same direction. One, xenophobic-conservative in orientation, came into being at the turn of the century in the northern region, first expressing itself through a combination of messianism and 'social banditry', later to take on the characteristics of an anarchistic rebellion with strong eschatological overtones. Another form of protest is that which developed in central Rwanda in 1957–58 and which first manifested itself through the so-called *Bahutu Manifesto*. Though aiming at the abolition of caste privileges, initially the movement had none of the xenophobic overtones of its northern counterpart. It was essentially a social reform movement which drew its inspiration from egalitarian-democratic ideals. By 1960, however, these originally very different manifestations had coalesced into a more or less unified revolutionary movement aiming at the wholesale elimination of Tutsi elements from all positions of influence. No doubt this convergence of trends can be explained by reference to the contiguity of the geographical areas in which they have originated. A kind of political osmosis seems to have developed between the northern and central regions, in part through the movement of ideas

Table 3.1: Typology of Protest Movements in Rwanda, 1898–1961

Chronology	Type of Protest	Orientation	Target	Localisation	Origins
Before 1900	Messianism-cum-Social Banditry*	Xenophobic and Messianic	Tutsi chiefs	Northern Region (Rukiga)	Northern Kiga ('Social bandits'; Nyabingi priestesses; *bakonde*)
1900–1920	Same	Same	Tutsi chiefs and Europeans	Same	Northern Kiga (same as above)
1957–1958	Social Reform Movement	Egalitarian-Democratic	Tutsi elites (modern and traditional)	Central Region (Gitarama)	Hutu intelligentsia from Central Rwanda (former seminarists)
1959	Jacquerie	Anomic-Restorative (pro-monarchical)	Tutsi-Undifferentiated	Country-wide	Hutu peasantry
1960	Social and Political Revolution	1. Xenophobic-Conservative 2. Xenophobic-Jacobin	Tutsi chiefs and subchiefs Tutsi-Undifferentiated	Northern Region (Rukiga) Central Region	1. Northern Bakonde families (Kiga) 2. Communal authorities (Hutu)
1961	Coup d'Etat	Republican	Tutsi monarchy	Gitarama	PARMEHUTU leadership and Belgian administration

* The term 'social banditry' is borrowed from E. J. Hobsbawn's classic study of archaic protest movements in nineteenth and twentieth century Europe. It refers to a rural, one might say 'pre-political' form of protest, identified with a Robin Hood-type figure who poses as the champion of an oppressed peasantry. In Rwanda, this type of protest is perhaps best illustrated by the peasant revolts which occurred in the northern region around the turn of the century under the leadership of Ndungutse. That Ndungutse happened to be of Tutsi origins is perfectly compatible with the general characteristics of social banditry. 'Social banditry', writes Hobsbawn, 'though a protest, is a modest and unrevolutionary protest. It protests not against the fact that peasants are poor and oppressed, but against the fact that they are excessively poor and oppressed. Bandit-heroes are not expected to make a world of equality.' J. E. Hobsbawn, *Primitive Rebels*, Praeger, New York 1963, p. 24.

and influences across regional boundaries, and in part as a result of the organisational ties forged during the early stages of the revolution. But perhaps even more decisive in bringing these various strands together was the overwhelmingly negative attitude of the Tutsi elites of central Rwanda in the face of the reformist demands voiced by certain Hutu politicians. Quite apart from the accelerating factors already mentioned, the radicalisation of the social reform movement in central Rwanda came about in reaction to the persistent obduracy of the ruling oligarchy, or what is usually referred to in the literature on revolution as 'elite intransigence'.

This process of radicalisation—here meaning a shift from reformist to revolutionary orientations—is perhaps best understood in the light of the different phases, and corresponding forms of protest, that have shaped the birth and maturation of revolutionary sentiment in central Rwanda. Historically, these various types of manifestations form a closely woven texture, whose separate strands are sometimes difficult to unravel. Nonetheless, and pending further elaboration, the following four stages can be distinguished.

(i) Social Reform Movement: The Bahutu Manifesto of 1957

The *Bahutu Manifesto* can be regarded as the first open revelation of a fundamental social disharmony in Rwanda society. By focusing attention on the gap between the democratic-egalitarian aspirations of its signatories and the oligarchical structure of Rwanda society, it laid bare the nature of the social and political tensions that ultimately led to the revolution. Characteristically, the tone of the *Manifesto* was not that of a call to revolution, but that of a plea for democracy. However, the connection between the objectives of the *Manifesto* and subsequent developments is clear enough. To a considerable extent the revolution developed in response to the failure of moderate Hutu politicians to bring about the social and political reforms expressed in the *Manifesto*.

(ii) Jacquerie: The So-Called 'Revolution of November 1959'

Though usually referred to as a 'revolution', the events of November 1959 are better seen as a jacquerie directed against the authority of the chiefs, and *not* against the legitimacy of monarchical rule. Insofar as it had any specific aim, it was to change political personnel rather than to seek a fundamental alteration of the constitutional order. The aim was to appeal to the crown to evict those chiefs and subchiefs who, because of their exactions, appeared to have betrayed their mandate. In line with most jacquerie ideologies, the Hutu peasants rose against their chiefs in the name of their king—'for the ideal of the just king

1. Mwami Yuhi Musinga of Rwanda (1896-1931); on his right, his uncle and chief confidant, the famous Kabare.

2. Mwami Musinga and his court *c.* 1916; seated to the right of Musinga, wearing almost the same headdress, is the Queen Mother, Kanyogera.

3. Mwami Mutara Rudahigwa (1931-59).

4. Mwami Kigeri Ndahindurwa (1959-62), in exile in Kenya.

who, if he only knew, would punish the transgressions of his underlings and lords'.[19] By and large, however, the jacquerie of November 1959 was a largely unstructured, anomic manifestation. The only exception to the rule was found in the north, where the aim of the movement was not only to displace the chiefs in office but to replace them with descendants of traditional Kiga lineages. Here we find in germ many of the ideas which later found expression among the northern Kiga elites: a conspicuous hatred of Tutsi chiefs, a tendency to revive an idealised past, and a marked aversion towards all forms of centralised authority.

(iii) Social and Political Revolution: November 1959–January 1961

This form of protest differed from the previous one in these respects: (a) the aim was no longer to change the personnel in office but to bring about a more fundamental change in the structure of society; (b) the aims of the revolutionaries were couched in ideological terms—they posed increasingly as 'black Jacobins', articulating their goals for the future in terms of democracy, freedom and equality, holding up to their followers the vision of a brave new world free of discrimination and constraints; (c) the associated ethnic violence was more deliberate and widespread than before. Indeed, by now, violence had become one of the prime 'accelerators' of social change. Acts of terrorism against Tutsi elements became so numerous that the administration could no longer repress them (assuming it ever had the inclination to do so seriously and effectively); in turn, Tutsi-instigated counter-terrorism picked up momentum, leading to a situation where ethnic antagonisms penetrated the whole of society.

(iv) The Coup d'Etat of Gitarama: January 1961

Though by no means the first step taken by the revolutionaries to relieve social and political inequities, the coup of Gitarama was certainly the most drastic. The coup was revolutionary in at least two senses: it destroyed the old monarchical regime and led to a de facto republican system of government, and it created the conditions for further accelerating the revolution 'from below'. In January 1961 the social system of Rwanda was already deeply shattered, but not to the point of having everywhere lost its basis of legitimacy. There were pockets of monarchic sentiment in the west and the east, and in many parts of the country abuses committed by the insurgents had led to considerable disaffection within their ranks. After the coup of Gitarama, however, the Hutu elites were able to gain partial control over the levers of the administration. And now that they enjoyed virtually unlimited discretion to use violence as they pleased, they had relatively little difficulty in carrying the revolution to its ultimate stage, to the stage where the republic would receive official, de jure recognition from the United Nations.

The foregoing typology of the phases that led to the seizure of power 'from above' reveals a characteristic widening of the 'targets' selected by the insurgents. These targets were, in chronological order, the chiefs, the crown, and the Tutsi community as a whole, each representing a different level of the traditional Rwanda society, i.e. the personnel in office, the regime, and the dominant ethnic minority. Inasmuch as the end result has been the systematic exclusion of the representatives of the Tutsi community from participation in the political institutions of republican Rwanda, one reaches the conclusion that democracy in contemporary Rwanda means, at best, democracy for the Hutu rather than democracy per se. By refusing liberty to the enemies of liberty, the Hutu elites have seriously undermined their claims to democracy; for if one takes democracy to mean equal access to opportunities and life chances, irrespective of caste or race, it is just as remote an ideal in republican Rwanda as it ever was under the monarchy.

As we shall see, the context in which the republican government of President Grégoire Kayibanda is compelled to operate is in some respects very similar to that of other independent African states, and in others a very different one. The similarities lie in the functions devolved upon the dominant party to ease the transition towards independence (from both Tutsi and Belgians), and to create the conditions of a new society. In Rwanda as elsewhere the party was to serve as the main integrating agency. Yet its apparatus proved too anaemic for this task. What has emerged in the meantime is a type of political system which shares many of the structural characteristics of the ancien régime —a kind of presidential *mwami*-ship in which authority is concentrated at the top and flows down into the local capillaries of the administration through appointed officials whose position in the system is not so different from that of former chiefs.

The newly emergent system reflects the same kind of cultural disparities between north and south as existed during Tutsi hegemony. Rwanda continues to incorporate within its geographical boundaries two distinctive subcultures. Though no longer reducible to caste differences, these polarities are just as threatening in terms of their disruptive potential as the old ones. Now that the 'steel frame' of Tutsi over-rule has been cast away, the northern enclave has reasserted its cultural distinctiveness with a vengeance, once more raising the familiar problem of national integration. There is nothing new, of course, about the 'northern question'. Of all the regions of Rwanda, the northern districts have always been the Achilles' heel of the administration. The element of novelty is that the methods which the Tutsi once used against the northerners are no more compatible with republican institutions than the continued survival of a 'feudal' enclave in the north. The northerners were, after all, among the most active participants in the revolution, and any threat to their indigenous institutions could well trigger off a counter-revolution, and perhaps convert Kigaland into another Vendée. Thus it is one of the ironies of Rwanda's history that, in destroying the old monarchic order, the republican revolution also created the conditions for a partial revival and perpetuation of 'feudal' institutions.

4. The Background to Revolution

HAVING identified some of the sources of strain in Rwanda's traditional social structure, a change of focus is necessary at this point to emphasise the relationship between the potential for change inherent in the traditional society and the part played by modern socio-economic forces in converting it into a revolutionary situation. As has already been discussed, the release of revolutionary potentialities was effected largely through traditional modes of social organisation. By shifting the base of clientage away from the Hutu-Tutsi nexus to their own ethnic stratum, the Hutu counter-elites were able to use the solidaristic ties of clientship to build up a political clientele of their own, and, later, to manipulate this following for revolutionary ends. But this substitution of 'horizontal' for 'vertical' solidarities could not have occurred, at least on a nation-wide scale, unless some new and unsettling influences had already penetrated the traditional society, and unless processes were beginning in the more modern sectors which in time would reverse the traditional inter-caste relationships.

At one level of analysis, one can identify certain changes in the traditional base of social prestige and political power which have generally predisposed the peasantry to challenge the authority of the chiefs and repudiate their conventional bonds to the ruling caste. The bureaucratisation of the chieftaincy and the abolition of cattle-contracts (*buhake*) were certainly among the more significant of these predisposing factors. Yet there is another level at which social change held even more obvious revolutionary implications, the level at which a growing incompatibility could be observed between the rigidities of the caste structure and the conditions of social mobility created by colonial rule. While the latter undoubtedly favoured the emergence of a potential counter-elite, the former consistently conspired to deny these new social and professional elements entry into the political arena. Each facet of the problem is intimately related to the other: the greater the rigidity of the existing pattern of stratification, the higher the degree of anomie* on the part of

* In the context of this discussion, the term 'anomie' is used in the Durkheimian sense and refers to a lack of clear-cut norms to regulate individual social behaviour. It should be clearly distinguished from the usage which Hollingshead

those individuals who could no longer fit themselves, socially and psychologically, into the caste system, and, by implication, the greater the revolutionary potential released by social disorganisation.

The Bureaucratisation of Chieftaincy

'The revolutionary mood and temper', Eric Hoffer has said, 'are generated by the irritations, difficulties, hungers and frustrations inherent in the realization of drastic change. Where things have not changed at all, there is the least likelihood of revolution.'[1] The changes that took place in Rwanda in the years preceding the revolution, while not drastic, were sufficiently deep and extensive to cause a major alteration of traditional relations between the chiefs and their subjects. In a sense, most of the 'irritations, difficulties and frustrations' which lie in the background of the Hutu revolution stemmed from the bureaucratisation of chieftaincy brought about through the exigencies of indirect rule. Even though the position of the chiefs in traditional Rwanda society was already partially bureaucratised, insofar as it involved a division of labour along functional lines and a corresponding role differentiation, their rule was not inevitably harsh and impersonal. Certainly, it was less harsh and impersonal than when they were forced to behave as the agents of the colonial administration, and when, for reasons of administrative convenience and economic necessity, they were asked to enforce upon their subjects a host of obligations and corvées which they had never known before.

The Belgian version of indirect rule as evolved in Rwanda forced upon the chiefs new standards of performance, elaborated in accordance with norms of efficiency and rationality. In most cases this spelled the gradual dissolution of affective ties between the chiefs and their subjects, and the substitution of a new set of obligations for those in existence in the traditional society.

The impact of indirect rule has been, first of all, to destroy the old balance of forces between cattle chiefs, land chiefs and army chiefs, which in previous times had served to protect the Hutu peasantry against undue exactions. The concentration of power in the hands of a

---

and Redlich make of the term, equating it with psychopathology (see *Social Class and Psychopathology*, Wiley, New York 1958). Before the latter usage can be said to apply to the Rwanda situation, considerably more research needs to be done on possible relationships between stratification and mental illness. The only study along these lines pertaining to the area under discussion, albeit a rather superficial and inconclusive one, is J. Vyncke, *Psychoses et Névroses en Afrique Centrale*, ARSC, Vol. v, No. 5, Brussels 1957.

single chief, exercising unfettered control over his people, was bound to lead to abuses: not only did it deprive the Hutu of opportunities to play one chief off against another, but it also eliminated the channels of appeal offered by the previous arrangement. As one student of Rwanda perceptively observed, this reduced 'the likelihood that the Hutu would think of the Tutsi as protectors';[2] moreover, the incumbents were given a greatly reinforced confidence in themselves, both as chiefs and as representatives of the ruling caste. Having experienced virtually unlimited powers, the chiefs were understandably reluctant to divest themselves of their authority in favour of the Hutu once the latter decided to challenge their claims to supremacy.

Along with these structural innovations, there occurred a simultaneous shift of accountability from the crown to the Belgian administration, which made it mandatory for the chiefs to 'meet the needs of the system' as defined by the administration, and to behave like functionaries of the colonial oligarchy. The chiefs were expected to discharge a wide range of functions for which there was no equivalent in the traditional society: to transmit administrative orders and regulations to their subchiefs; to preside over the local tribunal, and on occasion attend the proceedings of tribunals outside their chiefdom; to collect taxes, to take a regular census of the population, and to hold a record of births and deaths; to go on an inspection tour at regular intervals to watch over the crops and the anti-erosion works, and see that roads were kept in proper condition; to supervise vaccinations and other health measures prescribed by the local administrator; to provide such labour as the administration might request; and, last but not least, to give regular accounts of their work to the local administration. Not only did this redefinition of the chief's role play havoc with the traditional nexus of relationships between the chiefs and the crown; now that the chiefs were solely responsible to the European authorities, their rule was rendered all the more unbearable for their subjects. Complaints brought against them by their own people were usually dismissed by the Belgian administrators as imaginary or ill-founded. Even in cases of gross injustices the administration at first preferred to ignore the charges on the grounds that any attempt to redress the situation might destroy the 'social ballast' of traditional society. Social injustice became a corollary of indirect rule.

The bureaucratisation of chieftaincy was accomplished by a judicious mixture of financial incentives and administrative sanctions. In addition to his basic salary—1,000 Belgian francs per annum, plus an extra 100 francs for every 1,000 tax-payers in excess of the normal ceiling of

3,000 for every chiefdom—a chief could draw a yearly bonus, or *prime*, of several hundred francs calculated on his rating as 'elite', 'excellent', or 'very good'.* This meant that, on average, an efficient chief would receive an increment of 15 to 20 per cent of his basic annual salary. Conversely, the penalty for negligence or laziness was a fine taken from his salary, or, more often, from the cash payment ('rachat de prestations coutumières') he received from his own people. If his negligence became too manifest, or if his attitude showed no signs of improvement, dismissal inevitably followed. In short, the whole system of sanctions and rewards devised by the administration was overwhelmingly weighted in favour of bureaucratic standards, so that whatever obligations of a traditional nature the chiefs owed to their people tended to be superseded by their obligations toward the administration.

To make the chiefs fully aware of their obligations, and of the penalties they would incur for not meeting these obligations, was a major concern of the European administrator during his tour of inspection. Indeed it is difficult to imagine a more rigorous and harassing surveillance than the one exercised by the Belgian authorities over the chiefs and the subchiefs. To 'meet the needs of the system', the chiefs were led to ask considerably more of their subjects than had been the case at any time before the advent of colonial rule. Thus it was not only the structural changes wrought by indirect rule, and the resulting shift in the locus of accountability, which made the rule of the chiefs so burdensome, but the fact that the 'weight' of chieftaincy increased in proportion to the new obligations imposed upon the peasantry in the name of administrative efficiency and economic viability.

At first, the expression 'prestations coutumières' served as a magic label under which a multitude of chores were thrust upon the peasantry, on the assumption that custom conferred immediate legitimacy to all forms of work. The official thinking of the Belgian administration was

* These salary figures are for 1951, and do not include the cash payment received from tax-payers in lieu of customary dues in kind and corvées. For further information on this, see *Compte-Rendu des Travaux du Séminaire d'Anthropologie Sociale Tenu à Astrida en Juillet 1951*, IRSAC, Astrida 1952, p. 74. One must note in passing that this type of financial incentive was largely inoperative in Burundi: because of the greater number of tax-payers from whom the chiefs (*ganwa*) collected revenue, their financial position was already very comfortable, and no amount of administrative laxity could hurt either their financial standing or traditional claims to authority. Administrative harassment was unnecessary in these conditions. Thus, in 1944, Chief Nduwumwe (the Mwami's uncle) 'reigned' over 26,640 tax-payers; his total annual salary, accruing from various taxes and customary dues, amounted to 198,492.50 Belgian francs, i.e., nearly the equivalent of $ (US) 4,000.00. See *Traitement des Chefs et Sous-chefs*, mimeo., n.d., n.p.

121

made abundantly clear by the comments of Halewyck before the Permanent Mandates Commission, in 1928: 'The upkeep of the main roads and secondary roads was entrusted to the chiefs, who used their own labour for this purpose. . . . There was no need to pay them for their work since such work was a form of public service consecrated by custom.'³ Meanwhile, little effort was made to ease the weight of customary taxes and corvées. Indeed, in some respects, the system was made even more burdensome by the laissez-faire attitude of the colonial authorities. Thus the 'land tax' (*butaka*), which traditionally involved one day's labour out of five, was raised by the chiefs to two or even three days out of six; new corvées were introduced which had never before existed, such as the construction of houses in durable materials for the *mwami* and the chiefs; the regular taxes were often supplemented through the most arbitrary methods: 'Where there is a predominance of "small" Tutsi', wrote Mgr Classe in 1916, 'the chief or his wife take anything they please [from the tax-payer]—bananas, yams, etc.—and the Hutu must comply lest he be expelled from his fields.'⁴ Not until 1933 was an attempt made to regularise the whole system of traditional dues in kind and labour. Thus, from now on, the tribute owed to the *mwami* (*ikoro*) was to be replaced by an annual payment in cash, and the land tax was to consist of three days' work a year for the chief and ten days for the subchief. Yet, if the changes brought considerable relief in the system of customary obligations, their effects were largely nullified by the introduction of new types of administrative corvées, involving, among other things, the compulsory cultivation of food crops, reafforestation work and anti-erosive terracing.*

* After the famine of 1928–29, during which thousands of people died of hunger, each adult Hutu male was obliged to cultivate 20 acres of food crops in addition to those already being used for his own crops. Despite this, some 36,000 people died of starvation during the famine of 1943, caused by the conjunction of a severe drought and the sudden spread of an epidemic of phytophtora. (The worst of all famines was that of 1916, called 'Rumanura' by the Rwandese, which caused an estimated 50,000 deaths). By 1947, in order to prevent the recurrence of seasonal food shortage and famine, compulsory cultivation was extended to 24 acres, and each family head was required to keep a stock of 120 lbs of subsistence crops to tide over the critical period between each harvest. About the same time, legislation made compulsory the cultivation of cotton in the plains, and reafforestation work in the regions of higher altitude to prevent soil erosion, on the basis of 16 acres of cotton or 0·40 acres of forest land for every 300 tax-payers. A special effort was made after the Second World War to extend this system to the cultivation of coffee. In time the maintenance of anti-erosive works destined to assist the cultivation of coffee became a major preoccupation of the administration—and the nightmare of both the chiefs and their constituents. The demands on native labour created by these innovations exceeded by far the exigencies of all customary taxes put together.

The general impression conveyed by the record is that the lot of the Hutu masses was unquestionably worse under Belgian rule than at any other time in the past. To be sure, few Belgian administrators would have conceded this fact without drawing proper attention to the positive side of the record, without emphasising the advantages derived from the imposition of the Pax Belgica, from the construction of roads, hospitals and dispensaries, from improvements in the quality and quantity of food crops and the margin of economic security this provided for the peasant masses. But if these were indeed appreciable gains, their cost in terms of human labour, taxation and regimentation was extremely heavy. When added to customary tithes, tributes and corvées, the 'civilising' aspects of the Belgian presence made the rule of the chiefs a singularly uncivilised one.

For a measure of the ruthlessness of chiefly rule one can do no better than point to the evidence contained in the following account of an interview conducted by a member of the first UN Visiting Mission to Rwanda in 1948. The interviewer was told by a group of Rwandese of predominantly Hutu origins that 'before the Europeans came any man could go anywhere he wanted to find good soil' but 'now our people must stay in one place and are beaten in order to grow certain crops'. The dialogue continued as follows:

Q. Who beats you?
A. The chief or the subchief.
Q. Does the chief himself do the whipping?
A. No, he designates someone to do it.
Q. Have you, yourself, been beaten?
A. So many times I cannot count them.
Q. How often?
A. Once or twice a month.
Q. Is this because you are lazy?
A. I am not lazy. It is because I cannot finish my work in the time demanded. I have to go to Astrida for roadwork also.
Q. How many days do you work on the roads?
A. Every Friday.
Q. During the entire year?
A. Yes.
Q. How much are you paid?
A. I am not paid for roadwork.

(The interviewer then asks each of ten men picked at random how often he has been beaten.)

1st man:	Too often to be counted.
2nd man:	Twice this month.
3rd man:	Only twice since I returned from work in the mines.
4th man:	Once in my entire life.
5th man:	I cannot count the number of times I've been beaten.
6th man:	More than forty times.
7th man:	I cannot say how many times. But many times.
8th man:	Four times.
9th man:	Many times.
10th man:	Many times.

Q. How many strokes did you receive each time?

A. In previous times twelve strokes were administered. Now only eight strokes.

Q. How many of you have been in prison?

(Of the group of approximately 250, five raised their hands.)

Q. How many of you have been whipped by a chief, a subchief, or a European?

(Of the group, all but two or three raised their hands.)[5]

Clearly, this image of the chief's behaviour is difficult to reconcile with his traditional role as the benevolent protector of the weak and the ultimate source of assistance to the needy. Although it would be inaccurate to conclude that all chiefs behaved like tyrants, those who exercised their authority with leniency were exceptions, for a lenient chief was generally regarded as a 'bad' chief and was, therefore, likely to be penalised or dismissed. A case in point was Chief Kayondo, who once held office in northern Busanza. In his *Escapade Ruandaise*, the Hutu writer Saverio Naigiziki describes Kayondo as 'the providence of the lowly and the idol of the gentry and the ordinary people alike'; 'Kayondo paid court without acting like a courtier, rendered justice without cruelty, loved the missionaries but failed to be loved by them, and throughout Musinga's troubled reign managed to maintain his prestige and popularity. . . . He asked for and obtained baptism, distributed cows, and was the first to buy and drive a car.'[6] In spite of this, Kayondo 'received his dismissal without a murmur of complaint, as if it were a stroke of fate'. 'He was blamed for everything', adds Naigiziki, 'including his old age, as if it were a crime. . . . In fact his only wrongs were his ostentatious show of wealth and a certain lack of education, both of which were further aggravated by the cockiness of his sons and followers.'[7] Kayondo, like many other great feudatories, simply refused to accommodate himself to the new standards of performance that were expected of him. He was kind and generous but too easy-going to stay in office. It is not a matter of coincidence, therefore, that those chiefs whom the administration rated as 'elite' or 'excellent' were also those who became the object of the greatest resentment from their own people.

The role conflict inherent in the position of the Rwanda chiefs is by no means a unique phenomenon in Africa. Lloyd Fallers has drawn attention to similar disharmonies in the Busoga district of Uganda, showing how the Busoga chiefs found themselves in a cleft stick because of the specific expectations of the European administration and the very different ones of the chiefs' subjects.[8] The uniqueness of the situation just described lies in its ethnic dimensions. One cannot fail to note the overwhelming preponderance of Tutsi who held office as chiefs and subchiefs. On November 1, 1959, 43 chiefdoms out of a total of 45 were in the hands of Tutsi, the remaining two being described as 'vacant'; 549 subchiefdoms out of 559 were held by Tutsi and only 10 by Hutu. Similarly, the vast majority of auxiliary personnel (judges, assessors, agronomical and veterinary assistants, etc.) belonged to the Tutsi caste. On the eve of the revolution only 12 per cent of these subaltern positions were filled by Hutu.[9] This Tutsi monopoly of chiefly position has exacerbated racial tensions in two ways: their awareness of both the advantages and inconveniences of their role made the Tutsi chiefs and subchiefs remarkably status-conscious as a group, vis-à-vis the Hutu masses; and because they were looked upon as the agents of the European administration, the Tutsi chiefs were generally held responsible by the peasantry for all the hardships and sufferings associated with colonial rule.

The animus which the office-holders attracted to themselves was bound to reverberate, sooner or later, not only on the Tutsi chiefs but on the Tutsi as a group, who came to be regarded by the Hutu leadership as the target of the revolution. This is where the 'caste context' of Rwanda politics differed fundamentally from that of Burundi. As in Rwanda, chiefly rule in Burundi was the source of considerable popular discontent, but as long as the chiefs were looked upon by the masses as a separate ethnic group—as *ganwa*—the ethnic quotient of popular discontent remained relatively low. In Rwanda, on the other hand, the abuses of the chiefs were inevitably identified with the abuses of the Tutsi as a group.

Moreover, as a consequence of the foregoing, the bureaucratisation of chieftaincy has contributed to the creation of a significant potential for revolt among the peasantry, a kind of 'rural radicalism' which predisposed the peasants to challenge the rule of the chiefs if not the legitimacy of the monarchy. This is by no means a unique situation in Africa. Similar phenomena have been observed by Martin Kilson in Sierra Leone, P. C. Lloyd in Western Nigeria, and V. Thompson and R.

Adloff in Chad; in each of these cases, as in Rwanda, 'manifestations of rural radicalism', as Kilson points out, 'seldom entailed demands for the destruction of the existing system of traditional authority (what Gluckman would call a revolution) but instead aimed at ameliorating aspects of its uses (what Gluckman would call a rebellion)'.* Yet in a stratified society such as Rwanda 'rural radicalism' held special implications. More than a case of individual or collective resentment against specific policies or chiefs, the strains and stresses which it has created between the chiefs and the masses were the expression of an incipient struggle between different castes and ethnic strata. The resulting opportunities for revolutionary action were virtually unparalleled elsewhere in Africa.

Granting that the effect of indirect rule has been to inaugurate a system of rewards and demands in which administrative efficiency was more often than not synonymous with sheer brutality and arbitrariness, why is it that the revolution did not occur at an earlier date? One possible answer is suggested by Lucy Mair's comment that 'resentment against the rule of chiefs is something more than a protest against injustice. It is part of a wider demand: the demand for full participation in the institutions which control the destinies of Africans.'[10] However, this demand could not become fully articulated unless and until a new set of relationships had begun to take shape outside the traditional system of authority. That these relationships did not emerge on any significant scale until the mid-'fifties, if not later, is one major reason for the long period of incubation preceding the birth of revolutionary sentiment. Moreover, the rise of a politically-conscious Hutu intelligentsia was a precondition to the launching and organisation of a Hutu revolutionary force; and the birth of this intelligentsia, as well as its capacity to aggregate support for its goals, presupposed a break in the chain of subordination between Hutu and Tutsi. It presupposed, specifically, the sundering of vassalage ties at some points in the social hierarchy, and an earnest desire on the part of at least some Hutu peasants to liquidate whatever links of dependency still operated in the chain of vassalage.

* See Martin Kilson, *Political Change in a West African State*, Harvard University Press, Cambridge 1966, p. 61. Kilson's contention that the relationships between the masses and the chiefs were inevitably coloured by 'ambivalence toward traditional authority' applies equally well to Rwanda. This ambivalence found expression not only in the dual image projected by the chiefs (as patrons and as chiefs) but in the ambiguity inherent in the very notion of traditional authority. At first, resentment of chiefly rule did not necessarily imply rejection of the *office* of chief; and when the office came to be challenged, the monarchy as an institution continued to retain considerable legitimacy among the masses.

THE SUNDERING OF VASSALAGE TIES

No other aspect of traditional society has had a more inhibiting effect on the expansion of democratic norms and processes than the clientage system. The very nature of the client-patron relationship, based on ties of reciprocal allegiance and personal loyalty, obstructed all possibilities of change in the direction of individualism and equalitarianism. As long as the place of the individual in society was wholly determined by the strength, or vagaries, of a strictly personal relationship, one could hardly conceive of individual rights, only of obligations. But with the development of a money economy and the concurrent growth of a cash nexus, with the spread of Christian ethics and the internalisation of egalitarian values, a new situation was engendered which brought about a reversal of traditional roles. As the stratification system became more fluid and diversified, as new social groupings emerged, status became increasingly dissociated from authority. For the old corporate categories of patrons and clients were substituted new social aggregates based on personal achievement; a growing number of individuals came to be identified not only as patrons or clients but as clerks, catechists, carpenters, innkeepers, traders, etc. Once this had happened, the old system began to crack. It was the rupture of vassalage ties, resulting from the surge of modern economic and social forces, which brought about the collapse of chieftaincy and the kind of social order for which it stood.

Since vassalage was so intimately linked to the *buhake*—the institution through which a client pledged his allegiance to a patron, who then acknowledged the homage of his future vassal by entrusting him with one or several cows—a brief consideration of its recent evolution is needed here. If anything, the history of the *buhake* shows that the adjustment of traditional norms to the demands of a modernising society can be a very long and arduous process, one which in Rwanda has yet to run its full course. That it took so long for this process to get underway is because of the understandable reticence of certain Tutsi diehards to give up their traditional rights and privileges. But this is not the sole reason. Strangely enough, the abolition of the *buhake* was sometimes resisted by the 'victims' of the system, while some of its presumed beneficiaries were among its most outspoken opponents.

As early as 1926 there were signs that the *buhake* no longer served its intended purpose; by mutual agreement, a number of patrons and clients were reported to have severed their clientage ties.[11] At the time, however, the administration could respond to this initiative only in the most negative terms, for the *buhake* was still, literally and figuratively, the 'sacred cow' of the whole system of indirect rule. Any attempt to tamper with this age-old institution was bound to be regarded as an almost sacrilegious and potentially dangerous initiative. Even as late as 1945, when the Mwami suggested that the institution be abolished once and for all, the Vice-Governor General urged the greatest caution. It was not until the early 'fifties, with the inauguration of the Ten-Year Plan, that serious consideration was given to the suppression of the *buhake*. The immediate purpose of the reform was to discourage the acquisition of cattle, to avoid overstocking and to expand the supply of land that could still be brought under cultivation. But the rationale underlying this momentous decision was that the institution had fallen into desuetude because it no longer provided the central axis of an individual's social and economic life. To quote from the Mwami's circular: 'The profound transformations that have occurred in all walks of life have necessarily had some perceptible repercussions on the *buhake*, and in many respects this institution has lost its imperative and regulatory character.'[12] The procedure for the sharing of cattle between patrons and clients was stipulated in the decree of April 1, 1954, as follows: the rights and obligations attendant upon the *buhake* could be waived by common consent or unilaterally; the cattle would then be distributed on the basis of two-thirds to the client and one-third to the patron, or three-quarters to the client and one-quarter to the patron, depending on the duration of the contract, with the understanding that a client could, if he so desired, retain all the cows and redeem the patron's share in cash. Any litigation regarding this procedure would be settled by the local tribunals, all of which, be it noted, were under the control of Tutsi chiefs and subchiefs. Finally, the conclusion of new cattle-contracts was, from that time, strictly prohibited.[13]

The significance of the reform, in terms of its social and psychological consequences, lies as much in its positive achievements as in its shortcomings. To the extent that it did promote a genuine emancipation of at least one segment of the peasantry, not only did it contribute to an undermining of the legitimacy of the old feudal nexus, and the creation of a kind of moral and psychological crisis among those individuals who had not yet been able to internalise the norms of the new social order; it also set the stage for an intensification of this crisis, by releasing new energies, now seeking alternative channels of action and self-gratification. But insofar as it failed to achieve the intended result, it has generated considerable resentment from those Hutu elements who ardently hoped to free themselves from the shackles of the system but who, for a variety of reasons, were denied this opportunity.

Two preliminary observations must be made at the outset. One is that there was no exact correlation between the ethnic background of clients and patrons and their respective attitudes to the reform. Many Tutsi chiefs welcomed the reform, either because their political rank provided them with alternative sources of wealth and prestige, or because they sincerely thought the *buhake* had outlived its usefulness, or because they preferred to sell their share of cattle rather than hang on to their clientele. For example, the record shows that even in 1945 many of the more prominent chiefs were categorically opposed to the *buhake*. One of them, Chief Rwigemera, asked: 'Since democracy has abolished slavery, why should an institution which smacks of slavery be allowed to survive?'; for Chief Haguma, only by suppressing the *buhake* could one hope to free the Hutu from 'this form of slavery'; and Chief Kayumba bitterly lamented the fact that 'the *shebuja* [patron] has no consideration whatsoever for his clients, whom he treats as his slaves'.[14] Conversely, there were a number of Hutu clients for whom the rupture of clientage ties was inconceivable, for economic or psychological reasons. Indeed, cases were reported in 1954 of some clients who, after dividing up their cattle, would remorsefully offer one of their remaining cows to their former patron as a token of continued allegiance. Quite apart from the threat of social sanctions, many of these clients saw a distinct economic advantage in maintaining vassalage ties. As one of them admitted in 1954: 'When my cow gives birth to a calf, I can sell it and use the money to buy clothes and hoes. My monthly salary is only 345.50 francs [$7.00.] I need the money to send my children to school. If you want to suppress the *buhake* you've got to find something else to replace it with.'[15] These differences of attitude explain why in some districts 70 per cent of the total stock of cattle had changed hands by 1956, while in others only 13 per cent was exchanged. However, it is only fair to concede that, on the whole, the most fervent supporters of the reform were found among the Hutu, and particularly among those Hutu who were already engaged in commercial activities and for whom the *buhake* constituted an abhorrent reminder of their continuing servitude. These were the people who, shortly after the passage of the reform, could be seen 'dancing with joy and shouting "*Nakazize Umusaraka*" (I have got rid of my cross)'.[16]

The next point to be stressed is that a good many of those clients who thought they had 'got rid of their cross' once and for all were subsequently reinfeudated through the peculiarities of the land tenure system (of which more in a moment). As one might expect, it was among these 'involuntary clients' that the Hutu revolution recruited its most dedicated adherents. Their numerical importance is impossible to determine, because the proportion of voluntary to involuntary clients was bound to fluctuate with the political climate and consequent shifts of political expectations, but there can be little question that by 1959 they represented a sizeable proportion of the Hutu peasantry. By that time many of the Hutu who in 1954 opted for a continuation of their client status no longer faced their condition with the same equanimity. As years went by, their vulnerability to the appeals of the revolution increased proportionately.

As a social category, these 'involuntary clients' can best be defined by reference to the position of their patrons, who, by and large, stood at the lowest echelon in the vassalage hierarchy. Unlike their more wealthy peers, who could always expect aid and deference from their entourage, this lesser gentry was largely dependent, economically and socially, on the services of their Hutu clientele.* Thus, in an effort to retain their privileges, many of them decided to resort to dilatory measures. A favourite tactic was to launch a long palaver before the local tribunal and to leave the matter pending for weeks and months on end; or else they would insist on a payment in cash for all the services which, they claimed, their former clients still owed them from previous years, knowing full well that they could not afford such payment. The standard trick, however, was to reassert one's feudal rights by claiming control over the grazing lands.

In Rwanda, as in many other societies in Africa, control over the land was traditionally linked to the exercise of political rights. Belgian occupation brought no substantial changes in the system of land tenure; no effort was made to introduce individual land holdings along the lines of the *mailo* system of Buganda (Uganda). (This system, introduced by the Buganda Land Law of 1908, made it possible for the Baganda peasants to acquire individual freehold and to buy or sell land at will. As a result of the *mailo*, Buganda saw at a relatively early date the emergence of a

---

* Yet there were notable exceptions to the rule. For example, considerable resistance to the reform was also encountered among: (i) those patrons who disposed of certain categories of cows that were inalienable, such as the *inyambo* cattle (the *mwami*'s cows) and the *ingabo* cattle (cows which had been given to the descendants of a royal army in reward for their feats of courage); (ii) those patrons whose clients had only one or two cows and who were too poor to redeem the patron's share in cash; (iii) those patrons whose clientele was interchangeable with their political entourage. More often than not in this case patrons and clients shared not only the same vested interests but the same aristocratic background. A case in point was Chief Kamatari, in the territoire of Ruhengeri, who, as late as April 1959, still owned 258 head of cattle, most of which had been 'leased' to a dozen Tutsi subchiefs who also happened to be his clients. This state of affairs is reported in an anonymous document entitled *Situation du Buhake dans le territoire de Ruhengeri*, Ruhengeri, April 1959. See also, R. Bourgeois, *Banyarwanda et Barundi: L'evolution du contrat de bail à cheptel au Ruanda-Urundi*, ARSC, Vol. IX, fasc. 4, Brussels 1958, passim.

class of independent land owners, who also gained a dominant position in local conciliar organs.)[17] Except for the northern region of Rwanda, which presents an altogether different situation, the traditional system of land tenure was characterised by two major types of holdings: agricultural holdings (*amasambu*) and pasture lands (*ibikingi*).[18] Both types were allocated by the chief or subchief to his clients, who received usufructuary rights over the land in return for their services. But whereas the rights of the Hutu over the *amasambu* came to be recognised after the Second World War as individual rights of a permanent nature, thereby introducing something approaching a freehold tenure, no such de facto situation developed with regard to the *ibikingi*. Thus a number of former patrons, by asserting their claims over these grazing areas, in effect compelled hundreds of theoretically emancipated cattle-owners either to accept reinfeudation or to give up their cattle. The absurdity of this situation is shown by the shocking disproportion existing in some regions between the total grazing area controlled by former patrons and the actual size of their remaining herds. In Kibungu, for example, one patron was reported to control 40 acres of grazing land for only two head of cattle; elsewhere the situation was just the reverse —40 cows herded in a couple of acres.[19] As a result, in most instances, the Hutu peasant continued as before to graze his cattle in his patron's *ibikingi* and to render him whatever services he was asked to perform in return for the favour.*

The reason why this whole question of the *ibikingi* acquired such urgency, and why it has justly been regarded as one of the key issues in

---

* Another source of conflict inherent in the retention of grazing rights came from the juxtaposition of grazing and arable lands, and from the seasonal conversion of *amasambu* into *ibikingi*. Because of the shortage of adequate pasture during the dry season, some cattle owners allowed their clients to graze their cows in the arable areas which lay fallow. This right (*igisigati*) was carefully regulated by custom. It could be exercised only during the dry season, and then only over the sorghum stubble or those rare patches of land where nothing was grown. But as we already noted, these *amasambu* had, in many cases, become the property of Hutu peasants, and thus the landed patrons no longer felt the obligation to protect their tenants against the encroachments of cattle herders. Customary prescriptions suddenly lapsed into desuetude. Not only did the exercise of *igisigati* imply an indiscriminate use of grazing rights (because many clients were forced out of the *ibikingi* by their former patrons after 1954) but a constant effort on the part of the *amasambu* owners to keep the cattle from destroying their crops. The *igisigati* issue became a serious source of friction between Hutu and Tutsi as well as among the Hutu. 'Wherever the right of *igisigati* exists', wrote Father A. Adriaenssens in 1962, 'the *abanyamasambu* [owners of *amasambu*] forcefully demand its suppression. They consider it to be obsolete, unjust and humiliating.' J. Adriaenssens, *Le Droit Foncier au Rwanda*, Kabgaye 1952, mimeo., p. 63.

the background of the Hutu revolution, s that it made the Hutu peasants more conscious than ever of their continued dependence on the ruling oligarchy. Not that the peasantry as a result was worse off economically in 1959 than in any previous year, but their level of expectations had never been so high. The psychological uplift provided by the 1954 reform suddenly gave way to a profound disappointment which, in turn, strengthened the conviction of some Hutu that nothing short of a revolution could possibly loosen the Tutsi hold over the peasantry.

Looked at from a broader perspective, however, the abolition of clientage ties was the symptom rather than the cause of the disorganisation of the traditional social system. It was but the outward manifestation of the gradual erosion of socio-political ties engendered by the spread of new metaphysical beliefs, new types of economic activity, new patterns of mobility. However limited these changes may have been at the beginning, they unleashed a host of disturbances in the traditional social order, not the least of which was the assault on the body of traditional beliefs and practices, on what Emile Durkheim called the collective conscience. 'As the conditions of life are changed', wrote Durkheim, 'the standard according to which needs were regulated can no longer remain the same. . . . The scale is upset; but a new scale cannot be immediately improvised. Time is required for the public conscience to reclassify men and things. So long as the social forces thus freed have not regained equilibrium, their respective values are unknown, and so all regulation is lacking for a time. The limits are unknown between the possible and the impossible, what is just and what is unjust, legitimate claims and hopes and those which are immoderate. Consequently there is no restraint upon aspirations.'[20] This absence of restraints upon aspirations, which Durkheim found to be typical of anomic situations, lies at the root of the social malaise which characterised Rwanda society on the eve of the revolution.

This state of affairs carried several implications, the most obvious being the sense of frustration and bewilderment felt by an increasing number of Hutu peasants in the face of a situation they did not fully comprehend. Secondly, the ideology of the revolution rapidly moved in the direction of a racist ideology, aiming at converting the more or less anti-Tutsi sentiments of the peasantry into a psychological scapegoat designed to provide, in T. W. Adorno's terms, 'a means for pseudo-orientation in an estranged world'.[21] Finally, this normlessness also accounts for the subsequent tendency of some Hutu politicians to reactivate clientage relationships within their own group of origin, as if they wished to resuscitate the system they once publicly condemned.

In so doing they were able to provide the peasants with a kind of compensating mechanism for the psychological disarray engendered by the abolition of vassalage ties between Hutu and Tutsi. But before these revolutionary potentialities could be capitalised upon, a new elite had to be born, whose skills and aspirations marked them off sharply from the unacculturated and half-acculturated rural masses.

THE RISE OF A COUNTER-ELITE

One of the Hutu characters in Naigiziki's play, *L'Optimiste*, after commiserating aloud on the injustices of the *buhake*, asks his companion, 'How long shall we have to wait until our injustices are redressed?', to which his interlocutor replies, 'Until the Hutu no longer has the soul of a serf. For that he must be reborn.'[22]

The rebirth of the Hutu caste—its reintegration into a new moral and psychological framework—became one of the primary goals of Hutu intellectuals in the years preceding the revolution. They were all the more willing to engage in this task as they themselves had already experienced a kind of spiritual rebirth from their close and continuous association with Christianity. To these men, Christianity came to denote the equality of all men in God—equal rights and opportunities for all, irrespective of caste. Through their corporate membership in the Church, they acquired a whole new set of values and expectations about human nature, as well as the manipulative skills with which to bring reality in line with their expectations.[23]

As an instrument of socialisation, nowhere else in Africa did the Church play a more critically important role than in Rwanda. Nowhere else did the inculcation of Christian ethics carry such potent revolutionary implications. Yet the history of Rwanda shows that Christianity has not always been a source of political instability. Depending on the time, period and denomination* that one chooses to consider, one could easily show that it has contributed alternately to stability and instability, continuity and change, acquiescence and revolt. Thus it is important at the outset to call explicit attention to the dual role played by the Church in Rwanda. Insofar as it lent its support to the principle of indirect rule and deliberately favoured the ruling caste in matters of education and

---

* Although we are here primarily concerned with the Catholic Church, by far the most important denomination in terms of its following and educational responsibilities, attention must be drawn to the very different policy adopted by the Anglican missions of Rwanda during the terminal phase of trusteeship. Unlike the Catholics, Anglican missionaries continued to give unrelenting moral and material support to the Tutsi group.

evangelisation, the Church has undoubtedly contributed to the preservation of the status quo; but to the extent that there were significant exceptions to this rule, as was the case after the Second World War, its role has been just the opposite. These variations in the attitude of the Church have led to the emergence of two distinctive types of elite, associated with different periods of history, different ethnic backgrounds and orientations.*

The first of these groups, consisting in the main of educated Tutsi chiefs, subchiefs and auxiliaries, represented an 'upper crust' whose claims to superiority were based on a combination of caste privileges and educational qualifications. Each of these factors so strengthened their position in the political system as to lead to a situation of cumulative inequalities, with wealth, power and prestige concentrated in the same aristocratic hands. Thus, instead of loosening the rigidity of the caste structure, the initial impact of modernisation (here understood as synonymous with the acquisition of a Western education) has tended to increase the weight of traditional sanctions, by extending 'the premise of inequality' to an entirely new field of human endeavour. This meant that social differentiation between Hutu and Tutsi was actually greater in the postwar years than at any time during the pre-colonial period. Not until the mid-'fifties, with the extension of secondary and higher education to members of the Hutu caste, did modernisation become a major factor in upsetting the traditional pattern of social stratification.

Given the ethnic composition and educational qualifications of this upper stratum, there is nothing surprising about the sense of solidarity displayed by its members. Yet there were substantial differences of attitude among them, owing in part to their different levels of educational achievement and particular age groups, and in part to status differences based on descent. At one end of the scale stood the elder generations of Tutsi chiefs, most of them products of the old government schools of Nyanza and Ruhengeri. Profoundly attached to tradition, unswerving

---

* In this context the term 'elite' includes traditional and non-traditional elites, the latter comprising both Hutu and Tutsi. P. C. Lloyd's definition of an elite as 'those men and women who have received substantial Western education and are (almost in consequence) relatively wealthy', however useful, does raise some obvious difficulties. There were in Rwanda, on the eve of the revolution, a small number of chiefs and many more subchiefs who were almost totally lacking in education, while a number of educated Hutu were almost totally lacking in wealth. Perhaps the only valid criterion here is the awareness which these people had of themselves as an elite, no matter how different their standards of evaluation. See P. C. Lloyd, "Class Consciousness Among the Yoruba", in P. C. Lloyd, ed., *The New Elites of Tropical Africa*, Oxford University Press, London and New York 1966, p. 328.

in their loyalty to the crown, they represented the 'old guard' of the monarchy. Next came the younger chiefs and auxiliaries, graduates of the Groupe Scolaire d'Astrida and collectively referred to as 'les anciens d'Astrida'. From the early 'thirties onwards, they provided the Belgian administration with a large reservoir of skilled manpower to replace 'backward', 'incompetent' or 'refractory' chiefs.[24] In 1933, one administrator described the graduates of the Nyanza school as representing 'a cadre of intelligent chiefs who have made a genuine contribution to the evolution of the country'; they were, he said, 'invaluable elements, trained by us and therefore influenced by our methods and our ideas'.[25] But this was even more true of the subsequent generations of Astridiens. While their attitude was unquestionably 'progressive', in that most of them recognised the need for social and political reforms, their brand of 'progressivism' implied nothing as drastic as the wholesale rejection of their cultural heritage. No matter how genuine their attraction to Western education and technology, their enthusiasm for the West was usually tempered by a very keen consciousness of, and appreciation for, their traditional values. In their minds there was nothing wrong in learning how to read and write, how to drive a car, how to increase soil productivity, since these new skills and techniques not only did not interfere with but positively encouraged the maintenance of Tutsi supremacy. As long as this body of knowledge remained the exclusive property of Tutsi elements, it gave them a new sense of superiority and prestige over their cloddish and illiterate serfs, and hence a renewed confidence in the legitimacy of their claims to power.

Eventually, their psychological commitment to the traditional culture of Rwanda found expression in a consuming urge to resurrect and adapt certain traditional political institutions. Their position on the eve of the revolution can be summarised as follows: (i) the traditional institutions of Rwanda were remarkably flexible and hence could have been easily adapted to the requirements of political modernisation; (ii) by making a tabula rasa of this heritage the Belgian administration bears full responsibility for the racial impasse facing the government; (iii) only through the achievement of independence will the Rwandese nation be in a position to restore this ancient legacy, for only then will it be possible to extract from the past solutions for the present.* 'Progressivism' in this sense was also typical of the attitude of university students,

---

* Consider, for example, the following statement, from a memorandum submitted by the secretary-general of UNAR to the UN: 'If the Crown Council had been given proper recognition, the Mwami would not have appeared as an absolute monarch; moreover, since it drew its membership from each racial group, the Council would have had an integrative function of the first importance

at first few in number but who nevertheless exercised considerable influence in later years on certain segments of the Tutsi refugee population. As time went on, their sympathies for the Communist left became increasingly apparent, yet seldom reached the point of a total renunciation of their traditional culture.

More than anything else, it was their growing awareness of the threats to their privileges posed by the emergence of a Hutu counter-elite which gave cohesion and solidarity to these various social groupings. But this was not the only factor. A major source of solidarity stemmed from their shared consciousness of belonging to a cultural elite whose claims to superiority were inscribed in the history of Rwanda. Admittedly, this peculiar form of cultural nationalism, associated with the idea of caste supremacy, would have expressed itself under any circumstances; but perhaps not with the same degree of intensity had it not been for the contributions it received from certain members of the Tutsi clergy.

As members of the ruling caste, the Tutsi priests inherited the well-endowed intelligence of an elite group whose early life experiences and traditional upbringing were highly conducive to the development of one's mental faculties, and these predispositions were further enhanced by a subjective feeling of being the prime possessors of *ubgenge* (intelligence). Like many of the younger chiefs, their adherence to Christianity stemmed from their deep conviction that it was inextricably bound up with other forms of Westernisation: 'For the Tutsi nobility', Father Louis de Lacger once observed, 'European culture is at one and the same time science and faith, and this culture is that which is being practised by the White Fathers.'[26] Unlike the chiefs, however, whose education never went beyond the secondary level, they were given far better opportunities to develop their natural aptitudes. Thus, if the possession of a higher education strengthened their claims to deference, it also gave them the means to write about their own culture, to evaluate it in the light of other cultures and, ultimately, to give it a new meaning. In this

---

for the future of Rwanda. . . . The brutal suppression of the cattle chiefs and the land chiefs has singularly complicated the task of setting up future ministries and destroyed the possibility of forming an independent native executive broadly representative of native interests. . . . By doing away with the army chiefs, the Belgian authorities deprived the country of the basis of its future army and of a source of civic education for the young. . . . The systematic elimination of the heads of the kinship groups has demonstrated a real lack of political sense [on the part of Belgium], as they included many Hutu chiefs and constituted the basic cells and future building blocks of a democratic government.'
Mémorandum de l'Union Nationale Ruandaise à la Mission d'Enquête des Nations Unies, Dar es Salaam, January 20, 1960; mimeo., p. 2.

fashion they were able to inculcate a sense of cultural pride and unity among various sections of the Tutsi stratum, which in time also provided a basis of legitimacy for its nationalist, anti-colonial claims.*

Not the least of the ironies of this situation is that, while the Tutsi priests were generally among the most outspoken supporters of the monarchy, and in specific instances actively participated in the decisions of the crown, their formal association with the Church gave them the benefit of political immunity. The indigenous clergy of Rwanda is still overwhelmingly Tutsi in origin, and this, as we shall see, lies at the root of one of the most burning issues in contemporary Rwanda.

Thus it is not by pure coincidence that the members of the Tutsi clergy were among the first to publicly express concern over what one of them referred to as 'certain egalitarian tendencies'. 'Certain egalitarian tendencies', wrote the Abbé Kagame in 1945, 'are advocated in front of those elements who are sometimes referred to as "child-like grown-ups", without proper intellectual formation, which are bound to run counter to the commonsense principles of most if not all of them. . . . The path of progress cannot stray away from our traditional heritage. . . . Regardless of the type of socio-political system adhered to, one must avoid humiliating traditional authorities, either by disregarding their claims to leadership or casting discredit upon them in front of their subjects under the pretext that everybody is equal. The conclusion the masses are likely to draw from all this is that progress, freedom, in short everything, implies contempt for the traditional authorities.'[27]

As early as 1945, there were unmistakable signs that the traditional authority structure might not be able to withstand forever the assault

---

* A case in point is Abbé Alexis Kagame, one of Rwanda's most talented and learned historians, whose writings, insofar as they reflect the official Tutsi interpretation of Rwanda's history, have undoubtedly served to strengthen the claims of the monarchy. See for example his *Inganji Karinga* (*The Victorious Drum*), Kabgaye 1959, and particularly his *Isoko Y'Amajambere* (*The Sources of Progress*), n.p., n.d., a compendium of epic poems purporting to show that Rwanda traditions are the only coils of energy from which any sort of progress can be generated. Equally revealing is his *Code des Institutions Politiques du Rwanda Précolonial*, IRCB, Vol. XXVI, fasc. I, Brussels 1952, in which Kagame tries to 'select' historical facts with a view to glorifying Tutsi traditions. The date of publication is worth noting, for it was in 1952 that the Belgian administration drafted the text of the 1953 decree on the democratisation of local councils. Kagame's presentation of the political institutions of traditional Rwanda, in the form of a legal code, was clearly intended to provide the Belgian government with a convenient frame of reference for the elaboration of the impending legislation. Even though the book did not receive the official attention he had hoped for, it was avidly read by Tutsi intellectuals, some of whom found in it justification of their supremacist claims.

of egalitarian ideas. Western values had already loosened the existing bonds of caste and clientage. Their corrosive effect on traditional conceptions of authority was already apparent—and so was the incipient sense of alienation of those whom Kagame called 'child-like adults'. Yet grievances and disorganisation, though necessary, are not sufficient to produce a revolution. Far more decisive than the mere existence of a social upheaval is that it usually occurs in conjunction with the rise of new elite groups who, unlike the masses, possess the skills with which to forge new symbols of allegiance as well as new collective ties to replace the old communal bonds.

Table 4.1: Ethnic Distribution of Student Enrolment at the Groupe Scolaire (Astrida), 1932–54

Year	Tutsi	Hutu Rwanda	Burundi	Congolese
1932	45	—	9* —	14
1933	21	—	— —	—
1934	26	—	13* —	—
1935†	41	—	11* —	—
1945	46	—	3	—
1946	44	1	8	—
1947	44	2	10	—
1948	85	2	11	2
1949†	85	5	9	—
1953	68	3	16	—
1954	63	3	16	3

* Territorial origins unavailable.
† Enrolment figures for 1936–44, and 1950–52, unavailable.
Source: Enrolment Records, Groupe Scolaire, Astrida (now Butare).

As shown by the figures in Table 4.1, until 1955 the extension of indirect rule to the realm of education resulted in the virtual exclusion of Hutu from the Groupe Scolaire. In 1956 the proportion of Hutu students began to increase substantially, and, by 1959, 143 Hutu students, against 279 of Tutsi origin, were enrolled at the Groupe Scolaire. Meanwhile the first Hutu student—and indeed the first Rwandese— to claim something approaching a university education graduated from the Centre Universitaire of Kisantu (Congo-Kinshasa) in 1955. That the first blows against the ancien régime happened to coincide with the emergence of this small educated Hutu elite is not altogether surprising; nor is it by accident that the first Hutu who openly dared to challenge the caste system were also the first to claim more than a smattering of education. Just as in other African territories the birth of nationalist movements coincided with the rise of intellectual elites who had reached the top of the European educational ladder, yet found themselves deprived of the status and recognition ordinarily accorded to Europeans with similar achievements, in Rwanda the first salvos against Tutsi supremacy were fired by a small minority of Hutu intellectuals who were denied the influence and material rewards to which they thought themselves entitled.

From about 1956 onwards an increasing number of qualified Hutu began to hit the job market, but under the conditions of indirect rule few posts other than mere clerkships were available to the new aspirants. The feelings of denial experienced by these men is perhaps best illustrated by the case of Anastase Makuza, who later became one of the leading figures in the government of President Kaybanda: after studying at the Grand Séminaire of Nyakibanda, Makuza attended the Centre Universitaire of Kisantu, where he completed a degree in political and administrative sciences. Upon his return to Rwanda, in 1955, he paid a visit to Mwami Mutara to explore with him the possibility of employment in the administration. As was to be expected, his request was turned down. He next went to the Institut pour la Recherche en Afrique Centrale (IRSAC) at Astrida, to seek a job as a research assistant; but here again the result was negative. According to Makuza, 'the IRSAC was 150 per cent Tutsi and the few Hutu informants employed by the European staff were all carefully selected by the court to make sure they would not feed the wrong information'.[28] After this rebuff he went to see the Directeur de l'Enseignement, in Bujumbura, only to be told that his diploma could not be recognised by the administration. He ended up as a typist ('candidat commis') in Kibuye, with a monthly salary of 750 francs ($15.00). In 1957 he was promoted to the rank of administrative assistant, first in Cyangugu, and subsequently in Kigali. By then, however, Makuza was already a potential revolutionary. Like other educated Hutu, he derived a burning sense of grievance from the monopoly exercised by the Tutsi caste over all sectors of the administration and the economy; to break the hold of this monopoly became a central objective of the Hutu intellectuals on the eve of the revolution. For this they relied principally on the closeness of their relationships with the Church. Although none of them enjoyed a formal position in the Church hierarchy, they all maintained informal contacts with the European clergy. Most of them became intimately acquainted with Mgr Perraudin, and at least two—Grégoire Kayibanda and Calliope Mulindihabi—at one point served as his personal secretaries. It is indeed a fact of no small significance that most of the leading personalities of the

Hutu movement happen to be former seminarists, having at one time or another studied for the priesthood either at Kabgaye or Nyakibanda. At least until 1956, the priesthood was not only the sole avenue to higher education but also the only field of human endeavour free from racial discrimination, and thus it held additional attractions for those few fortunate Hutu who managed to catch the eye of the missionaries.

As we shall see in a subsequent chapter, it would be misleading to assume anything like a common political orientation on the part of these nascent elites (see chapter 8, page 230 ff.). Just as there were 'conservatives' and 'progressives' among the Tutsi, there were 'moderates' and 'radicals' among the Hutu. The Hutu moderates were usually those who, after a brief stay at the seminary, joined the Groupe Scolaire with a view to eventually securing a post in the administration. The more intransigent were those still at the seminary on the eve of the revolution: lacking the necessary qualifications to gain entry into the administration through the normal channels, they saw little attraction in the prospect of social reform. Only by a total commitment to the cause of the revolution, to the creation of an entirely new society, could they hope to make their mark in life outside the Church. As it happened, however, these divisions did not become fully discernible until after the revolution; as much as their common opposition to the privileges of the ruling caste, their unanimous adherence to the Christian values of equality and freedom initially contributed to hold in check whatever differences of outlook otherwise existed among them.

Here, then, was a group of individuals who could best be described as an alienated counter-elite: 'alienated' because of their intense feelings of frustration from being denied participation in the political institutions of their country; a 'counter-elite' to the extent that they stood as the creators of a new ideology, aimed at a total restructuring of society (at least in theory). They were, in Karl Mannheim's terms, 'utopian' intellectuals—in short, iconoclasts. But if the emergence of an alienated counter-elite was all that was needed to achieve a successful revolution, the birth of the republic would not have occurred in 1961 but in 1957, perhaps even earlier. Quite apart from the role played by the obduracy of the incumbents in driving this counter-elite down the road to violence, an equally vital element in creating a revolutionary situation was their ability to broaden their bases of support in the countryside, and to forge connecting links between themselves and the masses.

If somehow the lines of cleavage within the Hutu community could have been reduced to a mere juxtaposition of an alienated intellectual elite on the one hand, and the peasant masses on the other, there would have been no revolution. The agents of revolutionary action in the countryside were neither the intellectuals nor the peasantry, if by peasantry one has in mind the rural masses, or the 'menu peuple', to use the favourite expression of the Hutu leadership. The rural organisers of the revolution belonged to a middle sector, which might be described as a 'middle class'. To speak of a Hutu middle class, however, implies a far greater uniformity of educational and occupational achievements than these people could actually claim for themselves.* While some were literate, others were at best semi-literate; while some had actually freed themselves of clientage obligations, others had not; and if most of them were gainfully employed, their occupations varied: some were employed as primary school teachers; a few served in the administration in the capacity of clerks or 'plantons'; most of them belonged to a kind of rural proletariat consisting of petty traders, inn-keepers, truck-drivers, brick-layers, etc. Yet to a greater or lesser extent they all shared genuine grievances against their traditional masters. Because of their close contacts and psychological affinities with the rural populations, they were ideally situated to act as intermediaries between the intelligentsia and the masses. In fact, in many instances, they acted as surrogate patrons for those peasants who could no longer expect aid and protection from their traditional overlords. They supplied the middle-leadership necessary for carrying off the revolution in the countryside.

Yet in trying to pry loose the peasantry from its traditional moorings, these middle elites were faced with several obstacles. For one thing, the conditions which governed the behaviour of the 'peasantry' varied enormously from one region to the next. The most vulnerable areas were Ruhengeri in the north, and Gitarama (near Kabgaye) and Butare in the central and southern regions, where economic and missionary activities combined to produce the most rapid and extensive socio-economic changes. Elsewhere, the rate of social change lagged far behind the expectations of the Hutu leadership.

Generation differences also played a part in limiting the scope of their

---

* One is faced here with a definitional problem similar to that which plagues the historian of the French revolution. To argue that the French revolution owed its origins to the emergence of a 'revolutionary bourgeoisie', as Georges Lefebvre claimed, overlooks the diversity of economic elements who participated in the overthrow of the monarchy; furthermore, the term 'bourgeoisie', somewhat like the term 'middle class' in Rwanda, insofar as it refers to a segment of society associated with nineteenth–century capitalism, tends to anticipate the chronology of social and economic changes. For an illuminating discussion of this problem see the article by Jeffrey Kaplow and the rejoinder by Elizabeth Eisenstein in "Class in the French Revolution", *The American Historical Review*, Vol. LXXII, No. 2, January 1967, pp. 497–522.

activities. An enquiry conducted in 1959–60 shows that even at this late date many Hutu (especially among the older generations) continued to identify thoroughly with the dominant ideology.[29] Typical of this attitude was the comment of a 70-year-old Hutu peasant in response to the statement that 'Tutsi and Hutu are racially different'. 'The Tutsi will always be the dominant race and the Hutu the dominated race', said the respondent; he added, '[the Tutsi] always knew how to do well by their servants. The Hutu ought to be dominated. The one who is the strongest and the most intelligent dominates.'[30] Another typical comment was: 'The Tutsi were good to many people. To keep them from having power when they once had it without question would be to commit a crime.' For many Hutu peasants, Tutsi rule, though undoubtedly unpleasant, continued to be part of the natural order of things. Yet among the younger generations, and particularly among the more educated, traditional beliefs no longer held firm, as indicated by the response of a 25-year-old cowhand: 'As long as the Tutsi are rich they will rule. Now rich Hutu will also rule.' Again to cite the words of a 34-year-old educated Hutu: 'With evolution and education the Hutu and the Tutsi will find positions according to their ability without regard to race, and the uneducated Hutu and Tutsi will be dominated by the educated Hutu and Tutsi.' A 24-year-old school-mistress went even further: 'The roles are going to be reversed and the dominant race will become the dominated one.' These various shades of opinion reflect a characteristic progression in the degree of radicalism and race consciousness.

Finally, even among Westernised or semi-Westernised elements, habits of submissiveness continued to prevail. However real their grievances, these potential revolutionaries at first lacked the self-confidence necessary to launch a frontal attack on the regime. They were sullen and withdrawn, as if the mental and social isolation which accompanied their change of status inhibited their involvement in political activities. Their whole deportment seemed to confirm the contention that 'closely linked with economic underprivilege is psychological underprivilege: habits of submission, little access to sources of information, lack of verbal facility. These things appear to produce a lack of self-confidence and increase the unwillingness of the low status person to participate [in political life].'[31]

In short, although the impact of new economic forces did bring about a partial restratification of society, it did not automatically lead to the obliteration of the value system of the dominant caste.* Nor did

*An interesting example of the extent to which the values and preconceptions of the ruling caste continued to predominate even among certain Westernised

it produce an instantaneous revolutionary consciousness. To this day Rwanda remains deeply immersed in a residue of traditional beliefs. What has been decisively challenged is the exclusive claim of the Tutsi oligarchy to positions of power and influence.

As one reflects on the nature of the social forces in the background of the Rwanda revolution, one is inevitably confronted with a choice between two distinctive theoretical traditions, one associated with Durkheim, the other with Marx. One might argue with Durkheim that the traditional society derived its cohesion from the system of reciprocities inherent in the patron-client relationship, that this network of reciprocities was torn to shreds by the new system of stratification brought into existence by European colonisation, and that in the process certain pervasive values were violated, thereby engendering profound disturbances in society as a whole. The anomic situation produced by the disruption of the traditional value system in turn created a revolutionary situation. Although Durkheim did call attention to the inequalities inherent in the existence of social classes, his emphasis was clearly on the normative aspects of inequality, on the fact that the violation of certain moral expectations was bound to have unstabilising consequences. For Marx, however, economic exploitation was enough to produce social instability. From this perspective the Rwanda revolution falls in the familiar pattern of a bourgeois revolution unleashed by the struggle between a feudal aristocracy and a bourgeois middle class, or, to use the Marxist formula, a 'capitalist bourgeoisie'.

The link between Marx and Durkheim in this case would seem to lie in the relationship between anomie and social mobility. A possible connection has already been suggested between the rigidity of the caste system and the degree of anomie felt by those individuals who managed to escape the constraints of the caste system. What must be stressed here is that anomie could not have become so manifest unless certain fundamental changes had taken place in the traditional social structure, unless the old status society had begun to give way to a new pattern of

---

Hutu is offered by Saverio Naigiziki in his autobiographical novel, *Escapade Ruandaise*. After telling the reader why he happened to fire his houseboy—'he was too intelligent and hence annoying'—Naigiziki, like a repenting Tutsi, goes on to admit his preference for '*boy-machines*, who run when I call for them, who dare not deny when I affirm, who bow when I wish, who tremble when I scold, in short who never argue, knowing beforehand that my reasonings, true or false, will prevail' (page 64). Elsewhere the author is at pains to conceal his uneasiness at the sight of a market place. The rapacious self-centredness he sees in the sordid bargaining of buyers and sellers prompts him to lament 'the clash of self-interests, the wounds of egoism, hearts which suffer under the lash of the ego' (page 79).

stratification, no longer based on 'orders' but on 'classes'. This is not to say that the class structure of Rwanda had achieved any degree of permanence or consistency, let alone that a capitalist bourgeoisie had appeared. The Marxist terminology has implications that are clearly irrelevant to an understanding of Rwanda society at this particular stage of its evolution. Nonetheless, the growing differentiation of Rwanda's social structure, taking place within the context of a political system which continued to operate in accordance with the norms of a status society, was bound to produce profound psychological disturbances among those Hutu who no longer 'belonged' to the caste system.

Because this process of social differentiation proceeded with extreme slowness, and then was confined to specific localities, the task of mobilising the peasantry was rendered all the more arduous. Although the peasantry was often described by certain Hutu personalities as the only revolutionary force, until 1960 the peasant masses of Rwanda remained conspicuously amorphous. As the Hutu leadership became increasingly conscious of the enormous lag between the very slow rate of social change in Rwanda and the increasing pressures brought to bear upon Belgium to give the country its independence, organised violence became the chief instrument with which they tried to accelerate the pace of social and political change. Even though the initial outbreaks of violence were anything but organised, they nonetheless opened a whole new set of expectations that lent themselves to exploitation by the revolutionary counter-elites. In the end, therefore, it is neither to Marx nor to Durkheim that one must turn for a clue to an understanding of the origins of the revolution but, rather, to Sorel.

5. The Road to Violence

LIKE MOST genuinely revolutionary movements, the real origins of the Rwandese upheaval will probably always remain something of an enigma. The opening moves of what was to become a massive demonstration of protest against the monarchy shared many of the qualities of the early peasant riots and disturbances that swept across the northern marches during and after the imposition of Tutsi rule. In part, also, the events of November 1959 were clearly due to the failure of the monarchy to democratise its political institutions. They were the tangible expression of unresolved tensions between the forces of change introduced by the European coloniser and the forces of monarchical absolutism.

Considering the nature of the oppositions involved and the numerical discrepancy between them, there is a temptation to view the phenomenon of revolutionary change in Rwanda in somewhat mechanistic terms—as if the revolution was bound to propel itself unfailingly from one stage to the next, as if its final denouement, like that of a Greek tragedy, was foreordained in the initial confrontation. Although the element of predictability looms larger here than in most other examples of pre-revolutionary unrest,[1] one major difficulty with this approach is that it completely ignores the unintended consequences of specific historical events. Moreover, it assumes a situation of simple bipolarity between incumbents and insurgents, thereby ignoring altogether the incidence of external variables, such as the role played by the Belgian administration during the revolution. As will be seen, although the Belgian presence could presumably be relied upon to prevent or at least minimise the incidence of violence, the administering authorities were led, through a series of events, to throw their full weight on the side of the insurgents, decisively altering the balance of forces between Hutu and Tutsi.

These considerations are not meant to invalidate the arguments presented in the previous chapter, nor are they meant to suggest that the Belgian authorities had intended the revolution. The only point here is that the pressure of 'objective' social conditions—of increased cramp and restlessness in the countryside, of social alienation and caste antagonisms, etc.—may not have sufficed to bring about a successful revolution. The decisive factor was that the Belgian authorities reacted to these 'objective' conditions in such a way as to make the success of

145

the revolution a foregone conclusion.* Once the Belgian administrators on the spot had decided that the peasant uprisings of November 1959 were a revolution (which they obviously were not), the real revolution could no longer be averted.

THE RISING EXPECTATIONS

Commenting on the 'great changes' which took place in Rwanda during the five years preceding the jacquerie of November 1959, an Anglican bishop who had spent many years in Rwanda wrote that 'the traditional feudal system of master and servant had been broken by giving every servant his share of cattle as his personal property and by abolishing the duties usually attached to the possession of cows. . . . Government obligatory labour—a long-standing grievance—had been ended. . . . Local councils have been given powers previously exercised by the chiefs and the administration. . . . There were elections in 1956 to the Mwami's Council which has considerable powers.'[2]

These changes, however, were more apparent than real, and in no way altered the position of supremacy traditionally held by the Tutsi oligarchy. The abolition of the cattle-contract was quickly circumvented by the perpetuation of clientage ties through land tenure; certain forms of compulsory labour continued at least until 1959; the local councils remained purely advisory and the chiefs could, if they so desired, ignore the desiderata of their constituents; the powers of the Mwami's Council were likewise advisory and its membership remained almost exclusively Tutsi, with a clear majority of chiefs. The crucial point here is not that social and political conditions were substantially different from what they were, say, in 1949, but rather that a whole series of expected changes had failed to materialise. Thus conditions which were still considered tolerable in 1949 were no longer so by 1959.

Beginning in the mid-'fifties there occurred a decisive heightening of expectations among Hutu intellectuals which in time led them to formulate their grievances in explicitly political terms. This change of attitude could not have taken place unless they had become aware of a legitimate alternative to the status quo, and this was scarcely conceivable

* Although, in my opinion, the Belgian presence played a determining role in accelerating the revolutionary process, an endorsement of the conspiracy theory of history is not intended. The latter type of explanation—once made fashionable by Abbé Barruel's unconvincing attempt to reduce the history of the French revolution to an international conspiracy by freemasons—must be categorically rejected. However, that the role of the Belgian administration came to be interpreted in precisely these terms by the Tutsi oligarchy is directly relevant to an understanding of their attitudes during the revolution.

5. The coup d'état of Mwima, July 27, 1959.
From left to right: François Rukeba, who became leader of the Union Nationale Rwandaise: the newly-invested Mwami Kigeri Ndahindurwa; the Resident of Ruanda, M. Preudhomme, M. Preudhomme; the Governor-General of Ruanda-Urundi, J-P. Harroy; and Chief Kayumba, head of the *biru*.

6. The Conseil du Pays of Rwanda, October 1959, whose membership became largely synonymous with the UNAR leadership. *From left to right: Front row*: Kabagabo, Ndamage, Mwami Kigeri, Kimonyo, Bwanakweli, Kayihura, Kimenyi, Abbé Mbandimwifura; *Second row*: Biniga, Mbanda, Rwabulindi, Munyakazi, Kabagema; *Third row*: Kaberuka, Karekezi, Rwagasana, Runuya, Ncogoza, Ndahiro, Bagirishya, Mfizi, Makuza, Kayumba; *Fourth row*: Rwabukamba, Rwigemera, Rwangomba, Gashugi, AT Pochet, Abbé Bushayija, Segikwiye, Abbé Kagiraneza, Mungalurire.

in the climate of 'immobilisme' that still characterised Rwanda in the years immediately following the Second World War. Not until 1956 did one begin to notice a significant change in the attitude—if not in the official thinking—of the European oligarchy. The challenge to the legitimacy of the established order originated from three separate sectors of colonial society: from the 'colonat' (white settlers), the Church and the administration. These pressures for change carried different implications; they expressed themselves through different channels and, depending on the period considered, with varying degrees of vehemence. The result, nonetheless, was to release forces which struck ever more fiercely against the traditional barriers separating caste from caste, while at the same time prompting the Tutsi oligarchy to redouble their efforts to shore up these barriers and restore the lost social equilibrium.

It was in 1956 that a European settler named A. Maus, member of the Council of the Vice-Governor General, took advantage of the debate on the reorganisation of the Council's membership to introduce a proposal aiming at separate representation for the Hutu. After the proposal was turned down by the administration, presumably under pressure from Mwami Mutara himself, who was reported to have said on this occasion that 'there were no objective criteria whereby one can distinguish Hutu from Tutsi', Maus reacted by handing in his resignation. He later explained his decision in a long and hard-hitting letter to Vice-Governor Harroy, in which he took Mutara to task as 'having by his statement revealed his anti-democratic spirit', and stigmatised the administration for its seeming indifference to what he described as 'the most pressing social problem and the most poignant human drama in the Territory'.[3] The response of Harroy to Maus's letter illustrates better than any official document the still hesitant, indeed almost paralysing, attitude of the administration at the time: 'If you can state your views high and loud', said Harroy, 'and offer your resignation whenever you dislike the decisions that are made, I, for one, must take a longer view of things. I must set for myself a policy line—the art of the possible—and try to implement it'; after emphasising the need for caution by way of some dubious metaphors ('Je n'ai pas le droit de casser les vitres; et encore moins de le faire en jetant le manche après la cognée'), Harroy conceded that Maus had nonetheless scored an 'incontestable victory' and that the 'door remained open for giving the Hutu the representation that he [Maus] rightly considered indispensable'.[4] Although Harroy's answer was not disclosed until 1961, the publication of Maus's letter in the local press evoked an enthusiastic response from the Hutu elites, who saw in the incident a clear proof that they did not stand alone.[5]

147

By then, however, signs of an incipient and ever more fruitful co-operation between the Catholic Church and the spokesmen of the 'menu peuple' were already apparent. Indeed, that the Maus letter happened to be reproduced in a Church-controlled newspaper was enough to indicate where the sympathies of the European clergy really lay. Kayibanda had become editor-in-chief of *Kimanyateka* in 1956. An important organisational step followed in December of the same year, with the foundation of the Coopérative Travail, Fidélité, Progrès (TRAFIPRO). Founded in Kabgaye, under the guidance and inspiration of Father Pien, and at first entirely financed through Church subsidies, TRAFIPRO served as the basic cell from which the Hutu movement developed. The leaders of the co-operative went far beyond their original goals of 'promoting, through the application of co-operative principles, the social and economic interests of its members'.[6] Insofar as it provided them with a meeting place, made possible the acquisition of certain basic clerical and administrative skills, and invited them to establish links with the countryside, TRAFIPRO also served their immediate political interests, long before the emergence of organised political groups. This initiative could hardly have succeeded without the unrelenting moral and material support it received from the European Catholic clergy, and in particular from Mgr Perraudin.*

Far less successful, and hence all the more significant in terms of the relative psychological deprivation it entailed, was the initial attempt of the administration to end the practical inequalities between Hutu and Tutsi through constitutional reforms. Except for the very timid experiment of 1953, not until 1956 was a serious attempt made to introduce popular elections at the level of the Conseils de Sous-Chefferies (councils of subchiefs). The importance of the reform, however, as noted earlier, lay not so much in the positive gains of the Hutu elites as in their bitter disappointment upon realising that so many of their hopes had failed to materialise. For if the proportion of Hutu to Tutsi councillors did show appreciable gains in the lower councils, and especially so in the north,† the result of the elections at the higher echelons was to bring a further predominance of Tutsi elements.

* Perraudin's personal acquaintance with the history of the co-operative movement in Switzerland (one of the most successful experiments of its kind in Europe) may have had a determining influence on the decision of the Church to launch TRAFIPRO. This is all the more plausible in view of the very active role currently played by the Swiss Coopération Technique in the financing and development of TRAFIPRO. See *infra*, p. 251 ff.

† Interestingly, the electoral gains of the Hutu in the northern region initiated an attempt to resuscitate certain traditional forms of government. Thus by 1957 the practice among the Abagesera, Abasinga and Abazigaba clans in the vicinity

As a result of these various initiatives, a growing disaffection developed among the spokesmen of the peasantry, accompanied by a vague recognition that the traditional value system was beginning to crack. Never before in the history of Rwanda had there been a greater sense of expectancy among Hutu intellectuals. Never before had they felt so deeply the need for fundamental social and political changes. The crystallisation of ethnic loyalties, which had been proceeding for some time behind the monolithic façade of Tutsi supremacy, was now beginning to take a more coherent shape, and would soon be further accelerated by the efforts of the ruling caste to stem the tide of these new and as yet barely understood revolutionary forces.

THE BAHUTU MANIFESTO

The turning point came in March 1957, shortly before the arrival of the UN Trusteeship Visiting Mission, with the publication of the *Bahutu Manifesto*.[7] In it, for the first time in the history of Rwanda, a group of nine Hutu intellectuals, all former seminarists, systematically challenged every conceivable feature of the feudal system. The heart of the matter, they said, 'lies in the political monopoly of one race, the Tutsi race, which, given the present structural framework, becomes a social and economic monopoly'. After citing specific examples of political, social, and cultural injustices, they concluded: 'From this to a state of "cold" civil war and xenophobia, there is only one step. From all this to the popularity of Communist ideas there is only one step.' To remedy the situation they proposed a series of measures designed to achieve 'the integral and collective promotion of the Hutu': the abandonment of caste prejudice, the recognition of individual landed property, the creation of a rural Credit Bank (Fonds de Credit Rural) to promote agricultural initiatives, the codification of customs, the promotion of Hutu to public office, and the extension of educational opportunities at all levels to Hutu children. Never before had such a devastating critique of the ancien régime been publicly set forth by its opponents.

The *Manifesto* was the response of the Hutu intelligentsia of central

---

of Ruhengeri was to hold 'clan meetings' on a more or less regular basis, to refer matters of local interest once a week to the arbitration of a clan tribunal composed of the heads of the leading families on the hills (*bakuru bimiryango*), and for each adult male to make an annual contribution of 20 francs to a 'clan treasury'. Thus, in 1957, the treasury of the Abasinda disposed of a total of 2,820 francs (about $56.00). See *Territoire de Ruhengeri, Rapport Administratif, 1957*, passim. While showing the part played by electoral processes in bringing into being a new political consciousness, it also throws into sharp relief the persistence of primordial attachments among the northern populations.

Rwanda to the Statement of Views (*Mise au Point*) drawn up in February 1957 by the Conseil Supérieur du Pays, whose membership was overwhelmingly Tutsi. Evidently prepared to 'inform' the UN Visiting Mission of the prevailing situation, the *Mise au Point* insisted on a rapid transfer of power to the incumbent authorities. Special emphasis was placed on the need for extensive reforms, aimed at the promotion of an elite 'technically capable of participating in the direction of the affairs of the country', at the implementation of economic reforms and the reduction of racial tensions and prejudices between whites and blacks.[8] As the UN Visiting Mission subsequently pointed out, the *Mise au Point* was 'as much a reflection of the ineluctability of a profound transformation of Rwanda society as of a desire to accelerate the race to self-government in order to strengthen, through a premature autonomy, the vacillating prerogatives of the dominant class'.[9]

No matter how shaky the prerogatives of the dominant caste, this was by no means a reflection of the organisational strength of its adversaries. The authors of the *Manifesto* had few organisational ties to hold them together. They formed a loose network of young people who knew one another, had attended the same seminary, and who, in some cases, belonged to the same chiefdom or subchiefdom council. Of these various personalities, Grégoire Kayibanda was the one who possessed the greatest ambition and the surest touch for politics.

Born in 1924 in the vicinity of Kabgaye, some say of a Mushi father from the Congo and a Hutu mother, Kayibanda attended the petit séminaire of Nyakibanda and subsequently found employment as a primary school teacher at the Institut Classe, near Kigali, where he stayed until 1952. While serving at the Institut he showed sufficient initiative to become Secretary of the Literary Committee in charge of awarding prizes for the best literary essays written by Rwandese students; to this function he then added that of Secretary of the Amitiés Belgo-Congolaises, a cultural association founded in Kigali by a Belgian settler named J. F. C. Goossens (who later became fanatically pro-Tutsi, perhaps as a result of having married a prominent Tutsikazi). In 1952 Kayibanda went to Kabgaye as a prospective seminarist, and two years later became the editor of *L'Ami*, a modest newspaper printed at Kabgaye, which ceased publication after 1956. In 1956 he assumed the functions of president of the board of directors (président du conseil de gestion) of TRAFIPRO, with Father Pien acting as 'adviser and animator'.[10] By then, in addition to looking after the affairs of the co-operative, Kayibanda was editor-in-chief of *Kimanyateka*, personal secretary to Mgr Perraudin, and member of the chiefdom council of Marangara, three roles which he apparently exploited with consummate skill—the first to propagandise his ideas, the second to enlist the support of the Church, and the third to recruit potential adherents to his cause. Thus, when in June 1957 Kayibanda launched the Mouvement Social Muhutu (MSM)—an all-Hutu party whose programme was indistinguishable from that set forth in the *Manifesto*—he had already established valuable contacts and gained considerable respect from the local peasantry as well as from the literate Hutu elites.

Yet the MSM remained a rather weak and ineffectual organisation, which failed to generate anything like grass-roots support in areas other than Gitarama and Kabgaye. The main asset of the Hutu leadership was the almost unconditional support they received from the Catholic Church, which enabled them, among other things, to gain control over the vernacular press and to use the daily newspaper *Temps Nouveaux d'Afrique*, published in Bujumbura, as a vehicle for the diffusion of their ideas among Europeans and literate Africans. As it happened, it was principally through their journalistic activities that they first sought to enlist support for their crusade against the feudal system.

From the very beginning the Hutu leadership was faced with several obstacles. One of the most serious was the absence of cohesion among the various personalities who claimed to represent the Hutu masses, for there were fundamental divergences of opinion about the goals and tactics to be employed against the Tutsi oligarchy. 'The only point of divergence among the Hutu', one petitioner stated in mid-1959, 'is whether the campaign [for equality] should be directed against all Tutsi without distinction, against the high aristocracy, or against the specific abuses committed by certain representatives of the Hamitic race. Hence it is mainly a question of tactics rather than of doctrine.'[11] Actually, this 'only point of divergence' turned out to be a source of major disagreements among the Hutu elites, and these were further aggravated by cultural and personality differences between the leaders of the north and those of the central and southern regions. The former, deeply attached to their own cultural institutions, seemed uncommonly brash and undisciplined compared to their confrères from Kabgaye, Gitarama and Butare. But even among the latter tensions quickly arose between 'moderates' and 'extremists'. This is why a man like Joseph Gitera— one of Rwanda's most erratic personalities, once described to this writer by a missionary who cannot be suspected of Tutsi sympathies as 'a veritable fanatic'—found it expedient in November 1957 to leave the MSM and set up his own organisation, the Association pour la Promotion Sociale de la Masse (APROSOMA). This splinter group shared with the MSM a deep commitment to the democratisation of Rwanda's institutions, yet unlike the MSM, whose appeal was restricted to the Hutu,

151

APROSOMA sought to enlist the support of the 'common folk', regardless of caste affiliations. Gitera's attempt to pre-empt the themes, if not the tactics, of the MSM was partially successful in and around Butare, but on the whole his party achieved no significant results, save perhaps that of weakening the still very fragile bases of support of its parent organisation.

Another problem confronting the Hutu leadership was their lack of contact with the rural communities on the hills. Furthermore, there was little they could do to break the rigorous surveillance of the chiefs and subchiefs. In some areas they took advantage of the so-called 'réunions de colline' (the judicial and administrative meetings held on the hills at the request of the local ruling families) to propagate their ideas; but this practice appears to have been limited to specific areas, mainly to the vicinity of the mission stations and principal commercial centres. Thus, while claiming a great many potential sympathisers, until 1959 the Hutu movement had relatively few adherents outside the Ruhengeri-Gitarama axis.

A third obstacle was the apparent indifference of the administering authorities. Although the *Manifesto* had urged the Belgian administration to take 'more positive and unambiguous measures to achieve the political and economic emancipation of the Hutu', at first nothing of substance was achieved to mitigate racial tension. Not until December, 1958, did Harroy finally concede that 'the Hutu-Tutsi question posed an undeniable problem', but even so one may wonder whether the proposed solution—the abolition of the official usage of the terms Hutu and Tutsi—did more than provide a convenient way to dodge the issue. As one reflects upon the attitude of the Belgian authorities during these years, one cannot fail to be struck by their utter lack of foresight and imagination, by their unseeing passivity in the face of the impending crisis. Although many Belgian officials probably sensed the gravity of the situation, it seems that they simply did not know how to handle it. Undoubtedly, the calculated silence of Belgian officialdom added significantly to the atmosphere of tension and uncertainty of this transitional period. Though naturally arousing the anxieties of the Hutu leadership, the attitude of the Belgian authorities was readily interpreted by some Tutsi as a tacit approval of their claims to supremacy.

In retrospect, the significance of the *Manifesto* lay not so much in the organisational steps which followed its publication—these, as we have seen, were little more than symbolic gestures—as in the psychological climate it created among the Hutu masses. The issues raised in the *Manifesto* became a staple news item in the local press and a prime subject of discussion on the hills. Only a spark was needed to transform this still incipient conflict into a more dramatic dispute. That spark was provided by the rioting of November 1959. Before we turn to a discussion of these events and their consequences, something ought to be said of the attitude of the Tutsi elites in the period immediately following the publication of the *Manifesto*.

THE MONARCHIST REACTION

The non-committal attitude of the trust authorities did not last very long. Before the end of 1958, serious tensions developed between the indigenous Tutsi elites and the European administration. At the root of the conflict lay two radically divergent estimates of the Hutu-Tutsi problem, and hence two basically incompatible approaches to its solution. By late 1958 the consensus of opinion among Belgian administrators was that a profound transformation was taking place, one that should be activated and controlled through appropriate institutional reforms; implicit in this view was the assumption that the Belgian presence should be maintained in Rwanda for as long as the exigencies of the situation required. In the minds of the Tutsi elites, on the other hand, a social transformation of the scale envisaged in the *Manifesto* was inconceivable. By and large they felt that the demands voiced by the Hutu leadership were representative of the views of only a tiny minority of hotheads, and that most of the trouble came from errors made by the administration in the application, or misapplication, of indirect rule. Such being the case, only through 'full independence' could a lasting remedy be found to the social ills generated by the Belgian presence. The strategy laid out by the Tutsi oligarchy, in brief, was to seek the eviction of the trust authorities at the earliest possible date, so as to reassert their control over the destinies of the country. Once this was done, the future of the monarchy seemed assured.

In spite of their quasi-unanimous agreement on the desirability of self-government within the shortest possible time, the Tutsi elites did not constitute a monolithic group. They had different social backgrounds, different degrees of commitment to traditionalism and different conceptions of the future character of the Rwandese polity. As already noted, the 'old guard' Tutsi traditionalists were decidedly more conservative in outlook than the younger generations of Astridiens, and among the latter some were more 'progressive' than others. Though deeply conscious of the virtues of their cultural heritage, these younger elements recognised the need to adapt their traditional institutions to the requirements of democracy; very few, however, had any clear idea of how this could be done, or even of what democracy really meant.[12] A

153

third group, at the other end of the scale, found the bulk of its support-ers among university students, and claimed as its leader Chief Bwana-kweli, one of the most intelligent and progressive of the Rwanda chiefs. While none of these groups can be said to have held a controlling posi-tion during the years preceding the revolution, subsequent develop-ments propelled the more conservative elements into the foreground.

The gradual eclipse of the more progressive of the Tutsi chiefs by the more conservative led to significant tactical shifts between 1956 and 1959. At first there seems to have been a genuine desire on the part of certain chiefs who had received their education at the Groupe Scolaire to avoid the worst by easing the burden of the peasantry through social and constitutional reforms. Such, at least, appears to have been the intention of Chief Bwanakweli in 1956, when he decided to initiate some drastic social reforms in his chiefdoms, thereby reportedly 'filling the Bahutu with hope'.[13] Apprised of this initiative, however, Mwami Mutara reacted by transferring Bwanakweli to Kibuye, a remote locality in western Rwanda. While the policies of the court came to reflect the views of the more 'reactionary' elements, in subsequent years a number of 'moderates', including Bwanakweli, were pushed into the camp of the conservatives under the pressure of circumstances. Simultaneously, the tactics of the monarchists underwent a significant change of emphasis. From an almost exclusive preoccupation with the reassertion of tradi-tional values, the Tutsi elites veered in early 1959 to a position of in-creased hostility towards the administration, and eventually to one of active involvement in party politics. These tactical shifts came about in response to the cumulative impact of a variety of factors and circum-stances, the most important of which were: (i) the mounting tensions provoked by the repeated attacks on the monarchy by the Hutu press; (ii) the appointment of a parliamentary commission (Groupe de Travail) by the Belgian government in April 1959, to investigate the conditions under which a transfer of authority could be safely accomplished; (iii) the news of Mutara's death, in July of the same year.

To the rising crescendo of Hutu attacks, the ruling oligarchy res-ponded in 1958 by a hardening of its position on the issue of race rela-tions. In May 1958, a group of elderly Tutsi at the Mwami's court— the so-called *bagaragu b'ibwami bakuru*, the Mwami's clients—issued a statement in which they said that the ancestor of the Banyiginya, Kigwa, came to the throne by reducing the indigenous Hutu tribes to a state of servitude, and thus 'there could be no basis for brotherhood between Hutu and Tutsi'. Then, to sum up the argument: 'Since our king con-quered the country and the Hutu and killed their petty kings, how can they claim to be our brothers?'[14] While causing considerable embarrassment to the younger and more moderate Tutsi politicians, if only because it seemed to suddenly unmask their pretence of racial tolerance, the statement was bound to invite a violent reaction from the Hutu elites. Indeed, from then on the race issue lay at the core of the debate. Ironically, although the statement represented the views of a small, ultra-conservative minority, the issue it raised eventually contributed to strengthen caste solidarity among the Tutsi as a group. By asserting the historical claims of the Tutsi over the Hutu, the statement prompted the Hutu to challenge the historical symbols of Tutsi supremacy; and so, by late 1958, the Karinga drum, the supreme symbol of monarchy, became the target of violent criticisms in the Hutu press. More than its symbolic association with the crown, it was attacked for its conjuring up a vision of permanent Hutu inferiority. As the Karinga contained in its external trappings the sexual organs of defeated Hutu kings one can easily see why the emblem of kingship should have caused such deep revulsion among the Hutu elites; why, in October 1958, Joseph Gitera appealed to Perraudin to bring to an end 'the idolatry surrounding the Karinga'; and why, a few months later, the same Gitera referred to the controversy as 'a matter of first importance'.[15] By focusing their attacks against the Karinga, the Hutu struck at the most sensitive aspect of Tutsi political culture. Not only did this cause a vigorous reassertion by the Tutsi of the legitimacy of their traditional institutions, but it also heightened the fears and hence the sense of solidarity of the ruling elites.

Another cause of Tutsi solidarity was that they had now gained the firm impression that the administration was tacitly supporting the 'menu peuple'. This feeling was first conveyed to the Mwami during his visit to Brussels in 1958. In the words of a UN report, 'it was rumored that the Mwami had been displeased by the way he had been treated in Brussels in 1958, which was alleged to be so different from the cordial reception he had been given on previous visits. Whatever the reasons, relations with the administrations became very strained.'[16] With the announcement of the forthcoming visit of the Groupe de Travail, shortly after his return from Belgium, this impression became a certitude. Given its terms of reference, one can easily see why the commission's arrival in Rwanda should have caused such deep anxieties among the ruling elites. The introduction of democratic processes implied the organisation of popular elections and the substitution of majority rule, ascertained through the ballot box, for the rule of the minority. In the climate of racial tension which had prevailed since the publication of the *Manifesto*, this initiative was bound to further increase the suspicions of the Tutsi as a group.

155

What brought these suspicions to the point of near-explosion was the news of the death of Mwami Mutara, on July 25, 1959, in circumstances that were never clearly elucidated. On that day, Mutara happened to be in Bujumbura; after attending a film, he suddenly felt ill and asked to see his doctor. It is said that, as he was being examined, Mutara was administered a shot of antibiotics and died shortly thereafter. The official explanation proffered by the Belgian authorities—that he had died of a heart attack—did not sound very convincing to the Tutsi, and to this day most Tutsi believe their Mwami was assassinated by the Belgians— 'like Rwagasore of Burundi, and Lumumba', as one of them told me. That Mutara's death should have occurred shortly after an exchange of views with Belgian officials, and only two days before he was scheduled to issue what everyone expected to be an important policy statement, seemed to confirm this opinion. Predictably, the immediate reaction of the ruling caste took the form of a bitter denunciation of the alleged duplicity of the Belgian authorities. Commenting on the 'painful, mysterious and instantaneous death of our Mwami Mutara', Laurent Nkongori undoubtedly spoke for many when he wrote: 'They killed the father, and now they have killed the son.'[17] Belgium's past policy towards Musinga suddenly found a new echo in Mutara's death, as if, by virtue of this policy, the son had been fated to the same destiny as his father. Once the historical connection had been established, it was only natural for the Tutsi to engage in a systematic onslaught against every aspect of Belgian policy, and to blame indiscriminately the settlers, the missionaries and the administration. With Mutara went the last vestiges of collaboration between the administration and the chiefs.

But Mutara's death did not signify the death of the monarchy. During the burial of Mutara, on Mwima hill, the name of his successor was first revealed to the public, in what will probably go down in history as one of the most dramatic episodes in the annals of Rwanda. What came to be known as the coup d'état of Mwima marked the beginning of a new phase in Rwanda politics, with a sudden upsurge of organised political activity, and a further deterioration of relations between the crown and the administration.

The burial took place in the vicinity of Nyanza, on July 28, in an atmosphere of great suspense. Attending the ceremony were the Vice-Governor General, Jean-Paul Harroy, accompanied by the Resident of Rwanda and a few other Belgian officials, and most of the chiefs and sub-chiefs, the latter surrounded by a vast crowd of Hutu and Tutsi on-lookers who had come from various parts of Rwanda to pay a last homage to their Mwami. After the funeral cortege reached the burial site, Harroy conveyed King Baudouin's message of condolences and then went on to deliver a graveside oration which, according to some, 'was interrupted by murmurs from the crowd'.[18] Then came the turn of Chief Kayihura, Vice-President of the Conseil Supérieur du Pays, who read a statement prepared by the custodians of the esoteric code, the *biru*. 'According to custom', said Kayihura, 'we have the authority to designate the king's successor. . . . Custom prescribes that the *mwami* shall not be buried until a successor has been chosen. . . . Custom prescribes that the head of the *biru*, of the Abatsobe clan, must introduce the new king to his people. Therefore Chief Kayumba must acquit himself of this mission.'[19] As he read the statement Kayihura seemed visibly ill-at-ease; according to some eye-witnesses, he was literally pushed before the microphone by a younger chief named Bideri. After Kayihura's hesitant performance things suddenly took a different turn. A man named François Rukeba stepped forward and began to harangue the crowd, and with far greater self-confidence and persuasiveness insisted that the name of Mutara's successor be disclosed at once. At this point, the head of the *biru*, Chief Kayumba, stepped forward and called the name of the new Mwami, Jean-Baptiste Ndahindurwa, son of Musinga and half-brother of Mutara, who from now on became known under the dynastic name of Kigeri v. The proclamation of his name was received with a thunder of applause from the audience, and with utter consternation by the Belgian officials nearby. Not only had they been left in total ignorance of the *biru*'s role in assuring the succession (although the Residency had admittedly been told of the possibility of 'unexpected developments'); even assuming that they knew that such a decision was being contemplated, they had no notion of when, where or how the ceremonial would take place—let alone who was to be designated as successor. If all this secrecy was perfectly in line with customary prescriptions, the immediate effect upon Belgian officials was little short of shattering.

Confronted with the fait accompli, the Vice-Governor had little choice but to ratify the choice of the *biru*, which he did, with the proviso that the prerogatives of the Mwami would be decided upon at a later date. Whether or not the choice of the *biru* was, as some Belgians later admitted, 'an excellent choice' is beside the point. The important fact was that the Belgian authorities had acted as if they were knuckling under to monarchist pressure, which not only caused the administration to suffer a considerable loss of face but also conveyed the impression that real power now lay in the hands of the monarchists.

The new Mwami could not possibly hope to play the unifying role that circumstances and natural ability had conferred upon his predecessor. At the time a 21-year-old youth, Kigeri lacked the intellect, experience and prestige of his brother. He lacked Mutara's adeptness at reconciling divergent viewpoints and tendencies, at giving a measure of harmony and unity to his following. As the need for unity became all the more pressing, an alternative source of cohesion had to be found: the Union Nationale Rwandaise (UNAR) was founded on August 15, 1959. Though ostensibly dedicated to 'the union of all Rwandese for the purpose of achieving true progress in all spheres', and under the nominal presidency of a Hutu, François Rukeba,* UNAR was clearly intended to serve as the instrument of Tutsi supremacy.

From the very outset the doctrine, tactics and leadership of UNAR seemed to reflect the circumstances that led up to its foundation. The party doctrine was consciously fashioned to extol the values of kingship, as if to reassure the masses that the passing of Mutara in no way compromised the strength and continuity of monarchic institutions. The theme of king ship found expression in a multitude of manifestos, tracts and newspapers, in which the notion of kingship was consciously related to the unit of all Rwandese—Hutu, Tutsi and Twa—thus suggesting that all three castes had always lived in total harmony with each other, and that the existence of racial tensions could only be attributed to the evil hand of the administration.

Though incarnating the continuity of monarchic institutions, Kigeli was only a figurehead. The most dynamic, if not the most influential, personality in the UNAR leadership was its president, Rukeba, the man who had dramatically revealed himself at Mwima as a potential leader by boldly stepping forth in front of the assembled crowd to urge the proclamation of Mutura's heir. Besides having shown on this occasion considerable courage and initiative, as a declared Hutu Rukeba was an ideal choice to give credibility to the ideological claims of the party; but it was justly said that he represented 'the emotional and prophetic

---

* Though commonly regarded as a Hutu by most Rwandese, Rukeba, like Kayibanda, is a man of mixed origins, his father being a Congolese and his mother a Hutukazi. Rukeba's commitment to the cause of the monarchy, and his profoundly anti-Belgian inclinations, must be seen in the light of his previous embroilment with the administration when he held office as subchief in the vicinity of Cyangugu. After being accused of having falsified the entries of a court register, Rukeba was dismissed by the administration in 1944. In 1947 a deportation order was issued against him which led him to submit a petition to the first UN Visiting Mission, in 1948, to the effect that he had been unjustly treated by the administering authorities. It is interesting to note in passing that Rukeba maintained very close relations with Mwami Musinga, after his deposition. It is said that it was during his exile in Kamember, a stone's throw from Cyangugu, that Musinga wrote his political testament, a copy of which he entrusted to Rukeba. In this testament, which Bwanakweli claimed to have seen, Musinga mentioned the name of his son Subika as a possible successor to Mutara.

element in the party, whereas some of the important chiefs of Rwanda constituted its braintrust'.[20] These were Michel Kayihura, chief of Bugoyi, Pierre Mungalurire, chief of Ndorwa, and Chrysostome Rwangombwa, soon to replace Mungalurire in Ndorwa after the latter's transfer to Bwanacyambwe in place of Etienne Gitefano. Gitefano is said to have abandoned his post and left the country shortly after his son, Joseph Rutsindintwarane, was appointed secretary of UNAR. That these men did in fact constitute the core of the UNAR leadership was made abundantly clear by subsequent events; as we shall see, it was in response to the administrative sanctions taken against them that, in November 1959, a group of young members of UNAR decided to resort to 'direct action'.

THE JACQUERIE OF NOVEMBER 1959

The eruption of violence which suddenly swept through Rwanda in November 1959 was the logical outcome of the enormous tensions that had been building up in previous months. The dramatic events following Mutara's death, culminating with the birth of UNAR and the spread of a militantly anti-Belgian, neo-traditionalist ideology, brought political agitation to a new level of intensity.

Already a number of pro-monarchist tracts had been circulating around Nyanza, all deliberately playing up the sacredness and invincibility of the monarchy; as a further warning to its enemies, UNAR organised a mass meeting at Kigali on September 13, 1959: there, before a crowd estimated at 2,000, Rukeba, the first of nine speakers, read out the party's programme and then launched into a long panegyric of the Rwandese monarchy, punctuated with repeated attacks on Belgian colonialism. 'The whole of Africa', roared Rukeba, 'is struggling against colonialism, the same colonialism which has exploited our country and destroyed our ancestral customs in order to impose alien ones upon us. The goal of our party is to restore these customs, to shake off the yoke of Belgian colonialism, to reconquer Rwanda's independence. To remake our country we need a single party, like UNAR, based upon tradition and no other ideology. He who does not belong to this party will be regarded as the people's enemy, the Mwami's enemy, Rwanda's enemy.'[21] Similar themes were echoed in subsequent addresses by Kayihura, Rwangombwa and Mungalurire.* After the singing of a song

---

* As pointed out by the UN Visiting Mission in its *Report on Ruanda-Urundi* of 1960, 'the speeches were made in Ruandese, which is extremely difficult to translate into French if all shades of meaning are to be rendered. The Ruandese are fond of hints and innuendoes, so that words which might seem harmless

which was to become the national anthem of UNAR, Rukeba again addressed the crowd and urged each and every one to join the ranks of the
party. The Kigali meeting opened the gates to a veritable frenzy of
political activity, and led to further organisational moves on the part of
both Hutu and Tutsi.

On September 14, 1959, a new party sprang up, labelled Rassemble-
ment Démocratique Ruandais (RADER), which had as its stated objective
'to work towards the realisation of a social, economic, political and
cultural order based on authentic democracy and harmony among the
constituent groups of Rwanda'.[22] Despite the personal efforts and
prestige of its leader, Chief Bwanakweli, RADER never attracted more
than a marginal following, primarily among Tutsi students. As a Tutsi,
Bwanakweli naturally aroused the suspicions of the Hutu; and as a
'progressive' democrat, who once openly challenged the authority of
Mutara, he earned the contempt of a great many conservative Tutsi.
Perhaps its most serious handicap, from the Tutsi viewpoint, is that it
had been founded with almost indecent haste after the Kigali meeting,
as if to challenge the entire programme of UNAR.

About a month later, on October 19, 1959, Kayibanda converted the
MSM into a new and more tightly knit organisation, the Parti du Mouvement de l'Emancipation Hutu, better known as PARMEHUTU, and today
officially labelled MDR-PARMEHUTU, i.e., Mouvement Démocratique
Rwandais-PARMEHUTU. Unlike RADER, PARMEHUTU was to emerge as a
fairly robust and militant organisation, fully committed to the Hutu
cause and with considerable support in and around Gitarama. At first
the party did envisage the possibility of a constitutional monarchy for
Rwanda, but insisted on a genuine democratisation of all existing institutions before the granting of independence. This in itself would have been
enough for UNAR to denounce the move as 'officially' inspired. What
gave this accusation a peculiarly convincing ring is that the birth of the
party had been predicted in a UNAR circular of September 16, which
warned 'the people, friends and children of Rwanda' that 'in a few days
a new party will be born, supported by the government and the priests.
This movement will be said to have come from Christ and to preach
charity. Its first meeting was held in Kigali, on September 14. Its

---

to anyone not familiar with Rwanda assume a very different meaning to anyone
who knows local conditions' (p. 13). A case in point is the use of the expression
'the Mwami's enemy', which even then sounded to many Rwandese far more
injurious, indeed sacrilegious, than one might think. Many Hutu had no qualms
about calling themselves 'enemies of the Tutsi', but few cared to call themselves
'enemies of the Mwami'. The expression implies a degree of moral degradation
which cannot be properly conveyed through a literal translation.

adherents went to pay homage to Mgr Perraudin on September 15. Each of these meetings was held at night, the first in Kigali, the second in Kabgaye.'[23] The circular continued: 'Rwandese! Children of Rwanda! Subjects of Kigeri, rise up! Let us unite our strengths! Do not let the blood of Rwanda be spilled in vain. There are no Tutsi, Hutu, Twa. We are all brothers! We are all descendants of Kinyarwanda!' If the tone of these exhortations is any index, the foundation of PARMEHUTU only served to exacerbate the hatred of UNAR towards 'the enemies of Rwanda'.

That the opinion of UNAR was probably not without foundation is shown by the contents of a confidential circular, dated September 24, addressed by Perraudin to all Catholic priests. Without in any way contesting the rights of Rwandese leaders to organise political groups, the spokesman of the Church cautioned his audience against UNAR's tendency 'to seek a monopoly of patriotism, a tendency which closely resembles national socialism'. The circular went on to criticise the party for its attempt to insulate the schools from the influence of the Catholic missions 'on the pretext that they can better be administered by the state', and for 'its plans for enrolling the youth into an ultra-nationalist youth movement in order to remove them from the influence of their families and the Church'. Finally, UNAR was said to be under 'pro-Communist and pro-Islamic influences', a fact which, allegedly, was supported 'by irrefutable evidence'. Whether or not these charges can be substantiated, the content of Perraudin's circular was surprisingly inconsistent with the directives which he and four other Apostolic Vicars had circulated earlier in the month among the indigenous clergy, which said: 'We must respect the commitment of our laity to the formation and development of political parties. The priests must be careful not to transpose on to the political plane the dogmatic attitude which they are permitted to adopt on the spiritual plane. In this fashion they will avoid an otherwise merited stigma of clericalism and the reprobation of laymen who know that the authority of the Church should not extend to the temporal realm.'[24]

It is against this background that one must view the decision of the Belgian authorities to take disciplinary sanctions against Chiefs Kayihura, Mungalurire and Rwangombwa, on the grounds that their participation in the Kigali meeting of September 13, 1959, was in flagrant violation of the instructions issued by the Residency. At first they were told that they would be dismissed from office but, after revision of the sentence by the Resident, they learned that they would simply be transferred to other chiefdoms. As much as the decision itself, the timing and procedure employed by the administration were critical elements in the chain of events that led to the riots.

One must note, in the first place, that the decision of the administration was not made final until October 12, exactly a month after the Kigali meeting. In the meantime, as we have seen, important developments had brought racial tension to a new high. The administration had no legal grounds on which to bring charges against the chiefs at the time of the Kigali meeting. Indeed, what made the decision so patently unfair is that the Residency's instructions on the extent to which indigenous authorities could participate in political activities had not been issued until well after the UNAR meeting; it was especially harsh on the chiefs for all three held important chiefdoms and enjoyed considerable prestige among their own people, including the local Hutu peasantry. In the words of a UN report, 'the affair of the three chiefs was a decisive turning point, indicating a break between the administration and UNAR. It led to the voluntary exile of the three chiefs and made it extremely difficult for talks to be resumed.'[25]

In this highly volatile atmosphere, only the slightest provocation was needed to set off an explosion. When, on November 1, the news broke that a band of young UNAR militants had attacked Dominique Mbonyumutwa, a Hutu subchief of the vicinity of Gitarama, the incident was the signal for a violent reaction from the local Hutu population. Being one of the very few Hutu holding the position of subchief, and one of the leading figures of PARMEHUTU, Mbonyumutwa enjoyed considerable popularity among the Hutu population of Gitarama. On the day after the assault on him, a large crowd of Hutu began to demonstrate in the Swahili quarter of Gitarama, where UNAR was known to count many ardent supporters, and on November 3, as the rumour spread that Mbonyumutwa had died of his wounds, a group of Hutu assembled in front of the house of the local chief, in Ndiza, to voice their anger. While the crowd was becoming increasingly restive, a subchief named Nkusi, well known for his anti-PARMEHUTU attitude, openly expressed his contempt for the party and threatened to kill its leaders. The reaction of the Hutu was instantaneous. Brandishing their sticks and long-handled sickles, they ran after Nkusi, who found temporary asylum in the chief's house. After urging the chief that Nkusi be let out, they seized him and hacked him to pieces, along with three other Tutsi notables who happened to be visiting the chief.

From then on, violence spread like wildfire through the entire country. In the weeks that followed, roving bands of Hutu could be seen on the hills, pillaging and setting aflame literally thousands of Tutsi huts. In less than a day, from the locality of Ndiza, where Mbonyumutwa had been attacked, the jacquerie engulfed the whole region of Gitarama. On November 6, the territoires of Ruhengeri and Gisenyi were the scene of violent clashes between Hutu and Tutsi. The bloodiest incidents occurred on November 7, in the territoire of Kibuye, where the local populations inflicted heavy casualties on the incendiaries; of approximately 200 Kiga who descended on the town of Rubegngera, near Kibuye, at least 38 were massacred. On November 8, fires were reported in the Rwankeri and Mulera regions, in the extreme north, and on November 9 and 10 the revolt spread into the predominantly Tutsi district of Nyanza.

With few exceptions, the methods employed by the arsonists were everywhere the same: 'Incendiaries set off in bands of ten. Armed with matches and paraffin, which the indigenous inhabitants use in large quantities for their lamps, they pillaged the Tutsi houses they passed on their way and set fire to them. On their way they would enlist other incendiaries to follow the procession while the first recruits, too exhausted to continue, would give up and return home. Thus, day after day, fires spread from hill to hill.'[26] Despite the striking uniformity of the methods used, there is every reason to believe that the revolt was more in the nature of a spontaneous uprising, triggered off by the force of example, than the result of a master plan. There was little evidence of planning and co-ordination in their activities, save perhaps in the immediate vicinity of Kabgaye. Most of them were the victims of a bandwagon psychology which led them to do what others did, sometimes without even realising what they were doing. 'They burned and pillaged because they had been told to do so and because the operation did not seem to involve great risks, and enabled them to seize the loot in the victim's hut.'[27]

For some, the revolt had the qualities of an inexplicable cataclysm. A British CMS missionary, resident of Shyogwe, near Gitarama, gave the following account of the sense of haplessness and bewilderment felt by many Hutu in the face of what some referred to as 'the wind' (*muyaga*)—a wind which suddenly transformed itself into a hurricane:

I live and work at Shyogwe, about 8 miles from the hill near Kabgaye where the uprising started on November 3–4. We were thus right at the centre of things and saw the bands going out to loot, burn and kill, totally unopposed for two days before any Tutsi counterattack developed. We know therefore how completely the mass of the population, even in our strongly Hutu area, were taken by surprise by the attack. Very many were compelled by terrorist tactics to join the bands (indeed these were the majority). Many we saw were stunned and ashamed that such things could be. Many were resentful but dared not show their resentment. They called the war *muyaga*—

the wind, something that comes you know not whence, and goes you know not whither: unlike any other war they had ever heard of, they said. In every raiding band was a hard core of trained PARMEHUTU leaders generally coming from a distance. The mass of the followers did not know what it was all about or else were just out to avenge private hates or gain spoil [sic]. I have heard Hutu speak tremblingly of *lyvily*—the 'movement', i.e. the PARMEHUTU, the strong government-backed organisation which has them in its clutches. Many make much of the fact that the word *muvumo* (another way of describing the movement) in their language means a 'curse'. Indeed what a curse it has been![28]

Strange as it may seem, many of the Hutu who took part in the jacquerie seem to have acted with the conviction that the Mwami himself had ordered the huts of the Tutsi to be burned: 'for that reason, some of the incendiaries sought him out on his tour of the country after the disturbances and asked to be paid for the work they had done for him. . . . When the military reconnaissance aircraft flew over the scene of the disturbances to track down the incendiaries, the latter thought that the Mwami was in the aircraft and that its course indicated the direction in which they were to start more fires.'[29]

The persistence of popular attachment to monarchic institutions in periods of social unrest and violence is by no means a unique phenomenon. One only needs to look at the attitude of the French peasants in the late seventeenth and eighteenth centuries: in 1674, the French peasants revolted against the salt-tax ('gabelle') in the name of the King, and in 1789 they claimed that it was Louis XVI himself who had given legal sanction to their plundering of the landlords' estates. As George Rudé points out, in his discussion of European protest movements in the eighteenth and nineteenth centuries, 'in countries of absolute monarchy, the King was both the symbol and the fount of all justice and legislation, and the belief in his paternal benevolence persisted even through periods of revolution and peasant revolt, when the king's ministers may already have long been discredited and the royal power itself was on the wane'.[30] Such, also, appears to have been the case in Rwanda, for, despite Tutsi claims to the contrary, few signs of organised political insurrection can be detected in the initial wave of disorders set off by the Ndiza incident; where violence did carry some political implications, as in the north, it was aimed against individual chiefs, not against the monarchy.

In contrast with this rather unstructured, amorphous quality of the Hutu uprising, the Tutsi repression was not only better organised but more specifically related to political aims. The main target of the repression was the Hutu leadership, widely regarded by the incumbents as the principal agents of subversion. Before the administering authorities had a chance to intervene, a veritable manhunt was under way, organised from the Mwami's palace in Nyanza. Heavy reliance was placed at the outset on traditional military organisation: the traditional army chiefs, the border guards (*abahevyi*), the Twa-led commandos, all played their part in organising the repression. On the actual conduct of military operations, the UN Visiting Mission had this to say:

> Each commando party amounted to some hundreds of persons or more, *and included a majority of Hutu* [italics added], but the leaders were generally Tutsi or Twa. The group would set off on missions with very definite instructions. In other cases emissaries were sent out from Nyanza with verbal orders instructing them to bring back or kill certain persons, and permitting them to appeal to local authorities for armed forces to be assembled on the spot to help them in their mission. It seems an established fact, moreover, that in many cases a commando group set out with orders to arrest a person, but in effect killed him, either because he resisted arrest or because some attackers had the instinct to kill.[31]

Thus, with no immediate relief or protection to be expected from the administration, on November 6 the UNAR leaders organised a series of raids against certain Hutu leaders. The first victim was a certain Secyugu, who was killed in his home, near Nyanza, by a commando party led by a Twa chief named Rwevu. The next day, several other Hutu personalities were killed in similar circumstances in the Nyanza and Gitarama regions. While some were killed on the spot, others were taken to the Mwami's palace, to be judged before an improvised tribunal. One survivor, Sagahutu, who owed his life to the unexpected arrival of the local administrator, related the scene in these terms:

> I was standing on the barza, before a window. . . . Inside were Rwagasana and Sendanyoye, with several other persons who took part in the interrogation. Each one asked questions that I did not have time to answer. . . . Then Sendanyoye asked me to write down on a piece of paper that Mgr Perraudin was the President of APROSOMA. I answered that this was false and that I would not write such a statement. . . . From time to time I would faint and fall on the floor. Then I was kicked and asked to get up. At one time Sendanyoye fetched me a bottle of beer. I came back to consciousness and the interrogation went on. Sendanyoye asked: 'Give us the documents concerning the convention made by APROSOMA with the Belgian government to

forestall independence.' I said I had never seen or heard of such documents, to which Nicolas, the electrician, along with Rugenza and Rwangombwa, replied: 'You're a liar! If you go on fooling us as you have until now you will be massacred by the mob!' This crowd was like a pack of dogs and was getting more and more excited. Everyone cried: 'Kill him! Kill him! Let us kill him!' It was awful.[32]

Awful, too, was the assassination on November 10 of Kanyaruka, secretary-general and treasurer of APROSOMA. After escaping into Burundi, a few miles away from the Rwandese border, Kanyaruka was captured by the *abahevyi* of Chief Mbanda and killed. His body, like a sieve, had been speared 53 times, hacked nine times with a machete, and knifed once. His relative and host, Renzaho, died in similar circumstances, his body bearing traces of 51 stabs.[33] On the same day, raids were organised against the APROSOMA leader, Gitera, in the district of Astrida. But when the news reached the administration that a mob of several thousand was converging on Save hill, where Gitera lived, the district administrator quickly dispatched a platoon of gendarmerie to disperse the crowd of assailants. The failure of the attack on Save marked the first serious attempt at military intervention by the Belgians and the end of the Tutsi repression.

According to the Commission of Enquiry appointed by the Belgian government to investigate the origins of the revolt, '[Belgian] military action was carried out with the greatest possible rapidity, precision, coolness and effectiveness, and with a constant concern to avoid useless bloodshed'.[34] A five-stage plan of action had been drawn up before the outbreak of disturbances, which involved (i) the immediate mobilisation of three mobile units of 20 men each, (ii) the deployment of the platoons stationed in Kigali (five police platoons of 51 men each), (iii) the transfer of two additional platoons from Goma and Bukavu, (iv) the transfer of a company and a reconnaissance unit from Rumangabo to Kigali, and (v) the transfer of another reinforced company from Rumangabo. On October 24, the first phase of the plan was put into effect, and on November 4 the second, third and fourth stages were implemented. On November 6, as the situation showed no sign of immediate improvement, the Mwami sent an omnibus cable to the Vice-Governor, the Belgian parliament and the King of the Belgians to ask permission to restore order on his own initiative. The Vice-Governor categorically rejected the request and instead took additional security measures—first, by issuing a decree placing the entire country in a state of military emergency; second, by putting all civil and military authorities under the command of Colonel Bem Logiest and proclaim-

ing a curfew and a ban on all meetings; and third, by ordering the transfer of four new companies from the Belgian Congo, including two
companies of Belgian paratroopers. However, it was not until November
14 that temporary calm was finally restored to the country.

That it should have taken so long to restore peace and order cannot
be ascribed to a deliberate failure to act on the part of the administering
authorities, as some UNAR leaders repeatedly claimed. On the other
hand, the statement of the Commission of Enquiry that military operations were conducted with 'maximum rapidity, precision, coolness and
effectiveness' does not detract from the fact that, given the circumstances,
these operations could not be conducted with all the desirable speed and
efficiency. For one thing, the security forces available on the spot (346
men) were less than adequate to maintain peace and order, even under
normal conditions; then, as the Commission pointed out, the topography
of Rwanda, 'mountainous and with few means of communication',
was obviously ill-suited to the kind of military action needed. One
might also add that the cost of the repression was not equally shared by
the parties involved. By the time security forces had arrived in sufficient
numbers, the Tutsi, claiming to act in self-defence, were the chief
perpetrators of violence and therefore the chief target of military operations. Whether or not there is any truth to the assertion that the Force
Publique 'machine-gunned crowds of Tutsi that were on the defensive,
made arbitrary arrests and tortured arrested prisoners',[35] the record
shows that the number of Tutsi (919) arrested in November 1959 far
exceeded the number of Hutu (312) apprehended during the same period.

One can only resort to conjecture on the number of human lives lost
during the troubles. Even so, it is difficult to agree with a Belgian
authority, J. R. Hubert, that 'this was not a bloody revolution', let
alone subscribe to the statement that 'in the course of events the number
of people killed by the Tutsi amounted to 37 and those killed by the
Hutu to 13'.[36] On the basis of the information gathered by the UN
Visiting Mission, 'approximately 200 persons were killed'. But the
Mission goes on to note that 'the actual figure is surely much higher, for
the people, when they can, prefer to carry off their dead and bury them
silently. An official communiqué issued on November 23 stated that at
that date the number of persons wounded in the disturbances who
were hospitalised or given first aid in hospitals had reached 317, but
probably many wounded had left without seeking attention.'[37] To this
must also be added thousands of huts destroyed and an undetermined
number of plantations plundered, livestock killed and personal belong-
ings pillaged.

The revolt, as noted earlier, was not a political revolution, but rather

167

a series of spontaneous uprisings triggered off by a localised incident. Like the French rural riots of the eighteenth century, 'far from being a simultaneous eruption touched off at some central point of control, they were a series of minor explosions, breaking out not only in response to local initiative but to the force of example'.[38] In Rwanda as in France, however, the rural riot was the midwife of the revolution. A major connecting link between these uprisings and the revolution proper is that they came to be officially interpreted (or misinterpreted) by the Belgian administration as a nation-wide manifestation of revolutionary discontent. By viewing the revolt as a massive display of revolutionary fervour, Belgian officials tended to impute to the Hutu masses a degree of revolutionary consciousness which was as yet limited to very specific areas—to the Kabgaye and Ruhengeri regions, essentially—and to a specific category of individuals—to the more Westernised elements of the Hutu population. Yet, as a result of the administrative measures initiated in the wake of the revolt, popular discontent was given a specific focus, revolutionary activity picked up momentum and a new mythology gained currency among the rural masses, associated with republican ideals. At this point the Hutu revolution passed from the initial stage of uncoördinated and unformulated restlessness to the stage where social contagion and popular excitement leads to the formulation of a revolutionary ideology.

The events of November 1959 caused the Hutu leadership to engage in a fundamental reappraisal of their ultimate political objectives. It may be that some Hutu leaders were committed to republican ideals long before the outbreaks; until then, however, they looked more like radical reformers than revolutionaries. Their commitment to egalitarian ideas did not necessarily presuppose the obliteration of the monarchy as an institution. Now that they had lost most of their illusions about the monarchy, instead of looking for a common ground on which elementary social justice could meet the requirements of tradition, they looked forward to the birth of a republic as the only viable solution to their ills. Not only the leaders but a substantial segment of the Hutu peasantry was now about to be converted into potential supporters of a republic. As noted earlier, economic grievances, personal animosities, a desire to get rid of the 'bad' chiefs, and a vague levelling instinct, were the various elements which formed the backcloth of the Hutu uprisings. These motives had nothing to do with anti-monarchist sentiments, yet this is precisely what the Hutu leadership claimed. After November 1959, a conscious effort was made to harness popular grievances to the cause of republican ideals and to force into the same republican mould a variety of social, economic and political motivations.

Finally, the revolt led to a further polarisation of attitudes and expectations. Until then, a major issue confronting the Hutu leadership was whether the target of the Hutu movement should be the Tutsi community as a whole or only some of its representatives. Although this issue continued to preoccupy and divide the Hutu leadership, a major consequence of the rioting was to make the prospects of 'peaceful coexistence' between Hutu and Tutsi all the more remote. Typical of the attitude bred by the events of November was the tenor of the statement issued by Kayibanda on November 27—in which he made a strong case for 'segregating' Hutu and Tutsi into two separate zones as a first step towards a 'confederal organisation'. Citing Disraeli, Kayibanda compared the communities of Rwanda to 'two nations in a single state. . . . Two nations between whom there is no intercourse and no sympathy, who are as ignorant of each other's habits, thoughts and feelings as if they were dwellers of different zones, or inhabitants of different planets.'[39]

Subsequent events showed this estimate of the situation to be starkly realistic. The shock waves of the peasant uprisings had barely died when a new political storm gathered. With the approach of the communal elections, the Hutu revolution moved into its next phase, the contagion spreading to previously inert peasant communities, leading to a new outbreak of violence.

6. The Birth of the Republic

ON NOVEMBER 10, 1959, Rwanda was a country torn by violence, with thousands of refugees fleeing their homelands—a country in the grip of a bitter civil strife, facing political chaos. Under the circumstances one cannot fail to discern a touch of grim irony in the self-congratulatory tone of the official statement issued on that day by the metropolitan government:

> Since 1917, Belgium has carried out in Ruanda-Urundi a disinterested mission, which has brought this disinherited and isolated region of Central Africa to a stage of evolution which leads us to believe that we have, indeed, according to article 76 of the UN Charter 'favoured the political, economic and social progress of the indigenous populations, as well as the development of their education and the progressive evolution to self-government and independence'.[1]

No less disconcerting was the underlying assumption that the pace and direction of Rwanda's political evolution would, from now on, be regulated from Brussels, in the manner of a controlled experiment. In fact, the initiative now lay almost entirely in the hands of the local administration. Even though the constitutional reforms that paved the way for independence originated from Brussels, in the last analysis much would depend on how these would be implemented.

Not only did the administration 'fix' (in both senses of the word) the procedures of the communal and legislative elections in such a way as to permit the Hutu to score a maximum success at the polls, but when it appeared that not even this would suffice to put his protégés in command, the Special Resident did not hesitate to connive with the Hutu elites to engineer an illegal seizure of power from above. This is what led to the coup of Gitarama, on January 28, 1961. Thus, while the monarchy was not legally abolished until the UN-sponsored referendum of September 1961, conducted jointly with the legislative elections, it is well to remember that Rwanda had been under the control of a de facto republican government since January. It is perhaps a commentary on their indebtedness to the Belgian administration that the Rwandese authorities should have chosen January 28, 1961, rather than July 1, 1962 (when the country acceded to self-government), to celebrate their 'real independence'.

To draw attention to the determining role played by the administration is not meant to underestimate the importance of the revolutionary potential created by previous years of Tutsi hegemony and by the legacy of mutual hatreds left by the riots of November 1959. In a sense, the forces which propelled the revolution from one phase to the next— from the stage of anomic violence to that of organised political action— were self-generating. The mere experience of violence was enough to set the stage for further violence, as well as for the emergence of a new set of psychological orientations for both Hutu and Tutsi. But even so, and somewhat paradoxically, one wonders to what extent the circumstances and motives which bred violence cannot be imputed to the very measures taken by the trust authorities to restore 'peace and order'. As the Special Resident, Colonel Bem Logiest, stated, in January 1960: 'By virtue of the situation we are obliged to take sides. We cannot stay neutral and sit.'[2]

The Aftermath of the Crisis

In the months following the jacquerie the trust authorities were confronted with three problems of great urgency, but for which there were no ideal solutions. One was to attend to the material needs of the Tutsi refugees, whose dwellings had been burned down and crops devastated; another was to find suitable candidates to fill the vacancies left by the flight or 'removal' of Tutsi chiefs and subchiefs; then, additional security measures were urgently needed to maintain a modicum of peace and order throughout the country. To a considerable extent, the effectiveness of the security measures adopted by the Belgians would depend on the adequacy of the solutions applied to the other problems. As it happened the latter proved utterly inadequate.

The Refugee Problem

Of all the consequences of the November riots none was more tragic than the forced exodus of thousands of Tutsi families from their native homelands, with all the material hardships and emotional pangs that such a massive uprooting is liable to entail. Though the element of human tragedy cannot be ignored, the political implications of the problem are no less worthy of consideration. Besides adding substantially to the prevailing atmosphere of mutual fear and suspicion, the revanchist attitude which this situation was bound to foster among the refugees contributed in no small way to the rapid deterioration of Hutu-Tutsi relations in the months preceding independence. Its ultimate repercussions, however, were by no means confined to the pre-independence period, or, for that matter, to Rwanda alone.

From about 7,000 at the end of November 1959, the total number of refugees rose to 22,000 by April 1960. Of these, about 7,000 were installed at the Nyamata camp for refugees, in the Bugesera, while the remaining 15,000, distributed through the territories of Biumba, Gisenyi and Astrida, found temporary asylum in mission stations and government buildings or wandered over the countryside in a vain quest for food, shelter and security. Only a small percentage of the total refugee population was allowed to return to their homelands after the events of November 1959, and many of those who did lived to regret it. Most of them eventually chose to resettle in neighbouring countries— Burundi, the Congo, Uganda and Tanzania. From a mere trickle, the number of refugees who sought asylum abroad grew rapidly after 1960: from approximately 1,500 in late 1960, approximately 130,000 Tutsi had left the country by the end of 1963.[3]

Among the refugees were many Hutu, some of whom are now living in exile with their former lords. It is symptomatic of the persistence of traditional ties within the Hutu community that so many of them would rather go into exile than shift their allegiance to the new regime. Their exact number is impossible to determine. By way of an illustration, however, one could cite the case of Chief Bideri, admittedly one of the most popular of the young chiefs, who, in an interview with this writer, claimed to have been followed into exile by a retinue of about forty Hutu. Similarly, Rachel Yeld reports the presence of a 'group of about fifty Twa families among the main groups of refugees in Tanganyika, who had been dancers and court servants of the Mwami'. Yet there can be little doubt, as she goes on to point out, that 'the majority of refugees can be said to be at least marginally in the Tutsi group in terms either of ethnic origin or of previous political, economic or social position'.[4]

For all the efforts of the Belgian administration to meet the needs of the refugees as promptly and efficiently as one could hope, little could be done to assuage their burning sense of grievance and to prevent UNAR from making political capital out of the situation. Deliberately ignoring the more creditable achievement of the administration, the spokesmen of UNAR constantly reminded the refugees of 'their brutal uprooting', of 'the devastation of their crops, the killing of their cattle, the destruction of their dwellings, the rape of their wives and daughters'. Likewise, attention was drawn to 'the enforced promiscuity of the refugee camps', to 'the criminal expulsion of the old and the young from their salubrious native regions and their parking [sic], without shelter of any sort, in a region . . . infested with tse-tse flies'.[5] Every effort was made to keep alive the grievances of the refugee population, and to relate these to allegations of racial bias on the part of the Belgian authorities. Before long the refugees were converted into ardent supporters of UNAR.

To appreciate the depth of their rancour towards the Belgian authorities, and ultimately the nature of the external commitments of their leadership, one has to bear in mind not only the thoroughly inhuman conditions in which some of them lived, both within and outside Rwanda, but, even more importantly, their unanimous conviction that they owed their fate to a deliberate racial bias on the part of the administration. True, a sizeable number of refugees left their homelands to escape the violence unleashed by the November riots, but the overwhelming majority began their exodus well after the rioting, when they suddenly found themselves confronted with Hutu chiefs and subchiefs, all appointed by the administration. Although these appointments were intended to placate the local populations, in the hope that calm would thereby be restored, the sheer arbitrariness, indeed the ruthlessness, with which many of these chiefs used their authority resulted in a further exodus of Tutsi families. To a large extent the refugee problem was the consequence of the 'interim appointments' of Hutu chiefs and subchiefs in those areas where the actual or presumed hostility of the local populations caused the eviction of Tutsi authorities.

The Installation of Interim Authorities

In the period immediately following the disturbances no less than 21 Tutsi chiefs and 332 subchiefs were either killed by the security forces, arrested, or forced to resign in the face of the local Hutu opposition. Of these, well over half held office in the northern region, a fact which also explains the predominance of Tutsi elements from the north among the refugee population of Nyamata. By the end of 1960, no less than 5,043 refugees out of a total of 6,732 came from the territoire of Ruhengeri.[6] While in some cases the administration had no choice but to bow to the popular verdict, it is equally true that Belgian officials sometimes encouraged the local population to get rid of their chiefs. Certainly, no effort was made to restore the authority of the Tutsi chiefs, in spite of the fact that the arbitration of the administering authorities still carried decisive weight.

The appointment of over 300 Hutu chiefs and subchiefs, in late 1959 and early 1960, to occupy the posts which the Tutsi authorities had left vacant, inaugurated a period of profound instability, marked by considerable administrative inefficiency, mutual provocations and recurrent violence. In making these appointments the administration showed remarkably little concern for procedural niceties. The text of one of the procès-verbaux illustrates the summary character of the procedure: 'Considering that x has left his post, that the population of the sub-chiefdom is opposed to the maintenance in office of subchief x, we declare this office to be vacant. Considering the vacancy of office, and considering the wishes of the population, we hereby designate y as subchief.' In an effort to explain its policy the administration made a great play of the fact that the revolt had created 'a practical situation which sprang from the very depths of popular will'; it also pointed out that 'these were not final appointments but interim appointments', pending the verdict of the communal elections. Moreover, the choice of interim appointments 'had the advantage of allowing some 200 Hutu the chance to show their aptitude for political office, and yet of not making commitments for the future since the elections would always provide an opportunity to repair unfortunate choices'.[7]

Countless examples of administrative incapacity were reported by administrateurs de territoire (AT) in early 1960, all of them involving Hutu chiefs and subchiefs. Of the Hutu chief of Rukiga, AT Ducène said in May 1960 that he was 'absolutely incapable'; of the Hutu chief of Ndorwa that he was, likewise, 'incapable', and that the situation there was rapidly getting out of hand.[8] 'They have created a Committee of Public Safety', Ducène added, 'with ministers, etc.' In Bunyambiri, AT de Jamblinne reported that, although the 'situation was good . . . it was necessary to clamp down on the Hutu subchiefs'.[9] In the Budaha, Buhoyi-Lac and Cyesha regions, the interim authorities were either unable or did not even try to prevent acts of incendiarism. In the Budaha alone, more than 500 huts were set aflame between May 16 and 18, 1960. In an attempt to absolve the arsonists, AT Nijs said that 'the actions of the incendiaries were primarily directed against violent [Tutsi] elements who were already implicated in different affairs', but one wonders if in this case Tutsi violence was not the result of previous Hutu provocations. This indeed is what one gathers from the comments of the same AT on January 11, 1960, when he voiced his satisfaction at the fact that in the Budaha 'the Hutu movement is well underway', that 'political meetings were held against the wishes of the Tutsi', and went on to note that 'the Hutu regret that they had not yet accomplished their revolution'.[10] Although the Hutu subchief of Budaha was said to have been put into office 'at the request of the local Tutsi inhabitants, as a measure of safety', this conciliatory move apparently did not prevent him from grossly abusing his authority. One can reasonably infer from the record of the 'réunions de cadres' (held under the auspices of Colonel Logiest, with the participation of the ATS) that this was not an isolated case.

To understand why the trust authorities should have allowed this state of affairs to develop, it is essential to recall that, in their minds, the exigencies of the situation made it absolutely imperative to hasten the politicisation of the Hutu masses, no matter how high the cost. The official viewpoint of the local Belgian authorities is nowhere better illustrated than in the declaration made by the Special Resident, Colonel Logiest, in the course of the 'réunion de cadres' of January 11, 1960:

> What is our goal? It is to accelerate the politicisation of Ruanda. In Urundi politics are avoided; one would like to have elections before political parties are brought into being. This may be all right for Urundi, but here the situation is different. Not only do we want elections but we want everybody to be aware of this. People must go to the polls in full freedom and in full political awareness. *Thus we must undertake an action in favour of the Hutu, who live in a state of ignorance and under oppressive influences. By virtue of the situation we are obliged to take sides. We cannot stay neutral and sit* [our italics].[11]

Far from being neutral or passive, the Belgian administration became the prime legitimiser of Hutu rule.

This commitment must be seen in the light of at least two different types of considerations. There was, to begin with, the practical aspect. The climate of unrest engendered by the November riots made the task of the administrators on the spot an extremely arduous and dangerous one. The consensus among local officials was that only through a genuine transfer of authority to the Hutu elites could one expect a return to normalcy, and this presumably implied a commitment in favour of PARMEHUTU. Commenting upon the attitude of the administration in the months following the disturbances, a spokesman of the Church Missionary Society (CMS) with over twenty years of missionary experience in Rwanda observed that 'one of the misconceptions of the [Belgian] government is that this PARMEHUTU-APROSOMA movement is a popular revolution—a spontaneous uprising of the downtrodden masses against Tutsi tyranny. . . . Since the government feels, mistakenly, that this is a popular uprising, they feel compelled to do nothing to thwart it and everything to implement it.'[12] The truth of the matter, however, is that this 'misconception' was a deliberate one, intended to rationalise the surgical steps necessary to bring to an end as promptly as possible the anarchic conditions created by the riots, and eliminate at the same time the possibility of renewed disturbances.

By mid-1960, however, the attitude of the Residency came to reflect motivations of a different order. To be sure, the necessity of espousing and encouraging the 'rising expectations' of the Hutu was still foremost in the minds of the Belgian administrators. But this policy seemed even more imperative after the independence of Congo-Kinshasa, when new connections were established between exiled Tutsi elements and certain Congolese parties for which the administration had but slender sympathies. As it became apparent that the UNAR leadership-in-exile courted the support of the MNC-Lumumba, and as the rumour spread that the local MNC branches in the Congo (especially in Goma and Bukavu) were giving financial and military assistance to the Tutsi leadership—presumably to help them fight their way back into the country—Belgian suspicions of UNAR's pro-Communist leanings hardened into certainty. Addressing a 'réunion de cadres' on September 2, 1960, Logiest summed up the political equation in these terms:

> There are four elements with which we must cope: the Hutu, the Tutsi, the West (and especially Belgium), and the outside world (the MNC-Lumumba). It is easy to understand that there will always be an opposition between the Hutu and the West on the one hand, and the Tutsi and the outside world on the other. It may be that in five years hence the situation will be different, but this is what it is now, even if the Hutu do not like us. And if a pro-Western regime should come to power in the Congo, this could only reinforce the pro-Western position of the Hutu. I don't think this reasoning can be challenged.[13]

It could, indeed, have been challenged on other grounds; but for the purpose of this discussion it is enough to note that by the autumn of 1960 the pro-Hutu attitude of the administration could no longer be explained only in terms of the practical exigencies of the Rwanda situation. By then the Residency saw itself engaged in 'a grand strategy', involving political considerations which clearly transcended the immediate arena of the Hutu-Tutsi conflict, or for that matter the context of African politics. In short, in supporting Hutu against Tutsi, the Special Resident acted with the unshakable conviction that in so doing he was liberating the Hutu peasantry from the oppression of both feudalism and Communism.

Regardless of the motivations behind it, the policy of the administration was bound to have major repercussions at the local level. The main significance of these 'interim appointments' is that they afforded the Hutu leadership a unique opportunity to expand their activities to areas where popular support for their cause had yet to be awakened. In many places these authorities became the self-appointed leaders of local PARMEHUTU branches; elsewhere, they preferred to wait and see which of the major Hutu parties would come on top. But as a rule they seldom missed an opportunity to demonstrate their anti-Tutsi feelings. A CMS missionary whose words have already been cited commented: 'Certain Hutu leaders were acting openly and unashamedly, organising the grossest outrages, but nowhere have these leaders been arrested, and in very many cases it is they who have been promoted to positions of responsibility and put to replace the ejected chiefs.'[14] Since they did not conceive of their role as involving any particular obligations save that of promoting the interests of their caste, they naturally tended to act more like political agitators than civil servants, and in so doing hoped to establish political credentials that would enable them to hold on to their positions on a more permanent basis.

As a corollary of this situation, the monarchists suffered some major disabilities. Not only was the threatening posture of the Hutu chiefs and subchiefs enough to cower some of their opponents into an attitude of passive obedience; the massive transfers of Tutsi populations that took place in the months following the November crisis caused a rapid shrinkage of the territorial support which UNAR might otherwise have expected. In those regions where the Hutu parties were already solidly established (as in the Kabgaye-Ruhengeri axis) the consequences were not all that significant, but where neither PARMEHUTU nor APROSOMA claimed more than marginal support the flight of Tutsi elements could only weaken the prospects of a UNAR victory at the polls. As the situation continued to deteriorate, prompting an ever-increasing number of Tutsi families to seek asylum abroad, UNAR saw a further dwindling of its bases of domestic support. The next logical step was to use the adjacent territories as bases for launching border raids and armed expeditions into the country. From then on, violence became endemic.

Thus, contrary to what the UN Visiting Mission had hoped, the approach of the electoral campaign saw no let-up in the racial tension. If anything, the constitutional reforms envisaged by the government, together with the flagrantly biased attitude of the local administration, helped reinforce UNAR's conviction that Belgian officialdom was doing its best to crush the Tutsi and promote the Hutu. Although there is little basis for the view that all official actions were systematically aimed at destroying Tutsi hegemony, that these actions were inevitably regarded by the Tutsi as prejudicial to their own interests was enough to bring racial antagonisms to a new pitch of tension.

THE COMMUNAL ELECTIONS

In line with the official communiqué of November 10, 1959, the administration began in early 1960 to lay the groundwork for the communal elections scheduled for June and July of the same year. The commune, headed by a burgomaster assisted by a popularly elected council, was to take the place of the subchiefdom as the basic political unit; the existing chiefdoms would be converted into purely administrative entities; at the central level, legislative powers would be vested in an indirectly elected Legislative Council that would exercise its functions jointly with the Mwami, with the understanding that the administration would nonetheless retain a veto power over the decisions made at each level. The election of 229 burgomasters and 3,051 communal councillors, between June 26 and July 30, 1960, gave Rwanda its first taste of local self-government. For the first time in the history of the country the Hutu masses were given an opportunity to elect their own local executive authorities; for the first time political parties were allowed to compete among themselves for the votes of the electorate; for the first time a genuine effort was made to acquaint the populations of Rwanda with the mechanics of democracy.

To see the elections in this light, however, is to confuse theory and reality, free choice and intimidation, political education and propaganda. Above all, it assumes that the contestants agreed on the rules of the game. The electoral struggle was really a struggle for supremacy between Hutu and Tutsi, for democracy meant the advent of majority rule and majority rule necessarily meant Hutu rule. In the minds of the Hutu leaders, democracy meant the liquidation 'of the old customs of bondage and domination which gave the Tutsi a position of hegemony over the Hutu'; it meant working hand in hand with the administration, because, as one Hutu propagandist pointed out, 'it is the administration which has acknowledged the equality of Hutu and Tutsi, protected the Hutu, relieved him of his heavy burdens and freed him of his enemies, of the corvées and other merciless obligations'; it meant 'a decent salary for the workers, jobs for the unemployed, and the ownership of land',[15] none of which could be secured without the help of the Belgians. By urging the people to register and vote, by ceaselessly drawing attention to the virtues of democracy and the ills of feudalism, the Belgian administration correctly figured that the higher the electoral participation the greater the chances of a Hutu victory at the polls. Thus the Residency used the full weight of available communications media (local newspapers, news-sheets like the government-sponsored *Imvaho*, administrative circulars, radio announcements, etc.) to urge the people 'to vote in full freedom for those whom [they] trust . . . to denounce the saboteurs of democracy . . . to demand that government circulars be read out to them, for this is their right'.[16] One such circular cautioned the electorate against 'the propaganda, deceit, and flattery of certain politicians . . . of those individuals who have everything to lose from the democratisation of the country's institutions . . . of those who enjoyed absolute powers, of the feudal elements who once possessed all the land and who abused their *bagaragu* and *bagererwa*, of the bad chiefs and subchiefs who saw in their mandate an opportunity to exploit the people'.[17] The same circular continued: 'These are the men who demand immediate independence, knowing full well that after the withdrawal of Belgian authority they would all the more easily go back to their obscure feudal practices, to their devious intrigues, to corruption and complicity.' Even under the best of circumstances, the UNAR leaders could never hope to match the weight and pervasiveness of the official propaganda machine. What is more, after the Special Resident decided to ban all political meetings, on July 6, under the pretext that 'certain leaders had abused their freedom of speech by advocating a boycott of the elections', official propaganda became the only legitimate propaganda.[18]

In the face of this sustained campaign of advertisement for democracy, the exasperation of the Tutsi leadership soon reached the point of explosion. The first serious incidents occurred on June 6, 1960, in the region of Gikongoro. After a group of young Tutsi set fire to a Hutu hut, a dozen Tutsi huts were burned to the ground by the local Hutu population. By June 12, 1,165 huts had been destroyed in the region of Gikongoro and Cyanika.[19] Similar incidents were reported to have taken place in the vicinity of Kigali, where 70 Tutsi huts were destroyed during the same period. On June 22, the situation was already well out of hand in the chiefdom of Bufundu. There the security forces (250 men) sent by the administration opened fire on a group of about 100 armed Tutsi activists, killing 10 and wounding 30. On July 20, in Kigali, some 300 Tutsi prisoners went on the rampage when they heard of the medical authorities' decision to organise an anti-typhic vaccination; it was not until the arrival of 75 policemen, and only after they decided to use tear gas against the insurgents, that the Tutsi allowed themselves to be inoculated. The incident was typical of the all-pervasive climate of fear and suspicion which gripped the country at the approach of the elections—a phenomenon strangely reminiscent of the Great Fear ('la Grande Peur') which suddenly seized the French peasantry in late 1789 and caused them to engage in gratuitous acts of violence against the manorial lords. Fantastic rumours gained currency among both Hutu and Tutsi. Convinced as they were of the existence of a Belgian plot to exterminate each and every one of them, many Tutsi used the pretext of self-defence to 'cover' their actions; the rumour that 'the Mwami would kill those who have paid their taxes or inscribed their names on the electoral rolls' spread panic among the Hutu.

But if violence was often the product of panic and excited imagination, instances of planned violence were not infrequent. Since both sides were guilty of deliberate provocations, it is impossible to lay blame exclusively on either Hutu or Tutsi. But the initial challenge more often came from local Tutsi extremists who tried to keep their opponents away from the polls through intimidation and terrorism. In addition to the incidents just described, numerous acts of Tutsi terrorism were reported in the region of Gisenyi in July and August, and in the early part of July a band of Tutsi activists set fire to the polling booths in the commune of Rubengera, near Kibuye. The Hutu reaction was swift and tempestuous. Throughout the months of July and August, countless Tutsi huts were burned down in retaliation. In some areas, committees of public safety and militia units were organised. Before long, the whole southern half of the country was converted into a vast training ground for Hutu counter-terrorists, arsonists and criminal bands. As time went on the Hutu did not even wait for the challenge to occur. They simply went ahead and burned the huts of the Tutsi, as if it now were a mere routine duty.

The passing of the elections brought no immediate sign of relief. In fact, exhilarated by their electoral success, many Hutu felt that the time had come to rid the country once and for all of 'feudal elements'. The official Belgian news agency, *Rudipresse*, reported in October 1960:

> The audacity of the arsonists knows no bounds. Fire has spread to Kamembe and threatens to invade the airport. In the more remote communes, bands of terrorists are in control. They vanish as soon as security forces are signalled, but reappear just as promptly. Terror has reached the point where police action is often ineffective, for the population does not dare to denounce the aggressors lest they turn against them once the patrol has gone. Taken unawares by the importance of terrorists bands, the authorities have lost control of the situation and are obliged to use planes to drop hand grenades on those terrorists which the security forces cannot reach.*[20]

---

* I had a chance to verify the truth of these assertions in September 1960, when I happened to witness a raid of Hutu against Tutsi in the vicinity of Astrida. The Belgian paratroopers in charge of rounding up the assailants were assisted by helicopters, flying at low altitude over the surrounding hills. In the course of the operations one of the helicopters crashed against a hillslope, only 100 yards away from the main road. Less than five minutes after the crash a crowd of at least 500 Hutu was gathered on the scene of the accident. Apart from the compassion shown by the Hutu to the injured crew, particularly remarkable was the extraordinary swiftness with which hundreds of Hutu peasants suddenly appeared on the scene, virtually materialising out of thin air.

That so many of these outbreaks should have occurred after the elections raises some obvious questions. How much authority could the newly-elected burgomasters really claim for themselves? To what extent can it be said that they acted as accomplices? What fate could the Tutsi minority, both within and outside Rwanda, expect in the months ahead? Before we try to answer these questions, something ought to be said of the outcome of the electoral struggle.

As shown by the figures in Table 6.1, PARMEHUTU scored a landslide victory at the polls. With 2,390 seats out of a total of 3,125, it clearly held a dominant position in the communal councils; its nearest opponent, APROSOMA, which was also its closest ally, claimed only 233 seats. With a mere 56 seats, UNAR had no choice but to concede defeat.

Table 6.1: Party Strengths in Communal Councils

Territoire	Total Number of Seats	PARMEHUTU	APROSOMA	RADER	UNAR	Other
Kigali	378	280	—	87	—	11
Astrida	537	237	223	28	—	49
Nyanza	321	257	10	5	4	45
Gitarama	259	233	—	13	1	12
Cyangugu	237	190	—	11	12	24
Kibuye	190	158	—	13	—	19
Ruhengeri	367	359	—	4	—	4
Gisenyi	299	257	—	6	—	36
Kibungu	270	160	—	38	39	33
Biumba	267	259	—	4	—	4
Total	3,125	2,390	233	209	56	237

Source: Rwanda Politique 1958–1960, CRISP, Brussels 1961, p. 272.

On the basis of these results the three-man Electoral Commission appointed by the Belgian government to watch the electoral proceedings concluded: 'Considering the degree of evolution of Rwanda, the Commission believes that the electoral proceedings were carried through with a maximum of guarantees, that UNAR's propaganda to boycott the elections has had no appreciable over-all effects in the country, and that the results reflect the will of the population.'[21] A closer look at the conduct of the elections would suggest a somewhat different conclusion —in particular, that 'a maximum of guarantees' in many cases meant no guarantees whatsoever; that UNAR's boycott resulted in certain areas in massive abstentions; that, as a consequence, the results tend to attribute to PARMEHUTU a far greater popularity than it actually enjoyed. Moreover, it also leaves open the question of whether or not PARMEHUTU could really be regarded as a unified political movement. All the evidence available shows that this was not yet the case. At the time of the elections PARMEHUTU was divided into at least fifteen splinter groups. In the territoire of Gisenyi alone, the party was torn into nine different groups, and in some communes no less than three PARMEHUTU lists competed among themselves for the favours of the electorate. In some constituencies Hutu candidates ran on individual lists, with no reference to or connection with PARMEHUTU. Elsewhere the party labels tended to reflect the traditional statuses of the candidates, as in the territoire of Gisenyi where a number of Hutu entered the race on *bagererwa* or *bakonde* lists, while others simply used the name of their clans as a party label. Thus one of the major weaknesses of the Hutu parties (and in particular of PARMEHUTU) is that they did not possess the structure, organisation and programme that is ordinarily expected of a political party, except perhaps in certain 'core' areas like Ruhengeri and Kabgaye. Beyond these strongholds Hutu interests tended to centre on primary groupings like the family, the clan, or the feudal nuclear cluster—or tended to coincide with social and economic roles rooted in the clientage system. Ironically, it was through this traditional substratum of socio-economic roles (which the PARMEHUTU leadership so ardently wished to destroy) that a great many Hutu gained access to the political arena.[22]

That the elections were attended by gross irregularities was openly admitted by AT Schmit, on September 2, 1960.[23] Many of these irregularities arose because the polling officers were in most places chosen by the 'interim authorities', that is by Hutu politicians who for the most part belonged to PARMEHUTU. This, along with the use of official scribes (also appointed by the 'interim authorities') to help illiterate voters fill out their ballot, created a situation admirably suited to electoral fraud. According to official statistics, 21·8 per cent of the electorate abstained from voting; but the actual percentage of abstentions was probably much higher, as this figure does not take into account those potential voters who failed to register. Then, omitted from this figure is an unknown but substantial number of so-called 'undesirables' who were expelled from their homelands in the months immediately preceding the opening of the electoral campaign, presumably under pressure from the local Hutu population. Although one can only resort to guesswork, it is reasonable to assume that the total number of abstentions was at least 10 per cent higher than the official figure.[24] It is notable that these abstentions are heavily concentrated in specific areas, which gives us an approximate index of the regional strength and distribution of traditionalist sentiment. The highest rate of abstention is found in a broad strip of territory extending along the eastern border of Rwanda, in the region of Nyanza in the south, and in a few other enclaves around Shangugu and Kibuye. In these areas, a total of 39 communes, less than 50 per cent of the electorate went to the polls. It was reported by the government-sponsored *Imvaho* that in the region of Nyanza 'the saboteurs of democracy' managed to keep electoral participation down to 30 or 40 per cent, 'or even less in certain localities'.[25] In 32 other communes, located roughly on the periphery of these areas, the percentage of abstentions fluctuated between 80 and 50 per cent. The conclusion reached by d'Hertefelt, that 'electoral participation decreased in the measure to which traditional political conceptions and diffuse social pressure were liable to facilitate the campaign [of abstention] of the traditionalist parties',[26] receives further confirmation from the fact that the revolutionary strongholds of Kabgaye, Gitarama and Ruhengeri also saw the highest electoral turnout.

There is yet another conclusion to be drawn: despite the sharpening edge of racial conflict, there remained substantial pockets of Hutu resistance to the spread of revolutionary ideas. Certainly, the electoral process has tended to activate the drive towards Hutu rule, by stimulating the growth and development of Hutu parties and by tightening the lines of cleavage between monarchists and republicans. In this sense, the electoral struggle did play a decisive role in bringing forward the revolution to a more advanced stage—to the stage where pressure from below prepares the ground for a legalisation from above. But this was still an incipient stage. Revolutionary fervour was as yet felt unevenly throughout the country. Rwanda was still, formally speaking, a monarchy, and in many places the organisational apparatus of the revolution remained embryonic, if not altogether non-existent. The real significance of the elections is that they made it technically possible for the newly-elected burgomasters to achieve virtually unlimited control over local affairs, and thus to make full use of their prerogatives to hasten the tempo of revolutionary change.

THE BURGOMASTERS IN ACTION

'The revolution is over.' With these laconic words the Special Resident summed up the political situation in Rwanda exactly three months after the beginning of the communal elections.[27] What he actually meant is that, by the end of October 1960, the incumbents were everywhere in the process of consolidating their electoral gains, and that an entirely new structure of power was taking shape at the local level. This new situation was the logical consequence of the radical shift in the distribution of power brought about by the electoral victory of PARMEHUTU. Of the 229 communes set up under the terms of the Interim Decree of December 1959, 210 were headed by Hutu burgomasters. Of these 160 were members of PARMEHUTU.[28] Although the chefferie was still recognised as a formal administrative unit, the chief was now no more than a figurehead. Some chiefs were employed as 'agents itinér-ants', supposedly to assist the burgomasters; in fact, most of them simply abandoned their posts and fled.

Yet, no matter how far-reaching, this transformation of the old feudal power structure did not everywhere imply a corresponding shift of loyalties. In some areas serious conflicts developed between the newly-elected authorities and those Hutu who, for personal or other reasons, felt it was in their interest to support the old ruling caste; among those were generally found the chiefs' personal clients and landed tenants. A major source of tension in the north arose from the conflicting claims of traditional and political *bagererwa* over the land of the *bakonde*. Although the displacement of the chiefs from the northern region left their political clientele at the mercy of the *bakonde* and their traditional landed clients, the claims of the political clients did not automatically lapse with the eviction of their chiefly patrons; thus even where the burgomasters also held the status of *bakonde* and used their newly acquired political prerogatives to enforce their traditional claims over the land, their actions were often met with considerable resistance from the chiefs' former clientele. Finally, in those few areas where the numerical strength of the Tutsi was equal to or above that of the Hutu, the authority of the burgomasters was openly challenged by their constituents. 'Where we have an even percentage of Hutu and Tutsi', said AT Lees on September 2, 'the Hutu burgomasters are not accepted.'[29] By the end of October, however, there remained relatively few areas where this percentage obtained. Through a combina-tion of terror, intimidation and political clientelism, the burgomasters were about to become complete masters of their communes.

It is doubtful that this mastery could have been attained so promptly without the continued and increasingly active co-operation of Belgian officials. Addressing a meeting of ATs, the Special Resident flatly stated, on September 2: 'Whatever you do, I shall support you; but I want you to keep me informed so that I shall not be taken by surprise.'[30] Very much the same kind of attitude seemed to govern the relations of the local administration with the burgomasters; no matter what they did, they knew they could count on the firm backing of the administration. Taking full advantage of these friendly dispositions, they had few com-punctions against resorting to intimidation to assert their authority.

In some places they instigated local disorders to provoke the exodus of Tutsi families, and once this was accomplished they proceeded to sell the refugees' land and property to their supporters. Elsewhere, individual Tutsi were arrested on the flimsiest grounds, tried before an improvised tribunal and thrown into jail. Meanwhile the raids organised by isolated bands of Tutsi refugees became a pretext for retaliating in the most arbitrary fashion against the local Tutsi population. In the Kibingo commune, for example, thirteen Tutsi were massacred on October 14 and 15, following the molesting of a communal policeman by 'an unknown Tutsi who refused to show his identity papers'.[31] In Kigali, rumours of an impending Tutsi raid caused the local Belgian administrator to 'purge' the locality of 'all the unemployed and all those who had no reason to reside there'.[32] Commenting upon 'the intolerance of numerous burgomasters and councillors who abuse their powers and tend to interfere with the operation of technical services', AT Lees reported that in Kigeme the European medical doctor was 'quite discouraged to see the pressure that is being placed upon him to get rid of an important [Tutsi] auxiliary'.[33] While some administrators deplored 'the scabrous decisions of the burgomasters' and freely admitted that they had 'a tendency to go too far', others took a more optimistic view of the situation: 'The burgomasters enjoy considerable authority', said AT Nyssens on September 2, 1960; 'they are helping us magnificently and we have the impression of holding the hills well in hand.'[34]

They had indeed considerable authority, not only because they were given a blank cheque to use their authority as they deemed fit, but also because their powers were as yet undefined in any legal terms. It was not until two months after they were in office that a decree was passed, setting statutory limitations on the exercise of communal authority: until then, as one administrator put it, 'neither the burgomasters nor the councillors knew the exact limitations of their powers'. Moreover, the new incumbents now had control of reliable 'auxiliaries'. The main issue confronting Belgian officialdom after the elections was succinctly formulated by AT Ausloos when he observed, on August 10: 'Following the elections we shall be confronted with a Hutu government and an administrative personnel of Tutsi origins, the vast majority belonging to UNAR.'[35] The obvious solution, in the words of AT Nyssens, was 'to make a clean sweep of all the personnel in office prior to the elections'.[36] Accordingly, each burgomaster was given permission to hire three policemen, three 'agricultural assistants' and one secretary. In addition, it was decided that the Resident would exercise a 'selective' control over the admission of students to the Groupe Scolaire; that the recruitment of administrative personnel at the higher levels would also be controlled by the Resident; and that the administrateurs de territoires would co-operate along the same lines whenever new appointments had to be made. As a result of this massive administrative turnover, a whole new group of political aspirants gained entry into the local power structure, thereby giving the burgomasters a new base on which to rest their authority.

Finally, this shifting political situation brought about a change of heart among those few incumbents who were still undecided, or whose allegiances had not yet firmly crystallised; they, too, began to jump on the revolutionary bandwagon. This change of mentality is nowhere better illustrated than in Pierre Gravel's account of the political conversion of the burgomaster of Remera during his first months in office. Once a UNAR member, Burgomaster Ijeri at first avoided all commitments, refusing to take sides in local disputes.

> But after gathering a small band of opportunists . . . he tried out his authority—first by prohibiting hunting and then by forbidding people to leave their homes after 6.00 PM. Ijeri and his gang patrolled the hill at night to see to it that his orders were obeyed. He bragged that he was out to get the Tutsi, and he started to put pressure on them. He advised those Tutsi who had jobs with the administration that he would see that they lost them. . . . The administration, through fear of subversive political meetings, allowed the burgomaster to forbid hill and lineage meetings. This served further as a pretext for arrests. He arrested more and more Tutsi. It seemed that three Tutsi drinking together was a meeting. He pressured the Hutu into buying party membership cards by telling them they could profit by signing and suffer by not. . . . Eventually Ijeri began to trample on the people's customary rights, and yet they would not file complaints against him because, they explained, the administration would support Ijeri in any case. It was better to say nothing than to further be harassed. To obtain the burgomaster's favour, people brought him gifts of beer. Ijeri started to pressure the cow-keepers to bring him gifts of milk. . . . He was well on his way to claiming the prerogatives of the ancien régime's chieftain.[37]

Thus, as a result of changing political circumstances—the new sources of patronage made available to the burgomasters, the appointment of Hutu auxiliaries to man subaltern administrative posts, and above all, the growing climate of insecurity engendered by Tutsi terrorism—a situation developed where the burgomasters consciously cast themselves in the roles of political patrons. They used their positions as a

means of extending guarantees of protection as well as certain benefits
—essentially in the form of jobs and immunities from specific administrative rules and regulations—to a political clientele whose functions
were, in a sense, very similar to those performed by the traditional
clients upon whom the chiefs used to rely to establish their bases of
power and influence on the hills. Unlike the chiefs, the burgomasters
had no way of backing their claims to authority by appeals to tradition
—with the qualified exception of the northern region, where the status
of burgomaster in many cases corresponded to the status of *bakonde*.
And yet the burgomasters shared with the chiefs many of the 'elite'
characteristics normally associated with achieved status. Most of them
possessed at least a primary education or some technical skills which
marked them off sharply from the ordinary peasants. For example,
among the burgomasters elected in the territoire of Kibungu were
nine school teachers (*moniteurs*), one catechist, one judge, one clerk
(*secrétaire de chefferie*) and three carpenters. However fragmentary, the
evidence available from other areas indicates a somewhat similar
breakdown of occupational statuses, with a predominance of primary
school teachers. Looked at from the standpoint of their social origins,
the burgomasters were not unlike the sans-culottes of the French
revolution: like their historic counterparts, they formed a fairly disparate
and shapeless group—a 'plebs' of craftsmen, petty shopkeepers, school
teachers, artisans, etc. Like the sans-culottes, 'they were fired as much
by memories of customary rights or a nostalgia for past utopias as by
peasant grievances or hopes of material improvement; and they dis-
pensed a "rough-and-ready" kind of "natural justice" by breaking
windows, burning their enemies in effigy, firing hayricks, and pulling
down their houses, farms, fences.'[38] As in the revolutionary France of
1793, these African sans-culottes provided the main striking force of
the Rwanda revolution; and, as happened in some of the Parisian
faubourgs, their revolutionary potentialities stemmed to no small
extent from their ability to keep in tow and manipulate a political
clientele with whom they shared important social and psychological
affinities.

If the transference of political clientelism to the Hutu stratum must
certainly be regarded as one of the essential mechanisms through
which revolutionary change gathered momentum, this conversion of
clientage ties for revolutionary purposes carried many of the inconveniences encountered in the traditional society—and some that had never
before existed, inherent in the situation of extreme instability arising
from the sudden and massive reallocation of power at the grass-roots.
Like so many petty tyrants the burgomasters arrogated to themselves

unlimited authority over their constituents; through bribery and intimidation they managed to build up a group of trustworthy followers who acted towards them somewhat like clients towards their chiefs; and, like the chiefs, they abused the privileges of their office. The parallel can be pushed even further: just as the chiefs' intolerance caused disaffection among their subjects, the methods employed by the burgomasters were bound to backfire. Although there were decided differences from one region to another, depending on the ethnic make-up of the local communities, the burgomasters were everywhere faced with some degree of resentment or resistance from their constituents. A growing fear of disaffection, rumours of an impending aggression from Tutsi émigrés and a vague suspicion that the Belgian authorities might 'pull out' before the consummation of the revolution were key elements in the background of the coup of January 1961. Although these were by no means the only factors instrumental in precipitating the seizure of power from above, the pressures towards 'rural radicalism' emanating from the hills certainly played a determining role in touching off the events of Gitarama.

THE COUP D'ETAT OF GITARAMA

To the uninitiated observer the proclamation of the Republic in January 1961 might have looked like an act of conspiracy against the administration; but if the word conspiracy is at all appropriate to describe the event, the administration is better cast in the role of the accomplice. The sequence of events that led to the coup of Gitarama involved different sets of actors, moving in separate arenas and actuated by conflicting motives. For a preliminary insight into this tangled situation it may be useful at this point to draw a rough sketch of the principal dramatis personnae. These were: (i) the Special Resident, all along acting in connivance with the PARMEHUTU leadership; (ii) the United Nations, cast by the Residency in the role of a villainous yet harmless organisation; (iii) the Belgian government, striking a somewhat ambiguous pose, caught as it was between the joint pressures of the local administration and the PARMEHUTU leadership on the one hand, and the limitations inherent in its obligations towards the United Nations; (iv) the PARMEHUTU leadership, desperately seeking to tighten its grip on the emergent political structure, and, to this end, seeking to bring maximum pressure to bear upon the metropolitan government.

As PARMEHUTU had captured control of the local institutions, the next logical step, in the minds of its leaders, was to attempt to extend their power to the central organs of government. In presenting their case for holding legislative elections as soon as possible after the communal elections, they argued that since PARMEHUTU had so clearly revealed itself as 'the party of the masses', and in fact held a dominant position in almost every communal council, there was no reason to defer the legislative elections until early 1961, as recommended by the UN Visiting Mission after its visit to Rwanda in March 1960. To allow for a 'cooling-off' period that would pave the way for national reconciliation was, in their view, sheer utopia. Any attempt on the part of the metropolitan authorities to delay the installation of an autonomous government through popular elections would necessarily be interpreted as a sign of bad faith by the masses, and thus provoke new outbursts of violence. Yet a more candid look at Rwanda's political scene in the months following the communal elections tells a somewhat different story. Not the strength but rather the very weakness of their bases of support is what caused the PARMEHUTU leaders to press their claims for an accelerated transfer of power. As they saw their position being gradually undermined by internal dissensions and incipient popular resentment against the communal authorities, the temptation to consolidate their electoral gains 'from above' became increasingly difficult to resist.

Between August and November 1960 there occurred a radical shift in the balance of forces within the country. In November 1960, the leaders of APROSOMA, RADER and UNAR agreed to form a 'Front Commun' in opposition to PARMEHUTU; soon after, the spokesmen of the Front Commun unanimously denounced the 'dictatorial regime' of PARMEHUTU, which they went on to describe as 'racist, racial and anti-democratic . . . deliberately attempting to crush all other parties through corruption and intimidation'. 'This kind of feudalism', they concluded, 'is worse than the old one.'[39] Meanwhile, in a number of localities the communal authorities were faced with recurrent acts of terrorism instigated by groups of Tutsi refugees from Uganda and the Congo—the so-called *inyenzi*, or 'cockroaches'. Usually aimed at Hutu officials, these border raids led to a cruel repression against the local Tutsi population. Tutsi-instigated terrorism at first strengthened caste solidarity among the Hutu, but in time the sheer arbitrariness of retaliative measures caused considerable disaffection among the Hutu peasantry.

Nor was the international conjuncture all that encouraging. The presence at the United Nations of an extremely able and articulate group of UNAR petitioners, led by Michel Kayihura, coupled with the inherently anti-colonialist nature of their case, assured them a favourable hearing in the UN General Assembly. But perhaps the main source of anxiety for the Hutu leadership was the apparent unwillingness of the

Belgian government to recognise their case. Brussels' initial reluctance to yield to local pressures for a rapid transfer of sovereignty to the Hutu is to be explained in part by reference to the personal preferences and inclinations of the then Minister of African Affairs, Auguste de Schrijver, leader of the Parti Social Chrétien (PSC). Whether because of his own aristocratic background or because of his conservative leanings, de Schrijver had always felt a deep sympathy for the Tutsi culture; in fact, having once privately admitted to this writer his admiration for Tutsi artistic traditions, he went on to express strong misgivings as to whether such a magnificent cultural heritage could be allowed to be swept away in the name of a form of democracy whose merits, in any case, remained dubious. But the attitude of the metropolitan authorities was also conditioned by the nature of their international obligations under the UN Charter. So soon after the secession of the Katanga, at a time when the Belgian government was drawing considerable and well-deserved criticism from the United Nations, Brussels could ill afford to further antagonise international public opinion.

Under the circumstances one can appreciate the sense of frustration and bitterness felt by the Hutu leadership when they learned that the UN General Assembly, in its resolutions of December 20, 1960, had recommended the postponement of legislative elections to a date to be decided at the resumption of its fifteenth session, in the summer of 1961. The Assembly's resolution 1579 urged the administering authorities 'to implement immediately measures of full and unconditional amnesty, to enable political workers and leaders who are still in exile or imprisoned in the territory to resume normal, democratic political activity before the elections'.[40] In addition, it was suggested that 'a conference fully representative of political parties, attended by UN observers, be held in early 1961, before the elections, in order to compose the differences between parties and to bring about national harmony'. While noting that this unexpected turn of events placed the Belgian government 'in the very serious dilemma of having to choose between immediately satisfying the urgent request of the people under its trusteeship or taking into consideration the new General Assembly recommendation',[41] Brussels grudgingly decided to comply with the terms of the resolution. In Rwanda, however, PARMEHUTU reacted to the news by a violent denunciation of the United Nations, saying in effect that the postponement of the elections was nothing less than a deliberate attempt to delay the setting up of democratic institutions. What the party leadership failed to mention, however, was that the 'cooling-off' period envisaged by the United Nations would, in all probability, be used by their opponents to increase their following, while the measures of amnesty, if implemented, would surely turn to the advantage of the more conservative wing of the Tutsi population.

By then, however, the role of the United Nations in Katanga had caused diplomatic relations between Brussels and the United Nations to suffer considerable strains, and the Belgian government was prepared to adopt a somewhat more flexible stance toward both the Hutu leadership and the administering authorities in Rwanda. The determining element was the appointment of Count Harold d'Aspremont Lynden to the post of Minister of African Affairs, in September 1960. A staunch supporter of Belgian policies in Katanga, d'Aspremont had little sympathy for UN objectives in Africa. If only by way of a reaction against UN policies, he felt naturally inclined to give his support to the Hutu against the Tutsi, which, in practice, meant that the local administration would be given a virtually free hand in preparing the accession of Rwanda to independence under Hutu rule. Prior to the appointment of d'Aspremont to the Ministry of African Affairs, the Special Resident, Colonel Logiest, had gone to great lengths to persuade the Belgian government to satisfy Hutu demands for internal autonomy, but with little success. Already, on August 29, 1960, Resident General Harroy had sent a cable to the Minister of African Affairs in which he called attention to the gravity of the situation and intimated that the installation of a provisional government was the only way to restore stability and check Communist penetration of the country. About the same time Colonel Logiest went to Brussels to present the Hutu case before the Belgian government, but here again Logiest's démarche, as he himself put it, 'yielded no positive results'.[42] Upon his return from Brussels, in the course of an impromptu meeting of administrateurs de territoires, he gave the following account of the political conjuncture:

> The Hutu have asked us that a government or a parliament be set up, or in any case, the organs which would permit the achievement of internal autonomy. The Resident General, Harroy, and myself had agreed to this request. This was the purpose of my trip to Belgium, which, on the whole, yielded no positive results. You must remember that our delegate to the UN, in order to placate international opinion, had said that the communal elections would carry no political consequences and had no other purpose than to set up the communal infrastructure. . . . The objective of our government, drawing a lesson from the Congo, is to have before independence a UN representative in Rwanda. . . . It favours the presence of a Permanent UN Commission and a few 'blue helmets'. . . . It is purely and simply 'la politique du parapluie'. . . . All that we can expect is a Visiting

Mission from the UN, and nothing else. The action of the UN, though ill-intentioned, cannot harm us. Furthermore, we are going to set up a kind of government which will gain practical experience and will take up positions.[43]

Clearly, as anxious as they were to seize the initiative, the local Belgian authorities could not disregard entirely the views of their government; consequently the policy of the administration remained to a considerable degree subject to the limitations imposed from Brussels, and, to a lesser extent, from New York. After the appointment of d'Aspremont as Minister of African Affairs, however, a close working relationship developed between Brussels and Kigali, the result of which was to substitute what one might call a 'politique d'entente' for the 'politique du parapluie'. Yet until the very last minute the Belgian government carefully avoided showing its hand. It obligingly paid lip service to the decisions of the UN General Assembly, and stated in early January that it hoped to set up an autonomous government *after* the general elections, around June 1961.

Meanwhile, from January 7 to 12, 1961, the Ostend Conference was held, during which some forty delegates, representing each of the main parties of Rwanda, held 'round-table' discussions with representatives of the Ministry of African Affairs on the political future of the territory. Ironically, it was at these discussions, held at the request of the United Nations, that final arrangements were made to circumvent the obstacles raised by the UN resolution of December 20, 1960. Although the evidence is admittedly lacking, there seems little question that the metropolitan government did co-operate on a fairly close basis with the Residency in planning the coup of January 28, 1960; if nothing else, the Special Resident must have received unofficial assurance from the Ministry of African Affairs that Brussels would not interfere with the course of action upon which the Hutu leaders were about to embark, no matter how serious the legal implications.

What became known in the history of Rwanda as the coup of Gitarama took place in the town of the same name, in central Rwanda, on January 28, 1961. Although the events surrounding the coup attracted surprisingly little attention from the outside world, anyone who happened to be in Gitarama at the time could have sensed their significance. Since the early hours of the morning dozens of trucks, coming from every corner of the country, had brought to their final destination 3,126 communal councillors and burgomasters. Officially, the sole purpose of the meeting was to discuss matters concerning 'the maintenance of peace and order' during the first and last general elections before independence, but many of those present suspected with reason that a more momentous decision was in the offing. A sense of great expectancy lingered over the dense crowd assembled in the market place as a group of Rwandese officials, flanked by a handful of Europeans, made their way towards the improvised platform. The first speaker, Jean-Baptiste Rwasibo, Minister of Interior in Rwanda's provisional government, 'set the tone' of the meeting; after a long diatribe against Rwanda's monarchical regime, he held up the vision of a brave new world, in which democracy and equality would reign supreme. He asked: 'What will be the solution given to the problem of the monarchy? When shall we abandon the realm of the "provisional"? It is incumbent upon you, burgomasters and councillors, representatives of the Rwandese people, to answer these questions.' The stocky, bespectacled Joseph Gitera, President of Rwanda's Provisional Council, gave the definitive answer to the first question. Speaking in Kinyarwanda, Gitera calmly announced the abolition of the monarchy and all its symbols, including the royal drum, and went on to proclaim the birth of the 'democratic and sovereign Republic of Rwanda'. His words were greeted by thunderous applause from the crowd, punctuated by repeated cries of 'Vive la République!' Next came the turn of Grégoire Kayibanda, the provisional Prime Minister, who translated the news into French, immediately touching off new waves of enthusiasm from the audience. Then, sitting as a constituent assembly, the councillors and burgomasters proceeded to elect a President of the republic, Dominique Mbonyumutwa, called upon Grégoire Kayibanda to form the future government, and by 7.00 PM a new cabinet of ten members had been set up, headed by Prime Minister Kayibanda.* A new phase had begun in the history of Rwanda.

That the authors of the coup knew beforehand that they would enjoy complete immunity from the Residency, and indeed the active collaboration of certain European administrators, is beyond question. As the UN Commission for Ruanda-Urundi subsequently observed:

> The Commission cannot escape the impression that the local administration, finding itself no doubt too much bound by promises to its favored political parties, and considering that its prestige was at stake, was reluctant to comply with the decision (initially) taken by the Belgian government to co-operate in giving effect to the recent UN resolutions on Ruanda-Urundi. . . . It is hard to believe that the

---

* This constitutional set-up was later revamped along the lines of a presidential system, with Kayibanda assuming key executive functions as President of the republic.

coup d'état of Gitarama could have taken place without the knowledge of the Belgian authorities in the territory, and indeed without
certain European members of the administration taking part in it.
Without help from the administration, the actual organization of a
meeting of some 3,000 burgomasters and communal councillors, con-
vened by the Minister of Interior, as early as January 25, is barely
conceivable.[44]

If so, there is an element of deliberate distortion in the explanations
offered by the Resident General to the UN Commission, whose report
states:

> The Resident considered that the action had resulted in part from
> the feeling of the political leaders that they had been betrayed by the
> administering authority, from the conviction that the UN was hostile
> to them and from a fear that the disorders in the neighboring Repub-
> lic of the Congo might extend to Rwanda. The Resident General
> said he had to choose, on the one hand, between the use of force to
> suppress the new regime—a course that was inconceivable and, more-
> over, impossible in view of the very small armed forces which the
> metropolitan country had placed at his disposal—and, on the other
> hand, the possibility of advising the Belgian government to negotiate
> with the new authorities. Though characterizing the action of
> Rwanda's burgomasters and municipal councillors as illegal, he noted
> that such action was in accordance with the Interim Decree of Decem-
> ber 25, 1959, which, at the time, had provided for indirect legislative
> elections.[45]

Certainly, the motives invoked by the Resident General cannot be overlooked; the only thing he omitted to mention, however, is that the Hutu
leaders might not have resorted to such drastic action unless they had
some excellent reasons to believe that the administration was on their
side. This fact alone was enough to spell the difference between a
successful and an abortive coup.

For some, the coup of Gitarama marked the beginning of an entirely
new phase in the history of Rwanda, in effect symbolising the birth of a
new social and political order in which the forces of democracy finally
emerged triumphant from their fight against feudalism. Taking a more
realistic view of the situation, the UN Commission for Ruanda-Urundi
stated in March 1961: 'A racial dictatorship of one party has been set
up in Rwanda, and the developments of the last eighteen months have
consisted in the transition from one type of oppressive regime to
another. Extremism is rewarded and there is a danger that the [Tutsi]

minority may find itself defenseless in the face of abuses. . . . Taken as a whole, the political situation in Rwanda is distinctly disquieting.'[46] Subsequent events showed this prognostication to be depressingly accurate. The months preceding independence saw a further deterioration of Hutu-Tutsi relations and a recrudescence of violence. To give a detailed account of the campaign preceding the legislative elections, of the innumerable brutalities and acts of terrorism it unleashed from both sides, would be tedious if not nauseating. According to a UNAR spokesman, Michel Kayihura, 'more than 150 persons were killed and 300 wounded' in the month of September alone.[47] This, however, is probably a conservative estimate. According to Richard Cox, of the London *Sunday Times*, 'between August and mid-September . . . *in the Astrida region alone* [our italics] there were over 150 deaths, 3,000 huts were burnt and 22,000 refugees came into Astrida. The violence spread to Nyanza . . . to Kigali and finally, in a wave of terror on the eve of the elections, to the north-east region of Kibungu. Despite the vast troop reinforcements, despite armed police, despite every modern method of control, the administrators and officers on the spot were "unable" to bring the trouble to a halt until a few days—a convenient few days— before the elections.'[48] No one will ever know the exact number of human lives lost during this period. No one, however, can deny the seething undercurrents, the intimidations, the calculated arrests of hundreds of UNAR members, that took place during the elections. In these conditions, to speak of electoral fraud is almost a euphemism. In view of the repeated threats, admonitions and brutalities committed by the burgomasters, it is a question whether the right to vote can be said to have had any significance besides that of showing on which side coercion tended to predominate.

This much at least can be gathered from the letter written by a Rwandese to Max Dorsinville, Chairman of the UN Commission for Ruanda-Urundi, a week before the date of the legislative elections. 'In general', said the letter, 'the troubles of the months of August and September were organised by these politicised functionaries (burgomasters, prefects, and ministers) with a view to disorganise their political opponents. . . . [These men] used their prerogatives to arrest, torture and incarcerate their political adversaries.' Speaking of the attitude of the *tutelle*, the letter went on to note: 'One cannot describe otherwise than as odious the attitude of authorities who, once apprised of specific abuses, seem to behave as accomplices, making us believe or declaring that the situation in Rwanda is *normal*.' Turning to the question of the refugees: 'We have witnessed the sickening spectacle of thousands of men, women and children, expelled from their communes and herded in valleys and swamps, exposed to the heat of the day and the cold of the night, drenched under the rains, dying of starvation while their fields and banana groves are only a few yards away. By virtue of the burgomasters' instructions they cannot even gather food from their fields. To do so they must first declare their adherence to the burgomaster's party. . . . The burgomasters who are responsible for these odious misdoings use as their sole weapons illegality, and the impunity which they have been granted [by the administration].'[49]

Given the circumstances, the outcome of the UN-supervised legislative elections of September 1961 was a foregone conclusion. They merely confirmed the de facto supremacy of PARMEHUTU, while the referendum on the question of the *mwami* officially abolished a regime that had already been overthrown. With 35 seats out of a total of 44 in the Legislative Assembly, and with 1,006,339 votes in favour of the republic as against 253,963 for the monarchy, PARMEHUTU could proclaim the legality of the republic. But the human costs of the revolution, already apparent in the tragic situation of the refugees, did not become fully discernible until after independence, when thousands of innocent Tutsi fell victim of a repression they could neither foresee nor prevent.

7. The *Inyenzi* at the Gates

THE REPUBLICAN government which came to power on July 1, 1962, was established under the opposing pressures of the trust authorities and the United Nations, the latter valiantly seeking to offset the trend towards racial supremacy unleashed by the former's blatant favouritism. It was the Belgian administration which made it possible for the Hutu to rid themselves of Tutsi chiefs and subchiefs; which ceaselessly denounced the sins of feudalism while deliberately ignoring the murders, thefts and provocations of its protégés; and which, in the end, joined hands with the republicans to bring the downfall of the monarchy. It was the United Nations which insisted on the passage of amnesty measures before the legislative elections, and did its best to bring its moral suasion to bear upon the contestants. In particular it laid down the terms of the modus vivendi contained in the New York Agreements of February 28, 1962, according to which UNAR would secure two ministerial posts in the republican government, an equal proportion of secretariats of state, two posts of prefects and subprefects, and a senior post in the Commissariat for Refugees.[1] Thus the balance of forces at the time of independence was not quite as overwhelmingly one-sided as might be thought. The Ministries of Public Health and Cattle-Raising were held respectively by François Ncogozabahizi and Etienne Afrika, both UNAR members; some key posts in the administration were entrusted to Tutsi elements; and in the National Assembly seven seats out of a total of 44 were held by UNAR deputies. What is more, UNAR was allowed to set up its own local headquarters (in Kigali), to print its own newspaper (*Unité*), and to criticise the government at will. Clearly, to use 'racial dictatorship' to describe this state of affairs would be patently inaccurate.

However, this spirit of tolerance has since all but vanished. The present (1969) government is an all-Hutu government; the National Assembly is composed exclusively of Hutu deputies; and the only legitimate opposition is that which exists within PARMEHUTU. While there are still a number of Tutsi working in the lower echelons of the civil service, the higher posts are all controlled by Hutu. Not a single post of prefect or subprefect has been allowed to remain in the hands of UNAR. The local UNAR headquarters have been dissolved, its leaders executed, its newspaper banned. Today, when one wishes to establish contact with one of the rare Tutsi who can still be seen in Kigali one must inevitably resort to some stratagem to avoid suspicion. All this, of course, does not make Rwanda a dictatorship, but it does suggest a far greater degree of racial exclusiveness on the part of the republican government than existed at the time of independence.

To put these developments in their proper perspective, attention must be drawn at the outset to what must still be regarded as the two most vital objectives of the Kayibanda government: (i) to avert the danger of a Tutsi-led counter-revolution, instigated from the outside; and (ii) to build up support from within, so as to lessen the chances of a successful counter-revolution and at the same time strengthen the bases of legitimacy and solidarity of the new regime. The advent of independence brought something of a reversal of the roles heretofore played by Hutu and Tutsi. With the Tutsi leadership-in-exile actively seeking the overthrow of the republican government, the Tutsi émigrés (like the French émigrés after 1789) were cast in the role of insurgents. But like their French counterparts, the Tutsi leadership-in-exile was rent asunder by factionalism, personal animosities, and ideological divergences between 'absolutists' and 'constitutionalists'. Their repeated attempts to fight their way back into the country ended in a disaster just as bloody—and politically suicidal—as that which followed the abortive landing of the French royalists at Quiberon in 1795. And just as the Quiberon landing consolidated the First French Republic at a time when it threatened to disintegrate, the abortive raids launched by the *inyenzi** gave Rwanda's republican regime the cohesiveness it needed to survive its own internal dissensions. Whatever measure of stability the republican government can at present claim for itself must be credited to no small extent to the combination of political ineptitude, tactical blundering and gratuitous cruelty time and again demonstrated by the Tutsi counter-revolutionaries.

THE EMERGENCE OF FACTIONALISM

The most crippling of all the disabilities suffered by the counter-revolutionaries was their inability to reach a measure of political unity among themselves. The lines of cleavage tended to shift, depending on the circumstances and issues at stake, and on the degree of favouritism shown by the Mwami towards particular factions or personalities.

*Meaning, literally, 'cockroaches', the term *inyenzi* is currently used both within and outside Rwanda to refer to small-scale, Tutsi-led guerrilla units trained and organised outside Rwanda and varying in size from about six to twelve men.

Basically, however, these divisions can be traced to any of the following factors and circumstances, or a combination thereof: (i) some were but the carry-over of long-standing differences of outlook and political orientation among the chiefs—differences which tended to express varying degrees of commitment to 'progressivism' or 'conservatism'; (ii) others came to reflect the basic political options raised by the approach of self-government—whether to return to Rwanda and seek a temporary accommodation with the republican government, or stay abroad and carry on the fight for the monarchy; (iii) finally, within the exiled group there were important differences of attitude between the so-called 'activists', who took part in guerilla activities, and the 'politicians' in charge of providing political guidance and material support to the *inyenzi*. Even within each of these groups, cohesion was the exception rather than the rule, torn as they were between various ideological tendencies, which often reflected the divisive pull of the influences at work in the various 'sanctuaries' where they found asylum.

What made UNAR so vulnerable to factionalism in the first place is that it never acquired the characteristics of a tightly-knit, well-organised party. Even assuming that such had been the objective of its leaders, they never had a chance to achieve even a semblance of internal cohesion. The party came into being at a relatively late date and then was almost immediately nipped in the bud by the administration. The idea of organising a party never held much attraction for the Tutsi elites, possibly for fear that, since its leadership would necessarily have to be in Tutsi hands, it might develop into a sect apart and hence give further substance to the accusations brought against them by their adversaries. Besides, the traditional administrative superstructure, with its hierarchy of chiefs and subchiefs, already offered an excellent organisational network: as it happened, UNAR's leadership was almost interchangeable with the chiefs. Hence it is not surprising if the same kind of factionalism which once existed among the chiefs should have reappeared within the top echelons of the party. Just as there were 'progressive' chiefs and 'conservative' chiefs, the UNAR leadership included 'progressive' and 'conservative' elements, or, to quote the words of a security report, 'Mutaristes' and 'progressistes', the former in turn subdivided into 'fanatiques' and 'opportunistes'. The 'Mutaristes' differed from the 'progressistes' in their perceptibly deeper commitment to the crown as an institution, and their far greater sense of loyalty to the Mwami's person. As the 'Mutaristes' were generally drawn from the royal clan of the Banyiginya, the basis of their individual commitment to the monarchy was often reducible to the existence of affinal ties between themselves and the royal family. Although the death of Mutara and his replacement on the throne by an inexperienced youngster greatly weakened the ties of personal loyalty between the 'Mutaristes' and the crown, the latter remained a major source of solidarity for the more traditionalist of the insurgent groups.

But even where the leadership and social bases of the insurgents seemed to imply a rejection of traditionalism, the mystique of kingship was deliberately kept alive to strengthen the appeal of the movement. One insurgent group, for example, based in Burundi and led by a handful of Tutsi students trained in Communist China, called itself *Iganguraruge*, the name given to the warriors of Mwami Rwabugili, grandfather of Kigeri v; its members were individually referred to as *intore* ('the chosen ones'), the Kinyarwanda term for young men recruited by the king or his chiefs to undergo military training; and one of the 'ten commandments' to which every *intore* had to pledge allegiance, in the presence of ten witnesses, stated, characteristically: 'I swear before these witnesses that, for me, Kigeri comes before everything. I swear in the name of Kigeri that I shall obey the commandments of the *Iganguraruge*.'[2] A conscious effort was made to attune the methods of recruitment and indoctrination of the *inyenzi* to Rwanda's traditional political culture. Involvement in the movement implied a total devotion to the values of kingship, even when the leadership of the movement was less than totally committed to the virtues of traditionalism, and when disagreements over matters of tactics and strategy had already driven a deep wedge among the insurgents.

One of the most divisive issues confronting the Tutsi leadership on the eve of independence was the question of whether the regime should be subverted from within, through the use of Trojan horse tactics, or forcefully overthrown from the outside. A profound rift developed between the 'internal' leadership of the movement, based in Rwanda, and the leadership-in-exile. The seeds of conflict were already visible in 1960. Following the voluntary exile of Chiefs Kayihura, Rwangombwa and Mungalurire, serious disagreements must have occurred between the exiled group and the local UNAR branches in Rwanda, or else how should one explain the refusal of some of these local branches to go along with the decision of the exiled leadership to boycott the communal elections? Just how serious these disagreements really were is shown by the contents of the letter written on March 19, 1962, by Jovite Nzamwita, one of the leading figures of the *inyenzi* movement, to his 'bien cher Rutera', better known as the Abbé Ruterandongezi, one-time representative of UNAR in Cairo. Commenting on Michel Rwagasana's decision to seek a reconciliation with the Kayibanda government, Nzamwita insisted on the absolute necessity 'to stay outside Rwanda to avoid falling into the hands of the Belgian paracommandos and their Kayibanda':

Neither the good intentions of the UN nor Spaak's condescension can allow us to return to Rwanda. This is also the feeling of Shalita, Mungalurire, Goossens, of the paramount chief of Bugufi, Baramba, and of the TANU leaders. In short: (*a*) the Mwami will not return unless he has the power to overthrow Kayibanda; (*b*) UNAR cannot participate in the government—it will only sit back and follow the course of events. . . . By accepting the elections Rugaju has deliberately destroyed UNAR, in particular by agreeing to exclude militant Tutsi from the regional presidency of the party. . . . Before our trip to New York you were in complete agreement with me on all this, but gradually you have succumbed to the spirit of conciliation of your co-workers. That spirit has led us straight into the gully. Over the past two years we have spent three million francs to cover the expenses of often inopportune trips. . . . Rugaju wants only one thing: a portfolio; as for Grégoire's cousin,* Rwagasana, neither the refugees nor UNAR exist any longer. . . . Take your pick: you can either play Rugaju's black cards, or stay faithfully on the side of the 'orthodox', who are lightly referred to by some as extremists. Don't let yourself be swayed by nefarious influences. I am here with friends whose existence you do not even suspect. . . . They have been combated by UNAR and by the Belgians, mon cher, by Rugaju's UNAR which has dextrously sought to sap our strength. I assure you that never again shall I let myself be taken in, and that I shall fight for the liberation of my country regardless of the shabby diplomacy and pettifoggery of my colleagues. I shall close upon this counsel of wisdom: we must rid ourselves of all illusions concerning a possible entente with Grégoire or Brussels. You must choose like a man, between two things: look for a job abroad, or accept to fight and even die for your country.

The tone of the letter gives some indication of why the *inyenzi* showed such utter indifference for the fate of the Tutsi community of Rwanda; why they continued to engage in border raids even when they knew their actions would endanger the lives of innocent Tutsi; and indeed why some may even have secretly rejoiced at the news of the terrible reprisal that was about to fall upon those whom they contemptuously described as 'the pacifists'. It is equally plain from this and other passages of Nzamwita's letter that the exiled leadership did not form a

* An ironic reference to Rwagasana's presumed sympathies for Kayibanda's republican regime.

homogeneous bloc. Three major subgroups, or factions, can be discerned, whose influence in relation to each other varied from time to time depending on how much value the political conjuncture placed on their respective skills, on how much support they could extract from the refugee population at large and ultimately from the crown. One such faction is that which is commonly referred to in refugee circles as 'les monarchistes'. It includes individuals whose position in the traditional society provides them with a direct entrée to the court, but perhaps its most influential members are of 'plebeian' origins. Thus the most ardent supporters of the crown, and until recently the Mwami's most trusted 'clients', were François Rukeba, and his sons, the late Kayitare (alias Masudi) and Butera, all three of whom were also at the vanguard of the guerrilla movement. Another group, 'les progressistes', comprises the younger, Western-educated Tutsi chiefs, subchiefs and professional men. Their progressive outlook has expressed itself in a gradual weakening of their psychological commitment to the monarchy, and in some cases in a strong attraction towards socialist ideas. The latter tendency is best represented by Gabriel Sebyeza, of the royal clan of the Bahindiro, graduate of the Groupe Scolaire, former subchief in the chefferie of Bwishaza, near Kibuye, and founder of the short-lived Parti Socialiste Rwandais. Equally representative of this group, though not nearly as engagé as Sebyeza, are Michel Kayihura—by far the most able of all the Rwanda chiefs in exile—Pierre Mungalurire and Joseph Rwangombwa. Finally there are the 'activists', the hard-core *inyenzi* fighters. Within this last category there are several constellations, identified with different personalities and theatres of operation and held together by different organisational ties. How much freedom they actually enjoyed in the conduct of military operations depended on the amount of support they managed to extract from either one of the above-mentioned groups, and, more importantly, on the nature of their relationships with the host governments.

That these divisions seriously compromised the chances of success of the counter-revolution is obvious from the series of convulsions that shook UNAR's leadership-in-exile in the years following the November riots. Until February 1962, formal control over the party affairs was in the hands of the progressive faction, represented by Michel Rwagasana* and Kayihura. Both were relatively well-educated, with a

---

* At one time Secretary of the Conseil Supérieur du Pays, Rwagasana was born of a Hutu father (from Idjwi island) and a Tutsi mother, which once prompted him to remark that Kayibanda had no more 'right' than himself to take up the defence of the Hutu against the Tutsi. Contrary to general belief, Rwagasana never held a chiefly position.

greater political sophistication than most other Tutsi leaders. Above all, they were excellent diplomats, and since diplomacy was clearly of the essence at a time when so much seemed to depend on the verdict of the United Nations, it is not surprising that these two men were accorded such wide recognition. But as they tried to compromise and eventually gave their endorsement to the terms of the New York Agreement of February 1962, they became increasingly suspect in the eyes of the monarchists. The breaking point came on May 17, 1962, when, in a statement delivered before the Legislative Assembly of Rwanda, Rwagasana unilaterally committed UNAR to a course which, for monarchists and activists alike, seemed a rank betrayal. 'Our party', said Rwagasana, 'can assure you that it will spare no effort in working for the achievement of a genuine understanding between the majority and the opposition, which, by virtue of its entry into the government, can no longer be considered an opposition, but rather a partner. . . . My party will therefore give its support to the government.'³ By then the progressive faction had lost not only much of its credit at the court but a good deal of its cohesion. Some of its members went back to Rwanda, while others, like Kayihura, Rutera, Rwangombwa, presumably yielding to the advice of certain African delegations to the United Nations, preferred to stay abroad.

Meanwhile, as Rwanda neared its independence, a government-in-exile was formed, with Rukeba as Prime Minister, Mungalurire as Minister of Finance, Gabriel Sebyeza as Minister of Information and Hamoud Ben Salim as Minister of Defence. The new government constituted a fairly accurate cross-section of the main political tendencies, Rukeba representing the 'ultras', Mungalurire and Sebyeza the 'progressives', and all three committed to 'activism'. Nonetheless, that Rukeba now held the prime ministership was a clear indication of the growing strength of the monarchist-activist faction within the party hierarchy. A man of boundless energy, endowed with unusual courage and determination and with considerable talent for organisation, Rukeba was a born activist. But he looked upon himself as more than an activist. Had he not followed the old Mwami Musinga to Kamembe, after his deposition? Had he not received from Musinga's hands his own political testament? Was it not he, Rukeba, who saved the day at Nziza by proclaiming the name of Mutara's successor? Though Rukeba thought he had every good reason to aspire to this eminent position, his title deeds made little impression on other leaders. Moreover, his bid for power was bound to look distasteful to the younger and more progressive elements, who suddenly saw their authority challenged by a commoner working in cahoots with the Mwami. No longer the acknowledged or even the titular leader of the party, Kayihura went to the Congo. Alexandre Rutera, another young progressive, went to Cairo to seek diplomatic and material support for the *inyenzi*. Then, in October 1962, Gabriel Sebyeza left the government to set up his own organisation, the Parti Socialiste Rwandais (PSR), based in Kampala. The PSR was led by a group of young radical Tutsi intellectuals, like Théoneste Ahishize, Antoine Rugwizangoga and Simon Kamonde, who had grown increasingly estranged from the monarchy and in particular from the person of Mwami Kigeli. As Sebyeza, the president of the PSR, told this writer in 1964: 'We are categorically opposed to the monarchy. Under the present circumstances, it is impossible to wage a popular struggle without the support of the masses. Nor can we expect substantial support from the outside as long as we cling to the monarchy. Kigeli is nothing but a fat pig anyway.' By autumn 1964, Sebyeza had become identified with another body, the Organisation pour la Réconciliation Nationale, founded in Kampala in September 1964. Though ostensibly aiming at promoting national reconciliation, the organisation was intended to serve as a temporary 'front' to cover up the objectives of the PSR which by then had been officially banned by the Uganda authorities.

As the conflict between Rukeba and his ministers threatened to deteriorate into a major split, another government-in-exile came into being in May 1963. The sole survivor of the cabinet shake-up was Rukeba, appointed Minister of Defence after surrendering the prime ministership to Michel Kayihura. Once again the new government was an attempt at reconciling mutually exclusive tendencies: in addition to progressives, like Kayihura, and activists, like Rukeba, there were a few conservatives, like Hesron Sebabi, a former medical assistant who now held the Ministry of Health, and Barnabé Kikabahizi, Minister of State without portfolio. For a time Mwami Kigeri, head of state of a stateless government, kept a precarious balance among the various factions. But not for long. By the end of 1964, the UNAR government-in-exile was reduced to a small coterie of notables drawn from the Mwami's personal entourage, headed by a new Prime Minister, a Hutu named Cosme Rebero. Rukeba had lost virtually all contact with the Mwami. Kayihura, true to his peripatetic vocation, spent most of his time between Geneva and Brussels, in a vain quest for some external support for his newly-founded Rwandese Liberation Front. And Gabriel Sebyeza, no longer under any illusions about the chances of success of his PSR, was busy attempting to give an aura of respectability to his newly-born Organisation pour la Réconciliation Nationale. If none of the dissidents could publicly disown the Mwami, neither could they be expected to take up the cause of the monarchy with burning conviction. From all appearances, UNAR had virtually ceased to exist.

In sum, factionalism, intra-party intrigue and personal rivalries all played a part in the ultimate collapse of UNAR. Though much of this internal bickering can be attributed to genuine differences of opinion over matters of strategy and ideology, at least three special factors have tended to accentuate these divisions. First of all, the UNAR leaders had no fixed residence where they could set up permanent headquarters and meet within relatively short notice. Rarely did they spend more than a few weeks in any one place. A look at the different localities where Mwami Kigeri established his residence while in exile will illustrate the point: after a prolonged sojourn in the Congo, from May to November 1960, he went to Dar es Salaam, and then decided to accompany the UNAR delegation to the UN headquarters in New York, where he stayed several weeks. He came back to Dar es Salaam in early 1961, and in October 1962 he left for Kampala. He stayed in Kampala until August 1963, as the guest of the Buganda Minister of Finance, until suddenly faced with a deportation order from the Uganda authorities. He then headed for Ndaiga, near the Congo border, some 150 miles west of Kampala, and shortly thereafter, in November 1963, left for Peking.* He came back to Dar es Salaam later in the year, only to be told by the Tanzania authorities that he should leave the country. In early 1964 Kigeri made another trip to Peking and, after his return, was subsequently reported to be living in the vicinity of Nairobi, where he had rented a villa. Though the Mwami's presence alone might not have sufficed to prevent dissension, his extreme mobility made it all the more difficult for him to exercise his leadership effectively. Furthermore, the high cost of his travels and alleged profligacy while travelling were bound to provoke resentment and disaffection among other leaders.

This brings us to another source of intra-party haggling—the question of control over party funds. The issue came to a head in early 1963, after the formation of the second government-in-exile. Rukeba, then Minister of Defence, charged Kayihura and Jean Bosco Kayunga,

---

* It is worth noting in this connection that it was in October 1963 that Communist China reportedly offered 'technical' and financial assistance to Kigeli. Similar assistance, though on a smaller scale, was simultaneously offered to Gabriel Sebyeza, self-appointed leader of the PSR, to prepare for an eventual coup against Kigeri. Kigeri's trip to Peking coincided with the arrival in China of a first group of ten Tutsi, 'invited' to attend a short guerrilla training course. A second group of ten left shortly thereafter to attend a seven-month course in Peking, followed by a third group of ten, scheduled to attend a fourteen-month course.

respectively Prime Minister and Minister of Finance, with squandering some $100,000, which represented the total amount of cash which UNAR had collected over the years, directly or indirectly, from the Catholic Relief Fund, the Oxford Committee for Famine Relief and various Communist and neutralist countries. Thus, in October 1963, in an attempt to satisfy Rukeba, the Mwami reportedly gave $23,000 of the $120,000 he had obtained in Peking to his personal secretary, Papias Gatwa, with specific instructions to give this money to Rukeba, who then happened to be in the Congo. Whether or not the Mwami's instructions were actually carried out is beside the point: Gatwa and Rukeba were both suspected of having used the money to line their own pockets. In fact, it was widely rumoured that it was to 'justify' the use of these funds, which by then had allegedly been spent for other purposes, that Rukeba launched the ill-fated Bugesera expedition, in December 1964 (which will be discussed later). Though much of the information is still lacking, the whole question of the use and allocation of party funds intensified personal animosities at a time when the need for unity had never been more urgent.

But perhaps a more fundamental obstacle to unity, and indeed one of the most paralysing handicaps suffered by the UNAR leaders, was the denial of direct and continuous contact with the refugee population. As pointed out by Rachel Yeld in her excellent study of refugee settlements in Tanzania, 'the fact that the Mwami has in general been isolated by the host governments from direct communication with the main refugee centers, and the geographical dispersal of the UNAR leaders in various countries of asylum has, due to the possibility of independent action, given greater impetus to rival policies and to the resulting factionalism and intrigue within the refugee population of individual centers'.[4] Not only within the refugee population but within the leadership as well, if only because their enforced isolation deprived them of the opportunity to test their support among the masses, and use this as a lever against one faction or another.

THE DIASPORA

Scattered in different countries, and at times in different continents, thousands of miles from each other and with only limited facilities for communication, the UNAR leadership-in-exile lacked virtually all the resources and conditions necessary for co-ordinated action. By the same token, the legal restrictions arising from the application of the principle of 'non-interference in the internal affairs of member states', stipulated by article 3 of the Addis Ababa Charter, in most cases meant that the

UNAR leaders were denied the organisational freedom they needed to carry on a successful counter-revolution. But these restrictions were not always and everywhere equally inhibiting. Their severity varied substantially from one area to the next, depending on the degree of administrative co-ordination and efficiency existing within the host country, the nature of the relations of the refugee population with the local authorities, and the receptivity and accessibility of the opposition forces within each country of asylum.

Nowhere were the restrictions imposed upon the refugee leadership more confining than in Uganda, where more than 35,000 Rwandese had found asylum by early 1962. Overall administrative efficiency, the 'co-operative' attitude of the central Uganda government and the geographical remoteness of Buganda from the border areas were all instrumental in achieving this result. Another handicap, one may note in passing, lay in the now inordinately cautious, if not overtly hostile, attitude of the old Banyarwanda immigrants, most of whom were already permanently settled in and around Kampala, towards the activist leadership of UNAR. Organised in a cultural association known as the 'Abadehemuka',* these long-time residents of Uganda retained close psychological links with the Rwandese monarchy, and at one point were the staunchest supporters of UNAR against both the Belgian administration and PARMEHUTU. Indeed, after Mutara's death and until early 1962 the Abadehemuka converted itself into a virtual satellite of UNAR; petitions were sent to the UN Trusteeship Council to uphold the Tutsi cause; tracts were printed at the headquarters of the association which eventually found their way into Rwanda; collections were made among the members of the association to help finance the trips of UNAR leaders to the United Nations. After the independence of Rwanda, however, the association fell prey to internal rivalries and from then on ceased to play a significant role. Many of its leaders refused to compromise their life chances and security for the sake of a Mwami who, they thought, was ill-advised, ill-tempered and ill-educated. Furthermore, some of these immigrants had already acquired a far more prestigious and lucrative position in the Uganda government than they could ever hope to gain from their association with UNAR. A case in point is Frank Kalimuzo,

---

* 'Abadehemuka' is the name of a royal army founded by Mwami Rwogera in the 1850s to 'pacify' the Buyaga region. The association bearing this name was founded in late 1956 by Mwami Mutara Rudahigwa during one of his visits to the Kabaka, in Kampala. The Abadehemuka brought into a single entity the Ruanda-Urundi Association (once intended for both Banyarwanda and Barundi immigrants) and the Banyarwanda United Club, both of which had been founded in the early 1950s.

a Tutsi of the Abagunga branch, a subgroup of the Banyiginia, once heavily involved in the activities of the association and now personal secretary of Prime Minister Milton Obote. The result, however paradoxical, is that by 1962 UNAR could expect considerably more support from the Baganda—and in particular from the Kabaka, whose affection for the late Mutara Rudahigwa and his successor was only equalled by his sense of distrust towards Obote—than from the permanently-settled Banyarwanda immigrants. In the end, however, UNAR supporters found themselves completely isolated from their bases of support both within and outside Buganda.

In 1961 the British authorities had taken preventive measures designed to keep the refugees at a safe distance (one mile) from the Rwandese frontier. Then, in early 1962, the Ministry of Internal Affairs ruled that refugee settlements should be kept at least five miles from the border; at the same time a close investigation was undertaken by the Special Branch of the ministry, that led to the expulsion of twenty-four refugees suspected of organising *inyenzi* commandos. Upon discovering that Rwanda chiefs held unauthorised meetings with the local chiefs, and that the former had instigated border raids against the republic of Rwanda, specific instructions were issued 'to penetrate these meetings and find out exactly what goes on'.[5] The official thinking of the Uganda authorities on the refugee problem was made clear by the statement issued by the Ministry of Internal Affairs in May 1962:

> Firm discipline is absolutely necessary if these refugees are to be made to behave in a manner which does not prejudice relations between Uganda and her neighbours. It is important that the Uganda government should begin to look outside her own boundaries and not take decisions based only on possible political repercussions within Uganda itself . . . and it is important for the future of this country that she should do everything possible to maintain good relations with her neighbours, even though, by so doing, the government may alienate certain sections of the community within Uganda.[6]

When the news came that on July 5, 1963, a raid had been launched against Rwanda, Obote issued a categorical warning: 'I wish to make it clear that I will not tolerate this sort of activity. . . . We have no intention within the context of the Addis Ababa spirit and Charter of allowing Uganda to be used as a base for any attacks or subversion against any African state. . . . If [our] hospitality is abused, and refugees use or attempt to use Uganda as a base to attack our neighbours, we shall have no alternative but to withdraw the protection we have granted to these people.'[7] Thus, when it became apparent that the Kabaka of

Buganda had developed close ties of friendship with Kigeli, that the latter was in residence at the home of the Buganda Minister of Finance, and that the 'aid' he received from the Buganda authorities was probably used to finance the activities of the *inyenzi*, the Uganda government reacted with a deportation order against Kigeli.* From then on Uganda virtually ceased to be a 'privileged sanctuary' for the *inyenzi.*

Equally stringent were the measures adopted by the government of Tanzania, but in some areas the presence of ethnic affinities between the refugee population and the indigenous authorities made these measures somewhat ineffectual. This at least is the conclusion that one reaches from Rachel Yeld's description of the incident that took place in 1962 in the resettlement centre of Bugufi, in the Ngara district, near the Burundi border.[8] From the first the relations of the refugee population with the Area Commissioner were less than auspicious. Being of Muhangaza origins, a Bantu tribe ethnically related to the Hutu group, and with little sympathies for the indigenous Tutsi-Hima populations,† the Area Commissioner lacked all authority over the predominantly Tutsi refugees. The latter, on the other hand, enjoyed considerable sympathy from the former chief of Bugufi, a Tutsi. For personal and political reasons the Area Commissioner 'strongly supported various government

* Although the Uganda authorities did not specify the motives which led to this decision, Kigeli's personal connections with the activist group, and the unrest which this caused among the refugee population of Uganda, was enough to make him persona non grata. The decision, however, met with an instantaneous protest from both the Kabaka and the pro-monarchist Buganda-based party, Kabaka-Yekka. On September 29, 1963, the secretary general of Kabaka-Yekka, Masembe Kabari, called a joint meeting of the local sections of Kabaka-Yekka and the Abadehemuka association to ask the government to reverse its stand. It was during this historic meeting, held at the Clock Tower in Kampala, that the president of the Abadehemuka, Haje Gashegu, was voted out of office and replaced by a certain Stephane Gakara. As he began to explain why he did not share the views of Kabaka-Yekka on this particular issue, Gashegu told this writer that he was 'booed and shouted down and later accused of having collaborated with the majority party, the Uganda People's Congress, to expel the Mwami'. Based on an interview with Haje Gashegu, conducted in the autumn of 1964.

† Bugufi was at one time an integral part of the Burundi kingdom. It was annexed by Mwami Ntare, probably towards the middle of the nineteenth century, and thereafter administered by a Hutu retainer of Ntare. Most of the local ruling families, however, are now of Batare origin (i.e. descendants of the Ntare branch). In February 1946 the Mwami of Burundi, Mwambutsa, presented the trust authorities with a letter stating that since Bugufi was once part of Burundi, its cession to Tanganyika in 1923 was in effect a violation of the historical claims of the Barundi over the region. Interestingly enough, the letter, and the genealogy appended to it, were both written by the late Jean Ntitendereza, the most distinguished representative of the Batare branch.

proposals which were made in the course of 1962 to move them to the interior of Tanzania, or to scatter them in small groups'.[9] As it became apparent that the refugees had no inclination to move, the local authorities decided to withhold food rations and close down the dispensaries. The refugees still would not budge. The Area Commissioner then called upon the Field Force and gave instructions 'to use threats and if necessary physical force to move the refugees'. After the arrest of their leaders, the refugees finally decided to move—but not in the direction that was intended. Overnight, the entire refugee population fled to Burundi, only to be forced back across the border by the Burundi gendarmerie a week or so later. Owing to the physical location of the resettlement centre, a safe distance away from Rwanda, and to the unusually co-operative attitude of the Burundi gendarmerie, the incident did not have serious repercussions outside the area of settlement; but it clearly shows how local circumstances could at times affect the potential resources available to the counter-revolutionaries.

In the Congo this factor played an even more decisive role in the political and military fortunes of the *inyenzi*. Here, however, a distinction must be drawn at the outset between those settlement areas which throughout the eastern rebellion remained under the jurisdiction of the Congo Republic and those which passed under the control of the 'Armée Populaire de Libération', commanded by the 'rebel' leader Gaston Soumialot. In the former areas, the refugees had no chance to organise themselves effectively. Not only did the provincial authorities keep a close watch on their activities, but their existence was often rendered miserable by the incessant harassments, provocations and intimidations of the indigenous tribes, some of which harboured long-standing grievances against the immigrant Banyarwanda, both Hutu and Tutsi. This was especially true of those refugees who found asylum in the region of Goma, in the former Kivu province of the Congo, on the Rwandese border. Long before the flight of Tutsi refugees from Rwanda, indeed long before the inception of colonial rule, thousands of Rwandese had infiltrated the region, only to be joined in later years by a fresh influx of immigrants who came to Goma to seek better job opportunities. While many of these immigrants had already become the object of a latent resentment on the part of the local tribes (and in particular of the less advanced and politically less astute Bahunde), with the sudden arrival of thousands of Tutsi refugees in late 1960 and early 1961 there occurred a rapid polarisation of ethnic tensions.

What brought these tensions to the verge of civil war was the decision of the central government of the Congo Republic, in May 1963, to split the old Kivu province into two new 'provincettes', North Kivu and

Central Kivu. When the news came that the cities of Goma and Rut-shuru would be integrated into the Central Kivu province, that the government of North Kivu would be transferred to the village of Sake, a minor trading centre on the northern bank of Lake Kivu, and that, in addition to and as a result of all this, the indigenous Bahunde popula-tions of Goma and Rutshuru would be separated from their northern kinsmen, the Bahunde politicians in each province reacted by a violent campaign of intimidation against all Tutsi indiscriminately, as if they alone were responsible. They said the Tutsi would soon dominate the entire North Kivu province and would thereafter impose their domina-tion upon both the old Bahutu immigrants and the local Bahunde; that the Tutsi would inevitably gain control over the Sake government, because of their innate resourcefulness and greater political talent; that they would then seek to turn the entire province over to Rwanda after reinstating the monarchy; and that, in the meantime, they would join hands with the local MNC-Lumumba to foment all sorts of trouble. Before long the refugee centres of Bibwe and Ihula, both in North Kivu, with a total refugee population of about 13,000 in 1963, became the object of innumerable molestations on the part of the Bahunde populations. Countless incidents, sometimes accompanied by wanton cruelty, soon followed. François Preziosi* reported from Goma, on October 10, 1963, that in Sake—'where the government has established its headquarters in a small house, with the ministers sleeping on the floor in one single room, half of which serves as reception room and secretariat'—'there are daily outbursts of violence, with people ill-treated and killed. The day before three Banyarwanda had been beaten, maimed, castrated, and left on the road to die.'[10] Similarly, citing specific examples of 'victimization of refugees', Rachel Yeld reported after her visit to refugee centres in the Kivu, in March 1964, that in February of that year 'a refugee was arrested by a local agronome and forced (with threats) to sign a paper saying that he had been in Uganda collecting money for the *inyenzi* there. He was then imprisoned for 12 months. Another 14 refugees who had gone with travel documents . . . to work in a tea plantation were all put in prison for leaving the center. Many other cases of refugees being arrested—money from their pockets re-moved by the police—put in the lock-up for the night—and released in the morning but their money confiscated.'[11]

Preziosi also reported: 'The politicians of North Kivu hold [the Tutsi] responsible for all their difficulties. Whatever happens in the territory

* Preziosi was delegate of the United Nations High Commission for Refugees (UNHCR) in the Kivu until his assassination by a band of Congolese rebels in 1964, while on an inspection tour in the region of Lemera.

8—RAB * *

of Masisi is the Tutsi's fault. The refugees, who are peacefully resettled in the virgin forest, are accused of murder, arson, violence, etc. . . . That under the circumstances the refugees feel insecure and abandon their centres, if they can, to seek refuge in more hospitable surroundings is almost inevitable.'[12]

Actually, the attitude of the Congo refugees varied in accordance with local conditions. When faced with the overwhelming hostility of the host populations, they had either to accept their fate as best they could, or seek refuge in other areas. But when circumstances allowed, they preferred to play the game of local politics, in the hope of extracting for themselves whatever advantages the political conjuncture could offer. For this they needed few inducements. Again to quote Preziosi: 'The refugees cannot remain neutral. They have to take sides. If they do not take sides they attract upon themselves the enmity of the chiefs and populations where they are. If they do take sides they are accused of meddling in politics by their adversaries. They stand to lose in either case.'[13]

How the presence of the refugees came to affect local politics is perhaps best illustrated by the controversy that developed in 1961–63 over the paramount chieftainship of the Bafulero, a small tribe located west of the Ruzizi river, near the Burundi frontier. The conflict began in early 1961, when the paramount chief of the Bafulero, Mwami Henri Simba, saw his prerogatives threatened by a certain Simon Marandura, a provincial deputy affiliated to the MNC-Lumumba (MNC-L).[14] When in January 1961 Anicet Kashamura, one of Lumumba's most dedicated lieutenants, seized control of the Kivu government, Mwami Simba fled to Bujumbura. On February 28, 1961, Marandura was appointed 'Président de la chefferie des Bafulero', to replace Simba. Armed with this new mandate Marandura wasted little time in appointing his own politico-administrative cadres, for the most part of MNC-L obedience. But as the political situation in the Kivu reverted to the status quo ante and showed signs of greater stability, Simba decided to return to his chiefdom. By then, however, he was faced with considerable opposition, not only from the functionaries and notables appointed by Marandura but from the Tutsi refugee population, whose size increased to approximately 10,000 by early 1963. When, in July of that year, Preziosi took the initiative in convoking a meeting of provincial administrators and notables to explore the possibility of organising a new resettlement centre in Katobo, the administrateur de territoire, Prosper Shishi, expressed his dismay at the activities of the refugees, and, speaking on behalf of Mwami Simba, indicated that under no circumstances could the chiefdom accommodate new refugees. 'The social committees [formed by the refugees]', said Shishi, 'are misunderstood by the Bafulero. . . . They think that the committees have as their goal sooner or later to seize power in our chiefdom, and, especially, to install their own chefs de groupement and capitas.'[15] In part because of the growing hostility of the Simba faction towards the refugees, whom they suspected of plotting an illegal seizure of power, and also because of their political affinities with Marandura (and his son Antoine, in particular, whose sympathies for the MNC-L were even more pronounced than his father's), the Rwandese refugees of Lemera—one of the key resettlement centres among the Bafulero—did not hesitate to cast their lot with the Marandura faction. When, in May 1964, Marandura's Bafulero warriors rose against the provincial authorities and the Simba clique, routing two battalions of the Armée Nationale Congolaise (ANC) with their bows and arrows and subsequently capturing the border town of Uvira, the refugees of Lemera played an important auxiliary role, fighting on the side of the Bafulero and often providing them with guidance and leadership.

Once they had gained access to a 'liberated' area, the refugees' modus operandi underwent a fundamental change. In some places a fairly close symbiotic relationship developed between the activist leadership and the rebel-led Armée Populaire de Libération (APL), resulting in the occasional participation of exiled leaders in the deliberations of the MNC-L (the political arm of the APL on the 'eastern front'), and sometimes in their assumption of important military and administrative functions.[16] Thus François Rukeba took an active, though intermittent, part in the meetings of the provincial committee of the MNC-L in Uvira, in 1964, and it was a Tutsi émigré, Colonel Louis Bidalira, who temporarily held the post of Chief of Staff of the Eastern Territories. Another Tutsi émigré, Jerome Katarebe, was described as Soumialot's chef de cabinet. But perhaps the most positive aspect of this relationship, from the standpoint of the *inyenzi*, is that it involved reciprocal assistance in the course of military engagements. There was a common awareness of the advantages that either party would draw from the realisation of the other's objectives: if the Congolese were to gain permanent control over the border areas, the refugees would then enjoy the benefit of a 'privileged sanctuary' for organising border raids into Rwanda; likewise, if Rwanda's republican regime should fall before the completion of their task, the Congolese could expect similar advantages for themselves.

But the terms of the quid pro quo were never clearly defined. Or else they were defined unilaterally, with little regard for the immediate needs and resources of the other partner. This in turn led to occasional tiffs and misunderstandings, and at times to serious strains in the 'alliance'. On October 3, 1963, for example, Rukeba was arrested by the Burundi authorities, presumably at the request of the 'rebel' leaders in Bujumbura, on the charge of having stolen weapons and ammunition destined for Soumialot's men, including 18 machine guns, 9 Fal rifles, 17 Mauser rifles, 19 revolvers, 21 'home-made' guns and 6 crates of ammunition. He was released shortly thereafter, however, when pressure had been brought to bear upon the palace by certain deputies of the so-called 'Casablanca' wing of the Parti de l'Unité et du Progrès National (UPRONA). Ironically, it was the same Rukeba who, in the course of a meeting of the MNC-L, held in Uvira on July 5, 1964, preached honesty and collaboration and urged his audience to avoid 'divisions of all sorts'. To quote from the minutes of the meeting:

> On behalf of UNAR, President Rukeba explained the reasons which led his party to collaborate with the APL, and insisted that unity must reign among the partisans if the revolution is to have any meaning. He cautioned his audience against divisions of all sorts, and dis-abused them of the belief that victory was already within their grasp. It is because of this notion that the combatants are beginning to feel discouraged. He added that another reason for this feeling of discouragement is that some of the militants have shown signs of opportunism during the struggle and have tried to enrich themselves and acquire titles.[17]

That some of the 'partisans' did 'try to enrich themselves' received further confirmation during the meeting from the charges brought against Antoine Marandura: 'President Rusagara recounted to the assembly how a truckload of cloth for export was intercepted by Colonel Bidalira. Comrade Antoine Marandura was accused of being behind the deal.' At one point in the discussion, Colonel Bidalira openly admitted the existence of dissatisfaction among the troops:

> The Colonel then went on to explain the sources of discontent within the army. The troops are asking for: (*a*) financial aid; (*b*) regular food supplies; and (c) the participation in combat of all the officers. President Rukeba felt that it was important in view of the prevailing mood of discouragement within the army to multiply contacts with the villagers, so as to ensure the continued recruitment of other militants. President Rusagara stressed that all necessary measures should be taken to prevent further discouragement. According to him, the feeling originated from the fact that the leaders had fallen out among themselves and were trying to do each other in off-stage. He added that 'money deals' had also played a part in fostering this attitude.[18]

One cannot escape the conclusion that these were indeed important contributory factors in the ultimate failure of the rebellion in eastern Congo.[19]

Such pleas for unity have a strange ring, coming from Rukeba, whose alleged manoeuvrings and double-dealings were cited by some refugees as a primary source of division within their ranks. Yet his words were entirely justified, considering the seriousness of the bickerings that racked the Congolese rebel leadership. Nor were these dissensions restricted to the Congolese side of the rebellion: the same kind of jealousies and disillusionment with the character of their leadership could be discerned among the *inyenzi*. Above all, many were the refugees whose enthusiasm for the rebellion waned upon discovering the risks to which they were exposed by the incitements of their leaders. Theirs was indeed an impossible situation: those who refused to co-operate were faced with the possibility of a pitiless repression by the ANC. This in fact was the essence of the conclusion reached by the UNHCR delegate in late 1964: 'Many of the refugees remaining in the Kivu are in an extremely precarious position, affected on the one hand by the harassment of the insurgents, and on the other hand by the security measures of the local authorities.'[20] This unhappy state of affairs, together with the rebellion's internal disorganisation and very limited success in the two strategic border strips, near Bukavu and Goma, confronted the *inyenzi* leadership in the Congo with formidable obstacles.

The last of the countries of asylum, Burundi, is also the one about which evaluations are the most difficult, in part because of the policy shifts that have attended various changes of government, and because of Mwami Mwambutsa's own vulnerability to external pressures.* Yet it is safe to say that in no other country were conditions so eminently favourable to the conduct of counter-revolutionary activities. There were strong ethnic affinities between the bulk of the refugee population and the indigenous Tutsi elites, and, even when the government was headed by Hutu, there were still ample opportunities for activating such ties of ethnicity as might have existed at one echelon or the other of the central and provincial administrations. There was an utter lack of administrative efficiency and co-ordination at the local and provincial levels, which often meant the absence of serious administrative control over the refugees. Then, with recognition of Burundi by Communist China in late 1963, the *inyenzi* leadership secured an important source of diplomatic leverage upon the Burundi authorities, a leverage made all the more effective by the largesse which the Chinese diplomats

* The relationships of the Rwandese refugee population with the Burundi authorities are discussed in greater detail in chapter 15, pp. 384–90.

reportedly extended to various Barundi politicians. Finally, the very size of the refugee population, which by 1963 numbered approximately 45,000, together with the proximity of the two main refugee camps to the Rwandese border, made Burundi a choice sanctuary for the exiled Tutsi leadership. Indeed, under the circumstances it is not pure coincidence that the raids launched from Burundi should have brought the *inyenzi* so close to the realisation of their political and military objectives.

THE BUGESERA INVASION AND ITS AFTERMATH

In October 1961 a prophetic dialogue took place between the Special Resident and a European security officer. The exchange ran as follows:

Special Resident: The possibility of terrorist actions aided from the outside is not absolutely unthinkable, but the chances of success of an internal action are very slim. The xenophobic parties are disorganised.
Security officer: But one must recognise that an outside intervention [by UNAR] could trigger off an internal reaction. Tutsi terrorists organised outside Rwanda could infiltrate the country and instigate seditious movements among certain segments of the population.
Special Resident: If such a movement should emerge among the Tutsi it would be the signal for a massacre by the Hutu. I think the Tutsi are fully aware of this.[21]

The events of December 1963 gave tragic confirmation to this assessment of the Hutu reaction to a possible 'terrorist action from the outside'. Between December 1963 and January 1964, following the so-called Bugesera invasion of December 21, 1963, at least 10,000 Tutsi died under the blows of the Hutu. For several weeks, Rwanda lived through an unprecedented orgy of violence and murder. Never before—not even during the worst period of the revolution—had the killings reached such frightening proportions. Never before had racial hatred led to such bestial cruelty. The scars which the events left on the political institutions of Rwanda have yet to heal.

One obvious question arises immediately. If, as the Special Resident claimed, the Tutsi were 'fully aware' of the possible consequences of their terrorism, why did they continue their raids against Rwanda? The first thing to note is that the refugees were not all equally strongly committed to the idea of a forceful re-entry into the country. Some were categorically opposed to it, knowing full well what the consequences would be if it should fail. Those who led the abortive raid of December 1963 were the activists—people like Rukeba, Nzamwita, Kabalira and many others—whose dedication to the cause of UNAR and the monarchy was much too strong to be in any way dissuaded from their plans. Their fanaticism was intensified by the hardships of their life in exile, and by their vision of a better future. It was through the incitements and propaganda of these activists that a growing number of refugees came to be inducted into the ranks of the *inyenzi*, although it is equally pertinent to note that many of these potential counter-revolutionaries were already predisposed to join the *inyenzi*, if only because of their feeling that 'outside their country they will always be subject to pressures, vexations and hostility on the part of the populations where they have sought refuge'.[22]

Quite apart from the fanaticism of the leaders and the receptivity of the refugee population to the appeals of the counter-revolution, many of the refugees who joined the activists did so because of their firm conviction that they would ultimately succeed in carrying their plans. In view of the circumstances that led to the Bugesera invasion, this belief was not entirely unwarranted. But before we proceed any further, and in order to understand the motives behind the repression, attention must be paid to the general pattern of violence which developed in the years preceding the abortive invasion.

In the past, the indiscriminate use of the expression '*inyenzi* raids' to describe just about any form of violence instigated by UNAR has tended to obscure certain major variations in the overall pattern of violence associated with UNAR's strategy. At first, Tutsi violence took the form of isolated acts of terrorism against specific individuals and families. But, as the mobilisable refugee population became more numerous, a more systematic attempt was made to organise small bands of combatants, or *inyenzi* fighters, whose primary function was to make armed raids on specific localities. Finally there have been instances of organised attempts at invasion, involving a substantial number of well-trained commando units, acting under a single military command and clearly aiming at the overthrow of the government.

Beginning with the first massive flight of Tutsi refugees in early 1960, Rwanda became the scene of countless incidents. The initial pattern of violence was almost everywhere the same, involving the settlement of personal scores between individual refugees and Hutu officials. By early 1962, planned armed raids had become the standard form of violence. The aim was no longer the settlement of personal scores but the infliction of maximum harm to Hutu officials, regardless of rank or position, and regardless of the consequences that such actions might entail for the local Tutsi community. The cost of the reprisals, however, was probably higher than the *inyenzi* had at first anticipated. A case in point is the repression that followed the raid of March 25, 1962, on the

217

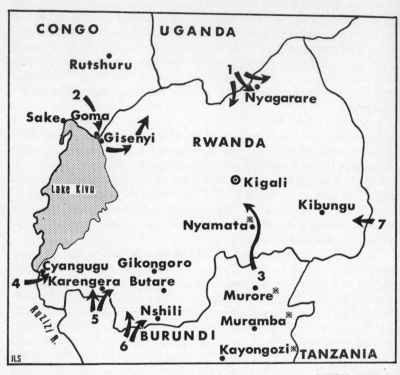

Map 2. Rwanda: Major *Inyenzi* Attacks, March 1961-November 1966

1. March 1961; July 1962
2. July 1962
3. December 1963
4. December 1963; June-July 1964; March-April 1964
5. November 1966
6. November 1966
7. July 1966

commune of Nkana in the prefecture of Biumba, when four Hutu (including one policeman and two civil servants) were killed and the communal cash box stolen.[23] About a month earlier, a similar raid on the communes of Mugira and Gatunda, also in the region of Biumba, had resulted in the death of two policemen. Apparently exasperated by these repeated acts of terrorism, the Hutu population of Biumba decided to teach the *inyenzi* a lesson. On March 26 and 27, between 1,000 and 2,000 Tutsi men, women and children were massacred and buried on the spot, their huts burned and pillaged and their property divided among the Hutu population. Commenting on the Biumba incidents, the pro-UNAR newspaper *Unité* described the massacre as 'the most agonising drama of the two nightmare years through which Rwanda has just passed'.[24] Compared to the reprisals provoked by subsequent raids, however, the massacre of Biumba looks almost trivial.

It was in November 1963 that the UNAR leadership in exile in Burundi decided to strike a decisive blow against the republican regime. In Rwanda, the communal elections of August 1963 had brought to light some serious dissensions within PARMEHUTU, and the local UNAR branches exploited this situation to consolidate its domestic support. Week after week, UNAR's official mouthpiece, *Unité*, denounced the 'intimidations, threats, and incitations to violence' which, it said, had figured so prominently in PARMEHUTU's campaign, and at one point the same newspaper paid a prophetic homage to those electors, who, by voting for UNAR, had become 'the martyrs of their convictions'.[25] The political conjuncture in Burundi seemed equally favourable. The Mwami was in Switzerland, thus allowing the refugee leadership to bring pressure to bear upon certain members of the government and the administration. Moreover, Gatwa and Rukeba had just received from Kigeri the financial support they so badly needed for the purchase of arms and ammunition. There had been unexpected windfalls: earlier in 1963 a group of *inyenzi* successfully attacked the police armoury at Ngara in Tanzania, and made off with a substantial quantity of rifles and small arms. By November 1963, a fairly effective liaison was established between Rukeba's headquarters in Bujumbura and various refugee camps in Burundi and Tanzania. The Kigamba camp, in Burundi, soon became one of the most active 'training centres' for *inyenzi*. Although the refugee camps in Tanzania never became fully 'operative', Rukeba paid several visits to these camps, each time doing his best to enlist the support of the local populations. Indeed, if anyone can be said to bear responsibility for the raids that were launched from Burundi, it was Rukeba, not only because of his feverish and partially successful efforts to 'keep the pot boiling' in the refugee camps but also because of his calculated attempt to co-ordinate the action of his lieutenants. As one refugee told Preziosi, explaining the circumstances that led to the first abortive attempt at invasion on November 25, 1963, 'Rukeba is responsible for these events. Before the abortive attack, Rukeba held a meeting in Bujumbura to ask all leaders to join in. However, most of these leaders rejected the proposal and in fact only the refugees in Burundi went ahead. The Mwami [of Rwanda] himself is said to have been against the venture and he sent the refugees a letter to that effect.' 'In spite of the opposition', wrote Preziosi, 'Monsieur Rukeba, who is a stubborn and illiterate old man with whom it is apparently impossible to argue, gave the orders for the attack, with the known results.'[26]

The results of the attack attempted on November 25 were far from encouraging. On that day, about 1,500 refugees from various parts of Burundi, most of them armed with spears, bows and arrows, began a three-day trek towards the Rwandese border. Alerted by missionaries and UN officials, the Burundi authorities, after considerable hesitation, finally decided to intervene and turned back the assailants before they had a chance to start the engagement. Besides the recalcitrance of some of the *inyenzi* leaders in Bujumbura, several other factors contributed to the failure of the November attack. For one thing, Rukeba was arrested by the Burundi authorities and thrown in jail shortly before the date on which the attack was to be launched. This decision was made after a substantial stock of arms and ammunition, apparently stolen from the Congolese rebels, was discovered in the house where he stayed in Bujumbura; at about the same time, or shortly thereafter, three truck-loads of rifles and ammunition were seized in the vicinity of Bujumbura. Thus, before the combatants had even had a chance to reach the border, their leader was locked up in jail and their arms confiscated. Ultimately, however, the decisive action came from the combined efforts of the UNHCR representative in Bujumbura, Jacques Cuenod, and a group of Protestant missionaries to forestall the attack, the former by desperately trying to persuade the Burundi government to halt the assailants before it was too late, and the latter by pointing out to the refugees that they were fighting a losing battle since the Garde Nationale Rwandaise (GNR) was probably waiting for them at the border. It was at this point that the Burundi gendarmerie finally showed up. According to one observer, 'all they did was to take away the refugees' spears, bows and arrows, and offer them free lifts back to their centres, which they took as there was nothing much else they could do'.[27]

These efforts met with only temporary success. On December 21, 1963, a second attack was launched from Burundi. This time the operations had been more carefully planned, and by then the attitude of the

Burundi authorities was far less co-operative, at least from the stand-point of the UNHCR. This change of attitude was in part the logical con-sequence of disagreements that led to the break-up of the conference, held in early December 1963 in Gisenyi in Rwanda, which had been called to discuss the terms of the dissolution of the customs and monet-ary union between the governments of Rwanda and Burundi. Agree-ments on economic co-operation between Rwanda and Burundi had been worked out at the Addis Ababa conference shortly before they became independent. Prior to the opening of the Gisenyi conference, a number of common services had already been dissolved—such as electricity, water, agronomy and telecommunications—and reconstitu-ted at the national level, thus leaving only three common institutions—the customs union, the Banque d'Emission, and the monetary union. The participants at Gisenyi failed to reach agreement on the agenda and the conference ended in total deadlock. They failed to find a mutually agreeable formula for the sharing of reserve currencies, Burundi insisting on 60 per cent for five years and Rwanda suggesting instead a 50–50 split, pending the recommendations of an inter-governmental commission of enquiry. The attitude of the Rwandese undoubtedly angered the Burundi delegates. As Dr Pie Masumbuko, then Vice-Prime Minister of Burundi, later told a Rwandese official: 'Rwanda is ungrateful. Recently we have arrested people who were about to attack you and now you decide to sever economic relations with us. Therefore you do not want collaboration.'[28] This lack of 'collaboration', however, was also a reflection of the increasing pressures put on the Burundi authorities by Chinese diplomats. If we are to believe the words of the same Rwandese official, the political climate of Burundi on the eve of the Bugesera invasion was distinctively pro-Chinese. We are told, for example, that on the morning of the attack Dr Masumbuko was 'found at home in the company of three Chinese who, after presenting him with a wedding gift, left immediately'. 'You do not have a sense of socialism', Masumbuko is reported to have told his Rwandese interlocutor, 'for you have refused to recognise Communist China; the fact that you have joined the Afro-Malagasy Union also shows that you only wish to serve the interests of the West.' The author of the document from which these words are taken went on to note:

At 6.00 PM, the President of the National Assembly [Thaddée Siryuyumunsi] came to see me at my hotel and invited me to join him at a table, with Papias Gatwa and a Chinese Communist named Kao-Liang and other persons whose presence I could not stand. I decided to retire to my room. . . . In general, during their off-duty hours, each Burundi minister is in the company of one of the terrorist leaders or a Chinese. The Chinese Communists, led by Kao-Liang, representative of the Hsinhua News Agency of the People's Republic of China, are always seen in the company of certain ministers. The government has appointed a certain Mubiligi, a Murundi and long-time resident of Tanzania, to teach them Kirundi. According to a high-ranking personality, these gentlemen make a point of purchasing expensive pieces of cloth in Dar es Salaam, which they offer to the wives of ministers. The ministers are so deeply immersed in luxury that they ignore what goes on in their own town.

This last statement does not seem exaggerated: as the Prime Minister of Burundi at the time, the late Pierre Ngendadumwe, candidly admitted to his Rwandese guest, 'he knew nothing of the attack [at the time of its occurrence], he had just heard about it on the radio'. This was on Monday, December 23, at 8.00 AM. By then, however, the assailants had already been routed.

According to reliable sources, the *inyenzi* leaders had hoped to organise simultaneous attacks from at least four different quarters: from the regions of Kabare (Uganda), Ngara (Tanzania), Goma (Congo), and Ngozi and Kayanza (Burundi). One group of assailants from Uganda, led by a certain Kibibiro, were reportedly intercepted by the Uganda authorities on December 25, before they reached the border; another, numbering about 600 men, entered Rwanda at Kizinga, on the Uganda border, on December 27, but was almost immediately repulsed by the Garde Nationale Rwandaise (GNR), after suffering heavy losses. About 300 invaders were killed and the rest turned over to the Uganda Rifles. Similarly, on December 21 and 22 a series of small-scale border raids were launched from the Kivu in the direction of the town of Cyangugu, across the Ruzizi, resulting in the intervention of the GNR and the subsequent execution of about 90 prisoners captured during the attacks. Although the projected raids from Tanzania somehow failed to materialise, during the same period a major attack was attempted from Burundi. The invading force, numbering approximately 200 or 300 men (some say only 80) armed, for the most part, with bows and arrows and home-made rifles, crossed the Burundi border at Nemba at 4.30 AM on December 21. An hour or so later they attacked and over-ran the Rwandese military camp at Gako. After stocking up on arms and ammunition they went straight to the refugee camp at Nyamata, where they received an enthusiastic welcome from the local Tutsi population. If we are to believe the accounts of certain observers, the invaders wasted some precious time when they decided to pause for a celebration, and the libations poured for the occasion probably did not improve their marksmanship either. Although their ranks had swollen to well over a thousand, by the time they reached the Nyabarongo river, at the Kanzenze bridge, about twelve miles south of Kigali, they were suddenly confronted with several units of the GNR armed with mortars and semiautomatic weapons and under the command of Belgian officers. Overwhelmed by the superior firepower of their opponents, the invaders were quickly repulsed. In the course of the engagement several hundred Tutsi lost their lives, including a handful of Congolese 'rebels'. On one of the 'rebels' were found the invasion plans of the raiders and the list of the ministers they had hoped to install.

After recuperating from the initial moment of shock, the first reaction of the Rwanda authorities was to round up and jail some twenty leading Tutsi personalities associated with the local branches of the UNAR and RADER parties, some of whom figured in the list of potential ministers. Less than a week later they were all taken to Ruhengeri and summarily executed. Among the victims were Etienne Afrika, one of the two UNAR members of the government, Ruditsitwarane and Rwagasana, respectively president and secretary-general of the local UNAR, Bwanakweli and Ndazaro, respectively president and vice-president of RADER. Some of them, like Bwanakweli, were well-known for their conciliatory attitude and enjoyed considerable respect from certain segments of the local Hutu population. (Asked why they should have been executed in Ruhengeri instead of Kigali, one Hutu official told this writer that Ruhengeri was 'the safest spot' for carrying out the execution.) Simultaneously, steps were taken to organise civilian 'self-defence' groups among the Hutu population, to counter possible attempts at internal subversion. For this task primary reliance was placed upon the burgomasters and the prefects. In addition, one minister was assigned to each of the ten prefectures (now converted into 'emergency regions') to supervise the organisation of the self-defence units. These arrangements were made within a few hours, in an atmosphere of panic, and therefore with little attention to procedural details or co-ordination. Meanwhile, Kigali Radio repeatedly beamed emergency warnings, asking the population to be 'constantly on the alert' for Tutsi terrorists. In this atmosphere of intense fear, saturated with rumour and suspicion, the worst was bound to happen.

The killings began on December 23, in the prefecture of Gikongoro, at the instigation of the local prefect, a certain André Nkeramugaba. Addressing an improvised meeting of burgomasters and PARMEHUTU propagandists, Nkeramugaba is reported to have said: 'We are expected to defend ourselves. The only way to go about it is to paralyse the Tutsi.

How? They must be killed.' This was the signal for the slaughter. Armed with clubs, pangas and spears, the Hutu methodically began to exterminate all Tutsi in sight—men, women and children. In the prefecture of Gikongoro, an estimated 5,000 Tutsi were massacred.* Soon the contagion spread to other areas, accompanied by wanton cruelty. One missionary later recounted how a group of Hutu 'hacked the breasts off a Tutsi woman, and as she lay dying forced the dismembered parts down the throats of her children, before her eyes'.[29] Robert Conley, of the *New York Times*, wrote that on one Tutsi hilltop the massacre went on all night, prompting one missionary to say— 'still stammering from shock': 'It was beyond belief—screams, they went on hour after hour.'[30] In one locality more than one hundred Tutsi women and children were reported to have voluntarily drowned themselves in the Nyabarongo river in a suicidal attempt to escape the clutches of attacking mobs of Hutu. The impression from various eyewitness reports is one of unspeakable brutality. Popular participation in violence created a kind of collective catharsis through which years of pent-up hatred suddenly seemed to find an outlet.

When the news of the reprisals finally reached the outside world— about a month and a half later—the general reaction was one of horror and shock. Commenting on the savageness which swept the country, Bertrand Russell said it was 'the most horrible and systematic human massacre we have had occasion to witness since the extermination of the Jews by the Nazi'.[31] The Holy See echoed Lord Russell's revulsion; in its broadcast of February 10, 1964, the Vatican Radio called the massacre 'the most terrible and systematic genocide since the genocide of the Jews by Hitler'.[32] A precise estimate of the number of persons killed during the repression, however, is impossible to establish. Certainly, the official figure of 750 casualties cited by the Rwanda Radio in its first mention of the massacre (subsequently raised to 870 in the white paper issued by the Rwanda government) is patently inaccurate. But it would be equally misleading to speak of genocide. Press reports alleging that

---

* That the reprisals should have been primarily in this area is not accidental. Besides having a very high density of Tutsi, the Gikongoro prefecture was the core area of the Tutsi opposition, a fact that is not altogether unnatural if one considers that it also contained within its boundaries the former royal residence of Nyanza. In an effort to weaken the Tutsi opposition, the Rwanda government had decided to break the former prefecture of Nyanza into two separate administrative units, one of which became known as the Gikongoro prefecture. But this did not prevent the Tutsi of Gikongoro from continually and defiantly expressing their hopes of returning to power. Under the circumstances one can better understand why the Hutu population should have been driven to such extremities.

thousands of Tutsi corpses were seen floating down the Ruzizi into Lake Tanganyika are not only false but reflect a total ignorance of the geographical location of the reprisals.[33] According to more reliable estimates, corroborated by the figures cited by the World Council of Churches, between 10,000 and 14,000 Tutsi lost their lives. Assuming that a total of approximately 200,000 Tutsi are now living abroad, this still leaves between 35,000 and 40,000 Tutsi living in Rwanda. Nonetheless one wonders whether such statistics are all that meaningful when seen in the light of the atrocities committed by the Hutu against innocent Tutsi.

To what extent can it be said that the reprisals were the result of a deliberate policy on the part of the Rwanda authorities? The answer given by the UN Secretary-General's Special Representative, Max Dorsinville, after investigating the situation on the spot, is categorical: 'It now seems clear that these brutal acts were in no sense dictated by the government in Kigali, but rather took place in areas over which the government had little control, due to lack of troops. In such areas a popular militia took reprisals on some of the Batutsi populations as a result of the raids of December 20–21 and the fear and panic which they inspired in the Bahutu population.'[34] On the other hand, according to certain observers, there is every reason to believe that at least *some* Rwandese officials were directly and actively involved in the reprisals. This is the view expressed by Denis Vuillemin, a Swiss professor sent to Rwanda under the auspices of UNESCO, in a letter to the French newspaper *Le Monde*.[35] A Belgian professor at the Université Libre in Brussels, Luc de Heusch, expressed a similar opinion in the course of a public debate organised in March 1964 under the auspices of the Belgian Ligue des Droits de l'Homme, adding that 'certain Belgian technical advisers have gone beyond the neutrality of their mission, by contributing to the hardening of governmental policies and precipitating the formation of a climate of racial hatred'.[36]

The truth, however, is that official responsibilities, though widely dispersed through the administrative and governmental hierarchy, are unevenly shared. At the root of the tragedy lies President Kayibanda's decision to entrust to each of his ministers emergency powers in each of the ten local prefectures, with instructions to take whatever measures they deemed appropriate. In many cases this mandate was interpreted as a licence to kill. Thus, next to the local prefect, the man who appears to bear most of the responsibility for the Gikongoro massacre is the Minister of Agriculture, Damien Nkezobera, who, along with the prefect and burgomasters personally supervised the 'operations'. When at the height of the troubles Nkezobera asked the Catholic Fathers of

Kaduha and Cyanika to surrender those Tutsi who had found asylum at the mission stations, the priests courageously refused, as to comply would have been tantamount to turning the fugitives over to their executioners. In some places the prefects and the PARMEHUTU propagandists saw in the reprisals a golden opportunity to solidify their bases of support among the local Hutu populations. Realising that a massive elimination of Tutsi would make their land 'available' to the Hutu, they saw distinct political advantages in encouraging the liquidation of the local Tutsi population. Thus one can better understand why the prefect of Gikongoro, André Nkeramugaba, after he decided to present his candidacy to the National Assembly, in 1965, was elected by an overwhelming majority of the votes in the prefecture of Gikongoro.*

The best proof that a number of high-ranking officials were directly implicated in the events is supplied by Kayibanda's reaction to the report of the commission of inquiry set up at the request of the Swiss government, partly in response to the accusations made by Denis Vuillemin.† As a result of this investigation—conducted under the auspices of the Procureur de la République, Tharcisse Gatwa—no less than 89 persons were found guilty, including two ministers, and a number of local officials, prefects and burgomasters. Kayibanda refused to acknowledge the evidence and ordered a new investigation. This time, as one might have expected, only a handful of individuals were incriminated. Most of them received light prison sentences. At this point the matter was laid to rest.

Perhaps the most baffling aspect of these tragic events is that they should have made so little impact beyond the borders of Rwanda. The most obvious reason for this was the general inadequacy of press coverage: the relevant facts were not reported in the American or European press until early February, and then in the most garbled fashion.[37] Furthermore, the deliberate black-out of the news enforced by the Rwanda authorities, together with the argument that this was essentially a domestic matter that lay outside the competence of the United Nations, were both instrumental in silencing criticisms from the outside.

---

* According to a reliable source, Nkeramugaba's electoral slogan in 1965 was: 'If I am not elected, charges may be brought against you; but if I am elected I shall do my best to prevent all investigations.'

† In February 1964, the head of the Swiss technical assistance programme, Auguste Lindt, informed President Kayibanda that his government would discontinue its aid to Rwanda unless an investigation was made. It was largely in response to this that the first commission of inquiry was appointed. The findings of the second commission of inquiry are contained in the White Paper released by the Rwanda authorities in March 1964, misleadingly entitled *Toute la Vérité sur le Terrorisme Inyenzi au Rwanda*, Kigali, n.d.

Although the UN Secretary-General twice sent his Special Representative to Rwanda, the Dorsinville Report tends to reflect the limitations inherent in the domestic jurisdiction clause of the UN Charter. 'Neither Rwanda nor Burundi', said the report, 'seemed to feel that a United Nations presence on its territory was necessary or desirable at this stage, or that observers or a commission of inquiry would contribute to the solution of current problems.'[38] The extent of UN intervention was a letter of the UN Special Representative to the President of Rwanda 'expressing the hope that his government would do its utmost to calm and pacify ethnic rivalries resulting from the events of December 20–21'.[39] Commenting on the general indifference of the international community, one American journalist observed: 'Not a single African state except Burundi raised a voice in protest. Not a word came from any other nation, western or eastern. Above all, not a finger was raised by the UN, under whose official tutelage the trusteeship region of Rwanda was given its independence.'[40] Thus the efforts of the UNAR leadership to make political capital out of the tragedy came to nought. Heavily decimated, and now deprived of the bases of internal support and relative freedom of action they enjoyed before the repression, the UNAR leaders found themselves more isolated than ever.*

The immediate result was to give the Rwanda authorities a new lease on life, or at any rate a far greater measure of popular support and internal cohesion than would have been the case otherwise. One Rwanda official freely admitted to this writer: 'Before the attacks of the *inyenzi* the government was on the point of collapse. We were faced with enormous dissensions among ourselves. Not only have we survived the attacks but the attacks made us survive our dissensions.' Whether the Rwanda government can devise alternative ways of bringing about national cohesion is an entirely different matter, which will be discussed in the following chapter. The main point to be stressed, in conclusion, is that UNAR in exile has thus far not only consistently failed to realise its objectives but in the end achieved precisely the opposite of what it had set out to do.

---

* However ruthless, the repression did not discourage the *inyenzi* from further attempts at invasion. Nor did it bring a lessening of the financial and diplomatic support of Red China. In June 1964, the Ministry of Foreign Affairs of Communist China transmitted £17,000 to Kigeli's personal account in Dar es Salaam, and the Chinese continued to supply the *inyenzi* with arms and ammunitions, most of them unloaded through Dar es Salaam, Mombasa and Zanzibar.

8. The Quest for Solidarity

THE PREVAILING mood after the declaration of the republic was one of great enthusiasm. Not only had the leaden oppression of the dominant caste been thrown off but electoral processes were simultaneously introduced at both the local and national levels, thereby providing institutional safeguards against further oppression. Communal elections were held in 1960 and 1963; legislative elections in 1961 and 1965, the latter held jointly with presidential elections. A genuine effort was made at substituting civil service norms of efficiency and neutrality for the ascriptive criteria associated with the old regime. A structure of accountability was established, in the form of a National Assembly, which presumably made the government answerable to groups other than itself. Finally, the interests of the population were aggregated through a 'mass' type of political party, intended to serve both as a channel of political recruitment and as a connecting link between the masses and the elites. Though none of these institutional arrangements was solidly anchored in the traditional norms of Rwandese society, they nonetheless symbolised a major attempt at eliminating the residual values and structures of the old regime.

Out of the contradictions between certain features of the old feudal order and the Jacobin aspirations of the revolutionary zealots serious conflicts have arisen. As the regime felt obligated to encourage the play of democratic forces, it has unwittingly favoured the expression of dissent, on an unforeseen scale. The mere tolerance of electoral competition was enough to produce conflict; but as the government saw its control over the state challenged by the rise of opposition forces, a conscious effort was made to turn back the tide—to accentuate the drive towards centralisation to repel attacks from within and from without, and to assert the primacy of the party over all other institutions. This has fostered profound misgivings among the masses as to the real meaning of the revolution. With the increasing stress placed on discipline, self-sacrifice and loyalty to the party, with the repeated exhortations to the people of Rwanda to remain 'tough, pure and competent',[1] enthusiasm gave way to disillusion. Today, to an increasing number of people, the government seems singularly lacking in at least two of the above-mentioned virtues, and only too often predisposed to display the third—toughness.

The psychological letdown which followed independence is nowhere more clearly revealed than in the comments of a Hutu informant, in a letter to this writer:

> The masses . . . are not, of course, for a monarchy, not even for a constitutional monarchy, but if you know how to approach them they will tell you of their disappointments. They long for a change of regime and sometimes regret, not without reason, some of the advantages they used to draw from the old regime; they become every day more painfully conscious of the fact that there are too many injustices in the allocation of offices; that parents no longer have any authority over their children; that there is no longer any harmony among families; that the school system is inadequate; that justice is no longer equitably administered; that pauperism and banditry run rampant; that security is everywhere lacking, day and night; that freedom of movement within and outside the country is stifled by the system of 'safe-conducts'; and that, consequently, the masses are neither socially, economically or politically more advanced than before the revolution. Only to the people of Gitarama and Ruhengeri has the revolution brought any tangible profits.

Before further elaborating on the contemporary political scene, we must first try to define the nature of the opposition. What are its social bases? How did it manifest itself? And with what results for the political system as a whole?

POST-REVOLUTIONARY SCHISMS

The withdrawal of Tutsi rule produced within the Hutu community a situation strikingly similar to that which followed the eviction of colonial authorities from other parts of Africa. No longer held in check by the 'iron grid' of Tutsi domination, a host of centrifugal tendencies suddenly came to light; and, as frequently happened elsewhere in Africa, parochial loyalties seemed strongest where the impact of 'alien' domination was least in evidence. In spite of the recurrent threats of counter-revolution, these divisions nonetheless persisted—an eloquent testimony of their depth. Addressing the National Assembly on April 30, 1964, Anastase Makuza launched into a bitter diatribe against divisions, factionalism and intrigue which, he said, had caused the parliamentary debates to reach a total impasse:

> Yes, this impasse is nothing but the work of an evil genius which embitters your debates and leads you to cut your own throat, abusing

the good faith of the vast majority of the people assembled here; this evil genius which whispers instructions into your ear and makes you pass watchwords around on little pieces of paper; this evil genius which presides over innumerable nocturnal meetings and underhand dealings of all sorts; this evil genius which leads some to take up contradictory positions and makes them the staunchest adversaries of those very measures they had advocated in the course of preliminary proceedings; this evil genius which has dictated public insults against your President; this evil genius which torments you with a quasi-pathological hatred against your President, with an obsessive desire to form cabals. . . .[2]

In typically Rwandese fashion, Makuza would rather invoke the presence of an 'evil genius' than call a spade a spade. But quite apart from such idiosyncrasies, and no matter how much they may complicate the task of the historian, any attempt to identify 'the opposition' raises difficulties. The term conveys a much greater degree of cohesion and programmatic consistency than one is ever likely to find within the Hutu community. The groups involved were never precisely delineated, never neatly organised. They often split into separate factions, each associated with specific regions, clans or personalities. Indeed, so great is the ascendancy of personal influences within each group that one often wonders whether factionalism was not at bottom a reflection of personal animosities. One is reminded of the situation in revolutionary France, in 1794, where the political struggle was 'the peculiarly intense and unabstract struggle of intimates'.[3]

Bakonde versus Bagererwa

On one specific issue at least, more was involved than just personalities. When the question arose of how to abolish the system of land tenure associated with the *ubukonde*, the old landowners (*bakonde*) fought tooth and nail to hold on to their privileges. Not only did they wish to retain the ownership of the land but they also insisted on getting rid of those clients—the so-called *bagererwa politiques*—to whom the former chiefs had 'leased' part of their holdings.

The root of the problem lies in the past. When the Tutsi took over the administration of the northern region at the turn of the century, they superimposed their own customs on those of the Kiga ruling clans. With regard to land tenure, the chiefs acted as if the rights of the *bakonde* over the land did not exist. Blissfully disregarding the traditional claims of the local ruling clans, the newcomers proceeded to expel the *bakonde*'s traditional clients—the *bagererwa coutumiers*—from their masters' estates, and allocated the land to their own people—who then became known as *bagererwa politiques*, having received their land from Tutsi political authorities. Though most of them were of local origin, these *bagererwa politiques* in effect became the clients of the Tutsi chiefs. Thus, after the flight of Tutsi authorities from the northern region in late 1959, some very thorny problems immediately arose. Could one still recognise the claims of the *bagererwa politiques* over the *bakonde*'s land? If so, under what conditions? More importantly, since the perpetuation of clientage ties was said to be incompatible with republican ideals, how could one reconcile the traditional claims of the *bakonde* over the land with the individual property rights of their clients?

To the first question the debates in the Conseil Special Provisoire (CSP), in July 1960, gave a seemingly unambiguous answer: 'The predominance of clanic customary law does not mean an a priori rejection of de facto situations born out of the exercise of Tutsi political rights over a great many years.'[4] But, as the subsequent debates in the National Assembly made clear, acceptance of this principle did not resolve the issue. For how many years should a *bagererwa* claim effective occupation of his land before he could be recognised as a bona fide *bagererwa*? At first the CSP fixed the period of effective occupation required to validate the claims of the *bagererwa* at a hundred years. Subsequently, this so-called 'prescription aquisitive' was reduced to sixty years, a move obviously designed to favour the claims of the more recently established clients (the *bagererwa politiques*), most of whom had secured their title deeds from Tutsi chiefs. This amendment led, in April 1961, to an extremely bitter exchange between the representatives of the *bakonde*—notably Balthazar Bicamumpaka, then Minister of Agriculture, and Banzi, deputy from Gisenyi—and the spokesmen of the *bagererwa politiques*. Anything short of a hundred-year prescription, said Bicamumpaka, 'will gravely compromise the prestige of our new political institutions, will dangerously delay the pacification of the country, and, on the social and economic plane, will only perpetuate the burning tensions at present existing in the *bakonde* regions'.[5] When Calliope Mulindihabi, then Minister of Armed Forces, pointed out the difficulty of establishing the validity of a hundred-year prescription in the absence of 'written documents prior to the arrival of the Europeans in 1900', Bicamumpaka sought refuge in the alleged complexity of northern traditions: 'The problem of the *ubukonde* will remain a mystery for anyone who is not a *bakonde* or a *bagererwa*.'[6] Banzi then asked: 'Who can ignore that the *bakonde* were the first to open the land for cultivation? Who can ignore that the *bakonde*, free before the infiltration of the Batutsi and oppressed thereafter, have never ceased to claim

231

their rights over the land? A testimony? One needs only to look at the history of the *ubukonde*, at the verdicts of the tribunals of the ancien régime, at the tenacity with which the *bakonde* hang on to their claims, and at the events of November 1959, of which we all know the underlying causes.'[7]

In the face of their obduracy, the views of the *bakonde* were bound to prevail upon the Assembly. Not only did the acceptance of the hundred-year prescription provide them with a blank cheque to expel from their estates whomever they pleased, but they also retained their full property rights over the land. Thus, no matter how distasteful the institution may look to some republicans, the *ubukonde* continues to spread its seamless web over clients and patrons alike.

Behind the complicated mosaic of inherited land rights lies a more fundamental issue, for this was not only a legal conflict between north and south but a conflict between two different and largely incompatible ways of life. Among those northerners who rose to eminent positions in the government and the administration—people like Callixte Habamenshi (former Minister of Justice and later a deputy), Balthazar Bicamumpaka (former Minister of Agriculture, then Minister of Interior and later President of the National Assembly) and Juvenal Habyalimana (Minister of Armed Forces and Police)—many are descendants of ruling families. Most are *bakonde* and own large tracts of land in the northern prefectures. They have a substantial clientele, upon whom they can always rely at election time, and the prebends they receive from their clients allow them to engage in lucrative commercial activities in places like Ruhengeri and Gisenyi. Habamenshi and Banzi, for example, are among the wealthiest traders in Gisenyi. Not only do they derive distinct political and economic privileges from their status as *bakonde*; they also feel a genuine nostalgia for their own traditional social order. Only if one has had occasion to come in contact with this class of 'patricians-turned-republicans' can one appreciate the sincerity with which one of them expressed his feelings to this writer—by citing an old Kiga proverb, 'The heart filled with sadness cannot speak clearly' ('*Umutima wuje amaganya ntusobanura amabambo*').

But if this is so, what has prevented the conflict from erupting into violence? In part, the very same factors which thus far have kept other conflicts within bonds: a shared consciousness of the external threats posed by the *inyenzi*; a skilful use of 'clanic' and regional arithmetic in appointments to key posts; and, of course, the very tolerance which the regime continues to show towards the claims of the *bakonde*. But one must also stress the incidence of a host of cleavages among the northern populations, cleavages so numerous and so persistent that it is doubtful whether one can really speak of a northern political consciousness. There are regional cleavages, as between the better educated and more resourceful Bashiru (in the Bushiru region of the Gisenyi prefecture) and the Bagoyi (in the Bugoyi region of the same prefecture); clanic cleavages, as between the Abasindi and the Basinga of the Ruhengeri prefecture; social cleavages of a traditional character, as between the *bagererwa* and the *bakonde*, between the better educated and politically influential large landowners—who tend to adopt a rather moderate position on the issue of land redistribution—and the small landowners, whose wealth and prestige depends on the continuation of clientage ties through the land, and between *bagererwa* and *bakonde* on the one hand and those who fit into neither of these categories. Thus, what is frequently regarded as a regional conflict between north and south actually conceals a multiplicity of local tensions and mutual antagonisms *within* the northern region. But the reverse is equally true: among non-northerners, unity is more an ideal than a reality.

PARMEHUTU *versus* APROSOMA

The conflict between *bakonde* and political *bagererwa* is not a conflict over formal political allegiances. No matter how 'retrograde' their position on matters of land tenure, the leading spokesmen of the *bakonde* are all members of PARMEHUTU. Many are known in Rwanda as 'first-batch revolutionaries', and this may well be the reason why the government ultimately yielded to their views. The government felt under no such obligation towards the APROSOMA 'rebels'. Thus, when the time came for PARMEHUTU to extend its hold to those areas still under the sway of Gitera's men—e.g. essentially, the prefecture of Butare—no effort was spared to ensure the liquidation of its opponents.

The conflict goes back to the period immediately preceding independence, when PARMEHUTU desperately tried to rally to its cause those Hutu already affiliated to RADER and APROSOMA. Behind this cleavage between 'moderates' and 'activists' lay an even more fundamental rift, centred upon two different categories of intellectuals—the ex-seminarists and the 'Astridiens'. The most important source of disharmony lay in the widely different career opportunities to which each group could aspire by virtue of education and training. Unlike the ex-seminarists, who lacked the necessary qualifications to hold administrative posts, the Astridiens knew that they would be the first to reap the benefits of constitutional and administrative reforms. Their reformist, gradualist outlook, the logical consequence of their professional training, gave them an overwhelming inclination to join APROSOMA.

The ex-seminarists, on the other hand, stood little chance of making their mark in life as long as the Centre Scolaire d'Astrida remained the only channel of recruitment to government posts. Faced with a denial of career opportunities, they were naturally predisposed to reject political reforms. Nothing short of a revolution of the kind advocated by the PARMEHUTU would enable them to satisfy their aspirations to leadership.

Thus, when independence became a reality, the first step taken by PARMEHUTU diehards to achieve republican unanimity was to weed out or neutralise their moderate opponents, most of whom belonged to APROSOMA. The operation began even before independence, when, in October 1961, Joseph Gitera—self-styled 'pioneer, martyr and champion of the cause of the Hutu of Rwanda'—was politely requested by a parliamentary caucus of PARMEHUTU to abandon all political ambitions and return to his commercial activities, which he did. At the local level, the elimination—or conversion—of the APROSOMA burgomasters was generally conducted by the prefects, acting hand in hand with the PARMEHUTU propagandists. True, in some places, burgomasters suspected of APROSOMA sympathies were purely and simply removed from office by the central authorities in Kigali. More often than not, however, these burgomasters simply switched allegiance under the combined pressures and intimidation of the prefects and their cohorts. They were converted willy-nilly to the cause of PARMEHUTU. The results were impressive: of the 41 burgomasters in office in the prefecture of Butare at the time of independence, 36 were affiliated to APROSOMA; by 1966, as far as this writer has been able to ascertain, the prefecture was entirely in the hands of PARMEHUTU burgomasters.

This, however, was not accomplished without some major squabbles and uneasy readjustments, the implications of which went far beyond the local arena. What has since become known as the 'affair of the Supreme Court' is illustrative of the way in which local conflicts can reverberate on the central institutions and in the process unleash major political convulsions. Although the full story has yet to be pieced together, enough is known about the affair to regard it as the most serious internal crisis faced by the Kayibanda government since independence.

The affair began in August 1963, in the prefecture of Butare, shortly after the communal elections. It can be traced back to a rather trivial electoral incident: the man who claimed the seat of burgomaster in the commune of Ndora, Silas Ntabomvura, was elected by a majority of one vote over his nearest opponent, Deogratias Misago. But the full story is very complex, and many elements are still missing from the record. On the basis of the information this writer was able to gather, it appears that Ntabomvura—a native of the region, relatively well-educated, with strong lineage connections and an excellent administrative record—entered the race with a considerable headstart over his opponent—a barely literate native of Kabagari (Gitarama prefecture). As it happened, Misago managed to secure the 'patronage' of a certain Amandin Rugira, native of Butare, who then combined the functions of President of the National Assembly and Regional President of the Butare branch of PARMEHUTU, and whose popularity in Butare was unrivalled. With Rugira's backing, and the efforts of the local PARMEHUTU propagandists—that is, of Rugira's local 'clients'—Misago scored an unexpected victory at the polls. What happened next is unclear. After a recount of the vote, presumably at the request of the President of the Supreme Court, but in any event involving the destruction of a number of Misago's ballots, Ntabomvura was officially said to have won the elections by a majority of one vote. Misago's defeat came as a stunning blow to the PARMEHUTU leadership in Kigali. Although both men belonged to APROSOMA, Misago was from Gitarama; he belonged to a wing of APROSOMA (the so-called APROSOMA-GASINGWA) well-known for its 'closeness' to PARMEHUTU; and he had successfully courted the support of a man who, in spite of his local origins, was a dedicated PARMEHUTU supporter. In these circumstances, his defeat could only be interpreted as a defeat for PARMEHUTU. Before the arbitration of the presidency could settle the controversy, local tensions reverberated upon the Supreme Court, driving a deep wedge among its members. As President of the Supreme Court, native of Butare, and known for having been a strong APROSOMA supporter, Isidore Nzeyimana was immediately suspected by PARMEHUTU of having deliberately falsified the results of the elections. At this point, the three Vice-Presidents of the Supreme Court—Claver Ndahayo, Jacques Hazikimana and Jean Sagahutu—all three ardent supporters of PARMEHUTU, began to manoeuvre for position, taking full advantage of their political entrées to discredit their adversary. Before long, Nzeyimana was looked upon as a 'renegade' by the entire PARMEHUTU leadership.

While the Ndora controversy continued to agitate the minds of the local populations, a more serious one was about to erupt in the commune of Nyabisindu (formerly Nyanza), which further embittered relations between Nzeyimana and his colleagues and soon threatened to extend the conflict to the very heart of the party apparatus. The facts, very briefly, are as follows. Prior to the communal elections, the National Secretariat of PARMEHUTU issued instructions that no deputy should be allowed to run for office at the local level, either as burgomaster or communal councillor. One PARMEHUTU deputy, named Jean-Baptiste Utumabahutu, decided to ignore these instructions. Utumabahutu was a former subchief in Nyanza, who later became Commissioner in charge of the Refugees. His well-deserved reputation as a moderate earned him the esteem of a great many Tutsi in and around Nyanza, and, since Nyanza was still very much under Tutsi influence (if only because of the density of the local Tutsi population), his candidacy seemed a logical choice if the commune was to be 'secured' to PARMEHUTU. The president of the regional committee of PARMEHUTU, Amandin Rugira, similarly decided to overlook the instructions of the National Secretariat. He and the local prefect, Charles Karanija, agreed that Utumabahutu should be allowed to present his candidacy. The result, unfortunately, was not what they had anticipated. Not only was Utumabahutu defeated; worse still, the post of burgomaster went to a noted member of UNAR, Augustin Munyanziza, who won 5,000 votes, 2,000 more than the PARMEHUTU candidate. Of the ten communal councillors elected in the commune of Nyabisindu, six were UNAR—two of them of Tutsi extraction—and only four PARMEHUTU. The government reacted to the news with utter consternation. The regional committee of PARMEHUTU was immediately dissolved. Soon after, an ad hoc congress of PARMEHUTU was called into session to take appropriate sanctions against Rugira and Utumabahutu. Their party membership was suspended, and in September 1963 Rugira was invited to hand in his resignation as President of the National Assembly. At the same time, to placate the more intransigent elements in the party and liquidate once and for all the 'Butare clique', Isidore Nzeyimana, long suspected of having displayed regional and political loyalties incompatible with his mandate as President of the Supreme Court, was forced to resign his post. Once bitter political enemies, Nzeyimana and Rugira were now thrown into the same camp. Their regional loyalties quickly superseded their previous animosities.

By late 1963 two bitterly antagonistic factions had emerged. One, represented by Isidore Nzeyimana, Amandin Rugira and Charles Karanija—all three from the prefecture of Butare—was openly accused by the other of fomenting subversion, of trying to launch a new opposition party allegedly called NZERUKA (after the first syllables of its leaders' names): in short, of doing their best to sap the strength of PARMEHUTU. The other faction, led by Claver Ndahayo, Jacques Hakizimana and Jean Sagahutu, was known to enjoy the full support of the secretary-general of PARMEHUTU, the rotund and boisterous Calliope Mulindihabi, and took advantage of its position to launch a violent campaign of intimidation against NZERUKA. The wildest rumours, slander and suspicion were all weapons in the arsenal of Ndahayo and his acolytes. For a while the conflict seemed on the verge of deterioration into a major fight for supremacy. A temporary resurgence of racial cohesiveness was created by the abortive *inyenzi* invasion of December 1963, but this did not prove sufficient to eliminate tensions once and for all. No sooner had the threats of counter-revolution evaporated than conflict reappeared. Although Nzeyimana had already tendered his resignation as President of the Supreme Court, his successor, Fulgence Seminaga, found himself immersed in a cesspool of intrigue and double dealings. By early 1965, the situation seemed hopelessly confused as there had been further splits among the Vice-Presidents of the Supreme Court (by this time four in number).[8] Not until August of that year was the drastic surgery made necessary by this advanced state of decomposition finally performed: the four Vice-Presidents of the Supreme Court—Ndahayo, Sagahutu, Hakizimana and Sakerere—were dismissed from office and replaced by five newcomers—Donat Murego, Antoine Ntashamaje, Apollinaire Nsengyumva, Sylvestre Kamali and Aloys Munyangaju.

The significance of this seemingly inextricable imbroglio is three-fold. First, the character of the factions involved throws into sharp relief the continuing importance of personality factors in Rwanda politics. Now, as before, politics remains an affair of cliques. It involves 'notabilities' whose influence, like that of the chiefs of the ancien régime, remains highly localised, contingent as it is on the building and retention of a local clientele. Secondly, underlying these personal animosities were strong regional antagonisms. The conflict between Nzeyimana and Mulindihabi was really a contest of influence between the Butare and the Gitarama elites, the former representing the interests of APROSOMA against PARMEHUTU. But it was also a contest between different types of elites, between a moderate intelligentsia and the hard-core, far more intransigent Jacobin faction. While much of the struggle took on the aspects of an intra-party squabble, part of it mirrored the growing disaffection of the moderate intelligentsia towards the aims of the party and its leadership.

The Intellectuals versus the Establishment

In recent times a new category of intellectuals has arisen whose position in society is in many ways reminiscent of their elders' before the revolution. They feel alienated and restless. Their radical outlook betrays the grievances they harbour against the incumbents, whom they blame for their present discontents. But, unlike their elders, they operate within a different political environment, the environment of an independent political system committed to democracy and social justice. This emergent class of 'angry young men' comprises at least three distinctive categories: the primary school teachers (or moniteurs), the junior civil servants and the students. Although the nature and intensity of their grievances vary with their respective qualifications, training and statuses, they are all critical to a greater or lesser extent of the alleged complacency and self-centredness of the elites in power. They all seem at pains to reconcile the official stress placed on social justice with the wide discrepancies between their standards of living and those of government officials. Hence they are all in some degree alienated from, or repelled by, the Establishment.

The material grievances of the moniteurs were first brought to the attention of the deputies in April 1964, in the course of the debates on the budget. Commenting on the 'deplorable material conditions of the moniteurs', a deputy from Ruhengeri, Nyirimpilima, described as 'scandalous' the salaries given to these 'zealous and devoted elements', and urged the government to take immediate steps to improve their situation.[9] As was pointed out in the course of the debates, the moniteurs earn on the average 750 Rwanda francs (RF) a month (about $ (US) 7.50), a salary out of all proportion with the innumerable chores that are expected of them.[10] Deputy Nzabonimpa undoubtedly spoke for many when he declared before the National Assembly—with more than a touch of melodrama: 'Les grandes douleurs sont muettes, dit-on; mais à force d'être contenues elles risquent un jour de dégénérer en désordre.'[11] What was never mentioned in the course of the debates, however, is that the conditions were made even more anomalous by comparison with the salaries earned by certain government officials. (To cite but one example, the monthly income of the Minister of Finance, Gaspard Cyimana, is said to total approximately $1,200, roughly 172 times a moniteur's salary!) As a result, a substantial number of moniteurs have abandoned their jobs to become PARMEHUTU propagandists, on the assumption that the gifts they would receive from their political 'patrons' would probably exceed their teaching salaries.

While many of these grievances are shared by junior civil servants, their resentment is primarily focused on the alleged corruption within the government and the administration. As one of them flatly told this writer, 'the government of Kayibanda is no less guilty of corruption than the previous regime'; the only difference is that 'there is more secrecy about it than before'. Indeed, anyone familiar with the savings bank scandal, the TRAFIPRO scandal and the illegal profits in real estate made by certain ministers is inclined to agree. Gone are the days when austerity was the hallmark of public life, and when a visitor to Rwanda could comment admiringly about 'President Kayibanda's shabby clothes and patched shoes' and the fact that the presidential car was 'only a Volkswagen'.[12] After a brief spell during which the virtues of thrift and self-sacrifice were not only extolled but practised, there has been a definite trend towards 'embourgeoisement'. No longer do Kayibanda and his ministers drive Volkswagens—now they have Mercedes; no longer does Kayibanda wear 'shabby clothes and patched shoes'— assuming that his earlier sartorial style was ever followed by his ministers, the present fashions seem closer to Savile Row. In short, the gap between revolutionary austerity and post-revolutionary embourgeoisement is getting wider and wider every day, causing increasing grumbles on the part of the less affluent and less corruptible.

Yet it is chiefly among students that feelings of disillusion are most noticeable. As elsewhere in Africa, a growing number of Hutu students are in the position of unemployed intellectuals. Many have left primary school for lack of resources, financial or intellectual, and are now vainly seeking employment in urban centres. Others, despite their degrees, are denied the career opportunities to which they feel entitled. Many claim that they are being discriminated against and that Tutsi students are unduly favoured by school authorities. All this has created a climate of agitation which did not go unnoticed by certain Hutu politicians.* Some went so far as to accuse the Church of deliberately seeking to foment troubles: 'In the Diocese of Nyundo', Deputy Mberabahizi told the National Assembly in July 1965, 'Catholic-inspired movements, acting under the cover of their juridical personality, have undertaken a vast campaign to systematically politicise our youth, and this in order to cast ridicule on PARMEHUTU.'[13] The same speaker went on to call attention to the existence of an Association des Etudiants Batutsi (AEB), also in the Diocese of Nyundo, which, he said, 'was obviously supported by the local clergy' and had 'political connections'. All this, he added, 'must be examined with all due circumspection'.[14] In fact, the Church has little to do with the students' increasingly restive mood. If anything it is the Church, through its various civic action programmes and recreational centres, which has contributed most to minimise student unrest. A case in point is the Maison des Jeunes (*Urugo Rwacu*), a 'home' for actual and potential juvenile delinquents set up under the

---

* According to the party newspaper, *Urumuli rwa Demokrasi* (Light of Democracy), the students fall into the following categories: (i) 'the PARMEHUTU zealots, imbued with the ideas of 1959'; (ii) those 'who are conceited and selfish and who only seek to accumulate honours, privileges and wealth'; (iii) 'the windcocks, who have one foot in PARMEHUTU and the other in the air'; (iv) 'those whose only objective is to destroy PARMEHUTU'—from the issue published on July 3, 1966.

auspices of various Church organisations, located a few miles from Kigali.[15] Resentment of bureaucratic privileges, a vague sense of alienation, a deep-seated hatred of all things—and men—reminiscent of the ancien régime, are the principal motivations behind the present unrest and dissatisfaction.

As noted earlier, it is not only in Rwanda that students and other second generation intellectuals have risen in protest against the vested interests and reactionary tendencies of the elites in power. But in Rwanda the oppositional bias of the intellectuals is more conspicuous than in most other African states, in part because the goals the regime has set for itself in the social and economic realms are more distant. Nowhere else in Africa has there been a stronger emphasis on democracy and developmental goals; but, because of the extreme paucity of the resources available, nowhere else has the fulfilment of these objectives seemed more remote. Thus, for many of these intellectuals, the revolutionary tune has a peculiarly hollow ring to it.

THE INSTRUMENTS OF SOLIDARITY

To counteract this revolutionary deflation the republican authorities have tried to convert the party into a genuine instrument of solidarity. At the time of independence, however, it was a very inadequate tool. It was rent asunder by factionalism, and its organisational armature was still pretty much in a state of limbo. Initially, therefore, primary reliance was placed on the administrative machinery, and in particular on the prefects. Although the word 'prefect' has strong revolutionary overtones, reminiscent of the highly centralised system of administration of republican France—which, of course, explains its special appeal to the republican elites of Rwanda*—the analogy with France, as we shall see, cannot be accepted unreservedly.

The Prefects

The installation of the prefects, in January 1961, is perhaps the only genuinely insurrectionary step taken by the Hutu elites towards the Belgian trusteeship, as it was the only step for which the trust authorities

---

* As Professor René David correctly points out: 'The Rwandese attach considerable importance to the term "prefecture". The reason for this, undoubtedly, is that the word "province" carries monarchical overtones whereas prefecture reminds one of republicanism; after all, the people of Rwanda are overwhelmingly republican, and the principles of 1789 and 1848 are very much in vogue.' (Personal communication.) Professor David, of the University of Paris, was one of the experts placed at the disposal of the Rwanda authorities by the French government to help them draft their civil code.

were utterly unprepared. When, in the course of the historic meeting at Gitarama on January 28, 1961, the decision was made by the 'conspirators' to convert the administrateurs adjoints—heretofore regarded as auxiliaries to the European administrateurs de territoires (AT)—into prefects, the Residency was taken completely unawares. This, as Jean-Baptiste Rwasibo, then Minister of Interior in the provisional government, later conceded, was clearly an 'insurrectionary decision'.[16] Once the decision was made, however, the Residency had no choice but to accept it. The administration was already much too deeply committed to the cause of PARMEHUTU to make an issue of this matter.

Nonetheless, this unanticipated turn of events at once raised innumerable problems which could hardly be ignored by the Belgian authorities. The essence of the dilemma, according to one AT, was that 'the duality of allegiances resulting from the regime of internal autonomy, coupled with the equivocal character of the institutions born of the coup d'état of Gitarama, had created a conflict of jurisdiction between the Belgian administration and the Hutu politicians'.[17] Specifically, attention was drawn to 'the absence of control of the administration over the political personnel'; the existence of 'parallel structures leading to a short-circuiting of the AT's authority by the ministers'; the 'inefficiency of the administrative personnel endowed with political responsibilities (burgomasters and prefects)'; the existence of 'conflicts between the ATS and the prefects' and the 'invasion of the AT's prerogatives by certain ministries'.[18] Clearly, the most pressing of all problems was to define the prerogatives of the prefects in such a way as to minimise the possibility of jurisdictional conflicts between themselves and the ATS. Should the prefects be given all the prerogatives of the ATS? Or should they be allowed only a partial delegation of authority? Could one give all prerogatives to certain prefects and only some to others? If so, how much authority should the latter have? According to Guillaume, Deputy Commissioner to the Residency, 'some prefects were incapable of exercising administrative powers, even partially, for they had been designated on the basis of their ascendancy over the masses, that is on the basis of qualities that were not necessarily accompanied by the intellectual baggage and moral courage which one must expect of a good administrator'.[19] In the prefectures of Biumba, Kibungu and Nyanza, the office-holders were described as 'incapable of exercising even part of the prerogatives of the AT', being all 'utterly worthless'.[20] In the end, and in line with Rwasibo's advice, the formula adopted involved a good deal of reliance on precedents as well as a fair amount of pragmatism. To cite Rwasibo's own words: 'We must base ourselves on previous practices; the prefect is the principal auxiliary of the AT, as well as his

241

partner, but the AT remains the senior partner—the active guide and the one who carries ultimate responsibility.'[21] At the same time, the AT was urged to display tolerance towards the prefects, even though, as Rwasibo went on to observe, 'the distinction between "commendable tolerance" and "culpable tolerance" was at times difficult to establish'.[22]

Whether commendable or culpable, the tolerance of the administration towards the prefects turned out to be even greater than Rwasibo himself had anticipated. By April 1961 the AT was no longer 'No. 1 in the tandem', as had previously been suggested; his role was now alternatively described as comparable to that of a chef de cabinet, and an adviser. The prefect, as the Resident put it, was from then on to be regarded as the only functionary 'responsible for what is to be done and what is not to be done in his prefecture', for 'in a newly emergent country, one in which political influences are beginning to come into play, and in which the prefect cannot be immune from attacks of a political nature, one must at all cost safeguard the unity of command represented by the person invested with governmental authority. . . . The comparison of a prefecture to a Belgian province cannot be sustained, for while the prefect may not be allowed to decide everything, he must nevertheless act as a channel through which all current administrative activities are co-ordinated, and the guide who supervises all activities liable to have political consequences.'[23] In legal terms, this meant essentially three things: (i) there would be 'a general transfer to the prefects of the powers heretofore enjoyed by the ATs'; (ii) the prefect would remain the chief co-ordinator of all technical services established at the prefectoral level; (iii) the prefect would be given control over the local security and information services, and the local police detachments, the role of the trust authorities at this level now being limited to one of 'assistance and co-ordination'.[24] Thus, by April 1961, the prefects were well on the way of becoming, in the Resident's words, 'the sole executive agents in their prefecture'. Indeed, not only did they exercise virtually all the powers heretofore reserved to the ATs but they enjoyed a far greater latitude in the making of political decisions than had ever been accorded to their predecessors.

With this broad sweep of powers the prefects were in an ideal position to 'promote' integration at the local and regional levels. Yet it was not until September 1963 that presidential instructions to that effect were issued by the central government:

The responsibility of the prefect for the democratic development of the prefecture is one of the key features of the administrative apparatus of the Republic. . . . Since we must orient ourselves towards a dynamic and efficient organisation [of our resources], we must clearly abandon the old administrative structure, far too reminiscent of the feudal regime. The administration of the prefecture will therefore become gradually, yet rapidly, technical in character. The prefecture must have as its head a man who is energetic and cautious, socially-minded and realistic, educated, and with a cool sense of organisation—a man unequivocally devoted to democracy and to the majority party, a man who will aid and control the development of democracy not only on the political and administrative planes but also on the social, economic and cultural planes.[25]

In addition, special emphasis was placed on the 'particular attributions of the prefect', ranging from 'the maintenance of public order and tranquillity' and 'the requisition of armed forces whenever troubles threaten to break out', to 'the watching over of the political life and activities of political parties in the prefecture' and 'the supervision and guidance of the communes, in accordance with the electoral law'. Finally, the functions devolved upon the heads of the various functional services (police, accounting, public works, agriculture, communications, etc.) were spelled out in considerable detail. The language of the instructions suggested a conscious attempt to use the French prefectoral system as a model.* Its application to Rwanda was bound to raise serious problems, however. If there is any truth to the contention that in metropolitan France 'the prefect is continually faced with conflicting duties and loyalties, and must have unusual political tact and administrative subtlety',[26] how much more true is this of a country like Rwanda, where loyalties are necessarily more numerous and parochial, conflict more intense, and political tact and administrative subtlety the exception rather than the rule.

Because of the extensiveness of their powers the prefects were faced from the very outset with considerable opposition from the burgomasters. The latter had been in office for a longer time; most of them had already built up a political clientele among their constituents, and in some places they had their own personal militia. Moreover, they made a great play of the fact that they had been elected by their own people, while the prefects were merely agents of the central government.

* This is not altogether surprising in view of the episodic contacts which have taken place between France and Rwanda since the latter's entry into the Afro-Malagasy Union (UAM) on March 5, 1963. A conference of the UAM Ministers of Justice was held in Paris from May 2 to 4, 1963; another from May 7 to 8, 1965. It was during the first of these conferences that the Rwandese delegation asked the assistance of French experts to help in the elaboration of their legal and administrative systems.

The prefects, in short, were looked upon by the burgomasters as their natural enemies. The prefects were widely suspected of political meddling, and some were openly accused of seeking the removal from office of the burgomasters. Asked what his relations with the local prefect were like, one burgomaster gave this writer a fairly typical answer: 'The man is dangerous. He has only one thing in mind: to bump me off!' Just as illuminating are the comments of the former prefect of Kigali, Noel Mbonyabaryi, in the course of a meeting of burgomasters, held on March 13, 1964:

> Certain burgomasters distrust the prefect, as if his only concern was to sabotage their work and pick quarrels with them. The instructions you get from the prefect come from way up above, from the prefect's own superiors. You must have complete trust in them, and put them into effect without the slightest hesitation. Those of you who think that the prefect bears a grudge against you are quite wrong. The prefect has nothing but good will. He wants things to go well in his prefecture. He has no interest in creating trouble. The prefect plays no favourite. He has no preference for this or that person as long as things work satisfactorily. I am not a native of this prefecture and have no parents here. Therefore, do not think that I am trying to get rid of a burgomaster or a functionary in order to put one of my relatives into office.[27]

Similar feelings of resentment were expressed by certain deputies over what one of them described as 'the dictatorial tendencies of the prefects'.[28] The potential for conflict was especially high where feelings of localism were most in evidence, as was the case in the prefecture of Gisenyi. We are told, for example, that in this locality, in April 1961, 'one deputy reacted against the prefect by circulating a petition demanding his removal. The deputy's main argument was that the prefect had not been elected by the population. Another deputy handed in his resignation, but then opened up the frontier to the Congolese. A third falsely alleged that he was the sub-prefect.'[29] Under the circumstances one can see why the rate of casualty among prefects was higher in Gisenyi than anywhere else, with five successive appointments between 1962 and 1966. While there are many local variations on this theme, the conflict between prefects and deputies remains a standard feature of Rwanda's political scene.* Readers of Bodley may note here a curious

---

* Ample evidence of this can be found in the 1965 proceedings of the National Assembly. To cite but one example—in response to the statement by the Minister of Interior that the prefects could only be impartial, Deputy Sebapolisi observed: 'How can the Minister seriously maintain that his prefects do not

resemblance between contemporary Rwanda and the third French republic; in each case, 'instances abound of the official favours of the prefecture being shown to one . . . candidate or group at the expense of another' and of 'an adroit prefect making himself a position which, if it fall short of that of grand elector . . . is one of commanding influence at election time'.[30]

However, to generalise about the effectiveness of the Rwandese prefectoral system as an instrument of solidarity is difficult, because of the widely different conditions prevailing from one locality to the next, and the similarly wide difference in the personal qualifications of the prefects. But if one is to trust the record, the situation seems to leave considerable room for improvement. The real dilemma confronting the prefects is that they cannot hope to rule effectively without taking sides. To remain neutral in a situation of cut-throat competition is often the safest policy; but, in Rwanda, this is seldom so. To remain neutral is, for a prefect, tantamount to exposing himself to criticisms from all sides. In most cases the prefects have become full participants in the game of local politics, a game which some have played with consummate skill, making sure all along that they were on the 'right' side. There have been cases where their calculations proved completely mistaken— for instance, Amandin Rugira's decision to back the wrong candidate during the communal elections of 1963, a move which cost him his job as prefect and also led to his suspension from the party. By and large, however, the prefects owed their political survival to their skill at playing one group off against the other. The result, as one might expect, has not been to eliminate localism but rather the opposite.

Since the prefects' presumed loyalty to the central government proved insufficient to ensure political solidarity, the next logical step was to bring the party into the picture. But instead of promoting harmony among local officials, the result has been to inject yet another element of conflict into an already very tense situation.

The Party

'Our political organisation', the President of the National Assembly, Anastase Makuza, told this writer in 1964, 'draws its inspiration from the errors of the feudal system. Abuses of authority had to disappear.

---

abuse their authority while knowing full well that in the Mukingo commune the prefect of Ruhengeri has imposed a burgomaster of his choice upon the population, and that the latter subsequently rejected him? If one only had a way of controlling the actions of the prefects some flagrant abuses would undoubtedly be brought to light.' *Assemblée Nationale, Document No. 216*, July 23, 1965, p. 1185.

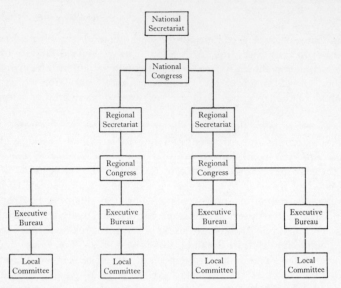

Table 8.1 Formal Organisational Chart of MDR-PARMEHUTU

1. *National Organisation*

   (a) *National Secretariat:* Composed of one secretary-general and seven deputy secretaries-general elected from a list of candidates drawn up by the regional secretariats; meets at least once every three months.

   (b) *National Congress:* Includes all members of the regional secretariats and of the national secretariat; elects a president from a list of three candidates drawn up by the national secretariat; the president is elected for a seven-year term; meets at least once a year and as often as the circumstances require.

2. *Regional Organisation*

   (a) *Regional Secretariat:* One in each prefecture; composed of all the communal 'responsables' of the prefecture; headed by a three man executive (a regional secretary, a deputy regional secretary and a treasurer); meets at least once every three months.

   (b) *Regional Congress:* Composed of all the members of the local committees included in the prefecture; headed by a regional secretary; meets at least once a year.

3. *Local Organisation*

   (a) *Executive Bureau:* One in each commune; composed of three members (a 'responsable', a 'rapporteur' and a treasurer); meets at least once every two months.

   (b) *Local Committees:* One in each commune; composed of all PAR-MEHUTU communal councillors plus an equal number of PARMEHUTU propagandists appointed by the regional secretariat; meets at least once every two months.

In the past, the accumulation of mandates in the hands of the chiefs led to innumerable abuses. The chief was a dictator. We do not want this to happen again. This is why our party watches over the functioning of the administration at all levels; this is why we have PARMEHUTU officials in each commune; this is why we have decided to circumscribe the authority of elected officials by the authority of party officials.' In line with these principles an attempt was made in late 1963 to bring under the same roof the communal councillors and the PARMEHUTU propagandists and to convert the prefects into regional party officials. From then on the prefects were ipso facto entrusted with the functions of regional secretaries of PARMEHUTU; and the burgomasters were made in every case members of the local PARMEHUTU committees, though not necessarily members of the local bureau.

The general organisation pattern outlined in Table 8.1 shows two distinctive trends. There has been a deliberate effort to extend the ramifications of the party to each level of the administrative hierarchy, so as to use it as an 'organisational weapon' for moulding the loyalties of the citizens; to further facilitate this task, the communal and prefectoral administrations were brought directly into the fold of the party. At each level of the governmental structure a kind of interlocking directorate was set up in order to achieve a genuine symbiosis of the political and administrative superstructures.

All this, of course, is pure theory. In practice the picture is not nearly as neat as one might infer from Table 8.1. The party officials almost everywhere challenged the authority of popularly elected officials (e.g. deputies and burgomasters) or vice versa, and considerable friction has arisen.

Nowhere have tensions been more prevalent—and violent—than between burgomasters and propagandists. As they saw themselves suddenly surrounded by swarms of PARMEHUTU zealots who told them what to do and what not to do, while secretly trying to build up a power base of their own, the burgomasters reacted vehemently. To be sure, there were notable exceptions, as in the commune of Mbago, in the prefecture of Ruhengeri, where, according to the burgomaster, 'everything was fine', and where 'the burgomaster, the communal councillors and the population got along beautifully with each other'.[31] Elsewhere, however, things did not go nearly as well. 'The main difficulty in my commune', said the burgomaster of Shyorongi, in February 1964, 'is that the population rejects the propagandists, accusing them of not having been elected regularly.' 'The population of my commune', added the local deputy, 'does not get along with the propagandists.' 'In my commune there is a propagandist with whom I do not get along at all', echoed the burgomaster of Gahengeri; 'his name is Sezikeze. He is absolutely unbearable. He never got along with any of the burgo-masters of this commune. With my predecessor things were even worse. He says I am a liar. The population hates him. All this because of his thirst for power; he wants at all cost to become burgomaster. He once inflicted a wound to himself and then went around saying I had struck him.'[32]

In some places conflicts between the burgomasters and the propagan-dists were further complicated by the presence of antagonisms among their constituents. The situation existing in the commune of Kambe, in February 1964, illustrates the point: 'There are in my commune several groups who are against me', said the burgomaster; 'first the UNAR-ists, understandably; then there are the people who engage in regionalist propaganda, accusing me of being an alien in the commune; finally there are those who ran for office [during the 1963 elections] on indi-vidual lists, who failed to be elected and subsequently turned against me.'[33] In such cases, the propagandists generally tried to exploit divi-sions to enhance their stature. This, in fact, is precisely what happened in the commune of Rubungo, where 'grave difficulties' were reported, apparently originating from the fact that at the time of the communal elections 'the party propagandists were divided by jealousies, each calling each other *Nkundabera*,* etc'. At that point, however, 'the regional secretariat intervened and the danger was averted'.[34]

While the regional secretariats did indeed intervene on many occa-sions, these moves were not always successful—least of all when, as seems to have happened in the prefecture of Butare in 1963, the mem-bers of the regional secretariat were themselves at daggers drawn over specific policy issues. The prefects, of course, had considerable powers: as prefects they enjoyed powers of tutelage over the communes and the decisions made at that level; and as regional secretaries of PARMEHUTU they had almost unlimited control over party activities in the prefec-tures. Moreover, they made full use of the 'réunions de cadres' (one of the most useful legacies of Belgian rule) to promote harmony between the burgomasters and the propagandists.† Sometimes they dealt with equal harshness with either group, as they deemed fit. But a cursory glance at the proceedings of the 'réunions de cadres' shows there was little they could do to eliminate the fundamental sources of disharmony. Caught in the vice of the local power structure, they had no alternative

* Literally, 'I like the whites', from *gukunda*, 'to like', and *abera*, 'the whites'; by extension, 'the friends of the Europeans'.

† The 'réunions de cadres' were attended by all the burgomasters of the pre-fecture, the prefect, the sub-prefect and the local deputies.

but to play the balance-of-power game as best they could. They seldom tried to alter the rules, only the outcome.

When dissensions finally emerged at the top, the entire party machinery suddenly threatened to collapse, and, because of the repercussions at the local level, not only the party machinery but the communal and prefectoral administrations were endangered. At this point the chief preoccupation of the prefects was to avoid being caught up in the power struggle that went on in the higher reaches of the party hierarchy.

Although tensions had long been apparent among certain members of the National Secretariat, these did not come into the open until September 1965, in the weeks immediately preceding the legislative elections. The crisis that was about to rack PARMEHUTU finds its origins, like many others, in an electoral dispute. The personalities involved were the corpulent and devious Calliope Mulindihabi, secretary-general of PARMEHUTU, and the frail-looking, Tutsi-like Jean-Baptiste Rwasibo, leading member of the National Secretariat. Both had come up the political ladder as 'chefs intérimaires'; they both won their spurs as two of the most vocal opponents of the ancien régime; and they both came from the same commune—Mushubati, in the prefecture of Gitarama— which explains their subsequent mutual antagonisms. Since they were both competing for the same electorate, they naturally eyed each other with considerable suspicion, all the more so as the burgomaster of Mushubati, Rwagahilima, was Rwasibo's younger brother and could presumably be expected to use his influence to favour Rwasibo at the polls. Ultimately, they each won a seat in the National Assembly, but the mere fact that Rwasibo received almost 30,000 more votes was taken as a personal affront by Mulindihabi. And since Rwasibo alone was thought responsible for this setback, Rwasibo would have to expiate his sin. In the best tradition of Tutsi politics, Mulindihabi decided to resort to poison; and, in a move similarly reminiscent of the Tutsi ways, he decided to act by proxy. He secretly enjoined Rwasibo's 'boy' to administer the poison; in return for his deed, the 'boy' was promised a brand new bicycle. At the last minute, however, Rwasibo's servant wavered. He remorsefully disclosed the plot to his master and gave him the poison (later identified by a local laboratory as strychnine). When the news of the aborted plot reached the National Secretariat of PARMEHUTU, it provoked the commotion that one can imagine. Before long, 'l'affaire du poison' became a prime topic of conversation in the corridors of the National Assembly, and eventually on the hills as well. Rwasibo and two other leading members of the National Secretariat, Anastase Makuza and Callixte Habamenshi, handed in their resignations

249

as national secretaries. In the meantime, the prefect of Gitarama, Servilien Karyango, was transferred to Cyangugu and demoted to the rank of sub-prefect, presumably because of his support for Rwasibo. The only way out of the impasse would have been to call a national congress of PARMEHUTU. Mulindihabi alone, as secretary-general of the party, could initiate such a procedure, and he carefully avoided doing so as he realised that it would have been tantamount to signing his death warrant as 'party boss'. Since President Kayibanda refused to commit himself one way or the other, for personal and political reasons, nothing was done to resolve the crisis.

Whatever cohesion once existed within the party had now evaporated. In theory, of course, the party never ceased to exist, but it survived only on paper. The state of suspended animation then afflicting PARMEHUTU was eloquently symbolised by the mortuary-like atmosphere, in August 1966, of the party headquarters, high on a hill overlooking the road to Gitarama, less than a mile from the mission station of Kabgaye. The only defenders left at that time were a 17-year old youth and a somnolent tomcat. The youngster, who introduced himself as Sigisbert Hategekimana, turned out to be the 'responsable' of the National Executive Bureau. His principal occupation at the time was the drafting of what he modestly referred to as a 'little project'; but judging from the items on the agenda for it, the tasks that lay ahead were not quite as picayune as the title seemed to suggest: 'Considering that the activities of the bureau of the PARMEHUTU are more or less paralysed, the only remedy is: (i) to recruit a completely new personnel—redacteur, secretary, accountant, typist; (ii) to delineate the functions of each service: each official has to mind his own business; (iii) to appoint a chef de service who will be recognised as such by the entire personnel; (iv) to prepare a programme of visits to the regional secretariats'.[35] What was involved here was actually nothing less than the reconstruction of the central party machinery.

Not until October 1966 was a concerted effort made to breathe new life into the party, as part of a more general counter-offensive against alleged threats of internal subversion—against 'all public or secret activities aiming at disintegrating constructive social groupings and legally established political institutions, or at simply sowing confusion and non-collaboration among those who are responsible for the democratic development of the nation'.[36] Now began a period of fraternalism and intransigence—fraternalism among the elect, intransigence towards the rest. Whether this new mood of Jacobin militancy can bring about the 'total reconversion' it seeks will be discussed next. But first something must be said of yet another instrument through which a partial reconversion of society has been attempted: the co-operative movement associated with the Coopérative Travail, Fidelité, Progrès (TRAFIPRO).

TRAFIPRO

The movement had its origins in 1950, when a group of moniteurs of the Kabgaye region decided to pool their meagre resources to set up a canteen in one of the buildings the mission had set aside for that purpose. The idea of transforming the canteen into a co-operative came from Father Pien, who drafted the statutes of TRAFIPRO and secured the approval of the Residency in November 1955. It was not until December 1956 that TRAFIPRO began its commercial activities, with the active collaboration of Father Pien, and the blessings of Mgr Perraudin. Judging from the circumstances of its foundation, the identity of its managers and the nature of its activities, TRAFIPRO was closely tied in with, and subject to the control of, PARMEHUTU. In his capacity as chairman of the board of directors, President Kayibanda became, as he himself put it, 'one of its initiators and first promoters'.[37] Despite or because of this, between 1956 and 1966 TRAFIPRO saw its commercial activities expand on a national scale. Its main assets in 1956 consisted of three general stores, all in the vicinity of Nyanza and Gitarama, and its membership of less than a hundred. Ten years later, a total of 27 branch stores were owned and operated by TRAFIPRO and its membership had risen to 70,000. No less impressive has been the impact of the co-operative in the social and political realms. While much remains to be done to make it a 'going concern', even at this stage TRAFIPRO can be described as one of the most imaginative and fruitful experiments attempted anywhere in sub-Saharan Africa.

Certainly, the harnessing of the co-operative movement to PARMEHUTU explains its popularity among the rural masses; but it also accounts for some of its shortcomings. Because so much of the money raised by the co-operative was in fact spent on the financing of political activities, its early development was slow and arduous. An even greater handicap was the continuing misuse and misappropriation of these funds by some of its managers, a fact which lends considerable justification to the often-heard quip 'TRAFIPRO Profitera'. No one profited more from the co-operative than Calliope Mulindihabi during the three years that he held the post of director-general of TRAFIPRO (1960–63): hundreds of thousands of francs are said to have been diverted by Mulindihabi for his personal use. So high was the level of corruption and incompetence that President Kayibanda decided to take advantage of his trip to Europe, in October 1962, to explore with representatives of the Swiss government the possibility of bolstering the co-operative, financially and otherwise.

These exploratory talks led in 1963 to the signature of a bilateral technical assistance programme providing for the extension by Switzerland of an annual loan of one million Swiss francs for the next ten years, to be spent exclusively on the development of the co-operative activities; in addition a team of experts in co-operative development were placed at the disposal of the Rwanda authorities by the Swiss government. At about the same time Mulindihabi handed the chairmanship of the board of directors (which he had inherited from Kayibanda in 1960) to Max Nyinzima, a long-time PARMEHUTU militant and one of the founders of the co-operative. The actual management, however, was placed in the hands of a Swiss citizen, R. Rebord. A man of boundless energy, properly tactful, and with a long experience of the Swiss co-operative movement as former director of the Coopératives de Neuchatel, Rebord is justly considered to have done a first rate job during his 'term of office' in Rwanda. Judging from the past record of the Swiss technical assistance programme, one cannot escape the conclusion that much of Rwanda's future evolution will depend on how much external aid is funnelled into the activities of TRAFIPRO, and for how long.

But what, exactly, is TRAFIPRO? Essentially, a consumers' and producers' co-operative. Approximately 20 per cent of the total production of coffee is bought and exported by TRAFIPRO. It imports a variety of consumer goods—oil, soap, salt, milk, matches, lamps, shirts, shoes, toothpaste, ballpoint pens, etc.—which are then sold at fixed prices throughout the country in each of the co-operative stores. During the coffee harvest, eighteen Mercedes trucks—all owned by the co-operative—collect coffee beans from individual producers at each of the 70 purchasing centres, and on their return trips to Rwanda deliver imported commodities to each of the 27 branches. Currently the co-operative has an invested capital of about 15 million Belgian francs, and an operating capital of about 3 million. The margin of its benefits for 1965— 8 million Belgian francs ($ US 160,000)—provides an eloquent testimony of its success as an economic venture.

TRAFIPRO is also an experiment in democracy, albeit a very timid one for the time being. Although the board of directors functions as a fairly autonomous body—except for the technical supervision of its European manager—the local executive committees are in theory directly responsible to the local assemblies. Each branch has its own assembly, composed of all the local co-operative members, and its own local committees of five, all elected by the assembly. The head of a branch is chosen from among the members of the local committee. Commenting upon the political functions of these local assemblies, the European manager of TRAFIPRO once drew this writer's attention to their resemblance to the

Swiss 'landsgemeinde', 'each', he said, 'representing a form of direct democracy'. Even though the comparison may seem unduly far-fetched, there can be little doubt that if democracy ever becomes a reality among the people of Rwanda this will be due to no small extent to the structures of accountability set up via TRAFIPRO—and also to the persistent efforts of certain Swiss advisers to acquaint the TRAFIPRO cadres with the meaning and principles of direct democracy.

Passing reference must be made in this connection to the Ecole TRAFIPRO in Gitarama, at present manned by twelve Swiss experts. Although its curriculum is primarily vocational in character, aiming at providing technical training for future accountants, secretaries, typists and so forth, its influence is by no means limited to the inculcation of technical skills. Swiss journalists have also been sent to Rwanda to help train Rwandese journalists associated with the TRAFIPRO newspaper. Indeed, nowhere is the Swiss presence more creditably felt than in the pages of the weekly newspaper *Trafipro*, written in French and Kinyarwanda. The relatively high standards of the editorials, the reportorial skills of its contributors, and the usually inspiring but inevitably hortatory column written by the European director of the co-operative have made *Trafipro* one of the most widely read and influential newspapers in Rwanda. In sum, the development of co-operative institutions, along with the political, educational and social transformations which they entail, may well bring Rwanda into the orbit of modern societies. But these are distant perspectives.

One can point to a good many tangible economic benefits for the rural masses, the training of technical cadres, the increased participation of the peasantry in the economy of the country, the emergence of a 'co-operative consciousness' and the beginning of 'a genuine decolonisation of the national economy'.[38] Yet, on the other hand, one can also point to the continuing existence of corrupt practices among certain TRAFIPRO officials, the lack of requisite skills and aptitudes to run the branches efficiently, and a vague sense of discouragement among certain Swiss experts when they find that their advice is frequently over-ruled at the local level. But by far the most serious difficulty is that TRAFIPRO still has to be accepted as a legitimate institution by certain politicians, and in particular by northern politicians. The economic wealth accumulated by the *bakonde* politicians as a result of the gifts they receive from their landed clientele has already been discussed; some of them have become prosperous independent traders, a nascent middle-class of entrepreneurs in their respective prefectures. Hence, many take a dim view of TRAFIPRO, accusing its leaders of trying to perpetuate the paternalism and authoritarianism of the old days; some have described the

253

co-operative as 'useless for society', as 'guilty of abuses and of exercising a de facto monopoly' over commercial activities; at one point certain deputies violently attacked the government for concluding a technical assistance agreement with Switzerland without first seeking the advice of the National Assembly.[39] Much of this hostility is a reflection of personal animus against the Gitarama politicians, who are accused of using the co-operative for their own political ends. It is one of the ironies of the co-operative movement that, while avowedly committed to the promotion of republican unity through economic democracy, it has become associated with one of the most divisive issues in contemporary Rwanda.

Clearly, the recurring disputes between *bakonde* and *bagererwa*, between PARMEHUTU militants and APROSOMA 'turncoats', between second generation intellectuals and the first batch of revolutionaries, all seem short of the original goals propounded for the republican revolution. This does not mean that the revolution has lost its momentum. Today there are many signs that a 'fresh start' is being attempted, one which will presumably lead to the replacement of the old revolutionary machine by a new one, bristling with zeal and revolutionary fervour. To these developments we must now turn our attention.

THE JACOBIN STRAND

'PARMEHUTU has again gathered its strength; a new blood flows in its veins, this very blood which the enemies of national progress, blinded with ambition, were sucking away like leeches. Its experience of previous divisions has forced our party to redouble its vigilance, and to work more efficiently towards the promotion of the interests of the masses.'[40] These are not the words of a Robespierre or a Saint-Just but of a minor PARMEHUTU official describing the political climate of Rwanda in April 1967. To speak of a 'Jacobin strand' to describe this new revolutionary mood is perhaps an abuse of language. After all, the element of revolutionary zeal in Rwanda is of rather small dimensions compared to that which poured from the Montagne in 1793; the control of the revolutionary apparatus over the country seems almost non-existent compared to that exercised by the Jacobin clubs; and the turgid rhetoric regularly spewed forth by the old party hacks cannot be compared with the fiery eloquence of a Camille Desmoulins or a Danton. Yet there are other aspects of the Rwandese political scene which need to be considered.

Like the Jacobins of 1793, the die-hard republicans of Rwanda are bent upon regenerating their society from top to bottom. This is to be a political, social and moral regeneration, aiming at a complete break with the past. The emphasis is placed overwhelmingly on discipline and secularism. The ultimate aim, of course, is the consolidation of the republic, but what really constitutes the republic remains unclear. Republican ideals are couched in the language of Saint-Just: 'What constitutes the republic is the destruction of everything that is opposed to it.'[41] For the Rwandese Jacobins, democracy is defined in a similarly negative fashion, meaning not so much government by consent as the eradication of dissent. More concretely, looking back from the beginning of the revolution to the present we perceive at least four distinctive phenomena, all typical of the Jacobin outlook: (i) a reign of terror; (ii) a reign of virtue; (iii) a trend towards secularism; and (iv) a trend towards increasing political centralisation and discipline.

Just as the threat of foreign intervention made the French revolution swerve to the left, resulting in the Terror, it was the fear of an impending attack by the *inyenzi* which led to the blood-stained excesses of December 1963 and January 1964. There is no need here to dwell at further length on the incredible ferocity with which droves of innocent Tutsi were massacred in the weeks following the Bugesera invasion, but it is worth pointing out in passing some of the parallels with the historic Jacobin Terror. The term Terror would seem to apply even more pertinently to Rwanda, from the point of view of numbers killed; indeed, in proportion to the total population of Rwanda, the 10–12,000 people slain by the Hutu convey an image of hysterical bloodlust infinitely more frightening than the 17,000 official executions carried out during the fourteen months of the French Terror. There is another parallel in the general 'inefficiency' of governmental authorities; for if, as Crane Brinton asserts, the French Terror 'was no steady and efficient rule from above as in an army or in Sparta, but a state of suspense and fear, a dissolution of the sober little uniformities of the provincial life', this was even more true of the Rwandese Terror. Describing the semi-anarchic conditions that prevailed in certain localities, the Minister of Interior, Balthazar Bicamumpaka, stated, on February 12, 1964: 'I deplore the attitude adopted by certain burgomasters. Some got carried away and took advantage of the situation to settle personal scores with their enemies or even totally innocent people.' In the commune of Kiyovu, one burgomaster reported: 'The population no longer has any respect for anything or anyone. People are arrested arbitrarily, on the grounds that they may be assisting the *inyenzi*. Cows are stolen.' In the commune of Kombe, a state of 'complete anarchy' was reported by the burgomaster: 'There are individuals, other than the burgomaster or the communal councillors, who have taken the law into their hands. They run everything in the commune. The burgomaster has been overtaken by events. People are dying, victims of acts of banditry. Yesterday seven persons were killed. In some places the accountant does what he wants; the secretary likewise; and also the police. Recently I saw a group of about fifty men go to a widow's plot and take her three cows away.'[42] As has already been noted, violence served as an outlet for the personal grievances, animosities and political ambitions of petty officials; and just as the disposition of the lands of the émigrés in France gave the Jacobins a choice opportunity to reinforce their waning popularity among the landless masses, in Rwanda the distribution of the lands owned by the Tutsi (émigrés as well as residents) enabled these officials to acquire a solid clientele among the peasant masses. A third parallel lies in the over-riding concern with political orthodoxy apparent in each manifestation. As in France in 1793, the Rwandese Terror was 'justified' by the existence of external threats to the republic, but in time internal opposition to the regime became so closely identified with the external menace as to make them almost indistinguishable. This is why, for example, various Hutu politicians with Tutsi wives—Anastase Makuza, Callixte Habamenshi, Jean-Baptiste Rwasibo, among others— were once suspected of subversion by their opponents. And this is why, today, 'every public or secret activity aiming at the destruction of constructive social groupings' tends to be regarded by the PARMEHUTU as evidence of subversion. Orthodoxy, in short, has been made to appear a sine qua non of national survival.

Virtue is no less essential; in fact it is the necessary adjunct of orthodoxy. 'Epuration' for the PARMEHUTU blowhards means really two things —'purification' and 'purge', the synthesis of the two being the achievement of virtue. One is reminded of Professor Apter's comments on the role of 'political religion' in what he refers to as 'the mobilization system', a type of polity which could just as well be described as 'the Jacobin system': 'The nations with political religions regard themselves as being without sin. This feeling stems from the notion of rebirth, that is, of new political units rising out of revolution and/or colonial status, with all the purity of the newborn.'[43] Echoes of this are found in official pronouncements as well as in the constitution: 'PARMEHUTU believes in the existence of an immortal soul'; 'Polygamy is forbidden'; and chapter IV, dealing with 'Religion and Religious Communities', warns that 'all Communist activities and propaganda are forbidden'.[44] But it is mainly in the realm of social values that virtue finds expression. Organised asceticism is regarded as the principal agent of moral redemption. Among the social rules which the party seeks to inculcate in the minds of its followers are 'devotion to the popular masses, austerity, personal and collective discipline, simplicity in everyday life and a constant vigilance over the ills of embourgeoisement'.[45] Like the French revolution, the Rwandese revolution has been invested with a puritanical quality that makes it all-encompassing and holy.*

Insistence on virtue also serves a practical purpose, and in recent times the enforcement of revolutionary ethics has become a formidable weapon in the arsenal of the republicans. If so far the results have not been too impressive, the methods are nonetheless significant. From the long and fiery parliamentary debates on the question of polygamy one can detect a curious combination of political subtlety and moral intransigence. Though declared unconstitutional since 1962, polygamy is still a common practice among many Rwandese politicians. Unlike concubinage, which is even more widespread, polygamy is inseparable from the socio-economic conditions prevailing in the north. It is a normal corollary of rights over the land. To have many wives, for these *bakonde*, is not only a mark of prestige—one which the Tutsi exploited with great skill, by offering them Tutsi wives to flatter their ego—but an economic necessity. As one of them explained to this writer, 'our wives look after our clients; they are expected to serve beer to our friends and clients, and to see to it that everybody is well-treated'.

If so, one can appreciate the dismay of *bakonde* politicians upon discovering that article 26 of the 1965 electoral law disqualified from seeking public office' people engaged in polygamy or concubinage'. The whole drift of the discussion that followed in the National Assembly seemed to confirm the tongue-in-cheek remark of the President of the National Assembly: 'The interference of the weaker sex with the destinies of mankind is a typical phenomenon of our times. History tells us that a woman—Eve—was the origin of Man's downfall. . . .'[46] In this case, however, as one deputy pointed out, the interference of the weaker sex in local politics was not merely 'a matter of sentiment', for 'in the old days polygamy served genuine social needs, and those who practised it also had considerable prestige'.[47] The irony of it all, said one *bakonde*, 'is that polygamy is being attacked by people who are themselves sons of polygamists. Why, then, should they disown the past which made them

* An interesting indication of the stress on puritanical values is found in the provisions of article 4 of the 1964 fiscal law, which sets the per capita tax on prostitutes at 6,000 Rwandese francs ($US 60.00), i.e. RF 5,600 above the normal rate. As one deputy observed: 'The objectives of this law are not only fiscal but social, insofar as it aims at eliminating prostitution. The proposed rate is perfectly suitable, for pleasure must be paid for.' Another deputy found this amount 'puny', considering that 'some of these prostitutes earn as much as RF 1,000 at a time, while others insist on being paid in hard currencies. Clearly, we should be pitiless with women of easy virtue who bring corruption into our society.' See *Assemblée Nationale, Document No. 161*, April 16, 1964, pp. 306 ff.

what they are?'[48] Although the issue, as another pointed out, should under no circumstances have been exploited by politicians 'for the purpose of serving the interests of their friends', this is precisely what it boiled down to.[49] The crusade against polygamy seemed to have been systematically planned and orchestrated by the Gitarama politicians to rid the regime of northern elements, which were widely regarded as 'traitors to the cause of republicanism'. Only after a long and heated discussion was a compromise finally hammered out which made the provisions of the electoral law retroactive only from the point when the constitution was adopted, a solution which, as someone said of hypocrisy, seemed like the homage that vice paid to virtue.

The third and by far the most perplexing aspect of the Jacobin offensive is the current trend towards secularism. The fashioning of a revolutionary gospel elevated to the rank of a secular religion is of course typical of most revolutionary upheavals; it is but the normal consequence of the devaluation of traditional ethics which usually accompanies attempts at national rebirth. In the context of Rwanda, however, this drive towards secularisation is doubly anomalous: not only is it directed against the one institution from which the revolutionaries drew their greatest support, but the men who were responsible for this initiative were precisely those whose connections with the Church had been the most intimate.

Thus one of the most burning controversies in contemporary Rwanda concerns the relationship between church and state. The issue came to a head in 1966, with the passage of the law of August 27 on national education. There is no room in this book for a detailed analysis of its 92 articles, most of them couched in a rather technical language.[50] Its key provisions, however, are as follows: (i) all school buildings constructed with state subsidies prior to the promulgation of the law on national education are ipso facto regarded as property of the state (art. 19); (ii) the hiring and firing of the lay and religious personnel of all subsidised private schools is supervised and controlled by the state (art. 54, 55); (iii) the admission, promotion and expulsion of students are no longer subject to the exclusive control of the school authorities (art. 47, 49, 51); (iv) the choice of textbooks and the content of the curriculum are no longer subject to the sole jurisdiction of the school authorities (art. 22). The aim, in short, is to bring the whole private (i.e. overwhelmingly Catholic) educational system of Rwanda directly under the control of the state—and since all existing schools (with the exception of three) are subsidised private schools, to secularise virtually the entire school system.

Predictably, the reaction of the Church was one of profound dismay.

On September 7, 1966, the bishops of Rwanda issued a pastoral letter reminding the government of the terms of a previous convention which, they said, could not be over-ruled unilaterally; furthermore, to national-ise in this fashion the property of the Church was contrary to article 23 of the constitution.[51] The ire of the Church was forcefully conveyed in the editorial which appeared in the October issue of *Kimanyateka*,* then very much under the influence of the European clergy: 'The rep-resentatives of subsidised private schools do not wish to become servants of the state. The *bugaragu* [clientage] is dead! They only wish to be the servants of your country, the servants of your children. Let there be no dictatorship in the schools of a country which praises liberty and democracy!'[52] A few days later, on October 23, PARMEHUTU circulated a manifesto in Kinyarwanda which bitterly condemned the position of the Church on this and other issues, pointing out that the law of August 27, 1966, was *not*, despite the allegations of the Church to the contrary, unconstitutional. The only aim of the Church, said the manifesto, was to propagate rumours (*gusopanya*) to discredit the policies of the govern-ment; in addition, the Church was openly condemned for its past neglect of the Hutu masses in the field of education, a state of affairs said to be responsible for the current dearth of competent administrative cadres.[53] The response of the Church, though presented as an objective 'mise au point', added new fuel to the controversy.[54] Typical of the present atti-tude of PARMEHUTU officials are the comments of one of the editors of the party newspaper, *Urumuli rwa Demokrasi*: 'The Church has never stopped discriminating against the Hutu. Its policy has never changed. Despite the national education law, the ecclesiastical authorities con-tinue to practise discrimination, do their best to incite the students to revolt, and create conflicts and misunderstandings between Hutu and Tutsi students—and all this to discredit the party and the government.'[55] Only if one remembers the unstinting support once accorded by the Church to the Hutu elites, its unflinching devotion to the cause of the revolution, its relentless efforts to diffuse and legitimise the aims of PARMEHUTU, can one grasp the cruel irony of the present situation.

But why this sudden transformation, this overturning of alliances? The reasons are social and political. It is not so much the Church as an institution which is being regarded as an enemy (as was the case in France during and after the revolution) as a particular segment of the clergy—the Tutsi clergy. It is worth remembering that the vast majority of the indigenous clergy, including some of those in control of the

---

* As a result of its continuing vigorous criticisms of governmental policies *Kimanyateka* ceased publication in May 1968, and its managing editor, Father Maida, was 'repatriated' to Belgium.

'commanding heights' of the Church hierarchy, are of Tutsi origins. Of the four bishops at present officiating in Rwanda, two are Tutsi, one is European (Mgr Perraudin), and the fourth is Hutu (Mgr Sibomana). To make things even worse, one of the Tutsi bishops (Mgr Gahamanyi) is the brother of a leading counter-revolutionary, former chief Michel Kayihura. During the revolution, the Tutsi clergy was widely suspected of UNAR sympathies, and some of its members did in fact rally to the cause of monarchy. This led to some very ungainly incidents. In September 1962, for example, following a search conducted by security officers in the diocese of Nyundo, one Tutsi priest suspected of harbouring pro-UNAR sentiments was charged with moral turpitude by an official and denounced to his European superiors as guilty of infamous behaviour, which in turn caused the Vatican to send a jury of inquest to Rwanda.* Tension between the Tutsi clergy and the republican authorities persisted long after the affair was settled, and to this day Tutsi priests continue to bear the stigma of UNAR sympathisers.

In recent times, however, the race issue has gone beyond the realm of party politics to become inextricably bound up with the school issue. As enrolment figures in primary and secondary schools continued to show a steady majority of Tutsi, with this majority reaching close to 90 per cent at the Université Nationale du Rwanda (UNR) in Butare, some school authorities were openly suspected of racial favouritism. This is unlikely to be true. The overwhelming majority of Tutsi students at the UNR is the natural consequence of *previous* discrimination—a situation reminiscent of the handicaps currently faced by many American Negroes seeking higher education. Moreover, in view of the very different patterns of socialisation affecting the Hutu, in view of their long consciousness of themselves as an inherently inferior people and of the psychological blocks thereby created, one can see why the Tutsi should fare better, on the whole, than the Hutu, and this at every stage of the academic cursus honorum. These arguments, however, smack of humbug to most republicans and are unlikely to receive much credence in official spheres.

* This move, initiated by the European Bishop of Kabgaye, Mgr Perraudin, occurred after the seizure by the Rwandese Security of the priest's personal diary. In it, the priest described how he nearly succumbed to the temptations of the flesh. After a preliminary investigation by the Bishop of Orléans, Mgr Riobé, the decision was made to grant the priest an extended 'leave of absence'. This decision, however, was reversed at the last minute by Mgr Bigirumwami, the Tutsi Bishop of Nyundo, after rumour had it that this 'punishment' constituted a proof of the priest's subversive activities, that he had been condemned by the Vatican as a heretic and that, consequently, President Kayibanda had decided to send him into exile. At this point the matter was laid to rest.

However important a part it may have played in shaping the outlook of certain PARMEHUTU officials, race is not the only factor behind the controversy. The current trend towards secularisation is part of a general process which can best be described by the French expression 'la levée des hypothèques', literally 'lifting the mortgages'. The political institutions of Rwanda had, in a sense, been 'mortgaged' by the Church by virtue of its past contribution to the revolution. While some Hutu privately acknowledge their debt to the Catholic Church, others find this indebtedness very burdensome, as it implies political obligations which they are not always prepared to accept. Indeed, on some occasions the advice proffered by the Church on specific policy issues seems to have been deeply resented by certain PARMEHUTU officials, including President Kayibanda,* for in so doing the Church gave the impression that it was trying to prolong its residual tutelage over the political life of the country. As long as it served the interests of the revolutionaries the tutelage of the Church was welcome, but it came to be viewed not as a prop but as an irritant once the revolution was consummated. The logic of the revolution made the liquidation of this once useful relationship a matter of necessity. One wonders whether the Church was viewed by the republican elites only as a convenient instrument for the realisation of a concrete political objective; if so, one can see why, once the objective was attained, the Church lost both its instrumental value and institutional standing.

Whatever aura of prestige and veneration once surrounded the Church has now rubbed off on the party. 'To impress upon all the strata of society a social and political life which draws its inspiration from democratic principles', once a key function of the Church, is now a formal prerogative of the party.[56] Socially, this means that the party alone has the right to promote 'the integral emancipation of the labouring and peasant masses from ignorance, poverty and complexes'; politically, that only the party may 'exercise control over public policies concerning the interests of the people, the recruitment of militants, the training of leaders at all levels, the control of administrative cadres with a view to developing among them honesty, initiative, discipline, efficiency'.[57]

---

* For example, after the troubles of January and February 1964, certain representatives of the Church, acting jointly with a Swiss close to President Kayibanda, drafted an official statement expressing regret over the abuses that took place during the repression. The statement, intended to be read publicly by Kayibanda, was flatly rejected by him on the grounds that the political circumstances left him no choice but to absolve the culprits. According to reliable sources, the initiative was bitterly resented by Kayibanda as it seemed an unwarranted interference with his prerogatives as President.

In line with these principles the party underwent a major face-lifting in October 1966. To supplement the National Congress a Council of Representatives has been set up, consisting of all the members of the regional secretariats; the National Secretariat has been replaced by a National Executive Bureau, headed by a national secretary assisted by one adviser, one propagandist, one administrator and two secretaries; seven specialised commissions—whose range of competence includes political and administrative affairs, economic affairs, infra-structural affairs, rural development, youth—act as auxiliaries to the central party machinery; finally, a National Committee of Arbitration has been instituted, made up of five members designated by the president of the party (Kayibanda) upon the advice of the Council of Representatives. Its principal function is 'to settle differences among PARMEHUTU militants ... and between the organs of the party and the agents of the administration'.[58] If the recent past is any index, the Committee of Arbitration is unlikely to remain idle for very long. While the general purpose of these structural innovations is clearly to ensure a better co-ordination of party activities at all levels, and to further accelerate the trend towards centralisation, for the time being this is little more than an act of faith.

Despite the existence of a formal party apparatus, Rwanda seems closer to the 'no-party state' than to the 'single-party state' model. A courageous attempt has been made to follow the example of other African nations by instituting a monopolistic party intended to provide new sources of legitimacy, a new impetus for economic and political modernisation, a new basis to solidarity among individuals. But the party has yet to get off the ground. The reason for this is two-fold. First, the task of revolutionary midwifery was largely pre-empted by the Belgian administration, thereby robbing the party of those very functions which, as they were being performed, could have strengthened its armature and reinvigorated its ideology. True, the revolution was a major crisis in Rwanda's history; no other historical experience could have instilled a greater sense of community among the Hutu. But if the effect of the crisis is clearly discernible at the level of individual attitudes towards the Tutsi as a group, though not without substantial variations from one individual to the next, it has yet to produce similar changes in the attitude of the Hutu towards each other. Despite the levelling influence of the revolution, Rwandese society remains deeply fragmented and apathetic. Residual cleavages of a traditional character tend to coexist with regional and social discontinuities to produce a host of fissures within society. As a result, innumerable obstacles stand in the way of national unification. These, of course, are the very obstacles the Jacobins are determined to overcome. Whether they shall ultimately succeed, or whether they shall meet the fate of the French Jacobins, is as yet unclear. But from the emergent shape of the political system one thing at least is reasonably clear: the present conjuncture seems much closer to Thermidor than to Prairial—more evocative of a presidential monarchy than of a Jacobin republic.

9. The Kingdom Reborn

IN A FAMOUS passage, de Tocqueville describes the gap between the aims of the French revolution and its subsequent realisations:

> No nation has ever before embarked on so resolute an attempt as that of the French in 1789 to break with the past, to make, as it were, a scission in their life line and to create an unbridgeable gulf between all that they had hitherto been and all that they aspired to be. . . . I have always felt that they were far less successful in this curious attempt than is generally believed. [For] though they had no inkling of this, they took over from the old regime not only most of its customs, conventions and modes of thought, but even those very ideas which prompted our revolutionaries to destroy it; they used the debris of the old order for building up the new.[1]

By substituting another date and another country for those mentioned above, one gets a fairly accurate picture of the present state of Rwanda politics. In Rwanda, the republican authorities are using the 'debris of the old order for building up the new'; and in so doing they remain in some ways tributary of those very institutions they had hoped to destroy. To put the matter in these terms, however, is a bit simplistic. As the word 'debris' makes clear, only fragments of the old order have survived the trauma of the revolution; but on which of these fragments is the new political order being built? More importantly, if tradition is that which belongs to the past, the question arises—to which past does neo-traditionalism refer? To the Tutsi past, or the pre-Tutsi past? To the past of pre-colonial Rwanda, or the past that has been crystallised through the structures of indirect rule imposed by Belgium?

Before trying to elucidate these questions, one needs to take a closer look at the meaning of neo-traditionalism in contemporary Rwanda. Does it merely signify the persistence of traditional group loyalties? Does it involve the strategic use of traditional symbols aiming at promoting national integration and political legitimacy? Or does it find expression in a traditionalisation of modern political institutions, i.e. in the perpetuation or resurrection of traditional norms and patterns of behaviour within a modern institutional framework? In varying ways neo-traditionalism in Rwanda refers to each of the foregoing phenomena. Our main concern, however, is primarily with the latter kind—with the process by which elements of the Tutsi culture have become reinvigorated and adapted to the context of republican institutions. This involves a re-patterning of behaviour which is thoroughly inconsistent with the ethos of republicanism. As already noted, this resurgence of traditional norms is violently combated by the more extremist of the Jacobins, being regarded by some as nothing less than an insult to republican ideals and by others as a justification of their commitment to the concept of 'permanent revolution'. Ironically, it is this very lack of consensus about the ultimate goals of the revolution (was it merely intended to destroy Tutsi supremacy? or was it also intended to effect a total redrawing of the social and political map of Rwanda?) which has stimulated the rebirth of tradition. But what tradition? And, even more appropriately, whose traditions?

THE AMBIVALENCE OF NEO-TRADITIONALISM

Anyone attending the celebration of the fourth anniversary of Rwanda's independence, in July 1966, could not fail to be struck by the traditional pageantry on display. The ceremony began with the familiar beat of the drums, a dozen or so altogether, lined up in front of the platform where the President and his retinue sat. Then came the turn of the famous *intore* dancers, wearing resplendent head-dresses, leopard skins, and anklets to which tiny bells had been fastened, all tinkling in unison at each of their footsteps. Like in the old days they would leap in the air, and whirl around, and wave their arms in a fashion consciously reminiscent of the flight of the crested crane. Although the grace of the few Tutsi performers was enough to tell the professionals from the amateurs, the typically Hutu dances that followed were more uniformly graceless. Clad in banana leaves, each man wielding a hoe, the northern dancers kept their time by a ponderous drumming of their feet, every so often interrupted by a curious ritual: at a given signal, each man would throw his hoe high into the air and, with luck, catch it before it could hit the ground. Occasionally the prefects would join in the act, insisting on demonstrating their physical prowess even at the risk of endangering the lives of the spectators. But why go on? The scene has already been described:

> When the performance is about to begin, the Sultan, his headmen and visitors of importance sit on mats placed across the platform, and an enormous audience of some thousands of natives from all over the country collect in a ring of humanity round the palisade, the middle being kept clear for the dancers. All eyes are on the far

265

door, through which, at first, come a troop of Bahutu peasants carrying hoes with which they dance, throwing them up in the air at intervals. Then there is, perhaps, a lively tattoo played on about eight drums, in which the Sultan himself joins; after that the drummers dance, balancing themselves with their drums and whirling round and round. Now comes the star turn when everyone awaits Musinga's special dancers. Every young man amongst them is a member of the royal clan and beautifully dressed in what looks like pure white calico, but which in reality is finely fretted cowhide in long strips which hang down from the waist. Their headdresses are plumes of long white hair, and jingling bells are tied to their ankles. There are thirty or forty of these splendid fellows dancing at one time, who form up in rows, jumping high into the air at intervals as the dance proceeds.[2]

The interesting thing about this passage is not only that it should have been written some forty years prior to the 1966 celebrations just described; even more significant for us is the author's reference to a mixed cultural tradition, here presented as a medley of Hutu and Tutsi folklore. Just as Musinga allowed the performance of a typically Hutu ritual at his court, today Kayibanda is willing to make similar concessions to certain features of the once-dominant Tutsi culture.

This ambivalence of attitudes toward the past underscores the mixed character of Rwandese cultural traditions. Repudiation of Tutsi hegemony did not entail a sloughing off of the acculturative influences of Tutsi rule, though, where these had been in operation for only a relatively brief period of time, the displacement of the Tutsi oligarchs has given way to a reassertion of pre-Tutsi traditions. Thus the political culture of Rwanda remains characteristically hybrid, incorporating within itself two distinctive legacies: whereas the central and southern regions reflect adherence to a predominantly Tutsi heritage, the northern region is still very much under the influence of indigenous Hutu traditions, by and large assimilable to the Bantu cultures of western Uganda. Because of their comparatively brief exposure to Tutsi rule, their persistent efforts to evade the tentacular drive of the Rwanda monarchy, and their sharing of certain common historical experiences, the northern populations to this day continue to display a distinctive sense of cultural aloofness. Now, as in the past, they tend to evince considerable pride in their own culture, which at times leads them to adopt an attitude of unmitigated disdain towards the people of the south and centre.

But if the threads of history and cultural evolution have undoubtedly helped to mark them off from their neighbours, within this northern complex there are sharp subcultural discontinuities, reflecting the different lineage or clan affiliations, patterns of stratification and narrow regional loyalties which continue to divide the northern populations. The centrifugal forces released by the abrupt removal of Tutsi over-rule have tended to cluster around kinship or residential affiliations in existence before the Tutsi conquest. Yet in some areas one also notices the continuing influence of lineage solidarities that were common to both Hutu and Tutsi.

Three types of kinship groupings have, at one time or another, played a part in shaping patterns of competition and processes of political recruitment in the north: the patrilineage (*umulyango*), the subclan (*ishanga*), and the clan or patriclan (*ubwoko*). Of these, both the patrilineage—the smallest of the three in terms of membership—and the clan—the largest—were also found in central and southern Rwanda. It seems clear, however, that the degree of control exercised by Tutsi elements over lineage and clan affairs was far less pronounced in the northern region, and that only in rare instances were the members of the dominant caste able to 'infiltrate and break up the clustering of households belonging to Hutu members on the hills',[3] as seems to have been the current practice elsewhere in Rwanda. Because the strength of these kinship groupings was inversely proportional to that of the vertical structures associated with the caste system, they still provide a major focus for the loyalties of the northern populations.

Depending on the level at which political competition occurred, and the area and time period considered, these groupings have assumed a different order of significance in relation to each other. During the communal elections of 1960, the *umulyango* was the primary grouping around which intra-Hutu competition centred. A very high proportion of elected burgomasters and not a few councillors claimed the status of *bakuru b'imilyango* (lineage heads). This is not too surprising considering the saliency of local issues during the electoral contest, and the very crucial role traditionally devolved upon the lineage heads in the settlement of such issues (especially those involving litigations over dowries, contractual obligations of the *buhake* type, and the ownership of land). Until a comparatively recent date, the *umulyango* remained the dominant form of political organisation in the north. 'Towards the end of the nineteenth century', writes d'Hertefelt, 'the lineage could still easily be identified in those regions of the north which had not yet been infeudated . . . where it constituted a residential, politically autonomous group that owned a collective estate.'[4] More than half a century later, its vitality was still very much in evidence. Its political significance rapidly waned, however, with the organisation of legislative elections, in 1961, and the adoption of specific administrative measures destined to curb the influence of the lineage heads on the hills. When, in 1963, a communal councillor of the Gatonde commune, in the prefecture of Ruhengeri, pointed out that 'the *bakuru b'imilyango* demand a salary, for it is they who "hold" the hills since the communal councillors are no longer responsible for the administration of a given sector', the Minister of Interior, Bicamumpaka, issued a strong rebuff: 'That the communal councillors are no longer responsible for a given sector within their commune does not give the *bakuru b'imilyango* the right to administer the communes. Or else they will soon transform themselves into *bilongozi*, and that is an office which is no longer accepted by the government.'[5]

Thus, by 1963, the clan and subclan tended to supersede the lineage as the most politically relevant form of solidarity. True, since no single individual can traditionally claim authority over a clan or subclan, lineage affiliations in some cases remained the dominant source of political identification. More frequently, however, it was on the basis of a clustering of lineages, that is of subclans and clans, that political aspirants tried to gain entry into the political arena. Thus, a recurrent source of tension in the prefecture of Ruhengeri lies in the conflict of interests and aspirations which continues to oppose the members of the Abagesera clan to those of the Abakuyane, subclan of the Abasinga. That the prefect who held office in Ruhengeri in 1964 happened to be an Abagesera, and the Minister of Interior an Abasinga, could have been the source of considerable potential discord between the two men had they not been so closely dependent upon each other's support, politically and administratively.

While political recruitment at the local level is often the affair of a dominant clan or subclan—of the Abasinga in Ruhengeri, Bagesera in Gisenyi, etc.—recruitment practices at the central level reflect a kind of 'clanic arithmetic' in the allocation of ministerial chairs, so as to give maximum satisfaction to the representatives of the major clans. In 1966, for example, the Minister of Co-operation and Planning (Thaddée Bagaragaza) was a Musigaba, the Minister of Postal Services and Communications (Otto Ruzigizandekwe) a Musinga, like the Minister of Interior (Balthazar Bicamumpaka), and the Minister of Education (Lazare Mpakaniye) was a Musindi. One finds here, albeit in a different guise, a replica of the technique elsewhere employed by African leaders to reconcile the conflicting ethnic claims of political aspirants.

It is not only at the level of political recruitment that the specificity of northern traditions finds expression, but at the level of political norms and institutions. Enough has already been said of the *ubukonde*, and of its political implications, to make it unnecessary at this stage to elaborate further. Yet this whole question of the *ubukonde* is directly relevant to our discussion: not only does it throw into relief the close interconnections between the social, economic and political aspects of the northern subculture—in particular the hierarchical ordering of socio-economic and political relations inherent in the *bakonde-bagererwa* nexus—but it also conveys a type of affective orientation to politics which is difficult to reconcile with the value system of non-northerners, whether they are Westernised or not. The *ubukonde* is more than a system of land tenure which the central government would like to abolish on account of its 'feudal' overtones; it also embodies the dominant political norms of the northern Hutu societies. There is positive value attached to the personalised, hierarchical, clientelistic type of relationships associated with the *ubukonde*, and politics in the north are more often than not an extension of this type of relationship.

In a sense, the northern region remains what it was under Tutsi rule—the Achilles' heel of the government. This situation is all the more unpleasant for the central authorities because they cannot rely on the application of naked force to bring the northerners to heel, as was often the case under Tutsi hegemony. But one must also remember that force was by no means the only instrument with which the Tutsi monarchy reigned and ruled. The Tutsi knew how to negotiate, how to appoint prominent Hutu to chiefly positions to ensure their collaboration, how to make tactical concessions to their demands, how to engage in alliances and counter-alliances. In the past the *mwami* had two major sources of strength: the sacredness of his office and his skill at political manoeuvring. Similarly, Kayibanda's strength lies not only in the sacredness of his office but in the skilful use he has made of various strategies of manipulation and bargaining. True, the exigencies of the political situation are such that bargaining becomes a sine qua non for anyone wishing to remain in office; yet the bargaining position of the officeholder is greatly strengthened by the aura of sanctity which surrounds the presidency. In David Apter's words, Kayibanda's position in the emergent political system can best be described as that of a 'presidential monarch', 'embodying both non-dynastic aspects of the role and dynastic aspects associated with the ceremonial and ritual functions of kingship'.[6]

A Presidential *Mwami*-ship

It may be that future historians will assign to President Kayibanda a place in the history of Rwanda similar to that which Robespierre occupies in the pantheon of the French revolution. Though the same cannot be said of his ministers, Kayibanda can make a valid claim to being called 'incorruptible'; like Robespierre, he is enigmatic, withdrawn, and, according to some, simple to the point of asceticism in his everyday life and personal habits; like him, too, he has in mind the ultimate goal of a moral and social regeneration of his people. For the time being this is as far as the parallel can be drawn. However, this may well be a very superficial analogy—at least judging from the gallery of royal portraits hanging from the walls of the Ministry of Foreign Affairs (now the Ministry of Co-operation and Planning). It is perhaps not for nothing that Kayibanda's portrait is surrounded by those of Queen Elizabeth of England, Queen Juliana of the Netherlands, King Constantine of Greece, King Frederick of Denmark, King Baudouin of Belgium, and—another regal figure—Charles de Gaulle of France. But of course this too can be regarded as very superficial evidence.

That the presidency has in fact taken on some of the qualities of *mwami*-ship is shown by the way in which Kayibanda defines his role in the political system of Rwanda. He embodies the ideal of Hutu solidarity just as the *mwami* once symbolised the ideal of Tutsi supremacy. But since Hutu solidarity is more apparent than real, Kayibanda must cast himself in the role of an umpire, in a fashion again reminiscent of the arbitrating powers of the *mwami*. Because he is the incarnation of moral values, his authority enables him to invest the presidency with special prerogatives, i.e. quasi-religious prerogatives. The religious character of his office is nowhere more evident than in public references to Kayibanda as 'the idol of the people',[7] a phrase which in the context of Rwanda is more than just a cliché. It evokes a kind of deference akin to that once accorded to the *mwami*. The President stands in relation to his people not unlike a divine king in relation to his subjects, and he uses the prerogatives of his position accordingly.

Under the circumstances the presidency cannot be made an object of political competition. One can challenge the *mwami*'s claim to power only at one's own peril. Since his authority is a grace of the gods, it can be taken away only by divine sanctions. Thus the whole purpose of presidential elections is not to provide opportunities for replacing the incumbent but, rather, to affirm his permanence in office. (In 1965, as in 1969, Kayibanda ran unopposed and received over 90 per cent of the votes.)[8] Like the *mwami*, the president is inaccessible, inviolate and unaccountable. His inaccessibility enables him to avoid taking up overt positions on specific issues, and thus to create around his person and his policies an atmosphere of ambiguity which makes them immune from criticism. The inviolability of his office acts as a further deterrent against political attacks. But, even when commitments cannot be averted, his decisions remain well beyond the pale of accountability. Just as in the past the *mwami* used his advisers as a cat's paw in order to deflect hostility towards his entourage, Kayibanda has consistently endeavoured to shift the onus of responsibility for his policies upon individual cabinet members. But since political office is still regarded as a gift of the sovereign, no amount of political pressure from the National Assembly or from anywhere else can force him to remove a member of his cabinet or prevent him from appointing a favourite.

These, however, are primarily defensive weapons. Sacredness of office may dull the edge of the opposition, but it cannot prevent heresy. Nor is it enough to ensure compliance with presidential orders. For this, a more subtle kind of weaponry is required, consisting of probes and withdrawals, of manipulation and negotiation, of appointments, promotions and demotions, as the circumstances may require. Kayibanda cannot disregard the established power structure. He is deeply indebted to the old-guard Hutu politicians—the first batch of revolutionaries—and although he probably feels the need to replace them with younger and better educated elements, he cannot always afford to do so. Many of these old-guard politicians (Calliope Mulindihabi is a case in point) have powerful political bases in the countryside, from which they cannot easily be dislodged. The same is true of the *bakonde* politicians: their position is so deeply entrenched at the local level that any move to suppress them is more likely than not to open up a Pandora's box of difficulties. Like the *mwami* under the former regime, Kayibanda must contend with a variety of political forces and personalities whose influence must be carefully weighed before any decisive move is initiated. His authority depends on his ability to reconcile divergent viewpoints and factions, but above all on preventing any one of these factions from gaining a permanent ascendancy within the governmental structure. More often than not this has meant playing one group off against the other—north against south, moderates against radicals, old-guard politicians against the younger generations. Ministerial portfolios are granted and withdrawn much as the chieftaincies were in the old days, on the basis of favour and political calculation. No formal vote has yet taken place in parliament to decide the fate of a minister, let alone of the cabinet. All parliament does is to serve as a seismograph of public opinion, the warnings of which may or may not be taken into account by the presidency. Of course there remains the party, but the party does what the president decides. The president remains the fount of all legitimate authority.

Rwanda

Whereas in other parts of Africa the legitimacy of the position occupied by nationalist leaders owes virtually nothing to political institutions and nearly all to the so-called 'charisma' of the office-holders, we find in Rwanda almost the reverse situation.* Whatever authority Kayibanda has rests largely on the perceived legitimacy of the office he occupies, a legitimacy which in the minds of the unacculturated masses is inextricably bound up with the legitimacy of *mwami*-ship. It is said that, in trying to mobilise support for his ideas, Kayibanda went about the countryside saying that the purpose of the revolution was to give the Hutu a *mwami* of their own. If this is true, his goals have been fulfilled beyond all expectations. In the long run, the incompetence and arbitrariness of some of the governing elites and the growing demands for increased political participation of those outside the government may bring insuperable pressure to bear upon both the office and the occupant. But until this happens the stability of the system will continue to depend to a large extent on the perceived legitimacy of Kayibanda's presidential *mwami*-ship.

THE REDEFINITION OF CHIEFTAINCY

Moving away from the top to the base of the political pyramid, one encounters a somewhat more complicated situation. The juxtaposition of two different role structures—one based on bureaucratic and the other on political standards of performance—was bound to create conflicts between prefects and deputies, deputies and burgomasters, burgomasters and propagandists, if only because the distinction between bureaucracy and politics is seldom clearly perceived or even accepted by most office-holders. Unfortunately, too little is known of the conflicts that must have arisen prior to the administrative reform of 1926 to draw a valid analogy between the present and the pre-1926

* This is not so, of course, if one considers charisma to be inseparable from the perceived legitimacy of traditional roles and the normative patterns they connote. Commenting on the sources and validation of charisma, Ruth Ann and Dorothy Wilner observe that 'the charisma of a leader is bound up with and indeed may even depend upon his becoming assimilated in the thought and feelings of a populace to its sacred figures, divine beings and heroes. Their actions and the context of these actions, recounted in myth, express fundamental values of a culture, including its basic categories for organizing experience and trying to resolve basic cultural and human dilemmas.' Ruth Ann and Dorothy Wilner, "The Rise and Role of Charismatic Leaders", in *The Annals of the American Academy of Political and Social Science*, Vol. 358, March 1965, p. 82. For a differing interpretation of charisma, see Carl J. Friedrich, "Political Leadership and the Problem of the Charismatic Power", *The Journal of Politics*, Vol. XXIII, No. 1, February 1961, pp. 3–25.

situation; but there is an obvious parallel between the previous division of authority between land chiefs, cattle chiefs and army chiefs and that which at present exists between various categories of bureaucrats and politicians.

Just as in the past the presence of several chiefs, each exercising specific authority within the same administrative unit, resulted in a system of checks and balances, today in Rwanda the existence of 'parallel hierarchies' seems ideally suited to provide certain institutional safeguards against possible abuses of authority. But this is not yet the case. For if the present structure of authority does resemble the pre-1926 situation, the roles of the incumbents are not so clearly defined as were the roles of the cattle chief, land chief and army chief. No such functional specificity is yet discernible. Viewed in functional terms, the present system seems much closer to the type of 'streamlined' chief-taincy inaugurated by Belgium.

Structurally, the organisation of prefectures approximates to that of the old provinces. The prefects, like the army chiefs before colonial times, are appointed by the central government and their powers are in theory circumscribed by those of the burgomasters, whose position in the system might be compared to that of the district chiefs in relation to the army chiefs. Like that of the district chiefs, the burgomasters' tenure depends ultimately on the grace of the presidential monarch. In theory, of course, they hold their mandate from the people who elected them, but in fact nothing prevents the central government from bringing their term of office to an end. As in the old days, when chiefly positions were given by the monarch to his favourites, today the appoint-ment and replacement of prefects and burgomasters depends entirely on the whim of the central authorities.

Looking at the situation from a functional standpoint, the analogy with the monarchical regime seems even more striking. Since chiefly rule was already bureaucratised prior to the beginning of European rule, and infinitely more so thereafter, it was perhaps inevitable that the role of the prefect should bear some resemblance to that of the chief. This is all the more understandable as chieftaincy is the only formal political role with which the majority of the people of Rwanda can identify in any meaningful fashion. Moreover, many of the prefects at present holding office did in fact act as 'chefs' or 'sous-chefs interi-maires' after the events of November 1959, and there is no reason to believe that a change of terminology automatically changed the beha-viour of the incumbents. No wonder, then, if the functions of the pre-fects (especially in the realm of rule enforcement, rule adjudication and communication) should resemble those of the chiefs. When litigation arises among the burgomasters, or between local officials and the citizenry, it is the prefect who has the last word. It is he who informs the central government of what sanctions to take or not to take against a recalcitrant burgomaster, who decides how many acres of coffee should be cultivated in each commune, how many people should be put to work on the roads, and for how long. It is he who has the authority to suspend 'the execution of ministerial orders when the circumstances require', and who alone is responsible for 'maintaining public order and tranquillity'.[9] It is the prefect who convokes the conseil de préfecture once a month to inform the burgomasters of his decisions. Like the 'chief-in-council', the 'prefect-in-council' supervises the debates, berating latecomers, congratulating others on their zeal and punctuality, distributing orders, reprimands and recommendations to each according to his due. The feedback from the prefecture to the central administration occurs intermittently and partially. Here again the parallel with the ancien régime is plain: the chiefs' past tendency to shield themselves from possible criticisms from above by withholding or distorting information can still be observed today.

Much of this is also true of the burgomasters, who stand in relation to the prefects not unlike the subchiefs to the chiefs. In fact it is at this level that, for the man on the hill, the parallel with the ancien régime is most painfully detectable. Exactions and injustices are still common, so much so that one prefect at least issued this categorical warning: 'The powers that have been devolved upon you', the prefect of Kigali told his burgomasters, 'do not authorise you to oppress your people. You must not behave like the old feudal authorities, who the regime, the absolute master, tacitly allowed to crush the people under all kinds of exactions and injustices.'[10] Like so many feudal potentates, the burgomasters have their own devoted followers among the communal councillors who perform for them the multitude of chores which the *bilongozi* once performed for the chiefs. Many are still using their influence to accumulate wealth: 'In order to obtain an administrative service, even a signature, the poor people of the hills must offer gifts to the burgomaster.'[11] Many of these gifts are the rewards they get for giving away the lands of the refugees: 'Certain burgomasters sell the land of the refugees to their own profit, not to the profit of the commune.'[12] How different are these methods from those the chiefs employed to build up their clientele?

Although traditional politics involved a fair measure of competition, the present situation has been rendered infinitely more competitive by the play of electoral processes. Not only has competition been extended to a previously inert stratum, it has been institutionalised through regular elections at both the central and local levels. The channels of political participation are more numerous, and so are the opportunities for becoming actively involved in politics; yet the style of politics remains unchanged. The political struggle continues to express itself in traditional forms; it is conducted obliquely, in an atmosphere of deceit and intrigue. It involves building up a clientele through a judicious dispensation of favours, bribes and 'benefices', and it also brings into play the familiar techniques of influence practised by the Tutsi, including *guhakwa* (paying court) and *ingorore* (tributes).

Just as in traditional Rwanda the offices of chief and subchief were inseparable from ties of clientship, today the tenure of local officials depends on how successful they are in building up a personal following among their constituents. This is not just a case of building up support for particular policies, or a reflection of a bargaining relation between voters and politicians; what is involved here is a personal commitment on the part of a group of potential 'clients' to do for their 'patron' whatever may be needed to serve his personal interests. Local officials in turn tend to acknowledge this commitment through prebends, i.e. tax exemptions, the allocation of landed property previously owned by Tutsi, and such other favours as may be expected of them. One is reminded of the 'prebendal organization' described by Max Weber, in which 'every sort of assignment or usufructs, tributes and services which are due to the lord himself or to the official . . . means a surrender of the pure type of bureaucratic organization'.[13] The result has been a blurring of boundaries between the administrative and political spheres, as well as a tendency for each set of roles to find a common denominator in the survival of feudal relationships.

Moreover, just as in feudal times access to office depended on 'proper connections', and on a perpetual probing of power relations, today local officials appear constantly manoeuvring for position, in a way re-enacting the traditional 'play for power' described by Pierre Gravel in his study of Remera. The key to an understanding of Rwanda politics lies in the relations of partnership (or reciprocity) which link various office-holders to each other.* To maintain or reinforce this relationship

---

* Because of the very personalised character of this relationship, empirical evidence is obviously difficult to come by. Nonetheless, I am willing to argue that the principle of reciprocity still has a controlling influence on the behaviour of political actors. This is so because the norm of reciprocity is by nature malleable and indeterminate in terms of the obligations it implies. It can be adapted to a variety of transactions and contexts while at the same time retaining its system-stabilising functions. As Gouldner put it, 'it can be applied to countless ad hoc transactions, thus providing a flexible moral sanction for transactions which might not otherwise be regulated by specific status obligations. . . . The

275

is the goal of every ambitious politician; to break it, that of his opponents. This kind of partnership is obviously reminiscent of the chain of vassalage which once tied the client to the subchief, the subchief to the chief, the chief to the *mwami*. Today, however, there is a double chain of reciprocities: one strand runs through the party hierarchy, and another through the administrative and social structures; one represents what one might call the 'pays légal' (legality as defined by the party), and the other the 'pays réel' (reality as defined by tradition).

Thus at the local level the burgomasters are dependent for re-election on the support of the heads of the local families on the hill (the *bakuru b'imilyango*); most communal councillors and communal police-men, likewise, feel that their tenure hinges on the ability of the burgo-master to retain the support of these families. Hence a triangular pattern of reciprocities tends to develop between the local family heads, the burgomasters and the communal policemen, which in turn may provide a basis for stability. But stability is often threatened by the party propa-gandists: sometimes they act as the agents of the prefecture, sent to 'break' the fiefdoms of the burgomasters; sometimes they are 'bought' by local aspirants who failed to be elected, or by a demoted burgomaster. The ramifications of political clientage can extend far beyond the local arena. In some cases there are ties of reciprocity between the burgo-masters and the deputies (especially at election time, as demonstrated by the Rwasibo affair discussed in the previous chapter), and in some cases it is the deputy who connives with the propagandists to eliminate the burgomaster. By and large, however, what goes on at the central level has little relevance to local politics, and this in spite of the recent trend towards increased centralisation.

Another notable feature of contemporary politics is the extent to which orientations to political action reflect the incidence of traditional directives to political action. The notions of *guhakwa* and *ingorore* are still basic to an understanding of the political culture of Rwanda. Holders of office are constantly solicited for personal favours, and just as in the old days favours were dependent upon gifts, today the acceptance of a cow or a jug of beer as a token of gratitude for the performance of certain administrative services is still expected from local officials. This can be inferred from the warnings issued by the prefect of Kigali, on April 30, 1965:

---

norm is like a plastic filler, capable of being poured into the shifting crevices of social structures, serving as a kind of all-purpose moral cement.' Alvin Gould-ner, "The Norm of Reciprocity: A Preliminary Statement", *American Socio-logical Review*, Vol. xxv, April 1960, p. 175.

There are a great many deficiencies. There is a widespread malady in our country which, unless it is quickly combated, may become an epidemic. This malady I shall call profit-seeking. Certain functionaries are preoccupied with furthering their own personal interest, to the detriment of the public interest. It is a shame to see that important stocks of Primus* are kept in the houses given to them by the government. What must one think of a man who has been in office for only three years and builds himself a palace worth a million francs? Where does the money come from?[14]

From the prefect's earlier comments about 'illegal remunerations', the answer is not far to find:

In several communes where people seem to ignore democracy, they let themselves be sucked passively as was the custom during the old feudal regime. . . . In the communes of Musasa and Rushashi, the local judges [*juges de canton*] refuse to handle litigations unless they first receive gifts. This has to stop. It is unworthy of democracy. The burgomasters who have also developed this habit of accepting gifts of cows and money are, of course, the last ones I would expect to make an effort to prevent these abuses. But I do want to remind them that they must beware of people who bring them gifts of cows and money, or else they will become so corrupt that they will behave like windcocks.[15]

In March 1964 the same prefect cautioned the burgomasters against 'feudal practices', and notably 'demands for gifts':

Alas!—Certain burgomasters insist on demanding gifts. In order to obtain an administrative service, even a signature, the poor people on the hills must present gifts to the burgomasters. Gentlemen, you should follow the example of the President of the Republic, the ministers and the prefects. You must act with benevolence and compassion towards the unfortunate ones who do not share with you the same easy circumstances and degree of civilisation.[16]

Gift-giving works in several ways: the acceptance of a gift by a burgomaster creates a relationship of reciprocal loyalty between the recipient and the giver; but the wealth thereby accumulated by the recipient also serves to duplicate this relationship at other levels.

This does not prevent certain burgomasters from trying other techniques, however, such as the spreading of false rumours: 'There are some burgomasters', one prefect observed, 'who, behind my back, go around the countryside telling people things which I never said. This

* Brand name of a local beer.

277

guhakwa method must stop, or else it is going to create a malaise.'[17] An even greater malaise is liable to arise from the politicisation of the local police detachments by certain burgomasters, as happened in the prefecture of Kigali in 1965: 'The head of the local police detachment', said the prefect, 'is accountable to me only. Today, however, transfers of police are decided without my consent. I am told of these decisions only after the departure of those concerned. Why, then, am I chief [sic] if I have nothing to say on these matters?'[18] To cite further examples of corruption, incompetence and administrative disobedience would be tedious. Nor is it necessary to go into other and far more distasteful types of behaviour such as spying and political assassination, both of which are still occasionally practised.* What should be stressed, however, is that the forms of behaviour just described are part of a normative orientation to politics which has persisted for a very long time and is likely to do so for many years to come.

The essence of my argument, then, is that behind the formal institutional framework of the republic lies a traditional role structure which continues to mould the attitudes and strategies of most political actors. It approximates to that of the ancien régime in that: (i) it has undergone relatively little structural differentiation since pre-revolutionary times— as we have seen, prefects and burgomasters cast themselves, or are cast by their constituents, in the roles of chief and subchief, with the communal councillors and party propagandists forming parallel hierarchies of clients and patrons; (ii) although local officials show greater independence of the central authorities than under the monarchy (in part because of cultural discontinuities within the Hutu community, and in part because the administrative apparatus of the republic is still too weak to enforce its rule in the countryside), the general trend is clearly in the direction of increased centralisation, and therefore of a lessening of sub-system autonomy; (iii) insofar as one's participation in the revolution remains a precondition to high office, recruitment to political roles is still based on very narrow, one might almost say 'ascriptive' criteria (and this, of course, is even more true of the situation prevailing in the north, where clan affiliations are still of decisive importance); (iv) it embodies a set of norms and expectations that are clearly borrowed from the value system of feudal Rwanda.

This is not to say that the political map of Rwanda is what it used to be before the revolution. Rwanda is at present going through a period

* I am told by a reliable informant that, in the prefecture of Kibungu, at least six people lost their lives during the 1965 legislative elections. They were all drowned in Lake Mohazi by party propagandists in the pay of their political adversaries.

of role search, in which the confrontation of republican and feudal norms inevitably leads to confusion. In trying to redefine their roles and self-images the elites of Rwanda are subject to contradictory impulses and motivations. At one extreme lies the ideal of a socialistic, austerity government, which draws its inspiration from the official motto, 'Liberty, Co-operation, Progress'; at the other extreme lies the reality of a neo-traditional polity, still very much ensconced in corruption and favouritism, rife with clanicism and regionalism. Although conflict has thus far been kept within reasonable bounds, this may not last forever.

ARMY MEN VERSUS POLITICIANS

In view of the pivotal role played by the army in traditional Rwanda, a discussion of military-civilian relationships seems an appropriate footnote to this chapter. The army may again become a prime mover in the political system of Rwanda; but if this should ever happen the relations between the civilian authorities and the military will no doubt deviate substantially from what they were under the monarchy.

That there are signs of a serious malaise within the army can be easily detected from the content of Kayibanda's speech, on March 15, 1967, to the Garde Nationale (the official title of the Rwandese army). As if to allay all possible misunderstandings about the meaning and legitimacy of the revolution, Kayibanda went to great lengths to differentiate between a coup d'état and a revolution. For the first time since the event occurred, the coup of Gitarama was officially described as 'a revolution, not a coup d'état', the implication being that revolutions alone are legitimate. 'It was the will of the people made manifest', said Kayibanda. 'Our objective was clear and honest, and our party was strong enough to avoid intrigue and bloodshed.' Such a revolution, he added, must not be confused with 'the subversive propaganda' of those who wish to foment military coups. Yet 'in one club or another the agents of subversion talk about military coups, trying to get people to work themselves up, and then slandering this or that officer, in an effort to weaken the moral cohesion of our Garde Nationale'. Like a man whistling in the dark, Kayibanda concluded on a note of faked optimism: 'These cabals will not work with us . . . for we know your fidelity and your honesty towards the republic, its institutions, its aspirations. Go ahead and set yourself as an example of discipline, competence and professionalism.'[19]

Much of the present uneasiness stems from a conflict of attitude between the army officers and certain politicians whose outlook and policies they find incompatible with their own modernising aspirations and professional expectations. But it also reflects problems of a more specific order, some having to do with the circumstances under which the army came into being, its ethnic composition, and, above all, its seemingly very impressive record as an instrument of national security against external invasions.

The Rwandese army was built from scratch, almost overnight, in the most improvised fashion. The operation began in May 1960, shortly before the communal elections. With the approach of Congolese independence, only short-term reliance could be placed on the Congolese Force Publique for maintaining order. In the absence of an indigenous military force, this task was to be temporarily entrusted to metropolitan units of para-commandos, but these, as the Special Resident pointed out, 'could not be expected to stay forever'.[20] All necessary steps were taken to organise a Garde Territoriale (later renamed Garde Nationale) worthy of the name. On May 19, 1960, the Special Resident issued special instructions for the recruitment of a military force of 650 men, whose ethnic composition would be 85 per cent Hutu and 15 per cent Tutsi. The recruits had to have completed their primary schooling, a requirement which could eventually be waived by the Special Resident. A year later the commander-in-chief of the Garde Territoriale, Major Vanderstraeten, summed up the result of the experiment:

(i) Collective reactions (among the Garde Territoriale), because of their racial solidarity and the incomplete character of their military training, are more intense and frequent than those of the soldiers of the ex-Force Publique.

(ii) The more or less satisfactory results thus far obtained reflect the greater or lesser ability of the European cadres.

(iii) The character of the soldiers is withdrawn. They have but few contacts with the local populations. Because they do not speak Kinyarwanda the European officers have few contacts with their men.

(iv) The soldiers attach a great deal of importance to political influences and think that they can have recourse to the first politician they meet—prefect, communal councillor or minister. These political personalities must show a greater sense of discipline. They must observe the usual chain of command.

(v) The soldiers evaluate everything by reference to the police. In some places tensions exist between the two outfits. They look upon themselves not as mercenaries but as Rwandese soldiers and this does create some difficulties when corvées are imposed upon them.

(vi) In conclusion, the over-all situation is satisfactory, but there remain some real problems: lack of funds, lack of European cadres.[21]

With independence just around the corner, the absence of an indigenous officers' corps was undoubtedly the most serious of all the handicaps then faced by the army: in March 1961 the officers' school in Kigali claimed only seven candidates, one of whom was a Tutsi.[22] After a year of preliminary training in Kigali, they would spend another year at the Ecole Royale Militaire in Brussels, and then another eight months in Arlon (Belgium) for further training. Only then would they be awarded the rank of second lieutenant. In practice this meant that Rwanda would cross the threshold of independence without having a single trained officer in its armed forces.

If one compares the record of the Garde Nationale in 1967 with what it was in 1961, the transformation seems almost miraculous. Given the rather dismal situation existing in 1961, progress was perhaps inevitable. That the Garde Nationale should have succeeded in repulsing the recurrent attacks of the *inyenzi* was far from inevitable, however. Today the Rwandese army can legitimately pose as the authentic champion of its country's national integrity. What is more, its tradition is not that of a colonial police force at the service of an alien power (as was the case of the Force Publique in the Congo), but one of armed struggle against foreign invasion. The Rwandese army now consists of approximately 2,500 men, commanded by a group of some 30 officers, all trained in Belgium. The officers' corps is made up of young, dynamic and competent individuals. They have indeed excellent reasons to consider themselves as competent as any local politician, and their outlook is decidedly more modern.

In such a situation it is not surprising if the officers' corps should feel somewhat dismayed by what they consider the retrograde and parochial attitude of certain politicians—and by the mobilising inadequacies of the political system. Manfred Halpern's comments on Middle Eastern armies would seem to apply equally well to Rwanda: 'Within the army, a sense of national mission transcending parochial, regional or economic interests or kinship ties seemed to be much more clearly defined than anywhere else in society.'[23] Thus an army intervention would probably be 'reactive' rather than 'designated', to use Morris Janowitz's terms—that is, 'a gesture of self-interested or public spirited despair against the obvious inadequacies of professional politicians'.[24] This, to be sure, is a fairly widespread syndrome in developing countries, especially when low economic development and particularistic modes of behaviour tend to breed civil disorder. The army frequently acts as a deus ex machina, to save the state from itself. In Rwanda, however, several additional factors further predispose the army to intervene.

To begin with, in the semi-anarchic conditions that prevailed from about 1960 to 1962 the army was involved in countless incidents with civilian authorities. Cases were reported of soldiers being arrested at the request of the public prosecutor for disorderly conduct, of occasional fisticuffs and bar-room brawls involving soldiers and politicians, and of a corporal being called an 'enemy of the *mwami*' by a Tutsi judge, in Nyanza in 1961.[25] Whatever ill-feelings these incidents must have generated between army men and civilians were also reinforced by a growing realisation among the troops that their contribution to national security was not properly acknowledged by Hutu politicians. The clear predominance of northerners (especially of the Bashiru) among the officers as well as the troops, owing to the fact that the northerners are generally taller and stronger than the Hutu of other regions, has also led to occasional frictions. While feelings of regionalism are rare among the officers, the troops often tend to display the prejudices and regional self-consciousness which generally colour the attitude of the northerners towards people of other regions. Finally, there has been considerable grumbling about the inordinately slow rate of promotions. In point of fact, President Kayibanda's recent decision to promote thirteen aspirants to the rank of second lieutenant is perhaps an indication of the feelings of dissatisfaction which otherwise would have arisen within the army.[26] Because the army is itself a very recent creation, promotions were necessarily slow, and the resulting lag in the Africanisation of the officers' corps continues to create a certain uneasiness between army men and politicians.

Clearly, these are powerful inducements in favour of an army take-over; yet there are some equally powerful disincentives. First of all, there are serious political dissensions within the army, which tend to reflect the cleavage already described between moderates and radicals, i.e. between the Mulindihabi and Rwasibo factions. This is illustrated by the incident which occurred in 1964 in the prefecture of Gitarama. Following an altercation between the prefect of Gitarama and Commandant Aloys Nserakije, the latter was severely reprimanded and temporarily demoted, by Calliope Mulindihabi, then Minister of the Garde Nationale. Although Nserakije reportedly asked the commander-in-chief of the Garde Nationale, Juvenal Habyarimana, to intercede on his behalf, Habyarimana refused to do so. Since then there has been latent tension within the officers' corps between the pro-Habyarimana and the pro-Nserakije groups. Moreover, there are regional tensions as well, as between the Bashiru majority and the non-Bashiru. Furthermore, the existence of a separate police force—the gendarmerie—acts as a formidable counterweight to the army. Numbering approximately

1,200 men and a dozen officers, the gendarmerie is looked upon with considerable suspicion by the army, partly because the gendarmerie has been in existence longer, and hence underwent a more rapid Africanisation of its cadres than the army. The promotions that have taken place within the gendarmerie seem somewhat unwarranted to those in the army who are still awaiting theirs, as they feel that the police is on the whole less competent and less disciplined than the army. Speaking of the gendarmes who graduated from the Ecole de Police of Ruhengeri in 1961, one Belgian administrator did not hesitate to describe them as 'vainglorious and undisciplined',[27] and one British visitor to Rwanda, mistakenly referring to the gendarmes as 'soldiers', spoke of them as 'exhibiting a strange combination of indiscipline and efficiency': 'At one road block on the Butare side of Kigali, three of the four soldiers were dancing to the music of a radio until we appeared. The fourth was holding an automatic rifle. After inspecting our papers and an exchange of pleasantries, the three accepted cigarettes and lit up. The fourth took the cigarette but would not light it while on duty.'[28] This very lack of discipline is perhaps a reflection of the daily involvement of the police with the local populations; that it should be so widely tolerated by the civilian authorities is also indicative of the political power it wields, a fact which goes far in explaining why the officers of the Garde Nationale have so far acted with such extreme caution in the sphere of domestic politics.*

The army's political prudence is further reinforced by the officers' realisation of their own inadequacy as potential candidates to the presidency. None could match Kayibanda's claims to legitimacy as a presidential *mwami* and revolutionary leader, and few seem anxious to cope with the enormous burdens of political and economic modernisation with which the regime is at present saddled.

---

* The politicisation of the gendarmerie must also be attributed to the special circumstances under which it came to be recruited. Until the communal elections of 1960 the gendarmerie included an overwhelming majority of Tutsi (according to AT Nijs, in the territoire of Kibuye nine gendarmes out of ten were Tutsi) and the remaining Hutu were generally predisposed to support the monarchy. As AT Nyssens declared, on September 2, 1960, 'the territorial police is one of the last nests of UNAR'. A drastic purge was conducted after the elections, under the supervision of the newly-elected burgomasters. The new recruits were almost everywhere selected on the basis of their sympathy towards the burgomasters. See *Procès-Verbal de la Réunion des Administrateurs de Territoire tenue à Kigali le 2 Septembre 1960*, mimeo., pp. 7, 9.

THE 'UNFINISHED REVOLUTION'

Though no longer running in a revolutionary direction, the cohesive currents of Rwanda society are still strong enough to dispel the threat of a major breakdown of political institutions. But this does not mean that the revolution has yet run its full course. Part of the dilemma facing the regime is that whereas its legitimacy depends to a considerable extent upon its ability to live up to the goals of liberty and equality propounded by the revolution, the exigencies of rapid economic development and social reform make it imperative to employ somewhat the same arbitrary methods as were once employed by the monarchy.

Proponents of the 'permanent revolution' thesis hold that constraint and regimentation are necessary evils at this stage of Rwanda's evolution. According to this view, the party is the sole representative of republican legitimacy. Its primary task is to substitute itself as nearly as possible for the old feudal power structure, so as to destroy it root and branch; to identify itself fully with the ideology and goals of republicanism and carry the task of psychological reconversion to its ultimate stage. The party must become the focal point of the political life of the nation, and convert itself into a 'party of solidarity'. It must not only act as a symbol of Hutu solidarity but as a mediator of the popular will. But this is more easily said than done.

The problem is fundamentally one of ideology. More concretely, the present political stagnation reflects a kind of ideological vacuum. Even though socialism and nationalism are two of the most powerful ideological forces at work in the African continent, two of the most powerful 'utopias' for infusing a sense of identity and solidarity among individuals, in Rwanda these themes are almost never voiced. Socialism has strange connotations to a people accustomed to think in terms of hierarchies of rank and privilege. There is no counterpart in Rwanda for Nyerere's concept of *ujamaa* socialism, or for that matter for any other form of socialism. National developmental goals have yet to be accepted as legitimate by the majority of the rural populations, and the presumed rationality of a socialist economy sounds singularly irrational to people whose lives are still overwhelmingly centred on personalised relationships. As an ideology, nationalism is in an even more ambiguous posture. Despite occasional attacks on neo-colonialism and imperialism, the Rwandese leaders have been understandably reticent about incorporating within their concept of nationalism the usual strictures against European colonialism. As we have seen, the Rwandese revolution was not a reaction against European colonial rule but a collaborative effort with the European coloniser, aimed at the abolition of an indigenous form of imperialism. In a sense, nationalism in Rwanda is little more than a misnomer for 'tribalism', a tribalism which drew its sustenance from an unholy alliance with Belgium. In these conditions, nationalism has some peculiarly freakish overtones.

What is there left in the way of alternatives? Essentially, the myth of Hutu solidarity, a myth which is invested with political as well as moral values. Because Hutu solidarity implies a common adherence to democracy it has become a major ingredient of progress; and just as in the past the myth of Tutsi supremacy tended to be associated with a normative view of society, Hutu solidarity is now regarded as the moral foundation of republicanism. Now, as before, the tendency is to twist the past in order to justify the future, in order to give an aura of legitimacy to the ideals of justice and equality, and, even more importantly, to conceal the fundamental differences of cultural and political orientation between north and south.* Again one is reminded of de Tocqueville's words: 'Though they had no inkling of this, they took over from the old regime not only most of its customs, conventions and modes of thought, but even those very ideas which prompted our revolutionaries to destroy it.'[29]

If the essence of a revolution lies not only in the overthrow of the state but in the fundamental transformation of the economic and social structure of society, the Hutu revolution is only beginning. Now that the initial phase has been completed, there remains the more fundamental task of social and economic reform, one which presupposes the alteration of age-old attitudes and modes of behaviour. Until this is done, the Rwandese revolution must be regarded, in Marx's terms, as 'a partial,

* Nowhere is this phenomenon better illustrated than in the story told by a Hutu leader to the parliamentary study group appointed by the Belgian government in April 1959. After commenting on the aspirations of his kinsmen, this leader stated: 'It is the second time in the history of Rwanda that the Hutu officially request de facto social and political equality with the Tutsi. The first petition of this kind can be traced back to 1890, at the time of the battle of Karagwe, during the reign of Mwami Kigeli IV Rwabugiri. The Hutu who fought alone against the enemy went beyond the line of defence drawn by the commander of the Tutsi armies in accordance with the auguries. The result was the defeat of the Hutu. They were condemned to be eternally dependent upon the Tutsi. The edict of the sovereign stipulated: "You will work for the Tutsi during the day and for yourself during the night." ' Although historical traditions confirm the existence of the battle of Karagwe, a battle which Kigeli lost after being overwhelmed by the combined armies of the kings of Karagwe and Buganda, there is not the slightest evidence in support of the contention that the outcome of the battle in any way sealed the fate of the Hutu. Apart from illustrating the mixture of fact and fiction that one is likely to encounter in oral traditions, the story shows a deliberate effort by Hutu politicians to give historical justification for their claims, in a typically Tutsi-like fashion.

merely political revolution, which leaves the pillars of the building standing'.[30] While Burundi has thus far escaped the trauma of a peasant revolution, Marx's verdict seems equally applicable to the Burundi situation. There, too, the social and economic revolution will undoubtedly prove the longer and more arduous of the two.

But this is another tale, which bears its own telling.

Part Three

Burundi

'The duration of the life of a dynasty does not as a rule extend beyond three generations. . . . The third generation has completely forgotten the period of desert life and toughness, as if it had never existed. They have lost the taste for the sweetness of fame and for group feeling, because they are dominated by force. Luxury reaches its peak among them, because they are so much given to a life of prosperity and ease. They become dependent on the dynasty and are like women and children who need to be defended by someone else. Group feeling disappears completely. . . . The ruler, then, has need of other, brave people for his support. He takes many clients and followers. They help the dynasty to some degree, until God permits it to be destroyed, and it goes with everything it stands for.'

Ibn Khaldun, *The Muqaddimah*

10. Burundi in Perspective: A Profile of Political Decomposition

IF THE HISTORY of Rwanda over the past decade inevitably calls to mind reminiscences of France in 1789, that of Burundi invites us to move even further back in time. In some ways, the social and political climate of Burundi in the years following independence reminds one of Renaissance Italy: the deliberate and calculated pursuit of power by individuals who use public office for private ends, the prominent place accorded in public life to the well-born and the well-endowed, and the conception of the state as a work of art—in the sense in which Jacob Burckhardt used this expression, to denote 'that which is deliberately contrived and wrought by individuals, as opposed to any unconscious process or natural evolution of institutions or styles of life'[1]—these are some of the obvious parallels which spring to mind. But perhaps the closest analogy between Renaissance Italy and Burundi lies in the nature of the conditions which made it possible for this style of politics to develop. Just as in Renaissance Italy the erosion of the old feudal order, dramatised by the struggle between pope and emperor, created a kind of political void which in turn encouraged internecine feuds between 'aspiring tyrants, factions, parties and social classes',[2] in Burundi, likewise, political life flourished—or decayed—in a situation of growing illegitimacy.*

Illegitimacy, to be sure, is a notoriously ambiguous concept: what one might regard as evidence of illegitimacy might not necessarily be so for others. But if we take the term to refer to a lack of popular acceptance of traditional values, one can detect a striking convergence of trends in Rwanda and Burundi. Today, the political evolution of Burundi has reached the point where a new constitutional order is set against the old one, and seeks to destroy it root and branch. As in Rwanda, the monarchy has been abolished, and is looked upon by the elites in power as a relic of the feudal ages. More than an anachronism, it is regarded as a major obstacle to social and economic progress, symbolising the dead

---

* One might perhaps better speak of 'conflicting principles of legitimacy', also bearing in mind the time-lag involved in the development of this situation. For a further elaboration upon this theme, see chapter 11.

289

hand of the past whose rigid grip on the institutions of the state prevented the release of modernising energies. Ironically, after emerging triumphant from the struggle for independence, at a moment in the consciousness of the Barundi when it stood as the supreme embodiment of their most cherished national values, the crown* has become for a growing number of politically-minded people the detested emblem of a by-gone era.

To conclude that history merely repeats itself would be misleading, however. Whereas in Rwanda the issue of monarchic versus republican legitimacy became inextricably bound up with the race issue, in Burundi the lines of political cleavage cannot be so easily identified. Ethnic tensions did occur, but they crystallised at a much later date, and then did not necessarily imply a commitment for or against the monarchy. Because it was relatively free of the stigma of caste superiority attached to its Rwanda counterpart, the crown in Burundi was, for a time, a stabilising force—but only for a while, and in the most superficial sense. Not only did the country experience one of the highest rates of governmental instability ever recorded in an independent African state (no less than six governments succeeded each other in power between 1962 and 1966), but the exclusion of the more modernised sectors of society from active political participation created a dangerous imbalance between the social and political systems, which could be redressed only at the expense of the crown.

In contrast with what happened in Rwanda, where the major point of tension lay in the opposition between Hutu and Tutsi, in Burundi the ethnic struggle tended to coexist with, and cut across, a social conflict between a privileged oligarchy—represented by the king and his relatives—and a newly-emergent elite of mixed origins whose grievances against the regime expressed their sense of revolt in the face of a socio-political order which denied them the opportunities for social, economic and political advancement to which they considered themselves entitled.

The Challenge of Modernisation

The resulting concentration of power in the hands of a traditional oligarchy that was largely indifferent to social and economic reform

---

* Here, as elsewhere in this discussion, the term 'crown' is used to designate the symbolic aspects of *mwami*-ship (i.e. the symbols of the *mwami*'s religious and political authority) as well as the institution associated with the office. Where the context does not otherwise specify the connotation, the term should be taken to refer to both the symbolic and institutional referents of the *mwami*-ship.

and concerned only with the perpetuation of its entrenched privileges, explains why, until recently, all efforts at modernisation failed conspicuously. Though possessing those very elements which some have singled out as the crucial determinants of modernisation[3]—i.e., relatively stable territorial boundaries; a fairly homogeneous national culture; a traditional ruler identified with the state as a whole, whose rule, far from being discredited by its association with the colonial administration, stood as a symbol of national unity—for as long as the monarchy remained in power Burundi was probably as far from realising the fundamental and manifold transformations which political modernisation implies as any other state in Africa. Whatever connotations one wishes to ascribe to the concept of modernisation, the record is anything but impressive: if, for example, one takes modernisation to imply a rational use of economic resources, the introduction of new methods of production, and priority to the more productive types of investments, Burundi has made little headway since independence. Indeed, the evidence shows that it has regressed. This explains, but does not necessarily justify, the hand-washing response of a French technical expert in a recent report to the Quai d'Orsay to the effect that Burundi is, economically speaking, a lost cause.

However pessimistic, this view is substantially confirmed by the statement issued by a group of junior civil servants in February 1966, in which they openly admitted being faced with 'a disastrous economic situation'.[4] The budgetary deficit for 1965 was said to have reached 100 million Burundi francs (approximately $(US)1,150,000), with prospects of an even greater deficit in 1966. Local enterprises produced only 25 to 50 per cent of their normal rate of production. Tax receipts had dropped sharply. Diagnosing future trends, the authors went on to point out that, unless drastic measures were taken, 'private enterprises will soon close down; custom duties will disappear; prices will go up'. The chief cause of this economic slump was said to be 'political instability': 'Because of the protracted political instability with which we have been faced, there has been no continuity to our decisions. All our projects could be implemented if only we enjoyed political stability, and if economic matters were given precedence over politics.'

To modernise the economy was hardly conceivable unless similar efforts were undertaken in the political and social realms. But here again, if by successful modernisation is meant the adaptation of traditional roles to a new socio-political structure, recent attempts to fit monarchic rule within the context of parliamentary institutions have been detrimental to both. For, if the failure of parliament to resolve its own inner contradictions was bound to invite the criticisms, and eventually the intervention, of the crown, discredit has also been cast upon the crown for its unwarranted meddling in the parliamentary processes. Only if modernity is identified with the emergence of new reference groups, with new values and attitudes, can a notable transformation since independence be discerned.

Here lies the essence of the dilemma faced by the Burundi monarchy in the years following independence: while the regime seemed to operate on the assumption that the norms prevailing in the traditional society had lost none of their legitimacy, in fact this legitimacy has been steadily eroded by the social transformations that have taken place during these years. New social groupings have come into being, which acquired a political consciousness of their own, a new perspective on the world as well as on the future destinies of their country, and which insisted on becoming full participants in the political system of Burundi. But, as the system proved utterly inadequate to accommodate their claims, it soon lost its basis of legitimacy. It unwittingly contributed to the surge of an alienated counter-elite, whose growing opposition to the crown was only temporarily checked by the self-limiting effects of ethnic dissensions in their midst.

THE ROOTS OF INSTABILITY

Basically, the process of decomposition that has taken place since independence is reducible to an extremely rapid politicisation of residual ethnic ties, and to a concommitant decline in the efficiency of party, parliament and bureaucracy. The ethnic crisis which tore asunder the Parti de l'Union et du Progrès National (UPRONA)—until its collapse, in late 1962, the main vehicle of nationalist assertions—gave a full measure of the depth of antagonisms between Hutu and Tutsi; but it also destroyed the only institutionalised source of authority which could conceivably substitute itself for the crown. Once the party had ceased to function as an autonomous political unit, the contagion quickly spread to parliamentary institutions. By then, the administrative machinery also threatened to collapse. In the absence of a viable institutional framework, the crown had no alternative but to step in and fill the vacuum as best it could. Just as the divisions between Hutu and Tutsi resulted in the collapse of the nationalist party, the persistence of these divisions among the Westernised elites seriously compromised their chances of concerted action against the crown, and therefore, also, their chances of fomenting rational change. As power passed into the hands of the traditional *ganwa* oligarchy, there emerged a type of polity which can best be described, in Professor Halpern's words, as a 'system of structured instability'—a system which 'lacks the capacity for orderly change responsive to the revolution of modernization', in part because 'the groups who share power in this manner avoid any action that would alter the existing system by removing the fundamental causes of cleavage that divide the groups'.[5]

At the root of this political immobilism lay a calculated attempt by the court to set itself up as the sole arbiter of conflict among competing factions. This did not necessarily mean a denial of political participation to the representatives of the new elites, but the extent and duration of their participation remained constantly subject to the court veto. Only the court had the authority to stipulate how much power a government could enjoy, and for how long. The political process was thus reduced to a protracted, and seemingly innocuous, game of musical chairs, accessible to all claimants as long as they accepted the rules of the game as defined by the court.

The only element of stability in the system was represented by those former chiefs, or *ganwa*, to whom the king entrusted key responsibilities. Though no longer claiming the status of chiefs, as a traditional elite they nonetheless retained considerable influence. Because of the family connections that linked the Bezi chiefs to the crown, and also because the king had no desire to manage the affairs of the realm single-handedly, the *ganwa* emerged as the real power behind the throne. But their power seldom manifested itself otherwise than in the most negative fashion—to stifle whatever initiative may have come from the government, to initiate sanctions against a 'rebellious' politician, or to induce the king to withdraw his confidence from his ministers. Although the king himself may not have been averse to change, nor unwilling to divest himself of his traditional prerogatives when the circumstances so required, once he had surrendered power to this entrenched patriciate Mwambutsa lost the capacity to act independently. As often happened in pre-colonial times, the king became the captive of his courtiers, who were, in turn, the victims of their continuing strong commitments to the political norms of the past.

Indeed, the kind of 'structured instability' brought to light during the latter part of Mwambutsa's reign is not without a certain similarity to the cyclical transformations that took place before the advent of colonial rule. In the past, the occurrence of dynastic rivalries among the princes of the blood produced considerable instability among office holders, but left the overall structure of the system virtually untouched. Similarly, the rapid turnover of political personnel in the post-independence period had little effect on the nature of political offices or on the traditional role structure within which they were embedded.

293

In each case, a new set of incumbents periodically came to power, but the structure of power remained unchanged. In each case, the game of politics was performed in a closed system, a system in which the continuing resilience of traditional roles served as a deterrent against structural innovations. Thus, while each new cabinet that came to power since independence brought promises of a fresh start, each time the fresh starts marked the beginnings only of new cycles of deterioration.

Among the factors which in recent times have contributed to perpetuate this state of affairs, none is more obvious—and yet more frequently misunderstood—than the so-called 'aura of legitimacy' surrounding the crown. That the crown happened to be part of the conventional myths, superstitions and mysteries associated with the traditional culture of Burundi is only part of the explanation. Even more significant is the central importance accorded to the symbols of kingship in the nationalist mythology of UPRONA. Although the recognised leader of UPRONA, Louis Rwagasore, was a chief, and indeed a *ganwa*, his unmatched popularity as a nationalist leader stemmed not from his chiefly status but from the fact that he happened to be the Mwami's eldest son. As such, he personified the growing attachment of the masses to the crown in reaction against the humiliations of colonial rule and the exactions of those who seemed to have acted as the agents of Belgian colonialism—the chiefs. The cruel irony of the situation is that, although the masses looked to the crown to bring the chiefs to heel, once the party had disintegrated the crown served as the instrument through which the chiefs regained authority and stature in the political system. Meanwhile, however, the crown continued to attract the solid loyalties of the peasant masses, binding them together around a common symbol and with a common mythology. The motto of UPRONA—'One God, one Mwami, one Country'—was also the slogan through which sentiments of loyalty to the monarchy found expression, irrespective of caste, region or occupation. In these conditions, any move against the crown was likely to be interpreted as an affront to UPRONA and its leader, and, by implication, to the goals and aspirations they symbolised.

Another source of strength for the monarchy lay in the gradual extension of kinship ties and family connections through the entire political system, and in the reciprocal obligations thereby incurred by various incumbents towards each other. Public office served as a screen behind which personal favours were extended and repaid. The civil service, in particular, was converted into a vast reservoir of sinecures, awarded on the basis of personal loyalty to the grantor; since loyalty was almost inevitably equated with kinship ties, nepotism was institutionalised on a scale which frightened even the beneficiaries of the system. The extensiveness of this chain of reciprocities was such that no one could possibly hope to dominate the system, let alone alter it from within. The sheer weight and pervasiveness of kinship obligations was enough to ensure compliance even from the most recalcitrant.

In these circumstances, the only serious threats to the regime were those originating from the outside—from organised political groups whose social bases were fundamentally different from those of the Establishment. Yet this is also where the strength of the monarchy resided, for, in the absence of any such form of political organisation, the position of the crown seemed almost impregnable. Since the party had long ceased to exist, where else could legitimacy inhere if not in the monarchy?

The problem of creating new political institutions which can either substitute themselves for, or at least impose enough pliancy on, the traditional ones to accommodate the forces unleashed by modernity is intimately linked to the social structure and environment within which these forces operate. The very complexity of Burundi's traditional social structure, divided as it is into a variety of different castes and status groups, coupled with the obstacles arising from the absence of an adequate communications network, greatly hampered social and political mobilisation and control. Further, this process of social mobilisation, however arduous and incomplete, so far from producing broad, over-arching solidarities, was the source of renewed tensions between Hutu and Tutsi. 'The process of modernization', as Samuel Huntington points out, 'induces not just class consciousness but group consciousness of all kinds: village, tribe, clan, religion, caste. Modernization means that all groups, old as well as new, become increasingly aware of themselves as groups, and of their interests and claims in relation to other groups.'[6] The supreme paradox, then, is that the impact of modernisation, while creating the conditions of a new social order, also contributed to generate new divisions within the modernised elite, making it all the more difficult for them to attain their objectives. For, in spite of their agreement that the monarchy had outlived its usefulness, this unanimity concealed some basic differences on the methods to be employed, and on which group should take the place of the traditional oligarchs. In short, the mere presence of ethnic divisions among its opponents gave the monarchy a new lease on life.

THE PROBLEM OF LEGITIMACY

The capacity of the monarchy to maintain itself in power, though intimately related to the factors just mentioned, also depended on the very nature of its policies. 'On the whole', wrote G. M. Trevelyan, 'social change moves like an underground river, obeying its own laws or those of economic change, rather than following the direction of political happenings that move on the surface of life. Politics are the outcome rather than the cause of social change.'[7] This statement cannot be accepted unreservedly, for if the influence of social change, or the absence thereof, is clearly of fundamental importance to an understanding of political events, the relationship between the two is not irreversible. The only point here is that the mistakes of the crown—its own ineptitude in the handling of the Hutu-Tutsi conflict, its lack of foresight and initiative, as well as the taint of ethnic favouritism which eventually coloured its policies—were just as instrumental in throwing discredit upon the institution as the changes of attitude induced by the thrust of modernity.

Initially, the policies of the crown were sufficiently free of deliberate constraints to discourage the rise of a stridently anti-monarchic opposition from either Hutu or Tutsi. Indeed, the political climate of Burundi between 1962 and 1965 was surprisingly tolerant, and refreshingly free of the 'mobilisation' features that one might have encountered during these years in other African states. When the crown intervened, it did so for seemingly excellent reasons—to curb demagogy, to mete out a deserved punishment, or to withdraw its mandate from a government which, from all appearances, no longer enjoyed popular support. Instead of taking sides with Hutu or Tutsi, the crown engaged in a complicated 'ethnic arithmetic' designed to give each faction an equal share of whatever power was left to the government. The diffusion of authority among the representatives of each group meant that neither side felt directly threatened by the system. Although feelings of dissatisfaction with the regime were undoubtedly widespread among both Hutu and Tutsi elites, for the time being at least the incentives to compromise were stronger than the inducements to revolt.

Quite different was the situation prevailing in mid-1965. From a situation of uneasy coexistence between two conflicting principles of legitimacy, in the summer of 1965 the system moved abruptly in the direction of monarchic absolutism. Worse still, this move occurred almost immediately after the crown had given unmistakable evidence of its desire to restore the legitimacy of parliament by calling new elections and by adding an upper chamber to the legislature, as the constitution prescribed. What is significant here is not only the abrupt change in the strategy of the court, but that it seemed so deliberately aimed at depriving the Hutu of their electoral gains. As opposition tides rose, the court fought back by a further curtailment of parliamentary institutions. By late 1965, the opposition to the palace had succeeded in rallying the support of a variety of discontented Hutu elements—intellectuals, deputies, civil servants, army and gendarmerie officers, all of whom felt that the policies of the court were not only despotic but clearly influenced by ethnic favouritism.

By then, the issue of monarchic versus parliamentary legitimacy could no longer be evaded. This was not only a conflict of legitimacy but a struggle for power between the Hutu elites and the crown. For the Tutsi, however, it was a choice not so much between traditional autocracy and parliamentary rule as between Hutu rule and a ruling monarchy, the latter being viewed for the time being as the lesser of two evils.

The main event, the knot in the skein from which the threads of all subsequent developments can be traced, took place on October 18, 1965, when a handful of Hutu army and gendarmerie officers unsuccessfully tried to overthrow the monarchy. Ironically, the consequences of the abortive coup were hardly less consequential than if it had succeeded. Indeed, the events of October 1965 brought to full light the extreme fragility of the institutional scaffolding built around the palace. Once the Mwami had fled the country, the process of government was reduced to a near standstill. For a while, Burundi seemed to exist in a period suspended outside time. A state of organised anarchy seemed to prevail, with the army as one of the few organising structures remaining available. Although the country still had a civilian government, in practice the normal functions of government were taken over by the army and the bureaucracy, both of which were now purged of Hutu elements. Not until July 8, 1966, was an attempt made to resolve the crisis, when a new 'government of Public Safety' was brought to power, under the protective wing of the army.

One of the most revealing aspects of the political life of Burundi at this crucial juncture lies in the relationship between the governmental crisis that followed the abortive coup and the succession crisis ushered in by Mwambutsa's precipitous flight to Europe. The army and the bureaucracy could, presumably, opt for one of two courses: either they could disregard the legitimacy of monarchic institutions altogether and set up a republican form of government, with or without the participation of the military; or else they could simply revert to the old system and restore the crown to its controlling position. The latter alternative, however, was quickly ruled out by the incumbents, as being largely incompatible with their psychological commitments. A republican regime was, at one point, very seriously considered, but was not without certain disadvantages. Given the profound attachment of the rural masses to the symbols of kingship, any such drastic alteration of

the established constitutional order could well trigger off a major upheaval in the countryside. On the other hand, the perpetuation of monarchic legitimacy offered opportunities for manipulation which otherwise might not be available. Thus a third alternative was eventually
chosen, which enabled the new power holders to 'have their cake and
eat it': by calling upon Prince Charles Ndizeye, then a teen-age prince,
to assume the burdens of *mwami*-ship, they hoped to minimise the
chances of further obstruction by the crown; and, by vesting all powers
in the hands of a civilian-military junta responsible to no one but itself,
they instituted a form of government totally in keeping with their
modernising aspirations.

In a way, the intervention of the army in July 1966 was intended, at
first, to save the monarchy from itself; but the end result was nothing
short of a political monstrosity. What emerged was a misshapen, hybrid
regime—a half-civilian, half-praetorian government, coupled with a
monarchy that struggled vainly to define its role in the political system.
The coexistence within this framework of such divergent interests as the
army, the bureaucrats and the crown was bound to result in serious
tensions.

Once again, the core of the dilemma lay in the combination of conflicting principles of legitimacy. When Captain Micombero took over the
prime-ministership, in June 1966, it was with the intention of redefining
the role of the crown along the lines prescribed in the constitution of
1962, which meant that the king would still reign but would no longer
rule. The crown was identified with an entirely new style of politics,
involving many of the features normally attributed to 'mobilisation'
systems. Authority was deliberately centralised at the top in order to
bring to fruition with maximum speed and efficiency all the latent
potentialities of society. The emphasis was on selflessness, abstinence
and thrift, and this, presumably, for the sake of a better future, associated with the vision of a 'brave new world'. In addition, heavy reliance
was placed on planning and rationalism as means of effecting rapid
social and economic changes. The prevailing atmosphere reminded one
of Professor Apter's contention that '[mobilization systems] are for the
young, not the aged; the future, not the past. . . . The atmosphere of
mobilization is one of crisis and attack. . . . All life becomes politicized.
. . . In the end, the state exerts its primacy over everything.'[8]

But, as the state tried to assert its primacy over the crown, the crown
insisted on asserting its primacy over the state. Although the roles
were now being played by different actors, the sequence of events
following the coup of July 1966 provided a curious re-enactment of
Mwambutsa's policies. Blissfully indifferent to the warnings of the

'king-makers', Prince Charles attempted to assert himself as the only legitimate source of authority. On the basis of the precedents established by his father, and with the help of his courtiers, he began to arrogate to himself full control over certain key ministries, by converting them into secretariats of state under the supervision of the court. He then proceeded to ask for the dismissal of the Minister of Foreign Affairs, but finally settled for a reshuffling of portfolios. When the government showed increasing signs of recalcitrance, the court tried to force its resignation.

Although the strategy of the crown in 1966 was no different from what it used to be under Mwambutsa, the circumstances then were entirely different from those which Mwambutsa had encountered when he first decided to reign and rule and ride roughshod over the constitution. In 1966, the game was being played against a far more serious adversary. Gone were the days when governments were torn asunder by ethnic dissensions and when the crown could still rely on the loyalty of the army to vouchsafe its rule. By now, not only was the prestige of the crown seriously dented by its failure to take appropriate measures to meet the modernising aspirations of the 'Young Turks' (civil servants, students, gendarmerie and army officers), but the military was now sharing control over the government with the civilians. The military, in other words, was now geared, like the government, to the goal of national redemption, against the forces of sectionalism, feudalism and monarchic absolutism. What had initially begun as a conflict of legitimacy between the crown and the government quickly transformed itself into a trial of strength between the crown and the army. As the crown renewed its bid for power, it unconsciously sowed the seeds of its own dethronement.

As one reflects on the events and circumstances surrounding the fall of the Burundi monarchy, one can hardly escape the conclusion that the legitimacy of the crown, though not identical with the legitimacy of the monarch, could not but be profoundly influenced by the personality as well as the policies of the monarch and his supporters. As it became apparent that these policies not only failed to satisfy the modernising expectations of the Westernised elites but in fact aimed at turning the political clock back to pre-colonial times—to a system in which politics were the prerogative of the court, and the spoils of power the rewards of the sovereign to his chiefs—part of the animus which the office-holder attracted to himself was bound to rub off on the office.

To go back to the analogy suggested at the beginning of this chapter, and by way of a post-mortem to the monarchy, one can do no better than quote Machiavelli's comments on "The Power of Fortune in Human Affairs":

> If a prince bases himself entirely on Fortune, he will fall when she varies. I also believe that a ruler will be successful who adapts his mode of procedure to the quality of the times, and likewise that he will be unsuccessful if the times are out of accord with his procedure. . . . These results are caused by nothing else than the nature of the times, which is or is not in harmony with the procedure of men. It also accounts for what I have mentioned, namely that two persons working differently, chance to arrive at the same result; and that of two who work in the same way, one attains his end, but the other does not.[9]

Though Mwambutsa and Ntare worked along much the same lines, neither succeeded in 'attaining his end'—and for basically the same reasons. Neither had the will or the capacity to attune their perspectives and procedures to 'the nature of the times'. Whether the army men, working differently, will reach different results, remains an open question.

11. *Mwami*-ship:
Ethos and Structure

ALTHOUGH THE MONARCHY is now a thing of the past, the long history of the Burundi dynasties, the symbolic significance attached to the office of *mwami*-ship, and the cultural heritage with which it has become associated, all bear testimony to the central role it has played in shaping the destinies of the realm. If the social and political forces set in motion by the advent of independence have often tended to operate in spite of, though not always independently from, the crown, the latter has nonetheless set the basic parameters within which the system functioned between 1962 and 1966. Until its overthrow, the crown acted as the single most important stabilising element in the political system, a role which it could not have played for so long and, up to a point, so successfully unless it had already acquired a legitimacy of its own.

Part of the peculiar dilemma of Burundi politics in the years immediately following independence was the difficulty of reconciling monarchic and governmental conceptions of legitimacy. Here we touch upon a fundamental paradox underlying the role of the crown, and in this paradox lies the clue to the seeming inconsistencies of Burundi politics during this period. The monarchy served as a legitimising formula* for the consecutive rise to power of a variety of elite groups whose rule, each time, came to be viewed as illegitimate by a potential counter-elite. As the incumbents, each in turn, steadily strengthened their identification with the crown—or vice versa—monarchical rule incurred a similar loss of legitimacy, in the end giving way to a republican regime.

The rapid and dramatic shifts of power that punctuated Burundi's evolution in the 1960s illustrate this only too well. In spite of his strong personal reservations about the usefulness of a ruling monarchy, Rwagasore owed his tremendous popularity as a nationalist leader to his unique title-deeds to eminence as the Mwami's eldest son, which

* The expression is here used in a sense largely synonymous with Mosca's 'political formula', referring to the abstraction through which the elites in power seek to justify their rule. For further information on Mosca's concept of the 'political formula', see Gaetano Mosca, *The Ruling Class* (*Elementi di scienza politica*), McGraw Hill, New York 1939, pp. 70–72.

301

at the same time conferred upon his party the 'aura of legitimacy' it needed to defeat its opponents. Similarly, only by spreading the mantle of royal authority on their political ambitions were certain members of the old *ganwa* aristocracy able to seize power from Rwagasore's party, after his death in 1961. And when, in October 1965, a group of discontented army and police officers, of Hutu origins, tried to overthrow the monarchy, it was again in the name of monarchic legitimacy that loyalist elements intervened to quash the mutiny and later decided to bring Mwambutsa's heir to the throne. By then, however, the kingmakers' perception of what constituted monarchic legitimacy differed fundamentally from the king's. While in theory the principle of kingship could still supply a source of legitimation for the pursuit of modernising goals, monarchical rule at this stage held political implications which could no longer be reconciled with the modernising aspirations of the new elites.

Thus, if the history of Burundi since independence is in a sense reducible to a protracted crisis of legitimacy, it is in point to note that the institutions around which the crisis initially revolved were *governmental* institutions. Only when monarchical and governmental institutions so reinforced each other as to become virtually indistinguishable was the fate of the monarchy directly involved. A preliminary distinction, therefore, must be drawn between the legitimising values of the monarchy and the political structures to which monarchical rule was harnessed, and which, so long as they allowed for a modicum of flexibility and mutual autonomy, constituted its best guarantee of survival.

The relative vitality of the crown, as an institution, stemmed in part from a certain conception of monarchic legitimacy which, for want of a better term, is referred to below as the 'ethos of *mwami*-ship'; moreover, the institutions of power surrounding the crown were at first sufficiently decentralised to allow political competition to take place without endangering its legitimacy. The structural weakness of the Burundi monarchy constituted its principal source of strength. Without in any way minimising the importance of the so-called 'modernising expectations' of the new elites as a source of conflict, the future of the monarchy was never so much in doubt as when, in response to a variety of pressures, it chose to depart from its more traditional orientation and transformed itself from a reigning into a ruling monarchy.

THE ETHOS OF *Mwami*-SHIP

'As long as the human heart is strong and the human reason weak, royalty will be strong because it appeals to diffuse feelings, and republics weak because they appeal to understanding.'[1] Whether Bagehot's phrase can be taken as a sure indication that Burundi has now passed from the primeval, pre-literate age into the world of scientific reason is beside the point; but it does call attention to the fact that every age, every civilisation, has its own peculiar way of looking at the world, its own patterns of thinking and modes of cognition—in short, its own ethos. What is meant here, specifically, by the 'ethos of *mwami*-ship' is that the institution of kingship has traditionally operated on the basis of certain symbols, and within the framework of a certain belief system, from which it derived a powerful, though largely irrational, support. As an institution, *mwami*-ship was not only a time-honoured symbol of national unity: it was also a source of religious sanctions which deferred possible threats to its legitimacy. Although the incumbent may have been regarded by some as unworthy of holding office, the office itself conveyed an image of virtue which clearly transcended the realm of human contingencies. It was part of a psychic whole which gave meaning and purpose to all members of society, regardless of social or ethnic origins. It was linked to the well-being of the nation through specific rituals (like those attending the celebration of the *umuganuro*, the sorghum festival) and symbols (like the royal drum, *Karyenda*), and thus acted as a mystic bond, unifying the dead, the living and the unborn, and, likewise, gave a sense of corporate unity to Tutsi, Hutu and Twa.*

Whatever else can be said of the concept of monarchic legitimacy, from the moment one tries to pin it down in the form of a reasonably precise formulation a host of difficulties immediately arises. The

* Illustrative of the complex of symbolism and magic surrounding the *mwami*-ship is the song, *Mwami wacu* (Our Mwami), until recently broadcast every day at noon over the radio, with religious punctuality. Though most of the historical references to Mwambutsa's prowess are patently false, they nonetheless suggest a strong mythical connection between royal authority and national power, and between the Mwami's personal well-being and the well-being of the nation as a whole:

> Our Mwami, Owner of the Drum,
> Our Mwami Mwambutsa,
> Thou, who defeated Biroro,
> Maconco,
> Kilima,
> Makaza,
> Triumph, triumph and reign in peace,
> Triumph over your enemies
> And let the sorghum ripen in Muramvya.
> O Mwami, Owner of the Drum,
> You are the Victorious Mwami.
> Triumph, triumph and reign in peace.

problem, in part, lies in the widely different connotations attached to the notion of kingship, itself a reflection of the variety of traditions and institutions with which it could conceivably be identified. On the eve of independence, for example, kingship could be taken to refer to a specific national cultural tradition, to a political institution, or it could be seen as the apex of a particular type of social stratification. The conceptual ambiguities involved in the definition of kingship become even more patent when one seeks to approach it from the perspective of a transitional environment. Is the national cultural tradition of Burundi that which is conveyed through oral traditions, or that which is pictured in the writings of modern politicians and literati? Is kingship as a political institution to be defined by reference to tradition or by modern constitutional norms? Is kingship to be viewed as the capstone of a traditional social pyramid or as the uppermost echelon in a modern social ladder alongside the traditional one? Here again there are a variety of possible interpretations.

Nor are the difficulties removed by leaving aside the 'transitional' dimension of the problem; even when replaced in its traditional context, there remains a peculiar ambivalence attached to the notion of monarchic legitimacy. To associate the monarchy with a 'national' cultural tradition suggests a degree of cultural uniformity for which neither the history of Burundi nor its political and social institutions supply conclusive evidence. In the absence of a cognitive map comparable to the *bwiru* of Rwanda, the historian is left with the alternative of consulting oral traditions; but these are notoriously unreliable, full of distortions and ambiguities, accidental or deliberate. Only in a very general sense, and by reference to specific symbols (like the *Karyenda*) and ceremonies (like the *umuganuro*) is it possible to speak of a 'national' cultural tradition, and even then there is still room for considerable disagreement as to the 'national' character and ultimate significance of such symbols and ceremonies.

One faces similar difficulties in seeking to elucidate the meaning of kingship as a political institution. Considering the frequency of the changes that have affected the format and structure of monarchical rule over the last century and a half, and when one remembers that there were times when not one but two or three different aspirants to the throne claimed legitimacy, each in turn claiming jurisdiction over the other's domains, one wonders whether there is any point in even raising the question. One possible way of coming to terms with the problem is to infer from oral sources the attributes which tradition conferred upon the *mwami* and *mwami*-ship in general. *Mwami*-ship as a supreme source of authority, a symbol of liberality, an object of inviolability: such are the themes succinctly expressed in proverbs like 'The Mwami protects your property' (*Umwami aguntugira mu vyawe*); 'The Mwami may be late in dispensing gifts, but he never fails' (*Umwami yimye niwe asaba*); 'The Mwami seeks no appeal' (*Umwami arateba ntaherana*); 'It is not the Mwami who kills, but his courtiers' (*Umwami ntiyica hica umusavyi*).[2] For each of these proverbs, however, others can be found which either restrict or negate whatever evidence each has to offer. Even the ubiquitous and more tersely evocative formula, '*Sabwa Ganza*', the royal motto—roughly translatable as 'The Mwami reigns and rules'—conveys a totally misleading picture of the nature of royal authority. For if one can entertain legitimate doubts as to the scope and structure of royal authority at any given point in time, most informed observers seem to agree that royal power was anything but despotic,[3] but in fact rested in the hands of a traditional oligarchy (*ganwa*) which ruled in the name of the monarch, or in spite of himself.

As regards the pattern of social stratification associated with kingship, one might have hoped to be standing on firmer ground. As noted earlier, the crown stood at the peak of a social pyramid in which the top positions, below the crown, were occupied by the descendants of the royal family (*ganwa*), with the lower orders, Tutsi, Hutu and Twa, constituting the base. This, however, is a rather superficial and in a sense inaccurate view. Not every member of the royal family claimed the same degree of 'closeness' to the king or the court, and these varying types of relationships, formal or informal, introduced a major variable in the hierarchy of rank and privilege. Moreover, the conferment of political or ceremonial functions upon the members of an inferior caste implied corresponding variations in the formal status positions established through the caste system. Finally, social prestige was more often than not the result of family connections or clan affiliations, which had very little to do with caste stratification. In these conditions, it is only with the greatest circumspection that one can equate monarchic legitimacy with the maintenance of a specific system of social stratification. This does not mean that it cannot be done, but the conclusions it would yield would probably not add significantly to what can already be inferred from the foregoing, namely that the concept of monarchic legitimacy remained an extremely vague, elusive concept, susceptible to a variety of interpretations. However trite and disappointing, this is also the most illuminating conclusion one can reach about kingship in Burundi.

The point here is *not* that kingship as such was unimportant, either as a source of legitimacy or an institution, but that its very loose connotations and structural malleability made it infinitely more adaptable to political change than was true of its counterpart in Rwanda. Kingship in Rwanda could only be described as 'despotic', and its normative implications as starkly inegalitarian. What is more, the symbolic referents of the institution carried an emotional effect profoundly detrimental to its capacity for survival in a democratic environment. In Burundi, by contrast, kingship implied a dispersal of power, and, because it was relatively free of the stigma of caste supremacy, its position seemed all the more secure.

The contrast with Rwanda is nowhere more obvious than in the different uses to which *mwami*-ship, as a legitimising formula, initially lent itself. Whereas in Rwanda the institution of kingship came to be regarded as the most formidable obstacle in the way of democratisation, in Burundi its role has been largely the reverse. Not only was *mwami*-ship seized upon by the nationalist elites to justify their claims to independence through democratic elections, but, as the masses became less and less beholden to the aristocracy, as they became increasingly resentful of the arbitrariness of chiefly rule and ever more conscious of the promises of democracy, they found in the concept of *mwami*-ship a meaning which they were not yet able to find in democracy—and a source of emotional identification which democracy has yet to supply. *Mwami*-ship, in other words, served as a focus for popular loyalties and sentimental attachments in an environment from which both seemed to be rapidly disappearing.

That much and even more can be inferred from the interesting pamphlet by the late Paul Mirerekano, *Mbire gito canje . . . (Listen my son . . .)*, published in 1961.[4] Written in the form of a political manifesto, which at one point became the Bible of every self-respecting UPRONA supporter, Mirerekano's work gives the closest approximation we have of what monarchic legitimacy meant at the time for the average Murundi. As one might have expected, Mirerekano's views on politics are intimately connected with his conception of *mwami*-ship. His initial exhortation is typical: 'Let the Owner of the Drum, the Mwami of Burundi, reign. Let *mwami*-ship be strong. Let it strengthen public order and the union of all Barundi in peace and justice!' Having paid tribute to the monarchy, he then goes on to elaborate on some familiar themes:

The *mwami* makes the law for all the Barundi. The *mwami* holds his power from God. As such he represents all the Barundi. Barundi! Do not follow the example of neighbouring countries (i.e. republics), or else you will disintegrate like flour scattered on the ground. Do not trip and fumble lest you lose the drumsticks and find yourself

7. Tutsi (Rwanda).

8. Tutsi-Hima (Burundi).

9. Hutu woman (Rwanda).

10. Twa (Rwanda).

11. Hutu terrorists under the surveillance of a Belgian paratrooper, near Astrida (now Butare), September 1960.

12. A Tutsi child lying near the spear that nailed him to the ground.

unable to get back on your feet. Say to yourself: 'We are the virgins who serve the Owner of the Drum.' The Drum is like the taste of honey to the lips of the Barundi! You must bend your energies around the Drum so as to make possible the strengthening of the established order and the union of all.

To help promote 'the strengthening of the established order and the union of all', Mirerekano's advice is simple: 'Remember the beautiful customs of the realm. . . . Too many people have forgotten the customs and traditions of the past, and therefore no longer know the proper behaviour to adopt towards others. . . . One no longer makes a distinction between an eminent guest, close relatives, a mere friend and ordinary people.' Above all, too many people have lost the sense of 'mutual aid', the key to good relations among neighbours: 'Solicit each other's help, respect each other, forgive each other. . . . The Barundi who are mindful of the established order know that to solicit each other's assistance is the basis of love and unity among men.'

To those who would object that to solicit aid from a superior is a form of subjection, Mirerekano's answer is that 'subjection has always existed, and here, as in other countries, the welfare of the people depends on reciprocal obligations'. To take but one example: 'If the cowkeeper deserts his master, the latter will sell his cows. No cowkeeper, no cows. No cows, no profit. There will be a shortage of milk, and a shortage of manure, and the crops will no longer thrive. Now, is it not true that when the cows disappear their owner is not the only one to suffer?' Throughout the book a deliberate emphasis is placed on the notion of reciprocity—expressed by the recurrent use of the term *kusaba*, meaning 'to solicit aid from someone'—as if to impress upon the reader the central importance of traditional hierarchical relationships among men. All along, in a typically Burkean fashion, Mirerekano seeks to justify tradition on the basis of its longevity, arguing that men must, on principle, obey their habitual social and political impulses.

However revealing from the standpoint of the institutions and style of life it portrays, Mirerekano's book aimed at something more fundamental. Its purpose was not only to extol the virtues of the past but to adapt the past to the present. Every page contains a prescription of some kind or another, but the dominant theme is that progress in one realm is no reason to overlook the sources of progress which tradition affords. Thus, if men 'have learned to fly like birds, and move underwater like fish', which, the author admits, is as much a proof of progress as 'spatial research', this does not mean that men can throw off all reverence for tradition and live unrestrainedly as if it did not exist. Despite his evident

307

Burundi

nostalgia for the traditional order, Mirerekano's precepts are not purely and simply 'reactionary'.

The emphasis placed by the author on the traditional bases of monarchic legitimacy was as much a reflection of his own emotional commitment to *mwami*-ship as a symptom of his anxiety over the passing of tradition. Although his views were undoubtedly representative of a large segment of public opinion, his interpretation of monarchic legitimacy was scarcely compatible with the ideological orientation of other and better-educated elites. Their intellectual background and predispositions were very different from Mirerekano's, as was their conception of the crown's position in the emergent polity. Rather than equating it with an idealised past, their inclination was to reinterpret the notion of kingship along the lines of a constitutional monarchy, taking as their frame of reference the examples of Belgium or Britain.

Even though, on the eve of independence, the legitimacy of the crown stood virtually unchallenged, there were already many signs of change and these became increasingly manifest as years went by. Indeed, that the book should have been written as a paean to the monarchy by a Hutu who was later shot for his presumed duplicity in a plot against the monarchy, bears testimony to fundamental changes of attitude among certain Barundi elites, and in particular among the Hutu elites. The crisis of legitimacy suffered by the monarchy was, to a considerable extent, a reflection of the very rapid social changes which have affected Burundi society in the years following independence.

Mirerekano's conception of the monarchy must be seen not only against the background of the changes that have taken place in society as a whole but in the light of the capacity of the monarchical institutions to accommodate the demands and expectations of new social groupings. At the time the book was written, it was still possible for the monarchy to maintain the belief—or the illusion—that the existing political structures were the most appropriate. But, as the system rapidly moved in the direction of royal autocracy, with the institution of kingship increasingly identified with the interests of a small group of feudatories, the issue of monarchic legitimacy was quickly pushed into the foreground of Burundi politics. The closure of opportunities for political participation at the top, combined with the surge of popular pressures from below, stripped the monarchy of whatever measure of legitimacy it still had. This situation calls attention to the continuing strength and vitality of certain traditional vested interests, whose grip upon the system was only temporarily released by the jerk they received from the thrust of modern nationalist forces.

308

THE CONSOLIDATION OF DYNASTIC RULE

The structural changes that shaped the form of the monarchy in the years preceding independence are just as crucial to an understanding of Burundi politics as the social changes which, after independence, threatened its survival. Colonial rule did not stop the motions of the system at a fixed point in time. In a sense, the political system of Burundi never stood still. Even under the constraints of colonialism, it continued to display a built-in tendency toward fission and consolidation, with the latter trend becoming ever more predominant in recent years.

As noted in an earlier chapter, the history of Burundi until the inception of colonial rule, and for some years thereafter, can be reduced to a long sequence of internecine feuds among the princes of the blood, with the monarchy surviving, as it were, within the interstices of the struggle. Only towards the close of the colonial period did the kingdom finally transform itself from a mere aggregate of more or less autonomous chiefdoms into a more unified political entity. This kind of structural transformation is a familiar one to the student of African history (as well as to the medieval historian), and one needs only to look back to the early history of Buganda to find a similar process of centralisation going on throughout the nineteenth century. What should be stressed here is that, in Burundi, this process took place very slowly and incompletely, and then not so much under the leadership of the king as under the guidance of a particular royal lineage, the Bezi.

Although the authority of the Bezi undeniably grew at the expense of their immediate rivals, the Batare, there was no immediate and complete elimination of the Batare from the political arena. Even after being relegated to the sidelines, they continued to display a remarkable vitality and resourcefulness, which not only set important limitations on the Bezi sphere of influence but also led to continuing rivalries within each clan. Thus, at no time before or after independence were the princes of the blood a monolithic institution. Princely feuds engendered cyclical tensions within the system which led to a dispersal of power between the contending factions as well as within each of these factions.

Insofar as the recent evolution of the kingdom has tended to shift the centre of power from the descendants of one family (the Batare) to another (the Bezi), the latter were able to capitalise upon their recently-acquired positions to strengthen their identification with the crown, as well as their personal ties with the Mwami. It is not only that, in Mosca's words, 'qualification for office . . . is much more readily acquired when one has had a certain familiarity with it from childhood',[5] but that the linkages thereby established between the Mwami and the Bezi family created a network of mutual obligations and reciprocities which continued to influence the policies of the court long after independence. After the elimination of the Batare from the political scene, on the very eve of independence, the strength of the nexus between the Bezi and the throne grew to such an extent as to lend retrospective justification to the view that the monarchy was little more than an instrument in the hands of 'feudal' elements.

However impressive the extent of dynastic consolidation achieved during the Belgian trusteeship, the Mwami of Burundi never achieved unfettered, personalised control. Even at the apogee of his reign, Mwambutsa did not possess the despotic authority which the Mwami of Rwanda once enjoyed. During the period with which we shall concern ourselves, Mwambutsa was far less than a primus inter pares among the princes of the blood. Because of his early subservience to elder members of his family, because of the troubled circumstances under which he acceded to the throne and his rather weak personality, the Mwami was a minor element in the equation of power at the court. Even though in later years he occasionally tried to assert his authority against certain members of his entourage, his writ, as in the past, ran only as far as the strength and influence of his feudatories permitted.

The roots of the Bezi-Batare conflict lie in the very nature of the distribution of power which characterised the traditional polity. In Burundi, as in most other African states where power tended to gravitate to unilineal descent groups, political competition took the form of a periodic struggle among the representatives of the different dynastic segments of the royal line. 'In this characteristic African version of the patrimonial struggle for power', as Professor Fallers points out, 'the unilineal descent groups [played] a decentralizing role, broadly analogous to that of the feudal houses of medieval Europe.'[6] This is not to say that these centrifugal forces could never be kept in check. In the interests of the wider political community, certain African rulers made an eminently successful use of certain devices and practices; while some relied principally on the coercive potential of their armies, others preferred to reassert the unity of the realm through the use of religious sanctions and institutions. In Burundi, however, these methods proved of no avail, and, as a result, each of the segmenting branches of the royal line have retained a sense of corporate identity to a degree almost unheard of in other African states at a similar stage of political evolution.

The historical dimensions of the conflict must be viewed against the background of conquests and territorial accretions which took place in the first half of the nineteenth century, under the reign of Mwami

Ntare Rugaamba, who acceded to the throne around 1795 and held it until 1852.[7] We have seen how, in order to consolidate his territorial gains, Ntare proceeded to appoint his sons to administer his newly-acquired provinces. It was at this point that the *ganwa* began to play a decisive role in the political system. Although the royal practice of delegating sovereign powers to the princes in their own domains had been inaugurated out of necessity or expediency, the practice later became institutionalised in the office of *ganwa*. From then on, the established policy of the *Bami* was to seek the eviction of their predecessor's kin in order to replace them by their own people. Thus, after the accession of Mwami Mwezi Kisabo, in 1852, his main preoccupation was to evict Ntare's descendants (the Batare) from their entrenched positions, to the profit of his sons (the Bezi). This struggle went on unabated during the colonial period, albeit at a more or less subterranean level, only to break out with renewed intensity in the months preceding independence. By then, however, the Bezi had finally managed to emerge on top, with the Batare holding a somewhat subsidiary position.

This result was not achieved overnight, and there was a serious cost in human lives on both sides. There is no point here in retelling the story of German pacification, with its countless contradictions and ineptitudes. Yet it is important to remember that the overall effects of German policies were decidedly more detrimental to the Bezi than to the Batare, despite the unification policy later pursued by von Grawert. The high point of this policy, it will be recalled, came in 1905, when, in an effort to consolidate the fledgling authority of Mwezi Kisabo, the German troops launched an extremely bloody expedition against Kanugunu, Ntare's great-grandson, at the time the most influential of all the Batare. The outcome was rather inconclusive. Despite von Grawert's good intentions, Kanugunu's son, the famous Mbanzabugabo,* and his cousin, Busokoza, continued to hold their ground in the north-east, defiantly frustrating the efforts of the German Residents. Evaluating the Bezi position at the close of the German period, Pierre Ryckmans concludes on this rather negative note:

> In his attempt to follow Ntare's policy, Mwezi Kisabo waged a long war against Kilima, but did not succeed. He succeeded in the north, but did not even try his hand in the north-east. He succeeded in the south but failed completely in the east; during wars conducted in this region against the most energetic of Ntare's sons [sic], Chief

---

* Father of André Muhirwa, later to become Burundi's first Prime Minister, after Rwagasore's death.

Kanugunu, the latter was killed with the assistance of the German troops, which has fostered an irreducible hatred between Bezi and Batare. A terribly bloody expedition was launched in 1908 against Busokoza, but came to nought.[8]

By then, the policy of the German Residency amounted to little more than a recognition of the status quo. The north-east was recognised as Mbanzabugabo's fief,* the north-west as Kilima's, and the southern fringes of the realm as the property of more or less independent chieftains of diverse origins. This was roughly how things stood in 1918, when Ryckmans assessed the situation.

The progressive 'easing out' of the Batare branch, under the Belgians, was not the result of a deliberate colonial policy. It occurred almost in spite of the authorities, partly as a result of the sheer astuteness of the Bezi, partly because of the exigencies of the situation created by the minority of Mwami Mwambutsa, and partly as the unintended result of a quasi-fetishist Belgian quest for 'administrative efficiency'. For the Belgians, administrative efficiency meant, essentially, the regrouping of smaller chiefdoms into larger and more viable ones. It also meant the appointment of intelligent, resourceful and, above all, authoritative chiefs. Thus, in many areas, this policy of regrouping consisted in bringing together a number of semi-independent chiefs or subchiefs under the authority of an influential *ganwa*, so as to consolidate several smaller holdings into a larger territorial and administrative entity. As early as 1929, the results of this policy had clearly worked to the advantage of the Bezi. The main beneficiaries were, in Muramvya, Chiefs Nyawakira and Bagorikundo, grandsons of Mwezi Kisabo; in Kitega, Chiefs Bakareke and Karabona, respectively grandson and son of Mwezi Kisabo; in Ngozi, Chiefs Nduwumwe and Bishinga, sons of Mwezi Kisabo; in Bururi, Chief Bararufize, grandson of Mwezi Kisabo. Although this policy was applied even more systematically in later years, in 1921 one 'délégué'† reported that the Bezi found themselves in roughly the same position as the Batare prior to the accession of Mwezi Kisabo: i.e., solidly entrenched in the peripheral regions, 'with Nduwumwe and Bishinga installed in the north, Ntarugera in the north-east, Bigoni in the south, Karabona and Kichogori in the east,

---

* Only in 1921 did Mbanzabugabo decide to make his peace with the Mwami. Following his submission, in 1922, Mbanzabugabo was admitted to the Regency Council; yet his authority remained unchallenged in his own province. See *Enquête Administrative Générale, Territoire de Muhinga*, 1929.

† Although their functions remained basically the same, in 1933 the title of 'délégué' was changed for that of 'administrateur de territoire', the equivalent of district commissioner in the British territories.

Matikagi and Yunzuguru in the north-west'.[9] The same report goes on to note that 'in order to implement this policy, it was necessary to expropriate the lands of the former occupants; thus we see this tendency, in itself a very wise one, take on the aspects of a veritable conquest'. The conquest, however, was only beginning.

This transformation, as noted earlier, was much less the result of a self-conscious, systematic pro-Bezi policy than the consequence of a de facto situation which the Belgians had to accept, whether they liked it or not. Although the official reports transmitted to the Belgian Parliament by the Residency suggest a carefully-planned policy, the reports from the local administrators have an entirely different ring. One gains the distinct impression that the délégués and their staff were often manipulated by the chiefs, and, while many were probably aware of what was going on in the wings, most of them unconsciously admitted that they could do little about it. It is difficult to see how it could have been otherwise, considering their lack of familiarity with the byzantine style of *ganwa* politics and the absence of a central 'native authority' worthy of the name, upon whom they could rely for assistance— the Mwami being constantly manipulated by his entourage. At the inception of the Belgian mandate, the Mwami was in his early teens and completely under the influence of his uncles—Ntarugera, Nduwumwe, Karabona and Bishinga, among others—and his grandmother, Ndirikumutima. Some of these, and in particular the formidable Nduwumwe and Ntarugera, already enjoyed considerable power in their own right, and it was they who most of the time reigned and ruled. To ignore their counsels would have been suicidal. Thus, for at least a decade after the Belgians took over the country, the policy of the realm was left largely to the descendants of King Mwezi, and they took full advantage of the situation to feather their own nests.

This state of affairs, however, did not always redound to the exclusive profit of the Bezi. For one thing, the Bezi were divided among themselves, so much so that at one point some of them did not hesitate to switch sides to join the Batare. These internal dissensions can be traced back to the early days of Mutaga's reign, at a time when Ntarugera, Mwezi's favourite son, became the object of a bitter hatred from his step-mother, Ndirikumutima, who felt that he represented a major threat to the interests of her own sons (Nduwumwe, Karabona and Bishinga). In order to weaken his position, his half-brothers found it expedient to enter into an alliance with their traditional arch-enemies, the Batare (in particular, Fyiroko, Bikino and Mpongo); similarly, a few years later, Nduwumwe decided to make his peace with Chief Baranyanka, by then the most eminent representative of the Batare, in order

313

to pull the rug from under the feet of his nephew, Nyawakira,* whose influence had now become a matter of grave concern for Nduwumwe. In 1930, Nyawakira was 'parachuted' by the administration into the territoire of Muhinga, the citadel of the Batare; though initially rejected by the local population and forced to leave his chiefdom, he was later reinstated by the Belgian Resident. He ended up commanding one of the largest chiefdoms of the realm, imposing his capricious will over some 35,000 people. Whether Nduwumwe's alliance with Baranyanka was motivated by a sense of revulsion against Nyawakira's arbitrary methods or by sheer jealousy is unclear; but that it should have happened at all is illustrative of the complexities of the political alignments during the Belgian period.

Moreover, the administration, in its quest for efficiency, at times did not hesitate to turn for assistance to the rivals of the Bezi. For historical and psychological reasons, many Batare caught the eye of the administration for their industriousness, initiative and good will. Chief Baranyanka is a case in point. Commenting on the reason why he was chosen to rule over one of the largest chiefdoms, one administrator tersely noted: 'Has risen by dint of his intelligence.'[10] Baranyanka, however, was much more than a brilliant Batare; he eventually became something of an institution all by himself. At the height of his career, he nearly eclipsed the Mwami's prestige (at least in the eyes of the Belgian administration), and he was openly regarded by the Bezi as a threat to the monarchy. Once the personal secretary of Richard Kandt, he was not only remarkably Western in outlook compared to most other chiefs but extremely well informed on a wide range of matters concerning the past and recent history of the kingdom. He became one of Pierre Ryckmans's chief informants (some Bezi might suggest 'informer' as more appropriate), and, in acknowledgement of his services, Ryckmans appointed him to the Regency Council in 1922, along with Mbanzabugabo (another famous Mutare) and five other lesser chiefs of mixed origins. Since apparently nothing in the traditions of the realm qualified either man to hold this rank, this move was interpreted as nothing short of an insult by the Bezi, and from then on their hatred of the Batare knew no bounds. To make things even worse, Baranyanka became the

---

*Nyawakira became one of the most powerful figures of the realm during the early years of Mwambutsa's reign. Grandson of Mwezi Kisabo, he has been described as 'fairly intelligent, energetic, authoritarian—without scruples or sense of righteousness, he is an intrigant of the worst kind, conceited and ambitious, and capable of the meanest actions', a description which fits equally well his son, Germain Bimpenda, who, after independence, stood as one of the most influential figures behind the throne. See Robert Schmidt, *Abatare et Abezi*, typescript, February–May 1953; in the Derscheid Collection.

protégé of several other Residents after Ryckmans, and in particular of Robert Schmidt, whose reputation as a high-ranking colonial civil servant is heavily tainted with partiality.

Which brings us to yet another element which occasionally played against the Bezi—the personal bias and preferences of certain colonial administrators. Unfortunately, we do not have a continuous record and thus cannot establish any precise relationships between attitudinal variations at the official level and actual changes of policy. For the period 1944–54, however, which corresponds to the term of office of Resident Schmidt, all the evidence suggests a systematic policy of favouritism towards the Batare, matched by repeated denigrations of the Bezi and '*their* king', Mwambutsa. What immediately aroused the suspicion of the Bezi was Schmidt's decision, in 1944, to hand over one of the chiefdoms contiguous to Nyawakira's—which he had long coveted—to Baranyanka's eldest son, Joseph Ntitendereza.* Whatever partiality Schmidt did show towards the Batare, there was no drastic alteration of the balance of power between the two families; but it did create a legacy of anti-European sentiment among certain Bezi elements which in turn contributed to the 'nationalist aura' of the crown. Evidences of personal bias are easily detected in Schmidt's description of certain Bezi personalities. In a 1953 report to the Ministry of Colonies, he said of Chief Nyawakira: 'conceited, ambitious, and capable of the meanest actions. . . . Has been responsible for numerous abuses, thefts and injustices'; Chief Bihumugani (better known as Biha) was presented as 'introverted and false. Could pass for a kind of Puritan but is actually secretive and hypocritical. Has few scruples, is anti-European and is getting very active behind the scenes'; Bigayimpunzi, son of Karabona, was said to be endowed with 'an average intelligence' and showed a tendency 'to flirt with all factions'. Ntitendereza, on the other hand, was reported to have 'a lively intelligence, an innate sense of command', as well as 'considerable loyalty, sincerity and self-control'.[11]

The impression one gets from Schmidt's estimate of Mwami Mwambutsa, who by then was a grown-up man, is that he simply did not qualify for the job. In addition to being woefully in debt—'which sets a very bad example for the native authorities of the country'—Mwambutsa was reported to have established some dubious liaisons with certain European social circles of Bujumbura for which Resident Schmidt had evidently very little esteem. After calling attention to what he referred

---

* This fact was confirmed to this writer in the course of an interview with Schmidt, in November 1964. Joseph Ntitendereza, one must note in passing, later led the pro-Batare Parti Démocrate Chrétien (PDC).

to as 'a rather special and not always commendable type of European society', Schmidt reported in 1953: 'It is becoming more and more apparent that he is interested only in women, and in catering to an entourage of favourites, most of whom tend to share his somewhat unstable personal life. . . . He criticises and persecutes those who are not among his favourites and who dare to pay a visit to certain European functionaries or members of the better class of European society. . . . The administration has been unable to react efficiently against the deportment which Mwambutsa publicly displays, which is all the more regrettable since the administration does all it can to enforce the laws concerning marriage and adultery.'[12] This last statement is perhaps even more revealing than the strictures against the Mwami and his entourage, some of which, one might add, seemed largely justified. That the Resident should have had certain reservations about the Mwami's behaviour is not in itself surprising; but the way in which they were expressed suggests that standards of morality were not the sole point at issue. References to the Mwami's private life were evidently brought up to draw attention to their political implications, so as to elicit a change of policy from Brussels. This at least is the impression one gets from Schmidt's semi-official note, characteristically entitled, *Répercussions Politiques de la Vie Privée de Mwambutsa*, written in 1953. 'It is therefore plain', Schmidt concluded, after turning a critical eye on the Mwami's behaviour, 'that Mwambutsa's private life carries political implications, and the repercussions thereof are much more consequential than one might think at first sight.' Mwambutsa's dissipation was interpreted as a source of considerable embarrassment for the administration as it 'hampered the smooth and normal functioning of local political institutions' and cast immense discredit on Belgium's 'civilising mission'.[13]

Behind this overwhelmingly critical attitude of the Residency towards the Mwami were several other motives and considerations, one being a quasi-pathological fear that if the Mwami should some day enjoy the official backing of the administration it might bring about a sudden change of heart among the younger anti-Mwambutsa (and hence generally pro-Batare) generations, who already enjoyed the favour of the trust authorities and were for the most part willing to co-operate with them. The possibility that the younger generations 'might deteriorate into an anti-Belgian party', and might, as a result, 'be forced into clandestinity' was Resident Schmidt's greatest source of anxiety; he could, therefore, take legitimate pride that 'he had done everything, and with a certain success, to prevent this situation from developing'.[14] Furthermore, great stress was laid upon the need for a 'healthy opposition', and any attempt to curtail one was regarded as 'contrary to the principle of progressive democratisation'. Finally, in advocating a withdrawal of support from the Mwami as a person, Schmidt was careful to point out that his policies would in no way undermine the crown as an institution, for the Mwami's personal prestige was, according to Schmidt, already at its lowest ebb, and 'solely dependent on the legitimacy of the Drum': 'Because of his association with the Drum, he [Mwambutsa] stands as a symbol of national unity, and for some—the abbés in particular—as a symbol of nascent nationalism.'[15] The Resident failed to appreciate —a surprising oversight, in view of the foregoing statement—that his policy could not but strengthen the prestige of the monarchy as a symbol of nationalism.

We have come rather far afield, and it is time to return to our starting point. Despite the obstacles raised by the Residency, the trend towards dynastic consolidation was already set, and in subsequent years an increasing number of Bezi were appointed to office, as chiefs or sub-chiefs. Among the specific events and circumstances which, directly or indirectly, have contributed to speed up this trend, the following three deserve mention. For the first time, in 1950, the Mwami took a trip to Europe, accompanied by two of his most devoted supporters, Bihumugani and Kamatari, and the result of his official contacts in Brussels was to greatly reinforce his self-confidence—as well as his leverage upon the Residency. As one former colonial civil servant told this writer: 'His visit to Europe had a tremendous impact upon him, because it made him aware of his strong bargaining power towards the trust authorities.'[16] Even more significant was the support he received from the local clergy —from the indigenous clergy, but also from certain European missionaries, like Father Grauls, whose voice carried considerable weight with the administration. With one or two exceptions, and in contrast with what happened in Rwanda, the European clergy of Burundi showed considerable respect for the crown, and even some for the incumbent. Despite the Mwami's cavalier attitude in matters of religion and morals (which many Barundi regarded as a fundamentally healthy attitude), he never incurred the same bitter animosity from certain members of the Catholic Church as Mutara Rudahigwa of Rwanda. Finally, the post-war years saw the emergence of a 'new wave' of young Bezi chiefs, trained at Astrida, whose administrative skills and personal dynamism greatly reinforced the position of the crown. Thus, by 1959, the Bezi controlled 17 chiefdoms out of a total of 37, and the Batare 9. But the total area controlled by the Bezi was more than twice the size of that held by the Batare. Not only were there significant differences in the size of the chiefdoms, but a number of chiefs and subchiefs whose origins were neither Bezi nor Batare were, in fact, committed to the Bezi cause.

As shown by maps 3 and 4 (pages 320, 322), the political transformations which have taken place since the turn of the century are best viewed as a series of contractions of the domains held by the Batare, matched by corresponding expansions of the Bezi-held areas. In 1913, the Bezi exercised control over the central region (i.e. Muramvya, Nkoma, Bututsi) but had virtually no influence in the peripheral regions. By 1929, however, their territorial holdings had increased substantially, partly at the expense of non-Batare elements but principally by taking more and more land away from their traditional arch-enemies. While still hanging out in nearly all the frontier regions, the Batare were in a much weaker position than a decade or so earlier. By 1959 their situation was even more precarious, as their influence was now almost exclusively confined to the eastern part of the territoire of Muhinga.

Two questions have an obvious bearing on the events just discussed. First, why did this long and still incomplete process of unification involve only two sets of contestants, and not four as the dynastic names of the *Bami* would suggest? In other words, what role did the Bataga and the Bambutsa play while the Bezi and the Batare competed with each other? Second, as Mwambutsa was the son of Mutaga, and hence a Mutaga by birth, why did he feel the need to identify himself with the Bezi instead of allying himself with his own people, the Bataga? The answer to the first question is a simple one: neither the Bataga nor the Bambutsa were sufficiently important in terms of number and influence. The Bataga were represented almost exclusively by Mwambutsa and his brother, the late Kamatari; the Bambutsa—the descendants of Mwambutsa II—were still too young at the time to exercise any significant influence, while their remote cousins—the descendants of Mwambutsa I—had long disappeared from the political scene. The answer to the second question is implicit in what has just been said: the Bezi were not only more numerous and influential than the Bataga but they were also much closer to Mwambutsa from the standpoint of parental relationships than the Batare, and were therefore the natural allies of the crown. According to Chief Barusasyeko, the Bezi managed to persuade Mwambutsa that he was of Bezi origins, a fact for which special credit is given to Chief Nyawakira.[17] This writer's own opinion, however, is that Mwambutsa was fully aware of his Bataga origins but deliberately chose to align himself with the Bezi, because they were the only ones whom he could trust to solidify his rule.

Yet, as the foregoing makes clear, the Mwami's rule was never so strong as to enable him to challenge single-handedly the influence of the Bezi. Even though the trend of the last fifty years has clearly been in the direction of increased centralisation, in no sense can it be said that there has been a concentration of authority in the hands of the Mwami. The process of dynastic consolidation initiated by the Bezi created a situation where power fell into the hands of a group of oligarchs who belonged to the same royal lineage, and were in that sense 'royal', yet this did not lead to a substantial increase of the Mwami's effective power. All it meant was a shift of power from one branch of the royal family to another.

This, of course, is not to suggest that the institution of *mwami*-ship did not play a significant role in keeping the society in operation, and indeed in promoting the interests of the Bezi. Its ultimate shape owed as much to the personality of the incumbent on the throne as to the character of the power structure associated with the monarchy. That the personality of Mwambutsa had an important bearing on the place *mwami*-ship held in the political system of Burundi, before and after independence, is a fact which most politically-conscious Barundi are prepared to recognise. The consensus of opinion is that the ultimate demise of the monarchy is in part attributable to Mwambutsa's own behaviour and personality—to his growing lack of concern for the well-being of his people, to his conspicuous deficiencies as a national leader, and to his lack of formal education—all of which meant, most of the time, an abdication of authority in favour of his courtiers. What is not always realised, however, is that Mwambutsa's failings as a leader were, in a real sense, a reflection of the environment in which he moved, an environment in which everything conspired to keep the incumbent on the throne in a subordinate and harmless position. It is interesting to recall, in this connection, the reasons advanced by Mwambutsa to explain the inadequacy of his formal education: 'In the old days', he admitted in a letter to the Resident, dated July 14, 1947, 'when I was a schoolboy, the former Resident of Urundi, Ryckmans, wanted to send me to Europe to pursue my studies. . . . But my uncles, Nduwumwe and Ntarugera, who were in charge of my education, refused to let me go, and the government bowed to their desire. When I remember this I suffer, for I might have been an educated man. I don't want my son to fall in the same predicament, for he would resent and regret this missed opportunity just as I do now.'[18] This does not mean that Mwambutsa was insensitive to the values of modernity—his letter suggests rather the opposite; yet it does help to explain his shortcomings in the realm of statesmanship. Had Mwambutsa acted with greater wisdom, had he possessed the qualities of mind and character necessary for strong leadership, had he shown less enthusiasm for European women and

319

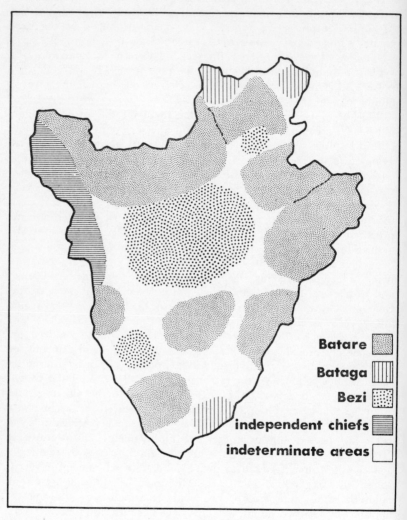

Map 3. Burundi: Distribution of *Ganwa* Fiefs, circa 1916
(map adapted from Hans Meyer, *Die Barundi*, Leipzig 1916)

more concern for other types of resources and skills available from the West, the history of Burundi might have been very different. As it turned out, much of the odium which the crown attracted to itself stemmed from Mwambutsa's well-deserved reputation as a 'roi fainéant' and a playboy.*

Just as Mwambutsa's behaviour can be explained in part by reference to the political environment of Burundi, the oligarchical structure of this environment goes far towards explaining the ultimate collapse of the monarchy. With the reactivation of feudal ties after independence, and the re-entry of *ganwa* elements into the political arena, the crown came to be viewed as little more than an instrument in the hands of a self-perpetuating oligarchy. For the newly-emergent educated elites, ever more anxious to take part in government, the monarchy seemed an anachronism, exclusively serving the interests of the king's men. Nor was this a mere rationalisation, based on ulterior motives. The persistence of the feudal nexus, with its strong emphasis on family ties and clientage relations, raised enormous obstacles in the path of social, economic and political modernisation. Thus, because of its failure to achieve or even attempt political modernisation the monarchy laid itself open to charges of corruption, nepotism and feudalism from those very elements who at one time claimed to be the most loyal supporters of the crown.

It was not only an institution that was eventually challenged but a whole style of behaviour, made increasingly obsolete by the spread of Western political concepts and ideas. It involved a carry-over into the modern age of the sub rosa manoeuvrings traditionally associated with the acquisition of power—ranging from the casting of discredit upon one's enemy to rumour-mongering, slander and political assassination, but always characterised by a fair measure of byzantine craft and tortuousness. The irony, as we shall see, is that those very groups who laid the stepping stones towards the republic were themselves engaged

---

* This argument is based on the assumption that the influence of personality in politics is in part function of the manipulability of the environment. In Rwanda, for example, where ethnic cleavages were much too rigid to allow fundamental restructuring, neither Mutara nor Kigeri could have significantly altered the course of events. In Burundi, on the other hand, the fluidity of political forces greatly enhanced the potential influence of Mwambutsa's personality as a political factor. Had Mwambutsa possessed the personal strength and political astuteness of a Mutara, his role may have been far more significant in shaping the destinies of the kingdom. For an excellent discussion of the personality theme in politics, see Fred I. Greenstein, "The Impact of Personality on Politics: An Attempt to Clear away Underbrush", *The American Political Science Review*, Vol. LXV, No. 3, September 1967, pp. 629–41.

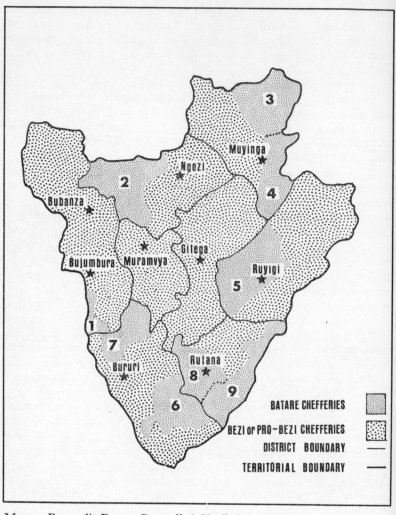

Map 4. Burundi: Batare-Controlled Chefferies, 1954

1. Mushasha-Sud: Chief Kisage
2. Kunkiko-Mugamba: Chief Baranyanka
3. Bwambarangwe-Busoni: Chief Ntidendereza
4. Busumanyi: Chief Muhirwa

5. Buyogoma: Chief Gashirahamwe
6. Buragane-Bukurira: Chief Hugano
7. Mugamba-Sud: Chief Ndakoze
8. Bunyambo: Chief Bujenjegeri
9. Moso-Sud: Chief Jean Kigoma

in similar manoeuvrings; certainly, among the younger aristocrats who tried to bolster Mwambutsa's heir through the awkward days of his ephemeral reign, many were those who looked to the past for a cue to the future. Nonetheless, there were notable exceptions, especially among the students and the army. For these men it was not only the principle of kingship that was objectionable but, even more fundamentally, the norms underlying the functioning of the monarchy. As they were soon to discover, however, their commitment to a new value pattern, symbolised by the advent of the republic, did not lead to a drastic alteration of the normative structures of society.

In trying to assess the relative strengths and weaknesses of *mwami*-ship, it may be that its potential vulnerability has been unduly stressed at the expense of its 'staying power'. If so, it is appropriate to remind ourselves that the forces which undermined the legitimacy of the crown did not develop overnight; they developed over an extended period of time, in response to changes in both the political environment and the policies of the crown. Meanwhile, the 'dynastic' structuring of conflict, by shifting the focus of competition away from the monarchy, placed the *mwami*-ship in the position of an umpire, high above the tumble of partisan politics. More, insofar as the cause of the Bezi came to be identified with the cause of the monarchy, the resurgence of the Bezi-Batare feud in the years immediately preceding independence undeniably contributed to the short-term popularity of the crown—if only because of the pro-Belgian label pasted on to the Batare by the accidents of history. At the same time, however, by focusing attention on a family feud, the conflict served to push into the background the more basic issues of how to achieve political stability and maintain constitutional legitimacy in conditions of rapid ethnic polarisation. When these finally came up on the agenda, they asserted their priority with vengeful urgency.

In this time-lag involved in the sequence and clustering of issues lies a major difference in the patterns of evolution of Rwanda and Burundi. In Rwanda, dynastic quarrels had been settled long before the country approached independence. The really critical issue, on which everything else seemed to depend, including the future of the monarchy, was that of the Hutu-Tutsi conflict. In Burundi, the issue arose at a later stage, and under such circumstances that it temporarily strengthened the position of the crown in the political system.

12. *Ganwa* Politics
in Modern Guise:
Bezi versus Batare

BECAUSE OF ITS cyclical tendency to fission, *mwami*-ship carried divisive implications. The reassertion of dynastic feuds in the guise of modern political parties is indeed the dominant theme of the transitional period; nonetheless, owing to the social conflicts and tensions at work as in any colonial situation, the traditional patterns of interaction between Burundi society and the institution of *mwami*-ship underwent certain major variations.

As the kingdom was about to 'recover' its independence, not only did princely rivalries reassert themselves with fresh intensity, but, through the cracks in the fabric of the traditional order, there emerged a host of political factions with new and somewhat revolutionary aspirations. By June 1961, twenty-three political parties were officially registered, running down the alphabet from APRODEBA to VPM.[1] Some, like the Parti du Peuple (PP)—founded in December 1959 by a group of Hutu politicians whose vision of the future was clearly influenced by recent events in Rwanda—based their appeal on ethnic solidarities; others, like the Parti des Jeunes Travailleurs du Burundi (PDJTB), sought support for their ideas from specific social categories; still others, like the equally short-lived Union Nationale du Burundi (UNB), confined their membership to specific regions. From the very beginning, however, Burundi politics were dominated by the struggle between the Parti de l'Unité et du Progrès National (UPRONA) and the Parti Démocrate Chrétien (PDC), whose leaderships were associated, respectively, with the Bezi and Batare families. Although the rules of the game were now drastically altered, the history of Burundi politics during the pre-independence phase of nationalist developments looks, on the surface, like a continuation of *ganwa* feuds, with the Bezi asserting themselves as the sole legitimate heirs to the crown.

Since parties are no more than the institutionalised expression of the social and ideological forces at work in any given environment, they are likely to assume different forms in different contexts. 'Even in an absolute monarchy', as Max Beloff reminds us in his discussion of

The Party System, 'where the ultimate repository of authority is in a single individual, his courtiers are likely to form groups in order to bring the maximum pressure to bear upon him when questions of interest to them come up for decision.'[2] In this sense, the Bezi and Batare families could be called 'parties' long before they decided to call themselves UPRONA and PDC. Yet there were obvious differences, in terms of doctrine, membership and organisation, between such 'archaic' parties, to use Professor Duverger's expression, and the kind of political organisation with which they later tried to become identified. From 'mere clienteles grouped around an influential leader',[3] the Bezi and Batare factions eventually aimed at transforming themselves into parties in the modern sense of the term, by incorporating into their membership a broader stratum of the population, by injecting an element of progressivism into their ideologies,' and by adapting their strategies to a system of government based on elections. That this transformation was not accomplished without enormous difficulties, and then in a very incomplete fashion, is what appears from a glance at the history of UPRONA.

The Birth of Uprona

UPRONA grew out of two separate phenomena, but which have consistently interacted upon each other: as a political party in the 'archaic' sense, UPRONA was the product of a pattern of differentiation and conflict endemic in the traditional society; as a nationalist organisation, however, UPRONA came into being in response to specific threats to the integrity of monarchic institutions and the social order they sustained. These threats emanated generally from the transformations of the traditional conditions of life engendered by colonial rule, and the partial dissolution of the psychological bonds that once existed between the chiefs and the masses; but also from the introduction of specific administrative measures believed to be prejudicial to the interests of the crown and its representatives, and from the announcement of constitutional changes that were bound to affect the prerogatives of the *mwami* and of the chiefs (*ganwa*) in some fundamental ways. Although the trust authorities were responsible for these various disabilities, actual or potential, in the minds of the Bezi the disabilities were consciously associated with the traditional infringements of the Batare upon their rule. Not only did the policies of the administration hold 'provocative' implications, which reminded them of the role and attitude of the Batare, but the Batare family—or, at least, some of its most influential members—did in fact express unqualified support for these policies. After all, having

325

themselves been reduced to such a marginal position as a result of the ascendancy of the Bezi during the colonial period, why should they be inclined to support a political order from which they had so little to gain?

These threats to the authority of the crown were, in a more fundamental sense, threats to the authority of the chiefs, and more specifically of the Bezi chiefs. In protesting against the limitations inflicted upon the crown by the administration, they were really protesting against the loss of status they would inevitably suffer as a result of the progressive democratisation of political institutions. This is not to say that the chiefs were all basically hostile to democracy, or that they all were determined to perpetuate the old feudal system in order to preserve their sinecures. While some of the older chiefs would have been content to preserve the status quo, the younger ones realised that the constitutional changes entailed by the advent of self-government could not be resisted. Many of them welcomed these changes, even though they spelled the disappearance of the chieftaincy as an institution. Thus, instead of 'bucking the tide', many were the chiefs who deliberately dissociated themselves from the traditional political order to join the nationalist crusade. In fact, these younger chiefs were themselves the founders and promoters of the nationalist movement built around UPRONA. But before the party converted itself into an openly nationalist organisation, there occurred behind the scenes a major conflict of leadership between the older generation of chiefs and the younger ones—a conflict far more intense than one might imagine from the presumed cohesiveness of the Bezi faction.

According to its founder, Chief Léopold Bihumugani (better known as Biha), UPRONA was founded in 1957, shortly before the arrival of the UN Visiting Mission, in protest against the decision of the administration to introduce a system of extra-customary centres—centres extra-coutumiers (CEC)—in Bujumbura, Kitega, Nyanza Lac and Rumonge.* Because of the system of administration associated with the CECs, the reform, if implemented, not only would have removed Bujumbura and these other localities from the jurisdiction of the crown but would have deprived the *mwami* of certain opportunities for 'patronage'. Thus,

---

* In 1941, in an effort to adapt the system of local administration to the conditions of a semi-urban environment, the Residency had set up two CECs in the vicinity of Bujumbura, known as 'Belge' and 'Village des Swahili'. This move, like the more recent one, represented an extension of the royal decree of July 6, 1934, which made possible the creation of CECs in the urban centres of the Congo. As in the Congo, these CECs were administered by a 'chef', assisted by an 'adjoint' and an advisory council, all hand-picked by the administration. See *Résidence de l'Urundi, Rapport Annuel*, 1950, passim.

what Lord Hailey once described as 'one of the most imaginative initiatives of the Belgian administration'[4] was readily interpreted by the chiefs who sat on the Conseil Supérieur du Pays (CSP) as a wholly unwarranted attempt to interfere with the *mwami*'s traditional prerogatives. The issue came to a head in early 1957, when the CSP members almost unanimously urged the Resident to reconsider the decision.[5] During the angry debate that took place between the Resident and the CSP, the former was frequently reminded of the historical claims of the crown over the town of Bujumbura, of the sacred character of kingship, and of the traditional identification of the *mwami* with the territorial integrity of the realm.[6]

Interestingly, the language of the petition addressed to the UN Visiting Mission by the CSP members, many of whom actually belonged to UPRONA, is shot through with nationalist overtones: to cast off the yoke of Belgian colonialism, so as to restore the integrity of the monarchy, was the message of UPRONA in 1957:

Here in Ruanda-Urundi, the Belgian government has reversed the order of things. . . . On the political and administrative plane they have only one thing in mind—to lessen the authority of our kings. So strong is our king's authority that they have launched a campaign of propaganda to annex Ruanda-Urundi to the Congo. . . . 'Sicilia amissa angebat Hannibalem' (The loss of Sicily angered Hannibal); likewise, the loss of Bugufi, Buha, Bunyabungo, Usumbura, and of all the areas about to be converted into CECs, against the will of the Murundi nation and the king, has tormented our people for many years.[7]

Another petition, presented at about the same time, in October 1957, reproduced the text of a resolution passed earlier by the CSP which the Resident had vigorously condemned for its 'crypto-Communist implications' and urged that it be 'thrown into the waste paper basket'.[8] The essence of the resolution, however, amounted to little more than a reiteration of previous demands: 'To deny the rights of the *mwami* over the CECs is contrary to the provisions of the UN Charter. . . . The *mwami* is and remains the real chief of the country.' 'To avoid the difficulties encountered by General Nasser over the Suez Canal', the petition continued, 'we lay claim to Usumbura, Kitega, Nyanza Lac and Rumonge; let these centres be returned as quickly as possible under the *mwami*'s authority.'[9]

Behind these occasional outbursts of nationalist rhetoric lay a basic conflict of interest between the more conservative chiefs and the administering authorities. By their attacks against Belgian colonialism, and by identifying the fortunes of the crown with those of the community they professed to serve, these chiefs struck a nationalist stance which, they hoped, might favourably influence the attitude of the UN Trusteeship Council. In so doing, however, they were really trying to defend their own prerogatives qua chiefs. For if the crown should lose its authority, to whom would they turn to secure their own? Here lay the basic weakness of UPRONA at this stage of its development: it was initially a 'party of chiefs', to use Biha's own words; secondly, it was the party of the Bezi chiefs of Muramvya, Biha himself being the most prominent member of this chiefly community; thirdly, it represented the interests of the more conservative elements among the chiefs. That the party should have succeeded in enlisting the support of the majority of the CSP members confirms its conservative tendencies: although not every member of the CSP was a chief, as a corporate entity it clearly represented the interests of the Establishment.

THE ARRIVAL OF RWAGASORE

By a curious twist of fate, the foundation of UPRONA coincided with the return of Prince Louis Rwagasore to Burundi. After completing his studies at the Institut Universitaire des Territoires d'Outre-Mer, in Antwerp, Rwagasore was given the chiefdom of Butanyerera to administer; but his new post evidently failed to satisfy his ambitions, and in 1958, anticipating the visit of the Groupe de Travail, he virtually took control of UPRONA. With Rwagasore at the helm, the party underwent something of a mimetic change.

Although his princely status debarred him from holding a formal leadership position within UPRONA, his prestigious personality had a determining influence on the political fortunes of the party. Officially, he was never associated with UPRONA other than in a purely advisory capacity. Although the presidency of the party changed hands several times, he remained an adviser until his death, in 1961. By traditional standards, his title-deeds to eminence were difficult to match: he was the Mwami's eldest son, the acknowledged representative of the Bezi (though himself a Mwambutsa) and a *ganwa*. But, in spite of his patrician origins, he had strong affective ties with the Hutu population, and his physical appearance (like that of his father) showed a greater resemblance to the average Hutu than to the Tutsi stereotype. Further, he had the advantage of a university education. Although he never attained a very high level of intellectual sophistication, his education made him sensitive to claims of the educated elite and gave him a 'progressive' outlook which marked him off rather sharply from most other chiefs.

328

His attitude was typical of what the administration referred to as 'progressive tendencies', characterised by 'a marked preference for a democratic regime', and represented in the late 'fifties by 'the former students of the Groupe Scolaire of Astrida and the former seminarists'. These young men, one administrative report stated, 'do not always enjoy the sympathy of the administration, because they lack moderation'.[10]

Among these young 'upstarts', few enjoyed less sympathy from the trust authorities than Rwagasore. His uncompromising commitment to 'immediate independence' earned him the perennial hatred of the administration; and at one point he and his party were openly accused of Communist proclivities. As he reportedly told Frank Moraes: 'The Belgians accuse us of being Communists. At the same time, they accuse us of being monarchist and feudal. They must make up their minds as to what we really are.'[11] The truth, however, is that Rwagasore sought to amalgamate within his platform the latent 'populism' of the masses, stemming from the cumulative discontents of the peasantry against the abuses of the chiefs, the subchiefs and the administration, and their residual attachment to the symbols of kingship. And while the 'populist' flavour of his ideas was viewed by the administration as a 'proof' of Communist sympathies, the anti-Belgian connotations thereby attached to his position merely served to enhance his stature as a nationalist leader.

Certainly, Rwagasore's insistence on self-government goes far to explain his popularity as a nationalist leader; but it is also in the measure of success he achieved in incorporating into his ideology elements of tradition and progress that one must look for the appeal of UPRONA. The traditional bases of its appeal were implicit in the Kirundi term to designate the party—*Abadasigana*—a term which reveals a dimension of belongingness that is totally missing from its French equivalent.[12] In traditional usage, *Abadasigana* refers to the group of individuals who formed the personal retinue of a *mwami*. More specifically, *Abadasigana* refers to the personal entourage of Mwami Mwezi Kisabo, and is usually translated by the Barundi as 'the followers of Mwezi'. The Kirundi appellation of the PDC, *Amasuka u'Mwami*, one may note in passing, also refers to the same category of officials, but is more closely associated with Mwami Ntare Rugaamba. In the popular consciousness of the Barundi, the term *Abadasigana* evoked a primordial focus of attachment to the Bezi family, and by implication to the crown, whereas the Kirundi label of the PDC, because of its pro-Batare connotations, carried a slightly anti-monarchic bias. Yet, as Peter Worsley correctly points out, 'nationalist sentiment is far more than cosy attachment to a reference

329

group, or a father substitute',[13] and Burundi is no exception. For all its efforts to identify its destinies with the crown, and to present it as the repository of the most precious of all national values, UPRONA also tried to live up to the progressive connotations of its French appellation. Thus Rwagasore made it plain at the outset that his devotion to the monarchy was conditional, and that his party was prepared to endorse a monarchic regime 'only insofar as this regime and its dynasty favoured the genuine emancipation of the Murundi people'.[14] 'UPRONA', according to the party's second manifesto, 'notes that the Burundi monarchy is *constitutional*, and wishes to see the constitution of the realm adapted to a *modern state*. . . . UPRONA favours the democratisation of institutions . . . and will firmly and tenaciously combat all forms of social injustice, regardless of the system from which they may come: *feudalism, colonialism or communism*. . . . UPRONA favours the election of the chiefs and subchiefs by the population, and will combat with all its forces those who seek to destroy the *unity* of the country [italics in the text].'[15] Far from advocating a return to the feudal era, or a complete break with the past, Rwagasore strove to modernise the kingdom by appealing to the traditions of the realm—by using the symbols of kingship as a means of absorbing and channelling change, in the best tradition of 'modernising autocracies'. It is this two-fold aspect of UPRONA's ideology that Mirerekano tried to make explicit in his *Mbwire gito canje*: when he urged his people to 'fight with the bow and arrows of Rwagasore and his *Abadasigana*', and reminded them that 'all Barundi, Tutsi, Hutu and Twa, are like grains in an ear of sorghum', Mirerekano was fully consistent with the ideological style of UPRONA, in effect invoking tradition with a view to inducing certain basic changes in the thinking and behaviour of the Barundi.[16]

To induce change, more was needed than just exhortation. From the very beginning, Rwagasore realised the need to convert UPRONA into a mass party, with ramifications extending through every segment of society, every caste, every locality. To do this, he employed several methods. He first resorted to a simplified version of 'ethnic arithmetic', and tried to incorporate into the formal leadership structure of the party an almost even proportion of Hutu and Tutsi. Thus, in 1961, the Central Committee of UPRONA comprised three Tutsi and four Hutu, with Hutu predominance compensated by the fact that the presidency and vice-presidency of the party were both in Tutsi hands (André Nugu and Théophile Rwuzuye). A similar effort was made at the local level to maintain an adequate dosage of Hutu and Tutsi, but again with the key positions generally entrusted to Tutsi.

At the same time, Rwagasore tried to build up support for his party via the co-operative movement. In June 1957, he launched his ill-fated Coopérative des Commerçants du Burundi (ccb), in the hope of using it as an instrument for enlisting the support of the so-called 'Swahili' population of Bujumbura. His motives were made clear by the letter he wrote in 1959 to a European firm in Bujumbura, to solicit its financial assistance: 'If the indigenous workers and traders are not helped and encouraged, the whole economic future of Burundi will be compromised, for it is precisely these courageous, labouring masses that we must help in order to improve the economic and political chances of the Burundi of tomorrow.'[17] Although the ccb never really got off the ground—partly because of mismanagement,* and partly because the administration refused to extend its financial backing to what it considered a 'front organisation'—Rwagasore's feverish involvement in the affairs of the co-operative was not completely in vain. If nothing else, it gave him wide renown among the urbanised masses of Bujumbura, whose grievances had until then received scant attention from either the European administration or the chiefs. Their sentiments were poignantly revealed in a petition submitted to the csp (signed 'les Barundi d'Usumbura') in 1958: 'Are we really to be abandoned like the scum of the earth? Here in Bujumbura we have our share of troubles. Our council has its hands tied; we never get what we ask for. We are commanded against our will, by people of bad reputation who are not even Barundi. The native authorities of Bujumbura do not care about us; we do not see them; we do not know them; we do not know even if they exist.'[18] To these people, Rwagasore's message was a message of hope, and theirs, in turn, one of complete faith in his ideas.

As conscious as he was of the need to alleviate the plight of the urban masses, Rwagasore also knew that he could not completely disregard the influence of the chiefs. By 1961, many of the old UPRONA chiefs had severed their ties with the party, in order to set up their own political organisations. Biha, for example, who never forgave Rwagasore his 'populist' leanings—nor his popularity—founded in 1961 a party of

*Although the ccb initially received some 6 million francs from various European firms of Bujumbura, by 1958 most of the money had vanished. According to one report, almost 2 million francs were lent to another co-operative (the Coopérative des Consommateurs et Commerçants du Ruanda-Urundi); 450,000 francs were lent to 'an influential TANU personality', and the rest 'to a number of businessmen who failed to observe the terms of reimbursement'. (See *Conseil Supérieur du Pays, Procès-Verbaux*, June 10–13, 1958, p. 17 ff.) A request for a 2 million loan was subsequently introduced on the floor of the csp, but was flatly rejected by the Belgian Resident on the grounds that the ccb was not 'viable financially'. (Ibid.)

his own which he called *Inararibonye*.* Pierre Bigayimpunzi, another famous *ganwa* of Bezi origin, founded the Parti Démocratique et Rural (PDR); Joseph Biroli and Joseph Ntitendereza, the elder sons of Chief Baranyanka, launched the Parti Démocrate Chrétien (PDC). But many were the younger chiefs (such as Léon and Michel Ndenzako, Pierre Barijane, Thaddée Siryuyumunsi, Gaspard Nkeshimana) who not only joined UPRONA but took full advantage of their influence in the countryside to strengthen the appeal of the party among the rural masses. Nor were these personalities all of Bezi origins: Siryuyumunsi was a Hima; Barijane, deputy chief of one of the CECs of Bujumbura, was a simple Tutsi; and André Muhirwa,—though admittedly rather a 'deviant' case from the standpoint of both age and origins—was a Mutare.† Relations between the chiefs and the peasantry were not always harmonious, and its courting of the chiefs could bring UPRONA more harm than good. But there were chiefs and chiefs. Those whom the population resented most were usually arch-reactionaries, who were unlikely to become ardent devotees of UPRONA. Furthermore, animosity against the chiefs was often deflected against the subchiefs and the auxiliary person-

* In Kirundi, the term *Inararibonye* refers to the Elders, and is associated with a famous legend about Mwami Mwezi Kisabo. The story goes that, having killed a lion, Mwezi removed the skin from the beast and wore it as a mantle. But the sun was hot and the skin shrank, threatening to choke him to death. At this critical moment came the *Inararibonye*. They took Mwezi to a nearby lake, immersed him in water and set him free. (Personal from Biha.)

† The case of Muhirwa is a prime example of the mixture of expediency and opportunism which governed the behaviour of the *ganwa* in their quest for power. As a Mutare—and, indeed, in his capacity as son of the famous Mbanzabugabo, Mwezi's arch-enemy—Muhirwa's political fortunes were seriously compromised at the outset. Nor was his position made any more comfortable by the sanctions taken against his family by the Belgian administration. After the death of his father, in 1930, he and his brothers were forced into exile by the Residency, apparently because of their vehement protests against the appointment of one of their former subchiefs, named Busego, to head their father's chiefdom. They spent a year and a half in Tanganyika and came back to Burundi in late 1931. Thanks to the assistance of a Catholic priest (Father Canonica), Muhirwa managed to be sent to the Groupe Scolaire at Astrida, from which he graduated in 1942. In 1944 he received the small chiefdom of Buhumuza, in the territoire of Ruyigi, many miles from his native homeland of Muhinga. As he later admitted to this writer, being so far from 'home', and from his father's clientele, Muhirwa felt as if he were still in exile. In 1953, he managed to be reinstated in the chiefdom of his ancestors—but only after he had made act of allegiance to the court, by marrying the Mwami's eldest daughter, Rosa. The 'deal'—for this is what it amounted to—was apparently concluded at the instigation of Chiefs Ntitendereza and Barusasiyeko, and it was the former who gave Muhirwa the half-dozen cows needed for the 'dowry'. From then on, Muhirwa became known as one of the staunchest supporters of the Bezi cause, and his presumed loyalty to the court later entitled him to a leading position in the inner circles of UPRONA.

nel attached to the chiefdoms, and these were in most cases supporters of the PDC (for reasons to be explained later). Many of the chiefs who cast their lot with UPRONA became vehement critics of the ancien régime, ceaselessly heaping scorn on 'feudalism and colonialism', as if they were two faces of the same coin. While openly antagonistic to the feudal system, there can be little doubt that UPRONA relied heavily on certain traditional authorities for solidifying its bases of support.

Because or in spite of all this, UPRONA remained basically an 'elite party', with an extremely weak organisational apparatus, and a rather low level of continuous, active, popular participation. In the countryside, the party cadres were generally recruited among the younger generation of chiefs, and loyalty to party supporters followed the traditional pattern of inferior-superior relationships. Only in the capital city was any effort made to give the party a mass base, through organisational links with co-operatives. Even so, this new synthesis of traditional authority patterns and modern forms of association never amounted to anything more than a loose amalgam of disparate elements, held together by Rwagasore's charismatic leadership.

This general organisational weakness of UPRONA must be attributed, first, to the personalised character of the party leadership. Since the central party machinery was almost entirely under the control of Rwagasore, the party fortunes naturally tended to fluctuate with the vicissitudes of his own turbulent career. Although the party statutes contained elaborate provisions about the functions devolved upon the central committee, its composition, and the procedures through which its membership could be altered, these were almost never observed. In the absence of established procedures, it was almost a foregone conclusion that endless litigations would arise among his presumptive heirs once Rwagasore had left the political scene.

Another handicap lay in the nature of the social context within which the party operated. Because of the absence of modern reference groups outside the capital city, the tasks of political mobilisation were made all the more difficult. Only in Bujumbura could Rwagasore address a crowd of several thousand; elsewhere, the gathering of a few hundred was a major enterprise. Not only did the physical environment of the country present enormous obstacles to effective political mobilisation, but the whole pattern of life of the rural masses, based on relationships of personal loyalty among individuals, interfered with the usual techniques of political recruitment. Physical isolation, social inertia, and the persistence of dyadic relationships among individuals, were (and still are) among the most important factors militating against the development of a mass-based organisational apparatus.

Finally, something must be said of the various disciplinary sanctions and restrictions taken by the trust authorities against the party leaders (most of whom, as noted earlier, were regarded as crypto-Communists) and which involved such measures as deportation, rustication to remote areas, and in the case of traditional chiefs like Rwagasore, prohibition from engaging in political activities. Already, in August 1960, Vice-Governor Harroy issued instructions to prevent the return of Paul Mirerekano to Burundi, at a time when the UPRONA leader was in Léopoldville, attending the Congo's independence celebrations; then André Muhirwa was declared persona non grata; then J. B. Kayabo, and many others. Most of them found refuge across the border, in the Kivu province of the Congo, where they established close contacts with local Centre du Regroupement Africain (CEREA) and MNC-Lumumba leaders. During their exile, they absorbed many of the radical ideas of these Congolese leaders and these eventually found expression in the diplomatic relations they later sought to establish with Communist China. But the most severe disabilities suffered by UPRONA stemmed from the administrative sanctions directed against Rwagasore.* Not only was every effort made to discredit his party in the eyes of the masses, but, when his popularity threatened to disprove the electoral prognostications of the administration, he was placed under house arrest. In view of what has already been said of the character of the party leadership, one can see why Rwagasore's arrest, shortly before the communal elections of November 1960, should have spelled the defeat of his party at the polls; another major reason for this temporary setback lies in the massive support the administration gave his opponents, a fact which further exacerbated antagonisms between Bezi and Batare on the eve of independence.

UPRONA VERSUS PDC

The historical dimensions of the Bezi-Batare conflict have already been discussed and need not be enlarged upon here, except to point out in passing the tenacity of traditional antagonisms and their historical tendency to flare up again with renewed vigour at the approach of self-

* In the eyes of the administration, these sanctions were justified by the resolution adopted by the representatives of the thirteen Burundi parties (including UPRONA) then in existence at the meeting held in Brussels, in August 1960, according to which: 'Relatives and connections of the *mwami*, within two degrees of relationship, may not receive an electoral mandate, hold political office or take part in any political activity.' One may wonder, however, if a resolution of this nature could have been adopted in the absence of strong pressures from the administration to hamper the political activities of UPRONA.

government. But there were other factors involved in the UPRONA-PDC fight which tended to fuse with, and reinforce, traditional animosities. To begin with, reference must be made to the differences of personality between Rwagasore and the president and founder of the PDC, Joseph Biroli. The two men disliked each other intensely, and made no effort to conceal it. Biroli was admitted to the Institut Universitaire des Territoires d'Outre-Mer in 1949, two years before Rwagasore, and turned out to be a much brighter student. After completing his studies in Belgium, Biroli attended Oxford and Harvard universities, and later found employment within the European Common Market organisation. Not only did he achieve far greater recognition in European circles, but his whole demeanour—his cosmopolitan outlook, his social graces, his poise—made Rwagasore look rather awkward and slow-witted by comparison. More importantly, Biroli's predispositions evoked a much greater sympathy from the European administration than Rwagasore could ever hope to earn for himself, quite apart from his political convictions.

These differences were bound to have important repercussions on the political plane. It is worth noting at the outset that, if UPRONA and the PDC were indeed the lineal descendants of princely families, their historical antecedents did not make their leaderships immune to the appeals of modernity. To say that the Bezi tended to look to the past for solutions to current problems, whereas the Batare were more conscious of the need to innovate in almost every realm, and particularly in the economic and educational realms, is not meant to suggest a fundamental clash of aspirations between the forces of tradition and the forces of modernity—but, rather, different ways of blending tradition and modernity. It is interesting, in this connection, to compare the abundant coverage given by the PDC programme to questions like 'the problem of youth', 'social security and public assistance', 'social relations', and the relative barrenness of the UPRONA programme on similar problems. Although Rwagasore was not unmindful of these problems, they were deliberately de-emphasised in the interest of what he considered the really critical issues: national unity, monarchical legitimacy, and independence.

While UPRONA seldom missed an opportunity to press its claims for 'immediate independence', the PDC never displayed such enthusiasm for the virtues of self-government. 'The most important thing we can say about independence', said a PDC spokesman on the occasion of the visit of the Groupe de Travail, 'is that it should not be hurled at us too quickly, without preparation. . . . Independence can only be conceived of as a long-run objective, not to be attained before the implementation of a double plan of progressive economic and political emancipation.

For, after all, we are a poor country, and while we do have a political structure of our own, by no stretch of the imagination can it be said that it has prepared us for democratic government.'[19] Either out of decency towards the administering authorities, from whom they received considerable support, or because they were too aware of how much still needed to be done before their country could stand on its own feet, economically and otherwise, the Batare never looked like a group of militant nationalists. After drawing so much from the West, they could no longer be weaned away.

These variations in the pattern of behaviour of the Bezi and Batare elites are in part attributable to an accident of history. Having been brought in contact with Western influence at a relatively early date, and having earned the respect and sympathy of a number of Belgian colonial civil servants, the Batare reacted very favourably to modernity. We have seen, for example, how Baranyanka became the protégé of the administration, and the object of boundless admiration from certain European visitors, as shown by the rhapsodic comments of Jules Sasserath: 'Paramount Chief Baranyanka is one of the coffee-kings of Ruanda-Urundi and a great connoisseur of Burgundy wines . . . owns his own chateau, drives an American car of the latest model, and is known to have a famous cellar. He makes a charming impression and has a refined intelligence. But if Baranyanka leaves an excellent impression, some of the other chiefs are full of deceit and deviousness, impregnated as they are with a typically oriental sense of duplicity.'[20] It is perhaps not too surprising, under the circumstances, that Baranyanka's sons grew up to gain a perception of the world, and of the West, which differed in some major ways from that of their peers.

But it is equally relevant to note that the psychological mechanisms which induced the Batare to behave as they did were intimately related to their relative loss of status before and after the inception of colonial rule. Just as in Tokugawa Japan, the samurai class, having lost their traditional power, tried to compensate for this withdrawal of status respect by taking full advantage of modernity, the Batare, in an effort to regain a measure of respect and prestige, were naturally attracted to the ways of the West.[21] The Bezi, after all, had every reason to feel relatively secure and satisfied with their lot, having achieved a position of virtual dominance in the country. Moreover, having done so through the existing social structure, and with the help of the crown, why should they be inclined to change the values of traditional society? Quite different were the motivations of the Batare. Although they did enjoy the blessings of the administration, they ended up surrendering most of their 'estates' to the Bezi.

There is an obvious correlation between the ideological predispositions and personality types associated with each of these traditional
elite groups and their ability, or inability, to generate support for their
ideas. Apart from the fact that the PDC leadership suffered a good deal
of discredit from its association with the Belgian authorities, its middle
leadership was generally drawn from those very elements whom the
masses tended to distrust, i.e., from those administrative auxiliaries
collectively known in Burundi as 'Astridiens' (after the Groupe Scolaire
d'Astrida, where most of them received their training), who formed the
lower stratum of functionaries against whom the masses inevitably
tended to deflect their diffuse hostility towards the Belgian administration.

UPRONA also included in its membership a substantial number of
Astridiens, but less so proportionately than the PDC. The bulk of its
middle leadership came from three distinctive social categories. First
of all, there were ex-seminarists—like André Nugu, Jean Ntiruhama,
Claver Nuwinklare—that is, from people who bitterly resented being
excluded from the more lucrative administrative posts available, while
in fact claiming a much higher degree of intellectual sophistication than
the Astridiens who filled most of these positions.* Even though
some of them probably disagreed with certain aspects of the UPRONA
doctrine, they were generally predisposed to endorse its nationalist
(i.e. anti-Belgian) orientation. Many enthusiastically rallied to the cause
of the monarchy, for if neither the PDC nor the administration would
consent to recognise their qualifications, at least the crown might, for
reasons of patronage. Because of their wide-ranging connections (especially with the Catholic hierarchy, both African and European), their
relatively high level of intellectual achievement, and their commitment
to a neo-traditionalist ideology, these former seminarists were a major
asset to UPRONA. In a second category were those evolués who had
already gained a smattering of education, either at the mission schools
or at the Groupe Scolaire. Some served on the CSP as 'notables'; others
held clerical positions in the administration or in the private sector; but
most of them were simply looking for a job in harmony with their

---

* According to the ordinance of October 24, 1953, relative to the status of the
so-called 'agents auxiliaires de l'administration', former seminarists with six
years of schooling in a seminary or a mission school were placed in the bottom
ranks of the civil service (fourth category). Their basic salary was 15,000 francs
a year, with possibilities of a 5 per cent increase; those who attended the 'grands
séminaires' were allowed 25,000 francs and could be classified within the next
category (third category). The Astridiens, on the other hand, were automatically
incorporated within this category and earned a basic salary of 31,500 francs.
See *Bulletin Officiel de Ruanda-Urundi*, 1960, p. 1663.

qualifications. Finally, there were the younger chiefs, or *ganwa*—people like the two Ndenzako, Gaspard Nkeshimana, Joseph Mbazumutima, Lorgio Nimubona—who formed the personal entourage of Rwagasore and secretly hoped for a share of the 'spoils' commensurate with their rank in the traditional society. In short, UPRONA included within its ranks a much broader cross-section of society than the PDC. The PDC was the party of the Batare and the Astridiens, and little else; UPRONA, on the other hand, was more than the party of the Bezi and the seminarists that its opponents claimed it to be.[1] It was really the party of both the masses and the elites (both the traditional and non-traditional Westernised elites), and for this reason the problem of maintaining a measure of cohesion within its leadership was all the more arduous. In the absence of a leader of Rwagasore's stature, it is indeed questionable whether the party could have capitalised on its other advantages with the same striking success, let alone preserve its unity during the period preceding independence.

THE VICTORY OF UPRONA AND THE DEATH OF RWAGASORE

Just how prominent a role Rwagasore actually played in the political fortunes of his party is shown by the electoral defeat suffered by UPRONA in the communal elections of November 1960, following the decision of the administration to place him under house arrest, and by his vigorous comeback during the legislative elections of 1961, after his release. The PDC emerged from the communal elections with 942 seats out of a total of 2,876, while UPRONA claimed only 545, and the PDC's lead over its opponent was duly acknowledged by the trust authorities when they set up the interim government, in January 1961: two ministerial chairs out of five went to the PDC, but not a single one to UPRONA. As might have been expected, this decision was bitterly contested by UPRONA, on the grounds that the results of the communal elections had been patently falsified by administrative pressure and intimidation. As a last resort, on January 28, 1961, the UPRONA leaders addressed a petition to the Mwami, along with an alternative list of ministers, in the hope that he might bring enough influence to bear upon the administration to change the composition of the provisional government.[22] But this proved to be of no avail. As the Resident told the UN Commission for Ruanda-Urundi: 'A decision by the Mwami to replace this government by one of his choosing would have been unacceptable to a large part of the people. For most of the political parties, the Mwami is only an august symbol. Any attempt to interfere with politics might result in

13. André Muhirwa.   14. Joseph Biroli.

15. Léopold Bihumugani ('Biha').   16. Paul Mirerekano.

17. Mwami Mwambutsa of Burundi (1916-66).

18. President Michel Micombero of Burundi.

a social revolution similar to that which occurred in Rwanda.'[23] In retrospect, this assessment of the political role of the crown seems singularly short-sighted: not only did the crown eventually become a force to be reckoned with, but, as subsequent events were to demonstrate, even as an 'august symbol' it could still wield considerable influence.

As the campaign for the legislative elections got under way, UPRONA made full use of its connections with the crown. Even though the Mwami repeatedly stressed that he was 'the Mwami of all Barundi', that 'he was above the parties and belonged to no party', in the popular consciousness UPRONA could not be anything else than the party of the monarchy. Certainly, Rwagasore's own personal campaign did much to foster this identification. Everywhere he went, he reminded his audience of his princely origins: 'I am the son of the Mwami. The man I want to introduce to you, and for whom you must vote, speaks for me. Everything he says is said in my name.'[24] But this is not the only reason for the landslide victory of UPRONA; the party could not have derived such a decisive advantage from its links with the crown unless Rwagasore already enjoyed considerable prestige in its own right.

Among the factors which indirectly played into the hands of the UPRONA leader, none was more important than the measures taken by the administration to substitute a new system of local government for the 37 chiefdoms which, until then, formed the basic administrative infrastructure of the realm. When, in September 1960, the Residency decided to abolish the chiefdoms and replace them with 18 provinces, each headed by a provincial administrator appointed by the administration, it created a political void which greatly enhanced the position of the crown. The point here is not that the Mwami arrogated to himself the prerogatives of the chiefs, but that the disappearance of the chiefs impelled the masses to turn to the crown for guidance, as if it were the only remaining symbol of authority they could trust. This situation was vividly described by a former administrateur de territoire, Jean Ghislain: 'The chiefdoms having been suppressed . . . the Barundi felt completely disoriented, and they all rallied around the Mwami's person (the only native authority who preached peace) like castaways around the mast of a sinking ship.'[25] And how could the masses better express their loyalty to the Mwami than by voting for the party headed by his son?

The irony, however, is that the Mwami never felt a great deal of attraction toward UPRONA, and certainly did less than one might expect of a father to help the electoral success of his son. Rwagasore did not belong to the inner circle of the 'king's men'. As noted earlier, the latter went their own separate ways and many ended up forming their own

339

political parties. Pierre Bigayimpunzi and Léopold Biha are cases in point; both men enjoyed the blessings of the crown, and they both tried to make the most of their 'favoured' position during the electoral campaign, but in the end they, like the Batare, had to concede defeat. This confirms the judgment passed by Ghislain on the outcome of the elections: 'The legislative elections of September 18 constituted a severe setback for the *ganwa*, to the profit of monarchical authority, and of the Hutu and Tutsi evolués. In this sense, these elections marked at one and the same time the victory of tradition, the victory of the people and the routing of feudal elements.'[26]

With approximately 80 per cent of the votes cast, and 58 seats in the Legislative Assembly out of a total of 64, UPRONA's position seemed impregnable. As Prime Minister designate, Rwagasore could turn to the tasks of nation-building, free from major opposition to his policies. Fate, however, decided otherwise. On October 13, 1961, as he was having dinner at a lakeside restaurant, Rwagasore fell under the bullets of a Greek gunman, victim of a plot concocted by his political enemies.

There is no need here to recount in great detail the facts and circumstances surrounding Rwagasore's assassination, as these are available from other sources.[27] Suffice it to note, in the first place, that the PDC leaders were directly involved in the chain of events that led to Rwagasore's death. On this score the evidence available is crushing. That the assassin, Jean Kageorgis, was a mere tool in the hands of these leaders; that the crime was the result of a political conspiracy organised by Biroli and Ntitendereza, and that the ultimate aim of this conspiracy was to create disturbances throughout the realm that would then be exploited by the PDC to its own advantages—these are well-established facts. However, the PDC leaders might not have resorted to such drastic action unless they had been actively encouraged to go ahead with their plans by certain Belgian functionaries. According to the testimony of a certain Hubert Léonard, principal commissaire at the Residency, Resident Régnier held a meeting on September 21, 1961—which he and the European secretary of the PDC, Mrs Belva, attended—in the course of which Régnier was reported to have flatly stated: 'Rwagasore must be killed!' 'In Rwanda', pursued Régnier, 'there would be no problem. . . . Of course, what I foresaw did happen—the Front Commun* lost the elections, but nothing is lost if one gets rid of Rwagasore in time. . . .

---

* The Front Commun, founded in September 1960, was a loose electoral coalition, or cartel, including, besides the PDC, the Parti du Peuple, the Parti Démocrate Rural, the Parti de l'Emancipation Populaire, the Voix du Peuple Murundi and several other minor formations. See Michel Lechat, *Le Burundi Politique*, Service de l'Information du Ruanda-Urundi, Usumbura, p. 36.

Once the deed is accomplished, the lake is not too far away.'[28] The content of this conversation was apparently reported to Joseph Ntitendereza the following day, and, while Ntitendereza later denied having 'any knowledge of the circumstances of the murder', there is every reason to believe that he himself was the chief architect of the plot. Finally, although the crime was clearly due to a combination of motives—some political, others of a more personal nature—it also constituted a settlement of 'old scores' between two rival claimants, whose reciprocal hatreds reached far back into the pre-colonial past. Only if one remembers the historical dimensions of the conflict can one understand the feelings of rage of the Batare in the face of a situation which denied them once and for all the opportunity to make good their traditional claims to power.

This element of atavistic hatred, combined with the sacred obligation of seeking a blood-vengeance proportional to the offence, helps to explain the rather unorthodox procedure adopted by the Burundi authorities to punish those involved in the murder of Rwagasore. Although the case had already been handled and tried by the judicial authorities of the 'tutelle', a re-trial was ordered after independence which led to a substantial modification of the judgment issued in May 1962 by the Court of Appeal of Bujumbura. The judgment of the Court of Appeal had confirmed the death sentence earlier passed on Kageorgis by the Court of First Instance, but had commuted the death sentences passed on Joseph Ntitendereza and his accomplice, Antoine Nahimana, to twenty years penal servitude. Although the issue was res judicata, a law of September 26, 1962, established a Supreme Court with retroactive competence which, a month later, on October 27, quashed the decisions of the Court of Appeal and the Court of First Instance on the grounds that the absence of a jury during the court proceedings was in effect a violation of article 85 of the newly-adopted constitution. At this point, the case was taken back to the Court of First Instance for a re-trial, and on November 27 the court issued its verdict: five of the accused persons (Ntitendereza, Nahimana, Biroli, Iatrou and Ntakiyica, the last three of whom had earlier been condemned to various terms of penal servitude by the Court of Appeal) were sentenced to death. On January 5, 1963, the Court of Appeal confirmed the judgment of the lower court. Still hoping for a miracle, the accused tried to lodge an appeal to the Supreme Court, only to find that their request could not be entertained. They were told that, according to the terms of a royal decree of October 30, 1962—which, incidentally, had not then been published—'a new appeal to the Supreme Court for the same cause [was] subject to the approval of the Public Prosecutor'.

Last minute efforts on the part of the Belgian government to appeal to the Mwami for clemency proved similarly futile. On January 14, all five men were transferred to Kitega and were publicly hanged the following day, before a crowd estimated at ten thousand. In the words of the International Commission of Jurists, 'this was the first time that a country passing from the status of a trust territory to that of a sovereign state had considered itself authorised to reopen judicial proceedings closed prior to its independence. . . . It is a principle of law in all civilised countries that a change in internal or international political status has no effect on the validity of certain decisions which have become res judicata.'[29]

However disquieting for the future of the country, this bland disregard of the rule of law seems almost inconsequential compared to the political implications of Rwagasore's death. Not only did it constitute an irreparable loss of leadership, but it also destroyed whatever measure of racial cohesion the UPRONA leader had achieved during his brief and turbulent political career. Rwagasore's death, and the fact that the legitimacy of his role as a nationalist leader owed very little to constitutional niceties and virtually all to qualities of personality, including that of being the Mwami's son, were critical elements in the background of the Hutu-Tutsi problem.

13. The Displacement of Conflict: Hutu versus Tutsi

No SOONER had the kingdom crossed the threshold of self-government than storm clouds gathered anew on the horizon. From what appeared to be a kind of intra-mural rivalry among the descendants of royal families, the bases of conflict suddenly shifted along ethnic lines, substituting an opposition 'from within' for the dynastic threats heretofore faced by the nationalist elites. A new segment of society was arising, with a strong psychological commitment to democracy and a growing sense of racial solidarity—too weak as yet to push aside the 'patricians', but no less eager to assert their claims to equality. The Hutu awakening had begun.

It revealed itself on August 26, 1962, less than a month after independence, in what could have been a much more serious incident. On that date, the Hutu leader, Paul Mirerekano, called a mass meeting of the rank and file of UPRONA, at Rwagasore stadium, in Bujumbura, with the obvious intention of converting the meeting into a plebiscite. This time the author of *Mwbire gito canje* abandoned his customary innuendoes for a more direct pitch: skilfully exploiting the ethnic solidarities of his supporters, Mirerekano bitterly denounced the attitude of the government in power, a government which, he said, had on numerous occasions shown evidence of racial favouritism and nepotism. With visible emotion, Mirerekano went on to elaborate at some length on what independence meant for Rwagasore, and how its original meaning was betrayed by his successors, intimating that he alone could lay claim to Rwagasore's mantle. As the audience (estimated at about 2,000) gave increasing signs of restiveness, several detachments of gendarmerie were summoned to the stadium to arrest Mirerekano and disperse the crowd. Instead, a group of about 60 gendarmes rallied to Mirerekano and proceeded to act as his personal bodyguard, while the others just stood by, apparently stunned. The army was placed in a state of emergency by Zénon Nicayenzi, then commissaire in charge of the armed forces, and who, exactly two months earlier, had publicly vaunted the indissoluble union of Hutu and Tutsi, 'intimately linked to each other . . . and free of the obstacles which in Rwanda separate the two groups'. Although calm was eventually restored without the army's intervention, the incident must have prompted Nicayenzi to entertain second thoughts about the presumed harmony of Hutu-Tutsi relations.[1]

What happened? Why this sudden manifestation of ethnic enmity where none had seemed to exist previously? At a broad level of generalisation, one might argue that the events of August 1962 were but the consequence of the rapid politicisation of residual ethnic ties which usually affects multi-ethnic societies at the approach of independence. While not inaccurate, so vague an explanation necessarily leaves out a number of elements within the total environment of Burundi, including the international environment, which have had a direct impact on the crystallisation of ethnic tensions. Perhaps the most important of these conditioning factors has to do with the shift of attitude which took place among certain Hutu elites in response to the Rwandese revolution.

THE SELF-FULFILLING PROPHECY

Even in the absence of ethnic affinities with their Rwandese kinsmen, it is difficult to see how the Hutu of Burundi could have remained insensitive to the implications of majority rule. After the coup of Gitarama, however, a number of Hutu politicians, at first mostly outside UPRONA, began to feel the contagion of republican ideas. By identifying their political aims and aspirations with those of PARMEHUTU, they imputed to the Tutsi of Burundi motives which they (the Tutsi) at first did not possess but to which they eventually gave a substance of truth, a phenomenon which is best understood by reference to Merton's notion of self-fulfilling prophecy.[2] By giving the Burundi situation a false definition to begin with, these Hutu politicians evoked a new behaviour, both among themselves and the Tutsi, which made their originally false imputations true.

Nor was this phenomenon restricted to the indigenous Hutu elites. One may indeed wonder to what extent their attitude was conditioned by a genuine identification with the Hutu of Rwanda, and to what extent it reflected the inducements and proddings of the Belgian administration. For if the political conjuncture in Rwanda was bound to affect the expectations of certain Hutu leaders, it also set a precedent for those Belgian functionaries who saw in the victory of PARMEHUTU a prefiguration of things to come.

Two of the most ardent supporters of the Hutu cause were Resident de Fays and the court inspector, F. L. Asselman: they both actively participated in the launching of the pro-Hutu Association des Progressistes et Démocrates Barundi (APRODEBA), and when its vice-president, Boniface Kiraranganya, later joined UPRONA, they gave their full support to the Parti du Peuple (PP), by then the most outspoken of pro-Hutu parties.[3] One of the key personalities associated with the PP was a Belgian settler, Albert Maus, formerly a resident of Rwanda and a member of the Conseil du Vice-Gouvernement Général. Totally unsparing of his time, energy and financial resources, Maus became the 'éminence grise' of the PP, acting as the main intermediary between its leaders and the administration, writing countless petitions to the United Nations, and always prepared to give his financial backing to the Hutu cause. So pathologically anti-Tutsi was he that he committed suicide upon learning of the UPRONA victory. Though few Belgian functionaries were actuated by the same sense of personal commitment, like Maus they naturally projected into the context of Burundi politics their own experiences or estimates of the Rwandese situation, and acted accordingly.

That in spite of this the PP should have met with so little success during the legislative elections of 1961 is, of course, indicative of the far greater popularity of UPRONA; but this may also be accounted for by a shift of 'anticipated reactions' somewhat similar to that which initially prompted certain Hutu elements to cast their lot with the PP. A number of PP leaders switched sides at the last minute, anticipating a massive victory of UPRONA at the polls; others, obeying the same impulse, refused to take sides. Thus, racial animosities on the political level were initially confined to a tiny minority of hard-core Hutu politicians (perhaps half a dozen) who faithfully took their cue from PARMEHUTU, and these had virtually no hearing outside the capital city.

But if the political odds were clearly against the PP leaders, at least for the time being, they nonetheless could count on a substantial potential following, not yet mobilisable for political action but which could conceivably become so under more favourable circumstances. Among the most vulnerable to republican ideas were those few Hutu intellectuals employed by the administration or the Catholic missions who, on account of their education and status, had internalised to a greater degree than their rural kinsmen the values and promises of democracy. While some of them eventually joined the PP leadership, many also belonged to the still-embryonic Syndicats Chrétiens, a trade union organisation founded in 1958, under the auspices of its metropolitan parent organisation, the Confédération des Syndicats Chrétiens (CSC). Theoretically apolitical, the Syndicats Chrétiens in fact served as forcing grounds for the nascent Hutu leadership. In time, they emerged as the most vocal defenders of the Hutu cause, and therefore as the main target of the Tutsi wing of UPRONA.

Regional affinities also played a part in shaping the attitudes of the Hutu elites. Although there is nothing in Burundi comparable to the sharp cultural differences between northern and central Rwanda, the historical influences that have come into play in certain regions have profoundly influenced the dispositions of the local Hutu populations towards the crown, as well as their own feelings of solidarity as a group. It is not a matter of pure coincidence if the strongholds of the PP happened to be located in the northern provinces of Ngozi and Bubanza, which at one time constituted Kilima's fief. Whether because of Kilima's policy of recruiting his military chiefs from among the local Hutu population, or because of the legacy of protest movements created by subsequent attempts to instigate local revolts (such as the one which Kilima's son, Rwasha, sought to instigate in 1934),[4] or, again, because of the more stringent policies later adopted by local chiefs to discourage the recurrence of similar threats to their authority, the Hutu populations of the Ngozi and Bubanza provinces have remained distinctively race-conscious, if not openly anti-Tutsi. This is confirmed by the abortive Hutu revolt which apparently took place in Kayanza (once the 'headquarters' of Kilima) in early 1960, following the Rwandese jacquerie of 1959, and by the innumerable racial incidents (some assuming the proportions of full-scale revolts) which later occurred in this same area.[5]

There remained the vast reservoir of Hutu supporters of UPRONA, the overwhelming majority of the peasant masses, whose adherence to UPRONA was more a conditioned reflex to the appeals of kingship than the product of a conscious, well-reasoned political option. Wholeheartedly committed to the monarchy, and with little or no collective consciousness of themselves as a group, they were the least inclined to challenge the legitimacy of the powers that be, and, likewise, the least susceptible to the appeals of race-conscious republicanism. Even after the desertion of Mirerekano from the ranks of UPRONA, he was unable to detach his ethnic followers en masse from the party. The task of bringing together under the same roof the rural segments of the Hutu community proved infinitely more difficult than some had initially expected.

Because of these discontinuities within the Hutu community, expectations of a massive upsurge of racial solidarities, along Rwandese lines, remained unfulfilled. Nonetheless, the Rwandese situation did provide a powerful pole of attraction for the small Hutu intelligentsia of Bujumbura, and, while their own vision of the future had no perceptible impact outside the capital city, one can easily understand why they were viewed with such deep apprehension by the Tutsi wing of UPRONA. What the latter failed to perceive, however, is that the methods they used in dealing with the Hutu opposition outside the party were liable to arouse an even more formidable opposition within it.

THE JNR ON THE MARCH

Signs of an impending crisis were already discernible before the kingdom achieved its independence. In late 1962, a number of bloody scuffles took place in various localities, which set the stage for a more serious confrontation. In almost every case, these incidents were the result of deliberate provocations by young Tutsi militants, affiliated to the Jeunesses Nationalistes Rwagasore (JNR), against Hutu trade unionists and politicians. Joachim Baribwegure, president of the PP, Jean Nduhabike, president of the Syndicats Chrétiens, Jean Kandeke, PP supporter in charge of a local co-operative, among others, became the object of violent threats, often followed by molestations; one of them, Jean Kandeke, was almost bludgeoned to death by a group of JNR militants. That these acts of violence were all instigated by Tutsi elements does not mean that they were inspired exclusively by racial hatred. Indeed, there is every reason to believe that, in spite of its obvious racial overtones, the social and political dimensions of conflict were by far the more important. The JNR constituted a group apart, not only in terms of the generations from which it recruited the bulk of its adherents, but also from the standpoint of its ideology and political ties. The very youthfulness of its cohorts, the fact that some of its more prominent leaders first developed a political consciousness outside Burundi—and in an environment peculiarly conducive to an exalted, extremist brand of nationalism—and, more importantly, that so many of these young men happened to be excluded from the positions of prestige and influence to which they aspired, have all contributed to give the JNR a distinctive ideological bent.

The origins of the JNR—initially known as the Union Culturelle de la Jeunesse Africaine du Burundi (UCJAB)—can be traced back to 1959. The organisation was founded in Lubumbashi (then known as Elizabethville) by Prime Nyongabo and Gilles Bimazubute, both of whom were at the time attending the Université Officielle. Unless one recalls the social and political climate of Elizabethville in 1959, with its strong 'white supremacist' undercurrents, one cannot understand the political orientation of its leadership: its petulant nationalism; its rebellious attitude in the face of the entrenched patriciate associated with the ancien régime; its redemptive quest for a solidarist, fraternal ideology. 'Our movement', said the statutes of the UCJAB, 'aims at leading humanity towards a greater fraternity, a greater mutual understanding, a greater

347

peace and happiness. . . . Its goals are to orient our youth towards a more mature form of nationalism, through appropriate civic training; to inculcate in our future generations of leaders a sense of mutual understanding . . . and to affirm the ideal of equality among all citizens.'[6] If the language of the UCJAB was from the very beginning the language of nationalism, its organisational links with UPRONA did not materialise until much later. At first the statutes of the organisation made no reference to specific political groups but merely stated its willingness to be 'in the service of political parties and milieux, in one capacity or another, in order to co-ordinate, educate and civilise their action'.[7] Only *after* the legislative elections of 1961 did the organisation change its name to JNR, and it was only after many hesitations and considerable soul-searching that its leadership finally decided to cast its lot with UPRONA (presumably because, at the time, UPRONA was thought to include too many old-timers of the *ganwa* variety, and because of the obvious contradictions between the party's ideological commitment to the monarchy and the JNR's 'progressive' orientation). This wait-and-see attitude did not pay. By the time the UCJAB had become the JNR, the spoils of office had already been shared among the victors, and the JNR's leaders found themselves in the position of an alienated counter-elite.

To supply a palliative and prevent the JNR from joining the ranks of the opposition, the government decided shortly before independence to use it as a 'parallel structure' for maintaining peace and order in the native quarters of Bujumbura, a task for which the JNR leaders showed more than ordinary zeal. From then on, the JNR took on a decidedly activist coloration, which has remained its most conspicuous characteristic. Though formally affiliated to UPRONA, neither the government nor what was left of the party leadership succeeded in keeping its activities under control. The relationship of the JNR with the government was never clearly defined, and its organic links with the party never solidified. Even within the organisation itself, nothing like a coherent pattern of authority seemed to emerge. The JNR, in short, was little more than a gang of 'angry young men', boisterous, undisciplined and prone to violence.

In view of the explosive situation created by the terroristic activities of the JNR, one can better understand the indignant reaction of the Hutu leadership. In early January 1962, the Syndicats Chrétiens held a congress on the premises of the Collège du Saint Esprit, in Bujumbura, in the course of which they bitterly condemned the 'provocations and revanchist attitude of the JNR'. 'The so-called Nationalist Youth of Burundi', stated the communiqué released after the congress, 'has ceaselessly aggravated national tensions to the extreme, propagating hatred and aggression. . . . The congress denounces the fact that the governments of both Belgium and Burundi have so far turned a deaf ear to the complaints lodged by the members of the opposition. Unless these governments respond to our invitation and see to it that peace reigns in our country, we shall initiate a policy of self-defence and will do everything to initiate work-stoppages throughout our national territory and invite the workers to stage public demonstrations.'[8] Another motion adopted by the congress reiterated its concern in the face of the 'provocations of the JNR, whose organisation and actions are directed by the militants of the UNAR youth movement', this time suggesting the formation of a government of National Union 'to re-establish a peaceful and democratic order and insure national collaboration and understanding'. In what might have sounded like a call to insurrection, the motion ended by urging the masses to rely on no one but themselves: 'Direct action is needed in factories, workshops and offices, in every town and city, in the fields and on the hills.'[9]

The response of the JNR was almost instantaneous—and violent. On January 13, 1962, a young JNR militant named Pamphile Bikoboke, who falsely claimed to be a court official and said he had received his mandate from the burgomaster of Bujumbura, arrested two well-known Hutu personalities in the commune of Muzazi, in the province of Bubanza. The next day, the president of the JNR, Prime Nyongabo, held a tempestuous meeting on the premises of the Centre Educatif et Social in the Kamenge quarter of Bujumbura, attended by a score of JNR militants, and shortly thereafter launched a series of armed raids against local Hutu personalities associated with the Syndicats Chrétiens or the PP. A veritable manhunt was under way, accompanied by arson and murder. In Kamenge alone, four houses were set aflame. In the course of these incidents, four prominent Hutu personalities lost their lives; one of them, Jean Nduwabike, president of the Syndicats Chrétiens and national secretary of the PP, was savagely stoned to death by his aggressors. The other victims were Severin Ndinzurwaha, permanent secretary of the Syndicats Chrétiens and national secretary of the teachers' association, Basile Ntawumenyakarizi, PP militant and principal of the Ngagara secondary school, and a certain Baruvura. The 'external' Hutu opposition had now practically ceased to exist.[10] This new flare-up of militancy deeply shocked the Hutu leadership of UPRONA, and its repercussions were immediately felt within the party. What later became known as the Kamenge incidents presaged a deepening split along racial lines, which not only aggravated the long-simmering leadership crisis within the party but eventually brought the entire administrative machinery of the state to a near standstill.

THE PARTY CRISIS

In the highly volatile atmosphere created by the Kamenge riots, little was needed to spread racial divisions within the party. While the riots were in themselves a dramatic symptom of the absence of effective controls within UPRONA, the struggle for the leadership of the party gave a decisive push to the deterioration of Hutu-Tutsi relations.

The internal crisis that shook UPRONA in the months immediately following independence is, of course, directly related to the loss of leadership and guidance following the death of Rwagasore, a loss from which it never recovered. But it also involved several other factors, some accidental, others reflecting the structural transformations brought in the wake of independence. For one thing, the rapid absorption of party cadres into the central and provincial bureaucracies caused the virtual disintegration of UPRONA as an autonomous political unit. For example, the president of the party, André Nugu, was appointed provincial administrator of Muramvya in 1961; the vice-president, Théophile Rwuzuye, became assessor at the Tribunal de Résidence in early 1962; the national secretary, Zacharie Ntiriyca, became director of public works in November 1961; André Rufruguta and Onésime Budome, provincial presidents of the Bujumbura and Muramvya branches of UPRONA, were both appointed provincial administrators in 1961. Not only did this paralyse the party, but the mere fact that power was now in the hands of its former leadership made its revitalisation unnecessary. More, the likelihood that the party might again become an autonomous centre of power raised understandable fears among those who had finally gained power, and hoped to retain it. At the same time, the allocation of rewards to the party faithful was bound to create enormous jealousies among those who, for some reason or another, happened to be left out. Of these unlucky ones, none was more ulcerated than Paul Mirerekano. His unquestionable honesty had once won him the post of national treasurer of UPRONA, a position he gave up after being forced into exile by the trust authorities; and now that he was finally permitted to re-enter the country, it was only to discover that the spoils of office had passed him by.

To regain a measure of influence and recognition, Mirerekano had no choice but to reassert his claims to the presidency of UPRONA. Yet this is precisely where he ran into trouble—not only for the reasons just mentioned, but also because the man who now held the presidency,

André Muhirwa (who, incidentally, also assumed the prime-ministership at the death of Rwagasore), categorically denied the legitimacy of Mirerekano's claims. When Mirerekano correctly pointed out that he had been appointed interim president by Rwagasore, upon his return from the Congo in mid-1961, Muhirwa retorted that, since he had taken Rwagasore's place in the government, he was automatically entitled to Rwagasore's seat within the party. In an effort to settle the issue once and for all, a caucus of various UPRONA personalities, including a generous sprinkling of JNR militants, met on July 4, 1962; but the select few who, on this occasion, confirmed Muhirwa in office could not possibly claim to represent the rank-and-file of the party, and their decision naturally failed to satisfy Mirerekano. By then, there was no doubt in his mind that the Muhirwa government and the JNR were hell-bent on pursuing a 'racist' policy.

The Kamenge incidents had already given Mirerekano sufficient evidence of the feelings of racial hatred which seemed to permeate the attitude of the JNR, and the informal ties which linked certain personalities of the Muhirwa government to the JNR leaders served only to intensify his fears. Much of Mirerekano's suspicion towards the Muhirwa government, however, also stemmed from suspicion of Muhirwa's own personality. Muhirwa epitomised many of the behavioural and personality traits associated with the Tutsi. In fact, one could hardly conceive of two personalities more cross-grained than these two. A *ganwa*, a descendant of the Batare family, Muhirwa showed a peculiar combination of political astuteness and aristocratic distinction. His unmistakably patrician outlook, tinged with condescension, his tall stature and protruding eyeballs, his extraordinarily quick mind and prodigious ability to conceal his inner feelings behind a mask of indifference, made Muhirwa something of a caricature of the Tutsi type. Despite his lanky frame, Mirerekano was of Hutu extraction, and he possessed a sense of naive self-righteousness and a simplicity of manners that stood in sharp contrast with the inordinately polished and convoluted ways of his opponent. Until then, the subtlety of *ganwa* politics had never come within his ken. His six years of schooling at Astrida earned him the grade of agricultural assistant, but very little in the way of intellectual sophistication. He retained all his life the sturdy and simplistic outlook of a Hutu peasant, qualities which his followers could respect and appreciate but which could draw only sarcasm and contempt from a man of Muhirwa's class. Perhaps the only element they had in common was the strength of their convictions: each considered himself the spiritual heir of Rwagasore, and neither would concede the presidency of the party to the other.

351

In August 1962, thoroughly exasperated by Muhirwa's obduracy, Mirerekano decided to force the issue by appealing to the rank and file of the party. This is what led to the meeting of August 26, 1962, at Rwagasore stadium, and to the unexpected action of the gendarmerie. Although the incidents were by no means the first symptom of racial deterioration, they dramatised better than any previous occurrence the incipient war between Hutu and Tutsi.

By the time the government could recover from the shock of the stadium incidents, and before Mirerekano could capitalise on his tactical victory, the Mwami seized the initiative and announced that a new executive committee of UPRONA would be elected by the rank and file of the party in September 1962. These elections, held in Muramvya, were attended primarily by Muhirwa's supporters, however, for only a tiny minority of Hutu elements were given the official passes allowing them to travel to Muramvya to cast their votes. The resulting executive committee represented a lame compromise between the aspirations of the two rival factions. As a sop to the Mirerekano wing, the presidency of the party went to Joseph Bamina, a Hutu, while Mirerekano was elected to a vice-presidency, along with Thaddée Siryuyumunsi and Muhirwa. From the very beginning, however, Mirerekano refused to attend any meeting of the newly elected committee, and within weeks he had organised a separate UPRONA wing, of which, at least, he became president.

Despite subsequent attempts at reconciliation, the breach was never healed. The impasse between the two factions of UPRONA was brought to full light during the so-called 'summit conference' (*Inama Kaminuza*), held in Kitega in September 1964. Attended by a score of Hutu and Tutsi 'notables' drawn from each wing of the party, the conference set out to 'debate in common the means to achieve national unity ... and the total reconciliation of the UPRONA leaders', and, to this end, gave first priority on its agenda to 'the constitution of a single Executive Committee'.[11] After lengthy discussions, agreement was finally reached on the composition of a new committee, headed by Joseph Bamina, including several personalities previously affiliated to the Mirerekano wing.* This move, a credit to the conference, also marked the limits of its achievements. On the very day of the election of the committee, and despite the commendable suggestion made by the vice-president of the National Assembly that 'everybody kiss each other', five of Muhirwa's supporters (including two Hutu) wrote a letter to the chairman of

* Mirerekano did not attend the conference, having sought refuge in Rwanda following his implication in a plot against the Nyamoya government in May 1964. He did not return to Burundi until early 1965.

the conference to express their disapproval of the procedure employed to elect the new committee, stating that only a national congress of the party was legally competent to discharge this function. In response to the objections raised in the letter, the chairman of the conference meekly observed that it was 'impossible to call a meeting of the national congress because no one really represented the party any longer'.[12] The deliberations of the summit conference merely confirmed the truth of the statement. UPRONA remained what it had never ceased to be since Rwagasore's death—a party in search of a leadership.

What had begun as an intra-party feud now threatened to assume wider dimensions. The stadium incidents inaugurated a cycle of renewed provocations, retaliation and revenge which, by contagion, spread to the parliamentary and administrative arenas, and eventually penetrated the rural sectors of society.

THE INFLATIONARY SPIRAL

The rapid polarisation of ethnic feeling unleashed by the events of August 1962 was the result of factors and circumstances somewhat similar to those which, in other African states, have governed the relations between the ruling elites and their opponents. As elsewhere in Africa, the techniques used by the incumbents to neutralise their adversaries involved a considerable amount of coercion and arbitrariness, and this inevitably led to an even greater degree of mutual distrust between the 'ins' and the 'outs'. Unlike what happened in most other African states, however, the dividing line between the two groups was never very firmly drawn, at least not until recently. The very size of the Hutu opposition, actual or potential, as well as its strategic location within the political system, defied all but the most extreme forms of prophylaxis. Moreover, even when racial animosities were at their peak, political divisions were not always consistent with ethnic cleavages. Either because they simply did not fit into either one of the two major ethnic categories, or because they refused to let their origins govern their political allegiances, the political commitments of many Barundi ran counter to their ethnic affiliations. A third factor to bear in mind is that neither the Hutu nor the Tutsi were totally and permanently 'in' or 'out' of government; as we shall see, once the crown had decided to intervene, its policy consisted more in balancing Hutu against Tutsi, and vice versa, than in seeking the elimination of one group in favour of the other. This, of course, did not prevent the crystallisation of opposition forces along ethnic lines; but it made their containment (or suppression) all the more difficult.

The ramification of ethnic solidarities through the political system meant that nearly every institution was vulnerable to the spread of ethnic discontent, but, because of the very nature of its functions, parliament was the first to show signs of contamination. The carry-over of racial animosities into the parliamentary arena occurred shortly after, and as a result of, the Kamenge troubles. In June 1962, the Minister of Interior, Jean Ntiruhama, was violently criticised by a group of Hutu deputies for his alleged collusion with the JNR leaders during the Kamenge riots, and in time no less than thirty-nine accusations were brought against him, on grounds ranging from 'flagrant favouritism in the choice of provincial governors' to 'incitements to racial hatred'.[13] In particular, Ntiruhama was accused of having deliberately encouraged the JNR militants to violence, by providing them with jeeps and ammunition. Although the evidence is too scanty to permit a final judgment, the mere fact that the government was believed to be at fault decisively strengthened racial solidarities among the Hutu parliamentarians. Before 1962 drew to a close, the Hutu parliamentary group, representing roughly half of the total membership of the National Assembly, became known as the 'Monrovia group', while the other half, representing the Tutsi faction, called itself 'Casablanca'. These labels bore no relation to the inter-African groups to which they normally refer, except as regards the different shades of pro- or anti-Western sentiment which they presumably connote. The only real source of unity within each of the two groups has been a common racial affinity, and a profound distrust of the other group. There were some notable exceptions to the rule that 'Casablanca' and 'Monrovia' were mere euphemisms for Tutsi and Hutu;* but, because they gained such a wide currency and were used as synonyms for Hutu and Tutsi, these terms institutionalised a situation of ethnic cleavage between the two groups which in turn tended to reinforce their separate identities.

Within the bureaucracy, ethnic tensions never reached the same pitch of intensity, because of its relative insulation from the turmoil of party-politics, and because racial affinities were in some cases superseded by solidarities of a different nature, such as those which distinguished the Astridiens from the former seminarists. Yet to pretend that the civil service remained totally immune to the appeals of ethnicity would be grossly inaccurate. Largely because of the discriminatory implications of indirect rule in the field of secondary and higher education, the overwhelming majority of the new bureaucratic posts went to Tutsi, thus

* For example, the leader of the Monrovia group, Thaddée Siryuyumunsi, was a Tutsi-Hima, and some Hutu, like Pierre Mpozenzi and Pierre Ngunzu, were quite obviously aligned with Casablanca.

creating a new set of vested interests among the Tutsi elites. Ethnic disparities in the distribution of governmental, administrative, judicial and diplomatic posts were given special attention during the UPRONA 'summit conference', in September 1964; and, while the conferees immediately recognised the urgency of the problem, in the end nothing was done to redress the balance. According to the report of the commission set up by the conference to inquire into the origins of 'racial divisions among the citizens of Burundi', evidence of discrimination was found at every level of the governmental and administrative hierarchies; the figures cited by the commission[14] require little elaboration:

	Hutu	Tutsi
Ministers	5	8
Chefs de Cabinet	3	7
Directeurs Généraux	4	9
Directeurs	8	34
Provincial Governors	2	6
Commissaires d'Arrondissements	3	15
Directeurs de Parastataux	0	13
Parquets	2	unknown
Tribunaux de Province	0	11
Tribunaux de Résidence	3	66
Diplomatic Corps	5	22
Total	33	181

Even if an honest attempt had been made to come to grips with the problem (which does not seem to have been the case), one may wonder if it could have been solved on the basis of the formula adopted by the conference—'Given equal competence, UPRONA members first; to positions of responsibility, the most competent UPRONA members'— for not only was the distinction between UPRONA members and non-members totally meaningless at this particular stage, but the second principle involved in the above formula could only serve to perpetuate Tutsi dominance in the civil service. This is where most of the trouble originated: administrative competence automatically favoured one group against the other, and this was ipso facto regarded as evidence of racial discrimination. This, however, did not exclude actual instances of ethnic favouritism (as shown by the remarkable homogeneity of certain ministries); nor did it minimise the competitiveness of the scramble for jobs created by the sudden opening of a whole new range of career opportunities in the public and private sectors. In either case, the result was a further polarisation of racial feelings.

While neither the gendarmerie nor the army was by any means immune to the ferment of racial discontent, the former was the more seriously threatened by ethnic dissensions. This fact, dramatically brought to light during the incidents of August 1962, received further confirmation during the abortive mutiny of October 1965. For this, two explanations suggest themselves. The most obvious is that, by the very nature of its functions, which brought its members in close and daily contact with the civilian population, the gendarmerie was far more susceptible to political influences than the army. Less obvious, but perhaps even more important, was the decision taken by the Belgian authorities, shortly before independence, to incorporate Rwandese elements into the Burundi gendarmerie, a decision motivated in part by the dearth of adequate security forces at the time of independence, and by the fact that these Rwandese elements had already been integrated into the 'corps de police' stationed in Burundi.* Since the overwhelming majority of the men were of Hutu extraction, it is difficult to see how the Rwandese gendarmes (altogether about eighty) could have failed to respond to the appeals of racial solidarity. Indeed, the likelihood is that many of the men who rallied to Mirerekano's side on August 26, 1962, were of Rwandese origins. Whether in fact the Burundi gendarmerie was subsequently purged of its Rwandese elements, as one deputy recommended, is unclear;[15] but, even if this were actually the case, subsequent events demonstrated that the gendarmerie was not the most reliable force.

The army, on the other hand, at first seemed much more dependable. Its exposure to civilian influences was minimal, compared to that of the gendarmerie, and the involvement of its officers in the ferment of party politics was made all the more difficult by governmental controls on their activities. Moreover, in the months following independence, the Burundi National Army was systematically purged of its 'subversive' elements (for the most part of PDC obedience) by Zénon Nicayenzi, then in charge of the armed forces. Nicayenzi personally told this writer how the trusteeship authorities had tried to politicise the army, through 'selective' recruitment and indoctrination—a fact which other sources seem to confirm—and how he subsequently weeded out every single non-member of UPRONA from the officers corps (which, of course, did not imply the elimination of Hutu officers). Because the army seemed so much more reliable, in September 1963, Captain Micombero

* The Burundi gendarmerie was inaugurated in May 1962, less than three months before independence; until then, the only equivalent security force was the so-called 'corps de police', entrusted with constabulary functions, whose members served in Rwanda or Burundi irrespective of their 'national' origins.

made a strong plea before the National Assembly to incorporate the gendarmerie into the army: 'Otherwise the army and the gendarmerie will constitute two antagonistic forces, pitted against each other.'[16] But even if Micombero's suggestion had been put into practice, the army could not have remained neutral for very long. Given the political sympathies of certain gendarmerie officers, this move could have produced precisely the reverse of what had been intended. In any event, so rapid was the deterioration of the political climate during the intervening years, that whatever degree of 'neutrality' the army may have claimed in 1962 had almost completely vanished by 1965.

In addition to what has already been said, three specific factors have contributed to the spiral of ethnic claims and counter-claims. To begin with, many of the issues involved in the Hutu-Tutsi conflict raised a host of subsidiary questions which in turn added a kind of 'multiplier effect' to the already existing tensions. The Kamenge riots, for example, though not directly instigated by the government, led certain Hutu deputies to question the role of the Minister of Interior before and during the incidents, as well as the attitude of the provincial governor, Ildephonse Ntamikevyo, and eventually the judgment of the public prosecutor's office during the trial of certain JNR personalities implicated in the riots. In the atmosphere of mutual distrust prevailing at the time, these issues could hardly be dealt with on the basis of their own merits. Similarly, the events of August 1962 led the deputies to take issue on whether the Rwandese gendarmes should stay in the Burundi gendarmerie or be repatriated, which in turn brought the debate to a new pitch of emotional tension; while some argued that the presence of Hutu from Rwanda in the gendarmerie constituted a permanent danger to the security of the state, others replied that the reasoning also applied to those Tutsi refugees from Rwanda who were given asylum in Burundi.

Nowhere was this inflationary phenomenon better illustrated than in the course of the gradual deterioration of diplomatic relations between Rwanda and Burundi, itself a symptom of the worsening Hutu-Tutsi relations within Burundi. As it became evident that the ties of collaboration between the Tutsi refugee leadership from Rwanda and the indigenous Tutsi elites of Burundi were largely responsible for the recrudescence of border incidents between the two countries, domestic and international issues became so closely intertwined that they could no longer be dealt with independently, let alone objectively. When, in February 1964, shortly after the abortive invasion of the Bugesera, the question arose of what sanctions, if any, should be taken against the refugees to prevent the recurrence of similar incidents, the Hutu faction in parliament took a characteristically hard line, suggesting that those who had

357

taken part in the attack be surrendered to the Rwandese authorities. The argument that the proposed measures were dictated by Burundi's international obligations vis-à-vis Rwanda did not sound too convincing to the Casablanca group. The latter's viewpoint, expressed by Deputy Jean Kayabo, was that Burundi had indeed a moral obligation to assist the refugees and their brothers in Rwanda, 'victims of Kayibanda's genocide'. 'Furthermore', said Kayabo, 'that some of these refugees were apprehended with arms in their hands is not a sufficient motive to disarm them.' Besides, 'no one knows their real intentions . . . some are in the pay of certain colonialist and imperialist embassies, and send cables to Kigali via Colonel Hennequiau [the Belgian Ambassador], to inform the Rwandese government of refugees' plans'.[17] Although at this point the issue was laid to rest, the debates to which it gave rise provided an eloquent testimony of the pervasiveness and intensity of racial feelings.

Simultaneously, attempts by the incumbent Tutsi elites to eliminate their opponents through the use of legal or extra-legal coercion led to a nightmarish sequence of plots and counterplots, accompanied by widespread terrorism and assassination. Under any circumstances, this could lead only to a heightening of reciprocal hatreds and violence. Once driven underground, the opposition had no choice but to resort to terrorism to alter the existing situation. A substantial number of Hutu politicians preferred to seek refuge in Rwanda rather than face further exactions from their enemies. As already noted, Mirerekano fled to Rwanda in May 1964, after his participation in an abortive plot against the pro-Tutsi Nyamoya government, and was subsequently joined by several other Hutu leaders, mainly deputies and trade-unionists. During their exile in Butare, they kept close and regular contacts with Rwandese officials and politicians, and, by the time they finally returned to Burundi, in early 1965, against their better judgment, they had evidently absorbed many of the attitudes and predispositions of their hosts. Conversely, they could not be viewed otherwise than with utmost suspicion by the indigenous Tutsi elites of Burundi. In short, the stimuli emanating from the domestic and international environments—either in the form of specific actions on the part of the incumbents to suppress the opposition, or in the form of conditioning influences from abroad—produced a kind of revolutionary feedback which decisively aggravated racial tension.

Finally, a conscious effort was made by the leaders of each faction to politicise certain segments of society in order to reinforce their positions towards each other. At one time or another, and with varying degrees of success, pressures were brought to bear from each side upon the gendarmerie, the army, trade unions and student organisations. After the intervention of the crown, however, access to the security forces became difficult (though not impossible), and instead the Tutsi faction concentrated its efforts almost exclusively on the trade unions and student organisations. In time, the Fédération des Travailleurs du Burundi (FTB), led by Augustin Ntamagara, emerged as one of the most stridently pro-Tutsi and anti-Western pressure groups in Burundi; but the very smallness of its membership prevented its leaders from acquiring the leverage they needed to become an effective political force—and this, incidentally, applied even more to the Syndicats Chrétiens, as their leadership had by now been virtually liquidated. In the end, the most significant source of support available to the contestants was the students at the Université Officielle and the Collège du Saint Esprit, both in Bujumbura. While most students, whether Hutu or Tutsi, were already predisposed to become actively engaged in the politics of ethnicity, on the Tutsi side their involvement received a decisive impetus from the informal 'bull sessions' organised by Zénon Nicayenzi in late 1963 and early 1964 at the university. By way of a reaction, a number of Hutu students began to establish contacts with Hutu politicians, and, by May 1964, two of these students had become so deeply involved in a plot against the government that one was thrown in jail while the other barely made it to Rwanda. Their attitude is best illustrated by the terms of a letter which one of them wrote to the plotters:

After the ignominious massacres of Kamenge, in February 1962 [sic], it would be a matter of legitimate self-defence to organise resistance, or a coup d'état, and even a revolution. We are faced with a moral obligation to defend ourselves. 'All means are legitimate as long as one reaches the goal', said Machiavelli, Prime Minister of Italy in the early sixteenth century [sic]. The loss of human lives is necessary and indeed inevitable. If we falter, we shall be the ones to be sent to the gallows. Do you really want to see 85 per cent of the population thrown back into slavery? . . . Our case is not unique in history. One needs only to read about the liberation of the Roman citizenry from the yoke of the patricians. The French, to get rid of feudalism, didn't they have to set up gallows in 1789? Nearer to us still, in South Africa, the Boers [sic] are struggling and dying to regain their rights, and since 1959 President Kayibanda has never ceased to do likewise.

However original a slant the author's words may cast on history, they are nonetheless typical of the intensity of the psychological commitments felt by certain students, both Hutu and Tutsi. By 1964, the atmosphere was so heavily saturated with racial tension that one may indeed wonder why explosions of violence did not occur even more frequently, and on a wider scale.

The main reason for this situation of relative stability (from the standpoint of the established regime) is that the political equation was not quite as simple as the foregoing might suggest. One major complicating factor has to do with the role of the crown in the management of the Hutu-Tutsi conflict. Although on this score the verdict of history is plainly in the negative, that the crown ultimately failed to resolve the conflict does not mean that its role has been unimportant. As we shall see, whatever measure of stability was achieved during the crucial years following independence must be credited to the crown, if not always to the personal initiatives of Mwami Mwambutsa.

14. The Intervention of the Crown

'DIVIDED SOCIETIES cannot exist without centralized power; consensual societies cannot exist with it.'[1] Samuel Huntington's incisive formula is the clue to an understanding of the political fortunes of the Burundi monarchy after independence. Although Rwagasore was denied the opportunity to establish a pattern of relationship between the crown and the government that could be understood by the masses, there never was the slightest doubt in his mind that the Mwami would stay in office only by surrendering power to the government; and, as long as the nationalist fervour aroused by Rwagasore's charisma held sway over the masses, this assumption seemed to reflect the popular consensus. But, as the party crumbled into competing factions, the crown again became the central fulcrum of power around which Burundi politics swirled. Just as Tudor despotism, in sixteenth-century England, served as a guarantee of stability in the face of civil strife and baronial wars, in Burundi the revitalisation of the crown was the consequence of the disruptive forces released by the leadership crisis within the party.

Even more directly relevant to this discussion than the analogy with Tudor England are the parallel trends discernible in the recent evolution of the Burundi and Moroccan monarchies. While in the case of Burundi the denouement of the plot (both in the figurative and literal meanings of the term) deviates substantially from its Moroccan counterpart, the history of the Burundi monarchy since independence provides a curious re-enactment of the situation that has arisen in Morocco in the late 'fifties and early 'sixties. Commenting on this situation, William Zartman observed of Mohammed V:

He was the strongest proponent of democratic measures, leading to and including elections, whereas the rule of his governments has sometimes tended towards the authoritarian. In an absolute monarchy, he acted more as an arbitrating president in a parliamentary regime than an arbitrary sovereign in a traditional empire. . . . Yet, as the groups pushed to fill the functions as well as the form of their offices, and as the king saw the formidable result of the forces he so successfully cultivated, he curbed his parties, dissolved his assembly, and

361

took over his government in order to prevent approaching the goal from the wrong direction. To the end, the king governed, reigned and decided.[2]

Like Mohammed v, Mwambutsa iv was at first the staunchest supporter of democratic reforms. He repeatedly stressed his desire to insulate the crown from the political arena, and, when this attitude could no longer be reconciled with the divisive conditions created by ethnic strife, he tended to act more like an arbiter than an arbitrary despot. But as ethnic tensions increased in scope and intensity, the prerogatives of the crown increased in proportion, to the point where everything happened as if the Mwami 'governed, reigned and decided'.

The transition from an 'oligarchical monarchy', in which the Mwami played the role of an arbiter among competing interests and personalities, to a polity approximating the characteristics of a 'ruling monarchy' marks a watershed in the political evolution of the country.*

As will be shown in a subsequent chapter, this drastic shift in the structure of monarchical rule was the result of an equally fundamental change in the balance of ethnic forces in parliament, a change which, in theory, should have made the government directly responsible to the National Assembly. Until the legislative elections of 1965, the National Assembly was almost evenly split between Hutu and Tutsi. In the absence of anything like a common consensus among the deputies, the crown emerged as the main beneficiary of the ethnic stalemate. But this was little more than a Pyrrhic victory: the crown took advantage of the situation to bolster its position, but proved utterly incapable of resolving ethnic tensions. The decision to hold legislative elections, in

---

* The distinction between 'oligarchical' and 'ruling' monarchies is borrowed from Samuel Huntington's article, "The Political Modernization of Traditional Monarchies", *Daedalus*, Summer 1966. 'In an oligarchical monarchy', writes Huntington, 'the monarch reigns but does not rule; yet the monarchy remains the principal source of legitimacy in the political system. . . . Effective power rests in the hands of an upper-class, bureaucratic-military oligarchy which rules in the name of the monarch.' 'In a ruling monarchy, the crown is the principal source of legitimacy and the king rules as well as reigns. . . . The efficient powers of government may be shared with other institutions, but in all cases the monarch also plays an active, efficient political role in the governing process.' On the basis of this distinction, it is extremely difficult to say when, exactly, the Burundi moved from one type to the other; but, in that they connote differences in the extent and frequency of royal intervention, these terms have considerable relevance to this discussion. Thus, until August 1965, the political system of Burundi can be said to have functioned pretty much along the lines of an oligarchical monarchy; from then on, however, and until the coup of October 1965, the system clearly moved in the direction of a ruling monarchy.

1965, was intended to create a consensus where none was previously forthcoming; however, ironically, the fostering of a new consensus by holding general elections invested parliament with a new basis of legitimacy, and this in turn made its coexistence with royal autocracy all the more difficult. Once it had moved into the political arena, the crown refused to move out. Thus, by changing the rules of the game in a way which could only turn to the advantage of its adversaries, the crown became the architect of its own undoing.

Here we shall concern ourselves with the initial phase of this transfer of power (1962–65), concentrating for the time being on those aspects of the political system which best illustrate the pluralistic nature of Burundi's 'oligarchical monarchy'.

The Mwami as an Umpire

Hints of the direction in which the crown was about to move could be detected as early as February 1961, when, faced with the alternative of choosing between the interim government appointed by the trust authorities and the slate of candidates submitted by UPRONA, the Mwami opted for a compromise solution. 'At this delicate juncture of my reign', said Mwambutsa, 'I hope that public opinion both in Belgium and in Burundi will allow me to play the role of an impartial chief and arbiter.'[3] Although the Belgian authorities denied him this privilege, the Mwami's gesture clearly showed his willingness to act when the circumstances required.

Once freed of the restraining influences of the tutelle, Mwambutsa rapidly cast himself in the non-partisan role of an umpire, subsequently gathering to himself the principal lines of governmental control. It was the Mwami who, in August 1962, after the stadium incidents, seized the initiative by announcing that a new committee of UPRONA would soon be elected by the rank and file of the party. Similarly, when the Minister of the Interior, Jean Ntiruhama, came under fire from the Monrovia parliamentary group for his failure to take sanctions against the JNR, and for his subsequent decision to dispatch the gendarmerie to the stadium while Mirerekano renewed his bid for the presidency of the party, it was the Mwami who released Mirerekano and then used his influence to have Ntiruhama ousted. Again, when, on June 1, 1963, the Prime Minister, Muhirwa, issued a communiqué announcing the appointment of Zénon Nicayenzi as Minister of Public Works to replace Ignace Ndimanya, just dismissed from office for his alleged involvement in a plot against the security of the state, the Mwami responded by categorically denying the news, specifying that the ministerial chair remained at the disposal of the court, to be granted to whomever it pleased. Meanwhile, apprised of the arrest of three well-known public figures (Ignace Ndimanya, Thaddée Siryuyumunsi, President of the National Assembly and acknowledged leader of the Monrovia group, and Pie Masumbuko, General Counsellor to the government), the Mwami immediately intervened and ordered their release. Rather than face further infringements from the court, Muhirwa handed his resignation to the Mwami on June 7, 1963.

Among the interplay of forces which caused the fall of the Muhirwa government, those emanating from the court were the most decisive. As one anonymous commentator shrewdly observed: 'Contrary to all expectations, [the Muhirwa government] did not succumb to a massive attack by the opposition during an important parliamentary debate which closed with the adoption of a vote of censure. No; it had not strength enough to deserve even the honours of a fine fight for prestige. Disgusted by the continuously increasing number of votes strengthening the opposition, and of being publicly made to look like a fool by the Mwami and his close advisers, the government, tired of fighting, saw itself forced "spontaneously", if one can say so, to hand in its resignation to the Mwami.'[4] Besides signalling a major departure from the figurehead role the constitution had assigned to the Mwami,* the circumstances of Muhirwa's fall were also a portent of the increasingly active role the crown was about to play in the political life of the kingdom. As one better-informed Murundi told this writer: 'The escalation began with the fall of Muhirwa. From then on, the governments were all appointed by the Mwami, whose grip on the system never ceased to tighten.'[5]

The appointment of Pierre Ngendadumwe (a Hutu) as Prime Minister, on June 18, 1963, marked the beginning of a new phase in Burundi politics, in which the machinery of the state became more directly vulnerable to the scheming of the court. From then on, the Prime Minister and his cabinet were answerable only to the king. While parliament retained its legislative functions, the king, in fact, became the chief initiator and executor of legislation. With the deputies now serving, almost literally, in the capacity of *bashigantahe*, and the govern-

* Article 51 of the constitution states specifically: 'The King is constitutional.' On the other hand, article 57 reads: 'The King names and appoints his ministers', almost an exact replica of article 65 of the Belgian constitution. In the absence of constitutional traditions and usages of the kind which in Belgium limit the powers of the king, this article became the basis on which certain deputies defended the intervention of the crown (see for example, *Assemblée Parlementaire, Procès-Verbaux de la Session Parlementaire du 20 Septembre au 19 Octobre 1962*, p. 87 ff).

ment's role reduced to a shadow of its constitutional self, the system suddenly seemed to slip back into the feudal ages.

Many of the tactical moves employed by the court to solidify its power base clearly belong to the realm of intrigue; others, however, were far less disingenuous. To begin with, a deliberate attempt was made to shift the locus of power away from the government to the court. Thus, on June 8, 1963, the army and the gendarmerie were converted into secretariats of state and brought under the exclusive jurisdiction of the court. A few days later, after calling upon Ngendadumwe to form a new government, the Mwami let it be known that a formal investiture by parliament was no longer necessary as long as the cabinet had received the prior blessings of the court. Having divested parliament of its most significant prerogative, the Mwami proceeded to further emasculate the powers of the government. In December 1963, he served notice to the Minister of the Interior that the provincial governors were the sole representatives of the crown in their provinces, and consequently that the Minister should from now on consult them on any matter likely to affect the local and provincial administration. Simultaneously, control over the radio station was entrusted to the Secretary of State for the Army. All public meetings were prohibited, and the provincial governors given a free hand to arrest anyone guilty of contravening these orders. 'By then', said the man who held the office, 'the Minister of the Interior had ceased to exist.'[6]

Not unnaturally, since the government was headed by a Hutu, the strongest reactions to the intervention of the court came from Hutu elements. On February 15, 1964, the bureau of the National Assembly —composed exclusively of Hutu, except for the President of the National Assembly, Thaddée Siryuyumunsi, a Hima—sent a letter of protest to the Mwami in which they expressed the strongest reservations about 'the current tergiversations of the court'. After pointing out the unconstitutionality of the measures adopted by His Majesty—and 'their extreme concern over certain actions and omissions [of the court] in violation of article 61 of the constitution'—they ended their remonstrance in these terms: 'To speak frankly to His Majesty, we dare draw His attention to the fact that for months on end certain intriguing politicians, among them the agents of the royal court, have been boasting about the success of their interventions—interventions which, sooner or later, cunningly, will lead to the overthrow of the government in the economic realm.' Again, on March 12, 1964, the same petitioners warned the Mwami that 'the institutions of the state have been turned into a parody of democracy'. 'In fact', they said, 'the separation of powers between the executive, the legislative and the judiciary,

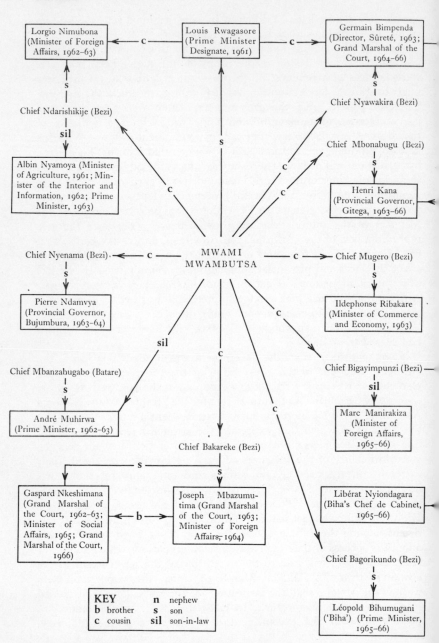

Family Connections and Political Relationships in Burundi, 1961–66.

prescribed by the constitution, has lost its raison d'être, as well as the respect which each branch normally owes to the other.' They continued, more outspokenly:

> In Burundi, where dictatorship has acquired a character all of its own, there prevails a kind of easygoingness, in that the administration does not give a hoot about what goes on. In other words the powers that be are totally ineffectual. . . . Where are we going? Economically, nowhere; politically, towards competition. . . . We are at present in the grip of a political and economic crisis, but those who should care seem to ignore it. They merely content themselves with uttering pious statements which never come across, not even at decisive moments. The docility of the people should not be mistaken for imbecility; and the calm they display should not be mistaken for passivity.

Interestingly, the person of the Mwami was still immune from all criticism. Instead, the blame was put on 'the agents of the court', and, while bitterly resentful of the meddling of the court, the signatories continued to identify themselves as the Mwami's 'totally devoted servants'. But how long could their devotion last? As the Mwami showed nothing but indifference to their demands, not only his person but even the role of the monarchy in the political system was eventually called into question.

Along with this drastic curtailment of executive and parliamentary powers, there was a tendency to entrust key posts within and outside the government to members of the royal family—that is, to *ganwa* elements of Bezi origin. Thus, no sooner was Ngendadumwe appointed Prime Minister than he found himself surrounded with a pleiad of former chiefs and sons of chiefs, nearly all of whom had gained access to their new positions under the protective wing of the court. Except for Lorgio Nimubona and Ildephonse Ribakare, who held respectively the posts of Minister of Foreign Affairs and Minister of Economy and Commerce, most of these 'notabilities' were found outside the government, and principally around the palace. Léopold Biha left his post at the Caisse d'Epargne (savings bank) to serve as the Mwami's personal secretary; Joseph Mbazumutima was appointed Grand Marshal of the court; Henri Kana, from a mere magistrate, became provincial governor of Gitega; Pierre Bigayumpunzi was promoted to the post of director of the Institut des Sciences Agronomiques du Burundi (ISABU); last but not least, Germain Bimpenda was now in charge of the Sûreté, a job which he reportedly handled with consummate skill, alternately 'feeling the pulse' of the government and relaying his diagnosis to the court, and acting as a transmission belt between the court and the government. So well did he acquit himself of this task that he was later appointed Grand Marshal of the court, when Mbazumutima became Minister of Foreign Affairs in the Nyamoya government. This sudden infusion of *ganwa* blood into the sinews of the administration profoundly altered the relationship of the government to the court: no longer at the mercy of a vote of confidence, the cabinet began to look to the palace for guidance and leadership; no longer the originators and formulators of policy, the ministers began to look and act as the obedient servants of the court.

Finally, and within the limits of the phenomenon just described, the court went to great lengths to insure a parity of representation in government. Each of the five governments appointed between 1963 and 1965 contained an almost even proportion of Hutu and Tutsi, all of them chosen because of their presumed loyalty to the monarchy. The policy of the court, moreover, was to give each group a 'fair chance', which meant that every government headed by a Tutsi was automatically followed by a Hutu-led cabinet once the former had lost the confidence of the court.

THE COURT AS AN ARENA

How much personal influence did the Mwami exercise? How much of his influence did he confer upon his courtiers? What kinds of links existed between the court and the formal institutions of government? And how did this affect the decisions of the court? To these all-important questions there are no precise answers. Nonetheless, on the basis of the evidence available, the outlines of the system can be sketched and possible modes of interaction among the political actors suggested.

The first thing to bear in mind is that Mwambutsa never had the stuff of a strong leader. Zartmann's description of Mohammed v of Morocco applies equally well to Mwambutsa: 'He was a constitutional monarch at heart, ready to arbitrate, suggest, restrain, but not to lead.'[7] As Resident Schmidt never tired of reminding his superiors, Mwambutsa's main interest was in women, and preferably European women. His innumerable trips to Switzerland, his great zest for social outings and night life, his tendency to select his friends from among the European café society of Bujumbura—all this contributed to establish his reputation as a playboy king.* The playboy aspect of his personality must not be

---

* This should not be construed to imply a necessary correlation between Mwambutsa's predilection for women and his lack of strong leadership and general indifference to power per se. Indeed the case of Henry VIII supplies abundant contrary historical evidence against this all-too prevalent type of assumption.

exaggerated, however, for if Mwambutsa had little taste for power, there were times when he did assert his authority in the most categorical fashion. That the Mwami did not always shy away from his responsibilities is shown by the extent to which every event of some political significance seemed to occur when he was away in Switzerland—'for reasons of health'—and by the deliberate efforts of certain members of his entourage to prevent him from having contacts with 'outsiders'. Yet there is no gainsaying that the very weakness of Mwambutsa's personality made it possible for certain aspiring politicians (both European and African) to exercise a far greater influence than might have been the case otherwise.

Often referred to as if it were an abstraction, the court is more accurately portrayed as an aggregate of personalities who stood in relation to the Mwami not unlike the *ganwa* of pre-colonial times in relation to the crown. This meant, first of all, that some of these personalities wielded considerable authority in their own right; and furthermore, that some were 'more equal than others'. An examination of the identity of the king's courtiers shows that their influence was, to a large extent (though not exclusively), a function of their family connections. Two of the most prominent and influential personalities in the entourage of the king were Germain Bimpenda and Léopold Bihumugani, both descendants of Mwezi Kisabo. As *ganwa* of the Bezi clan, they used their kinship affiliations with the royal family to strengthen their leverage on royal decisions and, directly or indirectly, on government policies. This, of course, is not to imply that there was always perfect agreement between them. Although their counsels were carefully heeded, it was the Mwami who had the ultimate word in the making of important decisions.

This was also true of a second category of courtiers, represented by a handful of European advisers. Some, like the ineffable Dusoulier de Saint Simon, who claimed the dubious title of aide-de-camp to His Majesty, never carried much influence. Others, like Simonian, did enjoy considerable authority. The scope of their influence, however, was severely circumscribed: they had relatively little say in decisions affecting the internal policies of the realm. Though some acted as if they were the real power behind the throne, their functions were primarily those of 'brokers' between the palace and expatriate enterprises or international business interests, but seldom those of policy-makers.

Finally, a word must be said of those who really did not belong to the Mwami's 'inner circle', but whose influence was nonetheless recognised by the court. Many of these 'outsiders' held a seat on the

369

Crown Council, an advisory body whose membership was in part elected by parliament, in part appointed by the Mwami. Antoine Bakareke, Boniface Simvura, Pie Masumbuko, Thaddée Siryuyumunsi, for example, all belonged to the Crown Council at one time or another. Their real source of power, however, did not lie in their formal roles as members of the Crown Council; that they happened to fill these roles was the result, rather than the cause, of their popularity. As public figures of considerable renown within or outside parliament, they already claimed substantial authority, and their counsels could be ignored by the Mwami only at his own peril. Yet, in some cases, the situation seemed to be just the reverse. It is indeed a tribute to the manipulative skills of the Mwami (or those of his more trusted advisers) that so many of these public figures wound up serving the interests of the court rather than their respective publics.

What all this amounts to is a fairly complex situation, in which patterns of interaction among political actors never became fully stabilised. One may, of course, discern several layers of influence within the arena of the court: first in rank and influence was the old *ganwa* group, representing the inner caucus of trusted advisers; next came the Mwami's cabinet, whose membership, like its policies, were never clearly defined; and finally, there was the Crown Council, accurately described as 'a kind of miniature Senate . . . whose role was limited to giving advice of a purely consultative nature.'[8] Beyond this, however, any detailed investigation of the decision-making process is at best a risky endeavour. Once a favourite pastime in Bujumbura, speculation about the interplay of rank and privilege which governed the thoughts and actions of Mwambutsa on any given issue seems a rather futile exercise.

But this much, at least, is clear: just as the behaviour of political actors was bound to be influenced by the policies of the court, the latter was also subject to influences from other arenas. In spite of the vagueness and fluidity of the relationships between the court and formal governmental institutions, one can distinguish at least three levels at which decisions were made: the government, the administration, and the court. We have seen how, from the very beginning, tensions arose between the government and the court, which led to a progressive paralysis of the governmental machinery, and ultimately to a situation where even the bureaucracy had its prerogatives drastically curtailed. The pattern of interaction which seems to have developed can best be understood in terms of a dialectical process, involving, on the one hand, a continuing tug-of-war between the government and the opposition (marked by alternating efforts by Tutsi-led governments to eliminate or restrain the Hutu opposition, and vice versa), and, on the other hand, a parallel struggle between the crown and the governments in power. Almost every attempt made by the incumbents to neutralise the opposition was met by a counter-move on the part of the crown. As the sphere of government autonomy shrank in proportion to the frequency of royal intervention, the point was reached where a change of government no longer held much practical significance. At this stage, the political system took on the characteristics of a patrimonial order, in which the relations of the government to the crown tended to approximate the old pattern of clientage relations.

POLITICAL OFFICE AS A PATRIMONY

In its ideal form, as Max Weber reminds us, patrimonial government was a mere extension of the traditional ruler's household. In such a system, the allocation of public offices resembles the doling out of 'benefices' from a chief to his clientele, and the resulting obligations tend to reinforce the pre-existing ties of loyalty between the two. In Weber's terms, 'the person exercising authority is not a "superior", but a personal "chief". His administrative staff does not consist primarily of officials, but of personal retainers. Those subject to authority are not "members" of an association, but are either his traditional "comrades" or his "subjects". What determines the relations of the administrative staff to the chief is not the impersonal obligations of office, but personal loyalty to the chief.'[9]

However illuminating, this picture cannot be accepted unreservedly as a description of Burundi politics. To begin with, not every government, nor every minister, behaved towards the crown like retainers towards their sovereign. Or, if this were really the case, why did the crown feel the necessity to withdraw its confidence from one government after another? Furthermore, the mere presence of a bureaucracy, along with the legal-rational norms of conduct associated with bureaucratic structures, introduced occasional restraints upon the Mwami's whim, pushing the system in the direction of a greater neutrality and efficiency of performance than would have been the case in the absence of such counteracting pressures. Finally, there were noticeable differences in the degree to which the system approximated the ideal form noted above, depending on the capacity of the governments in power to capitalise on the existence of countervailing centres of power, and on the circumstances prevailing at any given time.

Bearing these qualifications in mind, one can nevertheless detect some striking similarities between the type of polity described by Weber

371

and the political system of Burundi. These are perhaps best identified by reference to three major variables: (i) the extent to which birth and family connections influenced political recruitment; (ii) the degree of saliency of clientage relations; and (iii) the extent to which prebends, or 'gift-giving', tended to institutionalise clientage relations. Even though these variables operated in different ways, depending on the institutional level and time period selected for analysis, their cumulative impact on the political system cannot be ignored.

Unless proper attention is paid to birth and connubial relations, Burundi politics are bound to remain something of an enigma. Indeed, Gus Libenow's comment on Liberian politics, that 'exact knowledge of the ancestral and connubial relationships of one's associates is essential for survival and advancement in the political fray', would seem to apply with even greater cogency to the Burundi situation. The importance accorded to birth was made apparent from the very beginning by the appointment of descendants of *ganwa* families to key cabinet posts. Rwagasore's cabinet, for example, included two prominent *ganwa* personalities, André Muhirwa and Pierre Ngunzu, and when Jean Ntiruhama was called to replace Muhirwa as Minister of the Interior and Information, after Rwagasore's death, it was another *ganwa*, Gaspard Nkeshimana, who replaced him as Minister of Social Affairs. Still another *ganwa* was added to the cabinet when, shortly before independence, Lorgio Nimubona was appointed Minister of Foreign Affairs, a post which he held until his accidental death in late 1963.

The *ganwa* became a permanent fixture of each successive government. Ngendadumwe's first cabinet, for example, included, besides Nimubona, Ildephonse Ribakare, great-grandson of Mwezi Gisabo, as Minister of the Economy and Commerce. Nyamoya's cabinet, likewise, included two *ganwa*, one of whom, Joseph Mbazumutima, was the cousin of the man who later served as provincial governor of Bujumbura (Pierre Ndamvya), and the brother of the man who held the post of Minister of Social Affairs in the Muhirwa government (Gaspard Nkeshimana). Nyamoya himself, characteristically, came from an excellent Tutsi family (Munengwe) and also happened to be Lorgio Nimubona's brother-in-law. Similarly, Pierre Mpozenzi, Minister of the Interior in Nyamoya's government, belonged to the important Bajiji clan, a clan from which the *mwami* traditionally recruited a great many court dignitaries, as well as his sorcerers. Mpozenzi's father once presided over the annual *umuganuro* (sorghum festival) ceremony. Under the circumstances, one can perhaps better understand why Mpozenzi should have shown so little reticence about appointing provincial governors from among the relatives of the king's 'men', like Henri Kana, for example, governor of Gitega and nephew of Germain Bimpenda.

Indeed, one of the striking characteristics of the patrimonialisation of offices is the extent to which family connections tended to penetrate not only the court and the government but the administrative hierarchy as well. This, of course, reflects the intense pressures to which certain members of the government (and especially those of *ganwa* extraction) were subjected by their friends and relatives, and their sense of personal obligation towards them. But it was also part of a more general strategy designed to insure maximum co-operation among the various layers of the governmental-administrative hierarchy. Thus, a vast network of family ties spread over the entire governmental structure, which not only made nepotism a ubiquitous phenomenon but also paved the way for the reactivation of clientage ties.

In some cases, the patron-client relationship was merely transferred from the private to the public sphere; although the evidence on this is admittedly scanty, cases were reported of civil servants being appointed to office by their former patrons, and this for no other reason than that the latter owed them certain favours in return for their previous services. More often, however, the client-patron nexus was nothing more than the adaptation of an age-old relationship to the context of a modern bureaucratic structure. While certain ministers did not hesitate to relate themselves explicitly to the Mwami and his men, like clients vis-à-vis their patrons, a similar situation often prevailed between the ministers and their subordinates within their respective departments. The result has been to substitute a highly personalised, nepotic type of administrative behaviour, based on ties of reciprocal loyalty, for the conventional civil service norms of anonymity and efficiency. The administrative and governmental processes were thus converted into a kind of social bargaining in which co-operation among individuals depended ultimately on the congruity of their roles towards each other, as traditionally defined by the patron-client relationship.

Because of the personalised character of this relationship, it was inevitably combined with the time-honoured custom of gift-giving (*igiturire*). 'To ask for a gift', say the Burundi, 'is to honour; to give a gift is to like.' 'In order to receive, it is necessary to obey, but everything depends on the will and affection of the superior. He will give if he wants to; if not, he will not give and, if he wishes, will take back what he has already given, in order to give it to someone he likes better.'[10] Similarly, appointment to public office involved the dispensation of gifts, not only in the form of relatively high salaries and perquisites, but also of what in the West would be regarded as graft, bribery and corruption. How much of this corruption can be legitimately regarded as a reflection of traditional gift-giving, and how much was really contravening traditional standards of behaviour, is difficult to say. But it seems clear that the scale on which corruption was, and is still, being practised has many parallels with the traditional society.

Among the various incentives which corrupted the official purposes of offices and institutions, at least two must be mentioned. The salaries paid to public officials were relatively low, and, consequently, there was an inclination to seek alternative sources of income through bribery, extortion and the private spending of public money. (One may cite in this connection the case of Albert Nyakazina, at one time ambassador to Bonn, who was reported to have spent 100,000 marks on the purchase of curtains for the Burundi embassy, a figure difficult to reconcile with the actual dimensions of the building.) An even more decisive inducement stemmed from the fact that many of these officials had no security of tenure, as they occupied their posts at the pleasure of the sovereign and his favourites. They realised from experience that fickleness is a necessary adjunct of love, and thus tried to make the most of a situation which they knew would probably not last forever. In other words, the mere anticipation of a possible disgrace phenomenally increased the scale of corruption. A more general source of corruption, obviously not limited to Burundi, has to do with the general indifference and cynicism generated among public officials by the advent of independence.[11]

Corruption, one might add, always involved an element of reciprocity. Just as in the old days the granting of a chiefdom was a source for revenue (in the form of tribute) not only for the chief but also for the Mwami, the allocation of public offices by the court generally entailed some sort of 'kick-back' from the beneficiaries to their benefactors. One example will suffice: in 1965 Belgium promised to give the Burundi authorities some 14 million Burundi francs to build a new complex of army barracks, as part of its regular technical assistance programme. Having accepted the offer, the government, in co-operation with the Secretariat of State to the Army, began to lay the groundwork for the project. But no sooner had the news of these preliminary steps reached the ear of the court than the Grand Marshal of the court, Germain Bimpenda, reportedly told the government that there was no need to build new barracks for the army, and instead suggested that the government could just as well rent the houses owned by a local Greek resident, a certain Vassilikos, and convert them into housing quarters for the army. The savings involved would then be split between the court and various government officials. Although the Secretary of State refused to agree, the incident was typical of the kind of questionable practices that went on in the higher reaches of the government hierarchy, but of which one also heard at lower levels.

Ultimately, the interference of the court was bound to generate considerable disaffection among certain cabinet members, and especially among the 'plebeians'—Hutu, Hima or Tutsi. Frequent complaints were heard in private that 'the system was rotten to the core', and that nothing constructive could be expected from the government as long as the court meddled in the affairs of the country. Yet it is interesting to note the extent to which many of these critics actually went along with the system. When out of office, they continued to keep in close touch with the court, anticipating a possible change of fortunes in their favour if and when the incumbents should fall from grace. And, if they happened to be reinstated in office, they proceeded to engage in the same kind of corrupt behaviour they had so vehemently attacked when practised by others. It would seem that the relations of many of the ministers with their subordinates were just as personalised, affective and corrupt as those of the court with government officials.

Woefully inefficient, top-heavy, and riddled with corruption, the Burundi bureaucracy shares many of the familiar ills which plague the civil service of other African states, and in addition some that are sui generis. As elsewhere in Africa, the Burundi bureaucracy has absorbed within its ranks a number of former politicians whose qualifications are at best open to question. At the same time, many of these young functionaries have acquired a distinctive outlook which marks them off sharply from ordinary politicians—'they are generally claiming a better education than the politicians, with a subtler awareness of their own position . . . and they have a greater security of tenure, which creates a totally different outlook'.[12] One also finds in Burundi the now familiar syndrome of an enormously inflated bureaucratic structure, whose efficiency seems to obey Parkinson's law. In mid-1964 the central bureaucracy comprised 1,239 functionaries; over half of these were incorporated in the middle ranks of the civil service—the so-called 'cadres de collaboration' (i.e., as chefs de direction, chefs de direction adjoints, chefs de subdivision, etc.), offices which in Burundi are usually regarded as sinecures. Approximately 72 per cent of the national budget for 1964 was spent on personnel—a fact which goes far to explain the near-catastrophic state of Burundi's public finances, as well as the somewhat worse situation which seems to prevail in the economy.

Among the more specific defects of the system, one of the most paradoxical is that governmental instability tended to increase rather than diminish the strength of clientage ties within the upper echelons of the bureaucracy. As the official in charge of the Department of

Administrative Affairs in the Ministry of the Interior, Aloys Buzungu, stated in 1964, in a memorandum misleadingly entitled *Santé de la Fonction Publique*: 'The lack of stability in government has meant that the higher functionaries (directeurs-généraux, directeurs, sous-directeurs) are not always sure to stay in office. Hence they are all the more easily subject to influences of all kinds, political and administrative . . . and they generally feel that their tenure in office depends on their ability to display a certain opportunism.'[13] At the same time, however, Buzungu lamented the 'rebellious attitude' of 'certain subordinates towards their superior', a fact which he went on to attribute to the catapulting of certain job applicants into relatively high offices, even though their qualifications were no better if not worse than those of their subordinates.

Another difficulty came from the 'depth' of clientage ties. Take for example the case of a lower-ranking civil servant who gained his position through the favour of a minister: knowing that he could always turn to his 'patron-minister' for support and protection, this official naturally had few compunctions about challenging the directives of his immediate superior; for, if worst came to worst, his protector would most probably intercede on his behalf. Just how far this could lead is shown by the following incident, related by Buzungu: after being informed by the director of one administrative department that one of his subordinates had quit his job, Buzungu took appropriate steps to stop the payment of his salary. The man immediately appealed to his minister, who reversed Buzungu's decision. Even after he deserted his job, the man in question continued to receive a salary from the government—which prompted Buzungu to meekly raise the question: 'What kind of authority can a director still claim for himself in these conditions?'[14]

The authority and efficiency of the civil service were further restricted when the government was 'forced' by the court into assuming the functions of the bureaucracy. In February 1963, an administrative circular was issued by Buzungu which spelled out, in considerable detail, the sphere of competence of the ministers; among the matters 'reserved to the ministers' were: '(i) the exercise of functions which have been specifically assigned to them by the law; (ii) matters of considerable importance, or which raise a major question of principle; (iii) matters involving decisions taken by their subordinates; (iv) matters involving divergences within the administrative services of the same ministry, or conflicts of competence between the services of different ministries.'[15] By April 1964, however, the author of the circular freely admitted that 'in spite of these instructions, certain ministers continue to paralyse the action of the department heads by turning their attention to matters of minor importance, such as the hiring of clerical personnel, attending to the complaints of a civil servant regarding his salary, routine correspondence, etc.'. 'It has also been observed', added Buzungu, 'that, as a result of this unfortunate interference, the ministers completely discourage the administrative authorities in charge of enforcing discipline.'[16] The ministers, deprived of their political functions by the court, had been pushed into the position of mere functionaries, and this inevitably involved an invasion of the prerogatives normally assigned to the civil service. But, in many cases, this phenomenon was also the outcome of the extension of the client-patron relationship into the administrative sphere, a relationship which, at this level, underwent a bifurcation along racial lines. Thus, stories were heard of certain ministers who felt obligated to attend to the needs of their ethnic protégés at almost every level of the administrative hierarchy, even if this meant short-circuiting the normal channels of command, and bringing total chaos to the administrative machinery.

Commenting on this situation, Gilles Bimazubute, then chef de cabinet of the Minister of External Affairs and Commerce, wrote, in March 1964:

> The party, the parliament, and the government fell prey to the rivalries which you all know, and this marked 'the beginning of the end'. Every functionary guilty of some wrong-doing could always find an excuse—worse still, a safe protection. It was said that it was because he was 'Casablanca' or 'Monrovia' that a minister was being persecuted. . . . Thus, functionaries who, under normal circumstances, should have been dismissed, found refuge in one camp or the other, albeit without much conviction and out of sheer opportunism, and they still hang on to these high-ranking positions and continue to betray their responsibilities in their respective departments. . . . From then on, incompetent elements have been retained or recruited into certain administrative departments, despite their incompetence and bad faith. . . . Friendship or parenthood have become the most constant and determining criteria for the recruitment of functionaries. The foreseeable result is that, once we are all contaminated, our administration will become so corrupt that it will collapse, like a house of cards.[17]

It is not so much the content of these strictures as their source which gives them a particular significance. Considering that the author of this diatribe was himself a member of the Establishment against which it was directed (until he finally decided to hand in his resignation), one can appreciate how deep the feelings of frustration and discouragement

377

ran among certain functionaries. Their sense of frustration stemmed from the contradictory requirements of a civil service which in theory aimed at a performance based on efficiency and neutrality and a political system riddled with corruption and nepotism. And from the realisation of their own impotence in the face of this situation came a profound feeling of discouragement. Caught between the dictates of the court and the inertia of the local baronies, they felt increasingly alienated from the system. While some merely retreated into an attitude of indifference and cynicism, others eventually joined the ranks of the opposition.

Although the Mwami and the bureaucracy needed each other, in the end the functional requirements of their respective offices introduced a host of tensions between them. As the Mwami tried to reign and rule, dominance over the bureaucracy became a sine qua non of monarchic rule; at the same time, and even though they realised that their survival in office depended upon the Mwami's favour, many were the functionaries who felt the inclination to disengage themselves from this relationship.

The conflict between the crown and the bureaucracy finds an interesting parallel in the struggle between the central bureaucracy and the local power structures. The situation at the 'grass roots' was in many respects reminiscent of the ancien régime, with the provincial governors and the burgomasters quite naturally fitting themselves into the role structure associated with the office of chief and subchief. Like the 'native authorities' who held office during the colonial days, they formed alliances with local officials, built up a following of loyal retainers, and, in the end, displayed towards their people the same combination of arrogance and arbitrariness which had done so much to discredit the authority of the chiefs. The local administration, in other words, looked like an aggregate of semi-autonomous units, operating more or less independently of the central bureaucracy.

This state of affairs was the logical outcome of the growing concentration of power around the palace. As the dominance of the crown increased at the expense of the government, the patrimonialisation of offices also began to penetrate the local administration. The provincial governors came to look upon themselves as the loyal retainers of the Mwami, the burgomasters as the 'sub-chiefs' of the provincial governor, and the communal councillors as the *bilongozi* (assistants) of the burgomasters. Thus the familiar chain of vassalage was re-established at every level of the governmental hierarchy, each level interacting with the other in a circular fashion.

Several factors have reinforced the patrimonial character of the local administration, some of which have been mentioned earlier in this chapter. Firstly, the incidence of family connections between the court and the local oligarchies not only made it possible for the Mwami's courtiers to influence the field officers of the central government agencies, but, in turn, enabled these local oligarchs to blandly disregard directives from the central government.* Another concerns the use of tax-tribute as a means of strengthening clientage ties. Under Belgian rule, the customary pattern of clientage relations involved the allocation (or reallocation) of prebends, in the form of cattle, beer and foodstuffs, while control over tax money rested with the Belgian authorities. Under the new dispensation, however, much of the local revenue was turned into prebends, giving rise to an unprecedented misuse of public funds. Monopolising part of the revenue from tax sources was not the only form of corruption; in addition, the burgomasters found it convenient to siphon off into their own pockets the public funds destined to pay the salaries of the communal employees. Thus the newspaper *Ndongozi* reported, in September 1963, that in certain areas roadmenders had been working for a whole year without receiving a salary.

*This particular aspect of the system was brought to my attention by an incident which I unwittingly provoked while doing field work in the province of Gitega, in the summer of 1964. After securing the required safe-conduct from the Ministry of the Interior, I went to Gitega to establish contact with the local provincial authorities, and in particular with the provincial governor, Henri Kana, nephew of the Grand Marshal of the Court, Germain Bimpenda. On the day I arrived, I paid a visit to the provincial governor, just as he was about to leave for Bujumbura, and, although he did express interest in my work and told me to go ahead and contact the personalities whose names I had mentioned, I sensed a certain suspicion on his part. A couple of days later, at 8.00 AM sharp, the commissaire d'arrondissement of Gitega called on me with a cable from the Sûreté of Bujumbura, which instructed him to drive me back immediately to Bujumbura under military escort—which he did. Once in Bujumbura, I went to see the directeur in charge of the Sûreté, Mélance Mbugu-Mbugu, brother of the former Minister of the Interior, Jean Ntiruhama, to ask for explanations. Much to my surprise, Mbugu-Mbugu said this was the first he had heard anything about my case, and suggested that I see the Minister of the Interior. After waiting a couple of hours to see the Minister, Pierre Mpozenzi, I was finally told that he was too busy to see me, and, besides, knew nothing of the circumstances under which I had been taken back to Bujumbura. As I finally discovered, it was the provincial governor, Henri Kana, who had taken upon himself the decision to send the telegram (assuming for the purpose of the occasion the title of directeur of the Sûreté), and this without even informing the Sûreté officers in Bujumbura, or the Ministry of the Interior. His move, however, worked beautifully, for I never returned to Gitega. Meanwhile, the Minister of Foreign Affairs had been told of the presence in Burundi of 'a strange individual travelling under cover of a French passport', and before long the question was taken up by the Council of Ministers. At the close of this ministerial session, the Prime Minister, Albin Nyamoya, called up my ambassador to check on my identity, and at this point the matter was finally laid to rest.

The road-menders said: 'The people who work on the roads beg His Majesty to see to it that they are paid like in the old days. . . . When the communal accountants ask us: "Why don't you pay your taxes", we reply: "Pay our salary and we'll pay our taxes!" Then we are thrown in jail. The next day we are set free and told to go to work and pay our taxes. Here in our commune of Muzinda the system has started all over again. . . . If Rwagasore could see what's going on, he would be appalled by the dishonesty of our authorities.'[18] Dishonesty took a variety of forms besides those already mentioned, but probably one of the most effective for gathering support from potential retainers was the allocation of jobs to minor officials, by which extra earnings might become available to them. Thus one of the most powerful means of pressure in the hands of the burgomasters was the use they made of 'influence peddling' in the granting or withdrawal of communal jobs.* How this could affect the attitude of public officials is made clear by the story which appeared in the November 24, 1964, issue of *Ndongozi*, told by a communal councillor from Shinya. At first, one learns, the burgomaster took his decisions in accordance with the views expressed by the majority of the communal councillors; but 'upon realising that this method was not entirely to his satisfaction, he proceeded to give jobs to some of the councillors, without asking anybody's advice'. 'He picked out those who seemed most willing to play the game, and gave them the jobs which others already held. The rest of the councillors he treated like his slaves.'[19] In time, the pattern of extra-legal reciprocity which underlay the relations of the burgomaster with the councillors meant that co-operation was almost always forthcoming: just as the burgomaster needed the co-operation of his underlings, the latter needed the protection of their 'patron' if they wished to hold on to their jobs. '*Nta wanka uwumugize ne za*', runs the Kirundi proverb—'One cannot hate one's benefactor'.

Equally instrumental in maintaining the system was the absence of appropriate channels through which popular demands could be articulated and converted into public policies. Partly because of the inadequacy of available news media (represented almost exclusively by the bi-monthly *Ndongozi*, printed in the vernacular) and partly because of the

*In American usage, 'influence peddling' has a somewhat different connotation. It usually involves the participation of an intermediary who 'peddles' his influence to a third party, as happens when pressure is brought to bear upon public officials by an influential 'broker'. In the context of this book, the term 'patronage' might be technically more accurate; but, on the other hand, patronage does not always imply the deliberate misuse of public funds for private ends, or the kinds of reciprocal obligations and clandestine understandings which in Burundi linked certain officials to their political 'clientele'.

obstacles raised by illiteracy, the only way the average peasant could possibly communicate his grievances to the authorities was on the basis of face-to-face contacts. But such contacts as could have taken place between the local population and the Mwami, during the latter's visits in the countryside, were systematically discouraged by the communal and provincial authorities. As one Murundi complained: 'When we ask if we can present a letter to His Majesty, we are told that the provincial governor must first see the content of the letter—otherwise, impossible! And when we ask to address our complaints verbally to His Majesty we are told that our name is not mentioned on the list of audiences. . . . Similarly, when a minister happens to pay us a visit, only the deputy and the governor have the right to speak, or perhaps the "comaro" [commissaire d'arrondissement]. . . . In Bubanza we tried to present a petition in which we asked for new communal elections, but the comaro and the communal councillors tore it up!'[20] As a last resort, local petitioners could always turn to their deputies; but this proved utterly futile as the parliamentarians' attitude was one of total co-operation with the local authorities. Again to cite the words of one petitioner: 'Whenever the Mwami honours us with his presence, our member of parliament declares to His Majesty that Burundi merely needs economic progress, and that there is no need for the provincial governor to allocate time for us to speak to His Majesty.'[21] Since approximately 40 per cent of the deputies also held the functions of burgomaster, any effort to dislodge the burgomasters from their entrenched positions implied a similar threat to their status as deputies. Above all, the deputies feared that if the demands of the local population for communal elections were met, legislative elections would automatically follow, which for many almost inevitably spelled the end of their mandate. Thus, despite repeated demands that communal elections be held in November 1963, as prescribed by the communal law, the deputies turned a deaf ear to the wishes of their constituents, meanwhile prolonging their parliamentary mandate for two extra years. Here again one finds a striking duplication of traditional interlocking status positions, with the deputies working hand in hand with the local authorities to perpetuate their sinecures.

But one must also take into account the pressures militating against the maintenance of the status quo. Certainly, the system never remained completely static, if only because of the way in which ethnic polarities reverberated upon local politics. Where the local oligarchs and the deputies happened to be of the same ethnic origins (which in most cases meant of Tutsi origins), rumours of 'ethnic conspiracy' quickly spread among the local community; and when they each belonged to a different ethnic group, the resulting tensions inevitably found an echo among the local population. In either case, ethnic conflict imposed considerable stress on the fabric of community relationships.

By far the most crucial aspect of this situation lies in its relationship to the total environment within which it has arisen. Because of the linkage of domestic and international issues brought about by concommittant changes in both the domestic and international environments, a new ideological dimension was added to the Hutu-Tutsi conflict, which made its peaceful resolution all the more problematic.

It is impossible to say how much longer the monarchy might have lasted in the absence of external threats to the system. As the foregoing discussion makes clear, the monarchy's main weakness was its structural inability to cope with and assimilate the new social forces released by modernity; and its principal source of strength was its capacity to capitalise upon the existence of ethnic divisions within these new social groupings. In order to successfully practise what amounted to a policy of 'divide and rule', two preliminary conditions had to be satisfied: the instruments of power had to remain loyal to the crown, and ethnic tensions had to be managed in such a way as to maintain the illusion that the crown was still an impartial arbiter. On each of these counts, however, the part played by the intrusion of Cold War issues has played a major, if not a determining, role in hastening the fall of the monarchy. Not that ethnic antagonisms were in any sense a product of the Cold War; but the Cold War has operated to give these polarities a scope and a degree of intensity which made the position of the crown all the more precarious.

15. The Intrusion of
External Influences

IF FURTHER evidence were needed to substantiate the view that monarchical rule was in fact the rule of an oligarchy, relatively free of centralising tendencies, the incongruous character of the kingdom's foreign
policy in the years following independence could be cited. Though by
domestic standards one of the most conservative polities in the whole
of Africa, Burundi came to be regarded, from 1963 to 1965, as one of
the most 'progressive', (i.e., leftist-oriented) in terms of its foreign
policy commitments. Nor is the incongruity in this case reducible to a
perfunctory exercise in diplomatic role-playing. Rather than expressing
a unilateral, calculated attempt to strike a militant stance on the international plane in order to compensate for whatever deficiencies might
have existed in the domestic realm, the situation is better seen as
involving different sets of actors, operating on the basis of different
motives and at different levels. Only if one remembers the pluralistic,
fluid character of the environment in which the game of politics was
initially played is it possible to understand its final outcome.[1]

Hutu and Tutsi politicians were led to cast about for external sources
of support because they both felt equally frustrated in the face of continued royal interference; but the mere fact that each should have perceived the possibility of an alternative to the status quo, and indeed that
some should have come so close to realising their objectives, shows that
it was royal interference rather than royal omnipotence that faced
them. In the absence of a single discernible point in the political system
from which power originated, decision-making processes left ample
room for manoeuvre, while at the same time offering considerable
opportunities for the play of exogenous forces, African and non-African.
This is where the system generated the seeds of its own transformation.
Its vulnerability to outside influences placed additional pressures upon
the crown to further restrict the area of latitude heretofore allowed the
indigenous protagonists, and in so doing the crown eventually deflected
on to itself the animosities which this very move purported to contain.

To emphasise the relevance of domestic factors and issues is not meant
to minimise the contribution of such obviously important elements as
Burundi's strategic geographical position, its contiguity to the then

rebel-held areas of the Congo, and the determined efforts of Communist agents to draw maximum advantage from this situation to further their objectives in the Congo and elsewhere in Africa. Alone, however, these other factors are of little help in explaining why Burundi became a focal point of East-West rivalries. The part they played in drawing the kingdom into the vortex of the Cold War cannot be properly understood otherwise than in the light of the domestic context of Burundi politics, a context of acute ethnic competitiveness in which neither contestant stood much of a chance to gain ascendency over the other without courting the support of external forces.

THE REFUGEE PROBLEM:
INTERNATIONAL ECHOES OF ETHNIC POLARITIES

Of all the issues that have affected the course of Burundi politics, few have had, and may still have, as far-reaching consequences as the refugee problem. According to official statistics, by early 1965, Burundi was host to 72,977 refugees, of whom approximately 52,000 came from Rwanda.[2] Of these, the vast majority were of Tutsi extraction. Brutally uprooted from their native habitat, for the most part ill-equipped to live productive lives in their adoptive environment, and in many cases still nursing hopes of repatriation, the Tutsi refugees were overwhelmingly predisposed from the outset to engage in politics of the most emotional kind. Here, as in the case of many other refugee communities, the tragic human dimensions of the problem were inextricably bound up with its political aspects. What gives the refugee problem of Burundi a special character is the existence of strong ethnic affinities between the indigenous Tutsi minority of the host country and their 'guests' from Rwanda. While substantially adding to the emotional quotient of the issues involved, it has also led to increasingly close ties of interdependence between the two communities, each tending to rely on the other's help to attain its own political ends.

The concurrence of interests between the two groups can be easily exaggerated however, and the nature of their relationships, as a result, grossly oversimplified. Despite their close affinities with the Tutsi of Burundi, relatively few of the Rwandese refugees identified themselves with their new environment to the point where they regarded Burundi as their home. By and large, their hope was to secure enough support from the Burundi authorities to enable them to successfully fight their way back into Rwanda, a strategy which some Tutsi in Burundi initially regarded as incompatible with their international obligations as well as dangerous from the standpoint of race relations in their own country.

Many complex internal problems have coloured the attitude of the Tutsi of Burundi towards the refugees, including the extent to which their presence in Burundi might conceivably threaten their own economic interests. Ethnic affinities were not always sufficient to allay the sense of grievance felt by some Tutsi of Burundi towards those refugees who, thanks to their skills, family connections or political credentials at the court, managed to occupy relatively lucrative positions in Bujumbura, in both the private and the public sectors. In specific instances, social and economic differences have aggravated pre-existing tensions not only between the indigenous and refugee communities but among different political factions within each of these communities.

But these are by no means the only relevant considerations. Equally decisive, from the standpoint of the indigenous Tutsi leadership (the so-called 'Casablanca' leadership), was the extent to which their immediate political objectives could be furthered by the manpower potential and political aspirations of the refugees. By and large, the closeness of their relationships varied in accordance with the internal political conjuncture of the kingdom. When the representatives of the indigenous Tutsi minority were in the opposition—that is, whenever the government in power was headed by a Hutu—their sense of ethnic solidarity with the refugees received an additional stimulus from the feeling they both shared of being at the mercy of a Hutu government, even though this government inevitably included some Tutsi elements.

Since in the minds of the refugees their chances of realising their political aims were so heavily dependent upon the good-will and logistic support of the government in power, they regarded it as a matter of vital importance that this government be as much under the control of Tutsi as could be hoped under the conditions of limited autonomy stipulated by the court. And just as the refugees saw that it was in their interest to aid the accession and maintenance in power of the Tutsi faction, the latter quickly understood the tactical advantage they could reap from a proper manipulation of the refugee movement.

The benefits which the refugees had come to expect of the advent of a Tutsi-led government were clearly brought to light in the course of the tortuous negotiations which took place in 1964 over the Mwezi Resettlement Scheme between UNHCR officials and the representatives of the two governments which succeeded each other in power in that year, the first led by a Hutu (Pierre Ngendadumwe) and the other by a Tutsi (Albin Nyamoya). Had it been implemented, the scheme would have transfered some 15,000 refugees from the Murore area of Burundi to a relocation camp in the Mwezi highlands of Tanzania. Most of the refugees had left Rwanda after the massacres of January 1964, and their unexpected arrival had caused a rapid oversaturation of the Murore area. Since a permanent resettlement of these newcomers into the country seemed economically unfeasible—as well as politically unsafe—Ngendadumwe promptly appealed to the UNHCR to organise their evacuation and resettlement in Tanzania. After preliminary inquiries, agreement was finally reached between the UNHCR representative in Bujumbura and the Tanzanian authorities on the siting of the relocation camp and the modalities under which the transfer was to be accomplished. Meanwhile, however, a new government had come to power in Burundi, headed by Albin Nyamoya, a Tutsi of Casablanca obedience. From then on, endless complications arose. At first, the Minister of Social Affairs, Claver Nuwinklare, agreed to co-operate with the UNHCR in carrying out the scheme, but subsequently reversed his decision under the pretext that his government could not possibly force the refugees to leave the country against their will. As one UNHCR official explained: 'The present Burundi government would like to see 10,000 Rwandese refugees being resettled in another country but cannot see how to induce the refugees to accept the resettlement plan. While the former government (with a Hutu majority) would have used *all* means at its disposal to ensure the departure of the refugees, the present one (Tutsi majority) is in a very difficult position to force the refugees to accept such a solution against their will. This is the heart of the problem.' He added: 'Pressure is being exercised on the government by those who are in favour of the transfer as well as those who are against it. We can rely on the full support of the ambassadors who are representing the UNHCR Executive Committee. On the other hand, the Chinese [diplomatic] mission, which has now been promoted to the rank of an embassy with a staff of seventeen officials, is extremely active. Some circles in Bujumbura believe that the time has come to approach the Secretary-General with a view to requesting him to send a special representative again to this part of Africa.'[3] From all the evidence, the attitude of the Nyamoya government on the resettlement issue reflected the categorical opposition of the Tutsi majority in this government to a move which, they felt, could only prejudice the interests of their kinsmen, and eventually their own.

No less important in the minds of the refugee leaders were the guarantees of immunity they had come to expect of the Nyamoya government in their attempt to organise themselves, politically and militarily. In June 1964, with his morale apparently boosted by Chinese financial aid, Kigeli dispatched one of his emissaries to Bujumbura—a certain Come Rebero—with instructions to organise an Association Sociale des Réfugiés Rwandais, presumably to prepare the return to Rwanda of those refugees who so desired. During a meeting with the UNHCR representative in Bujumbura, Rebero said the primary goal of his association was to promote a climate of mutual trust between republicans and monarchists, so as to prevent further attacks against Rwanda and reach a final political settlement between the refugees and the Kayibanda government. The next day, however, on June 16, 1964, Rebero secretly met a number of exiled *inyenzi* leaders and proceeded to lay the foundation for a subversive, para-military organisation— the so-called Armée Populaire de Libération Rwandaise (APLR)—whose leaders were Jovite Nzamwita, François Sayiba, Anicet Ugirashebuja, Léopold Nkurikiye, all of whom, except Nzamwita, had received intensive guerrilla training in Red China. Although the 'Liberation Army' ultimately failed to free the homeland, and indeed never amounted to more than a few isolated bands of ragged, inexperienced guerrilla fighters, its presence in the countryside came to be regarded by the Casablanca elites as a major asset in case of a violent confrontation with the local Hutu populations. The possibility of such a confrontation became all the more real after the Mwami withdrew his confidence from the Nyamoya government, in January 1965.

As 1964 wore on, the relationships between the Casablanca and Monrovia groups grew worse, and, by early 1965, it was the turn of the Casablanca elites to seek the support of the refugees. By then, ethnic tensions had reached an unprecedented high, made worse still by the deepening involvement of Communist China in the internal affairs of the kingdom. That the support of the refugee leadership for the Casablanca group should have expressed itself so quickly—and brutally— after the crown withdrew its support from the Nyamoya government is indeed indicative of the extent to which the interests of both groups were now dependent on the continued involvement of Communist China—a point which will become clearer later in this chapter. At any rate, only three days after the Mwami had once again called upon Ngendadumwe to form a new cabinet, on January 15, 1965, the newly appointed Prime Minister was shot to death by a group of Rwandese refugees in front of the Rwagasore hospital, in Bujumbura, where his wife had just given birth to a son. Shortly thereafter, on January 2, about thirty *inyenzi* affiliated to the APLR, including most of its leaders, were arrested in Murore in connection with the assassination. Rukeba's son, Butera, was arrested in Rumonge on February 19; according to one ballistic expert, the bullet which killed Ngendadumwe came from the Luger revolver found on Butera at the time of his arrest. What is known of the circumstances of the assassination (including the fact that the man who fired the shots was a Tutsi refugee employed by the United States' embassy) in no way exonerates those Casablanca personalities who, behind the scenes, actively collaborated with the refugees in the planning and execution of the plot. Nor is there any evidence to disprove a possible collusion of the Communist Chinese embassy. One thing at least is clear: Ngendadumwe's assassination was both an act of revenge and an act of solidarity—an act of revenge against the crown, and the expression of a growing solidarity between the Casablanca elites and the refugee leadership.*

Although generalisations on this score are rendered extremely difficult by the sheer fluidity of Burundi politics, and the equally complex, unpredictable character of political alignments within the refugee movement, there are ample grounds for holding that the mere presence of Tutsi refugees in Burundi has directly contributed to heightened tension between the indigenous Hutu and Tutsi communities. Material hardships and renewed political disappointments crossbred to further increase the refugees' hatred of all Hutu, irrespective of national origins, and this situation was bound to reverberate on race relations within the host country, with continuing grim prospects for the future.

While the refugees often tried, and sometimes succeeded, in enlisting the logistic and financial support of the Burundi authorities in their raids against Rwanda, they were also used as a political and military tool by the Tutsi community of Burundi against its indigenous enemies. This, ironically, is where the immediate preoccupations of the Tutsi of

---

* After a temporary lull, another element of instability was injected into this already troubled situation by the arrival in Burundi of some 500 hard-core *inyenzi* fighters, in December 1965. Led by a Chinese-trained Tutsi named Joseph Mudandi, and accompanied by thirty Cuban technical advisers, they made their way into Burundi from the Congo, where they fought at the side of the Congolese rebels before being pushed back by the counter-offensives of the ANC. After a march of 300 miles from Bendera, a few miles north of Albertville, to the north-western tip of Burundi—a march which lasted seven weeks and which one *inyenzi* described to this writer as 'our long march'—they finally settled in the Bubanza province of Burundi, near the Rwandese border. Although they apparently came into Burundi at the request of certain members of the Burundi government, as a 'guarantee' against a possible Hutu uprising, their presence in the country eventually caused considerable difficulties to the Micombero government—which came to power in July 1966—if only because they seemed to favour the more radical elements against the army.

The first sign of a possible lessening of border violence came in March 1967, with the decision of the governments of Rwanda and Burundi to seek a compromise on the status of the refugees. Although Micombero agreed to disarm the refugees, not until several months later was he able to carry out his pledge. Reliable sources indicate that the disarming of the so-called 'Red Battalion' was accomplished with the unofficial assistance of ANC units from the Kivu.

Burundi were liable to come into conflict with the long-run objectives of the refugees. As ethnic antagonisms gained intensity, the strategic value of the refugee population was correspondingly enhanced in the eyes of the Casablanca group, so much so that, before long, the refugee came to be regarded as an indispensable manpower reservoir for repressive action in case of a showdown between Tutsi and Hutu. Under the circumstances, in the minds of the Casablanca politicians a permanent settlement of the refugees in Burundi was evidently preferable to the alternative solutions of a peaceful repatriation or a forceful re-entry into Rwanda.*

Besides serving as a tool of ethnic enmity, the refugees were also used as pawns in a power struggle whose ramifications extended far beyond the borders of Burundi. Though this is by no means the only explanation for Burundi's involvement in East-West rivalries, there is every reason to believe that the presence of certain refugee leaders served as a major vehicle of Communist penetration into the country and other parts of Africa. Admittedly, among those refugees who became attracted by Communism, ideological considerations played a relatively minor role. As noted earlier, their sympathies for the Communist world arose out of the exigencies of the Rwandese revolution: they courted the support of Communist China on pragmatic grounds, because they earnestly felt that the material support of Peking was their only hope of political salvation. Nonetheless, they did keep in close contact with Communist agents in East Africa, received secret Chinese payments and weapons, and occasionally travelled to Communist China (on passports delivered by the Burundi Ministry of Foreign Affairs), where some received intensive training in guerrilla warfare in late 1963 and early 1964. The effect on the political climate of Burundi was deeply felt, even in the rural areas. For a while, accusations of Communist sympathies gave the refugees and their Casablanca friends something of the prestige which similar accusations from the tutelle had once unwittingly conferred upon Rwagasore's party. In time, however, this identification gave way

---

* However, on this issue, as on many others, the Tutsi community of Burundi did not show complete unanimity. While Tutsi politicians were generally inclined to use the refugees as a weapon against their domestic foes, the army took a very different view. As the refugee militia gained strength, the possibility that they might substitute themselves for the army became a major source of anxiety to Burundi officers, Hutu and Tutsi. This, coupled with continuing attempts by certain refugee leaders to influence Burundi politics in a way which might have required the direct intervention of the army, explains the extreme suspicion shown by the Burundi army in general towards the refugees, as well as the subsequent and as yet unsuccessful attempt by Captain Micombero to negotiate their repatriation.

to an atmosphere of profound fear and uncertainty, reflecting the sense of dismay and apprehension of the rural masses in the face of a situation they could not fully comprehend. More important still, the strength of cultural affinities between the refugees and the indigenous Tutsi community, coupled with the support which Peking had already given to certain segments of the refugee leadership, made the Casablanca elites all the more receptive to Communist China's diplomatic overtures.

THE CHINESE SYNDROME

Burundi was, and still is, especially attractive as a base for Communist penetration in Africa because of its strategic location in relation to the Congo, a fact which takes on added significance when one remembers the opportunities for revolutionary 'armed struggle' offered by the Congo rebellion. The revolutionary activities of which the Congo became the scene in 1963–64 were indeed the crucial determinant of Peking's involvement in Burundi politics.

Already, in July 1962, on the occasion of the independence ceremonies, unofficial contacts had been established between certain Barundi politicians and Chinese diplomats,* but it was not until December 1963, after the Mwami finally yielded to the pressures of the Casablanca faction, that Red China received official recognition. What caused the initial exchange of courtesies between Peking and Bujumbura to crystallise into something approaching an alliance was the sudden deterioration of the Congo situation, in late 1963, and Peking's determination to take full advantage of what Chou En-Lai described in 1963 as 'an excellent revolutionary situation'. The motives which inspired Peking's policies in Burundi are well-known. They received their clearest formulation from a statement by Tung Chi-Ping, the Chinese diplomat who defected to the West while serving as assistant cultural attaché to the Chinese embassy in Bujumbura: 'Because it is the gateway to the Congo, this small, under-developed, over-populated nation is important in Mao's long-range plans to dominate as much of Africa as he can. Before I was sent to Burundi, I had been thoroughly briefed on the progress being made there and the plans for the future. Again and again my superiors repeated Mao Tse-Tung's statement: "When we capture the Congo,

---

* The initial probings, on the Chinese side, were conducted by Kao-Liang, the tough-minded, ubiquitous correspondent of the New China News Agency. Kao-Liang's most valuable 'contact' at the time was the late Lorgio Nimubona, then in charge of the Ministry of Foreign Affairs and well known for his leftist leanings. See Gilles Bimazubute, "Les relations diplomatiques entre le Burundi et la Chine", *Remarques Africaines*, February 17, 1965.

we can proceed to capture the whole of Africa. Burundi is the stepping stone for reaching the Congo".'[4]

What is not always appreciated is the extent and forms of Chinese involvement, not only in Burundi but in other areas contiguous to the Congo. While the roots of the Congo rebellion unquestionably lie in the internal conditions of the country after independence, the evidence supplied by the *Cahiers de Gambona* suggests the Chinese played a far more active supporting role than has generally been suspected. Discovered after the capture of Bolobo by the Armée Nationale Congolaise (ANC), in the northern Congo, the *Cahiers* give irrefutable proof of the role played by the Chinese in Congo-Brazzaville in organising training centres for the conduct of guerrilla warfare.[5] Even though the circumstances in Burundi did not permit a similar scale of involvement, that the country assumed a high order of priority in Peking's strategy is indicated by the substantial, though undetermined, sums of money which have been paid to various local politicians; by the very size of its diplomatic representation in Bujumbura;* and by the wide range of activities conducted through its local diplomatic network.

Of these different types of activity, few were more important than the establishment of informal contacts with local politicians. These were intended to serve at least two purposes: they enabled the Chinese to 'size up' their interlocutors, and provided Peking with a rough index of priority for the allocation of financial aid. Although the Chinese quickly discovered the venality of Burundi officials and reportedly distributed their funds with a lavish hand, they nonetheless concentrated their efforts on those whom they considered the most 'worthwhile'. Thus, in a confidential report entitled "L'action communiste au Burundi"—actually written by a Belgian priest to provide the Belgian embassy with background information on the origins and extent of the Chinese presence in Burundi—attention was drawn to the 'remarkable power of seduction of the Chinese Communists': 'They capitalise to the fullest possible extent on the anti-American and anti-Belgian sentiments of the Barundi, and thus elicit a reaction of tolerance towards their activities, even from certain members of the indigenous clergy.' Among the various targets of Communist propaganda, four were said to be particularly vulnerable:

---

* In November 1964, the Chinese embassy included twenty-four officials, of whom eight were registered as 'diplomats', the rest labelled 'auxiliary personnel'. One may perhaps guess the nature of their auxiliary functions from the fact that at least four of them lived in the peripheral district of Bujumbura known as 'Le Belge'. Communication with Peking was ensured by three broadcasting sets, each operating on a different wave-length.

(i) The politicians, to whom the Chinese never omit to present gifts in order to win their sympathy and support; (ii) the functionaries, with whom the Chinese keep frequent contacts, and many of whom do not conceal their sympathy for Communism; (iii) the Jeunesses Nationalistes Rwagasore (JNR), and the Fédération des Travailleurs du Burundi (FTB), on whose leaders the Chinese influence is profound and real . . . the secretary-general of the FTB, Ntamagara, just went to China and came back enthused . . . and the permanent secretary, Semahuna, is manifestly committed to Marxist ideas; (iv) the students attending universities and secondary schools, who also retain the attention of the Chinese.[6]

In addition to what has already been said of the role played by certain refugee leaders in conditioning the attitude of their hosts and facilitating the latter's contacts with Communist emissaries, several other factors have helped awaken the interest of Barundi politicians in Communist China. One of these is traceable to the informal connections established between certain UPRONA personalities and left-wing Congolese politicians in 1960 and 1961, following the administrative sanctions taken by the tutelle against those considered 'subversive' (see chapter 12, page 334). Clearly, no less than the circumstances of their exile, their sudden immersion in the 'radical' political environment of the Eastern Congo could only increase their sensitivity to the Chinese brand of radicalism. Furthermore, among the growing number of Barundi students who, after independence, attended institutions of higher learning in France and in Belgium, many came under the influence of left-wing European intellectuals and fellow-travellers; many of them, too, had occasion to travel in Communist countries—though, admittedly, few went to Communist China—and their exposure to Communist doctrine and propaganda had a noticeable impact on their attitude and general political orientation. Even more decisive were the strategic advantages which certain Tutsi elements had come to expect of an informal alliance with Peking. They felt that the Chinese brand of 'technical assistance' was far more effective, politically and militarily, in dealing with their internal adversaries, than the aid they received from Belgium, and, for some at least, it was financially more rewarding. What is more, in the minds of many Tutsi, the Chinese ideological 'model' evoked a type of political control which seemed ideally suited to the perpetuation of minority rule.

While these conditions were eminently favourable to the realisation of Chinese tactical objectives, the really critical question—to which neither the Chinese nor anyone else at the time could give a precise answer—was:

how far, and for how long, would the crown tolerate the intrusion of Chinese influences? It is all too facile, in retrospect, to lay blame for the setback eventually suffered by the Chinese Communists on their failure to comprehend the role of the crown in the political system of Burundi, and hence on their failure to properly assess its capacity to react when the circumstances required. Although there is considerable truth in this assertion, the initial response of the crown to Chinese manoeuvres was one of remarkable tolerance, if not total passivity.

From the triangular pattern of relationships which, by early 1964, had developed among Chinese diplomats in Bujumbura, certain Casablanca politicians and Congolese rebels, one could easily guess the nature of Chinese tactics. The first step toward the installation of a revolutionary base in the Congo was to convert Burundi into a kind of 'privileged sanctuary' from which the Congolese rebel leadership could lay out its strategy under the guidance of Chinese 'technical advisers'. As may be re-called, it was in late January 1964 that one of the leading figures of the Comité National de Libération (CNL), Gaston Soumialot, arrived in Bujumbura to organise the eastern branch of the 'liberation movement'.[7] Almost overnight, the Paguidas Hotel in Bujumbura, where Soumialot first established his headquarters, became the favourite hangout of stray refugees and JNR youths, as well as the scene of several nocturnal rendezvous between Soumialot and Chinese diplomats. After the fall of the Ngendadumwe government, on March 30, 1964, and the coming to power of a 'Casablanca' government, the nexus of influence between the Chinese embassy and the Congolese rebel leadership became increasingly evident.

The next logical step was to organise training facilities for guerrilla fighters, as had already been done at Impfondo and Gambona in Congo-Brazzaville. On June 16, 1965, the usually reliable correspon-dent of the *Libre Belgique*, J. Van Der Dussen, stated: 'The Chinese Communists encourage the rebellion, and perhaps supply its leaders with funds, *but they have not furnished any weapons* [our italics]. Their tactics are to instigate troubles so as to prepare the ground for a revolu-tionary situation through anarchy. Chinese intentions do not go beyond these tactics, which, they hope, will be enough to set the stage for subse-quent revolutionary actions.' In March 1964, however, the ambassador of Congo-Léopoldville in Bujumbura had reported differently—and more accurately—to his government: 'The intentions of the Congolese rebel leadership are to use Burundi as a training base for the youths of their party, who, after their military training, will attack the authorities [of the Congo Republic] and trigger off a revolution aimed at the over-throw of the present [Congolese] government.'[8] In point of fact, at the time these lines were written, certain Barundi authorities had already given Soumialot a house in a suburb of Bujumbura where, with the assistance of certain JNR leaders and Communist instructors, small groups of 'partisans' were given intensive training in the tactics of guerrilla warfare.[9]

After the hiring of exiled Cuban pilots by the US Central Intelligence Agency for military operations against Congolese rebels, and the stepping up of American military and logistic aid to the ANC, immediately following the fall of Stanleyville,* Burundi became a major entrepôt for arms and ammunitions of Communist provenance, most of which reached their destination through Dar es Salaam, Kigoma, and Nyanza Lac. In organising these shipments, the Chinese embassies of Bujumbura and Dar es Salaam could count on the tacit co-operation of the Tanzanian authorities and the active support of certain Barundi politicians. Little did they suspect, however, the reaction of the crown upon discovering the nature and extent of the trafficking.

In mid-December 1964, a convoy of fourteen trucks, containing 80 tons of weapons and ammunitions of Chinese and Russian origin, was intercepted by elements of the Burundi army under Belgian command on the road leading from Nyanza Lac, in the south, to Gitega. Among the weapons seized by the Burundi military authorities were 500 Kalashniko rifles, 30 Simonov rifles, nine 75MM cannon, nine 82MM mortars and an undetermined number of anti-aircraft guns. Despite the strenuous efforts of Zénon Nicayenzi (then directeur général in the Office of the Prime Minister) to let the convoy through, Captain Micombero, apparently yielding to the pressures of Belgian military advisers, ordered the confiscation of the entire cargo. At this point, rumours of an impending Chinese-sponsored coup quickly spread through the country. It was only a matter of days before the Mwami withdrew his support from the Nyamoya government and, on January 12, 1965, he asked Ngendadumwe to form a new cabinet. Whether the

---

* As will be remembered, Stanleyville fell to the rebels on August 5, 1964. Two days later, on August 7, the US Under-Secretary of State for Political Affairs, Averell Harriman, met in Brussels with the Belgian Prime Minister, Paul-Henri Spaak, to negotiate the terms of US military assistance to the Congo government. On August 13, the first deliveries of US matériel arrived in Léopoldville, in the form of three helicopters, four C-130 transport planes and an undetermined number of C-45 planes. Accompanying these deliveries were forty US paratroopers of the 820th airborne division from Fort Bragg, to serve, presumably, in a purely technical, non-military, capacity. The evidence available, however, does suggest a rather active involvement of certain US military personnel in the planning of military operations against Congolese rebels, especially in and around Bukavu in the crucial summer days of 1964.

weapons captured were specifically intended for the Rwandese refugees, as some have maintained, or for the Congolese rebels, or both, is immaterial. The important point here is that the news of their discovery was the decisive factor behind the intervention of the crown. The subsequent decision of the Mwami to call upon Ngendadumwe (a Hutu) to form a new government came as an additional shock to the Casablanca group and the refugee leadership, and this, as we have seen, lies at the root of the motives which inspired his brutal liquidation, on January 15, 1965.

If there is any trace of irony in this otherwise tragic turn of events, one could find it in the diplomatic repercussions of Ngendadumwe's assassination. By eliminating Ngendadumwe from the political scene, the authors of the plot had hoped to re-establish direct connections between the government and the Chinese embassy, as these had been temporarily suspended by the appointment of a Hutu Prime Minister. The end result, however, was precisely the opposite of what had been intended. Shortly after being apprised of Ngendadumwe's death, Mwambutsa served notice to the Chinese ambassador and his staff to leave the country within forty-eight hours, a move which, as one commentator observed, 'had the effect of ending alleged Chinese subversive activities and, more importantly, of isolating the leftist Tutsi from their presumed source of support'.[10]

Although one can safely impute responsibility for the severance of diplomatic ties with China to the court, this does not mean that the Mwami was impervious to outside influences, and least of all to the influence of certain Western embassies. Indeed, a major consequence of the Chinese involvement in the domestic affairs of the realm has been to release a variety of countervailing pressures from Western representatives in Bujumbura, for a while engendering something approximating a stalemate situation.

COUNTERVAILING PRESSURES

Beginning in early 1964, in an attempt to counteract Peking's manoeuvres, increasing pressure was brought to bear upon the court by Western diplomats in the hope of inducing 'from above' a disengagement from the Chinese orbit. Eventually, a situation was reached where East and West each endeavoured to balance with their own local 'clients' those of the other. Despite the element of symmetry resulting from the simultaneous involvement of Communist and Western powers, there were significant differences in the style of action and methods adopted by each of the protagonists. In part, these differences tended to reflect contrasting commitments to ways of fomenting change; in particular, the explicit rejection by Western powers of agitation, propaganda, sub-version or force as techniques of political action. But this is only a partial and, in a sense, misleading view of the situation. While there is no gainsaying the strategic advantages initially drawn by Communist China from the use of well-known, battle-tested 'agit-prop' methods, on the whole the balance of forces was not so heavily tilted to the 'left' as the foregoing might suggest.

For one thing, the channels of influence available to the West were far more diversified, thereby offering a much wider range of opportunities for exercising pressure on internal affairs. Not only were the Western embassies more numerous but the Western presence in general was mediated through a variety of agencies and institutions which, even though they may not have had any formal links with Western embassies, none the less considerably enhanced their influence. If only through the intelligence some of their representatives were able to relay to their respective embassies, Western technical assistance missions, UN relief agencies and the Catholic Church have all been instrumental at one point or another in shaping the course of Western policies in Burundi. Particularly significant, though of course largely unpublicised, has been the 'auxiliary' role played by the Belgian military assistance group, whose links with the Belgian embassy were made all the more intimate by Colonel Hennequiau's brilliant record in the Congolese Force Publique before being appointed ambassador to Burundi. The greater diversity of contact points available to the West implied a correspond-ingly larger scale of involvement in technical assistance, and therefore a relatively stronger bargaining position towards the recipient authorities. This was especially true of Belgium, by virtue of the preponderant role it continues to assume in shouldering the burdens of technical assistance to Burundi. Thus, even at the risk of laying themselves open to charges of economic blackmail, Belgian diplomats were in an excellent position to 'trade' on this relationship for political ends. Here, indeed, is the key to an understanding of the delaying tactics adopted by the court, in 1963, in the face of mounting pressures from the Ministry of Foreign Affairs to establish formal diplomatic relations with Communist China. The court, itself a major beneficiary of Belgian aid, feared that, if the government were to recognise Communist China, Belgium might dis-continue, or at least substantially pare down, its technical assistance programme to Burundi. Although this did not prevent the government from eventually recognising Communist China, one wonders whether renewed threats of economic sanctions, now rendered all the more legitimate from the Belgian standpoint, did not play a part in prompting the palace to sever diplomatic ties with Peking, in January 1965.

At all events, and in contrast with Peking's efforts to sap the system 'from below', a characteristic tendency of Western diplomats has been to try to make their influence felt 'from above', by applying maximum pressure upon the court, and, if need be, on the Mwami. In this, they were actuated by several motives: by their conviction (on the whole, justifiable) that the court was fundamentally pro-Western; by their belief that the crown still had an important role to play in the political system; and by a general reluctance to by-pass formal hierarchical channels. Yet, as they discovered that the policies of the crown were shaped at least as much by external proddings as by internal pressures, part of their influence was deliberately channelled into the political system through local politicians, most of them, predictably, of Hutu origins.

Thus, just as the Chinese presence was often mediated through the actions and statements of individual Tutsi politicians, many of the petitions submitted to the court by certain Hutu personalities echoed the views of Belgian and American diplomats. One needs only to glance at the letter sent by Paul Mirerekano to the Mwami, on August 28, 1964, to grasp the nature of his 'connections': 'Sir, realising that the peace of the entire world is often threatened by people of ill-will, I bow to Your Majesty to request: (i) the dismissal of the Nyamoya government, rejected by the majority of the parliamentarians; (ii) the permission to allow all UPRONA members to elect their president in full freedom; (iii) the expulsion of all these Chinese Communists from Burundi, and the infliction of a severe punishment on all their acolytes. Can you not see what is going on in the Congo as a result of their dirty propaganda? Show us that you are the Mwami of the Barundi and not of a certain caste.'[11] That the letter happened to be written from Butare, in Rwanda, where Mirerekano was occasionally visited by agents of the Central Intelligence Agency, strengthens the presumption of co-operative links between certain Hutu politicians and the American embassies in Kigali and Bujumbura. In these conditions, the struggle for power between the Monrovia and Casablanca factions became the outward expression of East-West rivalries.

The message of the Hutu leaders was also relayed to the court through the Catholic Church, and in particular through the European clergy. In a letter addressed to Mgr Grauls, Archbishop of Gitega, dated August 17, 1964, Mirerekano cautioned the Catholic hierarchy against the dangers of the Chinese presence in these terms:

It is beyond question that the Barundi are theist by nature; this is attested by their immemorial belief in *Imana*. . . . It is a public secret that the winds of Communism have already swept across the country for a certain number of years, and now these winds are becoming more impetuous. . . . Communism in Burundi manifests itself through organisations like the JNR and the FTB. Note that the FTB is affiliated to the World Federation of Trade Unions (WFTU), based in Prague, which is itself directly dependent upon Moscow. Communist countries, and the USSR and Communist China in particular, have regularly offered tours and scholarships to Barundi students, with a view to converting them into Communist agitators. Communist China has just made an offer to the government of Burundi to bring in 62 Chinese—30 Communist agitators ['formateurs de jeunesses'], and 32 technicians, who will also engage in Communist propaganda. Already, 22 Chinese move about day and night through the whole country.[12]

This letter could not possibly have been written by Mirerekano: anyone even vaguely familiar with his erratic mind and very limited skills of expression in a medium other than Kirundi can immediately sense the falseness of its authorship. Moreover, only a few weeks later, the bishops of Burundi issued an official letter which reproduced, and elaborated upon, the ideas expressed under Mirerekano's signature; here, however, the authorship of the Church seems authentic, if not necessarily reflecting the views of all the signatories.* The most significant passages run as follows:

1. Communism is against God. Lies, extortions, murder, assassination, all means are legitimate [for the Communists], and those who disagree are called 'enemies of the people'. All things spiritual, religious, moral, legal, are regarded as obstacles. God is the first whose presence must be eradicated from the people's minds and hearts. Yet the Barundi believe in God and no one has the right to make them lose faith in God, be it through lies or violence. . . .

2. Communism is opposed to kingship and seeks to destroy it. . . . A regime with a constitutional king is incompatible with the notion of a 'people's democracy'. Not only are 'people's democracies' seldom democratic but one is even less likely to find a king where Communism has implanted itself. You can check all the countries annexed by Russia: Lithuania, Estonia, Latvia, Poland, Bessarabia, Bukovina, Moldavia, Sub-Carpathian Ukraine, Eastern Prussia. . . . Communism is incompatible with kingship and Burundi will be no exception to

---

* One of them, Mgr Ntuyahaga, Bishop of Bujumbura, well-known for his UPRONA, 'pro-Casablanca' sympathies, had his signature appended to the document before he even had a chance to see it in print!

the rule; Communism threatens the peace of Burundi. As soon as Communists arrive in a country, their first preoccupation is to create conflicts. This is what Lenin preaches in the fourth volume of his *Complete Works*: 'Our task is to utilise all forms of discontent, to gather together and exploit all particles of protest, even the most embryonic.'[13]

The aim, in short, was to alert the Mwami to the threats to the survival of the monarchy posed by Communist influences, and to awaken him to the fact that the interests of the Church in this matter ran parallel to those of the throne. Such, also, was the intent of Mirerekano's letters of August 17 and 28. Even though the effect of these warnings and exhortations was not immediately felt, the conclusion one reaches is that Ngendadumwe's assassination was not the only factor behind the Mwami's decision to expel the Communist Chinese diplomats.

The foregoing suggests a pattern of cross-pressures whose actual workings can scarcely be reconciled with the image of an absolute sovereign, unperturbed by the play of outside forces. The vulnerability of the crown to these environmental pressures is certainly a major reason for the policy shifts that have characterised Burundi politics in the period following independence; but it also helps to explain the element of indirection which entered into the strategies of the 'pro-Western' and 'pro-Chinese' factions, their tendency to counteract each other's influence by seeking to apply maximum pressure upon the crown. In these circumstances, the position of the crown in the political system might be compared to that of a steering mechanism, whose ability to chart a reasonably safe course depended upon its sensitivity to the danger signals and warnings emanating from the total environment of Burundi politics. Thus, each time the Mwami withdrew his confidence from a government, it was in response to specific 'warnings'. In June 1963, the warning came from the election of Thaddée Siryuyumunsi to the presidency of the bureau of the National Assembly, by 33 votes to 31, which the Mwami interpreted as a vote of confidence in the Monrovia group, and hence led to the appointment of a 'Monrovia' government. Likewise, the interception of Russian and Chinese weapons, in December 1964, was the decisive warning which led to the fall of the Nyamoya government.

But there were times when the signals lent themselves to different interpretations, and times when the existing channels of communication failed to properly convey the stimuli of the environment to the court. Thus, as long as the Casablanca group justified their flirtation with Communist China on grounds of 'positive neutralism' and claimed that the asylum given to Congolese rebels was inspired by 'purely humanitarian' motives, the court was understandably reluctant to intervene. Similarly, the court had probably little reason to suspect the hand of the Central Intelligence Agency behind some of the petitions submitted by Hutu leaders, and, even if it did, the conflicting pressures emanating from each side tended to cancel each other out. The result, for a while, was to engender 'immobilisme'.

The possibility of a misinterpretation of the danger signals is perhaps nowhere better illustrated than by the incident which took place in March 1964, when mysterious tracts were circulated around Ngozi, some announcing the Mwami's intention to dismiss from office four members of the Ngendadumwe cabinet, all of Hutu extraction, and others accusing the Mwami of sowing discord among the Barundi and of hoarding his money in Switzerland. Was the distribution of these tracts a manoeuvre of the Casablanca opposition to discredit the government in the eyes of the court? Or was it an attempt by the incumbents to intimidate or blackmail the Mwami, so as to discourage him from further interfering with the policies of the government, or perhaps induce him to reverse his decision to fire the four cabinet members? One will probably never know. Either because he wanted to teach the unknown authors a lesson, or perhaps because he had already made up his mind and had no other alternative, Mwambutsa fired the four controversial cabinet members on March 31, and asked Ngendadumwe, the incumbent Prime Minister, to form a new government. Agreement could not be reached, however, and the Mwami then turned to Albin Nyamoya to head a new cabinet. Even though the Mwami's choice may not have had anything to do with the tracts, these nonetheless provided the 'feedback' which prompted him to form a new government. Whether his decision to revoke the four cabinet members reflected an accurate reading of the 'signals' is an entirely different matter.

This state of 'immobilisme' was further encouraged by the blocking of popular demands, either as a result of a deliberate policy on the part of certain personalities in the Mwami's entourage,* or simply because the Mwami's absence from Bujumbura made it impossible for the court to respond effectively and speedily to these demands. We have already noted how the Mwami's courtiers tried to shield him from outside pressures, to preserve for themselves a monopoly of influence at the

---

* For this the Grand Marshal of the court, Germain Bimpenda, deserves special credit; his tactics were brought to my attention in the summer of 1964, when, after having written him three consecutive letters to request an audience with His Majesty, none of which he deigned to answer, Bimpenda later said he had 'lost' the letters.

court. At no time were these limitations upon his authority more effective than during his travels outside the country; similarly, the government's authority seemed to increase in proportion to the distance separating the Mwami from Bujumbura.

A final point, implicit in what has just been said, is that the Mwami was by no means the only source of authority in the political system. Although the major decisions ultimately depended on his will, his role, as we have seen, was essentially that of an arbiter. While his veto powers were rarely questioned, at least in the beginning, the responsibility for every phase and aspect of the policy-making process was not his alone. If decisions were often unpredictable, this is because decisions inhered at several levels, and because the Mwami could not always control the decision-makers, especially those *ganwa* who gravitated around the palace, whose connections with the government and the administration gave them a much wider range of discretion than was generally assumed at the time. As in the old days, the Mwami was 'first among equals,' and, as often happened in pre-colonial times, his dictates were frequently over-ruled by his courtiers.

In trying to arrogate to himself increasing control over the government, and to tighten his hold over the system so as to minimise ethnic strife and governmental instability, Mwambutsa ended up transferring power from one oligarchy to another. By calling upon his relatives and protégés to reinforce his position vis-à-vis the government, he unwittingly gave birth to a host of vested interests whose stakes in the system became increasingly obvious as time went by. This, as we shall see, was to have fatal consequences for the future of the monarchy and for the stability of parliamentary institutions.

16. The Dialectics of Succession

THE MOST arresting fact about post-independence Burundi politics is not that the court ultimately failed to balance the claims of Hutu and Tutsi but that this balancing act could have lasted so long. Faced with the dilemma of either confining his role to the civilities of a constitutional monarch, at the price of letting his people sink in the maelstrom of a protracted ethnic strife, or of moving as far away from this role as seemed necessary to prevent the crisis from coming to a head, Mwambutsa chose the latter course—a course which, in effect, denied the 'new elites' opportunities for reform and vested almost unfettered control over the affairs of the realm in the hands of a traditional oligarchy.

By giving in to the demands of the traditional elements in society, and by seeking their support in the maintenance of a neo-traditional polity, Mwambutsa's policies were self-defeating. A neo-traditional polity must sooner or later come to terms with the demands of the modern educated elites, and, where no effort is made to accommodate their claims to power, or to slow down the pace of social change in such a way as to minimise the impact of modernising influences on society as a whole, conflict is bound to occur between the traditional oligarchs who support and identify themselves with the existing institutions, and the core of modern-oriented elites, whose view of the world and aspirations can no longer be reconciled with the continuation of the status quo. Thus a kind of dialectical relationship developed between the crown and this new group of aspirants, which inevitably compromised the chances of peaceful coexistence between them. Each time the latter tried to consolidate their position in the interstices of the royal Establishment, the crown responded by a further closure of opportunities for political participation and control. A total impasse was reached when the crown, yielding to the pressure of traditional vested interests, decided to reign and rule.

And yet, if the monarchy managed to gain temporary stability, this was not so much by virtue of its inherent strength as by the weakness of actual and potential opposition forces. A major source of weakness came from the extension of ethnic divisions to the new social groupings brought into existence by modernity. No matter how deep their grievances against the crown, so long as their hatred of each other equalled or surpassed their hatred of the monarchy, the latter's position remained

402

relatively secure. Without consciously resorting to a policy of divide and rule, the existence of an ever-deepening racial split among its opponents gave the monarchy a new lease on life.

In practice, then, not one but two main lines of political cleavage were discernible, partially intersecting but never completely cancelling out each other. From the combination of ethnic and occupational differences created by the coexistence of traditional and modern systems of stratification, a dual pattern of conflict and interaction came into being, involving, on the one hand, a persistence of ethnic polarities between Hutu and Tutsi, and, on the other, an incipient 'class conflict' between the new educated elites and the descendants of the old *ganwa* aristocracy. One of the most striking characteristics of this new elite has been their pervasive commitment to modernity, and their consequent aversion for what some of them contemptuously referred to as 'the feudal monarchy of Mwambutsa'. Even more remarkable is that, in spite of this common orientation and of their shared antipathies towards the crown, the majority should have evinced an even stronger loyalty to their respective subcultures. Rather than compromise the chances of success of their own group of origin, most of them preferred, for a while, to settle for the lesser of two evils, the maintenance of the monarchical status quo.

The reality of the situation was not quite as simple as this, however, if only because of the changing definition of the ethnic interests at stake, which tended to reflect changes in the policies of the court. Instead of looking at Hutu and Tutsi interests as fixed and immutable quantities, it would be more accurate to regard them as involving groups of individuals in competition with each other but depending for their chances of success on their capacity to manipulate factors external to themselves. In practice this meant that, in seeking to improve their relative position vis-à-vis each other, Tutsi and Hutu alike had to contend with the influence of the court, here expressing the probability that each set of players had to score a victory over the other. To put it somewhat differently, the contest between Hutu and Tutsi was not only a contest between themselves but a kind of game being played against the limitations inherent in the political environment, and, more specifically, against the limitations imposed by the court. These limitations varied from time to time, however, depending on the court's own evaluation of the threats to its interests and prerogatives alternatively posed by Hutu and Tutsi politicians. And these in turn were bound to affect the strategies of the contestants towards each other.

The effect of this triangular gamesmanship on the style and tenor of Burundi politics has already been noted. In particular, we have seen how each set of players sought to maximise its chances of winning by entering into coalitions with outside forces, even at the risk of over-playing its hand against the court. All along, the behaviour of the players seemed to comply with the tacit rule that the court alone had the right to arbitrate their moves, and to 'deal out' rewards and penal-ties accordingly. Compliance with this basic rule was not unconditional, however. Indeed, if any conclusion can be drawn from the tortuous sequence of events that led to the downfall of the monarchy, it is that the incentives to change the rule increased in proportion to the severity of the penalties imposed by the court. But before a description of the ultimate stages of the game, and of its outcome, is given, the players, and in particular those referred to earlier as the 'new elites', must be identified. Although the intensity of their involvement in the game, and the magnitude of their stakes, varied significantly from time to time, as well as in relation to their ethnic backgrounds and occupational statuses, they have played, and will continue to play, a determining role in the political destinies of their country.

THE EMERGENCE OF THE NEW ELITES

Among the new elites were four distinctive subgroups: the intelligentsia; the youth leaders; the bureaucrats; the gendarmerie and army officers. Insofar as they represented a group of individuals 'Western educated and wealthy to a high degree relative to the mass of the people', they were not untypical of the new elites that have sprung up in recent times elsewhere in Africa.[1] But these are by no means the only relevant criteria, for even among the traditional holders of office many were those who were 'Western educated to a high degree' in relation to the masses, and among this category of office holders were also found the wealthiest of the Barundi. If they came to look upon themselves as an elite, this is because several social and situational factors combined to make them a group apart. The nature of the socialising influences to which they had been exposed invited them to treat the monarchy as a more or less retrograde form of government, maintained in power by corruption and foreign intervention. Their extreme youthfulness reinforced their sense of belonging to an 'out-group' while at the same time making them all the more vulnerable to the appeals of radicalism. And for some at least, these predispositions were further strengthened by their socially and politically marginal position in their own society. Their ideological leanings, in any event, differed sharply from those of the elder generations of traditional elites, animated as they were by a strong reformist zeal and a concern for secularism, social progress and technical innovation.

Of all four categories, the intelligentsia was, and still is, the most receptive to modern influences. If their intellectual achievements are not always impressive, they nonetheless represent the most highly educated stratum in Burundi society, and some have already demonstrated considerable skill and determination in injecting modern ideas and values into the fabric of the traditional society. Most of them have attended or are still attending European universities and were at one time or another affiliated to the Union des Etudiants Barundi (UNEBA), an influential and vocal student organisation with branches in Bujumbura and abroad, whose principal spokesman, until his return to Burundi in late 1966, was the talented Gilles Bimazubute. From about 1964 onwards, in tracts and in the pages of the left-wing Belgian review *Remarques Africaines*, UNEBA lampooned and pilloried and cast considerable discredit on the monarchy. The anti-monarchic bent of this student intelligentsia is best revealed by the content of some of the resolutions adopted by UNEBA at its fifth congress, held in Bujumbura, August 26–31, 1964:

Conscious of the advantages of a constitutional monarchy . . . we none the less deplore the sad instability of our governments, owing to the weakness of the representatives of the nation and to the nefarious influences exercised upon the court by self-seeking nationals and foreigners. Sometimes a government is imposed upon us without preliminary consultations with the parliamentarians. . . . We condemn the existence of secretariats of state who are responsible to no one but the king. We protest with indignation against the attribution of public offices on the basis of nepotism. We condemn the tendency of the king to arrogate to himself absolute powers. And thus we request His Majesty to consider that a constitutional sovereign reigns but does not rule.[2]

Their sense of estrangement from the monarchy also found expression in a host of pressure activities designed to bring about social and economic reforms. These centred primarily upon three basic themes: 'economic austerity', a theme which also implied 'a diminution of the frequency and duration of His Majesty's trips abroad'; 'the expansion of educational facilities for women' through the organisation of social and recreational centres; and 'the expansion and improvement of news media', the existing ones being judged insufficient, inadequate or useless.[3] Every effort was made to emphasise the anti-colonialist and Pan-African vocation of UNEBA, and to proclaim its support of 'all the movements and all the organisations struggling for the development, dignity and welfare of mankind; of all the peoples who struggle against the yoke

405

of foreign domination; all of the movements which combat racial, social, religious, and political discrimination; of all that is likely to hasten the emergence of a United States of Africa'.[4] A growing sense of disillusionment with the monarchy, a tendency to espouse a levelling social ideology, and an open commitment to a radical brand of Pan-Africanism, were the hallmarks of this new intelligentsia.

These commitments and predispositions were also characteristic of the youth leaders and the bureaucrats, which is not unnatural considering that most of them at one time or another belonged to the intelligentsia. The case of Gilles Bimazubute, one-time founder of the Union Culturelle de la Jeunesse du Burundi (UCJB), then chef de cabinet in the Ministry of External Affairs, and for a time a law student at the University of Paris, is not untypical. One could also cite as examples Zénon Nicayenzi, Anicet Njangwa and Amedée Kabugubugu, all three of whom, before they became incorporated into the bureaucracy, had taken a very active part in their foundation of UNEBA, their initiative dating back to 1958, when they were attending Lovanium University, Léopoldville. In subsequent years, they continued to keep in close touch with the activities of the association; meanwhile, some of them went to Europe to pursue their education and helped organise new branches.

In the course of their studies abroad, they came in contact with left-wing European intellectuals from whom they borrowed many of the ideas they later incorporated into the doctrine of UNEBA. This was particularly true of those who happened to attend the Université Libre in Brussels, well-known for its anti-clerical bias, and to a lesser extent of those who went to the University of Liège. Once absorbed into the bureaucracy, however, many of these intellectuals felt the need to adjust their perspectives to the norms of the Extablishment of which they had become a part. While some, like Gilles Bimazubute, did not hesitate to hand in their resignation upon discovering that the realities of the 'system' could not be brought in line with their expectations, others were decidedly more cautious. No matter how deep their distaste for the ways of the court, they derived substantial benefits from their posts, and this naturally tended to mute their criticisms of the regime. That some of them saw no apparent contradiction in giving their support to the austerity programme of UNEBA while at the same time insisting that they deserved higher salaries and perquisites 'to keep up with the rising cost of living' epitomises the ambivalence of their position. Yet, as the court gradually invaded their prerogatives, they felt increasingly alienated from the main centres of power and grew bitterly resentful of the 'retrograde and obscurantist elements' gravitating around the palace. As one of them confided to this writer: 'Isn't the raison d'être of an intellectual to create? And how in the world can we create when the court insists on making decisions for us?'

Unlike the bureaucrats, whose hostility towards the crown was somehow tempered by their stake in the system, the youth leaders (most of them of Tutsi origins) were subject to no such restraints; and unlike the intelligentsia, whose physical and psychological insulation from the realities of Burundi politics often prevented them from playing an active part in the game, they showed a complete devotion to the virtues of 'the total praxis',* to borrow Frantz Fanon's phrase.[5] Like Fanon's 'damnés', their most salient characteristic was their wholehearted adherence to the Sorelian ethos of violence (a commitment which they expressed with particular savagery during the Kamenge incidents of late 1952). Again, in a way which reminds one of Fanon's gospel, to their minds the use of violence was necessary to bring about the total transformation of society to which they aspired. Even though the theme of violence has never been the object of systematic theorising on the part of the JNR leaders, one can easily see the relation of theory to practice in the lapidary formula which, in a nutshell, sums up their ideology: 'Independence must be a creative destruction.'[6] No doubt, the term ideology conveys a greater coherence and systematisation of ideas than could possibly be construed out of the rambling, loose-jointed doctrine of the JNR. Nonetheless, a number of significant themes emerged from what otherwise could be dismissed as mere rhetoric: a devotion to the total reconversion of society (à la Sékou Touré); a recognition of the need for a continued struggle against the forces of traditionalism; a sense of great self-confidence and faith in the future—these are some of the main themes set forth in the opening sentences of the document which later served as a profession of faith for every self-respecting JNR militant, significantly entitled *La Jeunesse après l'Indépendence*:

In our minds, this independence which we have today acquired has never meant anything else than a fundamental 'rite de passage', a transitory liberation and not an absolute denouement through which everything is settled once and for all. The essence of independence is what is at stake in our present and future combats. Our combat will go on forever, because the real meaning of independence will always be called into question. Our country is in a state of full evolution. . . . We are witness to the decolonisation of an entire nation, and we want this decolonisation to penetrate the innermost recesses of our souls, not merely the surface. Independence must be a creative

---

* I.e., a commitment to direct and sometimes violent action as a means of effecting change.

destruction. . . . We have faith in ourselves and we place great hopes in our youthful vitality. We want to educate ourselves and we know that, next to our daily bread, education is our first concern. We believe we shall succeed, because the restraining factors of colonialism have now disappeared. Independence means first of all the destruction of the forces which hold back the development of the country, its economic progress, its social, human and cultural development. But the problems with which we are faced are not only economic in nature . . . we must also create new ways of doing things, a new way of life, a new way of thinking. In order to build a nation, and at the same time safeguard the liberty of the people and individual freedom, each one must actively participate in the building of the nation. Youth knows that anything can be changed, and it knows it can do so. To meet the needs of our country will be the responsibility of our youth.[7]

Equally representative of this nascent, activist counter-elite, though moving in a somewhat different ideological direction, were the handful of trade union leaders associated with the Fédération des Travailleurs du Burundi (FTB). Despite the efforts of its secretary-general, Augustin Ntamagara, to build up a mass following, the FTB never really got off the ground. Although it is impossible to know the total membership of the FTB, 'the labouring masses' it claimed to represent probably did not amount to more than a few dozen at the peak of its recruiting drive. Yet, however meagre its membership, ineffective its organisation and limited its actual experience of direct political action, the FTB developed into an extremely vocal group, distinctively Marxist in outlook and openly committed to the liquidation of 'colonialism, neo-colonialism, imperialism, reaction and feudalism'.[8] Its main target was the Establishment, identified with 'a category of parvenus who in effect constitute a new feudal class, without any kind of national conscience, a corrupt class unsuited for any work'.[9] Stripped of its Marxist jargon, the position of the FTB tended to reflect the same feelings of revulsion towards the 'feudal oligarchy', whom they charged with corruption and nepotism, as did that of the JNR—and, indeed, the same inclination to forcibly manipulate the masses to make them collectively conscious of their role in society.

The fourth and most critically important category, the corps of army and gendarmerie officers, shares many of the characteristics of the other elites. They are modern-oriented and generally endowed with high administrative skills, at least by local standards. A number of army officers received their training abroad, at the Ecole Royale Militaire in Brussels, the Ecole d'Infanterie in Arlon (Belgium) or at the Saint

Cyr Officers' School in France. They came back to Burundi with new perspectives, new skills, and sometimes with unfortunate personal experiences, as exemplified by the case of Captain Damien Nkoripfa, expelled from the Arlon school after being judged 'unfit to become an officer'. Like the civilian elites, they are extremely young, roughly between the ages of 25 and 30, and derive considerable pride from their UPRONA background.

In spite of this, they form a distinctive subgroup in terms of their origins, occupational statuses and ideological ties. Most of the army officers come from the province of Bururi, where the country's first Ecole Militaire was set up in 1960, and they are for the most part of Tutsi extraction. In addition to sharing strong ethnic and regional affinities, they also displayed a sense of professionalism which marked them off rather sharply from other elite groups. At first, their loyalty to the crown seemed unquestionable, and this was further reinforced by the creation of secretariats of state for the army and the gendarmerie placed under the direct supervision of the crown, and by the spectacular promotions which this relationship sometimes involved. One only needs to look at Captain Micombero's meteoric rise: in April 1960, at the age of 20, Micombero entered the Ecole Royale Militaire of Brussels; in March 1962, he was promoted to the rank of second lieutenant; and, only eight months later, in November 1962, to the rank of assistant commander-in-chief of the Burundi National Army. Thus, even though many officers eventually came to entertain serious misgivings about the regime, they tended to look upon themselves as a privileged group and thus shared none of the bitterness and ideological radicalism of the activists and the intelligentsia. Like certain members of the government and the para-state organisations, they belonged to the Mwami's personal clientele, with the difference that they enjoyed a far greater security of tenure and higher salaries.

It is important to remind ourselves at this point of the differences of attitude noted earlier between the gendarmerie and army officers. The gendarmerie officers were not only distinctly less Westernised, so few having had the occasion to travel abroad, but not so well-educated, and not nearly as secluded from everyday political life. Moreover, the gendarmerie included a slightly higher proportion of Hutu officers than the army; out of a total of 38 in 1965, 20 were of Hutu extraction. Similarly, it is interesting to note that, in 1965, the Secretary of State for the Gendarmerie (Antoine Serukwavu) was a Hutu, while the Secretary of State for the Army (Michel Micombero) was of mixed origins. The gendarmerie, in short, was more directly vulnerable to political influence, and in particular to the influence of Hutu politicians.

But if the army officers were generally less 'politicised' than their confrères in the gendarmerie, and less radically committed than their civilian peers, they managed to keep close contacts with certain members of the intelligentsia and the bureaucracy. In some instances, they had known each other since their school days at the Collège du Saint Esprit, in the late 'fifties and early 'sixties; they met on social occasions— at parties, weddings and official receptions; and they paid occasional visits to each other to discuss matters of common interest, to exchange ideas about possible future developments, and to inform (or misinform) each other of the latest gossip about the court. Thus, through this informal network of friendships and comradeships, the army officers enjoyed a good deal of interaction with the local intelligentsia and the bureaucracy, and, just as the latter categories were predominantly Tutsi, the closest personal ties between army men and civilians were also found among the Tutsi elites.

Clearly, no matter how genuine their affinities, be it in terms of age, ideological orientation, educational experience or wealth, these various social groupings did not form a very cohesive bloc. There were, to begin with, different degrees of eliteness within the elite. The younger *ganwa* elements, for example, retained a much stronger sense of loyalty to the crown than their 'plebeian' peers, even though they shared the same educational background. Similarly, those who happened to occupy responsible or second-level leadership positions were naturally more conscious of their role as an elite than, say, the average JNR militant, or the university student who was vice-president of the local UNEBA branch. Another source of division tended to reflect the incidence of different environmental and socialising influences: thus the sections of UNEBA based in Europe tended to evince a much stronger sense of ideological commitment than the nationally-based association. Similar differences of attitude could be detected between those civil servants who represented their country abroad and those who found employment at home. Moreover, there was a striking contrast between those sedate and rather ineffectual youth movements developed under the auspices of the Catholic missions, and in particular of the metropolitan Catholic youth movement known as the Jeunesses Ouvrières Chrétiennes (JOC)—represented in Burundi by the still embryonic and largely apolitical CHIRO movement—and the flamboyant radicalism of the JNR.

But by far the most serious source of disunity came from the mutual suspicions, antagonisms and rivalries which, to this day, so prominently colour the attitude of Hutu and Tutsi towards each other. The resulting strains were occasionally subdued by their common resentment of the monarchy, but they constantly re-emerged on the surface in the course of competition for public office. Indeed, the real paradox of Burundi politics is that feelings of ethnic repulsion were probably strongest among these new elites, and this in spite of the fact that they generally shared the same vision of their country's future, the same misgivings about the monarchy, the same overt receptivity to Western influence.

Precisely for this reason, they also suffered from seemingly insurmountable handicaps. Beset by ethnic dissensions, they were unable to attain the minimum of social and political cohesion necessary to break the hold of the monarchy on the political system. Opposition to the monarchy thus expressed itself in a series of ethnic responses to specific threats from the crown, each set of responses in turn giving birth to a new pattern of relationships between Hutu and Tutsi as well as between each of these groups and the crown.

THE KING VERSUS PARLIAMENT

Not until 1965 did the situation begin to change drastically, and then, characteristically, in response to a shift in the crown's policies. Early that year, the palace gave evidence of an intent to restore the legitimacy of parliament by holding parliamentary elections and creating the upper chamber prescribed by the constitution. But the crown, in an unexpected turn about, moved instead toward royal autocracy, thus breaking the uneasy coexistence between itself and the National Assembly and increasing the tension between conflicting principles of legitimacy. More significant than the abruptness of the change was the fact that it seemed openly calculated to deprive the Hutu of their electoral gains. Occurring at a moment when expectations of change among the Hutu elites had never been so high, this sudden reversal of the crown's attitude could only intensify their feelings of rage against the system.

But if the crown never intended to restore the faintest measure of legitimacy to parliament, how should one account for its decision to hold new elections? In view of its previous disregard of constitutional provisions, one must obviously look elsewhere for an explanation. The answer, it seems, lies in the very nature of the political style of the Burundi monarchy at this stage of its evolution, a style which, however authoritarian, was not yet autocratic, and thus not basically hostile to certain limited concessions to democracy. In calling for new elections, Mwambutsa not only wished to satisfy the mounting demands of the electorate for new deputies and burgomasters, the incumbents by then being largely discredited in the eyes of the masses, but hoped that a new consensus might emerge in the National Assembly that would invest parliament with a new aura of legitimacy. As usual, he tried to find a

411

compromise solution, by combining elements of both monarchical rule and parliamentary government. What he apparently failed to anticipate is that the revitalisation of parliamentary institutions would require at least a partial destruction of the traditional bases of power and influence built around the court. At this stage, however, Mwambutsa was no longer in a position to turn the clock back, as he himself was now heavily dependent upon, and often manipulated by, these traditional interests. To avoid political suicide, he had no alternative but to reign and rule.

In any event, from the legislative elections of May 1965 the Hutu emerged in the National Assembly with 23 seats out of a total of 33. The party strengths in parliament were further evidence of the ascendency of Hutu elements: the pro-Hutu Parti du Peuple (PP), which had suffered a resounding defeat in the September 1961 elections, won 10 seats and UPRONA won 21, the remaining two being held by independents. By then, UPRONA had become a meaningless label: in some constituencies, no fewer than five different slates of UPRONA candidates competed among themselves for the favours of the electorate; but the main political tendencies were said to be the UPRONA 'populaire' and the UPRONA 'traditionaliste', representing respectively Hutu and Tutsi interests. If ethnic loyalties did not necessarily follow party lines, they were sufficiently strong to enable the Hutu to control the presidency and the vice-presidency of the Assembly, and later of the Senate.

Significantly, the President of the National Assembly (Emile Bucumi, one of the very few deputies to be re-elected) and the two Vice-Presidents (Paul Mirerekano and Patrice Mayondo) had all spent some time together in exile in Butare (Rwanda), and did not return to Burundi until shortly after the elections. Of the three, Mirerekano was undoubtedly the most popular among the Hutu masses, and his return to Burundi did more to arouse their ethnic consciousness than the combined efforts of all other Hutu politicians. Because of his enormous popularity among the Hutu, Mirerekano's candidacy became a source of grave concern to certain Tutsi army officers and public officials. Thus, shortly before his return to Burundi, the Secretary of State for the Army, Captain Micombero, and the Secretary of State for Justice, Immigration and Sûreté, Sixte Butera, had agreed to condemn him in absentia to a twenty-year prison sentence under the jurisdiction of a 'conseil de guerre' especially set up for this purpose, but they apparently changed their minds after Mirerekano won the overwhelming majority of the votes in the Bujumbura constituency.

In these circumstances, the ethnic issue became inextricably enmeshed with constitutional questions. How much power would the Mwami deign to devolve upon the National Assembly? The answer would inevitably affect the power which the Hutu, as a group, could claim for themselves in the political system. The initial response came, not from the Mwami, but from a Hutu official, Gervais Nyangoma, at the time directeur-général in the Prime Minister's Office, in the form of a devastating verbal attack on the regime. On July 1, 1965, the third anniversary of Burundi's independence, Nyangoma delivered a speech at the Rwagasore stadium in which he obliquely but firmly condemned the part played by the palace in creating 'governmental instability, administrative anarchy and political chaos', and suggested that the only solution likely to extricate the country from its mess was to set up 'a new party, a new economy and a new state'.[10] Without ever mentioning the Hutu by name, Nyangoma indicated quite clearly where his sympathies lay: 'The people are sovereign and their sovereignty is exercised by their representatives in the National Assembly, who enact legislation and control the action of the government. The participation of the people is a necessity if we wish to move ahead.' Having just returned to Burundi after several years abroad, first as a student at the Université Libre in Brussels, and then as Burundi's Ambassador to the United Nations, Nyangoma was out of touch not only with the realities of Burundi's political life, but also with one of the basic rules of his national culture—never to be too outspoken in expressing one's feelings. Nyangoma's attitude, one may note in passing, epitomises the paradox of Burundi politics: despite his Hutu origins, Nyangoma's radicalism was shared by a great many Tutsi intellectuals. His sporadic involvement in the activities of the Cercle Patrice Lumumba, a left-wing student organisation based in Brussels, earned him the reputation of a 'left-wing extremist', a label more frequently used to designate the younger Tutsi elites. None the less, while some Tutsi intellectuals openly admitted their sympathies for some of the ideas set forth in Nyangoma's speech, they also expressed great reservations about his ethnic loyalties. Nor were these misgivings totally unfounded: no sooner had Nyangoma arrived in Burundi than a crystallisation of ethnic interests began to take shape. In time, he emerged as the leading personality in a loose-knit coalition of Hutu parliamentarians, trade unionists, civil servants and activists, the latter represented by the Jeunesses Mirerekano— a fledgling youth organisation centred in Muramvya, and named after the Hutu leader Mirerekano, whose home base was Muramvya.

Nyangoma's speech had a bombshell effect in Bujumbura. Informed of the content of his diatribe, the Mwami, who returned soon afterward from one of his frequent visits to Switzerland, issued a heated rejoinder. He told his people that although it was 'not his intention to resuscitate certain obsolete customs', the formula by which the king reigns and rules 'could not be allowed to violate their ancestral traditions, the people having always known, appreciated and respected the supreme authority of their *bami*, exercised under the aegis of *Imana* [God]'. 'On the basis of the time-honoured adage "Ganza Sabwa" ', the Mwami continued, 'and on the basis of your unanimous support, I refuse to subscribe to a subterfuge of language that would deprive me of all control, of all authority, and of all possibilities to extend to you my protection.'[11]

If there were any doubts as to where power really lay, they were quickly dispelled by subsequent events. When, in its opening session on July 19, 1965, the Assembly objected to the creation of a second chamber, on the grounds that the court might use it to weaken the influence of the deputies, the Mwami told the deputies to reconsider their decision under pain of 'draconian measures, as the circumstances might require'.[12] Meanwhile, pending the naming of a government, responsibility for day-to-day administration was entrusted to a famous *ganwa* of the Bezi family and long-time protégé of the court, Léopold Biha. When Mwambutsa refused in August to accept the candidacy of Gervais Nyangoma for the post of Prime Minister, the news came as a shock to many Hutu deputies, and, when their alternative choices were turned down, their consternation gave way to rage. The next-to-last straw came on September 2, 1965, with the issuing of an 'arrêté-loi' that reduced the number of communes from 181 to 78, and transformed the elected burgomasters into mere functionaries appointed by and responsible to the Mwami and his ministers.[13] Not only did the substance of the decree deprive the Hutu of a chance to consolidate their position at the local level (assuming, of course, that the long-awaited communal elections were ever held, which they were not), but the Mwami's method confirmed what many Hutu already suspected—that parliament was to become a rubber stamp. On September 28, 1965, in protest against the arrêté-loi of September 2, a group of Hutu parliamentarians, including the officers of both chambers, addressed a strongly-worded letter to Mwambutsa, in which they reminded him that his initiative was a flagrant violation of the constitution, and therefore that 'they absolutely refused to accept the provisions of the arrêté-loi'. Moreover, they would do 'all that is possible to prevent the election [of communal councillors] according to the procedure of the arrêté-loi'. This letter subsequently served as a death-warrant for its signatories, all of whom were executed during the repression which followed the abortive coup of November 1965.

Meanwhile a number of incidents took place in the countryside which further reinforced the identification of the crown with Tutsi supremacy.

Most of these incidents involved cases of ethnic discrimination by burgomasters. But since these burgomasters held office at the pleasure of the provincial governors, whose decisions in theory required the sanction of the Ministry of the Interior, the taint of racial discrimination inevitably spread to the higher echelons of the administrative hierarchy. A case in point is the imbroglio which occurred in the province of Muramvya, shortly after the legislative elections: in the heat of the electoral campaign, the Hutu populations of Muramvya showed increasing signs of hostility towards certain burgomasters of Tutsi origins. One of these, named Mikobamye, who held office in the commune of Rutegama, became the object of such violent hatred that the local Hutu councillors petitioned the provincial governor, Etienne Miburo, who removed Mikobamye from office. But when the news of Miburo's decision reached Bujumbura, the directeur-général in the Ministry of the Interior, Jean Masabo, responded with a strong reprimand accompanied by strict orders to reinstate the burgomaster.[14] Miburo turned a deaf ear to the instructions of his superior, meanwhile allowing a group of Jeunesses Mirerekano to stage a public manifestation in Muramvya. In the end, Miburo was dismissed from office and the burgomaster reinstated. The incident, undoubtedly not the only one of its kind, illustrates the growing sense of ethnic solidarity discernible between the local and national elites; but it also explains why certain Hutu politicians reacted so bitterly to the decision of the court contained in the arrêté-loi of September 2, 1965: by vesting unfettered control over local affairs in the hands of functionaries, the court raised the spectre of continued Tutsi hegemony at the grass-roots level.*

News of the appointment of Léopold Biha as Prime Minister, on September 13, 1965, and the formation of a government composed of seven Hutu, two Tutsi and one Hima, was a meagre consolation for the Hutu parliamentary leadership. True, the Hutu had a clear majority in the government for the first time since independence; but what did it mean when, in fact, the ministers continued to act at the beck and call of the sovereign and his feudatories? By making a parody of the constitution, the Mwami increased the exasperation of the Hutu, who had already shown an unusually high threshold of tolerance for royal caprice, to a point beyond their endurance.

* According to the original provisions of the arrêté-loi, the burgomaster was to be chosen from among the secrétaires communaux, but, since the vast majority happened to be of Hutu extraction, this stipulation was subsequently eliminated. By December 1965, at least 55 burgomasters out of a total of 78 were of Tutsi extraction.

A COUP THAT FAILED

The explosion came on October 18, 1965, when a group of Hutu army and gendarmerie officers tried unsuccessfully to take over the royal palace, presumably as the first step toward the establishment of a republic. Late that night, the Secretary of State for the Gendarmerie, Antoine Serukwavu, left the suburb of Kamenge with a few jeeps and a score of armed men. Near the palace, he was joined by a small group of para-commandos, most of them Hutu, led by a non-commissioned officer of Hutu extraction named Budaga. Shortly thereafter they met a third group of mutineers, led by a couple of gendarmerie non-commissioned officers, François Rusake and Albert Harimenshi. While these two launched the attack against the palace, one of the Hutu army officers, a certain Banikwa, went back to his barracks, presumably to look for reinforcements.

From then on, things did not go according to plan. After shooting three sentries, the mutineers tried to penetrate the palace, but met unexpected resistance from the Mwami's personal guard. Meanwhile, upon reaching the entrance of the military camp, Banikwa was shot by one of the guards, and thus he and his men never reached the palace. Instead, a reinforcement of loyal troops under Captain Micombero arrived and the mutineers, caught in crossfire, quickly surrendered.

While the fighting was in progress, another group of gendarmes drove to the residence of Prime Minister Biha, summoned him outside and greeted the unsuspecting politician with a volley of bullets fired at point-blank range. The Prime Minister miraculously escaped, though not without suffering serious injuries. At about the same time, the Hutu troops stationed at one of Bujumbura's two main military camps, locally known as 'la base', revolted against their Tutsi officers. Loyal troops did not regain control of the camp until the next morning. By then, the Mwami, apparently panic-stricken, had fled from his palace to seek refuge across the border at Uvira, in the Congo. Only after a preliminary investigation of the situation by a group of white mercenaries in the Armée Nationale Congolaise (ANC) did he agree to return to Bujumbura, and then for only a few days. He left for Europe on November 2, 1965.*

* Compare this version of the events with that offered in an anonymous document printed in Brussels, in English, probably at the request of the Rwanda government: 'In the night of the 18th to the 19th of October the tension [between Hutu and Tutsi] resulted in a military putsch. Racial cases of injustice were also common in the army and the police: most of the soldiers are Hutu while practically all officers are Tutsi. The few Hutu officers are subjected to constant humiliations and persecutions either for racial reasons or because their democratic opinions are not tolerated. Faced with the threat of an outbreak, the

Calm was promptly restored in the capital city, but not in the country-side. Apparently heeding the call of Serukwavu, the coup leader, who had managed to escape to Rwanda unharmed, roving bands of Hutu terror-ists began to attack Tutsi families and set fire to their huts. Most of the troubles took place in the Muramvya province, where the Jeunesses Mirerekano went on the rampage almost immediately after the attempted coup. In the days that followed, at least five hundred Tutsi fell under their blows; about a thousand sought refuge at the Catholic mission at Bukeye, and another five hundred at the Muramvya mission. Similar unrest was reported in other areas, particularly in and around Cibitoke, near the Rwanda border. Though it would be wrong to speak of a mas-sive peasant uprising, the situation was extremely serious.

Whether it was serious enough to justify the brutal retaliation against the Hutu that followed is another matter. In some parts of the country, the repression was carried out by civilian self-defence groups of ten or fifteen 'spears', organised under the supervision of the army, which by then was purged of its Hutu officers. The army reportedly went about its task in a most ruthless fashion, summarily executing scores of inno-cent Hutu. At one point, rumour had it that 'popular tribunals' had been established, but these were probably informal gatherings of army men and local administrators assembled to segregate those Hutu who were to be executed from those who were to be placed in preventive detention. In some areas, however, the repression was carried out with no such procedural refinements. Thus, in Muramvya, a certain Tharcisse

extremist Muhirwa Tutsi group plotted to kill all Hutu officers and under-officers [sic] of the army and police. After having taken control of the army and police the group was to liquidate all civil [sic] Hutu leaders. On 11th of October, soldiers, led by an extremist Tutsi officer, Shibura, tried to kill a Hutu officer on guard, Joseph Banikwa. They failed, however, due to safety measures taken by Colonel Verwaeren, a Belgian officer of the Technical Assistance headquarters. The exasperated Hutu officers then resorted to a desperate move: a military putsch.' See *In Burundi, feudal Tutsi leaders methodically and ferociously exter-minate the elite of the Hutu race*, Brussels, November 18, 1965, mimeo. The reference to the plot allegedly concocted by 'the extremist Muhirwa Tutsi group', and to Shibura's attempt to kill 'a Hutu officer on guard', are pure fabrications. The same applies to 'the safety measures taken by Colonel Ver-waeyen' (and not Verwaeren), at least in the context in which they are presented. It is true, however, that an investigation had been ordered by Verwaeyen shortly before the coup, to dispel rumours that some army officers, presumably Hutu, had had 'mysterious contacts' with politicians after curfew hours. Although the results of the investigations are unknown, reliable sources indicate that a 'conseil disciplinaire' was to be held shortly after the date on which the coup occurred. It may be that the anticipation of possible disciplinary sanctions induced certain army officers to launch the coup before the date for which it had been planned.

417

Ntavyubuha, commissaire d'arrondissement, went trigger-happy and shot nearly every Hutu who crossed his path. His reasoning was simple: 'If they run away', he is reported to have said, 'this means they have a guilty conscience; if they don't, they probably want to attack me.' For his 'loyal services' during the repression, Ntavyubuha was later promoted to the post of provincial governor of Muramvya; from then on, the slightest trace of opposition to his whim was enough to justify immediate imprisonment—or worse. His methods are vividly described in the cable which the director of the prison of Muramvya sent to the Secretary of Justice, in early January 1966, in which Ntavyubuha was said to have personally arrested the judge of the provincial tribunal of Muramvya—'after a scuffle at the café'—and brought him at gunpoint into the prison. When the prison director asked to see the warrant of arrest, Ntavyubuha responded by striking him in public; adding insult to injury, Ntavyubuha then ordered that he be 'put into the black hole' for twenty-four hours. Had the situation not been so tragic in its consequences, one could have detected a further touch of irony in the jailer's protest: 'What are we going to do about this unjust governor? Legal charges must be brought against him.' No one will ever know how many Hutu were killed, the estimates ranging between 2,500 and 5,000. In Muramvya alone, reliable sources give a total of 232 executions between November 7 and 13. On November 14, after a group of Hutu attempted to escape from the local jail, 92 inmates were shot. Conditions inside the prisons were described to this writer by an International Red Cross representative as 'absolutely beyond belief'. In the prison of Muramvya, some 900 people were herded into an area designed to accommodate 90; by January 1966, over a hundred were reported to have died.

Meanwhile, in Bujumbura, after recovering from the initial shock, what was left of the government headed by Biha (shortly thereafter formally 'suspended' on the Mwami's orders) took repressive measures against culprits and suspects alike. On October 21, a 'conseil de guerre' issued thirty-four death sentences against the army personnel involved in the coup; they were executed by a firing squad the same day. Nine gendarmes, including four officers, were executed on October 25. Having dealt with the army and the gendarmerie, the government then turned to the politicians. Virtually every Hutu leader of some standing was apprehended, and ten of them were tried on October 28 before the conseil de guerre and shot. According to a statement issued by the International Commission of Jurists on January 8, 1966, some eighty-six death sentences were handed down by improvised military tribunals, set up under the joint auspices of the army and the Ministry of Justice, and carried out after October 1965.[15] Among the more eminent victims were Gervais Nyangoma, directeur-général in the Prime Minister's Office; Emile Bucumi, President of the National Assembly; Paul Mirerekano, second Vice-President of the National Assembly; Sylvestre Karibwami, President of the Senate; Paul Nibirantiza, President of the Parti du Peuple; Pierre Burarume, former Minister of Economy; Ignace Ndimanya, senator; and Bernard Niyirikana, chef de cabinet in the Ministry of Economy.

Although the share of responsibilities is impossible to establish in any precise fashion, the weight of evidence indicates that the army and the gendarmerie officers were by no means the only ones implicated in the coup. In addition to Antoine Serukwavu, Secretary of State for the Gendarmerie, who certainly played a major role in the planning and the execution of the coup, at least a handful of Hutu politicians and civil servants are believed to have participated—among others, Gervais Nyangoma, Paul Mirerekano and Paul Nibirantiza. Of these, Nyangoma was probably the most deeply and actively involved; in spite of the absence of any conclusive evidence, it is generally assumed that he was the one who initially conceived the idea of a coup against the monarchy. To argue, as an anonymous spokesman of the Rwandese government does, that 'the upheaval was an exclusively military affair', and that 'no civil [sic] political leader, no member of parliament had been informed of the conspiracy, which had been prepared without them and for reasons other than theirs [sic]', seems contrary to all available evidence.[16] Whatever the case may be, one must nevertheless emphasise that a substantial number of those Hutu leaders who were executed had nothing whatsoever to do with the events for which they were held responsible. The need to satisfy an ethnic vengeance, and a fear that anything short of a 'total punishment' might lead to further troubles, are the only explanations for the massive and arbitrary character of the executions—twenty-two of which occurred during the presence in Burundi of the observer sent by the International Commission of Jurists, Dr Philippe Graven. Commenting on the procedure employed by the Burundi authorities, Graven came to the conclusion that 'no responsible body could pass over in silence the executions of all the officers of both houses of parliament of a country and of many of the principal leaders of a racial group without some evidence that justice and legality had not been violated'.

Besides bringing about the physical liquidation of the entire Hutu leadership, one of the most significant consequences of the abortive coup was that it led to the near collapse of the government machine built around the palace. With the Mwami and most of his protégés outside the country, either in refuge or in convalescence, the kingdom was literally without a government. When the Council of Ministers met on November 23, 1965, to consider steps to restore a measure of peace and order, no one seemed to know exactly what to do; their helplessness is nowhere revealed more clearly than in the following exchange:

Minister of Information: I think the population should be better informed of what's going on in Burundi. Foreign radio stations are better informed than we are.

Minister of Economy: But if we tell the people that so and so has been arrested, and so and so has been killed, isn't this going to make matters worse? Information is good; but sometimes it is bad. The Mwami should deliver a long speech and try to reach the minds of the common folk.

Minister of Information: To distribute a document with the signature of the Mwami would be good, but it would be even better to use the radio.

Minister of Economy: There is no authority on the hills any longer. The only people left are the young, between the ages of 16 and 18. The remaining authorities are the provincial governors, the commissaires d'arrondissement and the *bashigantahe.*

Minister of Interior: Before we start distributing these tracts, we must see if we have the necessary credits; for this is going to cost us over 500,000 francs.

Minister of Economy: What we've got to do is get the politicians together and tell them: Now, please, Messieurs!

Minister of Interior: [I disagree] because the solution would not work.

Minister of Information: We must get these brave parliamentarians together and make recommendations to them, in line with His Majesty's counsels.

Minister of Interior: It's absurd to speak of His Majesty's counsels since His Majesty has himself become a target of protest. If we only knew who are the instigators of the revolt, we could meet with them, perhaps in a neutral country. That's the whole point; we must find the core of their organisation and arrange a meeting at some future date in another country.

Minister of Information: But if we can't find the instigators, are we going to let the country go up in flames?

Minister of Social Affairs: If we only knew who are the leaders of the rebellion. That's the whole question.

Minister of National Education: We are really paralysed. People make all kinds of suggestions, and none are retained. I insist on contacting His Majesty to persuade him to issue a statement. Then we can call a 'round table'. We could even release a few inmates for the purpose of the occasion and to limit the damage.

Minister of Economy: I am in favour of a 'round table' discussion, to be held in, say, the Congo.

Minister of Interior: I should like to remind you that the situation in the Congo is different. If we only knew the culprits we could ask them to stop making a shambles of the country, and then open negotiations. What's annoying is that if we quell the rebellion here it will flare up again tomorrow in another place. We must absolutely try to talk to the Mwami.[17]

The Mwami, however, was not only out of reach but utterly out of touch with the realities of the situation. Although on November 20 he had restored the Biha government, which had been temporarily suspended during the emergency, there was really no government to be reinstated, as the army and the bureaucracy had taken the law into their own hands. Since his wounded Prime Minister was physically incapable of discharging his functions, the Mwami at first tried to reign and rule from a distance; but he quickly discovered the shortcomings of government by remote control. Partly for this reason, but mainly because the attractions of power no longer matched the enticements of his European dolce vita, he decided, on March 24, 1966, to issue a royal decree entrust- to Prince Charles Ndizeye, his heir apparent, 'special powers to co-ordinate and control the activities of the government and the secretariats of state'.[18] By then, it was clear that the Mwami did not wish to return. The palace had become a stage-prison too oppressive for his old age, and Bujumbura a town too limited in the scope of its social whirl to satisfy his 'démon de midi'.

Mwambutsa's weakness of character, his rather debonair attitude and lack of interest in the affairs of the realm, doubtlessly facilitated the transition to the military regency inaugurated by the accession of Prince Charles to his father's throne. By the same token, the extreme youth of Charles Ndizeye, at the time a nineteen-year-old boy who had spent most of his adolescent years in Switzerland, also helps to explain his lack of success in trying to play the role of a ruling monarch. Had Mwambutsa been more seriously interested in the destinies of his kingdom, had he been more determined to stay in power, had he shown greater physical and moral courage, he may well have retained his throne. So also, if Charles Ndizeye had not been the teenage prince that he was. As it happened, Mwambutsa's precipitous departure proved a source of great discredit to the monarchy; it also created a political void which invited the emergence of a new set of aspirants on to the political stage.

THE PLAY FOR POWER

In conferring these important responsibilities upon his son, the Mwami did not make it clear whether he intended a de facto abdication from the throne. To all appearances, his heir was being groomed for the succession, and yet the Mwami did not want to abdicate unconditionally. The all-important question of his pension was not settled, and, moreover, certain members of his entourage seemed anything but willing to surrender their traditional claims to authority. In the classic tradition of *ganwa* politics, they began to feel their way around the prince without severing their connections with the old monarch, whom they might need if all else failed. They hoped that, if the succession crisis were settled in favour of the prince, they might secure a fresh entrée into the political arena and thus recapture a measure of influence.

In a manner again reminiscent of the old days, the potential kingmakers did not form a homogeneous group, in terms of age-group or politically, but were themselves subject to divisions and disagreements. There was, on the one hand, the old *ganwa* group, represented by Léopold Biha and Germain Bimpenda, and, on the other, the younger elements, also of the Bezi family, represented by Léon Ndenzako (the Mwami's son-in-law and one-time holder of a chieftainship in Rumonge), Gaspard Nkeshimana (also a former chief, appointed to the Crown Council in 1962 and Minister of Social Affairs in the Bamina government), Henri Kana (Germain Bimpenda's nephew and provincial governor of Gitega) and a few others. The former group would have been content to restore things as they used to be, while the latter had some interest in economic and social modernisation; the former tended to distrust the young 'hotheads' in the army and the civil service, while the latter seemed more willing to get along, if not to go along, with the 'Young Turk' elements. The manoeuvring suggested the cyclical feuds which, in the old days, pitted the young *bami* and members of their entourage against dissident chiefs. The youthfulness of the teenage prince, and his consequent obligations to the 'kingmakers', created a situation ripe for social and political intrigue. His position recalled the state of affairs which Hans Meyer witnessed in 1912, when Mwambutsa's predecessor on the throne, Mutaga, found himself utterly dependent on the princes of the blood. 'Since the present king is a youngster', Meyer wrote, 'approximately 20 years of age, and totally lacking in will-power, he is entirely under the influence of some of his elder brothers, who live in the vicinity [of the royal capital], and who, along with their followers, are the true rulers of Urundi.'[19] In early 1966, the true rulers of Burundi were no longer psychologically committed to the ideal of kingship; their organic relationship with the crown was far more distant, and their bargaining power infinitely greater than that which the *ganwa* once possessed. Strange as it seems, however, the behaviour of the court in 1965-66 reflected little awareness of the changes that had occurred since the days of Mutaga.

Difficult though it may be to identify these 'new men', given the extreme fluidity of the situation engendered by the coup of November 1966, by and large they fell into three categories. The first and most important group was the young army officers who, however ruthlessly, managed to restore a semblance of order to the kingdom. Although the overwhelming majority are of Tutsi origins, Captain Micombero, as already noted, is of mixed origins—a factor which may help to explain his meteoric rise to power. Another group was made up of those junior civil servants who served as directeurs-généraux in various ministries before and after the coup. Like the army men, they carried heavy responsibilities during the troubled times which followed the rebellion; like them, they are extremely young and for the most part of Tutsi extraction. Finally, there are the youth leaders. They too are notable for their tender years and ethnic homogeneity, yet they stand as a group apart, because of their pronounced radicalism and because their ideology is typically structured along 'mobilisation' lines. Their radical outlook undoubtedly influenced the attitude of the army officers, and, because their organisational base had been in existence for a longer time than that of either the army or the bureaucracy, and showed none of the traces of the disruption which plagued the party, they could make available to the regime the organisational infrastructure and skills it needed to consolidate its rule.

In this mixed group of army men, bureaucrats and activists, something of a consensus began to emerge in early 1966. It dawned on them that they were operating a government where none had existed before. They came to realise that they were no longer dependent on the royal whim; if anything, the reverse was becoming true.

The inertia of the crown was made manifest during the repression which followed the coup. The Mwami made no attempt to use his authority to restrain abuses, to exhort the population to calm and obedience, to initiate steps to restore peace and order; not until early 1966 did he decide to delegate part of his authority to his son. By then, however, power had already passed into the hands of the new elites.

423

That they did intend to use it independently of the court was demonstrated by the decision of the Foreign Ministry, in December 1965, to order the recall of the American ambassador, Donal Dumont: on January 9, 1966, the US State Department was apprised of the news by way of an air mail letter, posted from Bujumbura, which said that 'rightly or wrongly' the ambassador was suspected of having had contacts with, and provided assistance to, the instigators of the coup. While most commentators were understandably shocked, or amused, by the unconventional character of the procedure, a more important point to note is that the Mwami would almost certainly have vetoed the decision had he been in a position to do so. How little authority was left to him was further shown by the decision of the government to reinstate the JNR, in open defiance of his instructions. Banned by the court in January 1965—presumably because of the implication of some of its leaders in the assassination of Prime Minister Ngendadumwe—the JNR was brought back within the pale of legality less than a year later; and when the Mwami questioned the initiative of the government, in a cable sent from Geneva in early 1966, the latter's reply came like a rap over the knuckles: 'Misinformed regarding JNR objectives. Stop. Consider your cabled message null and void.'

Not only did they feel themselves emancipated from the tutelage of the court; they were under strong pressure to move even further away from it. The pressures emanated principally from UNEBA and the JNR. Their criticisms of the regime found an outlet in the recurrent diatribes penned by Gilles Bimazubute in the pages of *Remarques Africaines*, which by then seemed like the official mouthpiece of UNEBA. At first, Bimazubute's polemics were directed against specific aspects of the court's policies, then against specific personalities in the entourage of the Mwami, and finally against the Mwami himself. In October 1965, Bimazubute lamented: 'One wonders for how long the [Biha] government will preside over the destinies of the country. No doubt, for as long as it will be the pleasure of the king. The Mwami's decision to reign and rule, according to the age-old formula "Ganza Sabwa", cannot justify this move back into the past.'[20] By November, the tone had become more biting: 'I accuse! . . . principally UPRONA and its leaders. . . . I accuse secondarily the state and the government. . . . When will you decide that the time has come to give us something else besides demagogy? Independence? Why, certainly we have it, but precious little else. Of course, we have citizen status, but we are hungry, for we are still human beings.'[21] A month later, speaking on behalf of 'the millions of citizens, abandoned to their fate', 'the intellectuals, bullied by their elders who claim to be more deserving', and 'the young . . . who are no longer naive enough to balance their interests against those of a crown that has become ever more tarnished', Bimazubute openly identified the goals of the October rebellion with the aspirations of UNEBA: 'Let there be no mistake—*we* are the rebels.'[22]

Predictably, the local UNEBA leadership did not remain long unresponsive to these cues. Echoes of Bimazubute's taunts were found in the placards held by student demonstrators during the important public manifestation staged by the Bujumbura section of UNEBA on January 20, 1966: 'A bas les gastronomes, vous vous saoûlez du sang du peuple!'; 'A bas le gouvernement impopulaire!'; 'Genève n'est pas Bujumbura!'; 'A bas les courtisans!'; 'A bas les vieux cupides!', etc. The significance of the demonstration was clearly seen by Bimazubute when he wrote: 'For the second time since October 19, 1965, the citizens have dared bring into the picture the man who is responsible for, and the main beneficiary of, the state of crisis in which Burundi has lived for the last three years. They have told the king that he is not infallible and had made mistakes. . . . One thing is sure: a new feeling, a deep aspiration towards a rejuvenation and a restoration of the state, has been brought to light.'[23] Similar feelings and aspirations were discernible in the lengthy tract released on February 2, 1966, which said: 'The general physiognomy of the Biha government reveals the worst governmental team the country has ever known. The Biha team must be revoked. In it are found accomplices of the coup d'état of October 19, 1965 . . . valets of the Belgian trusteeship, unremitting foes of national independence.' There followed some typical characterisations: 'Biha: The prototype of reaction, the enemy of independence, vomited by the people, more mindful of the interests of his Bezi clan than of the interests of the nation, mentally short-sighted, semi-illiterate. . . . Ngowenbusa: Insouciant bourgeois, naively jovial. . . . Masumbuko: Doubtful morality, intrigant of the worse kind, opportunist. . . . Muhakwanke: Weighs heavily on the shoulders of the taxpayer . . .'[24] For the first time since the abortive coup, a powerful movement of opinion against the monarchy was beginning to make its voice heard: the voice of rebellion against established privileges, traditional sinecures and royal caprice; the voice of youth and, more specifically, of Tutsi youth.

Perhaps the most damaging blow ever dealt by UNEBA against the monarchy came in March 1966, in a tract which reproduced in toto a personal letter from Germain Bimpenda, Grand Marshal of the court, mailed from Switzerland to his younger *ganwa* friend, the worldly-wise Joseph Mbazumutima, then in charge of administering the Banque du Royaume. Bimpenda hinted at a 'family plan' designed to bring the Bezi back into the saddle. 'The moment has now come to jump into the fray', said the letter, 'for this is our last chance.' Which prompted the authors of the tract to describe the regime as 'a rotten monarchy . . . preoccupied only with advancing the interests of its own clan, the Bezi. . . . We demand that the Mwami's abdication become official; we demand a young and dynamic head of state capable of bringing to Burundi the era of peace and prosperity to which we aspire.'

Youth and dynamism Prince Charles could claim, but his investiture as head of the state, on July 8, 1966, certainly did not satisfy all of the 'kingmakers'. This at least is what can be inferred from some of the passages in Bimpenda's letter. Because of the light it sheds on the manoeuvrings and conflicts of interests which went on behind the scenes, it deserves to be quoted at some length:

Our plan, with Biha, is to disperse [the young upstarts] in all sectors. We do have some young elements on our side, but we must get to know them, and sift them out. . . . Others are plotting against us. They are afraid of the Hutu, but they are the ones who are responsible for this situation, whether they like it or not. . . . If they are honest, the Tutsi must recognise that we have never encouraged ethnic animosities. The Bezi have always been looked upon with a favourable eye by the local populations because they have never tried to generate conflicts of this kind among their subjects. Of this, Muhirwa cannot boast. He is our public enemy No. 1, for he always tried to get us into trouble. As far as I am concerned, Muhirwa is the great Pharisee of our times. . . . As I told the Mwami, we must go back to our system, as it existed before independence, when we used it against Schmidt and Co. The Baranyanka family was stronger and more intelligent than ours, because of all the support they got from the trust authorities, but with my father's plan, that we suggested to Rwagasore, we scored a victory which later turned to the advantage of the Tutsi-Hima and Muhirwa. Subsequently, whenever a government was to be formed, I always had to intervene on behalf of our family. . . . I hear that the prince will soon receive a triumphal welcome in Bujumbura, and that he will be forced into forming a new government, against the will of his father, and that he will be proclaimed king. The prince is proud of all this. Those who are the spearhead of the movement are well-known: Masumbuko, etc. Those who push him into this deal are not the friends of the monarchy. They are trying to deceive him, so as to set up a republic thereafter. We have tried to warn the prince of the devious manoeuvres of this bunch; but, personally, I think he has already gone too far, and, besides, he has a thirst for power. . . . Also, look into the diamond business; Mr Israel is worried about it.

The Hima and others are pushing this business to the point where the boy can no longer resist the lure of money. We are worried about all this. . . . I must also warn you that Nkeshimana has been chosen to replace me temporarily at the court. Nyankiye and Léon Ndenzako are suspect. . . . This is what I wanted to tell you. Biha and I have worked a lot. He wants to safeguard the interests of our family. He no longer has the ideas that we suspected him once of entertaining. I am waiting for your answer. Give my regards to everyone.

Insofar as it acknowledges the determining role which he and his acolytes played before and after independence, though unfortunately not with all desirable precision, Bimpenda's letter is a document of great historical significance; and, insofar as it hints at possible future developments, one cannot fail to note its prophetic ring. But the letter is also significant for the light it throws on the divisions which had begun to appear among both the actual and potential holders of power. It is clear, for example, that some entertained serious doubts as to the usefulness of maintaining a monarchical form of government, while others were not nearly as committed to republican ideas. That Bimpenda had sufficient trust in Mbazumutima to make him his confidant—together with the fact that the content of the letter was divulged through an indiscretion and not by the recipient—suggests that the court could still count on the support of a few of the younger *ganwa*. At the same time, however, some of these younger elements were busy ingratiating themselves with the prince. Nor were they the only ones gravitating around the prince, and those who lacked the family ties necessary to obtain the favours of the future Mwami were now approaching him with gifts. Hence Bimpenda's reference to 'the diamond business', which involved the illegal sale of diamonds smuggled in from the Congo and sold under the cover of a 'certificate of origins' granted by the court. From what one can infer from the letter, it also involved the 'good offices' of a well-known local middleman, named Israel, presumably helped in this venture by Simonian's connections in Switzerland. Now that Mwambutsa had left the country, and could no longer get his share of the proceeds, the diamond business had fallen into the hands of 'the Hima and others', and among them no one was better placed than Rémy Nsengyumva, Minister of Economic Affairs, to use this traffic for political ends.

In retaining the symbols of kingship and calling upon the prince to become the new Mwami, the 'kingmakers' had an essentially preventive motive—to avoid a flare-up in the countryside, and perhaps also to win over the allegiance of the elders (*bashigantahe*), who, along with the provincial governors and the commissaires d'arrondissements, formed the armature of the local administration. In a more positive sense, they also hoped to redefine the monarchy in a way that would permit the effective mobilisation of the masses. Although some may have foreseen certain difficulties from the court, for the time being at least the advantages of maintaining the monarchy seemed to outweigh the liabilities of a republic. Subsequent events showed this to be little more than wishful thinking.

NTARE'S INTERREGNUM

The seemingly endless manoeuvrings triggered off by the abortive coup of October 1965 culminated, on July 8, 1966, with the proclamation of a new head of state, followed by the announcement that a 'new era' had finally dawned. On that day, Prince Charles told his people over the radio that, in order to bring to an end 'four years of chaos and anarchy, of nepotism and corruption', in order to 'bring about a revaluation of the Murundi personality in the context of a continuous and harmonious economic development', he had decided to take over the destinies of the kingdom.[25] Consequently, he said, Prime Minister Biha and his government were dismissed, and the constitution suspended. The next day, he called upon Captain Micombero to form a new government, and, on July 12, Prime Minister Micombero presented the members of his cabinet to the king.

The mixed reactions which followed Prince Charles's initiative testified to the momentous changes expected by friends and foes alike. On July 9, while throngs of people publicly manifested their enthusiasm for the new regime in the streets of Bujumbura, apparently moved by an irrepressible wave of popular sympathy for the young prince, Mwambutsa voiced his sharp disapproval of what he termed 'an usurpation of power'. His scorn was made explicit in a statement issued by Germain Bimpenda from Geneva, which said that 'he [Mwambutsa] had warned the prince against certain intriguing politicians [who had] decided to deceive his youthfulness and profit from his inexperience', and that he still 'considered himself the Mwami of Burundi'.[26] Undaunted, the prince let it be known on the same day that he, and he alone, had assumed the position of head of state, and that he rejected categorically the message of his father 'who claimed to contest his rights in this matter'. On September 1, 1966, to allay all possible doubts as to his intentions, he allowed himself to be formally proclaimed Mwami of Burundi under the dynastic name of Ntare III.

The coronation ceremonies were held in the ancient capital of Muramvya, before an estimated crowd of 100,000, in an atmosphere of religious awe. Some 40,000 eucalyptus trees were felled to erect triumphal arches along the road taken by the royal cortège, and it was with the royal spear in hand, and coiffed with the traditional beaded headdress, that Charles Ndizeye took the oath of office that promoted him to the dignity of Mwami. Yet, for all the traditional regalia summoned for the occasion, and indeed despite the reassertion of monarchic legitimacy implied by the spectacular coronation rites, the social and political climate of September 1966 was without parallel in the annals of the Burundi monarchy. Never before had the country experienced such a pervasive atmosphere of social stress, not even during the tumultuous days preceding independence. Never before had the youth of Burundi been so vulnerable to the appeals of revolutionary change, and so deeply committed to the forces of progress and political reform. Somewhat incongruously, Ntare's accession to the throne seemed to encourage belief in the sanctity of monarchic institutions at a time when anti-monarchic sentiment had seemed to have gathered an almost unprecedented momentum.

The subsequent strong reactions against Ntare by the same men who, on September 1, with great fanfare, had proclaimed him Mwami of Burundi, was in part the product of false and excessive expectations. The 'kingmakers' were not prepared to cope with a ruling monarch; and the king was not willing to be cast in the role of a ceremonial cipher. As it became apparent that the attitude of the crown was patently out of tune with the reformist zeal of the army and the bureaucracy, and its policies so basically at odds with those of the government that the latter would probably find itself perpetually stymied by the palace, the stage was set for a major test of strength: either the government would yield to the court, or the court to the government.

The government which came to power on July 12, 1966, represented a fairly accurate cross-section of the 'new elites' already described. The army was represented by Captain Micombero, who combined the functions of Prime Minister and Minister of Defence, and three other officers: Captain Martin Burasekuye, Captain Damien Nkoripfa, and First Lieutenant Sylvère Sota, who controlled, respectively, the Ministries of Postal Services and Telecommunications, Security, and Public Works. Agriculture and Social Affairs went to Anicet Njangwa and Prime Nyongabo, two prominent JNR personalities. The portfolio of National Education was given to Jean Chrysostome Mbandyabona, erstwhile president of the Bujumbura section of UNEBA, while the Ministry of Foreign Affairs went to the dapper and enigmatic Pie Musumbuko, who had been Minister of Health in a previous government. Significantly, a kind of liaison was established with the palace through secretariats of state for Diplomatic and for Economic Affairs, entrusted, respectively, to Léon Ndenzako and Rémy Nsengyumva. And, as before, the prince could count on the service of a Grand Marshal of the court, in the person of Gaspard Nkeshimana, who had held the job under Mwambutsa.

The personality of Ntare—his very youth and apparent dynamism—seemed wholly in keeping with the new regime, and a ubiquitous slogan —'for the new era, new men'—evoked the promise of a brighter future. For the time being, the tension between the government and the palace was concealed by enthusiasm for the change.

On July 20, the government had held a mass meeting at the Rwagasore stadium, attended by numerous officials, scores of JNR sections from every part of the country and a few detachments from the army and the gendarmerie. Royal drummers and dancers added a touch of traditional pageantry, somehow belied by the placards the JNR displayed as they marched into the stadium: 'Vive le gouvernement populaire!'; 'C'est Micombero que nous attendions!'; and 'Yankee go home!' When the king's dancers had performed their act, it was Micombero's turn to perform his. In a lengthy declaration read before a mesmerised audience, he outlined a programme which indicated that indeed a new era had dawned. In a typically Rousseauist vein, he proclaimed: 'The finality of the state is the general interest! The state is the instrument through which the collectivity, using all the means at its disposal, attains the objectives it has assigned to itself; the state organises society, power, the administration, men, and things, in such a way that the means of production are harmoniously combined to bear the maximum of fruit against a minimum of suffering, deprivation, pain and effort.'[27] He called for discipline: 'Of course, planning implies constraints from above . . . men and things must bow to this and mobilise themselves accordingly.' But planning, he said, also implies a dialogue: 'In order for the plan to be executed it must bathe in an atmosphere of mobilisation. . . . This implies a dialogue between peasant and minister, governor and minister, between Barundi and other Africans, between Europeans and Africans. . . . This dialogue must go on within the framework of mass organisations, such as UPRONA, youth organisations, unions of workers and peasants. . . . In our minds, the mass organisations will play the role of a vanguard, to make us aware of our real contradictions, of our real problems, and of our solutions.'[28]

A rather different kind of dialogue must have occurred among the new power elites in the weeks that followed—one that made them aware of their 'real contradictions' sooner than they had expected. The nature of these contradictions is best understood in the light of the answers they gave to three basic questions. How radical a revolution should the new regime seek to carry out? How should it go about it? And how much power should the palace retain vis-à-vis the government?

From the beginning, there was disagreement on the kinds of sanctions, if any, to be taken against persons who, in one capacity or another, had been associated with the old regime. On this point, the more intransigent voices seem to have drowned the moderates. In August, Henri Kana and Léopold Biha were arrested, and all who had been appointed minister of state under the previous regime lost their titles. Two of the more prominent figures affected by this measure were Albin Nyamoya and André Muhirwa, both of whom had been prime ministers under Mwambutsa, but whose reputations at the time were certainly not of moderation. Subsequently, half-a-dozen influential personalities—including Pierre Ngunzu, Minister of Education in the Muhirwa government, Mathieu Muhakwanke, Minister of Economy in the Biha government, and Apollinaire Sineremera, Vice-President of the first National Assembly —were placed under arrest. All were released within forty-eight hours, however, after the intervention of the court. This fact alone was enough to remind the government that, as long as the role of the crown in the political system remained undefined, the other issues would probably remain unresolved.

Nonetheless, the question of restructuring the institutions of the state could no longer be postponed, and thus, on October 7, 1966, the Council of Ministers met to discuss 'the delicate, complex, but fundamental problem of mass movements—parties, youth groups and trade unions'.[29] The Council of Ministers, 'heeding the wise counsels of Jean Jaurès who said that a multi-party system is not a sign of democracy and freedom but a symptom of the contradictions inherent in a society divided into conflicting classes and interests, gave its unanimous support to the idea of a general integration of the masses within the framework of the same revolutionary action'.[30] While a general consensus seems to have favoured the government's ultimate decision to divest the JNR of its party functions and regenerate UPRONA within a single party system, the choice must have antagonised important personalities within and outside the government. For, in choosing UPRONA as the single-party instrument, the incumbents, though acting on a sound principle, made a grievous error: UPRONA could offer them little real support since the party had long since ceased to be effective, and they risked alienating some of their initial supporters in the JNR. At any rate, a 21-member commission was eventually set up to 'endow the party with a well-structured charter, so as to permit the effective organisation of the masses, officered by a politically conscious elite', for 'the party is the number one fundamental option, and its charter must stipulate the options that will lead the people on to the path of progress'.[31]

Whatever ill-feelings the decision may have created within the ruling junta were initially blunted by the incipient struggle between the crown and the government. By mid-August, tensions were already apparent between the 'prince's men', represented by Léon Ndenzako and Rémy Nsengyumva, and the government. Ndenzako and Nsengyumva believed they were treated as nonentities by the government and denied their proper role in policymaking. The situation suddenly worsened on September 11, when the head of the FTB, Antoine Ntamagara, organised a meeting at the football stadium, at which he was reported to have said: 'Let the people's enemies—Ndenzako, Nsengyumva and Muhirwa— have their heads chopped off, and their bodies thrown to the dogs.' On the very same day—and possibly in response to a tract written in Kirundi accusing the Minister of External Affairs, Pie Masumbuko, of 'opportunism, corruption and theft'—the Mwami entered the struggle by attempting to force Masumbuko's resignation. During the night of September 11 to 12, rumours of an impending coup spread through Bujumbura. Micombero, still undecided, was not to be found anywhere. From all appearances, if the coup failed to materialise at this particular juncture, it is because Captain Rusiga, assistant commander-in-chief of the Burundi National Army, refused to comply with the orders of the more radical politicians that he lead his troops against the king, presumably because he was unwilling to run the risk of a mutiny. Nonetheless, the pressures against the court steadily mounted. On the morning of September 12, a tract of an extreme violence circulated in Bujumbura, demanding the physical liquidation of Ndenzako, Nsengyumva and Muhirwa, and causing a crowd of 10,000 to gather at the stadium to watch the executions. By noon, the crowd had disbanded, thoroughly disappointed.

As the tug-of-war between the government and the court seemed to approach a stalemate, the contestants agreed to negotiate. In a compromise reached on September 16, Masumbuko agreed to exchange portfolios with the Minister of Social Affairs, Prime Nyongabo. But this was only a temporary lull. Next, the Mwami, seeking always to be one jump ahead of the government, created three new secretariats of state, for the Army, Gendarmerie and Justice, which of course involved a transfer of jurisdiction from the government to the palace. The demoted Minister of Justice retaliated by having the three newly appointed secretaries of state arrested and thrown in jail.

There followed a period of relative calm, during which the adversaries cautiously eyed each other as they awaited a propitious occasion for

checkmate. The Mwami thought this moment had come with the departure to Addis Ababa of Burundi's delegation to the OAU heads of state
conference. In the evening of November 7, accompanied by one bodyguard and a Belgian gendarme, he went to the radio station with
the intention of broadcasting a royal decree suspending or dissolving
the government. The guard on the radio station refused to let him
in. The Mwami insisted, but withdrew when the troops raised their
rifles.

Three weeks later, the army seized its opportunity and brought the
game to a close. The Mwami journeyed to Congo-Kinshasa, as President
Mobutu's guest at the first anniversary celebrations of Mobutu's military
takeover. He learned by radio that, in his absence, the army had deposed
him and proclaimed the republic by way of a military coup similar to
that which he happened to be celebrating. Captain Micombero added
a warning to the Mwami that he would be treated 'like a common
criminal' should he return to Burundi.

Mwami Ntare and his men—or should the order read Ntare's men
and the Mwami?—apparently fell prey to a series of miscalculations. They
miscalculated their chances of winning against the combined strength of
the army and the bureaucracy. They miscalculated the amount of support they could reasonably expect from the masses. Above all, they overlooked the determination of the army to strike at monarchical institutions once these appeared to have outlived their usefulness. A more
fundamental explanation is that which is suggested by Machiavelli's
advice to another prince:

> I do not wish to omit a reminder to princes who have secured a brand
> new state by means of the favour of persons within it. They should
> consider well what causes moved those who favoured the change to
> do so. If it is not natural affection for the new ruler, but merely
> discontent with the government as it was, a prince will succeed in
> keeping them as his friends only with effort and great difficulty,
> because it is impossible for him to satisfy them. And if he will examine
> the cause of this . . . he will see that it is much easier to gain the
> friendship of the men who had been contented with the earlier govern-
> ment, and therefore were his enemies, than to gain that of those who
> became his friends and favoured his occupation merely because they
> were not contented.[32]

Whether Charles Ndizeye ever came across this counsel of prudence is
highly dubious; but he must have drawn a similar lesson from his own
unfortunate experience of Burundi politics. While 'securing a brand
new state by means of the favour of persons within it', he conspicuously

433

failed to 'consider what cause moved those men who favoured the change to do so'.

The men who had seized power in July 1966 were actuated by a variety of motives, but none was stronger than their aversion to monarchic absolutism. Not only did they seek to destroy the vested interests built around the court; they also wished to restore a wide measure of autonomy to the government, so as to breathe a new life into the political institutions of the realm and inaugurate 'a new era'. The populist flavour of their ideological commitments, their dedication to social progress and economic prosperity, the emphasis placed on political mobilisation and their consequent refusal to acknowledge differences between individuals —these were the motives and aspirations which Ntare failed to take into account. By refusing to adjust himself to the expectations of those who had brought him upon the throne, Ntare committed political suicide.

Nonetheless, the protracted nature of the struggle suggests a greater ambivalence of motives than might be inferred from the foregoing. Or else how can one explain the apparent reluctance of the new elites to set up a republic on July 8, 1966, when they initially took the destinies of the country into their hands, and their visible lack of such scruples only a few months later? Why, in other words, did Micombero bother to recognise Prince Charles as the legitimate heir to the monarchy, if he was to dethrone him ninety days later? Part of the explanation has already been mentioned: in retaining the outward symbols of kingship, the 'kingmakers' tried to gain the best of both worlds—they tried to combine the legitimacy of monarchic institutions with the élan of a mobilisation system, and hoped to redefine the role of the crown in a way that would facilitate political mobilisation. Only after discovering the shortcomings of this hybrid polity did they decide to abolish the monarchy.

In addition, attention must be drawn to the variety of views and differences of political orientation within the ruling junta. At one end of the political spectrum were the representatives of the JNR and UNEBA, by far the most radical in outlook and the least predisposed to put up with the royal whim; at the other extreme stood the younger *ganwa* elements, like Léon Ndenzako and Gaspard Nkeshimana, who shared a strong psychological commitment to the monarchy, and whose position in the political system depended on the continued existence of a monarchic form of government. Between these two extremes stood the army men, whose threshold of intervention seemed to oscillate back and forth between those of the radicals and the conservatives. The pivotal figure in this situation was Captain Micombero, who stood as an umpire, in a way re-enacting the balancing role of the crown.

To understand why the army should have had serious hesitations before eventually resorting to such drastic political surgery, another factor has yet to be considered: the army was not in a position where it could at any time purely and simply seize power and enforce its will on sectional interests by force alone. Besides finding himself politically captive of the Tutsi elites who hatched the conspiracy against Mwambutsa, Micombero also had to reckon with the presence of certain paramilitary organisations over which he had little control. One such organisation was the JNR, whose membership by September 1966 was said to have reached some 10,000, which in itself testified to the increasingly important role it was destined to play in the new polity. Another source of paramilitary support available to the politicians was the Rwandese refugee militia, including a 500-strong, battle-tested group of Rwandese *inyenzi* led by a Peking-trained Tutsi named Joseph Mudandi.* In this situation, Micombero had to tread warily. Had he tried to prematurely oppose the objectives of the more radical Tutsi politicians by transforming the army into a court of ultimate appeal to adjudicate the conflict between the government and the crown, he may well have precipitated a civil war between the armed forces and the combined strengths of the JNR and the Tutsi refugees, and perhaps between Hutu and Tutsi elements within the army.

Eventually, however, this is precisely the role which the army was called upon to play. The elimination of the Hutu faction from the political scene released a violent struggle for power between radical and conservative Tutsi politicians, between republicans and monarchists, and in this struggle the army played a determining role. It took a gamble, and won. But the question remains whether the alignment of the armed forces with the more radical elements in society is only a transitory phenomenon, dictated by reasons of opportunism, or whether it can lead to a permanent civil-military partnership.

* This group, better known as 'the Red Battalion', came into the country from the north-western border of the Congo, in late 1965, presumably at the request of certain Tutsi personalities in the Ministry of Foreign Affairs. See supra, chapter 15, p. 388n.

17. The Army at the Helm

AGAINST THE BACKDROP of the self-generating convulsions triggered off by the coup of October 1965, the overthrow of the Burundi monarchy seems to fit the melancholy pattern of political decomposition seen elsewhere in Africa. In view of the economic and political discontents that have agitated Burundi since independence, one might assume that Micombero responded to the same kinds of forces that led to army coups in, say, Upper Volta, Dahomey and Congo-Kinshasa: in all these countries, the attractiveness of military rule increased in proportion to popular dissatisfaction with the civil order. This assumption is, however, only partially true, and, unless an effort is made at the outset to clarify what actually constitutes the 'civil order', the analogy with other African states is likely to lead to a dangerously distorted view.

There are several possible definitions of the 'civil order', and at least as many types of 'civil order' as there are conceivable orders of political culture.* For the purpose of this discussion, however, the expression may conveniently be taken to refer to two different levels or types of political legitimacy—to the broad constitutional norms (in the Aristotel-

---

* One might indeed be inclined to regard civil order and political culture as two sides of the same coin, and, on this basis, to formulate a range of possible modes and levels of military intervention similar to that suggested by S.E. Finer in his discussion of 'mature', 'developed', 'low' and 'minimal' political cultures, using as key variables the degree of '[popular] attachment to, and involvement in, the institutions of the regime'. But if there is enough evidence in support of Finer's contention that 'the levels to which the military press their intervention are related to the levels of political culture of the society', the categories employed are far too general to be of any use for the investigation of individual African cases—a point implicit in Harvey Glickman's observation that 'Finer eschews distinctions among regions in regimes of "low political culture", all of which are vulnerable to military intervention'. See S.E. Finer, *The Man on Horseback*, Pall Mall Press, London 1962, p. 86 ff; cf. Harvey Glickman, "The Military in African Politics: A Bibliographic Essay", *African Forum*, Vol. II, No. 1, Summer 1966, p. 72. This said, Finer's work stands out as a pioneering contribution to our understanding of military politics in general; my own indebtedness to Finer's analysis is made plain by the concepts used in this chapter, including those which appear in the typology below. But as the article by Harvey Glickman shows, a serious comparative study of the role of military interventions in Africa has yet to be written; his is the best introduction to the bibliographical sources so far available on the role of the military in African politics.

436

ian sense) within which a government operates, or the institutions of government associated with civilian rule. As should by now be clear, the distinction between monarchical and governmental legitimacy is no less essential to an appreciation of the role played by the Burundi army after October 1965 than it is to an understanding of civilian politics in the preceding years. Just as the tug-of-war between monarchical and governmental institutions stands out as the dominant feature of Burundi politics until the proclamation of the republic, this duality of political structures has also set the key parameters within which military interventions have occurred.

The first thing to note is that the division of authority between the court and the government offered a wider range of possible levels of intervention than would normally be conceivable, had power been exclusively concentrated in one or the other. It is worth reminding ourselves in this connection that the curtailment of civilian rule did not, strictly speaking, coincide with the abolition of the monarchy. Rather it was part of a succession crisis that had been in the making since October 1965. Viewed in the perspective of the tortuous sequence of events triggered by the mutiny of Hutu gendarmerie and army officers, the republican coup of November 1966 appears as the completion of a partial army take-over begun on July 8, 1966, when the new Mwami acceded to the throne under the protection of a rather odd assortment of army officers and politicians, and then appointed one of these officers, Captain Micombero, as Prime Minister in a mixed government of officers and civilians. Only when the liabilities arising from the continued opposition of the court to the ruling group appeared to outweigh the advantages of retaining the formal trappings of the monarchy did the army officers turn against the regime they were hired to defend.

The seemingly irreconcilable roles played by the army during and after the abortive coup of October 1965 point to yet another anomaly in the Burundi situation. When the army first intervened, immediately after the abortive coup, it was to protect the monarchy against a Hutu conspiracy; but the army's ultimate move, a little over a year later, aimed at protecting a predominantly Tutsi government against what was interpreted as a monarchic conspiracy. The anomaly lies not only in the apparent contradiction in the attitude of the officers' corps but in the ultimate outcome of military intervention. For if there is any plausibility to the notion that 'in proto-dynastic societies, i.e. societies where allegiance is owed to the monarchy . . ., any military intervention would be exercised in the name of the dynasty—as it was in the revolt of the Ethiopian Imperial Guard in 1960',[1] the case of Burundi points to a rather different state of affairs. Although monarchic legitimacy did

437

serve, for a while, as a deterrent against military intervention, or as a means of limiting the extent of such intervention, in the end the mere existence of monarchical rule did not prevent the army from turning against the crown. A monarchy's capacity to resist military intervention is contingent upon the degree of legitimacy it can claim for itself, and where the familiar symbols of monarchical legitimacy no longer command the allegiance of the military-civilian elites, the likelihood of army rule increases accordingly.

A third point, implicit in the foregoing, is that military interventions in Burundi have taken different forms at different times, and in the series of coups, successful or abortive, that have punctuated the country's recent evolution one can discern a variety of motives, reflecting the varying ethnic interests and aspirations of the instigating groups as well as their changing position in the political system. As shown by the typology in Table 17.1, Burundi has thus far experienced three distinctive types of military interventions, each resulting in a different combination of military-civilian relationships. First, there was an *abortive coup*, on October 18, 1965, triggered by a mutiny of Hutu army and gendar-

Table 17.1. Typology of Military Interventions in Burundi, 1965–66*

1 : Date	2 : Origins	3 : Target	4 : Character	5 : Outcome
Oct. 18, 1965	Hutu army and gendarmerie officers	King and monarchy	Abortive coup	Limited, indirect military rule
July 8, 1966	Predominantly Tutsi army officers and politicians	King and government	Dynastic-governmental coup	Dual civilian-military rule
Nov. 28, 1966	Predominantly Tutsi army officers	King and monarchy	Revolution-ary coup	Direct military rule, quasi-civilianised

* The characterisations employed under heading No. 5 (referring to variable modes of civilian-military relationships) are borrowed from S.E. Finer, *The Man on Horseback*, op. cit., p. 165 ff; likewise, the distinction made under heading No. 4 between 'dynastic-governmental' and 'revolutionary' coups is adapted from Samuel Huntington's essay, "Patterns of Violence in World Politics", in Samuel Huntington ed., *Changing Patterns of Military Politics*, The Free Press, Glencoe, 1962, p. 32. For further clarification of these concepts, see below p. 446.

merie officers against the monarchy, and resulting in a situation where the 'loyalist' faction (i.e. primarily Tutsi) of the military, though not formally in power, in fact exercised considerable influence behind the scenes. Second, there was a *dynastic-governmental coup*, on July 8, 1966, instigated by a temporary coalition of Tutsi army officers and politicians, which brought a new king to the throne and a new government to office but left the constitutional framework virtually untouched; moreover, the army was invested with a formal political role it did not previously possess. Third, there was a *revolutionary coup*, accompanied by 'post-coup efforts to make basic social and economic changes and to alter the underlying distribution of power within the political system by eliminating or subordinating some groups and adding or strengthening others'.[2] This led to the proclamation of a republic, on November 28, 1966, and the emergence of a governmental structure approximating a situation of 'direct military rule, quasi-civilianised'.[3]

Besides highlighting the sui generis character of the Burundi case, the preceding sketch may provide a convenient frame of reference in seeking tentative answers to three major questions around which this chapter is constructed. What were the motives for military intervention? What types of civil-military relationships have developed in the wake of military interventions? To what extent have the army men the means and ability to live up to the revolutionary ideals they have officially set for themselves?

THE MOTIVES FOR INTERVENTION

On November 28, 1966, at 7.00 PM, while the army was in the very act of seizing power, Captain Micombero explained over the radio the motives which prompted him to strike against the monarchy:

> When in 1961 the Barundi people followed the footsteps of Prince Louis Rwagasore to claim their independence, it was with a view to securing a higher standard of living, and better opportunities for individual self-realisation in the context of a harmonious and continued economic development. Alas! as was said on July 8, 1966, the disappearance of the prince ushered in a long crisis of authority. . . . The so-called head of state, with the complicity of his governments, installed a regime aiming at the systematic exploitation of the masses. And that king, Mwambutsa, instead of staying among his people who ceaselessly clamoured for his presence, chose to leave the country, for the sake of his own selfish interest. Instead of trying to promote national unity, he embarked, at the instigation of a group of intrigants,

439

upon a policy of 'divide and rule' which led to the loss of numerous human lives. Instead of placing our national resources and the financial aid of friendly countries at the service of the common good, he preferred to use them for the exclusive satisfaction of his personal needs. It is to this crisis of authority, to this regime of corruption and nepotism, that the Barundi people said 'No!', on July 8, 1966. In his declaration of July 8, 1966, Prince Ndizeye took a solemn engagement over the radio to bring to an end this revolting situation, no matter how high the cost. . . . My government, in full awareness of the responsibilities entrusted to it by the people and the head of state, immediately set about the task of promoting national reconstruction and reconciliation. It immediately began to fight all forms of social injustice and particularly nepotism and corruption; but instead of being encouraged in this task by the head of state, the latter proved incapable of breaking with the precedents of the ancien régime. On several occasions, he tried to re-enact his father's policies. Like his father, each time a government was brought to power, he joined the ranks of the opposition. On September 11, 1966, he tried to dismantle the government by dismissing the Minister of Foreign Affairs; two days later he tried to further weaken the government by appointing independent secretaries of state. Far from assisting the authorities in their efforts to seize the conspirators, he set himself up as their defender and gave them asylum in the royal palace. . . . On several occasions he tried to instigate a mutiny in the ranks of the armed forces. Pursuing his policy of high treason in connivance with his father, he then proceeded to recruit foreign mercenaries, thus endangering the lives of our valiant soldiers. . . . People of Burundi, our fatherland is betrayed! The army is dishonoured! Mwambutsa and Ntare have sullied our honour and that of our ancestors! Fighting brothers, the time for the great struggle has come! Army officers, soldiers and corporals, do not abandon the noble cause which is yours to defend![4]

From this virulent indictment of the monarchy emerges a familiar theme. The army intervened because of its obligation to discharge a 'sacred trust', that of 'defending the independence and liberty of the people' against the devious manoeuvrings of a regime ensconced in 'corruption and nepotism'. As the supreme custodian and sole judge of the national interest, the army had a moral obligation to rid the country of its feudal parasites. Confronted with repeated attempts on the part of 'intrigants and courtiers' to sacrifice the 'common good' to their own personal interests, with a monarch who time and again demonstrated his blissful indifference to the welfare of his people and whose meddlesome dispositions were abundantly shared by his teenaged successor, the army had no choice but to move in and 'clean up the mess'.

The trouble with this plea is that it leaves a number of crucial questions unanswered. If the army was all along so deeply conscious of its role as custodian of national interest, why did it have to wait until October 1965 to assert itself as a significant political force, and then, curiously enough, as a pro-monarchical force? How can one reconcile Micombero's vitriolic attacks on the monarchy in November 1966 with his earlier decision to scotch an anti-monarchic coup? Even if we assume that the army was by then already aware of the need to end the reign of corruption and nepotism perpetuated by Mwambutsa's rule, why did it have to wait another thirteen months before it finally decided to overthrow the monarchy?

Whether the role of the army in Burundi politics can at all be explained in terms of its pre-existing commitment to a definable conception of the national interest is indeed very dubious. As noted earlier, one of the characteristics of the Burundi army (and of African armies in general) has been its relative immunity to the ferment of political life, its tendency to avert a commitment for or against either one of the two major ethnic protagonists: in short, its sense of professionalism. In theory, of course, as Samuel Huntington reminds us, professionalism implies a corporate loyalty to the virtues of technocracy and a corresponding devotion to the principle of civilian supremacy; in these conditions, the army becomes the servant of the state rather than the instrument of special interests.[5] In practice, however, the ethics of professionalism may have radically different consequences, for it may be that the only way the soldiers can be kept out of politics is for the army to engage in politics. As William Foltz perceptively emphasised, 'it may happen that the only way serious and conscientious officers can protect the integrity of the military against political pressures is for themselves to become actively engaged in politics; one of the classic reasons for the overthrow of a civilian regime by the army is precisely that the civilians tried to induce the army to become involved in politics'.[6] Burundi is a case in point. When the army first intervened, it was to thwart a conspiracy of factious officers, presumably acting at the instigation of Hutu politicians; similarly, if we are to give any credence to Micombero's testimony, his ultimate decision to strike against the monarchy was precipitated by Ntare's attempt to 'instigate a mutiny in the ranks of the armed forces'. Following a kind of dialectical process, the levels at which the army intervened in civilian life shifted according

441

to the source of attempted civilian interference with the armed forces, to the point where even the monarchy had to yield to the military.

To this general explanation, at least two qualifications must be added. First, the army may not have become actively involved in politics in the first place unless it had already shown some evidence of vulnerability to outside political pressures. Far from being a monolithic entity, socially and ethnically undifferentiated, the Burundi army, like most other African armies, contains within its ranks a variety of factions, clans, and ethnic interests, all of which have contributed to shape the political leanings of its men as well as their responsiveness to the political environment. To argue that the army intervened in spite of itself, as it were, to preserve its integrity in the face of continued political pressures, overlooks a key element in the background of most military interventions: the propensity to intervene increases in proportion to the degree of vulnerability of sectional interests within the armed forces to such pressures.

Second, no matter how sincere the military community may have been at the beginning in its avowed opposition to intervention, once the army becomes involved in politics its ethos of public service takes on a different coloration. Its functions are no longer solely the maintenance of law and order but the creation of new laws for the sake of a new order. At this point, the army tends to become invested with a political role of its own. Simultaneously, the bases of conflict tend to move away from the realm of civilian-military relationships to the more narrow sphere of intra-military politics.

Of all the factors that have made the Burundi army potentially vulnerable to the incitements of civilian politics, none has been and continues to be of greater importance than the presence in its midst of different ethnic interests. No matter how high their consciousness of themselves as members of a profession, the army officers are just as aware of their own cultural identity as members of a specific ethnic group. In these conditions, one may wonder whether the vicious spiral of ethnic strife which destroyed the party and drove the army to fill the vacuum will not have similarly disintegrating effects within the military community.

This point will be returned to later in this chapter. Suffice it to note for the time being that ethnic motivations within the army have expressed themselves with varying degrees of intensity, depending on the ethnic and educational background of the individuals involved and the exigencies of the political conjuncture. It is not enough here to acknowledge the greater vulnerability to political pressures of 'pure' Hutu or Tutsi officers as contrasted with the more ambiguous posture of those of mixed or *ganwa* origins. Ambiguity and indecision have also been characteristic features of the behaviour of certain Hutu and Tutsi officers, albeit for different reasons. Insofar as they had any inclination to intervene, their tendency has been to subordinate their moves to their own estimate of the threats posed to their respective ethnic interests by the political conjuncture. It is not by pure coincidence, for example, that the abortive coup of October 1965, staged by Hutu officers, took place at a time when the policies of the court had never been so flagrantly detrimental to the interests of Hutu parliamentarians; nor is it by accident that the co-operative links subsequently established between Tutsi officers and civil servants were never so strong as when they were suddenly confronted with the threat of an impending Hutu revolt in the countryside.

If the incidence of ethnic motivations increased in proportion with the saliency of ethnic competition in civilian life, with the temporary elimination of Hutu elements from the political scene, ethnic feelings gave way to a different set of motivations. As noted earlier, one of the unintended consequences of the abortive coup of October 1965 was to shift the focus of conflict away from Hutu-Tutsi relations to the plane of political, dynastic and regional rivalries within the Tutsi caste. Concurrently, the increasingly active participation of the army in the political life of the country meant that the attitude of the military would inevitably tend to reflect these incipient divisions and stresses within the Tutsi oligarchy. Thus, from October 1965 to July 1966, the preoccupations of the army officers veered away from the plane of ethnic politics to that of dynastic politics. This is what led to the installation of a new government and a new dynasty in July 1966, both of which seemed to mirror the political and generational affinities of a new group of reformist Tutsi officers and civil servants. The 'honeymoon', however, did not last very long; no sooner had the prince taken his oath of office than new conflicts developed among those who had initially supported the coup. On the one hand, an increasingly tense situation developed between the army and the crown, culminating in November 1966 with the overthrow of the monarchy; on the other hand, the expansion of the military into the sphere of civilian politics bred fresh grievances among the more radical Tutsi politicians, and before long they found themselves at odds with, and ultimately at the mercy of, the military.

As can be seen from its temporary dickering with the monarchists and its subsequent alliance with the 'Young Turk' elements of the Tutsi faction, the army has not always been unresponsive to sectional interests; in recent times, however, its corporate awareness of itself as an institution has come to the fore as an increasingly powerful motive for intervention. As long as the army understood its role to be that of a docile and primarily decorative instrument in the hands of the monarchy, its tendency was to align itself with the Establishment; but, when circumstances required that the army transform itself into a coercive apparatus, its relationships with the crown underwent a radical alteration. Not only was the army forced into the unenviable position of having to suppress an incipient revolt, and this largely as a result of the ineptitude of the court's policies; in addition, the state of near-paralysis created by Mwambutsa's flight to Europe, coupled with his subsequent decision to recruit West German mercenaries for the establishment of some sort of personal militia, were powerful inducements for the military if not as yet to abolish the monarchy at least to lend their support to the civilians to bring a new dynasty to the throne. By then, however, the army had become a major participant in the government. While this in itself might have been enough for the army to develop a political consciousness of its own, its tendency to assert itself as an autonomous force was further reinforced by Ntare's renewed attempts to hire foreign mercenaries, and subsequently, as we shall see, by the efforts of the more radical Tutsi politicians within the government and the administration to re-establish diplomatic relations with Communist China. After finding itself structurally and ideologically at odds with the monarchy, the army eventually turned against those very elements whose support it had initially courted.

To bring some sort of conceptual order to what might otherwise seem a hopelessly confusing situation, we should remind ourselves of the analogy suggested by Samuel Huntington in his discussion of military politics, and look upon this sequence of coups and counter-coups as the functional equivalents of party-electoral competition: 'In and of themselves, coups, like elections, strongly resemble each other. Coup is distinguished from coup not by the technique by which power is seized but by the nature of the groups that seize it and the uses they make of it.'[7] Viewed in this light, the motives for military intervention are inextricably bound up with the interests of the groups instigating the coup, and, in the case of an abortive coup, of those who carry out the repression. Thus the abortive coup of October 1965 signalled the defeat of the Hutu as an active political force and the triumph of the Tutsi faction; the dynastic-governmental coup of July 1966 confirmed the decline of the old Bezi aristocracy and the emergence on the political scene of a new leadership of Tutsi politicians and army men, categorically opposed to the claims of the previous dynasty and its government; finally, the revolutionary coup of November 1966—comparable to what Huntington would call, after V. O. Key, a 'critical election', in that it seemed to presage a fundamental change in the structure of the political system—eliminated once and for all the monarchists, irrespective of their dynastic allegiances, and further consolidated the position of the army in government. With the proclamation of a republic, the army emerged as the central source of power and legitimacy, the main sponsor of revolutionary change, and the key symbol of national unity.

This is not to imply that the army no longer needs the support of the civilians; only that, after having been used by the civilians for their own purpose, it is now the army's turn to use civilians to legitimise its rule. Nor does it imply the elimination of internal conflict and intrigue; in fact the continued reliance of the military on civilian elites has been the source of renewed frictions within the army as well as between army men and civilians. Yet there is no longer any doubt in anybody's mind as to where power really lies, and, if the recent trend is any index, the next step will probably be in the direction of a further restriction of the area of civilian autonomy.

EVOLVING PATTERN OF CIVILIAN-MILITARY RELATIONSHIPS: THE QUEST FOR A MODUS VIVENDI

Broadly speaking, Burundi politics since October 1965 might be compared to a game of changing partnerships between army officers and civilians, with the former quickly asserting themselves as the dominant partner. The closest parallel to this situation is that offered by Iraq from 1936 to 1961, when 'a loose group of politicians rent by rivalries confronted a loose group of ambitious officers. From time to time, a clique of politicians would link hands with a clique of officers and thereby get themselves installed in office. Then another clique from each side would momentarily combine to oust the first combination, and so forth.'[8] In the case of Burundi, however, the military clique of Captain Micombero remained a permanent fixture of each successive political combination after November 1965, the only noticeable changes being those affecting the composition of the civilian participation and its relationship to the army.

The direction of change in civil-military relationships is perhaps best understood by analogy with the changing relationship between the crown and the government in the period preceding the October 1965 coup. We have seen how, through a pattern of challenge and response, the position of the crown in the political system gradually shifted from that of an umpire to that of an active participant, to the point of virtually eliminating all traces of governmental autonomy. A somewhat similar phenomenon can be detected in the gradual invasion of the civilian

445

sphere by the military, culminating in the displacement and ultimately the partial supplanting of civilian authorities.

The operation was conducted in three stages. The first, lasting approximately from October 1965 to July 1966, saw the emergence of the army as the main domestic prop of civilian authorities. Indeed, the 'prophylactic' role played by the army during the repression, together with the judicial and administrative responsibilities devolved upon it by the collapse of governmental authority, gave the military a considerable measure of initiative. What seems to have developed during this period can best be described as a state of intermittent military intervention under the cloak of a fictitious government, a situation in many ways reminiscent of that described by S. E. Finer under the rubric of 'limited, indirect military rule'.[9] After the dynastic-governmental coup of July 6, 1966, with the army's assumption of formal governmental responsibilities alongside the civilians, came the second stage. A new kind of military-civilian tandem emerged, sharing the characteristics of a 'dual polity': 'Such a regime rests on two pillars. The army is one and the civilian party or some organised civilian opinion is the other, and the ruling oligarchy or the despot is the head of both.'[10] The system did not remain static, however; it was during this period that a fundamental change of relationships occurred, first between the army and the crown, and at a later stage between the military and civilian members of government. When Ntare took office, under the aegis of the army, the army was being used as a 'shield' by the supporters of the new dynasty to protect the investiture and maintenance on the throne of their candidate. By November 1966, however, the relationship had been reversed, and it was the army's turn to assert its control over the civilians. Thus with the proclamation of the republic, on November 28, 1966, a third stage was initiated which saw a very rapid transformation of the system in the direction of military autocracy. Although the regime retained some of its civilian trappings, the army clearly stood at the centre of the political system. The party and other civilian ancillary organisations formed the panoply that gave an aura of legitimacy to army rule, yet the dominant characteristic of the system, again to borrow S. E. Finer's terms, was its 'dependence on, or rather its emanation from, the ruling junta', a situation he goes on to describe as 'direct military rule, quasi-civilianised'.

But if government, as before, came from above, and if the military carried out the functions previously assumed by the monarchy in the same autocratic fashion, the instrumentalities were no longer the same. Unlike the monarchy, whose tactics consisted in playing one group off against the other without ever really trying to alter the machinery of the state (except for a very brief interval, in early 1965), the army's explicit commitment to revolution expressed itself through a series of sweeping institutional changes. Some of the previous structures—like the National Assembly—have been formally dismantled; others— like the party—have been remodelled; and new ones have been erected to help the regime consolidate its rule. A new façade has been substituted for the old one, which enables the army to cloak its rule in a new kind of civilian legitimacy. But, in spite of its civilian shell, the regime remains, in essence, a military regime.

The predominance of the army in civilian life is attested by the extent of military penetration of the central and provincial administration; by the growing subservience of the government to the armed forces, as personified by Micombero; and by the latter's determination to bring the party and its ancillary organisations firmly under his control. In the new pattern of control, ultimate authority at first rested with the National Revolutionary Council (NRC). Set up as a provisional organ pending the formation of a new government, the NRC consisted of twelve members, all army officers, with Micombero acting as chairman. Until its dissolution in early 1968, the NRC functioned as a supreme advisory body. All nominations to the upper echelons of the administration—including the appointment of army officers as provincial governors—in the end depended upon the collective will of its members. Although the boundaries of its jurisdiction were never clearly delineated, so far as one could tell the scope of its authority was constitutionally unlimited. The reality of the military component is further evidenced by the several key positions simultaneously held by Micombero. As Chairman of the NRC, President of the Republic and President of UPRONA, he provides the crucial link between the army on the one hand and the party and the government on the other. In his dual capacity as head of the state and head of the government, he places the army in direct control of the executive branch of government, a control further reinforced by his decision to bring the Ministry of National Defence and the Civil Service (to which, for a while, was added the Ministry of Foreign Affairs) directly under the purview of the presidency. In addition, several key ministries have at one time or another been entrusted to members of the NRC; although, by late 1967, only one ministry remained in the hands of a NRC member, this apparent demilitarisation should not be mistaken for a sign of political emancipation. Professor Cart's observation (to the present author) that 'the government seems relegated more and more to the role of an administrator and executor of the decisions taken by the NRC and the National Committee of the

UPRONA' aptly sums up the role of cabinet members in the months immediately following Micombero's coup.

The dependence of the government upon the army is paralleled by a similar relationship between the army and the party. As self-appointed President of UPRONA, Micombero has made clear his intention to assume the leadership of the new order; equally plain is that, by converting the party into a base for the military, he has taken away what little autonomy it previously had. The domestication of party activities began immediately after the proclamation of the republic, with the appointment by the NRC of an electoral commission to which were provisionally entrusted the prerogatives of the national committee of UPRONA. But here again the provisional has given way to what seems a permanent arrangement. The long-awaited elections of party organs were postponed sine die, with the electoral commission meanwhile serving as permanent directing committee, and the provincial governors as the provincial heads of the party. In an effort to further reinforce its control, the army for a while entrusted the management of party affairs to a special Minister in charge of Party Affairs, a post for a time held by Jean Ntiruhama, formerly Minister of the Interior in the Muhirwa government and whose loyalty to the junta was said to be surpassed only by his hatred of the JNR, the now-defunct youth wing of UPRONA.

As if the appointment of Ntiruhama to this post did not constitute a sufficient guarantee against a possible resurgence of the *jeunesses* as an autonomous political force, the JNR and the UNEBA were both dissolved. A new youth movement was created on February 3, 1967, labelled Jeunesses Révolutionnaires Rwagasore (JRR). Though much of its membership comprises former affiliates of the JNR and UNEBA, the directing organs of the JRR, like those of UPRONA, have passed to those known for their presumed loyalty to the regime. The same holds true of the Union des Travailleurs du Burundi (UTB), founded in March 1967 to serve as a single national trade union, and of the Union des Femmes du Burundi (UFB), a women's organisation in charge of promoting what is officially referred to as 'animation féminine'. There has been in short, a restructuring from above, but as yet little effort has been made to seek a genuine civilian endorsement of these new political structures. The substance of power unmistakably rests with the army.

Ironically, though intended to create a semblance of civilian legitimacy, a major consequence of this institutional revamping has been to arouse civilian opposition on a scale which made it necessary for the army to further consolidate its grip over the system. In part, the roots of the opposition lie in the structural inconsistencies arising from the circumstances under which the army came to power. When Ntare was brought to the throne, in July 1966, the army served as an instrument in the hands of the civilians; and, while Micombero did emerge as the central figure in the new government, a number of Tutsi politicians of varying ideological stripe came to power under the aegis of the military. Few, however, were prepared to surrender their prerogatives to the army. We have seen how, immediately after the installation of the new dynasty, Ntare and his supporters vainly tried to free themselves of the limitations imposed upon them by the army, and how, in the end, the destruction of the royalist opposition led to the downfall of the monarchy. At this point, the opposition moved from 'right' to 'left'. The elimination of the royalist opposition cleared the way for the republican opposition from the 'left', and before long it was the turn of the young radicals to challenge the army's monopoly of key governmental posts as well as its policies.

The opposition leaders can be easily identified. They are mostly of Tutsi or Hima extraction; many come from the province of Bururi, in the south-west, which is also the area of origin of a substantial number of army officers; partly for this reason, most of them acceded to office after the coup of July 1966. More important still, they belong to a narrow circle of intellectuals, or jeunesses-turned-politicians, whose record of involvement in the affairs of the JNR and UNEBA is matched, as one might have expected, by a strong commitment to the ideas of radicalism and revolutionary socialism. Summing up the attitude of his confrères before the army moved in, one former UNEBA member retrospectively noted, half-wistfully: 'Taking their desires for realities, and placing greater trust in their hopes than in an objective analysis of the situation, they all along went on the assumption that the regime that would replace the monarchy would be highly progressive, indeed socialist. . . .'

Given these ideological leanings, the rise of a radical opposition must be viewed as the direct result of the measures taken by the junta to solidify its rule. The issues around which the opposition crystallised itself were essentially three. By far the most divisive, within and outside the government, centres upon the character of the methods used by Micombero to reorganise the party. The parachuting from above of all party cadres at all levels of the hierarchy, including those in charge of ancillary organisations; the abolition of the JNR and UNEBA, once regarded by their members as the only repositories of revolutionary fervour, together with the ban on all UNEBA-sponsored activities abroad; and the persistent refusal to allow the replacement of provisional party structures by permanent, popularly-elected organs—such, in brief, are the sins of omission and commission of which the junta is found guilty. The extenuating circumstances invoked by the Minister in charge of Party

Affairs, on February 26, 1967, to the effect that 'the prompt and efficient installation of new political structures was deemed incompatible with electoral manoeuvres and the waste of time this would inevitably entail',[11] did little to absolve the army in the eyes of the radicals; rather the contrary, for, coming from a man like Ntiruhama, the argument had a peculiarly hollow ring. As one intellectual lamented, characteristically: 'Who are those elements parachuted into office by the government? Unless party leaders are elected by the people, they cannot validly express the people's will and aspirations. They cannot link themselves to the masses and elicit the creative enthusiasm that is needed.'[12]

The appointment of Ntiruhama to the post of Minister in charge of Party Affairs lies at the heart of another issue that bears directly upon the question of the opposition. It was received as nothing short of an insult by former JNR militants and UNEBA intellectuals, a reaction which the following statement by a former UNEBA member helps to explain: '[Ntiruhama] is as much a subject of fear as of controversy—of controversy because he is accused of clericalism by the revolutionaries, of fear because of his firmness and authority.'[13] Although Ntiruhama did keep close and amicable ties with the Catholic Church, having once served as the personal secretary of Mgr Grauls, the Bishop of Gitega, these connections were not nearly as objectionable as his previous anti-JNR record. Many of the sanctions taken against the JNR leaders after the Kamenge incidents, back in 1962, were initiated and authorised by Ntiruhama himself during his brief term of office as Minister of the Interior in the Muhirwa government; this, coupled with his unambiguously pro-Western attitude were sufficient reasons for the radicals—some of whom had suffered imprisonment at the hands of the man with whom they were now asked to collaborate—to look upon his re-entry into the government as proof of the regime's 'reactionary leanings'. Not only was Micombero's handling of party affairs ominously reminiscent of the ways of the ancien régime, but the trust that he temporarily placed in certain personalities seemed to confirm radical suspicions that the government was still captive of Mwambutsa's men.

For further evidence of 'reactionary' tendencies, the radicals could also point to the generally pro-Western character of Micombero's foreign policy commitments, and in particular to his persistent refusal to re-establish diplomatic relations with Peking. Thus, once again, the issue of diplomatic recognition of Communist China intruded itself at the centre of the stage, driving ever deeper the wedge between the army and the civilians. Like Mwambutsa a year or so earlier, Micombero firmly rejected all propositions of diplomatic rapprochement with Communist China; unlike Mwambutsa, however, he did not retreat into an attitude of passive retrenchment. After eliminating the remnants of the royalist faction, Micombero proceeded in early 1967 to systematically rid the government and the administration of the more troublesome of his civilian collaborators.

This civilian opposition to army rule manifested itself in a number of different ways. As early as February 1967, anonymous tracts were circulating in Bujumbura which bitterly attacked the regime for its lack of revolutionary ardour, intimating that nothing positive had been accomplished since the army had seized power and that its stated devotion to the cause of the revolution was little more than a clever manoeuvre to hoodwink the population. Another irritant was injected into this already tense situation when, a few days later, Gilles Bimazubute, the brilliant UNEBA spokesman, whose promotion to the rank of secretary-general to the Presidency on January 17, 1967, had in no way diminished his sympathies for left-wing ideologies, announced his intention of holding a press conference to define the government's position on the recognition of Communist China. Bimazubute failed to realise that, in view of the previous record of Communist China's intervention in the country's domestic affairs, the army had every reason to view this attempted move towards a diplomatic rapprochement as a stratagem to undermine its power and prestige; moreover, the possibility that Communist China might again be in a position to make political capital out of the refugee problem and trigger off a new series of border incidents was enough to bring forth a veto from Micombero. As might have been foreseen, the conference was called off at the last minute.

Undaunted, the radicals none the less insisted on forcing their diplomatic options upon the regime. On March 5, a North Korean delegation headed by the Vice-President of the People's Republic of North Korea arrived in Bujumbura for a ten-day official visit which had been secretly arranged beforehand by Prime Nyongabo, once a notable JNR figure and now holding the post of Minister of Foreign Affairs. Faced with a fait accompli, Micombero had little alternative but to bow to his minister's decision. By then, however, the strain between Micombero and the 'Young Turks' was more than he could bear. On March 13, a major reshuffling of the cabinet took place, accompanied by the dismissal of three familiar figures of the radical Tutsi faction: Prime Nyongabo, Gilles Bimazubute and Zénon Nicayenzi. While Nyongabo purely and simply lost his job as Minister of Foreign Affairs, Bimazubute was appointed to the post of directeur-général in the Ministry of Information, which he held until his incarceration on May 6, 1967; the third man, Nicayenzi, was sacked from the Ministry of Planning and Co-ordination (which he had hoped to convert into a key ministry) and sent back to his previous sinecure as vice-rector of the Université Officielle of Bujumbura. Simultaneously, with the transfer of the departments of Technical Co-operation and Civil Service to the presidency, there occurred a further centralisation of power around the presidential throne.

Opposition from the 'left' persisted, however, and by mid-April an extremely violent tract appeared in Bujumbura; among other things the authors of the tract claimed that 'the revolution has completely swung over to the right, to the profit of the Catholic clergy and Belgo-American neo-colonialism, thanks to the efforts of the perfidious intrigant, old Jean Ntiruhama, product of the ancien régime, congenital lackey of the Church, and champion of nepotism. . . . For this ignoble character nothing but capital punishment will do. . . . Furthermore, one must deplore the treasonable dealings, lack of ideology and general incompetence of the NRC.' A few days later, on April 19, a special ordinance was drafted by the Ministry of Justice, presumably at the request of the Minister of the Interior, which, had it been carried out, would have resulted in the imprisonment of half-a-dozen of the radically-minded Tutsi politicians. The reasons which apparently prompted Micombero to withhold approval of the ordinance are unclear; but, from the subsequent turn of events, one is led to assume that he was merely looking for a convenient pretext to justify his projected move. He did not have to wait long. On May 5, late at night, a violent scuffle reportedly took place in the so-called OCAF quarter of Bujumbura between members of a local section of the JRR loyal to Micombero and various and sundry politicians of extremist leanings. Altogether, about forty people were involved in what had initially begun as a bar-room brawl. Before the army had time to intervene, at least four of the participants were seriously injured and three of the JRR jeeps badly damaged.

Although the hypothesis of a deliberate provocation by 'loyalist' JRR elements is not to be excluded (especially if one considers the precedent of 'strategic violence' established by the JNR), there is no concrete evidence that this had been the case. The result, in any event, would have been the same. No sooner had the news of the incident reached Micombero's ears than five of the more turbulent left-wing civilian personalities were arrested on presidential orders and sent to jail, including Gilles Bimazubute and Prime Nyongabo; among the lesser casualties were Augustin Nkengurutse, substitut du procureur, Adolphe Binagana, in charge of the Department of Internal Revenue, in the Ministry of Finance, and a certain Kanyoni, at one time mayor of Bujumbura. Significantly enough, this time the purge penetrated the ranks of the army, though admittedly not with the same severity, and on May 6 a special presidential decree retired Major Albert Shibura of his command of the armed forces and dismissed him from the vice-presidency of the NRC; after being demoted to the rank of second lieutenant, Shibura was subsequently discharged from the army and appointed directeur-général in the Ministry of Finance. Another army officer, Sylvère Sota—a member of the NRC and at the time Minister of Public Works—and the Minister of Justice, Artémon Simbananiye, were also implicated; both were to be dismissed from office but subsequently managed to earn their rehabilitation by pleading their innocence to Micombero.

That certain elements of the armed forces happened to be involved in what Micombero later described as 'the foolish attempt of a small group of irresponsible personalities, acting with the complicity of the administration and the magistrature, to seize control of the republic', would seem to indicate a partial commitment of the military to the radical ideas of some of the civilians. While this may be partly true, the mere presence of political or ideological affinities between army men and politicians is not a sufficient explanation. However flimsy the evidence available, regional and kinship ties must have played a contributory part in sensitising certain army officers to the views of the civilians. Whether or not there is any substance to the rumour circulating at the time that Micombero acted to foil an impending counter-coup hatched by members of the Abasapfu clan is difficult to say; it is interesting to note, however, that three of the leading personalities affected by the purge—Nyongabo, Bimazubute and Shibura—are members of the Abasapfu clan; that it is possible to extract from the history and origins of the Abasapfu a tentative explanation for the anti-monarchical dispositions of its descendants and, by implication, for their uneasiness in the face of a resurgence of monarchical forms of government in the guise of republicanism; and, finally, that all three originate from Bururi, fief of the Abasapfu.*

* Father M. Rodegem gives the following interesting account of the origins of the Abasapfu: 'Tutsi of high-ranking status. They initially came from a Hima clan. But, for some reason which traditions have failed to ascertain, the king one day decided that they should all be exterminated. He entrusted this task to the Abongera clan, who made a clean sweep of the Abasapfu cattle, plundered their crops, set fire to their kraals and killed whoever stood in their way. One of the few survivors was a small boy, who had found refuge behind a reed screen. After the raiders had left, he was discovered by some passersby, who decided to take him to King Ntare. The latter kept him at his court under his protection and called him Musapfu to commemorate his adventure.' M. Rodegem, *Onomastique Rundi*, Bujumbura 1965, mimeo, p. 155. I am grateful to Professor Henri-Philippe Cart for drawing my attention to this source.

This said, it is as well to bear in mind that whatever kinship or regional ties may have existed among the conspirators—assuming this is the appropriate word to use in this context—have operated in conjunction with a variety of other factors, rooted in solidarities of a different order. To the close parental relationship—of the kind associated with the modern, nuclear family—existing between some of the key personalities involved,* one must add, so far as the civilians are concerned, the continuing strength of political affinities resulting from their previous record of militancy in the ranks of the JNR; the network of personal contacts established in the years preceding and following independence; and the profound sense of dismay and personal frustration experienced by the more radically-minded opposition leaders in the face of a regime increasingly committed to the virtues of technocracy, which many among the younger generations regard as the hallmark of political conservatism.

The aversion of the military for left-wing elements became even more manifest in the summer and autumn of 1967. As if the recent purge had not sufficiently narrowed the field for the opposition, a series of sackings and arrests took place, culminating in November 1967 with the formation of an almost entirely new cabinet. The first to join the inmates of the Rumonge prison was François Bangemu, a well-known JNR zealot, at the time directeur-général in the Ministry in charge of Party Affairs; then came the turn of Pie Masumbuko, arrested on July 6 on charges of seeking contacts with Congolese rebels and plotting against the regime. Next to fall from grace was Augustin Ntamagara, former leader of the FTB; on October 25, Ntamagara was politely invited to trade his post of secretary-general of the newly-formed UTB for the still more innocuous position of secretary in charge of External Affairs in the same trade union. A similar fate befell his sister, Léocadie Singirankabo, 'pasionaria manquée' of the Micomberist revolution, when asked three days later to surrender her post of president of the UFB. Finally, on November 4, A. Yulu and Artémon Simbananiye, respectively director of the Office des Cultures Industrielles du Burundi (OCIBU) and Minister of Justice, were both arrested on presidential orders and sent to Rumonge. According to reliable sources, Yulu is said to have appropriated for himself some 17 million Burundi francs from the receipts of the OCIBU, and, to supplement this 'cut', to have used the funds of the Sûreté Nationale for personal ends. The most plausible explanation for the sacking of Simbananiye is that it was part of Micombero's policy of placating the Hutu community, so as to soothe the wounds left by the events of 1965 and at the same time ward off possible

---

* To cite but one example, Sota and Simbananiye are first cousins once removed; similar ties are said to exist between Nyongabo and Simbananiye.

accusations of ethnic favouritism. Having taken upon himself a large share of the responsibility for the execution and jailings of Hutu leaders in 1965, and known for having done so, Simbananiye was the ideal expiatory victim. Disarming the opposition from above, therefore, is not only an end in itself but a means to other ends.

From the composition of the new cabinet, appointed on November 14, 1967, one reaches a somewhat similar conclusion. The weeding out of all actual or potential left-wing opponents from cabinet posts also meant the elimination of the most ferociously anti-Hutu elements (people like Simbananiye, for example, and Sota, to whom one might add the names of Shibura and Yulu). While the ratio of Hutu to Tutsi cabinet members remained fairly even (with five Hutu, five Tutsi and two of mixed or *ganwa* origins), the new team was predominantly 'technocratic' in character. Particularly significant in this respect was the abolition of the Ministry in charge of Party Affairs and the transfer of Ntiruhama to the Ministry of Telecommunications, a move which not only confirms the trend noted above but suggests an attempt to neutralise criticisms from the 'left'.

Reviewing the process as a whole, one may discern more clearly the nature of the analogy drawn earlier between the army and the monarchy. Just as the palace consistently tried to root out all forms of opposition, by alternately clamping down on Hutu and Tutsi, the army seemed determined to destroy all bases of resistance to its rule. The army's attempt at self-preservation was mainly at the expense of radical Tutsi elements, because the latter have thus far put up the most stubborn, though in the end unavailing, resistance; but this in itself does not make the Hutu, or for that matter the more conservatively-minded Tutsi or Hima elements, immune to the sanctions of the military. Similarly, the attitude of ethnic neutrality adopted by the army in the allocation of cabinet posts is but a re-enactment of the game of 'ethnic arithmetic' previously pursued by the monarchy. Now as before, parity of ethnic representation in the government remains a cardinal principle of Micombero's policy. By virtue of his mixed origins, however, Micombero has extended this principle to a pinnacle for which there is no precedent. Finally, and this is perhaps even more true of the army than of the monarchy, the emasculation of governmental powers reached the point where the army stood as the only significant source of authority in the political system. The army, like the crown, became the sole interpreter of what political legitimacy meant; yet, unlike the crown, and for as long as Micombero retains control over the guns, the army can force its own interpretation of political legitimacy upon the government and the population at large. Unlike the crown, the army can afford an air of complacency: 'No one need worry, the army is keeping watch.'[14]

The Army: New Caste or Revolutionary Force?

Army rule operates in an environment thoroughly saturated by its own revolutionary mythology. Along with the emphasis on what might be regarded as typically military virtues—efficiency, discipline, work, etc.—every effort is made to impart to the regime an air of revolutionary respectability. The official atmosphere is aptly summed up by the title of the party newspaper, *Unité et Révolution*, meaning in effect 'Unity *through* Revolution'; from all appearances, the theme of revolution is being used to exorcise actual or imaginary threats of civilian revolution. The least that can be said even at this early stage is that the revolution has promised more than it can possibly deliver. Not only is the regime committed to a fundamental restructuring of the state machinery; its ultimate aim is the restructuring of man himself: 'We want to create and give to the world a new type of revolutionary whose character traits will fit the motto of our party, a man for whom the notions of Unity, Work and Progress are fundamental.'[15]

So vague, in fact, is the content of 'Micombérisme' that it often sounds like a hodge-podge of empty formulas; nonetheless, stripped of its rhetoric, four basic themes have struggled to emerge from the obscurities of the ideology. One such theme is that of the 'permanent revolution'—a ubiquitous slogan designed to speed up the revolutionary momentum initiated by the army take-over of November 1966 and widen its social bases. According to the party newspaper, 'the Revolution never ends—our struggle must never end'. In a style reminiscent of Sékou Touré, the junta makes no bones of its determination to get rid of the 'essouflés' and punish the 'nocifs': 'To have been a revolutionary yesterday is not enough; one must also be one today, and remain one tomorrow.'[16] Presumably, only at this price can the revolution subjugate the forces of 'reaction, ambition and revisionism'. Secondly, the regime is explicitly committed to the doctrine of African socialism, i.e. to 'the adaptation of socialism as an economic social and political doctrine to African realities'.[17] The formulation is a familiar one, and so are its implications: 'African socialism is not a reaction against anything or anyone; there is no point in getting involved in a class struggle, since African society is free of antagonistic classes; what we must do is look back to our spiritual roots.'[18] Thirdly, and basic to an understanding of the official role of the party and of its relationships to the masses, is the notion of 'democratic centralism'. Here again the definition carries familiar overtones: according to the charter of UPRONA, democratic centralism means: (a) 'the election of all directing organs of the party from the base to the top'; (b) 'periodic accounts of party activities at each level of the hierarchy by the directing organs immediately below'; (c) 'the maintenance of a rigorous discipline within the party'; (d) 'a strict obligation for the lower party organs to observe and apply the decisions originating from the higher echelons'.[19] In this fashion, we are told, 'power becomes a two-way current in which everything comes from the people and goes back to the people'.[20] A final theme centres on the mystique of work. A good militant is by definition a diligent worker; conversely, hard work is the unmistakable proof of a man's aptitude to militate in the ranks of the party. The 'mobilisation of the masses into collective work' is regarded as a fundamental prerequisite of national development; if we are to believe official testimonies, the response of the masses to the so-called 'mobilisation directives' has been so great that UPRONA, in the course of a recent congress, unanimously adopted a resolution making it mandatory for each militant to 'devote each Saturday morning to collective work'. This way the permanent revolution becomes the expression of a permanent effort at mobilisation.

Despite these incantatory formulas and exhortations, the results, so far, have been minimal. The theme of revolution has not gone very far beyond the stage of verbalisation. The brand of revolutionary ardour advocated by the regime has yet to take roots in the countryside; it has yet to elicit a genuine and positive response from the masses and bring forth the kind of popular enthusiasm which might give a semblance of credibility to its long-term objectives.

Part of the problem lies in the internal contradictions of a doctrine which, like the structures it is supposed to bolster, is largely divorced from the environment in which it operates. To speak of a 'permanent revolution' while at the same time seeking to thwart or defeat all forms of political self-expression other than those tolerated or imposed from above is like squaring the circle. The links between government and governed, through which an authentic social revolution might be engineered, are largely missing, and so is the programmatic appeal of the objectives which the junta has set for itself. In these conditions, similar doubts may be cast on the value of 'democratic centralism' as an organising principle; not only has there never been the slightest effort to institutionalise anything remotely resembling this principle (at least as reflected in its theoretical formulation), but as long as the NRC's control over the party makes the work of UPRONA redundant, democratic centralism is bound to remain an empty formula, and at best a mere ritual. Official endorsement of the doctrine of African socialism also raises difficulties.

457

For if one accepts the contribution of the African past to the elaboration of socialism, where does one draw the line between those aspects of tradition that are considered positive for the implementation of the tasks at hand and those which, because of their association with the ancien régime, must be discarded? How can one advocate a 'return to sources' and at the same time (to quote the words of President Micombero) deny the merits of 'ancestral communism and of certain communal structures which have nothing to offer in the way of meaningful social, economic and political implications'?[21] How can one in the same breath extol the virtues of the past and condemn its symbols and political structures? The answers, it seems, are anybody's guess.

Another set of difficulties stems from the regime's continuing, though increasingly precarious, reliance on civilian structures which do not necessarily share the pliancy of their military counterparts. If their control of the government and central bureaucracy seems beyond dispute, the armed forces are nonetheless very thinly spread on the ground; there are not enough officers around to man the local administration, and thus the tendency has been, and still is, to rely heavily on former administrative cadres and jeunesses who—although they call themselves JRR, acknowledge their subordination to UPRONA and pay lip service to the regime—operate in a fairly autonomous fashion.[22] Administrative decisions at the local level are seldom referred for approval to the upper echelons, even when such approval would seem mandatory; in sum, the local JRR branches tend to function as an ultimate court of appeal in the provinces, with the local army men passively watching the proceedings.* So far, the only notable reaction has come from the Catholic

* Writing in late 1967, a Belgian journalist described the attitude and methods of the JRR in these terms: 'The single-party state upon which Micombero must perforce lean offers a slavish copy of certain all-too-familiar control methods. . . . The youth of Burundi, better known as Jeunesses Rwagasore or Jeunesses Révolutionnaires de la République, a social milieu of whom one hears a lot nowadays, deserve special mention. Though seldom armed, these young men stop the traffic on the roads, molest, insult or kidnap their political opponents, without eliciting any significant reaction from government officials, who seem to be rather afraid of them. Gradually they have managed to evade governmental controls. Hence they play in Burundi a role similar to that played in Congo-Brazzaville by the JMNR and in Congo-Kinshasa by the MRJP, and constitute a potential for political action which could conceivably be turned against their progenitors, and which in the meantime supplies various political leaders with the personnel they need for their dirty work. The youths are largely responsible for the recent wave of kidnappings in Bujumbura, of which the Hutu are the principal victims. Dressed in civilian clothes, operating preferably at night and with an unusual wariness, they are well supplied with jeeps, seem to enjoy all kinds of protection, and are now intent upon sowing terror.' *Le Soir*, September 16, 1967.

Church whose position, as a result, has become increasingly uncomfortable in recent times. Faced with repeated anti-clerical provocations from JRR zealots, certain members of the indigenous and European clergy have not hesitated to voice their apprehension in the face of a regime which, they said, 'openly violates the fundamental rights of men'.* That the Church should have aroused the growing hostility of the jeunesses is, of course, symptomatic of the predominance of Tutsi among the JRR cadres and of the special conditioning influences of the Rwanda situation on these same elements; but it also shows the extent to which ethnic and other prejudices continue to govern current political behaviour. What needs to be underscored here is that there can be no purely military rule in contemporary Burundi, for, even though the party and the administration have both suffered superficial purges, the stability of the regime depends in part upon the continued support of civilian structures over which it has but the most tenuous control. The emerging pattern is clearly reminiscent of the state of affairs prevailing under the monarchy: power in the provinces continues to gravitate into the hands of local elites, with the central machinery of the state operating as before in a political void. As one seasoned observer recently told this writer: 'The government machinery is out of control. People adhere to the party from fear. An increasing use is made of strong-arm methods to boost up the faltering enthusiasm of the crowds. Micombero

* Illustrative of the tension between the Church and the secular authorities is the incident which followed the sermon delivered by Mgr Nestor Bihunda, Bishop of Gitega, on November 28, 1967. Accused of having used the pulpit on this occasion as a platform to condemn some of the methods of the junta and its ancillary civilian organisations (in particular those tending toward the 'politisation of everything and everyone, including the children, as advocated by Mao and Lenin'), Mgr Bihunda was immediately placed under house arrest and the text of his sermon banned. Shortly thereafter, another incident, in the province of Muramvya, brought a further deterioration of church-state relations. Apprised of the news that a primary school teacher had been fired by the local Church authorities on the grounds that she had abjured her faith after marrying a Muslim, the Minister of Education insisted that she be reinstated in her post. Whereupon, disregarding official warnings, the Bishop of Bujumbura, Mgr Ntuyahaga, personally went to Muramvya to confirm the decision of the local Church authorities; on December 18, the Minister of Education travelled to Muramvya to reverse the Bishop's decision. At this point the rumour spread that, if Mgr Ntuyahaga should once more travel to Muramvya in connection with this affair, the JRR would see to it that he be arrested and thrown in jail. The feelings of the Church were made clear in a collective letter to President Micombero, signed by 'the priests of Burundi', dated December 13, 1967, which severely condemned the 'arbitrary sanctions taken against Mgr Bihunda', the 'repeated attacks against the Church made in the course of political meetings', and the general climate of 'uncertainty and insecurity facing the Burundi clergy as a result of the regime's wilful defiance of the fundamental rights of men'.

459

is very isolated. The cabinet hardly ever meets. Instead, cabinet members are called one by one by the President.'

The revolutionary drive launched by Micombero, far from generating its own momentum, is being stalled by the very methods employed to bring it under way. Rival political factions have been coerced into union or docility, but the effect of this on public life has been anaesthetising. The few positive responses the regime has been able to elicit are largely the result of patronage and intimidation. As already noted, by seeking ways and means of carrying off a revolution from above, Micombero is really trying to avert a revolution from below; these are not interchangeable formulas, however. The former has brought a new class to power, but the fundamental societal changes that one ordinarily associates with a revolution from below have yet to materialise. It may be, of course, that the present policies will eventually act as a goad to popular revolutionary action, and, by virtue of their own intransigence, bring about precisely the type of revolutionary situation which the authorities would like to avoid. The point has already been made, albeit in a different context: 'In intimidating the public as well as crystallising radical opposition, the military, which fears revolution from below, brings it on by its own disregard of constitutional norms'.[23] Although this may be a tenable proposition in the context of Latin American politics and elsewhere in Africa, in Burundi this kind of situation is unlikely to develop as long as the revolutionary potentialities of the masses remain fragmented into mutually hostile blocs, and, even more importantly, as long as the army has the will and the capacity to maintain itself outside the pale of ethnic antagonisms. Whether this condition can long remain satisfied is an entirely different matter.

Largely isolated from the masses, yet determined to force its own values and political institutions upon them, the army tends to take on the characteristics of a closed corporation, existing alongside but never really penetrating the fabric of the larger society. For this situation there are several possible explanations, some of which have already been alluded to. First, and most obviously, is the influence of its professional ethos: like other armies in Africa, the Burundi National Army (BNA) tends to view its role as that of a highly specialised and self-sufficient caste, and this conception inevitably colours its behaviour. Commenting on 'the fundamental reason for the lack of interaction between the civilians and the military', one Murundi student recently observed that 'the bulk of the troops is still under the influence of the apolitical mystique of its Western instructors'; thus, 'in opposition to the revolutionary, democratic conception of dialectical relationships between the civilians and the army, is being maintained the aristocratic, technical, apolitical and charismatic ethics of the military'.[24] Although the argument is more directly relevant to an understanding of the attitude of the officers' corps (and even then with the reservations noted earlier in connection with the influence of professionalism on the armed forces), it does suggest a type of professional conscience as well as a corporate self-awareness radically different from that which might be expected from the non-military elites. Several additional factors have encouraged the military to look upon themselves as a group apart—the existence among the officers of strong regional ties; a common experience of having undergone officer training overseas; the predominance among them of a distinctive age group; and, despite a clear majority of Tutsi elements a rather mixed ethnic background among the non-Tutsi, including three Hutu, two Hima, one *ganwa* and one so-called 'Swahili'.* Even more significant as a source of corporate solidarity is a growing realisation among the officers that any attempt to closely identify themselves with the ethnic components of their society would harm the military as much as any other group, and perhaps unleash a civil war of major proportions. Despite powerful pressures building up in precisely this direction, for the time being the army looks very much like an autonomous caste, having in a way pre-empted the role the *ganwa* used to play in the traditional society; like the *ganwa*, most of the officers refuse to openly identify themselves as Hutu or Tutsi; indeed, they seem to regard themselves as belonging to a privileged group, to a kind of favoured occupational stratum existing independently of all others. Above all, and not unlike the *ganwa*, they command the means of coercion with which to back their claims to authority.

Pushing the analogy a step further, one is tempted to ask whether the army will not eventually fall prey to internal tensions and sibling rivalries similar to those experienced by the *ganwa* in the course of history. In view of the continuing close links of dependence between the military and the civilian elites, what evidence is there that the seeds of ethnic strife will not penetrate the barracks and sow fresh and perhaps

---

* Among the 17 officers included in the NRC in 1968, eight were from the province of Bururi (five Tutsi, two Hutu and one Hima); eight were born in 1940—the oldest member being 33 and the youngest 24. All except three had spent some time abroad: ten had a six-month military training period at the Arlon officers' school in Belgium; three, including the recently demoted Albert Shibura, spent three years at the Saint Cyr officers' school in France; one (Evariste Karorero) spent a year at the Ecole de Gendarmerie at Melun (France). Four attended the Collège du Saint Esprit, in Bujumbura, for periods varying from four to six years, and one (Martin Ndayahoze) spent a year at Lovanium (Kinshasa). Significantly enough, except for Ndayahoze, a Hutu, the best educated among the officers were also of Tutsi extraction.

fatal dissensions in the armed forces? Although direct evidence on this score is naturally limited, by way of a speculative assessment attention must be directed to two different sets of conditioning factors, one having to do with the internal practices and policies governing the military establishment as a whole, the other with factors and contingencies external to the military.

Whether the officers can retain their grip on the army depends in part on their capacity to maintain formal and informal ties of loyalty between themselves and the troops, and the maintenance of similar relationships between senior and junior officers. Since the bulk of the troops is predominantly Hutu and the majority of the officers of Tutsi extraction, factors such as the rate and ethnic incidence of promotion to senior ranks, the amount and quality of esprit de corps among the troops and their officers, and the latter's ability to keep the barracks insulated from the ferment of ethnic politics would seem essential to the preservation of the army as a strong, independent and reliable security force. In this connection one must note, on the negative side of the ledger, the continuing disproportion of Tutsi in the officers' corps as compared with Hutu, the persistent tendency on the part of at least some officers to engage in sub rosa manoeuvrings and political intrigue, and, as a further source of potential conflict, the dangers of political 'contamination' arising from Micombero's decision in late 1966 to integrate the gendarmerie within the army. All this suggests a situation of considerable tension; and yet at the same time one is impelled to wonder whether factors such as these (with the exception of the last one mentioned) are really significant as a source of conflict in a society like Burundi, where traditional values seem to meet the organisational requirements of the military almost ideally. Indeed, the transfer of traditional behavioural norms into the military mould positively strengthens the solidarity of the armed forces as a whole. It would be grossly misleading to infer from the previous discussion of civilian politics conclusions directly applicable to the military; for, without in any way denying that the Burundi army shares the characteristics of a modern bureaucratic organisation, the central organisational principle around which it is built—hierarchy—makes it admirably suited to the traditional expectations and behavioural norms of the Barundi. As in the traditional society, where relations among individuals were embedded in a certain hierarchy of rank and privilege, the army provides an alternative framework for the maintenance of hierarchical status positions. In these conditions, the army draws its strength from those very elements which are found wanting in the more modernised sectors of civilian life, i.e. a sense of respect and loyalty to one's superior as well as a relative indifference to egalitarian values. As David Wilson observed in connection with the role of the army in Thai politics, because the military is particularly apt at 'framing unambiguously the relative rank of each', 'in a society which has such a socio-psychological taste for hierarchy, a military organization will very likely be a strong one, particularly in comparison to groups which seek to follow more egalitarian principles'.[25]

Whatever threats the army will have to face in the future will, in all probability, emanate from forces or individuals other than those associated with the army. Two distinct possibilities suggest themselves: the civilian structures planted by the military may in time acquire a degree of autonomy and vitality incompatible with the maintenance of army rule, in which case the regime may either re-civilianise itself, with the army voluntarily retreating into professionalism (as happened in Egypt after the coup of 1952); or else a trial of strength is likely to develop between the army and the civilian elites, with the latter seeking support from among the rural populations through a reactivation of ethnic ties accompanied by the use of guerrilla tactics and wanton terrorism. This latter alternative seems the more probable in view of the most recent attempt of certain Hutu elites to overthrow the government. Disclosure of a plan for a Hutu-led coup for the night of September 16–17, 1969, led to the arrest of about thirty persons, all of Hutu origins, including civilian and military elites as well as a score of soldiers, also of Hutu origins. Among those arrested were Barnabé Kanyaruguru, Minister for Planning and Economy, Jean-Chrysostome Mbandabonya, former Minister of Social Affairs in the first Micombero government, Cyprien Henehene, former Minister of Health (said to have died 'under questioning'), and Joseph Cimpaye, director of personnel of Sabena Airlines in Bujumbura. Although there are still a few Hutu in positions of responsibility within and outside the government, the trend towards Tutsi supremacy is clear: seven out of twelve cabinet ministers, including those in charge of such key posts as foreign affairs, defence and security, and interior, are of Tutsi extraction; six of eight provincial governors are Tutsi; enrolment figures at the Université Officielle of Bujumbura show an overwhelming majority of Tutsi. More important still, the army is now being recruited almost exclusively from among the Tutsi. In these conditions, the potential for ethnic violence remains as high as it has ever been in the recent past.

Another possible threat to the integrity of the armed forces stems from the potential for spontaneous ethnic strife present in both the urban and rural areas, and which, if it should explode into actual violence, might also cause an ethnic revolt within the army. Admittedly, the performance of the army during the abortive civilian insurrection of

1965 suggests a rather different conclusion. Yet there are limits to how far and how often Hutu troops can be relied upon to suppress their kinsmen. That the army has not yet broken under the stress of ethnic antagonisms is not in itself a sufficient proof that it will not do so at some future date. In the past, the officers could keep their troops in hand by telling them the monarch's life was in danger; in point of fact, it is said that the rebellious Hutu officers used this stratagem in 1965 to induce their men to attack the palace, and that the coup failed when the troops realised they had been deceived. Whether Hutu soldiers can be manipulated with the same ease in the name of the republic is uncertain.

The military junta can find more reasonable grounds for optimism, for the time being at least, in the pervasive sense of fear generated by the military presence among the rural masses, a fear for which the brutality of the 1965 repression gives ample justification. Fear has bred apathy and hopelessness among many Barundi, but particularly among the Hutu. Deeply traumatised by the events of 1965, deprived of political leadership, intimidated or anaesthetised by the joint efforts of official propagandists and JRR brigades, the Hutu had little to offer, in 1969, in the way of a potential for organised, sustained revolutionary action. How long this situation may last is impossible to say; that it will not last forever is about as safe a prediction as one can make under the present circumstances. With the re-emergence at some future date of a new Hutu leadership, the junta will again be faced with a challenge to its authority which may yet produce some startling realignments of civil-military relationships.

Meanwhile, behind the façade of the new republican institutions, traditional patterns persist. A new caste has come to power whose methods are strikingly similar to those of its predecessor. As before, the interplay of clique and factionalism constitutes the moving force of Burundi politics; networks of clientage ties and reciprocities spread their tentacles across the bureaucracy and the army, replicating the pattern of informal alliances which used to permeate the old monarchical order. Although the symbols of the monarchy have been destroyed, the patrimonial ties of loyalty between the monarch and his courtiers have reappeared in a new guise. The officers' corps partakes of the quality of a closed fraternal order whose relationships to the presidency are not unlike those which prevailed between the Mwami and his court. Even though Micombero speaks with the voice of a revolutionary, his role in the emergent polity is that of a presidential Mwami.

Thus, if there is any parallel between Burundi and Rwanda nowadays, rather than in the republican ideas written down in their constitutions, or the revolutionary mystique each has adopted, it is to be found in the persistence over time of monarchical norms which even today continue to reflect the specific characteristics of their traditional cultures.

But although both states are, in a sense, hybrid polities, in so far as they each represent a particular blend of traditionalism and modernity, the area of compatibility, or functional harmony, between the two is not the same in Rwanda as in Burundi. The difference, succinctly stated, is that, unlike Burundi, Rwanda has experienced a type of revolution which, by virtue of the cultural ambiguity of its provenance, redeems tradition and at the same time offers a genuine potential for achieving the promises of democracy and political modernisation. It redeems tradition in two ways—first, through the restoration of a pre-Tutsi tradition (at least in specific areas) whose roots are specifically Hutu; and, second, by transferring into the mould of Hutu supremacy the 'premise of inequality' that once gave sustenance and stability to the Tutsi monarchy. By the same token, and even though the principle of majority rule has yet to be institutionalised within the Hutu stratum, the revolution gave concrete expression to the aspirations of leaders and politicians whose claims to represent the majority of the population could hardly be doubted. Their involvement in revolutionary activities, as we have seen, came to be justified in terms of their commitment to the values of freedom, equality and democracy, and in reaction against the perpetuation of helotry, inequality and monarchical absolutism. Quite apart from the question of whether there is any basis for democracy in contemporary Rwanda, the fact remains that Hutu supremacy implies majority rule in opposition to Tutsi supremacy, parliamentary sovereignty in opposition to monarchic absolutism, individual equality in opposition to collective bondage. The seeds of a new ideology have been planted which carry within themselves the germs of new political institutions. That there are still enormous difficulties to be surmounted, and many divisive issues to be resolved, has already been stressed in an earlier chapter. The only point that need be emphasised here is that the ideology spawned by the revolution provides an auxiliary guide for modern political activities—i.e., for the enlargement of opportunities for popular participation, the harnessing of the masses to the tasks of political modernisation, the institutionalisation of a free parliamentary debate, etc.—while at the same time giving a new and more self-conscious dimension to the cultural traditions to which the Hutu, for the most part in spite of themselves, have become heir.

This carrying forward of traditional norms into the modern world, with the former acting as a prod to modernising endeavours, is what the Micomberist revolution has yet to achieve. It is not enough here to stress the structural obstacles which military rule places in the way of sustained modernisation (for example, its blatant disregard of the need for broadly-based civilian institutions through which a genuine mobilisation of collective energies can take place); what must be stressed, rather, is the contradiction which exists between the ethnic underpinnings of current revolutionary aspirations—even though these have not yet developed beyond the stage of revolutionary tropisms—and the imposition from above of a revolutionary ideology whose roots are still pretty much in the air. What brought about the extinction of the *ganwa* as a caste and a political elite was their failure to take into account, or, better, their inability to check the spread of, political ideas borrowed from the West, based upon the notions of majority rule and popular participation; this is also the reason why the monarchy had to bow to the military, and why the military may yet have to bow to the populace. For even though Micombero has the power to perpetuate himself in office, the present equilibrium has no firm ideological foundations. In due time, revolutionary practice, as defined by Micombero, may generate its own legitimacy, but this ideological millennium is not yet in sight.

At the root of all the problems currently facing the regime lies a fundamental hiatus between the revolutionary image it seeks to project and the kind of revolutionary praxis it would like to avoid. On the eve of the Rwandese revolution a Hutu leader is reported to have said: 'Pour éviter une révolution il faut la faire' ('To avoid a revolution, you must achieve one'). Micombero's dilemma is perhaps best summed up by reversing the formula: 'Pour faire une révolution il faut l'éviter' ('To achieve a revolution, you must avoid one'). As another example of the justly celebrated 'dialectic of the Barundi',[26] the proposition carries interesting cultural overtones; but, as a recipe for promoting what we have come to call 'nation-building', and what in Burundi is better interpreted as a seemingly perpetual effort to avoid political chaos, its value is not without certain obvious limitations.

Part Four

Rwanda and Burundi:
Conclusion

18. Revolutionary Change and Nation-Building

To DISMISS the changes that have occurred in Rwanda and Burundi as nothing more than interesting political pathologies would be just as unwarranted as to read into their recent histories generalisations applicable 'across-the-board' to the rest of Africa. No matter how wide the spectrum of social and political upheavals experienced by these two states, ranging from messianic movements and peasant revolts to social revolutions and coups, it is a relatively small inventory compared to the extraordinary diversity of protest movements encountered in the whole of Africa.[1] Nonetheless, there is more to be learned about revolutionary processes in general from an investigation of their political systems than from any other two states in Africa; this is so not only because of the divergent patterns of development each has exhibited in recent times, but, curiously enough, because both share those very features which some would regard as untypical of the 'newly-created state'.

In his discussion of the causes of 'internal war'—a genus of which revolution is a major species—Harry Eckstein hypothesises that 'a generalisation about the causes of internal war will certainly founder if it is expected to account simultaneously for such disparate phenomena as, say, the outbreak of political violence in late eighteenth-century France and ethnic strife in a newly-created contemporary state'. 'The French revolution', he adds, 'involved war-like and deviant social force for purposes of political competition, and it seriously disrupted settled institutional patterns. In the case of the new state, however, there was, in all probability, no previously shared system of norms from which to deviate, and, even more probably, no previously settled institutional pattern; there can, therefore, be no speaking of internal war in the proper sense.'[2] Implicit in this statement is the objection that Rwanda and Burundi so deviate from the usual pattern of haphazard ethnic juxtaposition encountered in most other African states as to make it well-nigh impossible to infer from their respective historical experiences generalisations applicable to the rest of Africa. This is true only up to a point, however. If Rwanda and Burundi were the only examples in Africa of stratified, hierarchically-organised societies, the only examples of polities sharing 'settled institutional norms', the temptation to treat them as sui generis cases would be difficult to resist, but one need only look at Zanzibar, Lesotho and Swaziland at the national level, at Ankole or Bukoba at the regional level, to realise that this type of polity is not without parallels elsewhere in Africa. Furthermore, even where the ethnic make-up and traditional social structure of the 'newly-created state' suggest different types of conflict than those exemplified in this book, the variations are not always so wide as to exclude similarities from which broader generalisations can be drawn.

Quite apart from the question of the relevance of these case-studies to the wider context of African politics, one may legitimately ask whether the range of variations between these two states justifies our initial contention that only in Rwanda has there been a transformation so violent and drastic as to deserve the name of revolution. There is of course no valid reason for making such an assertion, other than the definition that one wishes to give to the term revolution. If one accepts T. Geiger's very loose definition, equating the phenomenon of revolution with 'each basic transformation of an existing situation', but not necessarily synonymous with 'violent or precipitous change',[3] recent events in Burundi are no less revolutionary in character than those of Rwanda. But this is only one of a variety of possible definitions, and by no means the most widely accepted. While both countries have been subject to major transformations, there is no equivalent as yet in Burundi for the internal sundering and battering suffered by Rwanda, and for the accompanying sudden, drastic substitution of one category of incumbents for another. It is with some caution, therefore, that one must accept the thesis that revolutionary change is a likely concommittant of stratified, hierarchically-organised societies once they become subject to the corrosive impact of popular sovereignty.[4]

We must now summarise in general terms the factors behind the patterns of 'deviancy' described earlier in this book. On the basis of the empirical evidence gathered in the preceding chapters, an attempt will be made to provide tentative answers to such obviously basic questions about the causes and anatomy of revolutions as: What are the roots of revolutionary change? Under what conditions can the potentialities of a revolutionary situation be released with maximum effectiveness—or repressed? What kinds of social categories are most likely to become involved in the revolutionary process, and for what reasons? How far is revolutionary change likely to penetrate the fabric of society once a revolution gets under way?

THE ROOTS OF REVOLUTIONARY CHANGE

To the first of these questions, the Rwandese revolution has prompted at least two different kinds of answers from social scientists. The interpretation offered by J.J. Maquet is that the revolution in Rwanda was essentially the expression of a 'class struggle', in the Marxist sense, between a deprived peasantry and a property-owning, tax-collecting oligarchy.[5] According to this view, the traditional pattern of social stratification was so organised as to create a fundamental clash of economic interests between property-owning and non-owning groups— that is, between Tutsi and Hutu. Only through a violent upheaval could the conflict resolve itself. Somewhat at variance with Maquet's thesis, in that it proceeds from different assumptions about the character of the traditional society and then makes relatively short shrift of the economic dimension of the Hutu-Tutsi conflict, is Helen Codere's 'power interpretation' of the Rwandese revolution.[6] For Codere, the revolution was the logical consequence of a conflict-situation which had always existed in the traditional society, a society in which 'the more powerful oppressed the less powerful or the powerless, and [where] power was used to the hilt by those who possessed it, [so that] fear and insecurity perpetuated the system'.[7] In this perspective, traditional Rwanda appears to have been in no way different from the Hobbesian state of nature, but with this qualification that the very scale and arbitrariness with which power was used *within* the Tutsi stratum acted as a deterrent against possible Hutu revolts. By inference, one is led to assume that the extension of the pax Belgica, by virtue of the limitations it imposed upon the use of power among the Tutsi, deprived them at the same time of the most effective source of control they had over their serfs. Once this had happened, the revolution from below was a likely concommittant of the removal or lessening of colonial controls.

There is no point here in restating the objections raised earlier in this work against each of these interpretations. Suffice it to note that they can offer, at best, only partially satisfying explanations. Because they uncover only a fraction of the totality of forces and motivations at work, they each tend to exaggerate the importance of specific factors while others are left almost completely unnoticed. Whatever the reasons for this rather lopsided view of social realities, one suspects that some important correctives might have been introduced by the authors had they taken the trouble to test their hypotheses against the evidence supplied by Burundi: Is there any reason to assume that the potential for revolution released by the limitations imposed by the Belgian presence upon the use of coercion did not also exist in the case of Burundi? Were not the princes of Burundi, at least before the onset of colonial rule, just as ruthless among themselves as the Tutsi of Rwanda? And if the clash of economic interests between Hutu and Tutsi in Rwanda was bound to lead to a class struggle, and ultimately to a revolution, why did not a similar competition develop between *ganwa* and non-*ganwa*?

Varieties of Oligarchical Control: 'Ruling' versus 'Hegemonic' Caste

As a starting point for analysis, a common characteristic of the 'colonial situation' in both countries must be stressed: in each case the circumstances of culture contacts produced something amounting to a system of dual over-rule. Some crucial implications of this duality of control structures are hinted at in Balandier's statement that 'the colonizing power has created [in Africa] a situation involving profound changes, but the control which it exercises imposes an upper limit to these processes'.[8] In both countries this 'upper limit' was really two-fold: that which the colonial situation had imposed upon the indigenous society as a whole; and that which an indigenous African caste strove to maintain upon the masses. Presumably, only by removing first the 'upper limit' of the caste system could the masses or their representatives expect significant changes for themselves from the elimination of European colonial controls.

However simple it may be to identify an upper caste and show that it does in fact occupy key political positions, this is not enough to allow us to make valid predictions about the likelihood of revolution. Some preliminary questions must be answered first: How extensive and effective were the controls exercised by the upper caste? What were its relationships to the subordinate groups?[9]

The most convenient approach to a differentiation of the patterns of dominance between Rwanda and Burundi is the one suggested by the Italian Marxist, Antonio Gramsci, in his use of the term 'egemonia', 'hegemony'. For Gramsci, hegemony was characteristic of an order 'in which a certain way of life and thought is dominant, in which one concept of reality is diffused throughout society in all its institutional and private manifestations, informing with its spirit all taste, morality, customs, religious and political principles, and all social relations, particularly in their intellectual and moral connotations'.[10] In this sense, the Tutsi of Rwanda formed a 'hegemonic' caste, whose values were 'diffused throughout society in all its institutional and private manifestations', and whose power was at first so magnified by the colonial authorities as to acquire almost unlimited scope over subordinate groups. The *ganwa* of Burundi never possessed this plenitude of powers and all-pervasive moral legitimacy; they had the qualities of a 'ruling caste' but not of a 'hegemonic caste'. Their *moral* ascendency was comparatively limited.

In the case of Rwanda this distinction suggests a form of institutional control which made it virtually impossible for the monarchy to dissociate itself from the principle of Tutsi hegemony. Monarchic rule and caste hegemony were thus so intimately intertwined that any attempt to bring about a status reversal through democratic means was bound to be interpreted by the Tutsi as a threat to the institution of kingship. Conversely, the abolition of monarchic rule came to be viewed by the Hutu elites as a sine qua non of equality. In Burundi, by contrast, the absence of all-embracing moral connotations attached to *ganwa* rule, coupled with the recurrent divisions or feuds among the *ganwa*, had the effect not only of facilitating upward social mobility to a degree almost unheard of in Rwanda, but of placing the monarchy in a rather subsidiary position in relation to society as a whole. To repeat a point made earlier, the Burundi monarchy owed its staying power to the very weakness of its position in the overall socio-political structure of the country. As will be recalled, it was only when the monarchy departed from this perfunctory role which tradition and circumstances had forced upon it that its future really came into doubt.

The normative implications are no less essential to bear in mind. It is one thing to note that political control ultimately rests in the hands of an oligarchy, but another to demonstrate that specific interests, decisions and policies follow from this type of situation which would not have taken place had control been vested in the hands of another minority. The Tutsi of Rwanda were generally so imbued with their own sense of superiority as a caste that any effort to accommodate the claims of the peasantry were automatically ruled out as contrary to the nature of things. Suppression rather than accommodation was the essential dictate of their value system. In their consciousness of belonging to a superior order of human beings lies the key to an understanding of the rock-like obduracy of the Tutsi patriciate in the face of mounting pressures from lower-caste elements. Against this unshakable commitment to the 'premise of inequality', the attitude of the *ganwa* strikes one as distinctively more flexible on the issue of caste relations. Nor is this too surprising considering the absence among them of anything approximating the sense of moral superiority of the Tutsi oligarchy of Rwanda, their comparatively small size, and, perhaps as a consequence of their numerical weakness, the closeness of the contacts which some of them had with lower-caste elements. Thus the strategy of the *ganwa* in Burundi has seldom been one of overt, implacable resistance to the principle of equality and popular sovereignty, but consisted in the main

473

in drawing maximum advantage from the opportunities offered by the democratisation of traditional institutions. This is nowhere more clearly demonstrated than by Rwagasore's attempt to steal the long-vacillating thunder of the crown by courting the support of the plebeian masses, a compromise which no Tutsi holding a comparable position in Rwanda would have been prepared to accept with the same equanimity.

Moreover, the ethnic context of inferior-superior relations was profoundly different in Rwanda from what it was in Burundi. In Rwanda one notices an almost perfect coincidence of social stratification and ethnic divisions; in Burundi, on the other hand, social stratification and cultural or ethnic pluralism were anything but 'consistent' in the sense that one automatically replicated the other. The potential for ethnic violence was therefore relatively small by comparison with Rwanda. Unlike what happened in Rwanda, where the social underpinnings of the revolution coincided with the 'relative deprivation' of a single, ethnically homogeneous stratum, in Burundi the persistence of ethnic cleavages among non-*ganwa* elements implied corresponding strains and divisions at the base of the social pyramid. Without in any way denying that their common opposition to *ganwa* rule encouraged integration among ethnically divided communities (i.e. essentially among Hutu and Tutsi), this was never carried to the point of dissipating all traces of ethnic particularism. No matter how high the revolutionary potential created after independence, this potential could never be tapped effectively as long as ethnic polarities continued to divide the would-be insurgents more than they divided them from the incumbents. Here also lies the key to an understanding of the relative stability of certain *ganwa* elements around the throne in the years following independence. The length of their tenure in office was far less a reflection of their inherent strength as an oligarchy than a symptom of the relative weakness of their ethnic opponents.

The conclusion which suggests itself is that the vulnerability of a traditional polity to modern political change is perhaps less a function of the presence or absence of a national upper caste than of the relationships of this caste to the institutions of power, norms and ethnic referents of the modernising society. The fragility of Rwanda's traditional society in the face of rapid social changes stemmed from a conspicuously high degree of interdependence and consistency between the monarchy as an institution, the 'premise of inequality' as a regulative norm of the social system, and the fact of Tutsi hegemony. Far from being an autonomous machine to be steered at will, the monarchy was closely linked to subsidiary political institutions, which all tended to reflect the pre-eminence and predominance of Tutsi cultural traditions and a system of social relations based on inequality. Inasmuch as these structures and values were mutually reinforcing, any move in the direction of institutionalising egalitarian values was bound to pose a major threat to the institution of kingship. In Burundi, by contrast, the identification of upper-caste elements points to entirely different attributes of social reality, in particular to the absence of consistency between institutional, normative and ethnic cleavages. This very lack of integration and coherence between the monarchy on the one hand, and the ethnic and social sub-systems on the other, made for a much greater receptivity to democratic norms than was ever conceivable in Rwanda.

Given the over-riding importance of ethnic referents, it will be useful to pause briefly for a somewhat more detailed consideration of the types of ethnic cleavages and configurations encountered in each state.

'Consistent' versus 'Cross-Cutting' Cleavages

Despite the impression of social fixity conveyed by the use of the word 'caste', we have seen that even the most rigid of caste systems admits some measure of inter-caste mobility. Thus one may conceive of a situation of minimal upward mobility, where social prestige, economic wealth and political power all tend to gravitate into the same hands. Rwanda was clearly the case par excellence. But in contrast with this 'closed system', one could also cite the example of caste societies, like Burundi, where the boundaries separating various status positions are relatively open and flexible, and where several possible combinations and alternative channels of mobility offer themselves. In this type of situation, a caste may claim considerable deference for itself while in fact being powerless (as were the *ganwa* in many of the crown lands); conversely, in some instances, representatives of the lower caste may hold significant power but little social recognition (as was true of the Hutu chiefs appointed in the crown lands); or again a caste may distinguish itself by its economic wealth while being largely deprived of social prestige and political influence (as in the case of Hutu or simple Tutsi clients attached to wealthy patrons). In brief, whereas the Rwandese pattern tended to approximate the ideal of a 'closed society', with a relatively high degree of consistency among various cleavages, whether political, social or ethnic, in Burundi these divisions tended to cross-cut each other in such a way as to eliminate the presence of a single common denominator from the social pyramid.

To bring the picture into proper focus, however, it is well to remind ourselves of certain qualifications mentioned earlier. Firstly, the vertical relationships of dominance and subordination characteristic of the traditional Rwandese society in fact concealed two different types of

475

stratificatory phenomena. Whereas in the central and southern regions a situation had developed of optimum functional integration, typical of the more rigid versions of the caste system, in the north and the north-west socio-ethnic differences tended to approximate what Weber had in mind when he used the expression 'ethnic coexistence' to describe the feelings of 'mutual repulsion and disdain' which prevail where ethnically divided communities are each allowed to 'consider their honor as the highest one'.[11] Characteristic of this latter type of situation is a relatively low degree of institutional and cultural integration, reminiscent of the 'plural society' discussed by M.G. Smith.* Enough has been said of the general aloofness and distinctively regionalist outlook of the northern Hutu populations to appreciate the significance of this distinction: as we have seen, the northern upheaval was as much a war of independence against 'alien' intruders as a social revolution.

Secondly, within the northern Hutu subculture, hierarchical relations have tended to survive virtually up to the present time, in a sense duplicating at the regional level and within the same ethnic group the relations of dominance and subordination elsewhere institutionalised under the auspices of the Tutsi diaspora. Though much of this indigenous Hutu organisation remained hidden behind the façade of Tutsi hegemony during the colonial period, there is every reason to believe that it did retain considerable vitality; in a real sense, the northern Hutu tended to form a distinctive subsystem within the larger perimeter of Rwandese society, one which implied a degree of institutional and cultural autonomy far superior to that evolved through the establishment of a caste system.

These considerations bring into relief some major dimensions of the dynamics of revolutionary change in Rwanda; and because they focus attention on a set of conditions only rarely satisfied in other African societies, they may also help to explain why a revolution is likely to

---

* The dichotomy drawn by Weber between 'ethnic coexistence' and 'caste structure' finds an interesting parallel in Antonio Gramsci's distinction between the already mentioned concept of 'egemonia' and that of 'dominio'. For Gramsci, dominio is always associated with 'coercion, state power and the movement of forces'; egemonia, on the other hand, despite its inegalitarian implications, conveys an impression of 'equilibrium, persuasion, consent and consolidation'. Gramsci's point that the communal regime of Renaissance Italy failed to produce anything like egemonia and hence also failed to evolve an integrated society, is equally applicable, mutatis mutandis, to the characteristics of Tutsi rule in northern Rwanda. See Gwyn A. Williams, "The Concept of 'Egemonia' in the Thought of Antonio Gramsci", *Journal of the History of Ideas*, Vol. xxi, No. 4, October–December 1960, p. 590 ff. Cf. H. H. Gerth & G. W. Mills eds., *From Max Weber: Essays in Sociology*, Oxford University Press, New York and London, 1958, p. 189.

succeed in one context and fail in another. As much as a reaction of protest on the part of a socially and economically deprived stratum, the
Rwandese revolution was a case of localised, anomic and primarily
ethnic rebellion rapidly converting itself into a social and political
revolution. Even at this latter stage, however, ethnic solidarities played
a major part in the extension of socio-economic grievances on a nation-
wide scale. For if there can be little doubt that the decisive spark came
from the north, where feelings of 'mutual repulsion and disdain' between Hutu and Tutsi were rendered particularly acute by the persistence of cultural and regional particularisms, these were never so
pronounced as to eliminate altogether the play of ethnic affiliations on a
country-wide basis. Unlike what happened in, say, the Kwango-Kwilu
during the 1964 Congo rebellion (where the spread of revolutionary
violence was limited in proportion to its quotient of ethnicity, and therefore to the territorial domain of specific tribes), or in Burundi (where
ethnic and regional rivalries consistently hampered the emergence of a
unified revolutionary movement in the years which followed independence), in Rwanda ethnic solidarities acted as the main vehicle of revolutionary sentiment and activity. A somewhat similar phenomenon can
be observed in Zanzibar: despite major cultural differences between
mainlanders and Shirazi, the strains of ethnic or cultural unity among
those of African descent were sufficiently powerful in relation to
Arab supremacy to act as the vectors of a common revolutionary consciousness.

Another major element in the background of the Rwandese revolution
is that part of its impetus came from the transfer and activation within
the same ethnic group of hierarchical solidarities of the kind that link
a 'client' to his 'patron'. The roots of revolutionary change, therefore,
were of two kinds: in addition to the persistence of horizontal, ethnic
loyalties that could be quickly invigorated and communicated on a
national scale, a vertical relationship—a relationship of clientage—
between the revolutionary elites and the masses came into play.

The 'Class' Dimension of Revolutionary Change

Although the foregoing may suffice to discredit the notion of a
'class struggle' as the motive force of the revolution, at least in the sense
in which Maquet uses the expression, this is not to say that the status
reversal brought in the wake of new social and economic forces did not
have a direct bearing upon the rise of a revolutionary consciousness
among the Hutu. In the absence of some degree of social restratification,
in the absence of new reference groups defined in terms of income and
education instead of birth, it is questionable whether a revolution would

477

have taken place at all. On the eve of the revolution, the social trans-formations that had affected the traditional Hutu society were of a very limited scope, and of varying intensity within these limits, resulting in the juxtaposition of very different and unevenly shared social referents within the same ethnic group. This juxtaposition, in other words, was the consequence of the coexistence within the same society, and indeed within the same ethnic group, of a caste-like, ascriptive basis of stratifica-tion, and a class-like universe of achieved status.

To argue that something resembling a class structure had emerged among the Hutu is by no means synonymous with the contention that the Hutu as a group represented a class in the Marxist sense.* To the extent that one can speak of a class struggle in connection with the Rwandese revolution, the struggle was less a reflection of incompatible class interests between Hutu and Tutsi than of a persistent effort at bridging social gaps within the Hutu stratum.

The effect of social restratification on Rwanda's traditional order finds a striking parallel in the part played by the so-called 'African middle classes' in the emergence of nationalist movements elsewhere in Africa. Even if the term 'middle class' sounds somewhat arbitrary when used in the context of such different societies as, say, Ghana and Rwanda, in virtually all African territories, including Rwanda, political change was primarily the initiative and responsibility of forward-looking 'new' men, more or less uprooted from their traditional milieux.[12] Conscious as they were of the obstacles placed in the path of their own professional advancement and political ambitions, yet possessing those very skills which not only justified their claims to power but in time enabled them to seize it, these middle classes became the driving force behind the rise of nationalist movements throughout Africa. And just as African nationalist 'revolutions' often entailed genuine social revolutions of the indigenous social structures from which they sprang, in Rwanda those middle-class elements who became involved in the movement for independence were equally determined to achieve a drastic trans-

---

* Ironically, it is from Marx himself that one could borrow the most telling argument against Maquet's neo-Marxist interpretation of the Rwandese revolu-tion. In a classic passage, from *The Eighteenth Brumaire of Napoleon Bonaparte*, in which he depicts the European peasantry as 'an immense mass whose individual members live in identical conditions . . . [but among whom] there exists only a local connection in which the individuality and exclusiveness of their interests prevents any unity of interests, national connections and political organization', Marx emphasises the absence of class consciousness of the French peasants in a way which seems eminently relevant to the conditions of the Hutu peasantry on the eve of the revolution. See Karl Marx, *The Eighteenth Brumaire of Napoleon Bonaparte*, C. P. Dutt ed., International Publishers, New York, n.d., p. 109.

formation of traditional social structures and political institutions. In Rwanda, however, the order of priority was the reverse of what usually happened in other African territories: independence from European colonial rule was a secondary objective in relation to the immediate necessity of eradicating an indigenous form of imperialism.

That nationalism as an anti-European movement was never more than an epiphenomenon among the Hutu does not mean that the factors which elsewhere in Africa have propelled middle-class elements to the forefront of the nationalist crusade did not exist in Rwanda. Apart from the obvious fact that Tutsi hegemony carried implications of permanent bondage which did not exist in the case of the Belgian trusteeship (by definition a transitory arrangement), part of the explanation lies in the extreme weakness of the Hutu middle classes on the eve of the revolution, and their consequent realisation that the assistance and friendship of the trust authorities were a sine qua non of domestic emancipation.

Here, then, is a notable difference between the class structure of Rwanda and that of other African territories on the eve of independence. The Hutu middle classes were comparatively weak, not only in numerical terms (being but a tiny fraction of the total Hutu population) but also in terms of income and education. There was no equivalent in Rwanda, among the Hutu, for the scores of well-to-do, well-educated professional people (doctors, barristers, businessmen and entrepreneurs) who, in countries like Nigeria, Ghana, Dahomey or the Ivory Coast, strove to replace the expatriate ruling oligarchy, and in time became the 'ruling classes' of their respective countries. Moreover, whatever civil service posts were entrusted to Africans were predominantly in Tutsi hands. Apart from a mere handful of journalists and former seminarists, better thought of as representatives of the 'new elite', the Hutu middle classes were essentially manual workers (truck-drivers, bricklayers, inn-keepers, house boys, etc.) and primary-school teachers (moniteurs). In a way, they might more accurately be identified as a 'rural proletariat'. As the term implies, their class affiliations were extremely ambiguous; in view of the still indeterminate and rather flexible character of their social and residential ties, one might better speak of 'trans-class affiliations'—to borrow Ali Mazrui's felicitous expression*—to describe their position in the emergent social order.

---

* Mazrui's definition of 'trans-class affiliations' as involving a combination of vertical and horizontal class differences is worth emphasising: a 'trans-class' man is one who may claim 'lower' status by traditional standards and yet at the same time belong to the 'modern elite' as defined by Western criteria of income and education; in addition, however, an individual may combine 'horizontal' class differences, in the sense of sharing the characteristics of a poor peasant

Their inferior economic position in the modern economic sector and very limited educational background gave them a 'proletarian' outlook which marked them off sharply from both the intellectuals and the peasantry; yet they kept close psychological and residential connections with the rural sector. Thus, working in conjunction with the peasantry, they were able to provide the catalytic agent, or connecting links, for enlisting the support of the rural masses.

The part played by this rural proletariat during the revolution emerges most clearly in the light of their own psychological predispositions as marginal men, and the peculiar relationships which later developed between themselves and the peasant masses. Caught as they were between the authoritarian constraints of the traditional order and the pressures for change originating from their occupational milieux, they were exceedingly vulnerable to psychological strains and insecurities. Indeed, to a considerable extent, their involvement in revolutionary activities is reducible to an attempt on their part to evade or remedy the anomic conditions created by the assault of new social forces upon the traditional society. But this was scarcely enough to set off a revolution. To the extent that they were able to provide an element of direction and control in the countryside, this was not only because they themselves felt the urge to effect radical changes, but because they were in an ideal position to act as surrogate patrons to the peasantry, and to appropriate for themselves the leadership role heretofore assumed by the Tutsi oligarchs in relation to the masses.[13]

In many instances, this conversion of clientage ties into a revolutionary weapon was a more or less conscious, artificial creation of semi-urbanised politicians and intellectual elites; yet the question arises as to whether this operation was not directly facilitated by the Tutsi landlords' growing inability to fulfil their traditional roles as patrons. We have seen how the bureaucratisation of chieftaincy inevitably tended to transform the old patron-client nexus, until then based on highly personalised, affective ties, into an impersonal, standardised, increasingly harsh relationship. In these circumstances, what was more natural

---

and a wage-earning urban worker. Both types of class ambivalence were present in the Hutu society, for if the former was characteristic of the revolutionary elites, the latter was typical of the so-called 'rural proletariat'. They each correspond to a different aspect of the mechanism involved in the emergence of revolutionary aspirations and activities, vertical disharmonies providing the status reversal needed to instigate a revolutionary consciousness among the Hutu elites, and horizontal ones the status differences and psychological affinities that led to the mobilisation of the rural masses. Ali Mazrui, 'Political Superannuation and the Trans-class Man', unpublished MS, n.d., esp. pp. 7–9.

for the peasantry than to seek a more secure and meaningful relationship through a transfer of allegiance to new, and more reliable protectors?

In specific areas, however, more was involved than an artificial shift of allegiance to modern-day politicians, or a calculated disengagement from the protection of a superior. Where the roots of clientage were indigenous to the Hutu subculture—as in the north where the *bagererwa* coutumiers formed the traditional clientele of the ruling families (*bakonde*)—this forging of new links of dependency was perhaps less a 'new' form of patronage than the expression of a patron-dependent relationship that had never really disappeared from the traditional social landscape of the Hutu populations. In this case, the enlistment of the peasantry into the revolutionary crusade was a relatively simple and swift operation. This indeed is the main reason why the northern insurrection gathered such rapid momentum, and with such devastating results.*

If the northern Hutu populations were culturally predisposed to resuscitate a pre-Tutsi form of clientship, historically the recurrence in this region of messianic activities can equally be viewed as cyclical attempts by the local populations to evade Tutsi hegemony through the reactivation of an indigenous patron-dependent relationship. That peasant involvement in the revolution was greatly accelerated by the legacy of messianic traditions is a reasonably well-established fact. There is nothing especially novel or intriguing about this. As Yonina Talmon points out, messianism and revolution both involve the same predisposing factors—'a combination of frustration, disorientation and disintegration of primary groups', along with a certain 'inflexibility, unresponsiveness and ineffectiveness of the agencies of social control'. Moreover, they both share the 'same dynamic interconnections'. The vision of a religious millennium heightens expectations, strengthens solidarities and releases human energies in very much the same way as a

---

* Here again one finds a striking historical parallel with the phenomenon described by Karc Tonnesson in his analysis of the sans-culottes movement during the French revolution. His explanation for the exceptional surge of revolutionary sentiment in the faubourgs is that the 'indigents could become the political clientele of the sans-culottes masters': 'The special force of the popular movement', writes Tonnesson, 'would then be explained by the fact that in the world of the faubourgs the artisans and shopkeepers, who were the most active elements of the little people, occupied the position of a social elite, a position the less contested the weaker was the bourgeoisie.' See K. Tonnesson, *La défaite des Sans-Culottes*, Presses Universitaires, Oslo 1959; Clavreuil, Paris 1959, p. xv. No doubt a similar situation must have arisen elsewhere than in the northern Rwanda area; yet it was in the north that the elite-follower nexus was the strongest because of the survival in this region of traditional reference groups for which there were few counterparts elsewhere.

secular revolution. Insofar as they provide 'a connecting link between pre-political and political movements', millenarian manifestations undoubtedly facilitate 'the passage from pre-modern religious revolt to full-fledged revolutionary movement'.[14] Thus, the insertion of messianic aspirations into the fold of a revolutionary movement was not merely the result of a manipulative, propagandistic scheme for the furtherance of secular revolutionism, nor solely the expression of an age-old attempt to recapture a sense of cultural integrity in the face of external threats; both strains were present in the northern upheaval, thus making possible the transformation of a pre-political clientage relation into a genuinely revolutionary nexus between the elites and the masses.

The politicisation of the patron-client relationship also gives us a clue to an understanding of the impact of the land problem on the growth of a revolutionary consciousness. To put the matter in the simplest terms, the establishment or re-establishment of clientage ties implied a 'benefice' (in the medieval sense of the term) for the clients, and this could be secured only at the expense of their former patrons. Thus the expropriation of Tutsi lands was the price that had to be exacted for the loyalty of the peasantry to the cause of the revolution. While it is true that in most cases the shortage of land was the initial motive which prompted the peasantry to shift its allegiance from the traditional to the revolutionary elites—a phenomenon also encountered, albeit in a different guise, in Kenya on the eve of the Mau-Mau emergency, as well as in pre-revolutionary France and Czarist Russia prior to the occurrence of revolutionary outbreaks*—the crucial fact to bear in mind is that, once the peasants had transferred their loyalty to the revolutionary elites, new expectations were generated which sooner or later had to be satisfied. Sooner or later the lands of the Tutsi had to be ceded to the peasants, and violence was bound to occur if the Tutsi landowners resisted. This kind of tacit obligation was a major element behind the massacres of December 1963 and January 1964, one which also helps to account for the otherwise inexplicable 'laissez-faire'

---

* The issue of the 'cut-off' lands before the Bolshevik revolution would seem to have assumed revolutionary potentialities similar to those carried by the issue of proprietary rights over the pasture lands (*ibikingi*) prior to the Rwandese revolution. Just as the 'cut-off lands', as long as they remained in the hands of the landlords, 'deprived the peasantry of meadows and pastures, water courses and access to woods, which were all essential to the peasant economy', and in time became a source of 'deep and direct conflict', likewise, the control exercised by the Tutsi landlords over the *ibikingi* must be regarded as a major source of revolutionary sentiment among the Hutu. Other parallels can be found in China before the Communist take-over, as well as in India. See Hamza Alavi, "Peasants and Revolutions", *The Socialist Register*, 1965, pp. 241–77.

attitude of Hutu officials once the news of the outbreaks finally reached their ears. In these conditions, little effort was needed to transform the land problem into a source of revolutionary capital; and nowhere could this be done more easily than in the north, for there the land problem had social and political ramifications of a unique character. The explosion of hatred triggered off by the jacquerie of November 1959 might not have reached such intensity had it not been for the fact that the Tutsi presence there was made all the more unbearable by the recent and systematic expropriation of the lands previously owned by the local Hutu clans and their clients.

Once this is said, it is well to note that a considerable number of Hutu peasants were drawn into the ranks of the revolution, not by deliberate choice or manipulation, but in spite of themselves. Gil Alroy pinpoints the reality of the situation when he writes: 'The traditional conceptualization of peasant involvement in internal war, with its exclusive focus on essentially active, voluntary modes of participation, totally ignores the considerable involuntary involvement of peasants in such a war.'[15] Alroy's own study of the anatomy of the Cuban revolution demonstrates the over-riding importance of what he calls 'involvement by victimization', thereby demolishing the Sartrian myth of the Cuban revolution as an 'essentially peasant revolution', with the peasantry serving as the 'heart, head and muscle of the revolution'.[16] Much of Alroy's analysis is applicable to Rwanda. For even if the peasantry did at one point provide the 'punch' of the revolution, this was often as a result of terroristic activities directed against innocent Hutu peasants by *inyenzi* commandos. Far from invalidating what has just been said of the opportunities offered by the carry-over of clientage ties into the sphere of revolutionary politics, the atmosphere of obsidional fear and insecurity created by the very arbitrariness of repressive measures can be interpreted as a further inducement for the Hutu to look for alternative sources of protection. In any event, once the nightmarish sequence of terrorism and counter-terrorism had set in, a pattern of violence was initiated which, as its scope and intensity increased, brought into its fold an ever larger segment of the peasantry.

By way of a tentative reformulation of the interpretations thus far offered of the Rwandese revolution, the following propositions may be hypothesised. (i) More than the intelligentsia or the peasant masses, the crucial agents of revolutionary change were drawn from the ranks of the rural proletariat. To the former they offered the intermediary links needed for activating popular support for the revolution; to the latter they supplied the surrogate leadership which prompted the masses to turn away from, or against, their former protectors. Thus the

483

picture which emerges of the dynamics of revolutionary change in Rwanda abundantly confirms Thomas Hodgkin's contention that 'the whole conception of a militant-intellectual-elite-operating-upon-passive-masses is naive and remote from the facts. . . . If we want to take [African] political change seriously we must pay attention to . . . the various activities and contributions of different sectors, strata, groupings and organizations within a given African system.'[17] (ii) But at least as much attention ought to be paid to traditional institutions and values as sources of revolutionary change. No less naive or inaccurate than the 'militant intellectual-passive masses' dichotomy would be the assumption of an irreducible conflict between the 'immobilisme' of tradition and the dynamics of modernity. While there can be no denying that the revolution drew its inspiration from Western political concepts and institutions fundamentally alien to, and at odds with, traditional Rwanda society, much of the tactics and strategy of revolutionary change at the grass-roots can be understood only in the light of traditional symbols and institutions. We have seen how the clientage relationship was really a double-edged weapon, which lent itself both to the perpetuation of the status quo and the promotion of revolutionary change. The same was true of the symbols of kingship, in that they could presumably be redefined along ethnic lines to suit the goals of the Hutu elites, in which case the concept of *mwami*-ship could acquire genuinely revolutionary potentialities.* In brief, to no small extent, the success of the revolution is traceable to the skill with which modern-day politicians managed to extract from the institutional arsenal of the monarchy the weapons which served to destroy it. (iii) Although the revolutionary elites were by definition of rural background, the revolution can hardly be said to have been instigated by the peasantry per se. The initial push came not from bush peasants but from the educated Hutu elites and rural politicians; only at a later stage, partly through the manipulation of latent grievances, partly through what Alroy calls 'involvement by victimization', did the

---

* In the light of recent interviews with Rwandese informants, it appears that great care was initially taken by the revolutionary elites in the countryside *not* to identify the symbols of the monarchy with the issue of Tutsi supremacy. More than that, the inherent virtues of the monarchy, along with the supreme goodness of the Mwami, were consciously juxtaposed to the ills engendered by 'bad' chiefs, so as to emphasise their illegitimate, anti-monarchical character. And when it finally appeared that the preservation of the Tutsi monarchy was no longer compatible with the goals of the revolutionaries, the standard argument advanced by certain Hutu leaders was that the revolution aimed at giving the Hutu a Mwami of their own. The very high quotient of emotionality released through this type of manipulation constituted a major asset in the hands of the revolutionaries.

peasant masses become active participants in the revolutionary process. Rwanda provides a classic example of the potentialities and limitations inherent in the behaviour of the rural masses. As Hobsbawm reminds us, 'the peasantry never provides a political alternative to anyone; merely, as occasion dictates, an almost irresistible force or an almost immovable object'.[18]

THE PROBLEM OF OUTSIDE INVOLVEMENT IN REVOLUTIONS

Having laid due emphasis in the preceding chapters on the crucial significance of the assistance proffered by the trust authorities to the insurgents, the question arises as to how much weight ought to be given to external factors as against purely internal ones in the overall balance of forces. To what extent did the involvement of the Belgian authorities in the revolution determine its outcome?

As has already been suggested, the scale and circumstances of Belgian involvement made the success of the revolution a foregone conclusion; there is no point here in restating what has already been said of the attitude and policies of local Belgian officials, except to emphasise once again that the Residency's efforts to thwart all possibilities of effective repression by the incumbents, together with the various administrative measures, legal or illegal, taken to place the levers of political control in the hands of the insurgents, had a direct and determining effect on the outcome of the struggle. From the moment the Residency decided to throw its weight on the side of the Hutu, as happened in late 1959, the die had been cast; short of a miracle, the period of Tutsi rule was bound to come to an end. However, this does not mean that the revolutionary potential arising from the internal conditions of Rwanda would have been in any way diminished in the absence of external involvement. The revolution may not have occurred so early, and the delayed timing of the popular explosion may have invited different forms and patterns of external involvement, but the ultimate results may not have been so different. Given the 'objective' conditions of the Rwandese situation at the beginning of the revolutionary phase, it is not implausible to assume that, over the long run, the Hutu movement would have stood a far better chance of realising its objectives, through the external support it would almost certainly have received from the Communist bloc, than the Tutsi elites, once they happened to be placed under similar circumstances.

To state the problem in more general terms: just how important is outside intervention in the scale of factors that lie behind revolutionary upheavals? Under what kind of circumstances is outside intervention likely to succeed in tipping the scales in favour of the insurgents? Is there any way of reaching scientific accuracy in predicting the effects of such intervention on domestic conflicts? In the absence of reliable statistical evidence, what other criteria can one turn to in order to gauge the impact of external involvement?

These are questions which assume a very different order of priority, and command very different answers, depending on the type of environment in which they are raised. The general consensus of opinion among English-speaking scholars seems to be that external involvement, as distinct from massive outright intervention, has had relatively little effect on the outcome of domestic conflicts. In Africa and Latin America, on the other hand, this is generally considered the single most important determinant of such conflicts. Of course, to make such generalisations is extremely difficult because of the veil of secrecy which surrounds certain basic dimensions of the problem (like the scale and modalities of external involvement) and the scarcity of reliable data. Yet if there is any lesson to be learned from past experience, it is that few insurrections of any note have succeeded without significant outside help. As one commentator recently observed, in thirteen of the seventeen most notable examples of successful revolutions or internal wars fought since the American revolution, the ' "rebels" received significant assistance from outside the country'.[19] Not only are there few signs that the trend will taper off in the near future, but there is every indication that the intrusion of external influences into the arenas of conflict of the Third World will become a factor of increasing importance in years to come.

In what must be regarded as the most ambitious attempt so far to reduce the problem of 'external involvement in internal wars' to scientific analysis, Karl Deutsch has recently suggested that 'our judgement of the domestic or foreign-controlled character of an internal war [can] be made more precise and more clearly comparable by introducing some simple measurement of at least some of their relevant aspects'.[20] This would presumably require quantification of the duration and extent of internal wars as well as of 'the recruitment and attrition rates of each of the contending forces'. This, we are told, might be computed in terms of how much 'manpower, money, material, and specialized services' have been contributed from the outside, and by estimating 'what the rates of recruitment and attrition might have been if there had been no outside intervention on either side, or only on one side'.[21]

Whether these and other attempts at quantification can be operationalised in any meaningful fashion is very dubious, however; not only is the necessary data in most cases difficult to come by, but much of it is simply not amenable to quantification. To calculate variations in the rates of recruitment and attrition of a revolutionary movement would be taxing enough under any circumstances, but to do so under the conditions of fear and suspicion created by foreign intervention is a task which only the most naive, or the most foolhardy, would care to undertake with any serious hope of success. The kind of data one would need to have in order to pursue this line of investigation is most likely to rest in classified files, and these are rarely made available to social scientists.

Many of the dimensions of external involvement are too elusive to permit precise quantification. According to Deutsch, 'even some qualitative aspects of the performance of the contending sides in an internal war can be gauged with the help of quantitative indicators. Such qualitative aspects include co-ordination, style of behaviour, and the presence or absence of certain themes, practices, symbols and behaviour patterns.'[22] Yet, even if statistical evidence on such factors were available, which is seldom the case, the reliability of the findings might still remain questionable. To make plainer the nature of these objections, the case of the Congo rebellion, which lasted approximately from late 1963 to early 1965, might be taken as an example. No one would dispute the usefulness of statistical evidence about the rate of recruitment of the Congolese 'Liberation Army' prior to the involvement of mercenary elements on the side of the legitimate government of the Congo, and its subsequent rate of attrition as a result of external intervention. If it exists, such data will probably never become available to Western political scientists; but even if it were available one would still have to take several other factors into account before reaching a reasonably valid conclusion about the effects of outside intervention— for example, the leadership crises suffered by the rebel army, the influence of magic on the morale (and suicidal behaviour) of the troops, the ethnic and social contexts of the rebellion—not all of which is susceptible to quantification. Similarly strong evidence about the importance of non-quantifiable factors might be gathered from an examination of the Rwandese situation: neither the style of behaviour of the revolutionaries in relation to the masses, the co-ordination of their strategies with the policy of the 'tutelle', nor the use of traditional symbols and institutions, really lends itself to computer analysis.

All one can infer from the Rwandese 'experiment' are certain general hypotheses about the probable influence of such factors as the timing of external involvement, its relation to the depth of internal cleavages in the environment in which it occurs, and the pattern of symmetry discernible in the character and sources of external intervention.

If one can speak of an 'optimum' timing for outside intervention, it is not only in relation to the sequence of revolutionary developments in a given territory but also in the light of the international status which this territory may claim at any given time. In regard to the first of these variables it is clear that where the initial sequence of outbreaks is primarily anomic, unstructured, much will depend on the nature of the countermoves initiated immediately thereafter by the incumbents to restore 'peace and order'. It is at this juncture that outside forces and influences can decisively influence subsequent developments. Inasmuch as it may help prevent the application of effective security measures by the incumbents, or help accelerate the institutionalisation of the revolutionary flux (as was so obviously the case in Rwanda), outside intervention may become a critical asset in the hands of the insurgents; conversely, where the weight of outside intervention is wholly on the side of the incumbents, its 'prophylactic' value may be just as important. The next point is that outside intervention, in order to be effective, requires at least a partial surrender of the prerogatives of national sovereignty from the host community, a condition scarcely compatible with the facts of national independence. How much sovereignty, if any, ought to be surrendered may become an issue of central significance to both the 'host' and the 'outsiders', and, unless a mutually satisfactory formula is devised to meet this problem, the internal bickerings that are then likely to arise are bound to seriously compromise the effectiveness of outside intervention. The reverse proposition, illustrated by the case of Rwanda, is that under conditions of non-sovereignty, or limited sovereignty, these internal strains, in whatever form they may arise, can be more effectively managed.

The effects of outside intervention must also be evaluated against the backdrop of the social structure in which it takes place. Here again there are some instructive gleanings to be had from an examination of the situation in Rwanda. Although we did stress on several occasions the social obstacles militating against the emergence of a strong, unified revolutionary movement, we also tried to indicate why traditional Rwandese society, with its rigid caste structure, contained such an exceptionally rich revolutionary potential, and why, by contrast, the configuration of caste relationships in Burundi tended to dampen whatever revolutionary proclivities existed among the peasants. We have also noted the very different reactions of the Hutu leadership in each country to what were, after all, basically similar attempts by the Belgian administration to encourage and assist the 'emancipation' of the 'menu peuple'. One can hardly avoid the conclusion that, in Rwanda, outside intervention operated within the limits of a social environment eminently favourable to the growth of revolutionary sentiment, an environment in which an almost perpendicular split was beginning to emerge between Hutu and Tutsi and where the ratio of numerical strength between them overwhelmingly favoured the insurgents. In brief, the effectiveness of outside intervention is likely to increase in proportion to the depth of mutual antagonisms among domestic factions. Where these antagonisms are still superficial enough to be superseded by a common apprehension of outside intervention, a common resentment of the 'foreigners', as happened in Burundi, intervention is likely to have the opposite effect of what it set out to achieve.[23]

A third dimension of the problem relates to the degree of symmetry discernible in the incidence of external influences. As the case of Rwanda makes plain, where outside involvement is unilateral, or so heavily one-sided as to create a relationship of asymmetry between the insurgents and their adversaries, the effect will be to increase the superiority of one group against the other to a degree which would obviously be inconceivable were each side to receive equal support from outside sources. By contrast, the pattern of bipolarity that has developed in Burundi after independence shows the extent to which competing influences from the outside tend to cancel each other when the internal balance of forces tends to duplicate the symmetry of outside involvement.

Looking at the problem of outside intervention from a somewhat broader perspective, there is yet an additional point to be made. Although this is still the standard argument advanced by the European oligarchies in areas of residual colonialism, the all-too prevalent assumption that violent, revolutionary upheavals are generally fomented by Marxist or Marxist-inspired movements is difficult to sustain in the light of the Rwandese experience. The criterion usually employed to determine the Marxist coloration of any revolution is the tactics by which it is conducted, a fact which recently prompted one observer to describe as 'an irony of our day' 'that most movements and tactics involving violence are attributed to Communism while genuinely revolutionary attempts to alter the foundations of certain societies without the use of violence are practically ignored'.[24] In Rwanda, the Belgian authorities, by action and by omission, allowed the insurgents to use very much the same kind of tactics—ranging from small-scale guerrilla warfare to flagrant breaches of legality—as are ordinarily attributed to Communist-led insurrections. Even though the reverse is admittedly more likely, the assertion that some Western countries may at times find it profitable or desirable to encourage revolutionary activities in order to secure a political base compatible with their immediate political interests and ideological commitments is perhaps not quite as fantastic as some would like to believe.

The Dynamics of Political Modernisation

Bernard Lewis's characterisation of Ottoman Turkey—'What existed was not a nation but a domination'[25]—gives us a hint of the contradictions involved in political modernisation in Rwanda. In a sense, traditional Rwanda was both a nation and a domination, and whatever success it may have claimed in the building of a nation was owed to no small extent to the fact of Tutsi domination. Despite occasional instances of cultural syncretism, the Rwanda monarchy was a Tutsi creation, and on this point Tutsi oral traditions merely record a basic historical fact. Thus the passing of the monarchy in Rwanda was much less a symptom of its inherently 'traditionalistic', 'backward' properties, than the result of a fundamental contradiction between one crucial aspect of tradition (elitism) and one equally central feature of political modernisation (popular participation). Conversely, one might argue that the reason why Burundi was comparatively more receptive to the principle of popular participation, and hence more 'modern' on this score, is because it did not possess the same degree of social and political centralisation, and was perhaps more 'traditional' in this respect than Rwanda.

Besides highlighting the selectivity with which modernisation operates, the foregoing suggests that instead of regarding 'tradition' and 'modernity' as incompatible, polar opposites, it might be more useful for analytical purposes to assume some degree of complementarity between them. To conceive of tradition and modernity as mutually exclusive necessarily obscures the elements of continuity which link them together, or what some writers refer to as 'the modernity of tradition', or the 'tradition of the new'.[26]

Behind these seemingly contradictory juxtapositions of language lies a phenomenon which is basic to an appreciation of the complexity of the historical forces and social mechanisms involved in political modernisation; this phenomenon, at bottom reducible to the simple proposition that some traditions are more modern than others, helps us understand why neither in Rwanda nor in Burundi the severance of certain traditional ties can be taken as proof of a corresponding input of modernity, and why, in specific cases, the introduction of new political structures is liable to hamper the release of whatever modernising potential inheres in tradition.

If Rwanda has come anywhere near the goal of political modernisation, this is because the revolutionary elites are heirs to a centralising tradition that went on unabated for centuries prior to the revolution. As already noted, this tradition was an essentially Tutsi tradition, which gradually undermined the divisive, particularistic tendencies of the pre-Tutsi (i.e. Hutu) societies, culminating with the rise of a strongly centralised state-system. In this process, the universalist norms of the Tutsi invaders (that is, universalist in relation to themselves) were substituted for the parochial, inward-looking, familial orientations of the indigenous Hutu societies; a 'national' monarchical structure was instituted where only clan solidarities previously existed; and 'functional' divisions eventually replaced those previously based on family or clan affiliations. This, indeed, was 'nation-building': in a fundamental sense, the establishment of a Tutsi state in Rwanda laid the foundations of a modern polity. But this process of nation-building did not take place all at once. Pockets of parochialism persisted in the north for some time after the inception of colonial rule, and the resistance they offered to the Tutsi imperium was overcome only with the greatest difficulty. To the extent that the revolution was an attempt to reverse the course of history, so as to restore to the Hutu the independence they had had before the Tutsi conquest, a good deal of the modernising influences of the Tutsi monarchy was lost in the process, or rejected for the sake of a pre-Tutsi tradition in some major ways incompatible with the requirements of political modernisation.

Viewed in this perspective, an understanding of the phenomenon of modernisation involves more than an attempt to identify a checklist of variables and see whether they are satisfied by the modernising society. It involves delineating the boundaries of conflict between several types of traditions, some of which are more 'modern' than others: (i) pre-Tutsi traditions; (ii) Tutsi traditions; and (iii) the tradition of 'dual over-rule' introduced by Belgium.

At the root of the transformations wrought by the Rwanda revolution lies a fundamental ambiguity of political motives and cultural orientations. Inasmuch as it was a war of independence against an 'alien', modernising oligarchy, many of the difficulties at present confronting the incumbent Hutu elites are similar to those faced elsewhere in Africa by nationalist leaders. They tend to express a conflict or disjunction between the modern superstructure imported by a once-dominant oligarchy and the survival, or resurgence from below, of particularistic identifications. Inasmuch as it was a genuine political and social revolution against the perpetuation of minority rule and privileges, and expressed an irresistible urge on the part of the masses to become active participants in the affairs of their country, the revolution has raised in the path of modernisation the same kind of obstacles which elsewhere in Africa have often followed in the wake of democratisation—namely, a commitment to a form of government which, by virtue of the diffusion of power it implies, is more likely to hamper than aid the modernisation of society as a whole.

Which reminds us of Huntington's thesis that, insofar as modernisation implies a rapid increase in mass mobilisation and participation, it may lead to the very opposite of what it seeks to achieve—namely, a breakdown of political institutions and, ultimately, political decay. To put it differently, the development of a stable polity, itself a prerequisite of political modernisation, assumes a 'slowing down' of mass mobilisation, to permit a sufficient concentration of power at the top, and enough governmental autonomy to the modernising elites, to enable them to create stable, strong and efficient institutions. A corollary proposition is that, where a traditional regime possesses those centralising, étatiste features, while at the same time being faced with the obligation of making concessions to rising demands for popular participation, its life expectancy is necessarily short.[27]

Rwanda illustrates this dilemma better than any other modernising polity; better than any other traditional state in Africa, it confirms Huntington's hypothesis that 'the vulnerability of a traditional regime to revolution varies directly with the capacity of the regime for modernization'.[28] The question arises, however, as to whether the new regime born of the revolution can afford to reject the centralising features of the Tutsi monarchy (as it normally must, if only by the logic of its democratic commitments) for the sake of improving its democratic 'image', or whether the exigencies of rapid modernisation are such that monarchical despotism is bound to reappear in a new guise. Here lies the crux of the dilemma currently faced by the revolutionary elites: how to be authoritarian enough to ensure rapid modernisation and political stability, and yet not so starkly authoritarian as to conjure up memories of the ancien régime.

As we have seen, the Tutsi 'model' has all but disappeared. Now, as before, authoritarianism is the rule rather than the exception; consciously or unconsciously, the governing elites have borrowed from the past the tools to shape the future. Every effort is made to promote political centralisation to the maximum extent compatible with, but inevitably at the expense of, democratic norms and institutions. This is achieved largely by traditional means, by the extension of a chain of clientage relations between the central and local elites. The ritual of a presidential *mwami*-ship has been substituted for the ritual of the Tutsi monarchy, and the dogma of Hutu supremacy for the myth of

Tutsi superiority. True, the mystique of the revolution carries another logic, which prompts a re-evaluation of current practice in the light of revolutionary norms. New voices are being heard, which proclaim the pre-eminence of values that are inconsistent with the survival of a neo-monarchical order. But these have yet to make an impact on the masses. It is indeed questionable whether the average Hutu peasant has been stirred into a new political consciousness by the revolution; all the revolution meant for him was a shift in the direction of clientage ties, not a drastic alteration of the pre-existing authority system. This in turn makes it possible for the republican elites to seize upon the more authoritarian features of the traditional monarchy to complete and accelerate the process of modernisation begun under the auspices of Tutsi supremacy. The centralised character of the monarchy persists in the guise of republican institutions and furnishes the weapons necessary to curb whatever divisive tendencies exist among the masses. This is all the more feasible as the homogenisation of society accomplished through revolutionary surgery has at the same time eliminated the obstacles inherent in caste and ethnic divisions. In these circumstances, political mobilisation becomes a far less risky enterprise. To be sure, there is still the ever-present risk of alienating the new, up-and-coming generations of Hutu intellectuals, but this is a minor liability as long as ethnic solidarities between them and the incumbent elites can be manipulated to provide alternative sources of cohesion, and as long as the danger—real or imaginary—of Tutsi subversion can still be exploited for this purpose.

This is where current efforts at modernisation in Burundi carry entirely different implications. In recent times, the activation of ethnic solidarities has created enormous pressures for broadening political participation, pressures which, as we have seen, not only led to the downfall of the monarchy but continue to hamper the tasks of nation-building and modernisation to an extent unparalleled in contemporary Rwanda. Not that the Burundi monarchy was in any real sense incapable of bridging status distinctions between Hutu and Tutsi; the point, rather, is that these distinctions were never sharp enough initially to produce as violent and drastic a transformation as in Rwanda, but were sufficiently strong to create a rapid polarisation of ethnic loyalties once these were caught in the mill of democratisation. As we have seen, traditionally the continuity and interconnectedness of changes within Burundi society expressed themselves *not* at the level of Tutsi versus Hutu traditions, but at the level of cyclical feuds within the upper caste (i.e., the *ganwa* caste). Because of these divisions, the Burundi monarchy was a rather poor instrument for mediating changes through society as a whole; the

493

fragmentation of power among rival factions of the royal family produced similar discontinuities in the range and depth of social changes initiated at the top. As a result of these discontinuities, and because *ganwa* rivalries tended to encourage cohesion among the various ethnic sub-sections of society, what Burundi lost on the scale of centralisation it gained on the scale of integration, precisely the reverse of what occurred in Rwanda. Ironically, although the monarchy did manage to transform itself into a fairly centralised institution, ultimately this very centralisation of power at the top was enough to make it vulnerable to forcible overthrow.

Here again the contrast between Rwanda and Burundi is best understood in the light of Huntington's observation:

> In general, the more highly stratified a society is, and the more complicated its social structure, the more gradual is the process of political mobilization. The divisions between class and class, occupation and occupation, rural and urban, constitute a series of breakwaters which divide the society and permit the political mobilization of one group at a time. On the other hand, a highly homogeneous society, or a society which has only a simple horizontal line of division between an oligarchy that has everything and a peasantry that has nothing, or a society which is divided not horizontally but vertically into ethnic and communal groups, has more difficulty moderating the process of mobilization.[29]

Thus, if the mobilisation of the Hutu masses of Rwanda was unquestionably facilitated by the presence of a sharp, vertical split between the aristocracy and the peasantry, in Burundi, where the division between rulers and ruled was not nearly as easy to identify, and where the monarchy was relatively free of ethnic 'bias', the mobilisation of the masses along ethnic lines was at first rendered all the more arduous. As long as the key political issues remained centred on what looked like a continuation of *ganwa* rivalries, the prestige of the crown remained unimpaired. And, even after the crown had emerged triumphant, a host of subsidiary cleavages persisted, as between *ganwa* and non-*ganwa*, Tutsi and Hima, modern and traditional elements, which for a while tended to blur the incipient ethnic split between Hutu and Tutsi. Residual loyalties to the crown, along with the fact that no elections were held in the years immediately following independence, contributed to give the monarchy an air of stability. Yet, no sooner were elections held than ethnic loyalties were suddenly stirred into action; by then, moreover, whatever institutions or social structures had helped mitigate ethnic competition could no longer adequately serve this purpose.

The party had disintegrated; *ganwa* rivalries had ceased to be an issue; and the subsequent efforts of the crown to deprive the Hutu of their electoral gains was bound to cast further discredit upon the monarchy. Not the least of the ironies discernible in this situation is that the Burundi monarchy, at first so different from its Rwandese analogue, in time developed precisely the same type of centralised apparatus and with very much the same results. In its attempt to cope with the centralist requirements of political modernisation, the Burundi monarchy exposed itself to the same suicidal consequences as the Rwanda monarchy by its refusal to meet the demands for popular participation created by the surge of political democracy.

Whether Micombero can succeed where Mwambutsa and Ntare failed, whether the virtues of 'Micomberism' will prove sufficient to avert a duplication of the revolutionary trauma experienced by Rwanda, is impossible to say. Although the army has the guns, naked force alone may not be enough to keep the forces of ethnic particularism in check; and even if that much should be accomplished, one may still wonder whether the army possesses the skills necessary to promote rapid modernisation. Should this mean a surrender of power to the civilian elites, a new cycle of instability and revolutionary upheaval may very likely be the result. Whatever the case may be, and as the example of Rwanda suggests, this will not prevent the traditional society from renewing its claims upon the newly-emergent order, whether in the form of patrimonial ties or factional struggles. The crux of the problem is whether these can now be divested of their ethnic content, and whether the system can stabilise itself long enough to prevent it from disintegrating in the midst of ethnic strife.

No matter how deep the transformations to which it is subjected, no society can embark upon the creation of a new order in a total vacuum. Links which one thought had been severed once and for all are quietly re-established; in varying degrees, the tenaciousness of the past determines the shape of the future.

'Men who share an ethnic area', writes Erik Erikson, 'an historical era, or an economic pursuit are guided by common images of good and evil. Infinitely varied, these images reflect the elusive nature of historical change; yet in the form of contemporary social models of compelling prototypes of good and evil, they assume decisive concreteness in every individual's ego developments.'[30] No more than individuals, societies cannot claim immunity from the traumas of brutal, radical political change, and their collective ego may suffer similar maladjustments as a result of specific historical experiences. If there is any truth to the contention that 'therapy and guidance [on the individual plane] may

495

attempt to substitute more desirable identifications for undesirable ones, but the total configuration of the ego identity remains unalterable',[31] it is equally true that, no matter how traumatic a revolution may have been in its consequences, and all-embracing in its goals, the collective identity of a nation cannot be recreated from scratch. Political therapy in the form of constitutional devices, representative institutions, and so on, can and often does bring about new identifications, but seldom do these operate in isolation from previous values and historical experiences. Again, commenting on the 're-education of "bad" nations', Erikson writes: 'It can be predicted that no admission of having sinned and no promises to be good will make a nation "democratic" unless the new identity offered can be integrated with previous concepts of strong and weak, masculine and feminine, based on experiences in the geographical-historical matrix of the nation and the childhood of the individual.'[32] Similarly, resort to egalitarian therapy will not prove sufficient to exorcise the 'premise of inequality' from the collective identity of the Rwandese; nor is the Micomberist revolution likely to obliterate the patrimonial syndrome from the consciousness of the Barundi. In each case, a new synthesis will have to be devised, incorporating within itself at least some of the elements of the traditional society; how to operate this synthesis, so as to render possible the sublimation of atavistic tendencies into constructive, modernising, socially-acceptable modes of behaviour is one of the most crucial and perplexing aspects of the process of political epigenesis inaugurated in each state by the advent of democratic norms and institutions.

Thus, if there is any existential dimension to a revolution, only the most impenitent of contemporary existentialists would claim that it entails a total jump. Nor is it possible to postulate the redemptive force of violence as a sufficient condition of moral rebirth. These themes, of course, are familiar to the devotees of Sartre and Fanon: 'Violence is a cleansing force', writes Fanon. 'It forces the native from his inferiority complex and from his despair and inaction; it makes him fearless and restores his self-respect. . . . For the native life can spring up again from the rotting corpse of the settler. . . . Violence unifies the people.'[33] Yet the case of Rwanda illustrates better than any other example of large-scale violence how wide of the mark Fanon's analysis really is. That violence did help unify the Hutu is undeniable; but whether it did succeed in 'freeing [the peasant] from his inferiority complex', in 'making him fearless' and in 'restoring his self-respect' is what remains to be seen. Whether the only effective remedy lies in further violence also remains in doubt.

And yet it is here, perhaps, that the relevance of Fanon's thesis suggests itself, and, oddly enough, because each country in its own way deviates so markedly from Fanon's apocalyptic vision. In each country the peasantry is still in a state of near-bondage; in many instances the caste system has reasserted itself with a vengeance, with the result that inferior-superior relations still carry the traditional stigma of the master-servant nexus. In these conditions, social discontent is likely to persist. If so, the 'next round' may well be Fanonist in its inspiration. Fanon's call may yet provide the ideological arsenal which will enable the peasants (or, better, their spokesmen) to bring their existence in line with their aspirations. As one of Fanon's most lucid interpreters puts it, 'for quite some time to come, the new rulers of the African nations will be faced with the specter of peasant uprisings and disaffections—and Fanon's myth will haunt them, much as the Communist Manifesto and its myth haunted the mill owners of Victorian Europe'.[34]

Beyond this, it is impossible to make a reliable prophecy of what Rwanda and Burundi may look like in ten or twenty years. But this much at least is clear: it is not because a society refuses to let itself sink into the formless chaos of a cultural revolution of the Maoist type that it must necessarily shut itself to all possibilities of internal change. All revolutions are to some extent cultural revolutions, and because of the crises they engender in the minds and lives of individuals, and the way in which they survive in the memories of subsequent generations, they belong to a unique range of historical experiences. They express a fundamental challenge to accustomed ways of thinking and modes of behaviour, and thus inaugurate a process of self-renewal that goes on uninterrupted from generation to generation. Whether the Rwandese revolution will acquire its permanency through a process of cultural regeneration or through a new round of violence—whether the Micomberist revolution can provide a viable substitute to ethnic violence, and in so doing combine the integrative functions of the traditional monarchy with the leadership and guidance of a modernising polity—is as yet unpredictable.

APPENDIX I

Chronology of the Kings of Rwanda and Burundi

RWANDA

Name	Date of Accession to Throne
Ndahiro Ruyange	?
Ndoba	1386
Samembe	1410
Nsoro Samukondo	1434
Ruganzu Bwimba	1458
Cylima Rugwe	1482
Kigeri Mukobanya	1506
Mibambwe Mutabaazi	1528
Yuhi Gahima	1552
Ndahiro Cyaamatare	1576
Ruganzu Ndoori	1600
Mutara Seemugeshi	1624
Kigeri Nyamuheshera	1648
Mibambwe Gisanura	1672
Yuhi Mazimpaka	1696
Karemeera Rwaaka	1720
Cyilima Rujugira	1744
Kigeli Ndabarasa	1768
Mibambwe Seentaabyo	1792
Yuhi Gahindiro	1797
Mutara Rwoogera	1830
Kigeri Rwabugiri	1860
Mibambwe Rutalindwa	1895
Yuhi Musinga	1896
Mutara Rudahigwa	1931
Kigeri Ndahundirwa	1959

BURUNDI

Name	Date of Accession to Throne
Ntare Rushatsi	1675
Mwezi I	1705
Mutaga I Seenyamwiiza	1735
Mwambutsa I	1765
Ntare II Rugaamba	1795
Mwezi II Kisabo	1852
Mutaga II	1908
Mwambutsa II	1916
Ntare III Ndizeye	1966

Source (for both tables): Jan Vansina, *L'Evolution du Royaume Rwanda des origines à 1900*, ARSOM, Brussels 1962, Vol. XXVI, fasc. 2, p. 56; and "Notes sur l'Histoire du Burundi", *Aequatoria*, No. 1, 1961, p. 4.

Genealogy of the Kings of Burundi,
1795–1966

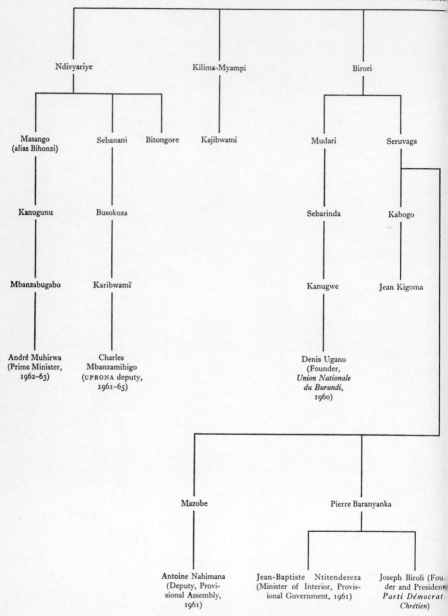

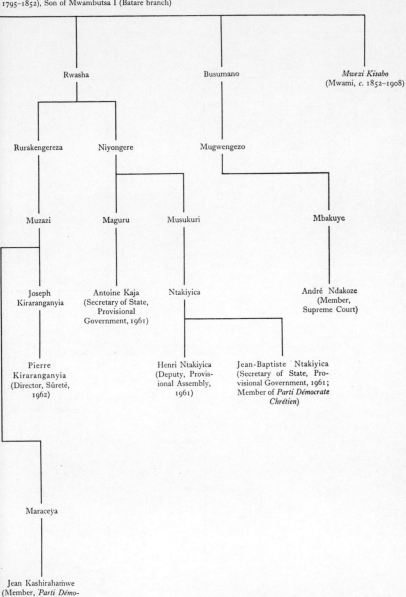

r. 1795–1852), Son of Mwambutsa I (Batare branch)

Rwasha   Busumano   *Mwezi Kisabo*
(Mwami, *c.* 1852–1908)

Rurakengereza   Niyongere   Mugwengezo

Muzazi   Maguru   Musukuri   Mbakuye

Joseph
Kiraranganyia

Antoine Kaja
(Secretary of State,
Provisional
Government, 1961)

Ntakiyica

André Ndakoze
(Member,
Supreme Court)

Pierre
Kiraranganyia
(Director, Sûreté,
1962)

Henri Ntakiyica
(Deputy, Provis-
ional Assembly,
1961)

Jean-Baptiste Ntakiyica
(Secretary of State, Pro-
visional Government, 1961;
Member of *Parti Démocrate
Chrétien*)

Maraceÿa

Jean Kashirahamwe
(Member, *Parti Démo-
crate Chrétien*; Deputy,
1961, 1965)

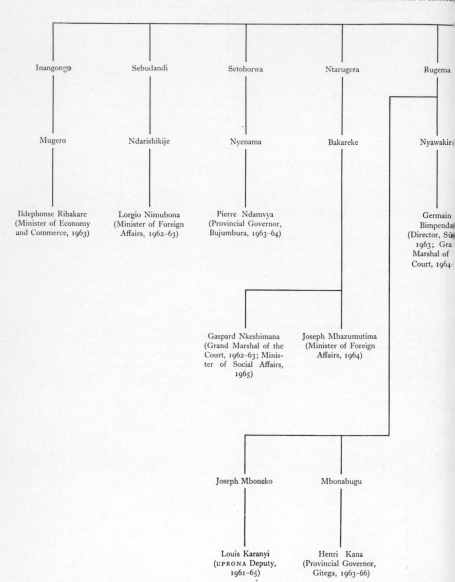

Inangongo — Mugero — Ildephonse Ribakare (Minister of Economy and Commerce, 1963)

Sebudandi — Ndarishikije — Lorgio Nimubona (Minister of Foreign Affairs, 1962-63)

Setoborwa — Nyenama — Pierre Ndamvya (Provincial Governor, Bujumbura, 1963-64)

Ntarugera — Bakareke

Rugema — Nyawakir — Germain Bimpenda (Director, Sû 1963; Gra Marshal of Court, 1964

Gaspard Nkeshimana (Grand Marshal of the Court, 1962-63; Minister of Social Affairs, 1965)

Joseph Mbazumutima (Minister of Foreign Affairs, 1964)

Joseph Mboneko — Louis Karanyi (UPRONA Deputy, 1961-65)

Mbonabugu — Henri Kana (Provincial Governor, Gitega, 1963-66)

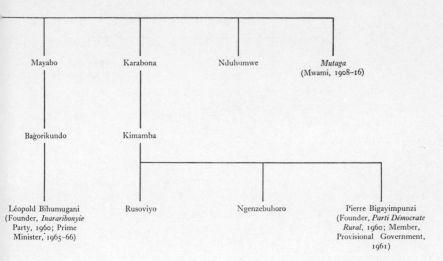

Mayabo   Karabona   Nduhumwe   *Mutaga*
                                        (Mwami, 1908-16)

Bagorikundo   Kimamba

Léopold Bihumugani   Rusoviyo   Ngenzebuhoro   Pierre Bigayimpunzi
(Founder, *Inararibonyie*   (Founder, *Parti Démocrate*
Party, 1960; Prime   *Rural,* 1960; Member,
Minister, 1965-66)   Provisional Government,
                                                        1961)

3. MWAMI MUTAGA II (1908–16), Son of Mwezi II (Bataga branch)

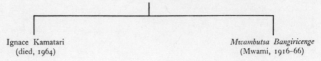

Ignace Kamatari
(died, 1964)

Mwambutsa Bangiricenge
(Mwami, 1916–66)

4. MWAMI MWAMBUTSA II (1916–66), Son of Mutaga II (Bambutsa branch)

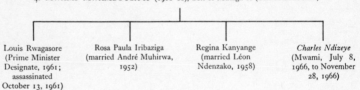

Louis Rwagasore
(Prime Minister
Designate, 1961;
assassinated
October 13, 1961)

Rosa Paula Iribaziga
(married André Muhirwa,
1952)

Regina Kanyange
(married Léon
Ndenzako, 1958)

Charles Ndizeye
(Mwami, July 8,
1966, to November
28, 1966)

5. MWAMI NTARE III (July–November 1966), Son of Mwambutsa II

Notes and References

Introduction

1. For a discussion of the differences and similarities between the Rwandese and Zanzibari revolutions, see René Lemarchand, "Revolutionary phenomena in stratified societies: Rwanda and Zanzibar", *Civilisations*, Vol. XVIII, No. 1, 1968, pp. 1–34. For an excellent background study of the Zanzibari revolution, see Michael Lofchie, *Zanzibar: Background to Revolution*, Oxford University Press, London and New York 1965.
2. See Rupert Emerson, "Nation-Building in Africa", in Karl W. Deutsch & William J. Folz, eds., *Nation-Building*, Atherton Press, New York 1963, p. 104.
3. See Claude E. Welch, "The Challenge of Change: Meiji Japan and Contemporary Africa", a paper prepared for delivery at the 1965 annual meeting of the African Studies Association, Philadelphia 1965.
4. For a further discussion of the patterns of deviancy between each state, and of the deviations which they both represent from Ted Gurr's predictions of civil violence, see Samuel P. Huntington, *Political Order in Changing Societies*, Yale University Press, New Haven and London 1968, pp. 173–4; cf. Ted Gurr with Charles Ruttenberg, *The Conditions of Civil Violence*, Princeton University, Center of International Studies, Research Monograph No. 28, Princeton University Press, Princeton 1967.
5. Gerald D. Berreman, "Caste in India and the United States", *American Journal of Sociology*, Vol. LXVI, 1960–61, p. 120.
6. M. G. Smith, *The Plural Society in the British West Indies*, University of California Press, Berkeley 1965, especially pp. 75–91.
7. J. J. Maquet, "La participation de la classe paysanne au mouvement d'indépendance au Rwanda", *Cahiers d'Etudes Africaines*, Vol. IV, 1964, p. 557.
8. P. C. Lloyd, *The New Elites of Tropical Africa*, Oxford University Press, London and New York 1966, p. 56.
9. René Dumont, *L'Afrique Noire est mal partie*, Le Seuil, Paris 1962, p. 63.
10. See Lloyd, loc. cit.
11. Crane Brinton, *The Anatomy of Revolution*, Vintage Books, New York 1957, p. 4.

1. The Lands and the People

1. Adolphus Frederick, Duke of Mecklenburg, *In the Heart of Africa*, Cassel, London 1910, p. 44.
2. Le Commissaire de District Adjoint, Resident au Ruanda, *Rapport*, Kigali, November 15, 1920; in the Derscheid Collection.
3. For further information, see *Le Ruanda-Urundi*, Brussels 1959, pp. 286 ff.
4. Ibid., p. 277.

5. Marc Bloch, *Feudal Society*, Routledge and Kegan Paul, London 1965, p. 145.

6. Drawing on the insights of Max Weber, Professor J. J. Maquet uses the terms 'state feudalism' and 'non-state feudalism' to differentiate the political system of Rwanda from that of Burundi, taking as his main variable the degree of control exercised by the central authorities over means of coercion; but it is a question whether his use of the term 'feudalism' strengthens the force of his argument. See J. J. Maquet, "Une hypothèse pour l'étude des féodalités africaines", *Cahiers d'Etudes Africaines*, Vol. II, No. 6, pp. 292–313. There is no point here in reopening the debate on the applicability of the concept of feudalism to African societies. Indeed, the term has been used in so many different ways as to make it applicable to a variety of situations. (See, for example, Jack Goodie, "Feudalism in Africa", *Journal of African History*, Vol. IV, 1963, pp. 1–18; and J. H. M. Beattie, "Bunyoro: An African Feudality?", ibid., Vol. V, 1964, pp. 24–36.) Suffice it to note that Rwanda and Burundi came as close to the ideal of a feudal society as any other two societies in Africa. In this discussion, the term feudalism is used to refer to a 'contractual relationship with a feudal overlord requiring the exchange of services and an oath of fealty', the definition used by G. Almond and B. Powell Jr. in *Comparative Politics: A Developmental Approach*, Little, Brown, Boston 1966, p. 252.

7. Mecklenburg, op. cit., p. 47.

8. Cited in Hans Meyer, *Die Barundi*, Otto Spamer, Leipzig 1916, p. 14.

9. Mecklenburg, op. cit., p. 47.

10. Meyer, op. cit.

11. See Jan Vansina, *L'Evolution du Royaume du Rwanda des Origines à 1900*, ARSOM, Vol. XXVI, fasc. 2, Brussels 1962.

12. Joseph Rugomana, *Les rois du pays Rundi et les hommes qui y sont venus les premiers*, mimeo, recorded by A. Coupez in December 1963 in Muramvya, for the Institut de la Recherche Scientifique en Afrique Centrale.

13. *Règne de Rwabugiri: essai par J. M. Derscheid, 1929, pour une conférence à l'Université Coloniale de Belgique;* in the Derscheid Collection.

14. Ibid.

15. A. d'Arianoff, *Histoire des Bagesera Souverains du Gisaka*, IRCB, Vol. XXIV, fasc. 3, Brussels 1952, pp. 88 ff.

16. The only detailed anthropological study of the Kiga is May Mandelbaum Edel, *The Chiga of Western Uganda*, Oxford University Press, New York and London 1957; but, as the title indicates, the book does not deal specifically with the Kiga of northern Rwanda. For a brief but enlightening discussion of the traditional political organisation of the Kiga populations of northern Rwanda before the Tutsi penetration, see Vansina, op. cit., pp. 77–81. The different patterns of cultural assimilation brought in the wake of the Tutsi conquest are discussed in René Lemarchand, "Power and Stratification in Rwanda: A Reconsideration", *Cahiers d'Etudes Africaines*, Vol. VI, No. 24, pp. 592–610.

17. See Jan Vansina, "Notes sur l'Histoire du Burundi", *Aequatoria*, No. 1, 1961, pp. 1–10.

18. G. Simmel, *Conflict*, trans. Kurt H. Wolff, Free Press, Glencoe 1955, p. 98.

19. Ethel Albert, "Women of Burundi: A Study of Social Values", in D. Paulme, ed., *Women in Tropical Africa*, University of California Press, Berkeley 1963, p. 180.

20. Meyer, op. cit., p. 167.
21. *Rapport sur l'administration belge des territoires occupés de l'Est Africain Allemand*, Brussels 1921, p. 16.
22. L. A. Fallers, ed., *The King's Men*, Oxford University Press, London and New York 1964, p. 98.
23. Lucy Mair, *Primitive Government*, Penguin Books, Harmondsworth and Baltimore 1962, p. 153.
24. Meyer, op. cit., p. 91.
25. Pierre Ghislain, *Territoire de Rutana: Note sur le Mosso*, n.d., unpublished document.
26. See "Essai de définition de l'institution historique des bashigantahe", in *Conseil Supérieur du Pays, Procès-Verbaux*, Kitega 1956, pp. 38 ff.
27. Ibid.
28. André Makarakiza, *La Dialectique des Barundi*, ARSC, Vol. XIX, fasc. 2, Brussels 1959, pp. 38–9.
29. Edward Shils and Michael Young, "The Meaning of the Coronation", *Sociological Review*, Vol. I, 1953, p. 79.
30. Bronislaw Malinowski, *Magic, Science and Religion and Other Essays*, Doubleday, New York, n.d., p. 146.
31. See A. Kagame, "Le Code ésotérique de la Dynastie du Rwanda", *Zaire*, Vol. IV, 1947, pp. 363–86. The text of the *ubwiru* will be found in Marcel d'Hertefelt and A. Coupez, *La Royauté Sacrée de l'Ancien Rwanda*, Musée Royal de l'Afrique Centrale, Tervueren 1964, in French and Kinyarwanda.
32. Jacques J. Maquet, *The Premise of Inequality in Ruanda*, Oxford University Press, London and New York, 1961.
33. Malinowski, op. cit., p. 126.
34. Cited in A. Kagame, "La Poésie au Rwanda", in *Compte-Rendu des Travaux du Séminaire d'Anthropologie Sociale*, IRSAC, Astrida 1952, p. 20.
35. Cited in M. D'Hertefelt, "Myth and Political Acculturation in Rwanda", paper presented at the XIVth Conference of the Rhodes-Livingstone Institute for Social Research, Lusaka, March 1960.
36. Ibid.
37. Helen Codere, "Power in Rwanda", *Anthropologica*, Vol. IV, No. 1, 1962, pp. 45–87.
38. See. L. A. Fallers, "Equality, Modernity and Democracy in the New States", in Clifford Geertz, ed., *Old Societies and New States*, Free Press, Glencoe 1963, pp. 162 ff.
39. J. J. Maquet, "The Kingdom of Rwanda", in D. Forde, *African Worlds*, Oxford University Press, London and New York 1954, p. 187.
40. Ibid.
41. H. H. Gerth and G. W. Mills, eds., *From Max Weber: Essays in Sociology*, Oxford University Press, London and New York 1958.
42. Pierre Gravel, *The Play for Power: Description of a Community in Eastern Ruanda*, unpublished PH.D. dissertation, University of Michigan 1962.
43. Ibid., p. 229.
44. "Le contrat d'ubugabire: Une coutume Murundi", *Bulletin de Jurisprudence des Tribunaux Indigènes du Ruanda-Urundi*, No. 3, 1947, p. 135.
45. Mecklenburg, op. cit., p. 54.
46. Meyer, op. cit., p. 14.
47. Ibid., p. 15.
48. Ibid.

49. Ibid.
50. Ibid., p. 16.
51. Interview with A. Makuza, September 1965.
52. *Conseil Supérieur du Pays, Procès-Verbaux*, Kitega 1957, p. 77.
53. Mgr Gorju, *Face au Royaume Hamite du Rwanda: Le Royaume frère de l'Urundi*, Vromant, Brussels 1938, p. 9.

2. HISTORICAL SURVEY

1. Roger Louis, *Ruanda-Urundi, 1884–1919*, Clarendon Press, Oxford 1963, p. 106.
2. Henry Morton Stanley, *Through the Dark Continent*, London 1878, Vol. 1, p. 455.
3. Graf von Goetzen, *Durch Afrika von Ost nach West*, Berlin 1895, p. 154.
4. This section bears innumerable traces of the author's indebtedness to Professor Roger Louis's masterful treatment of German rule in Ruanda-Urundi, *Ruanda-Urundi, 1884–1919*, op. cit.; the author has also relied very heavily on Pierre Ryckmans, *Une Page d'Histoire Coloniale: L'Occupation Allemande dans l'Urundi*, IRCB, Brussels 1953, Vol. XXIX, fasc. 5, as well as on his illuminating 'notes' and reports now available through the Derscheid Collection. Professor Louis's work remains the definitive one for information on this period.
5. Adolphus Frederick, Duke of Mecklenburg, *In the Heart of Africa*, Cassel, London 1910, p. 46.
6. Raymond Leslie Buell, *The Native Problem in Africa*, Macmillan, New York 1928, Vol. 1, p. 448.
7. Cited in Louis, op. cit., pp. 119–20.
8. Ibid., p. 114.
9. *Note concernant l'origine et les droits du chef Kirima et de sa famille*, from a report by M. L. de Lannoy, Substitut de l'Auditeur Militaire, Kitega, November 18, 1918; text adapted and condensed by J. M. Derscheid from the original communiqué by P. Ryckmans, Brussels 1934; in the Derscheid Collection.
10. Hans Meyer, *Die Barundi*, Leipzig 1916, p. 163.
11. Louis, op. cit., p. 115.
12. Ryckmans, op. cit., p. 8.
13. Eugène Simons, "Coutumes et Institutions des Barundi", *Bulletin des Juridictions Indigènes*, No. 7, Elizabethville 1944, p. 146. Though basically correct in his assessment of the situation that followed von Beringe's campaign, Simons inaccurately holds von Grawert responsible for the decision to recognise the independence of Kilima and Maconco, a decision which every other historian attributes to von Beringe.
14. Louis, op. cit., p. 117.
15. Ryckmans, op. cit., p. 13.
16. Pierre Ryckmans, *Note sur les Titres et Fonctions de la Famille Royale du Burundi*, extract from a report by Ryckmans, 1st quarter, 1918; in the Derscheid Collection.
17. Louis, op. cit., p. 118, note 3.
18. For a very different interpretation of German policies under the Residencies of von Beringe and von Grawert, see Simons, op. cit., esp. pp. 145 ff.
19. Meyer, op. cit., p. 169.

20. *Urundi Jahresbericht*, 1911–12, cited in Louis, op. cit., p. 132.
21. Ryckmans, *Une Page d'Histoire Coloniale* . . ., op. cit., p. 22.
22. Louis, op. cit., p. 133.
23. Ibid., pp. 128, 134.
24. See *Notes concernant l'origine du roi Mwambutsa et la mort du roi Mutaga*, from a report by M. L. de Lannoy, Substitut de l'Auditeur Militaire, Kitega, December 18, 1918; text adapted and condensed by J. M. Derscheid; in the Derscheid Collection.
25. Louis, op. cit., p. 137.
26. Ryckmans, *Un Page d'Histoire Coloniale*, op. cit., p. 46.
27. *Kolonialblatt*, XXI, September 1913, p. 752.
28. See Alexis Kagame, *Yuhi Musinga: Un Règne Mouvementé*, unpublished MS.; also, Pagès, *Un Royaume Hamite au centre de l'Afrique*, IRCB, Brussels 1933, Vol. I, pp. 195–232.
29. Kagame, op. cit.
30. J. M. Bessel, "Nyabingi", *Uganda Journal*, Vol. VI, 1938–39, p. 78.
31. Félix Dufays, *Pages d'Epopée Africaine*, René Weverbergh, Ixelles 1928, p. 58.
32. See ibid., 65–76; also Louis, op. cit., p. 178, note 7.
33. May Mandelbaum Edel, *The Chiga of Western Uganda*, Oxford University Press, London and New York 1957, p. 155.
34. Louis, op. cit., p. 156.
35. Ibid., p. 157.
36. Ibid.
37. Ibid., p. 180.
38. See especially, A. Van Overschelde, *Un Audacieux Pacifique: Monseigneur L. P. Classe, Apôtre du Rwanda*, Grands Lacs, Namur 1948, pp. 65–76.
39. Louis, op. cit., p. 204.
40. *League of Nations, Permanent Mandates Commission* (hereafter cited as PMC), 16th session, 1929, p. 56.
41. Louis, op. cit., p. 216.
42. PMC, 7th session, 1925, pp. 55 ff.
43. Ibid., 16th session, 1929, pp. 68–9.
44. *Rapport sur l'Administration Belge au Ruanda-Urundi* (hereafter cited as *Rapport*), *1925*, Brussels 1926, p. 64.
45. Ibid., *1921*, p. 7.
46. Richard Kandt, *Caput Nili*, Berlin 1905, p. 483.
47. *Rapport*, *1925*, p. 63.
48. Pierre Ryckmans, "Le problème politique au Ruanda-Urundi", *Congo*, Vol. I, No. 3, 1925, pp. 410 ff.
49. Ibid.
50. *Rapport*, *1925*, p. 64.
51. Sandrart, *Rapport sur le territoire de Kigali*, 1929; in the Derscheid Collection.
52. This version appears in a communication made to the UN Visiting Mission, in 1948, by John Lister. Nowhere else has the author seen it mentioned in the literature on Rwanda. For further details about the circumstances of Musinga's dethronement, see Louis de Lacger, *Ruanda*, Kabgaye?, n.d., pp. 531–8.
53. Kagame, op. cit.
54. Ibid.
55. PMC, 16th session, 1929, p. 66.
56. Lenaerts, *Rapport établi en réponse au questionnaire addressé en 1921 par*

M. le Gouverneur Général du Ruanda-Urundi à l'Administrateur de Territoire de Nyanza, p. 33; in the Derscheid Collection.

57. De Lacger, op. cit., p. 467.
58. Sandrart, op. cit., p. 4; cf. J. J. Maquet, *The Premise of Inequality in Ruanda*, Oxford University Press, London and New York 1961, pp. 96–128.
59. See *Historique et Chronologie du Ruanda*, Kabgaye?, n.d.
60. Alexis Kagame, *Le Code des Institutions Politiques de Ruanda Précolonial*, IRCB, Brussels 1952, Vol. XXVI, fasc. 1, p. 7.
61. For further information, see de Lacger, op. cit., pp. 522 ff.; and especially Van Overschelde, op. cit., pp. 105–8.
62. De Lacger, op. cit., p. 522.
63. Ibid., p. 524.
64. *Historique et Chronologie du Ruanda*, op. cit., p. 128.
65. Oger Coubeau, *Note au sujet des écoles du Ruanda-Urundi*, July 2, 1933; in the Derscheid Collection.
66. R. E. S. Tanner, "The Belgian and British Administration in Ruanda-Urundi and Tanganyika", *Journal of Local Administration Overseas*, Vol. IV, No. 3, 1965, p. 205.
67. *Rapport, 1928*, p. 53; see ibid., *1925*, p. 77.
68. PMC, 19th session, 1930, p. 133.
69. *Résidence du Ruanda, Rapport Annuel*, Kigali?, 1938, mimeo., Part II, chapter 2 (no page numbers).
70. Ibid., 1949, p. 78.
71. Anon., "Note sur les causes des troubles du mois de Novembre 1959 au Ruanda", unpublished document.
72. Lord Lugard, *The Dual Mandate in British Tropical Africa*, London 1926, p. 203.
73. PMC, 37th session, 1939, pp. 54 ff.
74. Tanner, op. cit., p. 205.
75. PMC, 16th session, 1929, p. 66.
76. Ibid.
77. Ibid., 35th session, 1936, p. 51.
78. See ibid., 23rd session, 1931, p. 19. Cf. "Statement by R. Schmidt, Resident of Urundi, presented at Usumbura, 9 August 1948", MTRU/48/Inf. 13, August 10, 1948, unpublished document.
79. Ibid.
80. Ibid.
81. Ibid.
82. Sir Andrew Cohen, *British Policy in Changing Africa*, Northwestern University Press, Evanston 1959, p. 41.
83. J. J. Maquet, "The introduction of an electoral system for councils in a caste society", in Raymond Apthorpe, ed., *From Tribal Rule to Modern Government*, Lusaka 1960, p. 61. See also, J. J. Maquet and M. d'Hertefelt, *Elections en Société Féodale*, ARSC, Brussels 1959, Vol. XXI, fasc. 2.
84. Aloys Munyngaju, *L'Actualité Politique du Ruanda-Urundi*, Brussels 1959, p. 20.
85. Ibid., p. 64.
86. Ibid.
87. Pierre Ngendadumwe, *Réorganisation Politique Indigène au Ruanda-Urundi: Le décret du 14 juillet 1952 et son application*, Mémoire de Licence en Sciences Politiques et Administratives, Lovanium 1959, p. 58.

88. The text of the government declaration of November 10, 1959, will be found in *Rwanda Politique, 1958–1960*, CRISP, Brussels 1960, pp. 160 ff. Cf. John B. Webster, *The Political Development of Rwanda and Burundi*, Syracuse University, Maxwell Graduate School of Citizenship and Public Affairs, Occasional Paper No. 16, p. 51 ff.
89. *Rwanda Politique, 1958–1960*, op. cit., p. 207.
90. *Question of the Future of Ruanda-Urundi: Interim Report of the UN Commission for Ruanda-Urundi*, UN Doc. A/4706, March 8, 1961, p. 29.
91. See "Future of Ruanda-Urundi: Fourth Committee Considers Commission's Report", *United Nations Review*, Vol. IX, No. 2, 1962, pp. 10 ff. For the text of the resolution, see ibid., No. 3, pp. 63–4.
92. *Report of the UN Commission for Ruanda-Urundi*, 1962, UN Doc. A/5126, p. 42.
93. Ibid., Annex X, p. 48.
94. Ibid., Annex XIII, p. 54.
95. For the text of the preliminary draft of the federal constitution of the 'United States of Ruanda and Burundi' (sic), see ibid., Annex XV, pp. 55–6.
96. For the text of the Economic Agreement, see ibid., Annex XVI, pp. 56–7.
97. Ibid., p. 32.
98. "Future of Ruanda-Urundi: Fourth Committee Considers Commission's Report", op. cit., p. 10.

3. THE PEASANT REVOLUTION: MYTHS AND REALITIES

1. Frantz Fanon, *The Wretched of the Earth*, trans. by Constance Farrington, Grove, New York 1963, p. 48.
2. Helen Codere, "Power in Rwanda", *Anthropologica*, Vol. IV, No. 2, 1962, p. 63.
3. Ibid.
4. Robert Redfield, "The Folk Society", *American Journal of Sociology*, Vol. LXII, No. 1, 1947, pp. 293–308.
5. O. Mannoni, *Prospero and Caliban: The Psychology of Colonization*, trans. by Pamela Powesland, Praeger, New York and London 1964, esp. pp. 39–49, 132–51.
6. G. M. Foster, "The Dyadic Contract: A Model for the Social Structure of a Mexican Peasant Village", *American Anthropologist*, Vol. LXIII, No. 6, 1961, p. 1191.
7. Max Weber, *Wirtschaft und Gesellschaft*, cited in H. H. Gerth and C. Wright Mills, eds., *From Max Weber: Essays in Sociology*, Oxford University Press, New York and London 1958, p. 189.
8. J. S. Furnivall, *Colonial Policy and Practices*, Cambridge University Press, London 1948, p. 304.
9. Weber, loc. cit.
10. P. T. W. Baxter, "The Kiga", in Audrey I. Richards, ed., *East African Chiefs*, Praeger, New York 1962, p. 281.
11. J. E. T. Philipps, "The Nyabingi: An Anti-European Society in Africa ...", *Congo*, Vol. I, 1928, pp. 316–17.
12. J. M. Bessel, "Nyabingi", *Uganda Journal*, Vol. VI, 1938–39, p. 78.
13. Philipps, op. cit., p. 317.
14. Baxter, op. cit., p. 287.

15. Chalmers Johnson, *Revolution and the Social System*, Hoover Institution Studies No. 3, Stanford 1964, p. 42.
16. *L'Attitude de l'Administration Belge à l'égard de l'Unar*, Bujumbura 1960, mimeo.
17. Hanna Arendt, *On Revolution*, Viking, New York 1965, p. 21.
18. *Rwanda, Carrefour d'Afrique*, February 1965, p. 2; February 1966, p. 4.
19. E. J. Hobsbawm, *The Age of Revolution 1789–1848*, World Publishing, Cleveland 1962, p. 160.

4. THE BACKGROUND TO REVOLUTION

1. Eric Hoffer, *The Ordeal of Change*, Harper Colophon Books, New York 1964, pp. 4–5.
2. Alison Des Forges, "The Impact of European Colonization on the Rwandese Social System", a paper prepared for the 1966 annual meeting of the African Studies Association, Bloomington 1966.
3. League of Nations, Permanent Mandates Commission (PMC), *Minutes and Reports, 14th Session*, 1928, p. 121.
4. R. P. Classe, *L'organisation politique du Ruanda au début de l'occupation belge*, 1916, unpublished document.
5. "Notes on a tour of the UN Visiting Mission in Ruanda-Urundi, July 24– August 8, 1948", n.p., n.d. From the files of the UN Trusteeship Council.
6. Saverio Naigiziki, *Escapade Ruandaise*, Deny, Brussels 1949, p. 175. A more lengthy version of this work was published by the Groupe Scolaire d'Astrida under the title *Mes Transes à Trente Ans*, Astrida 1955. Naigiziki's novel won the literary prize awarded under the auspices of the Brussels Colonial Fair.
7. Ibid.
8. Lloyd Fallers, "The Predicament of the Modern African Chief: An Instance from Uganda", *American Anthropologist*, Vol. LVII, 1955, pp. 290–305.
9. See A. Makuza, "Le problème des cadres au Rwanda", in *Staff Problems in Tropical and Subtropical countries*, Report of the 32nd Incidi study session held in Munich, September 19 to 22, 1960, Incidi, Brussels 1961, p. 190.
10. Lucy Mair, "African Chiefs Today", *Africa*, Vol. XXVII, No. 3, July 1958, pp. 198–9.
11. R. Bourgeois, *Banyarwanda et Barundi: L'évolution du contrat de bail à cheptel au Ruanda-Urundi*, ARSC, Vol. IX, fasc. 4, Brussels 1958, p. 11.
12. *Circulaire No. 33/52 du Mwami du Rwanda: Projet de Suppression de l'ubuhake*, Nyanza, April 10, 1952, mimeo.
13. Bourgeois, op. cit., pp. 19 ff.
14. Ibid., pp. 13–14.
15. Runiga, *Ceux qui attendent la suppression de l'ubuhake*, n.p., 1954; from the files of the UN Trusteeship Council.
16. Cited in Bourgeois, op. cit., p. 23.
17. See Audrey I. Richards, "Some effects of the introduction of individual freehold into Buganda", in D. Biebuyck, ed., *African Agrarian Systems*, Oxford University Press, London and New York 1963, pp. 267–80.
18. See J. Adriaenssens, *Le Droit Foncier au Ruanda*, Kabgaye 1962, mimeo.; and J. J. Maquet & S. Naigiziki, "Les droits fonciers dans le Ruanda ancien", in *Zaire*, No. 41, April 1947, pp. 339–59.
19. Adriaenssens, op. cit., p. 62.

20. Emile Durkheim, *Suicide*, ed. by George Simpson, Free Press, Glencoe 1951, pp. 252–3.
21. Cited in Lewis Coser, *The Functions of Social Conflict*, Free Press, Glencoe 1956, p. 108. The analogy with the roots of anti-Semitism, as analysed by Coser, is obvious: 'Some types of anti-Semitism, as do other forms of prejudice, have important functions for those who suffer from "degrouping", that is, from a loss of cohesion in the society of which they are a part. Anti-Semitism provides "a means for pseudo-orientation in an estranged world". The Jew's alienness seems to provide the handiest formula for dealing with the alienation of society. The degrouped man, by directing his diffuse hostility upon a specific target and then attributing his sense of menace to this target group, attempts to find a solid point of repair in a world that otherwise makes no sense to him.'
22. Saverio Naigiziki, *L'Optimiste*, Astrida 1953, p. 10.
23. For an interesting discussion of the impact of Christianity in so-called 'primitive' societies, see Raoul Allier, *La Psychologie de la Conversion*, Payot, Paris 1925, esp. pp. 313–17 and 348.
24. PMC, *Minutes and Reports, 18th Session*, 1938, p. 17.
25. Oger Coubeau, *Note au sujet des Ecoles du Ruanda-Urundi*, July 2, 1933; in the Derscheid Collection.
26. Louis De Lacger, *Ruanda*, Kabgaye 1959, p. 519.
27. Alexis Kagame, "Le Ruanda et son Roi", *Aequatoria*, Coquilhatville, No. 2, 1945, p. 56.
28. Interview with Anastase Makuza, August 1954.
29. Helen Codere, "Power in Ruanda", *Anthropologica*, Vol. IV, No. 1, 1962, pp. 71 ff.
30. Ibid., p. 63.
31. Genevieve Knupfer, "Portrait of the Underdog", *The Public Opinion Quarterly*, Vol. II, No. 1, Spring 1947, p. 114.

5. THE ROAD TO VIOLENCE

1. See Rex D. Hopper, "The Revolutionary Process", *Social Forces*, Vol. XXVIII, No. 3, March 1950, pp. 270–9.
2. Bishop Brazier, "Ruanda's Fiery Trail", *Ruanda Notes*, No. 147, March-May 1960, p. 12.
3. Cited in *Ruanda Politique, 1958–1960*, CRISP, Brussels 1961, p. 14.
4. Ibid.
5. Ibid., p. 16.
6. *Trafipro*, No. 22, December 24, 1966, p. 3.
7. For the text of the *Manifesto*, see *Ruanda Politique, 1958–1960*, op. cit., pp. 20–9.
8. For the text of the *Mise au Point*, see *UN Visiting Mission to Trust Territories in East Africa, 1957; Report on Ruanda-Urundi*, T/1346, pp. 42–6.
9. Ibid., p. 19.
10. *Trafipro*, loc. cit.
11. Petition submitted to the *Groupe de Travail*, n.p., n.d. (1959?).
12. See for example, *Résidence du Ruanda, Réunion du cadre des chefs et des délégués des sous-chefs et du personnel judiciaire du Rwanda*, 3rd session, Nyanza, 1959, mimeo., pp. 3 ff.
13. *Ruanda Politique, 1958–1960*, op. cit., pp. 16–17.

14. Ibid., pp. 35–6.
15. See also *L'Aprosoma fête la liberation des Bahutu . . . à Astrida le 27 Septembre 1959*, n.d., n.p., mimeo., p. 1.
16. *UN Visiting Mission to Trust Territories in East Africa, 1960; Report on Ruanda-Urundi* (hereafter cited as *UN Visiting Mission, 1960*), T/1551, p. 17.
17. Laurent Nkongori, *Face à la mort mystérieuse de notre Mwami Mutara*, n.p., n.d., typescript.
18. *Rwanda Nziza*, August 1, 1959.
19. Ibid.
20. *UN Visiting Mission, 1960*, op. cit., p. 22.
21. Cited in *Mémoire sur la révolution Rwandaise de Novembre 1959 présenté à la mission de visite de l'ONU par la délégation Hutu au Conseil Provisoire du Rwanda*, Kigali, February 20, 1960, p. 15.
22. RADER, *Statuts*, p. 1.
23. *Mémoire sur la révolution Rwandaise . . .*, op. cit., p. 18.
24. See *Consignes et Directives des cinq vicaires apostoliques du Ruanda-Urundi*, Kabgaye, September 1959; mimeo.; for the text of the circular see *Mise en garde contre l'Unar*, Kabgaye, September 24, 1959; mimeo., partially reproduced in *Rwanda Politique, 1958–1960*, op. cit., p. 139.
25. *UN Visiting Mission, 1960*, op. cit., p. 27.
26. Ibid., p. 28.
27. Ibid.
28. P. D. Guillebaud, in a letter dated March 14, 1960, to Mason Sears, Chairman of the UN Visiting Mission to Trust Territories in East Africa.
29. *UN Visiting Mission, 1960*, op. cit., p. 28.
30. George Rudé, *The Crowd in History*, John Wiley, New York 1964, p. 228.
31. *UN Visiting Mission, 1960*, op. cit., p. 29.
32. *La maison du Mwami pendant les événements de Novembre 1959*, no author, typescript, n.p., n.d.
33. J. R. Hubert, *La Toussaint Rwandaise et sa Répression*, ARSOM, Vol. XXXI, fasc. 2, Brussels 1965, p. 37.
34. F. Peigneux, G. Malengrau, S. Fredericq, *Rapport de la Commission d'Enquête au Rwanda*, mimeo., January 1960, p. 82.
35. *UN Visiting Mission, 1960*, op. cit., p. 31 (citing the charges brought by UNAR against the Belgian authorities).
36. Hubert, op. cit., p. 40.
37. *UN Visiting Mission, 1960*, op. cit., p. 31.
38. Rudé, op. cit., p. 31.
39. Supplement to *Jya Mbere*, November 27, 1959, No. 3, mimeo.

6. THE BIRTH OF THE REPUBLIC

1. *Rwanda Politique: 1958–1960*, CRISP, Brussels 1961, p. 161; as the Communist deputy G. Moulin pertinently observed, on December 15, 1960, before the Chamber of Representatives: 'Recent events, sir, have given the lie to your statement that Belgium had fulfilled its obligations under the San Francisco Charter. If the present situation were not so tragic, such an affirmation would only provoke laughter.' Ibid., p. 173.
2. *Réunion des Administrateurs de Territoire*, Kigali, January 11, 1960, p. 2.
3. See *UN Visiting Mission, 1960*, p. 32.

4. Rachel Yeld, *Implications of Experience with Refugee Settlements*, Conference paper, East African Institute of Social Research, Kampala 1964, p. 5.
5. Laurent Nkongori, *L'administration tutrice cause de la révolution du Ruanda*, typescript, Astrida, n.d.
6. See J. R. Hubert, *La Toussaint Rwandaise et sa Répression*, ARSOM, Vol. XXXI, fasc. 2, Brussels 1965, p. 57.
7. See *UN Visiting Mission . . . 1960; Report on Ruanda-Urundi*, T/1551, p. 33. The text of the procès-verbal is excerpted from *Territoire de Ruhengeri: Procès-verbal de vacance de pouvoir*, Ruhengeri, n.d., mimeo.
8. *Réunion des AT*, May 19, 1960, p. 4.
9. Ibid., p. 5.
10. Ibid., January 11, 1960, p. 3.
11. Ibid., p. 6.
12. Petition from Rev. P. D. Guillebaud submitted to the UN Visiting Mission on March 14, 1960; unpublished document.
13. *Réunion des AT*, September 2, 1960, p. 11.
14. Guillebaud, op. cit.
15. The citations in this paragraph are taken from the electoral speeches by the Hutu leaders Alexis Baziyaka and Hasani Ndangari, delivered in Ruhengeri in May and June 1960. Translation from Kinyarwanda by Jean Rwigemera.
16. *Communication No. 6 à la population d'Astrida*, mimeo., n.d. See also *Imvaho* of June and July 1960. For other instances of blatant administrative interference, see *Communiqué No. 7*, issued by Colonel Logiest on February 8, 1960, in *Rwanda Politique, 1958–1960*, op. cit., p. 219.
17. *Circulaire No. 7 à la population d'Astrida*, mimeo., n.d.
18. See *Imvaho*, No. 14, July 15, 1960, p. 3.
19. The information in this paragraph is distilled from the local and metropolitan press, and in particular from *Ruanda-Urundi under Belgian Administration: Notes and Comments on the Trust Territories*, mimeo., for internal use only, United Nations, R-U 60/10, October 21, 1960.
20. Ibid., p. 29.
21. Ibid., p. 11.
22. For further information on the 1960 communal elections, see Marcel d'Hertefelt's excellent study, "Les elections communales et le consensus politique au Rwanda", *Zaire*, Vol. XIV, Nos. 5–6, 1960, pp. 403–38.
23. *Réunion des AT*, September 2, 1960, p. 7.
24. See d'Hertefelt, op. cit.
25. *Imvaho*, No. 14, July 15, 1960, p. 2.
26. d'Hertefelt, op. cit., p. 427.
27. *Réunion des AT*, October 27, 1960, p. 9.
28. See *Interim Report of the UN Commission for Ruanda-Urundi*, A/4706, March 8, 1961, p. 6.
29. *Réunion des AT*, September 2, 1960, p. 8.
30. Ibid.
31. Ibid., October 27, 1960, p. 10.
32. Ibid., September 2, 1960, p. 6.
33. Ibid., October 27, 1960, p. 11.
34. Ibid., September 2, 1960, p. 6.
35. Ibid., August 10 and 11, 1960, p. 15.
36. Ibid., p. 7.
37. Pierre Gravel, *The Play for Power: Description of a Community in Eastern*

Rwanda, unpublished PH.D. dissertation, University of Michigan, Ann Arbor 1962, pp. 263–4.
38. G. Rudé, *The Crowd in History: 1730–1848*, John Wiley, New York 1964, p. 6.
39. *Rwanda Politique, 1958–1960*, op. cit., p. 347.
40. *Interim Report of the UN Commission for Ruanda-Urundi, 1961*, op. cit., p. 6.
41. See ibid., Addendum 1, Annex xv.
42. *Réunion des AT*, September 2, 1960, p. 10.
43. Ibid., pp. 10–11.
44. *Interim Report of the UN Commission for Ruanda-Urundi, 1961*, op. cit., pp. 46, 48.
45. Ibid., pp. 29, 30.
46. Ibid., p. 51.
47. See *Statement made by Mr Michel Kayihura . . . at the 1268th and 1269th meetings of the Fourth Committee*, xvi–1962, UN Document 62–02112, mimeo., p. 13.
48. *Spearhead*, November 1961.
49. x, *Note sur l'aspect 'moral' des événements actuels au Rwanda*, typescript, Astrida, September 16, 1961.

7. THE *Inyenzi* AT THE GATES

1. See *Report of the United Nations Commission for Ruanda-Urundi, 1962*, A/5126, pp. 11 ff.
2. Ingangurago z'u Rwanda (Comité de Liberation Nationale), "Les dix commandements des Abatabazi", n.d., n.p., mimeo.
3. *Report of the United Nations Commission for Ruanda-Urundi, 1962*, op. cit., p. 79.
4. Rachel Yeld, *Implications of Experience with Refugee Settlement*, EAISR Conference Paper, Makerere 1964, p. 6.
5. "Notes for the Minister of Internal Affairs for discussion on Ruanda Refugees on Tuesday 29th May, 1962", Ministry of Internal Affairs, Entebbe, S. 5622/4, unpublished document.
6. Ibid.
7. "Prime Minister Warns Rwanda and Sudanese Refugees", Ministry of Internal Affairs, Entebbe, July 10, 1963, mimeo.
8. See Yeld, op. cit.
9. Ibid., p. 8.
10. François Preziosi, *Report on a trip to Goma*, Goma, October 10, 1963, typescript.
11. Rachel Yeld, *Notes made on a month's visit to refugee centers in Kivu*, March 1964, typescript. I am heavily indebted to Miss Yeld for sharing with me her first-hand acquaintance with the refugee problem, and for allowing me to consult her field notes and other documents—such as the one cited above —on the refugee situation in the Kivu. Much of the information in this and other paragraphs is drawn from Miss Yeld's personal files.
12. François Preziosi, *Conversation with refugee leaders for Central Kivu*, Bukavu, December 20, 1963. Letter to the High Commissioner, No. 280.
13. Ibid.
14. For a more detailed account of the controversy, see Benoit Verhaegen, *Rebellions au Congo*, Vol. 1, CRISP, Brussels 1966, pp. 268 ff.

15. Republique du Congo, Province du Kivu Central, *Procès-Verbal Administratif*, Bukavu, August 1, 1963, mimeo., p. 2.
16. *Procès-Verbal de la réunion de MNC-L tenue le 5 Juillet, 1964, au Bureau du Territoire d'Uvira et groupant les délégations du Comité Provincial, du Comité Territorial d'Uvira et celui de Fizi*, n.p., mimeo.
17. Ibid.
18. Ibid.
19. For an excellent, short discussion of the origins of the rebellion, and of the causes of its failure, see Crawford Young, "The Congo Rebellion", *Africa Report*, April 1965, pp. 6–11. One conspicuous omission from the reasons advanced by Professor Young to explain the failure of the rebellion is the determining role played by both European and South African mercenary units who fought on the side of the ANC, and the repeated strafings of the rebel-held positions by Cuban pilots in the pay of the Central Intelligence Agency, whose exploits, wrote the *Observer* correspondent Gavin Young, have won 'astonished admiration'.
20. UNHCR, Press Release No. REF/857, p. 5.
21. *Compte Rendu de la Réunion des Administrateurs de Territoire tenue le 27 Octobre, 1961, à Kigali*, Kigali, October 27, 1961, mimeo.
22. Preziosi, *Conversation . . .*, op. cit., p. 2.
23. See *Report of the United Nations for Ruanda-Urundi, 1962*, op. cit., pp. 18 ff.
24. *Unité*, April 15, 1962.
25. Ibid., September 1, 1963.
26. Preziosi, *Conversation . . .*, op. cit., p. 1.
27. Rachel Yeld, in a personal communication.
28. This and other quotations in the paragraph are from the report of a directeur-général in the Rwanda Ministry of Justice, following his visit to Bujumbura, December 21–3, 1963, to explore with the Burundi government the possibility of an extradition treaty between the two countries, and at the same time to inquire into the reasons why Rukeba had been let out of jail after his arrest in November 1963. The treaty was never signed. On the question of Rukeba's release, the official answer given by the Minister of Justice was that 'carrying weapons illegally is punishable only by a fine', and that 'since Rukeba, Kabalira and others have duly paid their 1000 francs fine, they had to be released'. *Rapport de Mission au Burundi*, Kigali, December 26, 1963, mimeo., p. 3.
29. As reported by Claire Sterling in "Chou-en-Lai and the Watutsi", *Reporter*, March 12, 1964.
30. *New York Times*, February 9, 1964.
31. *Le Monde*, February 6, 1964.
32. Cited in *Brève response à quelques grossières calomnies que l'on a lancées contre le Rwanda*, mimeo., n.d., n.p. This document, written by a group of European priests of Rwanda, was sent to the Vatican in protest against its broadcast of February 10, and more specifically to refute the charges brought against the European clergy by the UNAR leaders Kayihura and Kayonga in a letter to Pope Paul IV. On the day of the broadcast, a cable was sent to the Vatican by the bishops of Rwanda, at the instigation of Mgr Perraudin, which said: 'Protest against false news concerning Rwanda situation broadcast on Vatican Radio on July 10. Ask you to broadcast this telegram.' The bishops' telegram was never broadcast, nor did it receive an answer from the Vatican. The authors of the *Brève response* later referred to the Vatican's

description of the massacre as 'monstrous and gravely offending for a Catholic head of state' (p. 3).

33. Other instances of distortion and calculated sensationalism can be found in the French newspaper *France-Soir* of February 4, 1964; see also the grotesquely distorted account given by John Cohen in *Africa Addio*, Ballentine Books, New York 1966.

34. Cited in *Africa Report*, April 1964. For a complete version of the Dorsinville Report, see *Rwanda, Carrefour d'Afrique*, March 1964, p. 10.

35. *Le Monde*, February 4, 1964.

36. Ibid., March 27, 1964.

37. A notable exception is Aaron Segal's article, "What Happened in Rwanda?", *New Statesman*, February 21, 1964; reproduced in a more extended version in *Africa Report*, April 1964. Although the article contains a few factual inaccuracies—for example the highly exaggerated figure of 10,000 to 14,000 Tutsi slain in the prefecture of Gikongoro cited in his article in *Africa Report*, p. 6—it is by far the best account anywhere available in print. See also his more extensive treatment of the events in the Fabian pamphlet, *Massacre in Rwanda*, London 1964.

38. *Africa Report*, op. cit., p. 8.

39. Ibid.

40. Sterling, op. cit.

8. The Quest for Solidarity

1. From Kayibanda's speech on January 28, 1967; see *Rwanda, Carrefour d'Afrique*, February 1967, p. 5.

2. *Assemblée Nationale, Document No. 172* (hereafter cited as *A. N. Doc.*), April 30, 1964, p. 425.

3. Crane Brinton, *A Decade of Revolution 1789–1799*, Harper & Row, New York 1963, p. 138.

4. *Conseil Spécial Provisoire, Doc. No. 57*, July 18, 1960, Annex 33, p. 2.

5. *Assemblée Législative, Doc. No. 9*, April 28, 1961, p. 2.

6. Ibid., p. 6.

7. Ibid., p. 7.

8. For further details, see *Assemblée Nationale, Doc. No. 206*, July 8, 1965, p. 1,078.

9. *A. N. Doc. No. 171*, April 29, 1964, p. 400.

10. Ibid.

11. Ibid.

12. *West Africa*, February 15, 1964, p. 180.

13. *A. N. Doc. No. 210*, July 16, 1965, p. 1,113.

14. Ibid.

15. For an interesting discussion of the problems posed by delinquent youth, see *Kimanyateka*, No. 14, April 1967.

16. *Réunion Conjointe des 6 et 7 avril, 1961*, Kigali, April 1961, mimeo., p. 2.

17. *Procès-Verbal de la Réunion Tutelle du 14 mars, 1961*, Kigali, March 1961, mimeo., p. 2.

18. Ibid.

19. Ibid., p. 10.

20. Ibid., p. 12.

21. *Réunion Conjointe*, loc. cit.

22. Ibid.
23. Ibid., p. 6.
24. Ibid., p. 7.
25. *Instruction*, No. 04/01/639, Kigali, September 19, 1963, mimeo.
26. Brian Chapman, *Introduction to French Local Government*, Allen & Unwin, London 1953, p. 105.
27. *Compte-Rendu de la réunion des bourgmestres en date du 13 mars, 1964*, Kigali, March 1964, mimeo., pp. 1, 2.
28. See esp. *A. N. Doc. No. 219*, July 20, 1965, pp. 1,154 ff.
29. *Réunion Conjointe*, op. cit., p. 26.
30. John E. Bodley, *France*, Macmillan, London 1907, p. 362.
31. *Réunion du 12 février 1964, presidée par son Excellence le Ministre de l'Intérieur*, Kigali, February 1964, mimeo., p. 3.
32. Ibid., pp. 2, 9.
33. Ibid., p. 7.
34. Ibid.
35. *Petit projet*, n.d., n.p., typescript.
36. PARMEHUTU, *Secrétariat Général, Resolution No. d/094*, Kigali, October 22, 1964, mimeo., p. 4.
37. *Trafipro*, No. 22, December 1966, p. 3.
38. Ibid.
39. See *A. N. Doc. No. 199*, January 25, 1965, pp. 970 ff.
40. S.H., personal communications.
41. Cited by Leo Gershoy in *The French Revolution*, Holt, Rinehart and Winston, New York 1967, p. 61.
42. *Réunion du 12 février, 1964*, op. cit., pp. 10, 6.
43. David Apter, *The Politics of Modernization*, University of Chicago Press, Chicago 1965, p. 293.
44. See PARMEHUTU, *Statutes*, art. 3; *Constitution of the Rwandese Republic*, art. 29, 39.
45. PARMEHUTU, *Statutes*, passim.
46. Ibid., p. 1122.
47. Ibid., p. 1121.
48. Ibid., p. 1120.
49. Ibid.
50. See "Loi du 27 Août sur l'Education Nationale de la République Rwandaise", *Journal Officiel*, No. 19, October 1, 1966.
51. See *Kimanyateka*, No. 33, October 1966, p. 3.
52. Ibid.
53. See *Itangazo rya Parmehutu ku Kibazo cy' amashuli muli iki gihe*, n.p., n.d., mimeo.
54. See *Kimanyateka*, No. 38, November 1966, p. 3.
55. S.H., personal communication.
56. PARMEHUTU, *Statutes*, art. 4.
57. PARMEHUTU, *Secrétariat Général, Résolution No. b/092*, Kigali, October 22, 1966, p. 2.
58. Ibid., *Résolution No. e/095*, p. 5.

9. THE KINGDOM REBORN

1. Alexis de Tocqueville, *The Old Regime and the French Revolution*, Double-day Anchor Books, Garden City 1955, p. vii.
2. T. Alexander Barns, *An African Eldorado: The Belgian Congo*, Methuen, London 1926, pp. 51–2. I am grateful to Alison Des Forges for drawing my attention to this passage.
3. Pierre Gravel, *The Play for Power: Description of a Community in Eastern Rwanda*, unpublished PH.D. thesis, University of Michigan, Ann Arbor 1962, p. 153.
4. Marcel d'Hertefelt, "Rwanda", in J. Vansina, ed., *Les Anciens Royaumes de la Zone Lacustre Meridionale: Rwanda, Burundi, Buha*, Tervueren 1962, p. 41.
5. *Ruhengeri, Réunion de Cadres du 3 février 1964*, mimeo., p. 3. From 1960 to 1963, each commune was divided into a number of 'sectors' administered by a councillor acting under the supervision of the burgomaster. This situation was brought to an end in 1963 by a ministerial directive enjoining the burgomasters to assume direct control of the communal administration.
6. David Apter, *The Politics of Modernization*, University of Chicago Press, Chicago 1965, p. 307.
7. *Rwanda, Carrefour d'Afrique*, July 1965, p. 3.
8. See ibid., September-October 1965, p. 3.
9. *Instruction* No. 04/01/639, Kigali, September 19, 1963; mimeo.
10. *Préfecture de Kigali, Compte Rendu de la Réunion des Bourgmestres en date du 13 Mars, 1964*, mimeo., p. 2.
11. Ibid.
12. Ibid.
13. H. H. Gerth and C. Wright Mills, *From Max Weber: Essays in Sociology*, Oxford University Press, New York and London 1958, pp. 207 ff.
14. *Préfecture de Kigali, Compte Rendu de la Réunion de Cadres du 30 Avril, 1965*, mimeo., p. 1.
15. *Préfecture de Kigali, Compte Rendu de la Réunion de Cadres du 3 Août, 1964*, mimeo., p. 2.
16. *Préfecture de Kigali, Compte Rendu de la Réunion des Bourgmestres en date du 13 Mars, 1964*, mimeo., p. 2.
17. *Préfecture de Kigali, Compte Rendu de la Réunion de Cadres du 14 Juin, 1965*, mimeo., p. 1.
18. *Préfecture de Kigali, Compte Rendu de la Réunion de Cadres du 30 Avril, 1965*, mimeo., p. 2.
19. *Rwanda, Carrefour d'Afrique*, March 1967, p. 3.
20. *Réunion des Administrateurs de Territoire à Kigali, le 19 Mai, 1960*, mimeo., p. 9.
21. *Procès-Verbal de la Réunion de Tutelle du 14 Mars, 1961*, mimeo., pp. 16, 17.
22. Ibid.
23. Manfred Halpern, "Middle Eastern Armies and the New Middle Class", in John J. Johnson, ed., *The Role of the Military in Underdeveloped Countries*, Princeton University Press, Princeton 1967, p. 286.
24. Keith Hopkins, "Civil-Military Relations in Developing Countries", *The British Journal of Sociology*, Vol. XVII, No. 2, June 1966, p. 177. Cf. Morris Janowitz, *The Military in the Political Development of New Nations*, University of Chicago Press, Chicago 1964, p. 85.
25. *Procès-Verbal de la Réunion de Tutelle du 14 Mars, 1961*, mimeo., p. 17.

26. See *Rwanda, Carrefour d'Afrique*, March 1967, p. 3.
27. *Procès-Verbal de la Réunion Conjointe des 6 et 7 Avril, 1961*, mimeo., p. 28.
28. Philip Whitaker and Jonathan Silvey, "A Visit to Congo, Rwanda and Burundi", *Makerere Journal*, No. 9, March 1964, p. 76.
29. de Tocqueville, loc. cit.
30. Karl Marx, *The Critique of Hegel's Philosophy of Right*, in Lewis S. Feuer, ed., *Marx and Engels: Basic Writings*, Doubleday, Garden City 1959, passim.

10. BURUNDI IN PERSPECTIVE:
    A PROFILE OF POLITICAL DECOMPOSITION

1. Benjamin Nelson and Charles Trinkaus, "Introduction", in Jacob Burck-hardt, *The Civilization of the Renaissance in Italy*, Harper & Row, New York 1958, Vol. I, p. 10.
2. Ibid.
3. See Claude Welch, "The Challenge of Change: Meiji Japan and Contemporary Africa", a paper prepared for delivery at the 1965 annual meeting of the African Studies Association, Philadelphia, October 28–30, 1965.
4. *Note à Monsieur le Vice-Premier Ministre*, n.p., n.d., typescript.
5. Manfred Halpern, "The Revolution of Modernization in National and International Society", in Carl J. Friedrich, ed., *Revolution*, Atherton Press, New York 1966, p. 188.
6. Samuel Huntington, "The Political Modernization of Traditional Monarchies", *Daedalus*, Summer 1966, p. 769.
7. G. M. Trevelyan, *English Social History*, Longmans, Green, London 1947, p. x.
8. David Apter, *The Politics of Modernization*, University of Chicago Press, Chicago 1965, p. 359.
9. Niccolo Machiavelli, *The Prince*, Hendricks House, New York 1946, p. 175.

11. *Mwami*-SHIP: ETHOS AND STRUCTURE

1. Walter Bagehot, *The English Constitution*, cited in Kingsley Martin, *The Magic of the British Monarchy*, Little, Brown, Boston 1962, p. 167.
2. See Father Rodegem, *Sagesse Kirundi*, Annales du Musée Royal du Congo Belge, Tervueren 1961, passim. See also B. Zuure, *L'Ame du Murundi*, Gabriel Beauchesne, Paris 1937.
3. For a different and highly misleading interpretation, see Professor Ziegler's article, "Structures Ethniques et Partis Politiques au Burundi", in *Le Mois en Afrique*, No. 18, June 1967, in which the author describes traditional Burundi society as 'theocratic and totalitarian'. Not only does 'totalitarian' carry misleading connotations when applied to traditional Africa: its use seems all the more unwarranted when applied to the traditional context of Burundi.
4. Paul Mirerekano, *Mbwire gito canje* . . ., mimeo., n.d., n.p., translated by Jean Ghislain. The title of the book is derived from the proverb *Mbwire gito canje gito c'uwundi yumvireho*, meaning roughly 'I am addressing my good-for-nothing [son, but let others also learn a lesson'; see Rodegem, op. cit., p. 179, proverb no. 1621.

5. Cited in James H. Meisel, *The Myth of the Ruling Class*, University of Michigan Press, Ann Arbor 1958, p. 48.
6. Lloyd Fallers, "Max Weber's concept of 'Traditional Authority' ", a paper prepared for delivery at the 1966 annual meeting of the American Political Science Association, New York, September 6–10, 1966.
7. For further information, see J. Vansina, "Notes sur l'Histoire du Burundi", *Aequatoria*, No. 1, 1966, pp. 1–10.
8. "Note sur les titres et fonctions de la famille royale du Burundi", *Extrait d'un rapport de M. Pierre Ryckmans, 1er Trimestre 1918*, in the Derscheid Collection.
9. *Enquête Administrative Générale, Territoire de Kitega*, 1929, in the Derscheid Collection.
10. Ibid., *Territoire de Ngozi, 1929*.
11. Robert Schmidt, *Abatare et Abezi*, unpublished document, February–May 1953.
12. Robert Schmidt, *Répercussions Politiques de la Vie Privée de Mwambutsa*, unpublished document, February 1953.
13. Ibid.
14. Ibid.
15. Schmidt, *Abatare et Abezi*, op. cit.
16. Personal interview with Jean Ghislain, December 1964.
17. Personal interview with Louis Barusasyieko, August 1966.
18. From Robert Schmidt's personal files.

12. *Ganwa* POLITICS IN MODERN GUISE: BEZI VERSUS BATARE

1. For a complete listing of these parties, see Michel Lechat, *Le Burundi Politique*, Service de l'Information du Ruanda-Urundi, Usumbura 1961.
2. Max Beloff, *The Party System*, Phoenix House, London 1958, p. 5.
3. Maurice Duverger, *Les Partis Politiques*, Armand Colin, Paris 1951, p. 19.
4. Lord Hailey, *An African Survey*, Oxford University Press, London and New York 1958, p. 222.
5. See *Conseil Supérieur du Pays: Procès-Verbaux*, 7th Session, 1957, pp. 18 ff.
6. Ibid.
7. *Petition addressée à la mission de visite du Conseil de Tutelle de passage à Kitega le 23 Septembre, 1957*, unpublished document.
8. The words used by the Resident are instructive: 'I am surprised at the terms used in the motion that you just drafted—"spoliation" and "purloin" [soustraire;] these are terms which smack of Communism. You are free, gentlemen, to send a petition to the Trusteeship Council if you so desire, but remember that the latter will nonetheless continue to ask our advice. . . . I suggest you throw this motion into the waste-paper basket.' *Conseil Supérieur du Pays: Procès-Verbaux*, 10th Session, 1957, p. 8.
9. *Petition addressée à la mission de visite du Conseil de Tutelle des Nations Unies*, unpublished document, n.d.
10. *Résidence de l'Urundi, Rapport Annuel*, 1956, p. 64.
11. Frank Moraes, *The Importance of Being Black*, Macmillan, New York 1958, p. 244.
12. Personal communication from Professor A. Trouwborst.
13. Peter Worsley, *The Third World*, University of Chicago Press, Chicago 1964, p. 81.

14. *Deuxième Manifeste du Parti Politique "Unité et Progrès"* (UPRONA), n.d., n.p.
15. Ibid.
16. Paul Mirerekano, *Mbwire gito canje* . . ., mimeo., n.d., n.p.
17. I am grateful to Aim Israel for permission to consult the files from which this citation is taken.
18. *Conseil Supérieur du Pays: Procès-Verbaux*, June 10–13, 1958, p. 29.
19. See Joseph Ntitendereza, *Note à l'occasion de la visite du Groupe de Travail au Burundi*, Kitega, April 25, 1959, mimeo.
20. Jules Sasserath, *Le Ruanda-Urundi: Etrange Royaume Féodal*, Germinal, Brussels n.d., p. 74.
21. On the implications of 'withdrawal of status respect' for modernising societies, see E. Hagen, *On the Theory of Social Change*, Dorsey Press, Homewood, Ill., 1962.
22. See *Question of the Future of Ruanda-Urundi, Interim Report of the UN Commission for Ruanda-Urundi*, General Assembly, A/4706, March 8, 1961, pp. 34 ff.
23. Ibid., p. 35.
24. Cited by Jean Ghislain in his *Chronologie Politique du Burundi*, mimeo., n.d., n.p., p. 50.
25. Ibid.
26. Ibid., p. 51.
27. See, in particular, *Report of the UN Commission for Ruanda-Urundi on the Assassination of the Prime Minister of Burundi*, General Assembly, A/5086, January 26, 1961.
28. Cited in *Le Livre Blanc sur le Procès des Assassins du Prince Rwagasore*, mimeo., Bujumbura 1963. This 'white paper' was written at the request of the Burundi authorities by a European lawyer known for his UPRONA sympathies. This, and the fact that it never appeared in print, casts doubts on some of the statements contained in this document. Leonard's testimony, however, given in the course of a pre-trial investigation, has not, as far as I am aware, been falsified. Nor does the tendentious nature of this document exonerate the Belgian administration, or some of its representatives, of their heavy responsibilities in the death of Rwagasore.
29. "A Political Trial in Burundi", *Bulletin of the International Commission of Jurists*, No. 16, July 1963, p. 15.

13. The Displacement of Conflict: Hutu versus Tutsi

1. This account is based in part on unpublished press releases communicated to this writer by the Agence Poly in Bujumbura, and in part on personal interviews with Paul Mirerekano.
2. See Robert K. Merton, *Social Theory and Social Structure*, Free Press, Glencoe 1963, pp. 421 ff.
3. See, in particular, Boniface Kiraranganyia, *Mémorandum addressée aux Membres de la Mission du Conseil de Tutelle ONU par le promoteur et le Vice President de l'Aprodeba sur certains problèmes politiques de l'Urundi*, unpublished document.
4. On the origins of the 1934 revolt in Ngozi, see *Rapport de l'Administration Belge au Ruanda-Urundi pendant l'année 1934*, Brussels 1935, p. 73.
5. The Kayanza incidents are reported in Jean Ghislain, *Chronologie Politique du Burundi*, mimeo., n.p., n.d., p. 47.

6. *Union Culturelle de la Jeunesse Africaine du Burundi, Statuts.*
7. Ibid.
8. See *Mémorandum du Mouvement Populaire Chrétien*, mimeo., n.d., n.p.
9. See Motion Publique, *Appel à l'Union*, mimeo., n.d., n.p.
10. This account is based on the evidence presented during the trial, and on personal interviews.
11. See *Rapport de la Commission Elue pour la Conférence en date du 7 Octobre, 1964*, mimeo.
12. *Compte Rendu de la Conférence au Sommet de Kitega, du 8 Septembre au 6 Octobre, 1964*, mimeo., passim.
13. Based on interviews with Jean Ntiruhama and Apollinaire Sineremera, in September and August 1964.
14. *Rapport de la Commission Elue . . .*, op. cit.
15. *Assemblée Nationale, Session du 14 Mai au 1er Septembre 1963*, p. 100.
16. Ibid., p. 92.
17. *Assemblée Nationale, février 1964*, pp. 67 ff.

14. THE INTERVENTION OF THE CROWN

1. Samuel Huntington, "Political Modernization: America versus Europe", *World Politics*, Vol. XVIII, No. 3, April 1966, p. 405.
2. I. William Zartman, *Destiny of a Dynasty*, University of South Carolina Press, Columbia 1964, p. 2.
3. *Interim Report of the UN Commission for Ruanda-Urundi;* General Assembly A/4706/Add. 1, annex XXV, p. 1.
4. "Le Burundi à la recherche d'une stabilité", *Présence Africaine*, No. 47, 1963, p. 235.
5. Interview with Zénon Nicayenzi, August 1966.
6. Interview with Pascal Bubiriza, July 1964.
7. Zartman, op. cit., p. 41.
8. "Le Burundi à la recherche d'une stabilité", op. cit., p. 219.
9. Max Weber, *The Theory of Social and Economic Organization*, Free Press, Glencoe 1957, p. 341.
10. Ethel M. Albert, "Women of Burundi: A Study of Social Values", in Denise Paulme, ed., *Women of Tropical Africa*, University of California Press, Berkeley 1963, p. 189.
11. See Gilles Bimazubute, *Pour la Santé de la Fonction Publique*, March 1964, No. CAB/255/AE, mimeo. For an interesting parallel with Burundi, see Ronald Wraith and Edgar Simpkins, *Corruption in Developing Countries*, Norton, New York 1963; and Colin Leys's judicious comments in his review of that book, "What is the Problem about Corruption?", in *The Journal of Modern African Studies*, Vol. 3, No. 2, August 1965, pp. 215–31.
12. David E. Apter, *The Politics of Modernization*, University of Chicago Press, Chicago 1965, p. 167.
13. *Santé de la Fonction Publique*, Ministère de l'Intérieur, Fonction Publique, No. 092/2/682, April 17, 1964, mimeo.
14. Ibid.
15. *Circulaire No. 090/3 du 18 Février 1963 sur les compétences, les délégations de signature, les remplacements, les cumuls de fonction, et les intérims et les commissionnements*, Ministère de l'Intérieur, Fonction Publique, mimeo.
16. *Santé de la Fonction Publique*, op cit.

17. Bimazubute, *Pour la Santé de la Fonction Publique,* op. cit.
18. *Ndongozi,* September 15, 1963.
19. Ibid., November 24, 1964.
20. Ibid., January 1, 1965.
21. Ibid.

15. THE INTRUSION OF EXTERNAL INFLUENCES

1. For a different view, see Jacques Niqueaux, "Le Burundi à l'épreuve", in *La Revue Nouvelle,* Vol. XLIII, No. 2, February 1966, pp. 176–81.
2. *Rapport sur la Situation au 1er Septembre des Réfugiés au Burundi: Prévisions pour l'Année 1966,* Royaume du Burundi, Cabinet du Roi, Bujumbura 1965, passim.
3. *Resettlement to Tanganyika: Attitude of the Burundi Government and Refugees,* UNHCR, BUR/755, June 22, 1964, unpublished document.
4. See Quentin Reynolds' interview with Tung Chi-Ping in *Look,* December 1, 1964, p. 24.
5. See *Les Cahiers de Gambona: Instructions Politiques et Militaires des Partisans Congolais (1964–1965),* CRISP, Dossier Documentaire No. 3, Brussels 1965.
6. Anon., *La Pénétration Communiste au Burundi,* Bujumbura, n.d., mimeo.
7. See Benoît Verhaegen, *Rébellions au Congo,* CRISP, Brussels 1966, Vol. I, passim.
8. Ibid., p. 293.
9. Ibid., p. 319.
10. John B. Webster, *The Political Development of Rwanda and Burundi,* Syracuse University, Program of Eastern African Studies: Occasional Paper No. 16, 1966, p. 93.
11. Letter communicated to the author by the late Paul Mirerekano.
12. Ibid.
13. For the full text of the bishop's letter, see *Remarques Africaines,* November 11, 1964, p. 471; see also Zénon Nicayenzi's illuminating response in ibid., p. 470 ("Interview de M. Z. Nicayenzi à propos de la Note des Evêques sur le danger qui menace le Burundi").

16. THE DIALECTICS OF SUCCESSION

1. Peter C. Lloyd, *The New Elites of Tropical Africa,* Oxford University Press, London and New York 1966, p. 4.
2. *Cinquième Congrès Organisé par l'Uneba du 26 au 31 Août, 1964,* Bujumbura 1964, mimeo. See also, *Résolutions du Séminaire National Organisé par l'Union Nationale des Etudiants Barundi (Uneba) du 25 au 31 Août, 1963,* n.d., n.p., mimeo.
3. Ibid.
4. Ibid.
5. Frantz Fanon, *The Wretched of the Earth,* Grove, New York 1966.
6. *La Jeunesse après l'indépendance,* n.d., n.p., mimeo.
7. Ibid.
8. *Programme d'Action de la Fédération des Travailleurs du Burundi,* Bujumbura 1964, mimeo.

9. Ibid.
10. For the full text of Nyangoma's speech, see *Infor-Burundi*, No. 153, July 3, 1965.
11. Ibid., No. 155, July 17, 1965.
12. Ibid., No. 156, July 31, 1965.
13. For the full text of the arrêté-loi, see ibid., No. 159, September 4, 1965.
14. See *Decision No. 4/1965 suspendant une résolution du conseil communal de Rutegama*, ibid., No. 150, June 12, 1965.
15. See *Statement of the International Commission of Jurists: Events in Burundi*, press release, Geneva, January 8, 1966.
16. See *In Burundi feudal Tutsi leaders methodically and ferociously exterminate the elite of the Hutu race*, Brussels, November 18, 1965, mimeo.
17. *Procès-Verbal du Conseil de Cabinet tenu à Bujumbura le 23 Octobre*, unpublished document.
18. *Infor-Burundi*, No. 171, March 26, 1966.
19. Hans Meyer, *Die Barundi*, Otto Spamer, Leipzig 1916, p. 172.
20. "Le Gouvernement Royal VI", *Remarques Africaines*, October 6, 1965.
21. "Le 19 Octobre . . . et après?", ibid., November 17, 1965.
22. "1965: L'Escalade de la Détérioration", ibid., December 29, 1965.
23. "Le prix du silence", ibid., February 9, 1966.
24. *Contre le Gouvernement Royal Biha*, Bujumbura, February 2, 1966, mimeo.
25. See *Infor-Burundi*, No. 181, July 2, 1966.
26. See René Bernard's interesting article, "The constitutional crisis in Burundi", *The Nationalist* (Dar es Salaam), August 17, 1966.
27. *Déclaration Gouvernementale*, Bujumbura 1966, mimeo.
28. Ibid.
29. *Procès-Verbal du Conseil des Ministres tenu à Bujumbura le 7 Octobre, 1966*, unpublished document.
30. Ibid.
31. Ibid.
32. Niccolo Machiavelli, *The Prince*, Hendricks House, New York 1946, p. 162.

17. THE ARMY AT THE HELM

1. S. E. Finer, *The Man on Horseback*, Pall Mall Press, London 1962; Frederick A. Praeger, New York 1962; p. 89, note 2.
2. Samuel Huntington, *Changing Patterns of Military Politics*, Free Press, Glencoe 1962, p. 32.
3. Finer, op. cit., p. 184.
4. From a radio broadcast, Bujumbura, November 28, 1966.
5. Samuel Huntington, *The Soldier and the State*, Harvard University Press, Cambridge 1957, esp. pp. 1–18; 59–79.
6. William J. Foltz, "Psychanalyse des Armées Subsahariennes", *Le Mois en Afrique*, No. 14, February 1967, p. 37.
7. Huntington, *Changing Patterns* . . ., loc. cit.
8. Finer, op. cit., p. 157.
9. Ibid., p. 167.
10. Ibid., p. 165.
11. *Intervention du Ministre du Parti à la Réunion des Cadres Provinciaux du Parti en date du 16 février 1967 (Compte-Rendu en Kirundi)*, quoted in Gabriel Mpozagara, *Sociologie Politique du Burundi*, Mémoire des Sciences Politiques,

Faculté de Droit et des Sciences Economiques, Université de Paris, 1967, p. 175.
12. Ibid., p. 179.
13. Ibid., p. 175.
14. *Unité et Révolution*, No. 10, September 29, 1967.
15. Ibid., No. 1, June 23, 1967.
16. Ibid., No. 10, September 29, 1967; see also ibid., No. 8, September 9, 1967.
17. Ibid.
18. Ibid., No. 2, June 30, 1967.
19. Ibid., No. 19, December 15, 1967.
20. Ibid.
21. Ibid., September 9, 1967.
22. See *Le Soir*, September 16, 1967.
23. Irving L. Horowitz, "us Policy and the Latin American Military Establishment", *The Correspondent*, No. 32, Autumn 1964, p. 58.
24. Mpozagara, op. cit., p. 174.
25. David A. Wilson, *Politics in Thailand*, Cornell University Press, Ithaca 1962, p. 182.
26. The expression is borrowed from André Makarakiza's work, *La Dialectique des Barundi*, ARSC, Vol. XIX, fasc. 2, Brussels 1959.

18. REVOLUTIONARY CHANGE AND NATION-BUILDING

1. See, for example, Robert I. Rotberg and Ali A. Mazrui eds., *Traditions of Protest in Black Africa*, Oxford University Press, London & New York 1970.
2. Harry Eckstein, ed., *Internal War: Problems and Approaches*, Free Press, New York 1964, p. 13.
3. T. Geiger, "Revolution", in F. V. Vierkandt, ed., *Handwoerterbuch der Soziologie*, Stuttgart 1959, p. 43.
4. See, for example, Aristide R. Zolberg, "The Structure of Political Conflict in the New States of Tropical Africa", a paper prepared for delivery at the Seventh Congress of the International Political Science Association, September 18–27, 1967.
5. See J. J. Maquet, "La participation de la classe paysanne au mouvement d'indépendance au Rwanda", *Cahiers d'Etudes Africaines*, Vol. IV, No. 16, 1964, p. 557.
6. Helen Codere, "Power in Rwanda", *Anthropologica*, Vol. IV, No. 1, 1962, pp. 45–87.
7. Ibid., p. 82.
8. Georges Balandier, "Social Changes and Social Problems in Negro Africa", in Calvin Stillman, ed., *Africa and the Modern World*, Chicago 1955, cited in Martin Kilson, "Nationalism and Social Classes in British West Africa", *The Journal of Politics*, Vol. XX, 1958, p. 378.
9. Plausible answers to these questions are suggested by M. G. Smith's definition of pluralism: see M. G. Smith, *The Plural Society in the British West Indies*, University of California Press, Berkeley 1965. But see also R. S. Bryce-Laporte, "M. G. Smith's version of pluralism: The questions it raises", *Comparative Studies in Society and History*, Vol. X, No. 1, October 1967, p. 116. For an outstanding contribution to the theory of social pluralism, see Leo Kuper and M. G. Smith, *Pluralism in Africa*, University of California Press, Berkeley 1969.

10. See Gwyn A. Williams, "The Concept of 'Egemonia' in the Thought of Antonio Gramsci", *Journal of the History of Ideas*, Vol. xxi, No. 4, 1960, p. 587.
11. H. H. Gerth & G. W. Mills, eds., *From Max Weber: Essays in Sociology* Oxford University Press, New York 1958, p. 189.
12. See Kilson, op. cit.; also, by the same author, *Political Change in a West African State*, Harvard University Press, Cambridge 1966, pp. 68–93.
13. For a very similar phenomenon, in the context of Latin America, see Bertram Hutchison, "The Patron-Dependent Relationship in Brazil: A Preliminary Examination", *Sociologia Ruralis*, Vol. vi, No. 1, 1966, pp. 3–30. For an interesting historical parallel, see J. Russel Major, "The Crown and the Aristocracy in Renaissance France", *American Historical Review*, Vol. LXIV, No. 3, April 1963, p. 635.
14. Yonina Talmon, "Millenarian Movements", *Archives Européennes de Sociologie*, Vol. ii, No. 2, 1966, pp. 198–9.
15. Gil Carl Alroy, *The Involvement of Peasants in Internal Wars*, Princeton University, Center for International Studies, Princeton 1966, p. 7.
16. See Gil Carl Alroy, "The Meaning of 'Peasant Revolution': The Cuban Case", *International Review of History and Political Science*, Vol. ii, No. 2, 1965, pp. 87–100.
17. *New Statesman*, August 3, 1962, p. 148.
18. J. E. Hobsbawm, *The Age of Revolution: 1789–1848*, World Publishing, New York 1962, p. 63.
19. See John Randolph in *Saint Petersburg Times*, April 16, 1967.
20. Karl Deutsch, "External Involvement in Internal Wars", in Eckstein, op. cit., p. 104.
21. Ibid., p. 107.
22. Ibid.
23. For a theoretical formulation of this phenomenon, see Lewis Coser, *The Functions of Social Conflict*, Free Press, Glencoe 1956, p. 93.
24. T. V. Sathyamurthy, "Revolutions and Revolutionaries", *Transition*, Vol. v, No. 21, 1965, p. 26.
25. Bernard Lewis, *The Emergence of Modern Turkey*, Oxford University Press, London and New York 1961, p. 228.
26. See Lucian W. Pye & Sidney Verba, eds., *Political Culture and Political Development*, Princeton University Press, Princeton 1965, passim.
27. Samuel P. Huntington, "Political Development and Political Decay", *World Politics*, Vol. xvii, No. 3, April 1965, p. 422.
28. Ibid.
29. Ibid., p. 419.
30. Erik Erikson, "Ego Development and Historical Change", *Psychological Issues*, Vol. i, No. 1, 1959, p. 18.
31. Ibid., p. 26.
32. Ibid.
33. Frantz Fanon, *The Wretched of the Earth*, Grove, New York 1966, p. 35.
34. Lewis Coser, "The Myth of the Peasant Revolt", *Dissent*, May–June 1966, p. 303.

Select Bibliography

Excluded from the materials listed below are the documents contained in the Derscheid Collection and my own, both of which are available in microfilm from either the University of Florida Library (Gainesville, Florida) or the Hoover Institution (Stanford, California). Pending the publication of a more complete inventory of the contents of these collections, at least passing reference must be made to the following important materials. One of the most valuable sources available from the Derscheid papers is the nearly complete set of administrative reports prepared in 1929 in response to the questionnaire addressed by the Governor of Ruanda-Urundi to the administrateurs de territoires of both Rwanda and Burundi, listed alternatively under the title of *Enquête administrative générale* (1929), or *Rapport établi en réponse au questionnaire addressé en 1929 par M. le Gouverneur du Ruanda-Urundi.* Supplementary information on political and administrative developments at the territoire level can be gleaned from the *Rapports de sortie de charge* and the annual *Rapports politiques.* Unfortunately, many of these documents are missing and those that are available cover only a very brief, though admittedly crucial, span of time, 1929–33. Political developments at the hill level are available only for the Bugoyi province of Rwanda, in the form of 91 'fiches', each dealing with a separate hill and covering a period of time of approximately fifty years (1880–1929). Especially useful for the historian are, in addition to the material mentioned above, the several interviews conducted by local administrators with local chiefs on the history of their respective provinces. Very few of these, however, are available for Burundi; the nearest equivalent are the transcripts of the oral testimonies recorded by Resident Oger Coubeau in 1935 (See *Traditions sur le règne de Mutaga I; Traditions sur le règne de Mwambutsa I; Traditions sur le règne de Ntare II; Traditions sur le règne de Mwezi Kisabo* [*Renseignements obtenus du Chef Baranyanka par l'intermédiaire du Résident O. Coubeau, June 1935*]), and the personal notes of Pierre Ryckmans and Jean-Marie Derscheid, also based on interviews with local chiefs and court officials. More directly relevant to recent developments are the following additional sources, available from my own collection. The role of the tutelle during Rwanda's transition to independence is abundantly documented by the *Procès-Verbaux de Réunion des Administrateurs de Territoires* (1960–1961), and the *Procès-Verbaux de Réunion Conjointe* (March, April, 1961). For post-independence developments at the prefectoral level, see *Procès-Verbaux des Conseils de Préfecture* (Kigali, 1964, 1965); *Compte-Rendu des Réunions de Bourgmestres* (Kigali, Ruhengeri, 1964); *Compte-Rendu des Réunions de Cadre* (Kigali, 1965, 1966). An interesting discussion of the land problem in the prefecture of Gisenyi will be found in *Réunion des Premiers Occupants* (abakonde) *et les usufruitiers* (abagererwa) *à Kisenyi, le 17 Août, 1962,* and also in the parliamentary debates for 1961 and 1962. While there are fewer documents of this kind available for Burundi, mention must be made of the proceedings of the so-called 'Summit Conference' held at Kitega in October 1964 (see *Rapport de la Commission élue par la Conférence en date du 7 Octobre, 1964;* and *Compte Rendu de la Conférence au Sommet de Kitega du 8 Septembre*

533

au 3 Octobre, 1964); of a number of important administrative circulars issued by the Ministry of Interior in 1964 and 1965; of numerous tracts and statements issued by political parties, factions, trade unions, and student organisations both before and after independence. A particularly rare and interesting document on the meaning of kingship in Burundi is the late Paul Mirerekano's *Mbwire Gito Canje* ('Listen, My Son', n.p., 1961?), translated and communicated to this writer by Jean Ghislain, former administrateur de territoire in Muramvya. Ghislain's *Chronologie Politique du Burundi* (mimeo.) is indispensable to an understanding of the political events preceding Burundi's independence, and so are his remarkably detailed genealogical tables of the Burundi dynasties. Finally, there are the innumerable petitions submitted to the UN Trusteeship Council prior to 1962, unquestionably the richest source of information on the history of political parties of both Rwanda and Burundi. While many of these are available from official UN documents, others have never been made public. In this latter category of documents, one of the most illuminating is a 65 page memorandum presented by PARMEHUTU to the UN Visiting Mission, entitled *Mémoire sur la Révolution Rwandaise de Novembre 1959*.

I. BIBLIOGRAPHIES

By far the most comprehensive bibliography on Rwanda and Burundi is Joseph R. Clément's monumental *Essai de Bibliographie du Ruanda-Urundi*, Service des AIMO, Usumbura 1959. For a more recent survey, see John B. Webster's useful inventory in his monograph on *The Political Development of Rwanda and Burundi*, Maxwell Graduate School of Citizenship and Public Affairs, Occasional Papers No. 16, Syracuse University, 1966, pp. 101–21. For earlier sources, dealing primarily with the German period, see Wm. Roger Louis's excellent bibliographic essay in his *Ruanda-Urundi: 1884–1919*, Clarendon Press, Oxford 1963, pp. 261–71. Equally valuable is Louis de Lacger's bibliography in his *Ruanda*, Kabgaye?, n.d., pp. 643–50. See, in addition, T. Heyse's classic *Bibliographie du Congo Belge et du Ruanda-Urundi, 1939–1951* in *Cahiers Belges et Congolais*, Nos. 4–22, Brussels 1955. Supplementary coverage of materials on Rwanda and Burundi will be found in the regular bibliographic listings of *Africa, Etudes Congolaises*, and (up until 1960) *Zaïre*.

II. GENERAL WORKS AND COMPARATIVE STUDIES ON
RWANDA AND BURUNDI

1. Books and Monographs

Anon., *Décolonisation et Indépendence du Rwanda et du Burundi*, special issue of *Chronique de Politique Etrangère*, Vol. XVI, Nos. 4–6, July–November 1963

Bourgeois, R., *Banyarwanda et Barundi: L'Evolution du contrat de bail à cheptel au Ruanda-Urundi*, ARSOM, Vol. IX, fasc. 4, Brussels 1958

de Cleene, N., *Introduction à l'Ethnographie du Congo Belge et du Ruanda-Urundi*, Editions de Sikkel, Antwerp 1957

Durieux, André, *Institutions politiques, administratives et juridiques du Congo Belge et du Ruanda-Urundi*, 4th edn., Editions Bieleveld, Brussels 1957

Grandes Lignes du Régime des Terres du Congo Belge et du Ruanda-Urundi, ARSOM, Vol. XV, fasc. 1, Brussels 1947

Guillaume, H., *Les Populations du Ruanda et de l'Urundi*, mimeo., n.p., n.d.

Halewyck de Heusch, Michel, *Les Institutions Politiques et Administratives des Etats Africains soumis à l'Autorité de la Belgique*, Bolyn, Brussels 1938

Heyse, T., *Congo Belge et Ruanda-Urundi: Notes de Droit Public et Commentaires de la Charte Coloniale*, 2 vols., Van Campenhout, Brussels 1952–54

Hiernaux, Jean, *Analyse de la variation des caractères physiques humains en une région de l'Afrique centrale: Ruanda-Urundi et Kivu*, Annales du Musée Royal du Congo Belge, Anthropologie, Vol. 3, Tervueren 1956

Jadot, J. M., *Les écrivains africains du Congo Belge et du Ruanda-Urundi*, ARSOM, Brussels 1959

Jentgen, P., *Les frontières du Ruanda-Urundi et le régime international de tutelle*, ARSOM, Vol. XIII, fasc. 2, Brussels 1957

Kagame, Alexis, *Le Colonialisme face à la Doctrine Missionnaire*, mimeo., Butare 1964

Lefebvre, Jacques, *Structures économiques du Congo Belge et du Ruanda-Urundi*, Treuvenberg, Brussels 1955

Leurquin, Philippe, *Le niveau de vie des populations rurales du Ruanda-Urundi*, Institut de Recherches Economiques et Sociales, Louvain 1960

Louis, Wm. Roger, *Ruanda-Urundi: 1884–1919*, Clarendon Press, Oxford 1963

Maquet, J. J. & d'Hertefelt, Marcel, *Elections en société féodale*, ARSOM, Vol. XXI, fasc. 2, Brussels 1959

Mecklenburg, Frederick, Duke of, *In the Heart of Africa*, Cassel, London 1910

de Meyer, Roger, *Introduction au Congo Belge et au Ruanda-Urundi*, Office de Publicité, Brussels 1955

Michiels, A. & Laude, N., *Congo Belge et Ruanda-Urundi*, Universelle, Brussels 1958

Office de l'Information et des Relations Publiques pour le Congo Belge et le Ruanda-Urundi, *Le Ruanda-Urundi*, Brussels 1959

Ryckmans, Pierre, *La Politique Coloniale*, Rex, Louvain 1934; *Dominer pour Servir*, Universelle, Brussels 1948

Sandrart, Georges, *Ruanda-Urundi*, Dessart, Brussels 1953

Sasserath, Jules Simon, *Le Ruanda-Urundi: Un étrange royaume féodal au coeur de l'Afrique*, Germinal, Brussels 1948

Van Bilsen, A. A. J., *Vers l'indépendence du Congo Belge et du Ruanda-Urundi*, Brussels 1958

Van Kalken, F., *Histoire de la Belgique et de son expansion coloniale*, Office de Publicité, Brussels 1954

Van der Kerken, Georges, *La crise économique en Afrique Belge: Situation actuelle et perspectives d'avenir*, Bruylant, Brussels 1931

Vansina, Jan, *Oral Tradition*, Aldine, Chicago 1965

Vermeulen, V., *Déficiences et dangers de notre politique indigène*, Brussels 1952

Webster, John B., *The Constitutions of Burundi, Malagasy and Rwanda: A Comparison and Explanation of East African French Language Constitutions, with French texts and English translations*, Maxwell Graduate School of Public Affairs and Citizenship, Occasional Papers, No. 3, Syracuse University 1964; *The Political Development of Rwanda and Burundi*, Maxwell Graduate School of Citizenship and Public Affairs, Occasional Papers, No. 16, Syracuse University 1966

de Wilde d'Estmael, X., *Cours de Juridictions indigènes du Ruanda-Urundi*, Astrida 1957

2. Articles

Albert, Ethel, "Socio-political Organization and Receptivity to Change: Some differences between Ruanda and Urundi", *Southwestern Journal of Anthropology*, Vol. XVI, 1960, pp. 46–74

Baeck, L., "Quelques aspects sociaux de l'urbanisation au Ruanda-Urundi", *Zaire*, Vol. X, 1956, pp. 115–45

Balfour, Patrick, "Tanganyika and Ruanda-Urundi", *The Geographical Magazine*, Vol. VIII, 1938, pp. 42–8

Barakana, Gabriel, "L'unification des langues au Ruanda-Urundi", *Civilisations*, Vol. II, 1952, pp. 67–78

Bequaert, Maurice M., "La position actuelle de la préhistoire au Congo Belge et au Ruanda-Urundi", *Fifth International Congress of Prehistoric and Protohistoric Sciences, Hamburg 1958*, Berlin 1961, pp. 84–8; "Préhistoire et Protohistoire au Congo Belge et au Ruanda-Urundi de 1936 à 1950", *Third International Congress of Prehistoric and Protohistoric Sciences, Zurich 1950*, Zurich 1961, pp. 108–14

Boone, Olga, "Carte ethnique du Congo Belge et du Ruanda-Urundi", *Zaire*, Vol. VIII, 1954, pp. 451–66

Bragard, Lucie, "Vers l'indépendance du Ruanda-Urundi", *Les Dossiers de l'Action Sociale Catholique*, No. 8, 1959, pp. 643–76

Chauleur, P., "Les Etapes de l'Indépendance du Ruanda-Urundi", *Etudes*, Vol. 314, September 1962, pp. 225–31

Comhaire, J., "Le Ruanda-Urundi en 1952", *Zaire*, Vol. VIII, 1954, pp. 55–61; "Evolution générale du Ruanda-Urundi en 1953", *Zaire*, Vol. VIII, 1954, pp. 1067–74.

Gelders, V. & Biroli, J., "Native Political Organization in Ruanda-Urundi", *Civilisations*, Vol. IV, 1954, pp. 125–32

Gerig, B., "Political and Economic Developments in Ruanda-Urundi", *US Department of State Bulletin*, Vol. 34, March 12, 1954, pp. 438–40

Gildea, Ray Y., "Rwanda and Burundi", *Focus*, Vol. XIII, 1963, pp. 1–6

Harroy, Jean-Paul, "La lutte contre la dissipation des ressources naturelles au Ruanda-Urundi", *Civilisations*, Vol. IV, 1954, pp. 363–74

d'Hertefelt, Marcel, "Le Ruanda et le Burundi vers l'indépendance", *Archives Diplomatiques et Consulaires*, Vol. XXVII, August–September 1962, pp. 372–3

Hiernaux, Jean, "Note sur une ancienne population du Ruanda-Urundi: Les Renge", *Zaire*, Vol. X, 1956, pp. 351–60

Jentgen, P., "Ruanda-Urundi: The Mandate and International Trusteeship", *Geographical Review*, Vol. 49, January 1959, pp. 120–2

Jezic, B., "Psychologische Testerfahrungen bei den Barundi und Banyarwanda", *Afrika Heute*, No. 19, 1967, pp. 287–9

Kagame, Alexis, "Les Hamites du Ruanda et du Burundi sont-ils des Hamites?", ARSC, *Bulletin des Séances*, Vol. II, 1956, pp. 341–63

Latham-Koening, A. L., "Ruanda-Urundi on the threshold of independence", *World Today*, Vol. XVIII, July 1962, pp. 288–95

Lemarchand, René, "L'influence des systèmes traditionnels sur l'évolution politique du Rwanda et du Burundi", *Revue de l'Institut de Sociologie*, Vol. II, 1962, pp. 333–57; "Political Instability in Africa: The Case of Rwanda and Burundi", *Civilisations*, Vol. XVI, 1966, pp. 1–29

Leurquin, Ph., "Agricultural change in Ruanda-Urundi", Food Research Institute Studies, Vol. IV, 1963, pp. 39–89

Malengrau, Guy, "Chronique de Politique Indigène", *Zaire*, Vol. VI, 1952, pp. 34–41

Maquet, J. J., "Ruanda: Urundi: The introduction of an electoral system for councils in a caste society", in R. Apthorpe, ed., *From Tribal Rule to Modern Government*, Lusaka 1960, pp. 57–68

Marzorati, A., "The Belgian Congo and Ruanda-Urundi", *Civilisations*, Vol. I, 1951, pp. 149–54

Maus, Albert, "Le statut politique du Ruanda-Urundi et la situation des Bahutu", *Eurafrica*, Vol. III, 1959, p. 19

Moncheur, Charles, "Feudal Kingdoms in Central Africa: Ruanda-Urundi", *African World*, December 1947, pp. 14–15

Mulago, Vincent, "L'union vitale Bantu ou le principe de la cohésion et de la communauté chez les Bashi, les Nabyarwanda et les Barundi", *Annali Lateranensi*, Vol. XX, 1956, pp. 61–263

Neesen, V., "Quelques données démographiques sur la population du Ruanda-Urundi", *Zaire*, Vol. VIII, 1953, pp. 1011–25

Nicaise, Joseph, "Applied Anthropology in the Congo and Ruanda-Urundi", *Human Organization*, Vol. XIX, 1960, pp. 112–17

Peeters, Leo, "Le rôle du milieu géographique dans l'occupation humaine du Rwanda-Burundi", *Bulletin de la Société Royale de Géographie d'Anvers*, Vol. 74, fasc. 1 & 2 combined, pp. 29–47

Postiaux, H., "La colonisation du territoire du Ruanda-Urundi", *Les Cahiers Coloniaux de l'Institut Colonial de Marseilles*, Nos. 551–2, 1929, p. 332

Rhodius, George, "The evolution of the native woman in the Belgian Congo and Ruanda-Urundi", *African Women*, Vol. I, 1955, pp. 73–4

Roucek, Joseph, "Rwanda and Burundi", *African Trade and Development*, Vol. IV, 1962, pp. 12–15

Rousseau, R., "La dernière année de la tutelle belge au Rwanda-Burundi", *Vie Economique et Sociale*, Vol. XXXIII, 1962, pp. 306–12

Sears, Mason, "Trust Territory of Ruanda-Urundi", *US Department of State Bulletin*, Vol. 41, August 3, 1959, pp. 180–1

de Sousberghe, L., "Cousin croisés et descendants: Les systèmes du Rwanda et du Burundi comparés à ceux du Bas-Congo", *Africa*, Vol. XXXV, 1965, pp. 396–420

Van der Kerken, Georges, "L'évolution de la politique indigène au Congo Belge et au Ruanda-Urundi", *Revue de l'Institut de Sociologie*, Vol. I, 1953, pp. 25–62

Van Tichelen, H. E., "Problèmes du développement économique du Ruanda-Urundi", *Zaire*, Vol. XI, 1957, pp. 451–74

Whitaker, Philip & Silvey, Jonathan, "A visit to the Congo, Rwanda and Burundi", *Makerere Journal*, No. 9, 1964, pp. 71–82

III. RWANDA

1. Books and Monographs

Adriaenssens, J., *Le Droit Foncier au Rwanda*, mimeo., n.p., 1962

Anon., *Historique et Chronologie du Ruanda*, n.p., n.d.

d'Arianoff, A., *Histoire des Bagesera souverains du Gisaka*, IRCB, Vol. XXIV, fasc. 3, Brussels 1952

Arnoux, Alexandre, *Les Pères Blancs aux sources du Nil, Ruanda*, Grands Lacs, Namur 1953

Centre de Recherche et d'Information Socio-Politiques, *Rwanda Politique 1958–1960*, Brussels 1961

Czekanowski, Jan et al., *Wissenschaftliche Ergbenisse der Deutschen Zentral-Afrika Expedition (1907–1908)*, 8 Vols., Leipzig 1912–27

Dufays, Félix, *Pages d'Epopée Africaine*, René Weverberghe, Ixelles 1928

Edel, May Mandelbaum, *The Chiga of Western Uganda*, Oxford University Press, London 1957

von Goetzen, Graf, *Durch Afrika von Ost nach West*, Berlin 1895

Gravel, Pierre Bettez, *The Play for Power: Description of a Community in Eastern Ruanda*, unpublished PH.D. thesis, University Microfilms, Ann Arbor 1962

d'Hertefelt, Marcel & Coupez, André, *La Royauté Sacrée de l'Ancien Rwanda: Texte, traduction et commentaire de son rituel*, Musée Royal de l'Afrique Centrale, Tervueren 1964

Hubert, Jean R., *La Toussaint Rwandaise et sa Répression*, ARSOM, Vol. XXXI, fasc. 2, Brussels 1965

Kagame, Alexis, *La Poésie Dynastique au Rwanda*, IRCB, Vol. XXII, fasc. 1, Brussels 1951; *Le code des institutions politiques du Rwanda précolonial*, IRCB, Vol. XXVI, fasc. 1, Brussels 1952; *Les Organisations socio-familiales dans l'ancien Ruanda*, ARSC, Vol XXXVIII, fasc. 3, Brussels 1954; *La Notion de génération appliquée à la généalogie dynastique et à l'histoire du Rwanda des X et XI ème siècles à nos jours*, ARSC, Vol. IX, fasc. 5, Brussels 1959; *Histoire du Ruanda*, Bibliothèque de l'Etoile, Leverville 1958; *Histoire des armées bovines de l'ancien Rwanda*, ARSOM, Brussels 1961; *Les milices du Rwanda précolonial*, ARSOM, Vol. XXVIII, fasc. 3, Brussels 1963

Kandt, Richard, *Caput Nili*, Berlin 1921

de Lacger, Louis, *Le Ruanda: Aperçu historique*, Kabgaye 1939; *Ruanda*, Kabgaye?, 1961

Maquet, J. J., *Le Système des Relations Sociales dans le Ruanda Ancien*, Musée Royal du Congo Belge, Tervueren 1954; *The Premise of Inequality in Ruanda*, Oxford University Press, London & New York 1961

Mulenzi, A., *Etude sur Quelques Problèmes du Rwanda*, Imprimerie Tournaisienne, Brussels 1958

Munyangagu, Aloys, *L'actualité politique au Ruanda*, Brussels 1959

Naigiziki, Saverio, *Escapade Ruandaise: Journal d'un clerc en sa trentième année*, Deny, Brussels 1950; *Mes Transes à Trente Ans*, Astrida 1955

Nkundabagenzi, Félix, *Evolution de la Structure Politique du Ruanda*, Université Catholique de Louvain, Mémoire presenté pour l'obtention du diplôme en Sciences Politiques et Sociales, Louvain 1961

Pagès, R., *Un Royaume Hamite au Centre de l'Afrique*, IRCB, Vol. I, Brussels 1933

Pauwels, Marcel, *Imana et le Culte des mânes au Rwanda*, ARSC, Vol. XXVII, fasc. 1, Brussels 1958

Segal, Aaron, *Massacre in Rwanda*, Fabian Society Pamphlet, London 1964

Vanhove, J., *Essai de droit coutumier du Ruanda*, IRCB, Vol. X, fasc. 1, Brussels 1941

Van Overshelde, A., *Un audacieux pacifique: Monseigneur L. P. Classe, Apôtre du Ruanda*, Grands Lacs, Namur 1948

Vansina, Jan, *L'évolution du royaume Rwanda des origines à 1900*, ARSOM, Vol. XXVI, fasc. 2, Brussels 1962

2. Articles

d'Arianoff, A., "Origines des clans Hamites du Ruanda", *Zaire*, Vol. V, 1951, pp. 45–54

Belshaw, D. G. R., "Resettlement Schemes for Rwanda refugees in Uganda", *East African Geographical Review*, Vol. I, April 1963, pp. 46–8

Bessel, J. M., "Nyabingi", *Uganda Journal*, Vol. IV, 1938–39, pp. 73–86

Birnbaum, Martin, "Reception in Ruanda", *Natural History*, Vol. 44, 1939, pp. 298–307

Briey, Comte R. de, "Musinga", *Congo*, Vol. I, 1920, pp. 1–23

Bushayija, Stanislas, "Le Ruanda en état de révolution: Plaidoyer pour la démocratisation", *La Revue Nouvelle*, Vol. 31, May 1960, pp. 503–13

Cauwe, André, "The Problem of Rwanda refugees in Kivu", *Migration News*, November–December 1962, pp. 1–4

Classe, Léon, "The Supreme Being among the Banyarwanda of Ruanda", *Primitive Man*, Vol. II, 1929, pp. 56–7

Codere, Helen, "Power in Ruanda", *Anthropologica*, Vol. IV, 1962, pp. 45–85

Coupez, André & Kamanzi, Thomas, "Quelques noms géographiques Rwanda", *Zaire*, Vol. XVIII, 1959, pp. 149–68

Des Forges, Alison, *The Impact of European Colonization on the Rwandan Social System*, a paper delivered at the 1966 annual meeting of the ASA in Bloomington, Indiana, October 1966; "Kings without Crowns: The White Fathers in Ruanda", in *Boston University Papers in African History*, Vol. III, Boston University Press, Boston 1967

Gahungu, F., "De la suppression de l'ubuhake", *Servir*, Vol. XIII, 1952, p. 204

d'Hertefelt, Marcel, "Les Elections Communales et le Consensus Politique au Ruanda", *Zaire*, Vol. XIV, 1960, pp. 403–38; "Stratification sociale et structure politique au Ruanda", *La Revue Nouvelle*, Vol. XXXI, May 1960, pp. 449–62; "Myth and Political Acculturation in Rwanda", in A. Dubb, ed., *Myth in Modern Africa*, Lusaka 1960, pp. 114–35; "Le Rwanda" in *Les anciens royaumes de la zone interlacustre méridionale: Rwanda, Burundi, Buha*, Musée de l'Afrique Centrale, Tervueren 1962; "Mythes et idéologies dans le Rwanda ancien et contemporain" in Jan Vansina, Raymond Mauny & L. V. Thomas, eds., *The Historian in Tropical Africa*, Oxford University Press, London 1964, pp. 219–38; "The Rwanda of Rwanda" in James L. Gibbs, ed., *Peoples of Africa*, Holt, Rinehart and Winston, New York 1965, pp. 403–40

Huxley, Elspeth, "The Rise and Fall of the Watutsi", *New York Times Magazine*, February 23, 1964

Kagame, Alexis, "Le Ruanda et son Roi", *Aequatoria*, Vol. XVIII, No. 2, 1945, pp. 41–58; "Le Code ésoterique de la dynastie du Rwanda", *Zaire*, Vol. III, 1947, pp. 363–86; "Bref Aperçu sur la poésie dynastique du Rwanda", *Zaire*, Vol. IV, 1950, pp. 243–70; "La Poésie au Rwanda", *Compte-Rendu des Travaux du Séminaire d'Anthropologie Sociale tenu à Astrida en Juillet 1951*, IRSAC, Astrida 1951, pp. 19–27; "La structure des quinze clans du Rwanda", *Annali Lateranensi*, Vol. XVIII, 1954, pp. 103–17

Karemera, Athanase, "La campagne d'alphabétisation et service social", *Servir*, Vol. XXV, 1954, pp. 33–5

Latham-Koening, A. L., "Attempted Genocide in Ruanda", *World Today*, Vol. XX, March 1964, pp. 97–100

Lemarchand, René, "Power and Stratification in Rwanda: A Reconsideration", *Cahiers d'Etudes Africaines*, Vol. IV, 1966, pp. 592–610

Maquet, J. J. & Naigiziki, Saverio, "Les droits fonciers dans le Ruanda ancien", *Zaire*, Vol. XI, 1957, pp. 339–59

Maquet, J. J., "Rwanda: Supernatural and Ethical Conceptions", *Compte-Rendu des Travaux du Séminaire d'Anthropologie Sociale tenu à Astrida en Juillet 1951*, IRSAC, Astrida 1951, pp. 15–19; "Le problème de la domination Tutsi", *Zaire*, Vol. VI, 1952, pp. 1011–16; "Les groupes de parenté du Ruanda ancien", *Africa*, Vol. XXIII, 1953, pp. 25–9; "The Kingdom of Rwanda", in Daryll Forde, ed., *African Worlds: Studies in the Cosmological Ideas and Social Values of African Peoples*, Oxford University Press, London 1954; "La participation de la classe paysanne au mouvement d'indépendence du Rwanda", *Cahiers d'Etudes Africaines*, Vol. IV, 1964, pp. 552–68

Maral, Paul, "La révolution Bantoue au Rwanda", *L'Afrique et L'Asie*, No. 69, 1965, pp. 3–13

Mbogo, Djuma, "Le Drame au Rwanda", *Les Temps Modernes*, No. 215, April 1964, pp. 1821–32

Mineur, G., "Le Mwami peut-il modifier la coutume?", *Servir*, Vol. VI, 1945, pp. 50–2

Monheim, Francis, "La révolution ruandaise", *Revue Générale Belge*, Vol. 95, December 1959, pp. 53–60

Nothomb, D., "Notion rwandaise du temps et de l'histoire", *Servir*, Vol. XXIII, 1962, pp. 203–16

Pagès, A., "Au Ruanda: A la cour du Mwami", *Zaire*, Vol. IV, 1950, pp. 471–84

Pauwels, Marcel, "Le Kalinga, tambour-enseigne du royaume et de la dynastie des rois Banyiginya (Absindi) du Rwanda", *Annali Lateranensi*, Vol. XXVI, 1962, pp. 221–56

Philipps, J. E. T., "The Nyabingi: An anti-European secret society in Africa", *Congo*, Vol. I, 1928, pp. 310–521

Ruhara, C., Rwamasibo, C. & Sendnanoye, G., "Le Buhake: Une coutume essentiellement munyarwanda", *Bulletin des Juridictions du Ruanda-Urundi*, Nos. 3, 8, 1947–48, pp. 103–42; 245–58; 261–5

Schnee, H., "Ruanda", in *Deutsche Kolonial Lexicon*, 3 Vols., Leipzig 1920

Schumacher, Pierre, "Au Ruanda: Considèrations sur la Nature de l'homme", *Zaire*, Vol. III, 1949, pp. 257–78

Segal, Aaron, "Rwanda: The underlying causes", *Africa Report*, April 1964, pp. 3–6

Simmonds, John W., Jr., "How the Banyarwanda understand Man", *Practical Anthropology*, Vol. X, 1963, pp. 17–20

Thibaud, Paul, "Le Rwanda déchiré", *Esprit*, No. 7, July 1964, pp. 150–7

Vanhove, J., "Les juridictions indigènes au Ruanda", *Congo*, July 1939, pp. 2–16

Vansina, Jan, "Chronologie des Règnes du Rwanda", *Afrika-Tervueren*, Vol. VII, 1961, pp. 22–3

de Wilde d'Estmael, C., "Le Ruanda en état de révolution: La formation des élites", *La Revue Nouvelle*, Vol. 31, May 1960, pp. 496–503

de Woot, Pierre, "Le Ruanda en état de révolution: Aspects du développement économique", *La Revue Nouvelle*, Vol. 31, May 1960, pp. 486–96

"Rapport de la Commission d'études relative à la suppression de l'ubuhake", *Bulletin des Juridictions du Ruanda-Urundi*, No. 15, 1955, pp. 863–86

Yeld, Rachel, "Implications of experience with refugee settlement", EAISR Conference paper, Makerere 1964

IV. BURUNDI

1. Books and Monographs

Anon., *Prince Louis Rwagasore*, Imprimerie du Royaume du Burundi, Bujumbura n.d.

Baeck, L., *Etude socio-économique du centre coutumier d'Usumbura*, ARSC, Brussels 1957

Cart, Henri-Philippe, *Etudiants et Construction Nationale au Burundi*, unpublished ms., 1969

Chrétien, J. P., *Le Burundi, Notes et Etudes Documentaires*, Documentation française, No. 3364, Paris 1967

Coifard, J., *Soixante ans de colonisation au Royaume du Burundi*, Diplôme d'Etudes Supérieures, Université de Rennes, Rennes 1965

Gorju, Mgr J., *En zigzags à travers l'Urundi*, Namur and Antwerp 1926; *Face au Royaume Hamite du Ruanda: Le royaume frère de l'Urundi. Essai de reconstruction historique*, Vronmant, Brussels 1938

Hilgers, W., *Eglise et Développement*, Bujumbura 1967, mimeo.

Keuppens, J., *L'Urundi Ancien et Moderne*, Bujumbura 1959, mimeo.

Lechat, Michel, *Le Burundi Politique*, Service de l'Information du Ruanda-Urundi, Bujumbura n.d.

Makarakiza, André, *La Dialectique des Barundi*, ARSC, Vol. XIX, fasc. 2, Brussels 1959

Meyer, Hans, *Die Barundi*, Leipzig 1916

Mpozagara, Gabriel, *Sociologie Politique du Burundi*, Mémoire de Licence en Sciences Politiques, Institut d'Etudes Politiques, Paris 1967

Ngendadumwe, Pierre, *Réorganisation Politique Indigène au Ruanda-Urundi: Le Décret du 14 juillet 1952 et son application*, Mémoire de Licence en Sciences Politiques et Administratives, Université Lovanium, July 1959

Perraudin, Jean, *Naissance d'une Eglise: Histoire du Burundi Chrétien*, Presses Lavigerie, Usumbura 1963

Rodegem, F. M., *Sagesse Kirundi*, Annales du Musée Royal du Congo Belge, Vol. 34, Tervueren 1961; *Essai d'Onomastique Rundi*, Bujumbura 1966, mimeo

Ryckmans, Pierre, *Une page d'histoire coloniale: L'occupation allemande dans l'Urundi*, IRCB, Vol. XXIX, fasc. 5, Brussels 1953

Van der Burgt, *Un grand people de l'Afrique Equatoriale*, Bois le Duc, Holland 1963

Zuure, Bernard, *L'Ame du Murundi*, Beauchesne, Paris 1932

2. Articles

Albert, Ethel, "Une étude de valeurs en Urundi", *Cahiers d'Etudes Africaines*, Vol. II, 1960, pp. 147–60; "La Femme en Urundi", in Denise Paulme ed., *Femmes d'Afrique Noire*, Mouton, Paris and The Hague 1960, pp. 173–206; "'Rhetoric', 'Logic' and 'Poetics' in Burundi: Culture Patterning of Speech Behavior", *American Anthropologist*, Special Issue, Winter 1964–65, pp. 35–54

Anon., "A Political Trial in Burundi", *Bulletin of the International Commission of Jurists*, July 1963, pp. 5–15; "Burundi at Close Range", *Africa Report*, March 1965, pp. 19–24

Bureau Permanent du Tribunal du Mwami, "Le contrat d'ubugabire: Une Coutume Murundi", *Bulletin des Juridictions du Ruanda-Urundi*, No. 4, 1947, pp. 35–41

Cart, Henri-Philippe, "Conceptions des Rapports Politiques au Burundi", *Etudes Congolaises*, Vol. IX, March-April 1966, pp. 1–22; & Rousson, Michel, "Prestige et Connaissance des Professions au Burundi", *Revue de l'Institut de Sociologie*, No. 4, 1969, pp. 635–57

Cornevin, R., "Après le coup d'état à Bujumbura", *Le Monde Diplomatique*, August 1966, p. 5

Delacaw, A., "Le droit coutumier des Barundi", *Congo*, Vol. I, 1936, pp. 332–57; 481–522

Gille, Albert, "Notes sur l'organisation des Barundi", *Bulletin des Juridictions Indigènes et du Droit Coutumier Congolais*, No. 3, 1937–38, pp. 75–81

Goebel, C., "Mwambutsa, Mwami de l'Urundi", *Revue Coloniale Belge*, No. 115, 1950, pp. 510–11

Goffin, J., "Le rôle joué par le gros bétail en Urundi", *Bulletin des Juridictions Indigènes et du Droit Coutumier Congolais*, Vol. XIX, 1951, pp. 31–53; 61–86; 100–21

Lemarchand, René, "Social Change and Political Modernization in Burundi", *The Journal of Modern African Studies*, Vol. IV, No. 4, 1966, pp. 14–24; "The passing of Mwamiship in Burundi", *Africa Report*, January 1967, pp. 14–24

Leroy, P., "Stanley et Livingstone en Urundi", *Lovania*, No. 44, 1957, pp. 23–4

Paradis, J., "Le contrat d'ubugarabu", *Bulletin des Juridictions Indigènes et du Droit Coutumier Congolais*, No. 3, 1947, pp. 137–46

Rodegem, F. M., *Structures Judiciaires Traditionnelles au Burundi*, Bujumbura n.d.

Ryckmans, Pierre, "Organisation politique et sociale de l'Urundi", *Revue Générale Belge*, April 15, 1921, pp. 461–84; "Note sur les institutions, moeurs et coutumes de l'Urundi", in *Rapport sur l'Administration Belge au Ruanda-Urundi, 1935*, Brussels 1936, pp. 34–58

Sebiva, Gatti, "Burundi: Détente entre le Parlement et le Gouvernement", *Etudes Congolaises*, No. 8, October 1963, pp. 42–4

Shantz, Homer LeRoy, "Urundi: Territory and People", *Geographical Review*, Vol. XII, 1922, pp. 329–59

Simons, Eugène, "Coutumes et Institutions des Barundi", *Bulletin des Juridictions Indigènes et du Droit Coutumier Congolais*, No. 7, 1944, pp. 137–282

Smets, G., "Quelques observations sur les usages successoraux des Batutsi de l'Urundi", IRCB, *Bulletin des Séances*, Vol. XVIII, 1937, pp. 729–40; "The structure of the Barundi community", *Man*, Vol. 46, No. 6, 1946, pp. 12–16; "Les Institutions Féodales de l'Urundi", *Revue de l'Université de Bruxelles*, Vol. I, February–April 1949, pp. 101–12

Sohier, J. P., "Le Prince Charles a mis en Question le Principe même de la monarchie", *Le Monde*, August 2, 1966

Trouwborst, Albert, "La mobilité de l'individu en fonction de l'organisation politique des Barundi", *Zaire*, Vol. XVIII, 1959, pp. 787–800; "L'organisation politique et l'accord de clientèle au Burundi", *Anthropologica*, Vol. IV, 1962, pp. 9–43; "Le Burundi", in *Les anciens royaumes de la zone interlacustre méridionale: Rwanda, Burundi, Buha*, Musée de l'Afrique Centrale, Tervueren 1962; "Kinship and geographical mobility in Burundi", *International Journal of Comparative Sociology*, Vol. VI, No. 1, March 1965, pp. 166–82

Van der Burgt, J. M., "Land und Leute von Nord Urundi", *Petermans Mitteilungen*, 1912, p. 324

Van de Walle, E., "Chômage dans une petite ville d'Afrique: Usumbura", *Zaire*, Vol. XIV, 1960, pp. 341–59; "Facteurs et indices de stabilisation et d'urbanisation à Usumbura", *Recherches Economiques*, Université de Louvain, March 1961, pp. 97–121

Vansina, Jan, "Notes sur l'Histoire du Burundi", *Aequatoria*, Vol. XIV, 1961, pp. 1–10; "The use of process-models in African History", in Jan Vansina, Raymond Mauny & L. V. Thomas, eds., *The Historian in Tropical Africa*, Oxford University Press, London 1964, pp. 375–90

Weinstein, Warren, "Burundi: Racial Peace and Royalty", *Africa Today*, Vol. XII, No. 6, June-July 1965, pp. 12–15

Ziegler, Jean, "Un Royaume en Crise: Le Burundi", *Le Monde*, November 19, 1965; "L'intégration sociale et politique entre Batutsi et Bahutu dans la région extra-coutumière de Bujumbura", in Atteslander, P. and Girod, R., eds., *Travaux Sociologiques*, Vol. I, Bern 1966, pp. 267–90; "Structures Ethniques et Partis Politiques au Burundi", *Le Mois en Afrique*, No. 18, June 1967, pp. 54–68

V. OFFICIAL DOCUMENTS

To supplement the materials listed below, the reader is referred to the following sources. For the German period, Wm. Roger Louis's survey of documentary and archival materials, in his *Ruanda-Urundi 1884–1919*, Clarendon Press, Oxford 1963, pp. 261–271, remains unmatched. *Rwanda Politique 1958–1960*, Centre de Recherche et d'Information Socio-Politiques, Brussels 1961, provides one of the most useful compendiums of official documentary sources on Rwanda; a more recent compilation, on both Rwanda and Burundi, will be found in *Décolonisation et Indépendence du Rwanda et du Burundi*, special issue of *Chronique de Politique Etrangère*, Vol. XVI, Nos. 4–6, July–November 1963, pp. 536–708. See also the excellent documentation prepared by the UN in *Documentation: Territoire du Ruanda-Urundi*, 3 Vols., mimeo., n.d., n.p. For the post-independence period, one of the most useful sources of continuing documentation is the *Revue Juridique de Droit Ecrit et Coutumier du Rwanda et du Burundi*, published in Bujumbura by the *Société d'Etudes Juridiques du Rwanda et du Burundi*.

1. Pre-Independence Sources:

(a) UN Documents

United Nations, Trusteeship Council, *United Nations Visiting Mission to Trust Territories in East Africa, 1951; Report on the Trust Territory of Ruanda-Urundi*, UN Doc. T/1031, New York 1952; *United Nations Visiting Mission to Trust Territories in East Africa, 1954; Report on Ruanda-Urundi*, UN Doc. T/1204, New York 1955; *United Nations Visiting Mission to Trust Territories in East Africa, 1957; Report on the Trust Territory of Ruanda-Urundi*, UN Doc. T/1346, New York 1958; *United Nations Visiting Mission to Trust Territories in East Africa, 1960; Report on Ruanda-Urundi*, UN Doc. T/1538, New York 1960

United Nations, General Assembly, *Question of the Future of Ruanda-Urundi; Interim Report of the United Nations Commission for Ruanda-Urundi*, UN Doc. A/4706, and *Addendum*, UN Doc. A/4706/Add. 1, March 8, 1961, New York 1961; *Question of the Future of Ruanda-Urundi; Report of the United Nations Commission for Ruanda-Urundi on the assassination of the Prime Minister of Burundi*, UN Doc. A/5086, January 26, 1961, New York 1961; *Report of the United Nations Commission for Ruanda-Urundi, 1962*, UN Doc. A/5126, New York 1962

(b) Belgian Documents

Annales Parlementaires of the *Chambre des Représentants*, and of the *Sénat de Belgique*
Rapport présenté par le Gouvernement Belge au Conseil de la Société des Nations au sujet de l'administration du Ruanda-Urundi pendant l'année. . . . (for relevant years)
Rapport présenté par le Gouvernement Belge au Conseil de Tutelle des Nations

Unies sur l'administration du Ruanda-Urundi pendant l'année. .... (for relevant years)
Conseil Général du Ruanda-Urundi, *Procès-Verbaux*
Conseil Supérieur du Pays (Urundi), *Procès-Verbaux*
Conseil Supérieur du Pays (Ruanda), *Procès-Verbaux*
Bulletin Administratif du Ruanda-Urundi
Bulletin Officiel du Ruanda-Urundi
Bulletin Administratif du Pays de l'Urundi
Bulletin Administratif du Pays du Ruanda

2. *Post-Independence Sources:*

(*a*) *Rwanda*

Assemblée Nationale, *Documents*
Journal Officiel de la République du Rwanda
République Rwandaise, Ministère de la Coopération Internationale et du Plan, Direction de l'Office Général des Statistiques, *Bulletin de Statistiques*
Trafipro-Actualités

(*b*) *Burundi*

Assemblée Nationale, *Procès-Verbaux*
Bulletin Officiel du Burundi
Royaume du Burundi, Ministère des Finances et des Affaires Economiques, Service de l'Information, *Bulletin Economique et Financier*
Royaume du Burundi, Institut Rundi des Statistiques, *Bulletin de Statistiques*
Banque du Royaume, *Bulletin de la Banque du Royaume*

Ad hoc documents of special interest include, for Burundi, *Rapport sur la Situation au 1er Septembre 1965 des Réfugiés au Burundi: Prévisions pour l'Année 1966*, Royaume du Burundi, Cabinet du Roi, Bujumbura 1965; and, for Rwanda, *Toute La Vérité sur le Terrorisme Inyenzi*, Ministère de l'Information, Kigali 1964; *Conservation et Amélioration des Sols au Rwanda*, Ministère de l'Agriculture, Kigali 1966; and *Les Paysannats au Rwanda*, Ministère de l'Agriculture et de l'Elevage, Kigali 1963; the latter two were prepared by M. C. M. Van den Steen.

VI. Newspapers and Periodicals

1. *Pre-Independence Press:*

(*a*) *Metropolitan Press*

La Cité (Catholic)
La Libre Belgique (Catholic)
Le Soir (Liberal)
Le Drapeau Rouge (Communist)

(*b*) *Local Press*

L'Ami (Kabgaye)
Inforrésidence (Kigali)
Kimanyateka (Kabgaye)
La Dépêche du Ruanda-Urundi (Usumbura)
La Chronique Congolaise (Usumbura)

Ndongozi (Kitega)
Temps Nouveaux d'Afrique (Usumbura)
Soma (Shangugu)
Servir (Astrida)

2. *Post-Independence Press:*

(*a*) *Rwanda*

Kimanyateka (Kabgaye)
Rwanda, Carrefour d'Afrique (Kigali)
Trafipro (Gitarama)

(*b*) *Burundi*

Infor-Burundi (Bujumbura)
Ndongozi (Gitega)
Unité et Révolution (Bujumbura)

Index

Tutsi—*continued*
policies, 72–3; dominance in civil
service, 355; representation in
government, 368, 463; representation in army, 461, 461n, 463
Rwanda: hegemony, 19ff; geographical distribution, 25; and
official mythology, 33ff; and inequality, 35; traditional patterns of
behaviour, 42ff; and Catholic
Church, 73, 106–7, 133; elites,
134ff; solidarity among, 154–6
Twa, 19, 165
Twarereye, 23

Ubgenge, 136
Ubucurabwenge, 32
Ubukonde, 39n, 230ff; 268; *see also*
clientage, *bakonde, bagererwa*
Ubuletwa, 59; *see also* corvée
Ubwiru, 32
Ubwoko, 267
Uganda People's Congress (UPG),
209n
Ugirashebuja, 387
Umuganuro, 303, 304
Umulyango, 267; *see also* lineage
UNAR, 160, 167, 177, 185, 227;
foundation and leadership, 158–9;
and Catholic Church, 161; *vs.*
PARMEHUTU, 162; and refugees, 172,
207ff; and MNC-Lumumba, 176;
electoral gains, 181; and Front
Commun, 189; tolerance towards,
197; and factionalism, 198–206
passim; and leadership in exile,
206–16 *passim*; and Bugesera in-
vasion, 216ff; repression against its
leadership, 223; sympathies among
clergy, 260
UNEBA, 405, 406, 424, 425, 448
Union Culturelle de la Jeunesse
Africaine du Burundi (UCJAB), 347,
406
Union des Etudiants Barundi, *see*
UNEBA
Union des Femmes du Burundi (UFB),
448
Union des Travailleurs du Burundi
(UTB), 448, 454
Union Nationale du Burundi (UNB), 324

Union Nationale Rwandaise, *see* UNAR
United Nations, 85, 86, 188–9, 191,
205, 226–7, 345; as an accelerator
of change, 106; attitude of Special
Resident towards, 191–2; and future
of Ruanda-Urundi, 86; violation
of UN Charter, 109; petitions to,
108; and January 1961 referendum,
170; resolutions on Ruanda-
Urundi, 190, 192–3
United Nations Commission for
Ruanda-Urundi, 88, 109, 193–4,
338
United Nations General Assembly,
86, 189, 190, 192
United Nations High Commissioner
for Refugees (UNHCR), 215, 220, 221,
385–6
United Nations Trusteeship Council,
106, 108
United Nations Visiting Mission to
Ruanda-Urundi, 123, 159n, 167,
177
Université Coloniale de Belgique, 20
Université Nationale du Rwanda
(UNR), 260
Université Officielle, 359, 452
UPRONA, 214, 344–6, 392; origins,
325ff; and monarchy, 294, 339ff;
as archaic party, 325; as elite party,
333; as party of chiefs, 328, 332; and
Rwagasore, 328ff; bases of recruitment, 330ff, 337; *vs.* PDC, 334ff; and
elections, 378ff, 340, 412; and JNR,
430–2; internal rifts within, 343ff,
350–3; ideology, 329–30; and fact-
ons, 352ff; connections with Crown,
339; and local government, 339; and
patronage, 350; and 'summit conference', 352–3, 355; and army
rule, 448ff; and 'democratic centralism', 457; and JRR, 458
Utumabahutu, J. B., 236

Van Der Dussen, J., 393
Vanderstraeten, M., 280
Van Overschelde, A., 61n
Vansina, J., 18, 31, 32n
Vassilikos, 374
Vendée, 117
Verwayaen, 416